A WAR TO BE WON

WILLIAMSON MURRAY

ALLAN R. MILLETT

A WAR TO BE WON

Fighting the Second World War

THE BELKNAP PRESS OF HARVARD UNIVERSITY PRESS

Cambridge, Massachusetts, and London, England · 2000

Maps by Malcolm Swanston

Title page illustrations: U.S.S. *Bunker Hill,* 10 May 1945 (background);
American soldiers in Wernberg, Germany, April 1945 (inset).
U.S. National Archives.

Library of Congress Cataloging-in-Publication Data

Murray, Williamson.
    A war to be won : fighting the Second World War / Williamson Murray,
and Allan R. Millett.
      p. cm.
    Includes bibliographical references and index.
    ISBN 0-674-00163-x
    1. World War, 1939–1945.   I. Millett, Allan Reed. II. Title.
D767.98.M87   2000
940.53—dc21   99-086624

This book is dedicated to the memory of the men and women who served and sacrificed in World War II to enlarge the possibilities of freedom— freedom of speech, freedom of worship, freedom from want, and freedom from fear—as the human race enters the twenty-first century.

PREFACE

World War II was the deadliest conflict in modern history. It continued World War I's slaughter of soldiers but then added direct attacks against civilians on a scale not seen in Europe since the Thirty Years' War three centuries earlier. On the Eastern Front, its horrors surpassed the worst battles of the first global war. At times the death struggle between the forces massed by the German Wehrmacht and Red Army never seemed to stop. From the Battle of Kursk in July 1943 to the Crimea in early May 1944, military operations involving hundreds of thousands of soldiers continued day in and day out. Then, after a pause lasting barely a month and a half, Soviet forces attacked the German Army at the end of June 1944, and the ferocious fighting in the east continued without letup until the collapse of Hitler's regime. After 6 June 1944, a similar war began on the Western Front. The amphibious assault of the Anglo-American forces on the beaches of Normandy on D-Day initiated military operations in northern Europe that would not end until May 1945.

The ferocity of the war among the world's great—and small—nations mounted with the addition of racial ideology to the nationalism, lust for glory, greed, fear, and vindictiveness that have characterized war through the ages. Nazi Germany espoused an ideological world view *(Weltanschauung)* based on belief in a "biological" world revolution—a revolution that Adolf Hitler pursued with grim obsession from the early 1920s until his suicide in the Berlin *Führerbunker* in early May 1945. The Nazis' aim was to eliminate the Jews and other "subhuman" races, enslave the Poles, Russians, and other Slavs, and restore the Aryan race—meaning the Germans—to its rightful place as rulers of the world. By the end of the war, the Nazis had murdered or worked to death at least 12 million non-German civilians and prisoners.

In Asia, the Japanese did not adopt so coherent an ideology of racial superiority as the Nazis, but their xenophobic nationalism, combined with dreams of empire and deep bitterness at the dominance of much of Asia by the Western colonial powers, also led to vast atrocities. With the invasion of China in summer 1937, the Japanese embarked on a war that involved murder, rape, and devastation to a degree not seen since the Mongol conquests in the early thirteenth century. The Japanese added a new dimension to the slaughter when they used bacteriological weapons and poison gas against the Chinese people as well as soldiers.*

Faced with this unprecedented aggression by the Axis powers, nations espousing other ideologies, particularly Soviet Communism and liberal capitalist democracy, responded with a fury of their own. By the time the war was over, civilian deaths inflicted by both sides outnumbered combat deaths by a margin of two to one. The West's ideological and moral imperative to punish the Germans for their many crimes culminated in the Combined Bomber Offensive waged by the Royal Air Force and the U.S. Army Air Forces. Four years of battering air attacks, followed by invasion on the ground, destroyed virtually every major city in Central Europe except Prague and Vienna. Dresden, Hamburg, Warsaw, Berlin, and Cologne, among others, lay in rubble. Race-tinged revenge may have shaped the United States' decision to firebomb Tokyo and to detonate atomic bombs over Hiroshima and Nagasaki, Japan—killing hundreds of thousands of civilians and leaving those cities in ruins. Yet as distasteful as these bombing campaigns are today to most citizens of the liberal democracies under sixty years of age, the Combined Bomber Offensive in Europe and the bombing of Japan reflected not only a sense of moral conviction on the part of the West but a belief that such air attacks would end a war that daily grew more horrible for soldiers and civilians alike.

Nazi Germany, Imperial Japan, and Fascist Italy could not, in the final analysis, be defeated except by fighting. The United States, Britain, the Soviet Union, and their allies had to fight their opponents in air, ground, and naval contests across the globe. Moral righteousness alone does not win battles. Evil causes do not necessarily carry the seeds of their own destruction. Once engaged, even just wars have to be won—or lost—on the battlefield. Because of the Axis' operational and tactical skill, stiffened in battle by fierce nationalism and ideological commitment, as well as the controls of police states, winning the "Good War" proved a daunting task.

*Just when World War II began is a matter of interpretation. Western Europeans and Americans tend to ignore the Japanese incursion into China and to mark the war's beginning with the German invasion of Poland on 1 September 1939. For Austrians, Czechs, and Slovaks, the war also commenced two years earlier, when the Third Reich used military force to swallow up sovereign nations in Central Europe that the Western European democracies had abandoned.

Waging World War II required more than the mobilization and equipment of huge military forces. It required the deployment of those forces
over enormous distances—in the case of the United States, across two vast
oceans. And it required the creation of military power in three dimensions:
in the air over both land and sea; across great land masses; and on and beneath the sea. The Germans led the way toward combined arms warfare
with their *Blitzkrieg* of air and ground forces in May 1940, an assault of
weeks that enslaved Western Europe for four years. But the Allies adapted
and developed their own forces for air-ground warfare that eventually
proved superior. Equally impressive, Allied amphibious forces—a fusion of
air, land, and sea units—made possible the landings in Africa, Italy, and
France. The air-sea-undersea-amphibious naval campaign in the Pacific
doomed Japan.

Logistical superiority was crucial to the Allies' victory, and America's role
as the "Arsenal of Democracy" made a critical difference. Not only did the
United States carry most of the burden of the naval campaign in the Pacific
and an increasing load of the combat in Europe as the war progressed, but
its Lend-Lease program was essential to the military operations of its allies
and to the functioning of their wartime economies. In contrast, the Germans and the Japanese, undoubtedly misled by the successes their military
forces initially achieved, did not mobilize their own economies until the
tide had already turned against them in 1942–43. Their desperate efforts to
match the Allies soon attracted the assaults on their economic systems
launched by Allied air and sea forces.

While the Allies' economic strength weighed heavily in their eventual
victory, reinforcing and accelerating the tempo of military operations in
1943–45, material superiority never by itself proved decisive. Intelligence
about the capabilities and intentions of their opponents became increasingly important to the belligerents as the conflict deepened. In the contest
of intelligence, the Allied powers won handily. A complete misestimate of
the capabilities of the Royal Air Force cost the Luftwaffe what little chance
it had of achieving its objectives in the Battle of Britain. Worse was to
come. In planning the invasion of the Soviet Union, Germany misjudged
the Soviet ability to absorb defeats. The result was a catastrophic stalemate
in front of Moscow, despite a series of impressive earlier victories in Operation Barbarossa. This failure was followed by Hitler's decision to declare
war on the United States—an unnecessary strategic error based on a complete misunderstanding of America's economic and military potential to
wage war against two enemies. The Allies slowly achieved an intelligence
advantage over their opponents as the war continued. With information

gained by breaking German and Japanese codes, Anglo-American commanders were able to shape battles to their advantage and to mount deception campaigns that misled their opponents. The Russians used secret agents and signals intelligence to the same result.

With all their advantages in combined arms, logistics, and intelligence, the Allies still confronted the grim task of destroying their enemies town by town, island by island, in terrible killing battles that exhausted victor and vanquished alike. In that struggle, the greatest advantage the Allies enjoyed over the Axis was the capacity to make strategic decisions that balanced ends against means. At first the Allies were no better at strategic decision-making than their opponents. Perhaps the shock of their initial defeats provided the sobering learning the Allies needed to guide their strategy as the war continued. The Germans, by contrast, never questioned their confidence in their planning superiority—a bit of hubris that proved fatal.

In this book, we have concentrated on the conduct of operations by the military organizations that waged the war. We have not ignored the strategic and political decisions that drove the war, but what interests us most are issues of military effectiveness. We have attempted to explain the battlefield performance of armies, navies, and air forces; the decisions made by generals and admirals in the face of extraordinary difficulties; the underlying factors that shaped the outcomes of battles and campaigns; and the interrelationships among battles separated by hundreds or thousands of miles. Thus, we have written a history of World War II that examines the reciprocal influence of strategy and operations. We try to explain how military decisions were made, and how those decisions made a difference to the outcome of the fighting. We are aware that as historians, with access to documents and accounts from both sides, we can understand events as they unfolded in a way that the participants could not. In every case, we have attempted to judge the decisions of military leaders and statesmen on the basis of what they could reasonably have known at the time that they had to act.

We also believe that individuals at every level of leadership made a difference. From Lieutenant Richard Winters, whose squad-sized force captured a German battery and its protecting company behind Utah Beach, to the German panzer commanders like Irwin Rommel and Hans von Luck who destroyed the French Army in little over three weeks, to Dwight Eisenhower who kept a strong-willed group of senior commanders focused on defeating the Wehrmacht, individuals guided the course of events. We have attempted to identify and discuss those who made the decisions that turned the tide of the war. Although we have not written an everyman's history of the conflict, we have not overlooked the hundreds of thousands of men in arms who bore the terrible burden of carrying out those decisions.

To the best of our ability, we have incorporated the expert research that has become available over the last thirty years into a full analysis of the war. The revelations of Ultra intelligence in the early 1970s and its operational implications have only recently achieved a balanced place alongside other factors that contributed to the Allied victory. The partial opening of the Soviet archives following the collapse of the Soviet Union has altered the West's understanding of the war on the Eastern Front—a historical event too long told from the German perspective. As students and teachers of military history for much of the postwar period and as veterans who profited from our own modest military experiences, we believe that we have written a history of World War II that does justice to that war's complexity and meaning. This, then, is our account.

Williamson Murray
Allan R. Millett

CONTENTS

Illustrations follow pages 112, 240, 400, and 496

MAPS

1

ORIGINS
OF A
CATASTROPHE

High in the Bavarian Alps in August 1939, a group of Germans looked toward the heavens and beheld a spectacular display of the aurora borealis that covered the entire northern sky in shimmering blood-red light. One of the spectators noted in his memoirs that "the last act of *Götterdämmerung* could not have been more effectively staged." Another spectator, a pensive Adolf Hitler, commented to an adjutant: "Looks like a great deal of blood. This time we won't bring it off without violence."[1] Hitler, the author and perpetrator of the coming catastrophe, knew full well of what he spoke, for he was about to unleash another terrible conflict, first on Europe and eventually on the world. How had Europe again come to the brink of hostilities barely a quarter century after the start of World War I—a clash of nations that had tumbled empires and destroyed a generation? It was indeed a sad tale of fumbled hopes and dark dreams.

The war that Hitler was soon to begin brought a new dimension to the cold, dark world of power and states, for it combined the technologies of the twentieth century with the ferocious ideological commitment of the French Revolution. The wreckage of 1918 had certainly suggested the possibilities. But the democracies chose to forget the harsh lessons of that war in the comfortable belief that it all had been a terrible mistake; that a proper dose of reasonableness—the League of Nations along with pacifist sentiments—would keep the world safe for democracy. Instead, the peace of 1919 collapsed because the Allies, whose interest demanded that they defend it, did not, while the defeated powers had no intention of abiding the results. The United States, weary of European troubles, withdrew into isolationism, and Britain followed to the extent geography allowed. Only France, vulnerable in its continental position, attempted to maintain the peace.

1

From the first, the Germans dreamed of overturning the Treaty of Versailles, which had codified their humiliation. The Italians and then the Japanese, both disappointed by their share in the spoils, displayed little interest in supporting the post–World War I order, while the revolutionaries in Russia focused on winning their own civil war and then on establishing socialism in the new nation. The ingredients for the failure of peace were present from the moment the armistice was signed; the inconclusive end to World War I, with the German Army still on foreign territory, made another European war inevitable. The appointment of Hitler as chancellor of Germany in January 1933 and the ensuing Nazi revolution ensured war on a major scale, involving nothing less than a bid for German hegemony over the entire continent.

Adolf Hitler was crucial to the rise of National Socialism. Beyond his political shrewdness, he possessed beliefs that fit well with German perceptions and prejudices. Ideology was central to his message. Above all, he rejected the optimistic values of the nineteenth century, in favor of a worldview that rested on race and race alone. On one side were the Aryans, best typified by the Germans, who had created the great civilizations of the past; on the other side were the Jews, degenerate corrupters of the social order, who had poisoned societies throughout history. In Hitler's view, Marxism, socialism, and capitalism were all ills that flowed from the effort of Jews to destroy civilization from within. Hitler believed that he had uncovered in his race theories the fundamental principles on which human development and human history turned. He had no more evidence for his system than Marx and Engels and their successors, Lenin and Stalin, had for their illusions, but ideologies, like religions, do not rest on facts or reality; they rest on beliefs, hopes, and fears.

The "biological world evolution" to which the Nazis aspired married other nasty quirks to anti-Semitism. According to Hitler, a lack of "living space" (Lebensraum) thwarted Germany's potential; great nations require territory on which to grow. Consequently, Germany would have to either seize the economic and agricultural base required to expand or else wane into a third-rate power. Russia's open spaces beckoned; in Hitler's view, they were inhabited by worthless subhumans, whom the Germans could enslave. German conquest would begin with the elimination of the educated elites in Slavic lands. The remaining population would then be killed, expelled, or enslaved as Helots. On these conceptions rested everything that Hitler and his Germans, military and civilians, would do in the coming five and a half years of war. The success or failure of Hitler's program would depend on the ruthlessness with which the leadership acted and how effectively Hitler fused his fierce ideology to a civilian administrative structure and military machine capable of executing his wishes. In both endeavors he was all too successful.

It has become popular among some historians to suggest that the "internal" contradictions of Nazism would eventually have resulted in the regime's collapse. Such views are questionable. Admittedly, internal dynamics and economic strains pushed the Third Reich toward war, but saying that is only to underline that war and the destruction of other nations were part and parcel of Nazi ideology. Had Hitler won, his regime had already proved it could find and motivate the people required to keep the system working.

Most leaders and observers on the Left missed the demonic nature of the Nazi threat. Leon Trotsky contemptuously remarked that the Fascist movement was human dust, while Joseph Stalin argued that Fascism represented capitalism's last stage. The Communists busily attacked the Social Democrats as "Social Fascists" in the early 1930s, thereby shattering the unity of the Left, especially in Germany. Stalin's German stooges were as much the enemies of the Republic as the Nazis, just less skilled.

There were, of course, many who prepared the way for Nazism. A massive disinformation campaign by the Weimar Republic's bureaucracy persuaded most Germans that the Reich had not been responsible for the last war and that in November 1918 the army had stood undefeated in the field until Jews and Communists stabbed it in the back. A national mood of self-pity and self-indulgence fueled the Nazi Party's attractiveness.

Initial Moves

In strategic terms Germany had won the Great War. Its industrial base remained intact; it lost little territory of value; it now fronted on one major power (a debilitated France) rather than three (France, Austria-Hungary, and Russia). Its industrial strength, its geographic position, and the size of its population gave it the greatest economic potential in Europe, while the small states of Eastern Europe and the Balkans were all open to German political and economic domination.

However, these advantages remained opaque to a nation that felt humiliated by defeat in 1918. For the Nazis, Germany's postwar economic situation offered a considerable stumbling block to regaining the Reich's great position of power. The Versailles Treaty's restrictions on arms manufacturing left even the Krupp industrial empire with little capacity for military production. In 1933 the aircraft industry, for example, possessed only

4,000 workers divided among a group of bankrupt manufacturers known more for their quarrels than for the quality of their products. The only raw material the Reich possessed in abundance was coal; oil, rubber, iron, nickel, copper, and aluminum were in short supply or nonexistent. Consequently, Germany had to import these materials, and in the 1930s imports required foreign exchange, which Germany did not have. As with all armament efforts, German production did not immediately rise to meet expectations.

Hitler did warn the German generals in February 1933 that France, if it possessed true leaders, would recognize the German threat and immediately mobilize its forces. If that did not happen, Germany would destroy the European system, not make minor changes to the Versailles Treaty. Hitler's intuition was right; France did not have leaders willing to make a stand. In the years of preparation for war, Hitler managed German diplomacy with consummate skill despite the Third Reich's military weaknesses. In 1933 Germany withdrew from the League of Nations and then in the following year signed a nonaggression pact with Poland, removing the Poles as a threat in the east. These diplomatic moves thoroughly confused Hitler's opponents. With few exceptions, Europeans hoped that the Führer was *reasonable* and that they could accommodate the new Nazi regime.

In Britain, most were deceived. Only Churchill warned: "'I marvel at the complacency of Ministers in the face of the frightful experiences through which we have so newly passed. I look with wonder upon our thoughtless crowds disporting themselves in the summer sunshine,' and all the while, across the North Sea, 'a terrible process is astir. *Germany is arming.*'"[2] It was indeed a lonely fight that Churchill waged. Well might John Milton's words in *Paradise Lost* about the angel Abdiel have been applied to Churchill: "Among the faithless, faithful only hee; Among innumerable false, unmov'd / Unshak'n, unseduc'd, unterrifi'd."[3]

More in tune with the European mood was the *London Times*'s response to Hitler's purge of the SA (Sturmabteilung), the Nazi Party's paramilitary arm, when firing squads executed several hundred Nazi storm troopers: "Herr Hitler, whatever one may think of his methods, is genuinely trying to transform revolutionary fervor into moderate and constructive efforts and to impose a higher standard on National Socialist officials."[4]

The political Left warned of the danger of Fascism, but regarded the threat as internal rather than external. In Britain, the Labour Party urged aid for the Spanish Republic, which was fighting for its life, but voted against every defense appropriation through 1939. In France, the Popular Front government of Léon Blum denounced Charles de Gaulle's proposals for an armored force as a gambit to create an army of aggression. If Germany attacked, Blum argued, no armored force was required; the working class would rise as one man to defend the Republic. His government undermined France's defense industry with social legislation and kept the lid on defense spending so that even Italy outspent France in the 1935–1938 period.

Soviet foreign policy was equally irrelevant; Stalin encouraged formation of "popular-front" movements against Fascism, but his policy aimed more at encouraging a war among the capitalists than at stopping Hitler. A savage purge in 1937 which decimated the Soviet military was further evidence of Stalin's belief that war with Nazi Germany was unlikely.

In 1935 Benito Mussolini invaded Abyssinia and added that country to Italy's colonial domain. Using the Italian war in Africa as cover, Hitler remilitarized the Rhineland in March 1936, thus flouting one of the most important provisions of the Versailles Treaty. A political crisis in France that led to the fall of the government rendered French protests against the Germans meaningless. And all the British could manage to mobilize was vague talk about the Germans moving into their own backyard.

In July 1936 the civil war broke out in Spain, and that conflict furthered Hitler's interests by distracting Europeans from the German threat. While Hitler provided some help to Francisco Franco, the rebellion's leader, German aid remained limited. In December 1936 Hitler flatly refused Spanish requests for three divisions and remarked that it was in the Reich's interest that Europe's attention remain focused on Spain. The Spanish Civil War dragged on, living up to Hitler's expectations. Franco deliberately drew out the conflict to kill the maximum number of his loyalist opponents.

In addition to the suffering inflicted on the Spanish people, the war exercised a baneful influence on Germany's potential opponents, particularly France, which was almost torn apart by the war's political fallout. The British government moralized, but did little to prevent the rush of arms and men to both sides. Stalin provided military equipment but remained more interested in exporting the NKVD (Soviet Secret Police) and Soviet paranoia than in defeating Fascism. Aside from Spain, Italy lost the most, however. By providing "volunteers" and arms to Franco, Mussolini retarded the modernization of his own military. All that Italy got in return was promises which, in the harsh world of the 1940s, Franco failed to keep.

After his Rhineland success, Hitler's planning proceeded for two years without a major crisis. The performance of German Army units in autumn 1937 maneuvers, however, indicated that the day of reckoning was not far off. Observers such as Mussolini and Britain's General Edmund Iron-

GERMAN EXPANSION IN EUROPE
1935–1939

German territory in 1935

1	Reoccupation of the Rhineland March 1936
2	*Anschluß* (union with Austria) March 1938
3	Occupation of Sudetenland October 1938
4	Slovak territory to Hungary November 1938

5	Czech territory to Poland March 1939
6	Slovak territory to Hungary March 1939
7	Memel territory to Germany March 1939
8	Bohemia, Moravia, and Slovakia become German Protectorate March 1939
9	Albania occupied by Italy April 1939

FINLAND

Helsinki · Leningrad

Stockholm · Estonia

Baltic Sea · Latvia

7 · Lithuania

Königsberg

East Prussia

Warsaw

POLAND

Kiev

5

ZECHO SLOVAKIA · 6

8 · 4

Budapest

HUNGARY

ROMANIA

Odessa

Bucharest

Belgrade · Danube

YUGOSLAVIA

Sofia

BULGARIA

Istanbul

Adriatic Sea

ALBANIA · 9

Taranto

GREECE

Aegean Sea

Athens

U S S R

Kursk

Stalingrad

Black Sea

T U R K E Y

SYRIA

Cyprus

Lebanon

ily

Crete

Sea

Malta (to Britain)

poli
ibya
o Italy)

Benghazi

Libya
(to Italy)

E G Y P T

Alexandria

Palestine

Trans-Jordan

Suez Canal

Cairo

side left East Prussia impressed with the German Army's efficiency. But the Germans were having serious economic difficulties. There was simply not enough foreign exchange to pay for the imports of raw materials required to fulfill the massive rearmament programs. From September 1937 through February 1939, these shortages prevented German industry from completing over 40 percent of orders on schedule.

In November 1937 Hitler met with his chief advisers to discuss these strategic and economic problems. The minutes of the meeting emphasize the Führer's belief that the Reich must soon embark on an aggressive foreign policy. His predictions about possible future wars were far-fetched, but the immediate targets, Austria and Czechoslovakia, were clear enough. However, Hitler ran into opposition from General Werner von Fritsch (the army's commander-in-chief), Field Marshal Werner von Blomberg (the war minister), and Konstantin von Neurath (the foreign minister). All three agreed that Germany was not ready for war and that a premature move could lead to disaster. Discussions were inconclusive, although within the month, Blomberg ordered contingency plans recast.

The hesitation of his senior advisers upset Hitler deeply. At the end of January 1938 he made his move; Blomberg's misalliance with a woman who had "a past" provided the excuse. The generals demanded Blomberg's removal, and Hitler gladly accommodated them. Then, using trumped-up charges of homosexuality, he turned on Fritsch and fired him as well. To complete the purge, Hitler replaced Neurath with his protégé Joachim von Ribbentrop, at the same time that he retired or transferred a number of other senior officers. Hitler then assumed control at the War Ministry himself and appointed General Wilhelm Keitel—remarkable even among German generals for obsequiousness—as his chief military assistant.

The purge presaged a major turn in policy. Hitler now controlled both the military and the diplomatic bureaucracies. However, the triumph was short-lived. The case against Fritsch dissolved due to the incompetence of the SS (Schutzstaffel, the Nazi Party's security and secret police). By March 1938, shortly before the opening of Fritsch's court-martial, Hitler and the officer corps appeared headed for collision.

The confrontation never took place, because at the same time the SS case against Fritsch was unraveling, Hitler was pursuing his dream of *Anschluß*—union with Austria. At a mid-February meeting with Austrian Chancellor Kurt Schuschnigg, Hitler demanded concessions that undercut Austrian independence. In response, Schuschnigg declared a plebiscite to determine whether Austrians were for a "free, independent, and Christian Austria." Enraged, the Führer ordered mobilization against Austria; at the same time, the Nazis placed great diplomatic pressure on Vienna to capitulate. Austria collapsed, its destruction abetted by its indigenous Nazi movement and Europe's indifference. Schuschnigg surrendered to Hitler's demands that he resign and allow the Nazi Arthur Seyss-Inquart to assume the position of chancellor. A hastily mobilized German Army then marched into Austria. Ecstatic crowds welcomed their new masters, while others desperately sought to escape. Hitler, his emotions thoroughly aroused by the enthusiasm of his Austrian fellow countrymen, almost immediately announced the union of Austria and Germany. For the next seven years Austria disappeared from Europe's maps, more willingly than those who were to follow.

The *Anschluß* ended the furor over Fritsch's removal. The German Army had accomplished its first major operation since World War I with no substantial problems. Nevertheless, military weaknesses did show up: careless march discipline, mechanical and logistical problems with the armored forces, and inadequate mobilization measures. As in the past, the army readily set out to learn from its experiences.

Although the *Anschluß* failed to solve Germany's long-range strategic problems as a resource-poor nation, it did bring short-term help. The Austrians possessed considerable foreign currency holdings which immediately aided the Reich's rearmament programs. One estimate at the time calculated that financial gains from the *Anschluß* underwrote the costs of rearmament for the rest of 1938, while by 1939 Austrian factories were turning out Bf 109 fighters and contributing considerably to the Reich's production of high-grade steel. The Austrian campaign netted military and strategic gains as well. Germany now surrounded Czechoslovakia on three sides and possessed direct frontiers with Hungary, Yugoslavia, and Italy. The Austrian Army, though of mixed quality, added five divisions to the German Army (two mountain, two infantry, and one motorized).

The self-serving memoirs of German generals such as Heinz Guderian describe the atmosphere in which "their Austrian comrades" joined the new "Greater German" Army as being happy and light. In fact, the heavy hand of National Socialism fell on anti-Nazi Austrians, military and civilian alike. Thirty senior Austrian officers were incarcerated in Dachau, while the Gestapo (Ge[heime] Sta[ats]po[lizei], or secret state police) murdered General Wilhelm Zehner, Secretary of War in Schuschnigg's cabinet. However, all too many Austrians enthusiastically accepted the changes; the SS German paper *Schwarzer Korps* delightedly commented on the "honest joy" with which Austrians were managing to "do in a fortnight what we have failed to achieve in this slow-moving ponderous north up to this day."[5]

The Czech Crisis and Munich

The major European powers greeted the *Anschluß* with indifference. Neville Chamberlain, British prime minister, admitted to his cabinet that Germany's methods had shocked the world as "a typical illustration of power politics."[6] Nevertheless, three days later he told the Foreign Policy Committee that there was no reason for Britain to alter its diplomatic course. With Austria now firmly under German control, Czechoslovakia was obviously Hitler's next target. But here the strategic niceties were different: the Czechs possessed alliances with France and the Soviet Union. Thus, a sudden German move might precipitate a major conflict.

In spring 1938, gorged on Austria's loot and the bullying of defenseless Jews in Vienna, the Germans turned on the Czechs. A minority of over 3 million Czech citizens of German descent (close to 20 percent of Czechoslovakia's population) were living along the Czech frontier. Geography had placed this minority solidly within districts where the Czechs sited their defenses. Moreover, recent history provided a useful issue with which Hitler could berate British and French liberals: that of self-determination and minority rights. Hitler immediately began preparations to undermine Czechoslovakia, while isolating it from external support.

On the military side, the armed forces high command (Oberkommando der Wehrmacht, OKW) began work on 28 March to deploy German units against the Czechs from newly acquired Austrian territory. In mid-May the Czechs, alarmed by intelligence reports of German troop movements, mobilized and occupied their fortifications to protect the Sudetenland from a sudden German incursion. Hitler was furious, while the major powers took stock. Chamberlain and the French premier, Édouard Daladier, determined to appease the Germans, even if they had to abandon the Czechs, while the Führer decided to destroy the Czech Republic in a military campaign in fall 1938. Nine days after the crisis, Hitler signed new deployment plans that clearly indicated his intention to smash Czechoslovakia. On the same day he ordered army engineers to accelerate construction of the *Westwall*—fortifications to protect Germany's frontier in the west.

Hitler's aggressive policy met serious objections from Ludwig Beck, chief of the general staff, who insisted that a German attack on Czechoslovakia would start a European war that Germany could not win. However, Beck received scant support for his position from the new commander-in-chief of the army, General Walther von Brauchitsch, who was already deeply compromised by the fact that Hitler had bought him out of an unhappy marriage. Part of the problem lay in the fact that no mechanism existed in the German system of government for the military services to evaluate the strategic situation—a state of affairs that accorded not only with the Führer's wishes but with those of the services as well. Thus, the summer of 1938 found the German Air Force (the Luftwaffe) and Army hard at work preparing plans to destroy the Czechs, while Beck's resignation at the end of August occasioned no response from the generals.

By mid-September, Nazi preparations had moved so far along that Chamberlain embarked on a personal intervention to prevent war. On 14 September he flew to Germany to meet Hitler at Berchtesgaden. After listening to the Führer's monologue, Chamberlain asked for the German terms. The prime minister then returned to London, where he persuaded his British colleagues, the French, and finally the Czechs that surrender of the Sudetenland represented the only hope for peace. The French acceded because they had no desire to fight, while in despair the Czechs surrendered the territory—an understandable attitude given their nation's size but a significant contrast with the behavior that the Poles and Finns would display under similar circumstances a year later.

On his return to Germany to settle terms, however, Chamberlain discovered that Hitler had little sincere interest in peace. The Führer's refusal to slow the pace of military preparations angered many in Britain and France, but Chamberlain and Daladier had no intention of taking a strong stand. Despite Hitler's rejection of a settlement, the British prime minister argued that the Western powers should continue on the path of appeasement. As he told his countrymen on 27 September, "How horrible, fantastic, incredible it is that we should be digging trenches and trying gas masks on here, because of a quarrel in a far away country between people of whom we know nothing."[7]

While England and France dithered, Hitler's September had been busy. Despite disquiet in the officer corps, he had driven Germany toward military confrontation. His diplomatic efforts had attempted to separate the West from the Czechs, and within Germany he had manipulated public opinion through the lies of the Nazi propaganda ministry, run by his evil deputy Joseph Goebbels. Nevertheless, on the brink of war—probably due to Allied mobilization measures and a lack of enthusiasm among the German population—Hitler drew back and with Mussolini's help agreed to a conference of the major powers (the Soviet Union excepted) to achieve a settlement. At Munich on 24 September 1938, his minions and Mussolini bullied Chamberlain and Daladier into accepting all the German demands. Chamberlain, with an agreement in hand, returned to London a hero. Churchill alone stood firmly opposed. In early October before a hostile

House of Commons, he savagely summed up Chamberlain's appeasement: "Thou art weighed in the balance and found wanting."[8]

Munich was a strategic disaster for the West. An attack on Czechoslovakia in 1938 would have involved the Wehrmacht in a major European war for which it was unprepared. Admittedly, German forces would have crushed Czechoslovakia, while the French would have done little. But a campaign against the Czechs would have destroyed stocks of Czech weapons (all of which fell undamaged into German hands in March 1939) and might have destroyed the Skoda Works—the giant arms complex in Czechoslovakia. The real problem for Germany, however, was not the conquest of Czechoslovakia but what options lay open *after* Czechoslovakia. In the air the Luftwaffe was incapable of conducting a strategic bombing campaign against the British Isles, while on the ground the army was equally unready for war. Its mechanized force consisted of only three panzer (armored) divisions equipped with tanks that were already obsolete. The Eastern European situation was murky, but generally hostile to German interests. Finally, the pressures of rearmament had placed the Reich's economy in a desperate situation. Dislocations caused by mobilizations in the spring and fall, the massive costs of rearmament, and shortages of foreign exchange led German economists to note that in the last half of 1938 "the German economy had faced unheard of difficulties. The strong box was empty."[9]

With little prospect of a quick victory for Germany, a European war beginning in fall 1938 would have turned on the economic strength and staying power of the opposing sides. Allied economic resources, industrial capacity, and naval forces were overwhelmingly superior, whether Germany faced only Britain or France, or a larger coalition that included Poland and perhaps the Soviet Union. Even so, a war against Germany in 1938 over Czechoslovakia would not have been easy, but it would have been a lot less disastrous than the conflict that ensued over Poland and Finland in September 1939.

The Road to War

Chamberlain and the appeasers had not surrendered Czechoslovakia because of fear that Britain might lose a war against Germany. Rather, they pursued appeasement because of a desperate fear of war itself. Not surprisingly, Chamberlain refused to speed up the tempo of rearmament after Munich. The Royal Navy received an increase of a few destroyers. The government extended the Royal Air Force's (RAF) contract for fighters but ordered no additional fighters for the next two years. The army received nothing. Across the Channel, the French proved no more willing than the British to address the fundamental weaknesses in their military forces.

With the West floundering, Hitler moved to secure his gains in Eastern Europe. Within three weeks of Munich, he ordered the OKW to prepare plans to occupy the remainder of Czechoslovakia. At the same time, he lambasted the officer corps for its lack of faith and demanded that officers exhibit a higher degree of obedience to his leadership. The generals, having seen Hitler at work in Munich, abdicated strategic responsibility to the Führer. Beck retired, and the emerging leadership largely consisted of technocrats rather than strategists. Instead of being pleased about his diplomatic successes, Hitler was furious at losing his opportunity to smash the Czechs. Within the month he made a slashing attack on British anti-appeasers and warned that Germany would brook no interference in Southeastern Europe.

The economic difficulties that continued to plague Nazi rearmament provided a major incentive to seize the remaining territory of Czechoslovakia. When a political crisis erupted there in March 1939, Hitler struck. By seizing Prague, Germany gained Czechoslovakia's resources, industry, and military establishment. The Germans also acquired substantial foreign exchange with the occupation, and if that were not enough, the British facilitated the process by transferring Czech gold from the Bank of England to Berlin. Of particular value were the Skoda and Brünn armament complexes, while the booty from Czech arms dumps was immense. The Germans acquired 1,231 aircraft, 1,996 anti-tank guns, 2,254 field artillery pieces, 810 tanks, 57,000 machine guns, and 630,000 rifles—all of considerable help in furthering the Wehrmacht's rearmament.

Germany's seizure of the remainder of Czechoslovakia had serious strategic consequences, however. For the first time the West responded to German actions with anger. The reaction stemmed more from public outrage than from any governmental recognition that Germany had stepped beyond the pale. Chamberlain himself commented to his cabinet that Hitler's action was mostly symbolic. However, a storm of public protest in Britain forced the government to rethink Britain's diplomatic course. Unfortunately, that reevaluation did not change the basic premise that war was avoidable. Chamberlain turned to active diplomacy to fence Germany in; appeasement never died, and as late as the summer of 1939 the British were offering diplomatic concessions and major industrial loans, if Germany would only behave.

The seizure of Prague did force Chamberlain to address the unpreparedness of Britain's armed forces. The government at last fully funded rearmament programs and recognized the army's continental role as essential. By May the British had introduced conscription (a measure still opposed by Labour) and had decided on an army of over 30 divisions. That recognition, however, had come too late; the British Army would have a relatively minor role in the drama of May 1940. Britain's commitment to the continent, however, delighted the French. That alone explains their willingness to join the British in extending guarantees to virtually every Eastern European nation.

Hitler's reaction to Britain's guarantee of Polish independence (given in a moment of panic) was incredulity at first and then outrage. Coloring his perceptions was a general contempt for Western leaders. He commented to Admiral Wilhelm Canaris, director of German intelligence, that he would cook the British a stew on which they would choke. To others he remarked that he had seen his enemies at Munich and they were worms. Hitler now determined to eliminate the Poles.

On 3 April he ordered the OKW to draw up invasion plans for Poland under the codename Case White. Military operations were to commence on or about 1 September; this time Hitler refused all opportunities to negotiate. As he told his generals in August: "Now Poland is in the position in which I want her . . . I am only afraid that some swine or other will submit to me a plan of mediation."[10] The new chief of the general staff, General Franz Halder, enthusiastically endorsed the Führer's decision. In the meantime, the British, urged on by the French, dithered in dealing with the Soviets, and by July Hitler himself had reached out to Stalin. His overtures were warmly received.

From the Soviet perspective, the German occupation of Prague and the Anglo-French guarantee of Polish independence fundamentally altered the strategic situation. Now Stalin had an opportunity to play Germany and the West against each other, and in this game, for now, the Germans possessed important advantages. Hitler could promise Stalin not only Finland, the Baltic states, and chunks of Poland and Romania but peace as well. The Western powers, ostensibly protecting the rights of smaller nations, could not even offer Stalin territory. In the Kremlin in late August 1939, Stalin and Ribbentrop concluded the Nazi-Soviet Non-Aggression Pact. The British foreign minister, Lord Halifax, immediately discounted the agreement as being of little strategic importance, although he admitted its impact on public opinion in the world would be enormous.

For the second time in 25 years Germany was ready to embark on war. On 1 September 1939, Hitler launched the Wehrmacht against Poland in the belief that Britain and France, given the strategic situation, would not honor their obligations. He was, of course, willing to face the consequences if he had misjudged the West. His comments to his generals at the end of August suggest his line of thinking. He argued that the Reich had no need to fear a blockade, because the Soviets would deliver everything the German economy needed. Outside such simplistic calculations, there is no indication that anyone in Germany had calculated German options should war continue after the Polish campaign. The German generals were happy to equate the conduct of military operations with strategy and then to leave strategic matters entirely to the Führer.

The British and French did possess a strategy—one that attempted to weigh the military, political, and economic balance between Germany and themselves. The Western powers aimed at imposing a close blockade on the Germans which over the long run would strangle the German war economy. However, such a strategy demanded the undertaking of serious military actions that would force their enemy to expend scarce resources in marginal theaters. In the end, that strategy failed because of the unwillingness of British and French statesmen and generals to undertake *any* military action. Their inaction ensured that the Wehrmacht possessed maximum military capability in spring 1940.

There were in fact three areas—Italy, Norway, and the Western Front—where Allied pressure could have affected the Germans significantly. Even before the war began, Britain and France had botched the Italian opportunity. With Mussolini's concern delicately balanced between his obligations to Germany and Italy's strategic vulnerabilities, the Allies pursued appeasement. For one of the few times in his career, Chamberlain had calculated the strategic equation correctly, but the chiefs of staff persuaded him to maintain a course of appeasement toward Italy. He had argued in late June 1939 that Britain should not allow Italy to remain neutral in a future war but should push it into Hitler's arms. However, the chiefs argued that Italy's neutrality would be preferable to its hostile participation in any gathering conflict. They won the argument. The Italians would remain neutral until June 1940, when the desperate situation of the Allies would entice Mussolini to join the war on Germany's side. In passing up the opportunity to add the Italian albatross to Germany's responsibilities in 1939, the Allies also missed the opportunity to fight the Italians at a time when little German help was available.

On the morning of 1 September 1939, Chamberlain met with his cabinet to discuss the invasion of Poland. He remarked that "the event against which we had fought so long and earnestly had come upon us."[11] One minister went so far as to suggest that Britain should avoid a declaration of war. Not surprisingly, it required a political revolt in the House of Commons to force the government to declare war two days later. The French declaration followed.

Conclusion

By late August 1939 the strategic balance had swung significantly against the Allies. The German military were finally beginning to realize the potential of serious military innovation coupled with the input of enormous resources for over a decade. On the other side, by contrast, Allied rearmament had hardly begun. The Germans also possessed significant mechanized forces which the great Polish plain, where the first battles of World War II would be fought, would favor. Moreover, Hitler's run of military and diplomatic successes had solidified the support of the German people behind his regime to a degree that had not been true in 1938.

The German strategic advantage was further helped by the Nazi-Soviet Non-Aggression Pact. The two powers could now enthusiastically cooperate in the looting of Eastern Europe—the first step to bigger and better things for both. For Hitler, destruction of the Eastern European states would open the gates to invading the Soviet Union itself and seizing Germany's *Lebensraum,* after he had disposed of the Western powers. For the Soviets, the agreement represented the opening salvo in the great war among the capitalist powers that would inevitably lead to European and perhaps world revolution.

The rise of Nazi Germany represented a threat to the survival of Western civilization. Yet the shadow of World War I's slaughter exercised a powerful influence over statesmen guiding Western policy. On one hand, their analysis of the intentions and aims of the Third Reich minimized the threat of Nazi ideology. On the other hand, from 1935 to 1938 their military advisers wildly exaggerated Germany's capabilities on the battlefield, a misjudgment that undermined Allied confidence and buttressed a policy of appeasement. But in 1939, when British armed forces received substantially greater funding, British military advisers became more optimistic. There is some irony in this change of mood, because before 1939 the German military did not possess the capability to break out from the Reich's constrained position. But 1939 was the year when the Wehrmacht gained significant benefit from its massive rearmament, as well as the looting of Austria and Czechoslovakia. Allied policy, pressed by inflamed anti-Nazi public opinion, could not avoid the implications of the Nazi seizure of Prague. Thus, in unfavorable circumstances the Western powers took a stand over Poland. While the outbreak of World War II was a direct result of Hitler's aggressive policies, the date on which it began reflected as well the choices and mistakes made by Western statesmen, military leaders, and diplomats. The long road to 1 September 1939 was paved with good intentions, but in a world of Hitlers and Stalins, good intentions were not enough. Now only cold steel and the battlefield could defend the interests and hopes of Western nations.

2

THE REVOLUTION
IN MILITARY OPERATIONS

1919–1939

From the perspective of the late twentieth century there is a starkness to the period between 1919 and 1939. Coldly and with malice aforethought, the powers that history would term the Axis (Nazi Germany, Imperial Japan, and Fascist Italy) prepared for war, while the democracies pursued idle dreams. Yet even the German military could not perceive the magnitude of the war their leader would unleash in 1939. To those preparing military forces, the future appeared opaque, while the lessons of the past remained unclear. And when the war began, even the Germans discovered weaknesses in their preparations. Their opponents, the Western powers (Britain and France), were less well prepared, partially due to the constraints placed on rearmament by political leaders, partially as a result of the professional weaknesses of their officer corps. And it would be the military preparations and conceptual thinking that determined much of the outcome in the first clash of arms.

World War I had seen the invention of modern war. A battalion commander on the Western Front in 1918 would have understood the concept of combined arms—the coordinated use of infantry, tanks, artillery, and aircraft—that still framed the conduct of military operations in the Gulf War of 1991. But a battalion commander from 1914 would have barely recognized the battlefields of 1918. In the air and at sea, as on land, much of what formed the conduct of operations in World War II had made its appearance in the war of 1914–1918.

In the air, operations had seen fighter duels, air reconnaissance, close air support of the ground battle, interdiction (attacks on the enemy's lines of supply and communications), and even strategic bombing. Moreover, the air war had taught one unambiguous lesson: without air superiority, all other air operations resulted in unacceptable losses in pilots and aircraft.

Similarly, at sea, the submarine underlined that there were alternatives to the great naval battle strategy advocated by Alfred Thayer Mahan. Even in conventional naval combat, aircraft had gained a role by 1918; in October of that year, British aircraft, flying off the carrier *Glorious*, had attacked targets on land. By summer 1918 tanks had become an integral part of Allied ground operations.

The continuities between 1918 and 1939 are striking; to a historian, the lessons of the Great War pointed unambiguously to the future. Yet what is obvious today was not obvious in 1919. Few at the time, except among the defeated, could imagine that Europe would initiate another world war within two decades. The dark shadows of the Marne, Champagne, Verdun, the Somme, the Isonzo, Passchendaele, and 1918's climactic battles lay across Europe. As F. Scott Fitzgerald's hero noted in *Tender Is the Night:* "See that little stream—we could walk to it in two minutes. It took the British a month to walk to it—a whole empire walking very slowly, dying in front and pushing forward behind . . . No European will ever do that again in this generation . . . This took religion and years of plenty and tremendous sureties and the exact relation that existed between the classes."[1]

Reflecting their societies, most officers could not imagine reliving the horror through which they had so recently passed. Most looked elsewhere for answers and sought to return war to the Napoleonic brilliance they had diligently studied at staff colleges. In the democracies, the political leaders made clear they would not tolerate a replication of the last war. The pain and losses their nations had suffered were too great and the people too weary. The British refused to commit an army to the continent until March 1939, while French politicians argued against offensive capabilities, such as those proposed by Charles de Gaulle.

Success on the battlefield in World War I had depended on tactical, not operational, expertise.* For all General Erich Ludendorff's genius as the architect of tactical reform in the German Army in 1917 and 1918, his comment when asked the goal for the March 1918 offensive—"we will punch a hole in their lines and see what turns up"—speaks volumes for the lack of strategic vision and operational insight in the conduct of war. Effective generalship in World War I had more to do with managing great organizations and supporting tactical and mechanical innovations than with the

*In this volume we define tactics as the means and methods of using weapons on the battlefield to attack or defend against the enemy. We define operations as the use of tactical engagements to achieve larger goals; examples of operations would be exploiting a break in the enemy's front lines or encircling large enemy forces. For further explanations of these and other military terms, see the appendixes.

conduct of operations. The emphasis on management was particularly marked in the British and French armies as the war drew to a close. It reflected their narrow focus on the Western Front. Admittedly, Field Marshal Lord Allenby, the British commander in the Middle East, conducted operations involving sweeping maneuvers that took Jerusalem in 1917 and broke the Turkish armies in 1918. Nevertheless, T. E. Lawrence's adventures and the 1915 debacle at Gallipoli received far more attention in Britain than Allenby's solid operational achievements. And while much of the German Army's exceptional performance in World War II rested on a thorough reading of what had actually happened in the battles on the Western Front, their experiences in the East from 1914 to 1918 focused German attention on the possibilities inherent in using tactical successes to pursue larger goals, such as encircling and destroying enemy forces.

In the interwar period the Soviets displayed the most imagination in thinking about future operational possibilities. Perhaps it was the Red Army's relative independence from the past that allowed thinkers such as M. N. Tuchachevsky and V. K. Triandafillov to imagine mechanized battles conducted over hundreds of kilometers in what they termed "deep battle"—operations waged to wreck the enemy's equilibrium as much as to destroy his army. Deep battle would create greater potential for crippling the enemy's frontline forces by driving deep into his rear areas. The Soviets realized that great states possessed reserves of manpower and materiel that would make single battles, however triumphant, no longer decisive. Instead, armies would have to conduct a series of battles to erode the enemy's strength. However, in 1937 Stalin instigated a devastating purge of the military that not only liquidated much of the Red Army's leadership but attacked any imaginative ideas about warfare that were not associated with the great leader himself. Yet even after the defeats of 1941, enough of the innovative operational thinking remained for the next generation of Soviet military leaders to wage the most impressive ground campaigns of World War II.

For the navies involved in the Great War, the dismal stalemate in the North Sea, broken only by the inconclusive Battle of Jutland in 1916, offered little guidance for thinking about campaigning in the next war. The most imaginative thinking in Germany lay in appreciating the bankruptcy of Grand Admiral Tirpitz's maritime strategy, which had focused all of Germany's resources on creating a great battle fleet. In European waters, the next war seemed to offer only blockade. But in the Pacific, the United States and Japan confronted new logistical and spatial problems just in positioning their fleets to fight. The result, particularly in America, was the development of revolutionary innovations in carrier operations, fleet logistics, and amphibious warfare. World War I had provided the tactical possibilities, some of which, like Gallipoli, were failures, but the requirements in the Pacific demanded that naval planners address fundamentally new issues.

The interwar period saw strides in the conceptualization of tactics and operations, but progress was uneven and planners could rarely predict what would work in the next war and what would not. Some military organizations turned their backs on the past, some distorted the lessons of the past, and only a few made progress in bringing to fruition revolutionary changes. What made World War II so devastating was the tactical improvements that enlarged operational possibilities well beyond anything that had taken place in the last conflict. Improved technology certainly had a role, but intellectual conceptualizations that combined many tactical pieces into complicated operational capabilities were the key element in successful innovation. And at the heart of that intellectual process lay professional military education and honest experimentation.

Ground Forces

Over the course of World War I, constant technological innovation finally broke the territorial deadlock on the Western Front in 1918 and returned maneuver to the battlefield. Crucial to the invention of modern war was the development of indirect fire techniques—the use of artillery to attack and destroy enemy positions not in sight. That innovation allowed artillery—the dominant weapon of World War I—to support the infantry at much greater distances, while suppressing enemy artillery. But these increasingly sophisticated offensive tactics consistently ran up against increasingly sophisticated defensive tactics, leading to continued stalemate. The conceptual breakthrough of 1918 involved rapidly penetrating weak points in the enemy's defenses, while leaving isolated strong points for later. The aim was to disrupt the enemy's defensive scheme through fire and maneuver. All four major combatants on the Western Front were using such tactics by late summer 1918. But when the British added the tank to the equation on 8 August, their forces swept to a devastating victory that Ludendorff characterized as the German Army's "blackest day" of the war.

With the advent of an uneasy peace in 1919, armies on two continents set about preparing for the next war in a climate of uncertainty. For the Germans, the explanation of defeat was not a flawed national strategy but the *Dolchstoß* (stab-in-the-back) legend, which received both official and unofficial support in a massive disinformation campaign sponsored by the Weimar Republic. This campaign argued that the German Army had stood unbroken and undefeated in the field as of November 1918, until the machinations of Jews and Communists, or what Hitler termed the "November criminals," brought about the nation's downfall. Supposedly, the outbreak of revolution in the army's rear areas and on the home front had caused the defeat by denying the front the moral and material support it required. German officers came to believe that the Nazi Party would guarantee the underlying support at home that the *Frontsoldaten* had supposedly lacked in the last war.

But while ordinary German citizens and officers accepted these distortions of military history, the Reichsheer (the German Army) undertook to examine honestly the revolutionary nature of the 1918 battlefield, and therein lay the great danger for Europe. Two factors aided this analysis. The first was the demand of the victorious powers that the Weimar Republic reduce its army to a total of 100,000 men, including an officer corps of no more than 5,000. The second was the appointment of General Hans von Seeckt to oversee the army's downsizing. In reducing the officer corps, Seeckt chose the new leadership from the best men of the general staff, with ruthless disregard for other constituencies, such as war heroes and the nobility. The resulting emphasis on the serious study of the military profession, including its history, and on honest communication between different levels of command ensured that the new officer corps would not repeat the errors of the last war. General staff officers had been central to developing the revolutionary tactical conceptions of 1917 and 1918, and the new German officer corps accepted the values of the general staff in a way that it had not before 1914. Thus, by 1939 the Germans had developed impressively effective tactics and operational concepts based on their thorough study of World War I.

One of the great myths of military history is that military organizations prepare for the next war by studying the last war and that is why they perform badly. In fact, Seeckt established no less than 57 different committees to study the war. As he stressed: "It is absolutely necessary to put the experience of the war in a broad light and collect this experience while the impressions won on the battlefield are still fresh and a major portion of the experienced officers are still in leading positions."[2] Those committees produced the first edition of *Leadership and Battle with Combined Arms* in 1923. The 1933 edition, *Die Truppenführung*, written by Generals Werner von Fritsch and Ludwig Beck (soon to become the army's commander and chief of staff), provided the doctrine for the coming war. A military organization's "doctrine" spells out the conceptual framework that determines how the organization will fight. By 1933 the Germans possessed a military doctrine of combined arms that fully took into account the lessons of the last war.

The most radical aspect of this German approach to war was to reject the concept of hierarchical, top-down leadership on the battlefield. *Die Truppenführung* stated explicitly: "Situations in war are of unlimited variety. They change often and suddenly and only rarely are from the first discernable. Incalculable elements are often of great influence. The independent will of the enemy is pitted against ours. Friction and mistakes are everyday occurrences."[3] The new German approach to combined arms would emphasize surprise, judgment, speed, and exploitation of an enemy's momentary weaknesses.

Thus, in the 1930s German officers understood the principles of mobile, armored war long before they received their first tanks. Fritsch and Beck were the key players in the development of the panzer forces. In 1935 Beck conducted a general staff tour on how a panzer division might be employed, and by the next year the general staff was examining the potential of a panzer army. While the Germans drew heavily from the British armor experiments in the interwar period, tank innovators emphasized that panzer units must have more than armor; they must consist of an integrated force of motorized infantry, artillery, engineers, and signal troops. More important, armored divisions must operate within a combined-arms team, if the enemy's weaknesses were to be rapidly exploited. Thus, the new panzer divisions represented an evolutionary rather than a revolutionary development, by merely extending the basic principles on which the German way of war rested. The panzer forces remained solidly within the army's overall tactical framework.

The bulk of the German Army remained, however, an infantry force, patterned on 1918. This conservatism had several sources. First, the leadership could not risk all its scarce resources on a new, untested form of war. Germany possessed neither the industrial base nor the petroleum reserves to motorize, much less mechanize, more than a small portion of the army. As it was, the great program of rearmament nearly bankrupted the country in the late 1930s and drove Hitler to attack Poland and risk a major war in 1939. But whatever the incomplete mix of technology and equipment, the Wehrmacht went to war in 1939 with a modern doctrine that had prepared its officers to fight a war of maneuver, decentralized authority, and exploitation.

The British Army was not nearly so modern in its outlook, owing to a

number of political and institutional blocks to developing ground forces for
the next war. First, the politicians and voters wholeheartedly rejected any
idea of training an army for the purpose of fighting on the continent. A
wave of antiwar literature heightened the public's bitter disillusionment
with the sacrifices of World War I. Consequently, until February 1939 the
British government refused the army any role beyond policing Britain's
colonies. Even military reformers like Basil Liddell Hart enthusiastically
supported this strategic policy, and it is hard to see where innovative tank
forces might have fit in a defense policy focused on protecting the colonies.
As one army bureaucrat put it: "[There] is, of course, the salient difference
between us and Germany . . . They know what army they will use and,
broadly, how they will use it and can thus prepare . . . in peace for such an
event. In contrast we here do not even know what size of army we are to
contemplate for purposes of supply preparations between now and April
1939."[4]

Nevertheless, under the leadership of the CIGS (chief of the imperial
general staff) Field Marshal Lord Milne (1926–1933), the British carried
out a series of innovative experiments with armor that suggested paths for
future development. Unfortunately, these efforts occurred in isolation from
the rest of the army. Ironically, the Germans may have learned more in the
long run from these experiments than did the British, since they watched
the exercises with great interest and disseminated the results widely.

A real weakness in the British Army lay in the peculiar tribal culture of
its regimental system, in which each regiment was a law unto itself. But
the army's most serious problem was failing to develop a coherent combined-arms doctrine based on a thorough study of the last war. It was
not until 1932 that Milne established a committee to study the lessons of
World War I and to suggest whether those lessons had been incorporated
into the army's manuals and training procedures. Unfortunately, the subsequent CIGS, Archibald Montgomery-Massingberd, suppressed the committee's report because it was too critical of the army's performance.

The story in France is equally sad. The French too failed to study history
carefully and to develop a framework based on a thorough examination of
the issues confronting armies in the interwar period. Wishing to avoid the
level of casualties they had suffered in World War I, the French veered
away from combined-arms concepts altogether, whether based on armor
or more conventional tactics, when thinking about a future conflict. Their
approach to war rested on the so-called methodical battle, aimed at maxi-
mizing firepower and preventing heavy casualties by tightly controlling
the movements of the relatively untrained draftees and reservists who

made up the bulk of the army. Those responsible for developing this doctrine—particularly in the École Supérieure de Guerre (the French War College)—focused their retrospective gaze on a narrow set of battles in 1918 that confirmed what the French military leadership already believed. The French officer corps studied World War I for lessons that reflected credit on the army; it did not study the past to discover unpleasant truths. Moreover, there was a Cartesian tendency toward deductive reasoning in the approach of French military leaders, as well as a willingness to cook the books whenever empirical evidence from the last war or from results of recent military exercises did not agree with current doctrine and practices. The leadership was inclined to press on and "hope" that things would turn out well.

Yet, to understand France's military weakness in the face of the upcoming war, one must look beyond the doctrinal weaknesses of the army to the sheer complacency it exhibited in preparing for war. Its exercises provided little training and even less food for thought. The French trained lackadaisically, while their German opponents prepared with the Teutonic thoroughness that they brought to war.

In contrast with the French Army, the Red Army made a distinct effort in the 1920s to break with the past. Despite the backwardness of Russia's economy in the interwar period, exacerbated by World War I and the civil war, the Soviet state and its military pushed actively to address their difficulties. Enjoying an international climate that represented relatively little threat in the 1920s and that grew even more benign in the early 1930s with the collapse of European defense budgets during the Depression, Stalin embarked on a massive program of industrialization, the Five Year Plan, to provide the Soviet Union with the economic wherewithal to build a great military force.

At the same time, Soviet military thinkers displayed considerable imagination in pushing for innovations in the ground forces. There were, of course, traditionalists who held to the doctrine of mass armies, as in the past. But the Soviets established their first mechanized corps in fall 1932, three years before the first German panzer divisions, and Red Army paratroopers made the first mass jump in the 1936 Soviet maneuvers, again well ahead of the Germans. The weakness of this emerging modern army lay in a lack of education among the bulk of its forces. Nevertheless, by the mid-1930s Soviet industry was already producing vast amounts of materiel. When the Germans invaded in 1941, the Red Army's tank park contained well over 17,000 armored fighting vehicles.

Then in May 1937 Stalin's heavy hand fell on the Red Army, as the political purges that had already savaged the Soviet Union's professional elites arrived at the army's doorstep. Stalin ordered approximately half of his 70,000 officers either shot or sent to the Gulag. The NKVD, the Soviet secret police, liquidated 3 of 5 marshals, 14 of 16 army commanders, 60 of 67 corps commanders, 136 of 199 division commanders, all 11 deputy defense commissars, and all the commanders of military districts—in effect destroying the professional officer corps. The purge of the Red Army eliminated not only most of the competent operational and tactical expertise from the officer corps but it also savaged the ranks of the technical experts, such as the engineering officers, the experts in mobilization, and those who knew how to manage the Soviet Union's primitive rail system to the army's benefit. The Soviet destruction of a reinforced Japanese division at Nomonhan in August 1939 proved that some of the officers who survived the purge were skilled. But most of the Red Army fell into a pattern of mindless obedience. Moreover, Stalin's military advisers drew the same erroneous conclusion from the Spanish Civil War as did the French: armored formations would not play a significant roll in the future. Beginning in August 1939, the Red Army disassembled most of its armored units. It would take the catastrophes of 1941 to awaken the regime to the importance of military competence in a world that the Wehrmacht also inhabited.

If military ineptitude was the driving force behind the future defeat of the French, and political ineptitude was responsible for Soviet defeats, the Italians displayed both military *and* political incompetence. The difficulties of the Italians were not the result of a lack of courage among individuals; Italian dead in World War I had numbered over 600,000. The problem lay with an officer corps that by and large did not take its profession seriously. As one commentator has noted: "The *Duce*'s problem—which admittedly, he was slow to recognize and unable to remedy—lay in what one might term the Italian general staff tradition: Custozza, Lisa, Adua, Caporetto. On those occasions the military . . . distinguished itself by the lack of the sort of diligent study, careful planning, and scrupulous attention to detail which characterized the Germans, and by a tendency to confusion of responsibilities and of incessant intrigue among senior officers."[5]

Italy's strategic vulnerability, economic weaknesses, and lack of natural resources all made it a dubious ally. Although the Italians matched French defense spending over the last half of the 1930s, much of that effort went to support the conquest of Ethiopia in 1935–36 and Franco's struggle to overthrow the Republican government in Spain, neither of which did anything to improve Fascist Italy's strategic situation. The resources Mussolini provided the army were misspent attempting to support a force structure Italy could not afford. The army itself lacked a realistic military doctrine commensurate with its means, and this problem was compounded by sloppy training and exercises. Summing up the Italian approach to war, which was to cost the Axis powers dearly, Marshal Rodolfo Graziani announced in the last prewar meeting of the Italian chiefs of staff: "When the cannon sounds, everything will fall into place automatically."[6]

Separated from their European counterparts and from each other by thousands of miles, the armies of the United States and Japan shared some similarities and some striking contrasts. They certainly suspected that they would eventually fight one another and assumed that a Pacific war would turn on air and naval strength. Neither army had in modern times lost a war, but neither had experienced the full impact of modern war that had so traumatized their European allies. Japan and the United States might have global influence, but the military power they exercised was regional, far away from the mass armies of Europe. Both assumed they would have plenty of time and resources to mobilize a land army before a world crisis arrived at their doorstep.

Stung by what its officers regarded as European duplicity in depriving Japan of its conquests in China and of the opportunity to eliminate Russia from Asian affairs after the Bolshevik Revolution, the Japanese Army prepared for a war to gain control of China and Manchuria in the 1920s. Ultimately, Japanese strategists aimed at breaking the grip of the Europeans and Americans on Asia and the Western Pacific. In 1930 the Japanese Army numbered 200,000 officers and men in seventeen divisions, but the number of men with predraft and reserve military training was approximately four million. Military training was a requirement in secondary schools, technical institutes, and universities. The training combined military skills with nationalist and martial indoctrination. Every Japanese soldier believed that he owed his life to the Emperor and the *yamato*, the chosen people of his homeland.

The chain of command below the Emperor had less clarity. The army (much like the Prussian Army) had three professional leaders in Tokyo: the war minister, the chief of the general staff, and the inspector general of training. Although in theory the Emperor headed an Imperial General Headquarters, the service staffs existed in entirely segregated spheres of the army and the navy. The war minister and the naval ministers had equal status with the chiefs of staff, so it was never entirely clear who was in charge. Moreover, the army had developed strong regional centers of power in the territories occupied by Japan. The Kwantung Army of Manchuria was the best known, but the Formosan and Korean armies also had near-feudal autonomy. The Kwantung Army even had its own auxiliary, the Manchukuo Army, manned by Chinese and Koreans eager to fight the Soviets and their Communist countrymen.

In the 1930s Japan accelerated its defense spending, both in volume of Yen and percentage of public spending and national income, and the Japanese Army modernized its field forces, shifting from rifles to machine guns and artillery pieces to tanks. The weapons it chose often resembled European models but were already a generation behind their Western counterparts. While these weapons were rugged and easily maintained, their most obvious characteristic was their cheapness and simplicity of production.

Supposedly the skill and élan of the Japanese soldier would provide the battlefield superiority his weapons would not. Japanese doctrine stressed night operations, infiltration, ambushes, sniping, camouflage, field fortifications, and advantageous use of terrain. Although their tactics were simple, Japanese commanders sought surprise with high-risk schemes of maneuver. Such training made the Japanese formidable foes when on the defensive, but vulnerable when on the attack. Since the army did not encourage initiative at lower levels, plans that went awry stayed fixed in error and became lethal. Operations proceeded on a logistical shoestring and with few provisions for reserves. Against an inexperienced or demoralized foe, Japanese soldiers would produce astonishing victories, but they would prove less fearsome against seasoned troops.

The experience of World War I shaped the land forces of the United States to a greater degree than it did the Japanese Army. U.S. Army officers who saw the face of battle in France knew that another war between the industrialized states would require far greater mobility and firepower, if land forces were to influence the outcome. General "Black Jack" Pershing, commander of the American Expeditionary Forces in World War I, made sure that his forces carried out almost as extensive an analysis of the fighting in the last war as did the Germans. That effort culminated in the *Field Service Regulation* of 1923, the army's basic doctrinal manual, and explains why the U.S. Army was able to adapt so quickly to the tactical conditions of combat in World War II. At the operational level, however, the army simply translated the French manual in the early 1930s and consequently ran into considerable difficulties in exercising large unit operations.

The United States also needed to lay the foundation of a mass citizen-army in peacetime without conscription. For more than a decade after World War I the War Department had supported all the U.S. Army's components: its regular force, the reserves, the National Guard, and the Army Air Corps. But the Depression of 1929 ended that approach. Concerned about Japanese aggressiveness, two army chiefs of staff, Douglas MacArthur and Malin Craig, shifted investment to the portions of the army they thought could be brought to readiness for immediate war, which meant within eight months. That force might reach 400,000 soldiers, but its budget fell more than $1 billion short of necessary weapons and equipment. MacArthur stressed improving the force through motorization; if the U.S. Army had any claim to world-class expertise, it lay in motor transportation, a reflection of the mechanization of American society. MacArthur also wanted a mobile artillery force, which meant combining trucks, ammunition, and the M2A1 105mm towed howitzer, probably the single most effective weapon fielded by the army in World War II.

Craig took the modernization further by sponsoring the adoption of weapons such as the Garand M-1 semiautomatic rifle, the 105's only challenger as *the* American weapon of the war. The army also had the Browning family of automatic rifles and machine guns, dating from World War I; three very good mortars that ranged from 60mm to 4.2 inches; and, eventually, flame-throwers and anti-tank rocket launchers. The American anti-tank guns, which grew from 37mm to 75mm, had many admirable qualities against all sorts of targets except German tanks, whose armored protection stayed a step ahead throughout the war. American infantry weapons equaled or outclassed the weapons of their foes with the exception of the German light machine gun, the MG42.

The army's considerable innovations for land combat, which also included the streamlining of infantry divisions to three regiments and the pooling of specialized units at corps level, did not include a comparable commitment to mechanized warfare. Part of the problem was simply geopolitical; mechanized forces seemed useless in a Pacific War with Japan, and no other potential American foe required such a high-risk investment. The army had nothing against the tank per se; in fact, the infantry had two tank regiments and wanted more.

Experimentation in mechanized warfare went through three halting stages. The first test of two tank battalions (one commanded by Dwight D. Eisenhower, the other by George S. Patton, Jr.) ended with the abolition of a separate tank corps due to the conservatism of the senior leadership. The second test unit, the Mechanized Experimental Force of 1928–1930, disappeared with MacArthur's decision to allow all the combat arms—the infantry, artillery, and cavalry—to produce motorized units. In 1936, however, Craig allowed the cavalry to form a third experimental force, the 7th Cavalry Brigade (Mechanized), which conducted combined-arms exercises to determine the most effective combination of scout units, tank-armed cavalry, motorized and mechanized infantry, and mobile artillery. The most serious problem was tank design, which stressed *Blitz* (that is, speed for its own sake) rather than *Krieg* (effectiveness in combat). In good cavalry fashion, the armored force, created in 1940, emphasized exploitation and envelopment and minimized tank-infantry teamwork in pitched battle, a costly omission.

Maneuvers conducted throughout the American South in 1940 and 1941 resulted in several promising developments. The army learned that it needed more robust radio communications for every element, down to the infantry platoon. The logisticians found potential gas consumption nothing short of ravenous; a medium tank, for example, gulped four gallons for every mile. The most heartening innovation was the ability of the artillery to adjust and mass fires on unseen targets, either by map analysis or, more importantly, by the use of ground or airborne observers.

All of the War Department's plans, however, underwent dramatic reevaluation after Germany invaded Poland in 1939, then France in 1940, and the Soviet Union in 1941. In summer 1941 the War Department's general staff completed an analysis of the army's needs. In light of its prewar planning and policies, even with the call-up of National Guardsmen and reservists and the initiation of compulsory peacetime military training in 1940, the army's "Victory Program" set staggering goals: a ground army of 6.7 million men organized into 213 divisions (half armored or mechanized) and an army air force of 2.9 million organized into 195 groups of more than 400 flying squadrons, more than half of them bombers. The plans of 1941 set the conditions for the greatest problems the United States Army would face in World War II: what was the appropriate balance between ground and air forces, and how much logistical support would two separate American armies—one in Europe and the other in the Pacific and each embarked on a different strategic quest—require?

Air Forces

World War I provided considerable experience for airmen to mull over, had they been so inclined. Virtually all of the missions that would play crucial roles in World War II—establishment and maintenance of air superiority, close air support of ground troops, reconnaissance, air defense, interdiction, and strategic bombing—had appeared in the Great War. Even more explicitly, air operations had underscored two points. First, air operations of any sort (from support of ground troops to strategic bombing) demanded first and foremost that air superiority be achieved and maintained. Second, aircraft found it difficult to find and hit targets accurately. Yet, at the center of air power theories lay the belief that air power could prevent a repetition of World War I's terrible slaughter. The air theorists of the interwar period, such as the Italian Giulio Douhet, emphasized attacks on an enemy's population centers as the only proper path for air power, one that would bring victory cheaply and easily. Thus, even before technology significantly changed air capabilities, airmen were rejecting the two crucial lessons of the last war as irrelevant.

Sir Hugh Trenchard, the chief of air staff for much of the 1920s, molded the British Royal Air Force's approach to air power in the interwar years. Trenchard had commanded the British Army's Royal Flying Corps on the Western Front for much of World War I. In the 1920s he emerged as an unabashed champion of strategic bombing. Under siege from the other services, who wanted to absorb the RAF, Trenchard preserved its autonomy. But the price was high—a fanatical commitment to the bomber as the sole embodiment of air power. Yet he did foster a group of innovative and creative leaders within his service—some, such as Arthur Harris and Charles Portal, unabashed supporters of strategic bombing but a few, like Hugh Dowding and Arthur Tedder, open to other possibilities.

Well into World War II, RAF leaders were rejecting the possibility of long-range escort fighters not only as unnecessary but also as technologically infeasible. Moreover, despite evidence from both World War I and the interwar period that aircraft had difficulty identifying and hitting targets, RAF leaders clearly believed that enemy populations in cities would be particularly vulnerable to attack and that only a relatively few raids would bring the enemy to his knees. The weight of contrary evidence made little impact on those preparing the bomber force for war against Germany. By 1939, Bomber Command's leadership had still made little significant progress toward developing the navigational and targeting aids on which the strategic bombing of Germany would eventually depend.

There was one bright spot in British air power preparations: the development of the nation's air defenses. That success, vitally important to the maintenance of an Anglo-American presence in the war, fell largely to one man, Air Marshal Hugh Dowding. In the early 1930s he assumed command of the RAF's research and development effort and encouraged experiments in radar as well as setting the specifications for the Hurricane and Spitfire fighter aircraft. In 1937 Dowding lost out in the competition for the position of chief of air staff but took over Fighter Command, a new organization responsible for the air defense of the United Kingdom. There he integrated the technology and weapons he had supported in research and development into the tactics of air interception and created a system to defend British air spaces. The Chamberlain government's prewar decision to support a defensive rather than an offensive air strategy supported Dowding's efforts, an approach the Air Ministry firmly opposed. By 1939 Britain had a functioning air defense system that integrated aircraft, radar, and communications into a coherent whole.

Development of air power in the United States followed a similar path in many respects. As with the British, American air power advocates staked out an ideological position. By the early 1920s, General Billy Mitchell, commander of U.S. air units supporting the St. Mihel offensive in 1918, was proclaiming the need for an independent air force that would render the army and the navy redundant. Mitchell set a passionate tone for the debate that scarred relations among the services until well after World War II. But Mitchell had one substantial difference from Trenchard and Douhet: he believed that the enemy's air force itself must be the first target of any air campaign before air operations could attack other targets on the ground.

The most influential ideas about how to employ air power came from the U.S. Army's Air Corps Tactical School. Its instructors developed a number of interlocking assumptions that were to dominate the thinking of American airmen early in the war. They argued that large formations of heavily armed bombers could fight their way through the enemy's airspace without suffering unacceptable losses. As one text at the school suggested: "Bombardment formations may suffer defeat at the hands of hostile pursuit; but with a properly constituted formation, efficiently flown, these defeats will be the exception rather than the rule."[7] The American position on long-range fighters was that they were simply not needed.

Unlike the British, the Americans did not plan to target civilians; any such approach would have drawn heavy fire from the Congress. Instead, American planners argued that modern economies possessed vital nodes, the destruction of which would have wide-ranging and perhaps catastrophic consequences. They singled out oil, electricity, transportation, ball bearings, and other industries necessary for the successful functioning of a modern war economy. But American airmen failed to foresee either the complexity of the task of attacking an economic system or the strength that modern economies possess.

Given the fact that the air corps was a part of the army, it had to pay lip service to tactical support of the ground forces, but its actual force structure underscored where its priorities lay. In 1935 the army field forces had direct control of only 10 observation squadrons; of the 45 flying squadrons under General Headquarters Air Force (reporting directly to Washington) or overseas air commanders under a theater commander (such as in the Philippines), only 7 were committed to the ground attack mission. The rest of the Army Air Corps (15 pursuit, 15 bombardment, and 7 reconnaissance squadrons) had missions related to bombing enemy industrial sites or invasion fleets or protecting air bases and cities from enemy bombers. Even operations designed to achieve air superiority to protect ground forces received low priority. Moreover, the air corps seemed destined to capture more and more of the War Department's budget. Its share jumped above 10 percent in 1930 to 15 percent in 1935. Attracted by the thrill of flying, higher pay, better living conditions, and quicker advancement, many talented army officers sought aviation duty.

The traditional picture of air power in Germany has depicted the Luftwaffe as the "handmaiden of the army"—as a service uninterested in air missions beyond support for the panzer spearheads. In fact, the Germans attempted to build the Luftwaffe in accordance with the lessons learned from their analysis of what had actually happened in the air war from 1914 through 1918. Despite the fact that the Treaty of Versailles forced the Germans to disband their air units, General Hans von Seeckt, commander of the Reichsheer, kept a substantial number of air officers buried within the army's command structure. These officers were anything but narrow-minded devotees of a handmaiden philosophy.

After the Nazis seized power in January 1933, the Luftwaffe was created under the command of Hermann Göring, the second most powerful man in the Nazi state. The new service had a number of air-minded officers and substantial support from the German population. From the first, some German airmen had urged the Nazi regime to create a strategic bombing force. But in 1934 German industry was in no position to build such a force. Nevertheless, in the prewar period the Luftwaffe developed a broader and more capable bomber force than its competitors. The Luftwaffe's basic doctrinal manual, *Die Luftkriegführung* (Conduct of the Air War), emphasized that the Luftwaffe's main missions would be establishing and maintaining air superiority, close support for the army and navy, interdiction of the battlefield, and bombing attacks on the enemy's industrial power. Throughout the late 1930s, the Germans worked at developing these capabilities and providing the technological support required.

For the Germans, the first target in war would be the enemy's air force, and to handle that mission the Luftwaffe had the world's finest fighter, the Bf 109. As German ground forces moved forward into enemy territory, the Luftwaffe's ground structure would move forward by transport to support an umbrella of air superiority over the army. The Germans even came up with a long-range escort fighter, the Bf 110, although it lacked the speed and maneuverability required to survive against first-class fighters. The Luftwaffe was least capable when called upon to provide close air support. While the Condor Legion developed procedures in Spain for providing close air support on a static battlefield (as along the Meuse in May 1940), the Germans could not provide close air support for mobile forces on a consistent basis until 1941. But unlike the Americans and the British, German airmen were willing to work at providing support for the ground battle before the war.

Even in its strategic bombing capabilities, the Luftwaffe was better prepared than its counterparts in the RAF and the U.S. Army Air Corps. The Germans never assumed that bombers would get through to their targets without fighter support or be able to find, identify, and hit those targets at night or in bad weather. Instead, when reports from Spain confirmed that hitting targets accurately from the air was not going to be an easy matter, the Germans set about solving the problems. By the start of the war, the Luftwaffe's bomber force possessed radio navigation devices, blind-bombing devices, and a pathfinder force—technologies and capabilities that the RAF would not employ until 1942. The Germans also built a significant fleet of medium bombers (1,176 at the outbreak of the war) that could strike the capitals of Central and Western Europe. If that bomber force was insufficient to defeat the British in 1940, it still led every air force in the world at that time. The Luftwaffe's balanced set of capabilities would contribute significantly to the German victories of the first war years.

The Italians' famous theorist of air power, Douhet, became an influential propagandist for strategic bombing in the immediate post–World War I period. Given its poverty, Italy itself could never have developed the technological means and the industrial support for such a campaign, but Mussolini's Fascist regime nevertheless trumpeted Douhet's theories as a means of realizing its vision of Italy as a great power. The size of the Italian military budget—almost equal to the expenditures of Britain from 1933 through 1938—should certainly have prepared the Regia Aeronautica (the Italian Air Force) for a major role in the coming war. But Mussolini gained precious little return for those expenditures. Much of this was due to a series of megalomaniacal foreign policy adventures in Ethiopia and Spain that drained the Italian exchequer. It was not that the Italians were incapable of developing or producing modern aircraft. But significant resources were required, and they were not available because of Mussolini's foreign adventures. The result was that the Italians would go to war in June 1940 with an air force that was even more out of date than the French Air Force.

Though France already had an independent air force, the French confronted the same set of technological and force-structure issues that beset other air forces in the mid-1930s. The industrial base of the French Air Force was no more outdated and obsolete in 1933 than that of the Germans. But whereas the Germans made major investments in their aircraft industry, the opposite was the case with the French. The next generation of aircraft demanded a complete overhaul of design, plant, and production facilities, which the French government refused to make until 1938. Léon Blum's Popular Front government deferred increases in defense expenditures in favor of social and economic reform. The result was that, while the Luftwaffe made the transition to a new generation of aircraft in 1937–38 and the RAF followed their lead the next year, the French began the transition only in late 1939. When they finally did bring first-rate aircraft on line, French squadrons ran into the same pattern of problems with maintenance, accidents, inexperienced crews, and low operationally ready rates (the percentage of aircraft in flyable condition) that had plagued the RAF and the Luftwaffe in the late 1930s. But the French experienced these problems just as the great air battles in the Low Countries erupted in May 1940.

Throughout the interwar period, the Soviets displayed great interest in air power; after all, it was an obvious attribute of modernization. But the Soviet Union's technological base was substantially more primitive than that of the industrialized Western powers. Cooperation with the German military in the last years of the Weimar Republic undoubtedly helped the Soviets more than the Germans, and by the mid-1930s the Soviets were on the way to developing a sophisticated industrial base for air power, especially in regard to factories and engineers.

Then, the NKVD devastated the air force's officer corps, and the resulting paralysis delayed transition to a new generation of aircraft until 1941. When the Wehrmacht struck, the Soviets found themselves in a position similar to that of the French in 1940. The units that were making the transition to new aircraft possessed neither the training nor the maintenance to support those fighters and bombers. The combination of obsolete aircraft, ill-trained pilots, and a late transition to the next generation of aircraft proved even more deadly for the Red Air Force than it had for the French.

The Navies

Widespread innovation in naval technology and tactics between 1919 and 1939 had important implications for the conduct of naval operations in the upcoming conflict. Those new capabilities were emerging as World War I drew to a close. Yet in one area, submarine warfare, navies on both sides displayed an astonishing, almost obdurate, unwillingness to learn from the past. That refusal almost cost the Allies the war and also prevented the Germans from reaping the advantages that the possession of western France provided in 1940. On the other hand, rapid development of carrier and amphibious forces would dominate naval operations in the wide spaces of the Pacific in the years ahead.

With the end of World War I, the Royal Navy remained the dominant navy in the world despite its disappointment at Jutland and the submarine campaign that had almost severed Britain's vital sea lines of communications. Perhaps the most astonishing failure of the interwar period was the British Admiralty's general dismissal of the submarine threat posed by Germany. This was partially due to the arrival of sonar (the attempt to detect submarines by using sound waves) at the war's end, although there was not sufficient time to test its capabilities. Nevertheless, by the 1930s, senior naval leaders were so confident of the Royal Navy's anti-submarine capabilities that they raised little opposition when naval bases on Ireland's west coast were returned to the Irish Free State in early 1938. This confidence was entirely misplaced. The Royal Navy tested its anti-submarine tactics in daylight, in good weather, in limited areas, and for short periods of time. Anti-submarine forces also exercised only to protect fast-moving fleets, not slow-moving convoys.

A second failure of the Royal Navy during the interwar period was in underestimating the importance of aircraft carriers. For most Royal Navy officers, the true measure of naval power remained the battleship. There was some irony in this, because by the end of World War I the British possessed a fleet of 11 primitive carriers—at a time when no other navy in the world possessed a single carrier. The creation of the RAF in 1917 turned the Royal Navy's air assets over to the air force staff, which placed development of carrier aircraft at the bottom of its priorities. Consequently, naval pilots floated between the two services in an uneasy limbo which prevented the emergence of admirals with direct knowledge of air power, and carrier aviation in Britain never received the conceptual push from naval thinkers that was occurring in the United States.

Perhaps the most important ingredient missing from the Royal Navy during the interwar years was an innovator among its senior naval officers with the drive, imagination, and political acumen of William Moffett in the U.S. Navy. Nevertheless, if the Royal Navy in the interwar period did not prepare itself to meet the U-boat or aircraft challenges of the upcoming conflict, it did an outstanding job of training the next war's leaders in the traditions of the eighteenth- and nineteenth-century Royal navies. In the future there would be few of the egregious errors that had marked the Battle of Jutland. That superior leadership allowed the British to hold the Mediterranean against a larger Italian fleet early in the war and eventually, at terrible cost, to master the threat posed by the second great German submarine offensive.

Ironically, given the success of its submarine campaign in World War I, the German Kriegsmarine evinced little interest in a repeat effort throughout the interwar decades. Its focus remained on building a new High Sea Fleet of battleships. After Hitler rose to power in 1933, he gave the navy a blank check, and Admiral Erich Raeder, its commander-in-chief, immediately embarked on an ambitious program of battleship building. As justification, German naval leaders resurrected Tirpitz's pre–World War I aim of building a world-class navy around the battleship. Raeder himself characterized aircraft carriers as "gasoline tankers," while his chief assistant suggested that land-based aircraft could do everything that carrier aircraft could do.

Constrained by dockyard space as well as shortages in raw materials, the Germans finished the first two battle cruisers in 1939 and two battleships in 1941. But it was not a fleet that could challenge the Royal Navy on the surface, while its leadership proved itself anything but imaginative or innovative. The navy's leaders believed that the British had solved the problem of detection and that therefore submarines could serve only as a scouting adjunct to the fleet. By 1939 the Germans possessed only 26 oceangoing submarines; and in the first war year they added only 35, while losing 28 boats—as a direct result of setting a higher priority on surface-unit construction than on submarines.

But in the long run it was German submariners themselves who deserve the blame for their eventual defeat in the Battle of the Atlantic. As early as 1937, Karl Dönitz, leader of the submarine campaign throughout the war, was arguing that U-boats held the potential to sever Britain's sea lines of communications (slocs). But Dönitz's preparations envisioned a U-boat war against Britain's slocs on the 1918 model—a war that had concentrated largely in attacking commerce as it arrived near the British Isles. Dönitz settled on a trim 750-ton boat, a submarine design that was highly maneuverable close to shore but would prove to possess severe limitations when the war on British commerce moved out into the Central Atlantic and even beyond to the coasts of the United States and the Caribbean. In those distant waters the U-boat's small size limited its range and the number of torpedoes it could carry, while its lack of air-conditioning made for nightmarish living conditions.

Equally important was the fact that the Germans appear not to have anticipated the possibilities inherent in the operational conduct of such a war. Both in their prewar preparations as well as in their conduct of U-boat operations, they concentrated on tactical and technological issues. They had little sense of the possibilities open to British defensive forces in the wide-open spaces of the Atlantic, the need for clear operational intelligence, the requirement for air support, and the dangers that air power might pose for a submarine campaign. Thus, the Germans devised skillful tactics but failed to come to grips with the wider operational issues. In the end, it would be those larger issues, particularly the use of intelligence and code breaking by their British opponents, that would defeat the U-boat.

In number of warships and tonnage, the Imperial Japanese Navy ranked third only to the U.S. Navy and Royal Navy in 1941. It exceeded both in torpedo range and destructiveness and in the techniques of night fighting. Modeling itself on the Royal Navy, the Imperial Japanese Navy had a heritage of victory as well as a high standard in gunnery, ship design, and seamanship. Its officer corps were members of the most cosmopolitan, westernized, and technologically advanced segment of Japanese society; and 80 percent of the enlisted force were volunteers whose superior qualifications had allowed them to escape army service. In 1941 the navy numbered approximately 311,000 officers and men for a force of 391 commissioned warships and auxiliaries. Almost two-thirds of its personnel had seagoing assignments. The problem with having such a small, elite corps was that it could not expand rapidly in wartime without significantly downgrading its standards for personnel and hence losing efficiency.

No group was more elite than naval aviators, the Sea Eagles, who numbered 3,500. Astonishingly, in their training plans for war the Japanese anticipated adding only several hundred new pilots a year despite their own estimates that wartime needs could reach 15,000. When Japan withdrew from the Washington Treaties of 1922 that limited naval armaments, the navy started a measured shipbuilding program to bring it abreast of the U.S. Navy in fleet modernity and fighting power by the early 1940s. In addition, the Japanese began an emergency program of base development and fortification, formerly proscribed, centered on Truk and Palau in the Carolines, with subsidiary bases in the Marianas (Saipan and Tinian) and the Marshalls. These bases lay astride the direct route from Hawaii to the Philippines and provided sites for forward operations by submarines and reconnaissance aircraft as well as fleet support.

Whatever its success in drawing closer to the American fleet strength in the late 1930s, the Japanese Navy rested upon a fragile industrial foundation that could not sustain a protracted war, especially if scarce raw materials and limited skilled manpower had to be shared with the army. This weakness would prove deadly in a contest with the United States. By the time Pearl Harbor was attacked, the U.S. Navy had 10 new battleships and 11 large carriers under construction, thanks to programs designed to expand and modernize the American fleet. After Pearl Harbor, the Japanese added 171 major surface combatants to the fleet, 88 of which were under construction in 1941, but the United States added 500. The Japanese Navy expanded to 1.7 million men, but the U.S. Navy grew to 3.4 million. The Japanese fleet's air arm could not keep pace, either. It never lacked for aircraft, but it could not match American naval aviation in numbers of either aircraft or pilots.

Although the Japanese Navy thought it had stockpiled a two-year supply of oil for wartime operations, its consumption rates and losses produced a fuel shortage for ships and aircraft after little more than a year of war. More oil had to come from the Dutch East Indies, but the navy, which controlled merchant marine operations in wartime, failed to make adequate preparations to protect Japan's merchant fleet, especially oil tankers, from American submarines. Japan started the war with a merchant fleet of approximately 6 million tons, one of the most modern in the world. But merchant tonnage dropped rapidly from the outset of war, and after the U.S. submarine force solved a number of technological difficulties having to do with its torpedoes in summer 1943, Japan's merchant marine suffered a precipitous collapse. The Japanese exacerbated their logistical problems in combat by providing insufficient land-based air cover and surface escorts for supply ships and transports, thus making uncertain night operations imperative.

A dispassionate analysis of the U.S. Navy by any of its potential opponents and allies in the 1930s would have recognized obvious weaknesses in ship numbers, training, and personnel but would have acknowledged that it possessed a solid foundation for conducting a two-ocean war, provided it received the necessary resources. Like its potential adversary, the navy envisioned a future naval campaign waged across the distances of the Pacific by forces capable of fighting on, above, and under the sea.

A separate service within the Navy Department, the U.S. Marine Corps embraced an entirely new role in naval planning. Marines organized and trained exclusively for the mission of seizing enemy naval bases, which the navy could then convert into advanced bases for the fleet and for land-based aviation. By 1941, war plans even suggested army air force strategic bombers might use some of these bases to attack the Home Islands of Japan.

Working together, the navy and Marine Corps carried out an extraordinary set of innovations in the interwar period in the two areas of carrier and amphibious warfare. The Naval War College in Newport, Rhode Island, under Admiral William Sims conducted war games to test the possibilities of carrier warfare even before the U.S. Navy possessed a single carrier. The appointment of Admiral William Moffett to head up the Bureau of Aeronautics (BuAer) added an individual with drive, ambition, and imagination to develop the navy's fleet of air carriers. Congress encouraged innovation by legislating that only aviators could command naval air bases and carriers; these assignments were considered the equivalent of battleship command and thus crucial for promotion to admiral. This legislation guaranteed that admirals with aviation backgrounds would constitute an increasingly powerful lobby in the navy.

By the early 1920s, Newport's war games had indicated that carrier air power was most effective when the attacking aircraft were flown in massed formations. That in turn led to the realization that the number of aircraft available on carriers would be essential to their combat effectiveness. Experiments in the fleet aimed to maximize the number of aircraft available. Crash barriers, arresting hooks, and a number of other technological innovations cut down on the space required for the rapid launch and recovery of aircraft and enabled a considerable increase in the numbers of aircraft that U.S. carriers could deploy. By 1929 the *Saratoga* boasted a deck park of over 100 aircraft—a number simply inconceivable to Royal Navy officers. Experiments also resulted in larger carrier size.

These innovations in U.S. carriers had unintended spin-offs. While in the 1920s in-line engines appeared to offer greater power than radial engines, the navy discovered that radial engines were easier to service on the pitching decks of carriers, even large carriers. The development of radial-engined aircraft for the U.S. Navy (which, unlike the Royal Navy, had control of its own aircraft procurement) influenced the development of radial engines for U.S. civilian passenger aircraft, leading to the DC-2 and DC-3. The civilian manufacturers then transferred that technology into engine designs for Army Air Corps bombers and fighters. The army's B-17, the B-24, the B-29, the P-47, as well as navy aircraft such as the Hellcat and the Corsair, all possessed radial engines—a considerable advantage in maintainability over their European counterparts.

Innovations in amphibious warfare resulted from the U.S. Marine Corps' struggle to survive and grow in a defense environment where benign neglect from the navy was the best they could hope for, and active hostility from the army was what they usually got. In the Pacific, where distances were enormous, defended islands had to be attacked and seized to serve as bases for future operations. John Lejeune, commandant of the Marine Corps in the early 1920s, first pushed the development of the corps as an amphibious assault force. With the harsh realities of the Depression threatening the corps' very existence, its Schools at Quantico shut down in 1931 to write the first draft of what eventually became *The Tentative Manual for Landing Operations* of 1934. From that doctrinal start came a series of fleet landing exercises, beginning in 1935, which clarified the problems involved in ship-to-shore movement and in supporting ground forces engaged in fighting once ashore. Throughout this period, army leaders remained skeptical about the possibilities of amphibious warfare; only the strategic realities of 1942 would bring the army around.

As a signatory to the Washington arms limitation treaty in 1922, the United States agreed to tonnage limitations and numbers and characteristics of warships that essentially froze the navy for more than a decade. In the 1920s Congress proved unwilling to build up to those reduced numbers. But fear of Japanese expansion after 1931 changed congressional attitudes toward appropriations for shipbuilding. At first shipbuilding focused on cruisers, but in 1933 and 1934 Congress approved plans to build as many vessels as the treaty would allow, which meant construction of 134 new warships, including 8 battleships, 3 carriers, 8 cruisers, and 71 destroyers. By 1938 when Japan went to war with China, Congress had passed the Fleet Expansion Act, which abandoned treaty limitations and set a goal of a "Navy Second to None" within ten years. This $1.1 billion program authorized 3 battleships, 2 carriers, 9 cruisers, and 23 destroyers. The German invasion of France in 1940 resulted in Congress's passing another naval bill, this one aimed to double the navy's tonnage with 9 more battleships, 11 carriers, and 44 cruisers. Not all of the battleships were built, but all of the carriers and cruisers were.

Although the U.S. Navy remained uncertain about the exact role of carrier aircraft, which could either protect the fleet from air attack or go on the offense to attack enemy warships with bombs and torpedoes, it sought and built a well-trained and tactically effective aviation force, even if its operational aircraft in 1941 could not match similar Japanese models. The Navy Expansion Act of 1938 and the Two Ocean Navy Act of 1940 laid the foundation for a naval fleet air arm of 8,000 pilots and 15,000 modern aircraft, most of them earmarked for deployment on carriers. By the time of the attack on Pearl Harbor, naval aviation had 6,750 pilots and 5,260 aircraft. In the annual fleet landing exercises of the late 1930s, the navy's carrier admirals proved the offensive potential of aerial attack from the sea on warships and land bases, including a mock attack on Pearl Harbor. Senior officers wedded to their battleships remained skeptical about the effectiveness of air power under nighttime and foul-weather conditions, as well they should have, but even they approved the mass armament of warships with anti-aircraft guns and the development of radar not only for gunnery but also for air defense.

Despite this massive buildup, even as late as December 1941 the U.S. Navy was not ready for war. A major Navy Department assessment in 1938, and updated each year thereafter, identified serious weakness: undermanning, poor training due to a lack of ammunition and fuel, too few ships in the "fleet train," undeveloped naval bases outside the continental United States, obsolete ship types and aircraft, and too few ships and landing aircraft for the Fleet Marine Force. The board of admirals who conducted the study could not gauge other problems, such as a peacetime attitude toward military training that minimized risk and learning, unknown defects in the torpedoes used throughout the fleet, and the slow development of radar for ships and air operations. Furthermore, the U.S. Navy was ill-prepared, both tactically and operationally, for war against any power other than Japan. Planning for a second war against U-boats which the Navy might eventually have to fight in the Atlantic suffered from institutional neglect, an unwarranted confidence in the Royal Navy, and a failure to appreciate the demands of convoy protection and offensive anti-submarine warfare.

The U.S. Navy's most likely enemy was also its most challenging. In fleet exercises, the classrooms of the Naval War College, and the offices of the Naval Department, a generation of U.S. naval officers thought long and hard about what would be required to defeat Japan. Reflecting on this mental preparation after the war, Admiral Chester W. Nimitz, the senior commander in the Pacific, testified that only the attacks by *kamikazes*—suicide aircraft that simply crashed into their victims—surprised him and his colleagues. With some exceptions, such as the pitiful performance of American torpedoes, submarine commanders, and night-fighting warships, Nimitz's view is credible.

Conclusion

In the interwar period, military organizations on three continents worked out the operational possibilities presented by the tactical and technological adaptations of World War I. To succeed at this demanding task, combat theoreticians needed a clear understanding of what had happened in the last war and why. Whenever military institutions and innovators attempted to jump into the future with little regard for the historical record, their efforts proved to be dangerously misleading.

Innovation demanded military organizations that could translate ideas and concepts into reality through hard, unremitting training and work on the exercise fields. Here the contrast between the French and German armies is significant. Both armies embarked on war in 1939 with considerable weaknesses in the training and preparation of not only their reserve units but their regular units as well. The Germans recognized those weaknesses and, through a ruthless training program of six days a week, twelve hours per day, they corrected those deficiencies. The French did not.

There was, however, an obverse to the combat excellence of the German Army. Their almost exclusive focus on the battlefield led German generals to minimize the importance of strategy, to believe naively that logistics would take care of themselves and that intelligence was only of value in the immediate help it could provide combat units. In 1935 the Luftwaffe produced one of the most impressive doctrinal manuals on air war ever written, but at the end of the first part dealing with combat operations, the manual states that the sections dealing with intelligence and logistics had yet to be written. They never were.

The war broke out in Poland in September 1939 at a time when the military forces of the opposing sides were still struggling with the lessons of the last war. Admittedly, the Germans held a considerable lead in translating concepts into capabilities, and their successes in the war's first years allowed them to extend that advantage. Nevertheless, their inability to understand the need for balance between means and ends, as evidenced by their obliviousness to the importance of intelligence and logistics, would eventually impose a heavy penalty.

Meanwhile, the military organizations of their opponents—the nations that would become the Allied powers—embarked on the war mentally and physically unprepared for the conflict. As a result, Allied soldiers, airmen, sailors, and marines, as well as the civilians on the home front who supported them, would pay a terrible price to achieve victory in the end.

3

GERMAN DESIGNS

1939–1940

By spring 1939 Hitler had assembled the military organization and senior generals with whom he would fight the opening campaigns of World War II. In early 1938, after the Fritsch-Blomberg purge, he had replaced the old War Ministry with a personal staff. He had given this new organization the imposing title of Oberkommando der Wehrmacht (OKW, or armed forces high command) and appointed the obtusely loyal General Wilhelm Keitel as its head. But the OKW had at this time no command function, nor did it provide any guidance to the services, unless at Hitler's direction. Thus, there was no headquarters in the German command structure charged with strategy or the coordination of the various service efforts—a state of affairs that accorded with both Hitler's inclination and the proclivities of the services.

In effect, only Hitler would determine the strategy and provide the guidance for the larger framework within which the military operations of the three services would fit. Directly under Hitler, then, were the Oberkommando des Heeres (OKH, or army high command), the Oberkommando der Kriegsmarine (OKM, or navy high command), and Oberkommando der Luftwaffe (OKL, or air force high command). The three service chiefs, Generaloberst (Colonel General) Walther von Brauchitsch for the army, Admiral Erich Raeder for the navy, and Field Marshal Hermann Göring for the Luftwaffe, jealously guarded their own prerogatives and displayed little inclination to cooperate.

The army remained the dominant service. Brauchitsch regarded himself as a troop leader and was clearly happiest when visiting combat units. He was already firmly within Hitler's grasp; the Führer had bought him out of an unhappy marriage and provided the financial support to make possible his new marriage to a fanatical Nazi. On the few occasions when he argued with his master, the result was usually a complete collapse before the Führer's ire. The chief of staff of the German Army, General Franz Halder, a bookish Catholic Bavarian, talked much after the war about his resistance to the Nazi regime, but he provided Hitler with competent and often imaginative military advice in the early war years.

The other two service chiefs could not have been more different. Göring had served as a fighter pilot in the last war; in the Nazi Party's struggle for power he had provided a crucial bridge to the political elites of the Weimar Republic. Underneath his bonhomie, he proved to be one of the Third Reich's most ruthless and murderous political barons. A major patron of the Luftwaffe's buildup, Göring retained the outlook of a fighter pilot and never gained the wider logistical and technological perspectives so necessary for command of an air force in the 1940s. A drug addict since his wounding in the Munich beer-hall putsch of 1923, when Hitler had attempted to overthrow the Weimar Republic, Göring's attention span and competence were already in decline as the war broke out. Raeder, by contrast, was one of the most conservative naval officers of his time. This did not prevent him from making the navy as avidly supportive of Nazism as the Luftwaffe, but his strategic conceptions for the German Navy were the least innovative of any of the German military leaders.

The Campaign Against Poland

The Anglo-French guarantee of Poland's independence in late March 1939 had infuriated Hitler and led him to decide to eliminate the Poles by military action the following September. Since a campaign against Poland would be largely an army matter, the OKH assumed responsibility for the planning of operations in the coming campaign. Halder threw himself and his staff into the project in early April; he certainly indicated his enthusiasm for a war against Poland to a number of senior officers at the same time, while entirely discounting the possibility of intervention by the Western powers. What is astonishing is that no one—neither Hitler, Brauchitsch, Göring, nor Halder—raised the issue of what long-range plans the Wehrmacht should make in case the Western powers declared war.

The initial concept for the attack on Poland involved two massive blows: the most powerful, by Army Group South, under Generaloberst Gerd von Rundstedt, would drive northwestward from Silesia toward Warsaw. Army Group North would close the Polish Corridor—the strip of territory separating Pomerania from East Prussia—and then swing southeast behind the Polish capital. Three armies were concentrated in Army Group South.

Eighth and Fourteenth Armies would cover the flanks of Tenth Army, which controlled a substantial portion of Germany's mechanized and motorized divisions. The Tenth would destroy the Polish Army in front of the Vistula River and prevent a prolonged resistance in the depths of the country. In the north, Army Group North's Third and Fourth Armies would cross the Polish Corridor and advance directly on Warsaw. Generaloberst Fedor von Bock, commander of Army Group North, argued, however, that Fourth Army's mechanized divisions should conduct a drive deep behind Warsaw after crossing East Prussia. The OKH eventually acquiesced.

Underlying the German plans ran the recurring theme that the Wehrmacht must execute operations with speed and ruthlessness. On the strategic level, this approach reflected Hitler's hope that quick military success would deter Britain and France from intervention. On the operational level, it underscored the German philosophy of war, one that aimed at destroying the Polish equilibrium at the start and, by the tempo of operations, ensuring the Poles would not recover.

In 1939 the Germans had not yet fully evolved the concept of *Blitzkrieg*— "lightning war." No panzer army existed yet, and the Luftwaffe was hardly a player in helping the ground forces advance. There was no headquarters responsible for coordinating the actions of the three services during the campaign. Luftwaffe plans called for a massive strategic bombing attack on Warsaw at the outset. This plan was aborted because of bad weather over Warsaw on 1 September, but direct support for the army remained at the bottom of the Luftwaffe's priorities. While the Germans devoted some resources to close air support, the only strategy the Luftwaffe and army had worked out was a coordination system for air support of ground attacks on static defense systems. Outside of these operations, neither service possessed the necessary communications, tactical doctrine, or practical experience to provide close air support for rapidly moving mobile forces. In 1939 and 1940 the tank-Stuka dive-bomber team existed only in Goebbels's imagination and Allied nightmares. The first experiments in such cooperation finally took place in April 1940, too late to support the army's mobile operations in Poland or subsequent operations against the French.

The deployment against Poland revealed significant improvements in training and readiness since the crisis of fall 1938. The Germans assembled approximately 54 divisions against Poland, all better armed than the 37 divisions concentrated against Czechoslovakia in September 1938. Six were panzer divisions, four were light divisions, and four were motorized infantry divisions. The rest were conventional World War I–style infantry divisions that marched to battle on foot and whose artillery and logistics were drawn by horse. Army Group North consisted of 630,000 soldiers; Army Group South, 886,000. Tenth Army contained two panzer, three light, and two motorized infantry divisions (in three corps) for the attack on Warsaw, while Fourteenth Army possessed one light and two panzer divisions for a push against Cracow in southern Poland. In the north, 10th Panzer Division remained in reserve, while General Heinz Guderian's XIX Panzer Corps controlled one panzer and two motorized infantry divisions for the drive across the Polish Corridor and the swing behind Warsaw. The Germans skillfully disguised the deployments, so that the Poles never picked up the start date.

The three most important commanders in the attack on Poland would be Rundstedt, Bock, and Generaloberst Walter von Reichenau, commander of the Tenth Army. Rundstedt was already old for a senior German military leader but was highly respected for his competence. Despite his postwar claims of having been uninterested in politics, he would loyally serve Hitler and the Nazi regime to the bitter end. Bock possessed a more acerbic personality, which explains why his career would terminate in summer 1942. He was particularly sharp with those he suspected of stepping beyond the bounds of "proper" behavior. During the march into Austria he had chewed Guderian out for the unmilitary state of his vehicles, many of which were bedecked with flowers. Reichenau was considerably younger than Rundstedt and Bock and was an overt, enthusiastic supporter of the Nazis. In the first years of the Third Reich, Reichenau, as Blomberg's chief subordinate, had done much to bring the army under the regime's control. In summer 1941 he would issue a proclamation to his troops that underlined his complete support for the regime's war of extermination against the Jews. As the Tenth Army commander, Reichenau showed himself to be an imaginative and driving commander at the operational level. In fact, all three of these officers, as well as most of their colleagues, were masters of their profession, at least on the battlefields of Central Europe.

By early August the Poles had recognized the outline of German deployments and had figured out where the Wehrmacht's drives might develop, but they were completely unprepared for the speed of German operations. Poland was, in fact, in an impossible position. Unlike Czechoslovakia, it possessed no natural borders. Its most important industrial region lay immediately adjacent to Germany, which surrounded Poland on three sides. In the east the Soviets were at best hostile. And the relative flatness of Polish terrain was ideal for mobile operations.

The Polish Army of 1939 consisted of 30 active divisions, 11 independent cavalry brigades, and 2 mechanized brigades. A further 9 reserve divisions would become available after mobilization. Overall, the Poles could put well over 1 million men in the field. Unlike the Czechs, the Poles maintained regular units on a reduced scale, which necessitated mobilization if active duty units were to reach full strength. Polish noncommissioned officers (NCOs) were well-trained, tough, and highly motivated, although too few in number. The quality of commissioned officers, however, varied widely. In addition to these problems, the Polish Army suffered from serious deficiencies in equipment; the Germans held considerable advantages in communications, heavy artillery, and fire support weapons, as well as logistics. Moreover, the Poles possessed no equivalent to the German mechanized forces, while their infantry lacked training, weapons, support, and doctrine for mobile operations. Completing the disparity, the Polish Air Force numbered only 313 combat aircraft, against the Luftwaffe's 2,085.

But the Poles enjoyed one priceless advantage: by skillful espionage and brilliant mathematical work, they had gained significant insight into the workings of the German Enigma enciphering machine. In summer 1939 they passed that knowledge along to their new allies, the British and French. On the basis of this intelligence, the British began to build their codebreaking effort (codenamed Ultra), which would play a crucial role in winning World War II.

The Poles' stubborn refusal to abandon their industrialized regions close to the German frontier made a difficult situation impossible. A sizeable portion of their forces deployed to defend this territory, which was for all practical purposes indefensible. Further dimming their prospects was bad timing: the invasion caught the Poles before their mobilization was complete. Here the Western powers were largely at fault. British and French statesmen, still actively attempting to appease the Germans, asked the Poles to delay mobilization so as not to offend Hitler. Domestic economic considerations also played a role in the decision to delay, but the end result was that Poland failed to mobilize until 29 August. When the invasion began on 1 September, only one-third of the Polish Army's units were at full strength. The other regular divisions were still integrating reservists, while reserve divisions were in the first stages of working up.

The German campaign was won in the opening days of the attack. In the face of fierce Polish resistance, clouds of dust, and the inevitable breakdowns that occur among troops exposed to combat for the first time, some of the German spearheads advanced 15 miles on the first day. Fourth Army sliced across the Corridor with Guderian's XIX Panzer Corps in the vanguard. Guderian then crossed East Prussia to join Third Army's drive on Warsaw. Cutting behind the capital, XIX Panzer Corps disrupted what little prospect the Poles had for prolonged resistance behind the Vistula River. In the south, Tenth Army achieved significant success. Reichenau's mechanized and motorized divisions broke through the defenses on their front in Silesia and into the clear, thus achieving operational freedom at the end of the second day. By 6 September Tenth Army's panzer units had destroyed Polish forces lying in front of them and were halfway to Warsaw. Polish divisions to the northwest soon found German troops between them and the capital. In the south, Fourteenth Army occupied Cracow, and Polish forces north of the Carpathians collapsed.

In the air, the Polish Air Force put up serious resistance in the first several days, and Polish pilots proved brave and skilled. But the Luftwaffe hammered the Poles, and German superiority in both the numbers and types of aircraft soon told. Strikes at Polish air fields on 1 September failed to catch the Poles by surprise; they had already deployed their aircraft to satellite fields. But relentless Luftwaffe pressure eventually destroyed the Polish Air Force. Meanwhile, strikes against the railroad system disrupted the ongoing Polish mobilization, while air attacks made it difficult for the Poles to move in the open. Efforts to break out of encirclements along the Bzura River collapsed under bombardment from the air, which so demoralized the defenders that they threw away their weapons.

The breakthroughs and relentless exploitation by German mechanized forces defeated the Poles by the end of the first week of fighting. On 7 September, Marshal Edward Smigly-Rydz, commander of the Polish Army, shifted his headquarters out of Warsaw because of the growing German threat. His decision completed the collapse of the Polish command-and-control system. Desperate attempts to fall back behind the Vistula foundered under continuing German pressure in the air and on the ground, and the Polish high command lost control of the situation. The rapid Polish collapse gave the Soviet Union an excuse to intervene on 17 September. Proclaiming that it was only protecting fraternal populations in Belorussia and the Ukraine, the Red Army crossed Poland's eastern frontier on 17 September. By then the course of the campaign had drawn the Polish Army to the west. German and Soviet armies now had only to round up the remnants of a beaten foe.

Warsaw, however, managed to hold out to the end of September, prompting a Luftwaffe general, Wolfram von Richthofen, to request permission to destroy the city completely, since it was only going to be a customs station. The OKW displayed more restraint; it ordered that the air bombardment eliminate only installations essential for the maintenance of life in the city. At the end of September the defenders of Warsaw surrendered, and Poland's armed forces ceased to exist on Polish territory. But the government went into exile, and its forces would continue to fight at the side of the Allies through to the end of the war. Polish losses were 70,000 killed, 133,000 wounded, and 700,000 taken prisoner; German losses were 11,000 killed, 30,000 wounded, and 3,400 missing in action.

Soviet-Nazi negotiations now established a "final" demarcation line. The initial line, haphazardly sketched in the protocols of the Nazi-Soviet Non-Aggression Pact of August 1939, had placed Lithuania within the German sphere, while some areas with Polish-speaking populations were to go to the Soviets. Alarmed by the invasion of Poland and smarting from the German seizure of Memel in March, the Lithuanians refused German overtures. The Soviets then proposed a change in the division of territory and people. Germany would receive all Polish-speaking territory, while Lithuania would fall within the Soviet sphere. Frustrated by Lithuania's failure to move into the German camp and worried that a division of the Polish population would lead to instability, Hitler agreed to the Soviet proposal. The strategic consequences of this rearrangement would play an important role in the outcome of the German invasion of the Soviet Union in 1941, since Hitler surrendered territory that would have significantly enhanced the Wehrmacht's geographic position. But no one in the German high command questioned the strategic consequences of ceding Lithuania.

From the first day of the war, the Germans embarked on the Führer's ideological program to remake Europe's demography. Cruelties unimagined by Europeans for four centuries descended on Jews and Poles alike, as the deliberate policy of the German government. Hitler demanded no less than the liquidation of the ruling and intellectual classes of Poland so that the Poles would never again challenge their masters. An entry in General Halder's diary, recording Hitler's comments, reads: "*Polish intelligentsia must be prevented from establishing itself as a new governing class.* Low standard of living must be conserved. Cheap slaves."[1]

But mass deportations, executions, and arrests by the Nazis in western and central Poland only matched what Stalin's security forces were doing in the east. A darker fate awaited the Jews. On 30 January 1939, Hitler had proclaimed his intention to punish "world Jewry" for the war he would soon unleash. From the start of the Polish campaign, SS Einsatzgruppen (special action groups) embarked on atrocities against the Jews, although the bulk of their work in 1939 aimed at savaging the Poles. The atrocities were severe enough to upset even the German Army, an organization not normally known for squeamishness. In fact, the senior general in Poland in charge of military administration, General Johannes Blaskowitz, actually complained to Berlin about the SS and the political authorities. If German atrocities in 1939 had yet to reach the horror of 1941, it was only because the Nazi leadership had yet to design an efficient system of extermination. In the occupied territories, German authorities concentrated Jews within restricted ghettos, where starvation, disease, and overwork would soon begin to take their toll.

Dilemmas of Strategy

Hitler's seizure of the remainder of Czechoslovakia in March 1939 had revived the Anglo-French alliance of World War I. Over spring and summer 1939 the two powers struggled to align their strategic and military policies, but underneath a layer of cooperation there remained a core of suspicion caused by the mistakes and carelessness of the past two decades. Popular opinion at home drove both Allied governments to support the Poles, but the prospects of the looming conflict terrified Allied leaders. Since the French were providing the bulk of the ground forces, they would determine the military strategy of the Western powers on the Continent, while the strength of the Royal Navy gave the British the preponderate voice in naval matters. But whereas the strategy of the Third Reich was largely a matter of the idiosyncratic will of one man, an almost infinite number of committees, inter-Allied agencies, and democratic institutions made it practically impossible for the Western powers to agree on any coherent decision or policy that involved action.

At the heart of this inaction-by-default strategy lay the hard fact that British and French politicians had no stomach for war. The German invasion of Poland had brought their worst nightmare to life. Appeasement had failed, but serious military action remained the farthest thing from their minds. At best, the Allied strategy rested on the hope that the Western powers could win by strangling the German economy without having recourse to the battlefield.

Their preferred tool would again be a blockade, an approach that had finally crippled Germany in 1918. Unfortunately for Allied prospects, the only possible way to make blockade effective was to embark on serious military operations that would damage German interests and force the Wehrmacht to fight at a disadvantage. Yet, such a course was precisely the one the Allied leadership, military as well as civilian, refused. In late August 1939, Mussolini had been poised on the brink of honoring his obligations to Nazi Germany. But a massive Anglo-French effort to appease the Italians succeeded, and at the last moment the Italians backed away from war. That successful bit of appeasement robbed Allied forces in the Mediterranean of the opportunity to achieve easy military successes against the Italians, at a time when the Germans were in no position to help.

Similarly, the French refused to undertake action on the Western Front in response to the attack on Poland. Since the Germans had deployed 35 divisions on the *Westwall* by 7 September, the French had little prospect for a major victory. Nevertheless, they could have attacked the Saar, a significant center of industry with nearly 8 percent of Germany's coal production, but did not. The French high command disregarded its prewar pledges to the Poles to attack the Germans in the west; French patrols did not even reach the *Westwall*'s outpost line. In mid-September General Maurice Gamelin, the French Army's commander-in-chief, replied to the Poles' desperate appeals for help by announcing that his army was in "contact" with the Germans, which it was not, while the French Air Force was pinning down much of the Luftwaffe in the west, which it also was not. He remarked to the Polish military attaché that France had thus already fulfilled his promise to launch an offensive within 15 days of mobilization. The French Army, he noted, could do no more.

At the same time he reported to the British that he did not envision heavy casualties in fighting on the Western Front, since the object underlying his operations then in progress (patrolling to the *Westwall*) was to distract the Germans. He had no intention of attacking the enemy's main defenses, let alone the Saar basin. In the end, Gamelin—suave, highly intelligent, a careful cultivator of political contacts—had not an ounce of real soldierly qualities, and this combination of traits was all too typical of Allied political and military leadership in 1939.

Allied strategy in Scandinavia also aided the Germans. Because French iron ore exports from Briey-Longwy stopped as soon as war broke out, the German war economy desperately needed high-grade Swedish ore. In summer that ore moved through the Baltic port of Lulea; in winter, when the Baltic freezes, through the Norwegian port of Narvik. In mid-September 1939, Winston Churchill, back in the British Cabinet as the First Lord of the Admiralty, proposed mining Norwegian territorial waters off Narvik. But he ran into opposition from the Foreign Office and the chiefs of staff. The former argued that such an operation would infringe on the neutral rights of a friendly small power, while the latter argued that such an operation might prevent Norway and Sweden from inviting Allied forces to aid Finland and occupy the ore fields.

The result of these Allied deliberations was *no* action. Military leaders rejected every avenue because of fears of Axis strength and exaggerations of their own weakness. At the same time that Allied leaders rejected moves against Germany, they were considering military measures against the Soviet Union for its invasion of Finland. The French Army's former commander, Maxime Weygand, urged air attacks on Soviet oil fields near Baku.

An RAF raid on the German Navy's base at Wilhelmshafen in December 1939 underlines the futility of the so-called Phoney War. Twenty-four Wellington bombers set out to attack the German fleet. Upon arrival, they discovered one battleship, one heavy cruiser, one light cruiser, and five destroyers. The Wellingtons took photographs, but, because the warships were tied up to docks where there might be civilian workers, the bombers did not drop their bombs. German fighters—less considerate—shot down ten Wellingtons.

Hitler had started the war in the belief that, given Poland's hopeless position and the craven Allied leadership, Britain and France would not intervene. Nevertheless, he was prepared to accept the consequences of a miscalculation. What he failed to anticipate was the shortfall in Soviet economic support and the impact of the Allied blockade on the German war economy. The tonnage and value of German imports fell by approximately 75 percent due to the blockade. Even more dangerous was a drop in fuel stocks between September 1939 and April 1940. In September German fuel reserves had stood at 2.4 million tons; by May they had declined to 1.6 million despite the almost complete absence of military operations. Moreover, fuel shortages over the winter caused serious economic difficulties and hampered military preparations. Supplies of gasoline fell from 300,000 tons in early September to 110,000 in April 1940; diesel fuel from 220,000 to 73,000; and bunker fuel from 350,000 to 255,000. Only supplies of aviation gas remained stable.

The economic situation explains why Hitler demanded in early October 1939 that the Wehrmacht undertake an immediate offensive in the West. An OKW directive of 9 October, written at Hitler's instruction, warned that "the danger in case of a prolonged war is in the difficulty of securing from a limited food and raw-material base [the necessary level of support] for the population while at the same time securing the means for the prosecution of the war."[2] Hitler's demand for an offensive in the west ran into considerable opposition from the generals. The result was a furious row. What lay behind Hitler's urgings was the economic pressure on the Reich. On the other hand, there was some justification in the army's claim that its tactical and operational weaknesses would impinge on its ability to execute a successful western offensive.

Arguments between Hitler and his generals focused entirely on operational and tactical matters. Yet the strategic conception behind Hitler's offensive in fall 1939 was fundamentally flawed, a reflection of the lack of foresight in the launching of the invasion of Poland. On 9 October, Hitler issued Directive No. 6 for the Conduct of the War. There he outlined his territorial goals and suggested his strategic expectations. The offensive would strike "the northern flanks of the Western Front, through Luxembourg, Belgium and Holland . . . at the earliest moment and in the greatest possible strength." Its purpose was "to defeat as much as possible of the French Army and the forces of the Allies fighting at their side." But its territorial goal was "to seize as much of Holland, Belgium, and northern France [as possible], to serve as a base for the successful prosecution of the air and sea war against England and as a wide protective area for the economically vital Ruhr."[3] Significantly, Hitler did not aim at the overthrow of France or its army but stressed the seizure of bases from which the Luftwaffe could prosecute an air and sea campaign against Britain. The Führer's emphasis lay on gaining leverage against the British. He was clearly estimating that the British appeasers would not stand up to hard blows and that France would collapse as soon as Britain crumbled. He suggested as much in a remark to Brauchitsch: "The British will be ready to talk only after a beating . . . We must get at them as quickly as possible."[4]

Halder began OKH planning for a western offensive on the basis of Directive No. 6. Thus, the resulting plan had limited strategic and operational goals: conquest of the Low Countries and northern France to give Germany control of the Channel ports. The plan was not a repetition of the 1914 Schlieffen Plan, which had aimed to destroy France by means of a great envelopment through the Low Countries into northern France that would sweep up the French Army. The OKW made clear from the start that the aim was rather to gain the Channel coast. Army opposition to the offensive was a result not of dissatisfaction with Hitler's strategy but rather of concerns about the combat performance of German troops in Poland. On the surface the Polish campaign had been a stunning success. Yet, the OKH analysis of unit performance revealed a number of weaknesses: the troops had *not* met the army's high standards. While major tactical and operational changes played a considerable role in coming German successes, training and institutional adaptation were equally important.

The searching reexamination and reassessment that the army went through after its victory in Poland suggests why the Wehrmacht would prove so devastating on the battlefield. By the end of October the OKH had gathered together large numbers of after-action reports. These suggested serious weaknesses in infantry and combined-arms training and in officer and NCO initiative and a lack of aggressiveness on the part of German troops under fire. Moreover, cooperation between the Luftwaffe and the army had not been satisfactory after panzer spearheads had broken into the open; on a number of occasions, Luftwaffe aircraft had attacked German armored units advancing through Polish rear areas. On the basis of these reports, the OKH instituted a thorough training program to raise the level of combat proficiency and to inculcate an aggressive spirit into the units preparing the offensive in the west. Over the next six months the German Army trained hard and long to correct its deficiencies.

The arguments between Hitler and his generals thus evolved around the army's readiness. In early November, Brauchitsch suggested to the Führer that the army was in as bad a state as it had been in 1918. Hitler exploded at the implication that National Socialism had not sufficiently motivated German youth; he bitterly reproached the generals, and Brauchitsch in particular, for not doing their job and demanded to know how many death sentences for insubordination army courts-martial had meted out. Thoroughly shaken, the army's commander-in-chief retreated to Zossen, headquarters of the OKH. A series of alerts in November and December moved German troops to jumping-off points in the west, but unsuitable fall weather, appalling even by European standards, resulted in postponements. Nevertheless, not until January, when a set of German plans fell into the hands of the Belgians due to the misflight of a courier aircraft, did Hitler finally postpone the offensive. He thereby allowed his generals four more months to bring the army up to uniformly high standards.

Throughout this period, the OKH abdicated its responsibility for the strategic and political conduct of the war and submitted totally to the Führer's. This abdication carried with it moral connotations as well. The army, in the words of its revered former chief, Fritsch, had come to regard "Hitler as Germany's fate," even though it possessed full knowledge of SS atrocities in Poland. One officer on the operations staff of the OKH wrote his wife in late November 1939: "The wildest fantasy of horror propaganda is nothing to the reality, the organized gangs who murder, rob, and plunder with what is said to be the tolerance of the highest authorities . . . It shames me to be a German!"[5] However, in neither strategic nor moral dimensions did the generals challenge Hitler. Even in the operational and readiness issues that the army regarded as its domain, it found Hitler oblivious to advice.

German Strategy in Scandinavia

While the German leadership squabbled about its next operation, the Soviets expanded their grip in Eastern Europe. NKVD squads terrorized eastern Poland. Lithuania, Latvia, and Estonia received peremptory ultimatums to admit Soviet garrisons "to protect" them from nameless enemies. Stalin then presented the same demands to Finland. The Finns acceded to some of the Soviet claims but refused concessions that placed their independence at risk. Seduced by his own propaganda, Stalin then attacked Finland in late November. Reservists from Leningrad found themselves deployed without the slightest preparations for Arctic warfare. Immediately after initiating hostilities, the Soviets recognized the Democratic Republic of Finland, consisting of a few Finnish Communists living in Moscow who had survived the purges. Obviously, Stalin expected the Finnish workers to welcome the Red Army with open arms.

However, Soviet forces ran into a unified nation, defended by some of the toughest and most skilled winter soldiers in the world. With less than four hours of daylight in southern Finland at year's end, temperatures of $-30°$ F, and violent blizzards, the ill-prepared Red Army met disaster. Attacks on the Mannerheim defensive line in front of the Finnish city of Viipuri collapsed, as did those north of Lake Ladoga. Two columns of Soviet troops, each of corps strength, pushed into central Finland. The northern advance fell back with heavy casualties. Finnish troops isolated, divided, and then destroyed the 16th and 44th Soviet divisions, which made up the southern advance. Along the entire front, the Red Army suffered a humiliating beating.

While these defeats suggested serious defects in the army, they were less representative of the quality of Soviet forces than the August–September 1939 battle of Nomanhan in Outer Mongolia. There, Soviet divisions under General Georgi Zhukov had smashed a reinforced Japanese division. However, on the basis of the disasters in the Winter War, European analysts deemed Soviet capabilities distinctly inferior. Such perceptions by the Germans would have a fateful impact on Nazi preparations for the invasion of the Soviet Union.

The Soviet invasion of Finland outraged the West. The League of Nations expelled the Soviet Union, while Britain and France began inept planning for intervention on Finland's behalf. Even Mussolini sent aircraft to the beleaguered Finns. Stalin, however, had no intention of involving himself in the wider European war, at least not yet. The first order of business was to persuade the Finns that Soviet defeats did not indicate the true balance between the nations. Soviet ground and air forces massed on the Karelian isthmus, and in early February approximately 45 divisions, backed by massive amounts of artillery and 3,000 tanks, battered the Finns back to Viipuri. By early March the Red Army had broken through Finnish lines, and on 13 March 1940 Marshal Carl Mannerheim, the Finnish commander-in-chief, persuaded his government to accept Stalin's territorial demands. Virtually the whole Karelian isthmus fell to the Soviets, while Stalin also gained Finnish territories farther north. But he backed off from demands that threatened Finland's independence; the Democratic Republic of Finland disappeared, and its membership returned to their shabby, fearful existence in Moscow.

Stalin's aggression against Finland upset an area of great economic importance to Germany. Despite considerable sympathy for the Finns among the German people, Hitler adhered to the treaty obligations of the Nazi-Soviet Non-Aggression Pact. The Reich even refused transshipment of Italian aircraft to Finland. Hitler's economic difficulties and hopes for Soviet help obviously played a key role in German policy. But while the two powers struck a grain deal in October 1939, they failed to reach agreement on larger trade issues until mid-February 1940. Although Hitler was annoyed at the Soviet invasion of Finland, he came to the conclusion that Allied intervention in Scandinavia would provide his enemies with control over the essential iron ore fields of northern Sweden. This attitude was precipitated by an incident on 16 February, when naval personnel off British destroyers boarded the German merchant vessel *Altmark,* which had served as supply ship for the pocket battleship *Graf Spee* in an ill-fated raid on British merchant ships in the South Atlantic in fall 1940. The British raid of the *Altmark* in February rescued British seamen that the *Graf Spee* had transferred to the *Altmark.* Since the incident occurred in Norwegian territorial waters, it convinced Hitler that the British would soon violate Norway's neutrality and that Germany must act preemptively.

This inclination was encouraged by the German Navy; since fall 1939, Admiral Raeder had advocated an aggressive policy toward Scandinavia to protect ore shipments and to establish naval bases in the area. However, Raeder was, as usual, not taking the long view. The western campaign, if successful, would provide Germany with the ore fields of northeastern France, as well as a more favorable geographic position, without putting Germany's surface fleet at risk. Moreover, Raeder failed to take into account the possibility that in the long run Norway's occupation might represent a burden to Germany out of all proportion to its strategic advantages.

Once Hitler had decided on the operation, planning proceeded for an attack on Norway in early spring. For virtually the only time in the war, the Germans mounted a joint-service operation, planned by a special staff established by the OKW. Denmark presented no significant difficulties, but Norway, with its long coastline accessible to the British Royal Navy, loomed as a serious problem. The Germans decided to commit their entire navy to transporting the ground forces required to seize Norway's strategic points. A small force of Luftwaffe paratroopers would seize the few air fields located in southern Norway. The battle cruisers *Scharnhorst* and *Gneisenau* would escort ten destroyers (2,000 troops) to Narvik; the heavy cruiser *Hipper* and four destroyers (1,700 troops) would attack Trondheim, while the light cruisers *Köln, Königsberg,* and *Karlsruhe* would strike Bergen (1,900 troops) and Kristiansand (1,100 troops). Finally, the heavy cruiser *Blücher,* the pocket battleship *Lützow,* and the light cruiser *Emden* would seize Oslo (2,000 troops). In addition, the Germans made provision to move supplies for the invading ground forces by merchant vessels. These supply ships left port six days before the scheduled attack in order to reach their destination concurrently with the warships.

The Scandinavian venture, codenamed Weserübung (Operation Weser), represented an enormous gamble. The operation hoped to catch the Royal Navy by surprise so that German forces could seize Norwegian ports and air bases before the British could respond. Control of the air fields would give the Luftwaffe control of the seas off Norway.

German Planning for Operations in the West

Weserübung, however, was to be a mere side show compared with Fall Gelb (Case Yellow)—the attack on Western Europe. The Germans assigned one mountain division, four infantry divisions, and a motorized infantry brigade to Norway, with three additional infantry divisions for Denmark. For Case Yellow no fewer than three army groups with 136 divisions deployed. Thus, while Halder and Brauchitsch did not participate in planning for the invasion of Norway, they were busy enough with Gelb.

The initial plan for the invasion of Western Europe, drawn up by Halder and based on offensive operations by two great army groups, Army Group A and Army Group B, had reflected Hitler's flawed strategy to force Britain out of the war early on. The plan pleased no one, including Hitler. At best, the German forces would seize the Low Countries, but they had little hope of destroying Allied armies with the first blow. Generaloberst Bock's Army Group B, driving through northern Belgium and Holland, might have gained Belgium, Holland, and the Channel ports, but the Germans would have had difficulty in advancing beyond the Somme.

The first alternative strategy came from Army Group A, which was to serve as a flank guard for the advance. General Erich von Manstein, chief of staff for Army Group A, commanded by Generaloberst Rundstedt, suggested moving mechanized forces to his army group to help speed its advance through the Ardennes. But Manstein's suggestion would have allocated only a relatively small portion of the panzer divisions to support that drive. Meanwhile, the initial plan was already undergoing revision. As early as 30 October, Hitler had suggested adding an armored corps to the advance through the Ardennes. By 20 November, Guderian was preparing his XIX Panzer Corps (one motorized infantry and two panzer divisions) to execute an Ardennes move, while a new OKW directive ordered that "all precautions be taken to enable the main weight of the attack to be switched from Army Group B to Army Group A should the disposition of enemy forces at any time suggest that Army Group A could achieve greater success."[6]

Throughout the remainder of 1939, Manstein and Rundstedt pestered the OKH to alter its plan. While Hitler was moving in a similar direction, the OKH could not make major alterations in plans because of the Führer's demand for an immediate offensive. Only the postponement of Gelb in January, owing to severe winter weather and the loss of plans to the Belgians, granted the Germans time for the massive redeployment and replanning that accompanied the shift in emphasis from Army Group B to Army Group A.

February 1940 was the critical time for recasting operational plans. At the highest levels, Halder redirected the emphasis in the German offensive on the Ardennes to a greater extent than Manstein had ever proposed. Yet considerable disagreements occurred between Halder and the panzer commanders as to whether armored forces should cross the Meuse before the infantry divisions closed on the river. In a war game at Koblenz on 7 February, Guderian argued that XIX Panzer Corps cross the Meuse on the fifth day. Halder noted after that meeting that Guderian's proposal made "no sense" and that a concerted attack across the Meuse would be "impossible before the ninth or tenth day of the offensive."[7] At this first discussion of the offensive, Hitler asked Guderian whether the thrust across the Meuse should head for the Channel coast or for Paris. The panzer general answered the Channel coast, but his choice reflected his belief that panzer divisions could cross the Meuse by themselves. Had they not been able to do so before the ninth or tenth day, then obviously Paris would have been the target because Allied reserves would have been deploying from the west and northwest.

Further disagreement over Guderian's proposal to cross the Meuse without waiting for the infantry occurred at a 14 February war game and then at a final game in mid-March. At the latter game, Halder recorded the following judgment: "Decision reserved on further moves after the crossing of the Meuse."[8] Contrary to Allied stereotypes, German planners and commanders agreed to disagree. In effect, there was no resolution of the Halder-Guderian argument; rather, the Germans would wait for events to determine which operational choices to make, depending on the actual situation. Instead of closing out operational possibilities because Halder outranked Guderian, the German planners allowed panzer commanders the latitude to try to make the crossing on their own. If they failed, Army Group A would then switch to the infantry option.

Thus, the new plan developed over a considerable period of time. It reflected a philosophy of operations that aimed at creating possibilities rather than limiting them and at allowing commanders on the scene to take full advantage of every opportunity. The German plan represented a considerable gamble. It rested on a number of assumptions, the failure of any one of which could have resulted in serious difficulties. For the Germans to achieve a decisive victory, the French would have to fail to defend the Ardennes, station weak forces along the Meuse, rush into Belgium with their mobile forces, and possess no reserves to deal with a breakthrough.

Fortunately for the invaders, the Allies played completely into German hands. Over the winter, General Maurice Gamelin, the Allied commander-in-chief, made his forces even more vulnerable to a thrust through the Ardennes by changing his plans and the deployment of Allied forces. The French worked under a number of disadvantages. Their army had no recent military experience, while its tactical and operational concepts were out of date. Not having the practical benefits that the Polish campaign had conferred on the Germans, neither the French nor the British could recognize their weaknesses, much less correct them. Across the Rhine, the Germans were gaining an edge because their training rested on realistic analyses of recent combat.

The Allies also ignored the lessons of Poland. One French general returning from Warsaw reported: "It would be mad not to draw an exact lesson from this pattern and not to pay attention to this warning. The German system consists essentially of making a breach in the front with armor and aircraft, then to throw mechanized and motorized columns into the breach, to beat them down to right and left in order to keep enlarging it."[9] Gamelin, however, had no intention of learning from the defeat of a second-class power. Since the 1930s he had clamped down on debate within the army and consistently played politics with defense policy. But his major contribution to the collapse of 1940 came in his preparations for meeting the German invasion of the west during the Phoney War. For starters, he established his headquarters in the ancient fortress of Vincennes, close to Paris but well removed from the front. There he possessed no radio communications. In January he further isolated himself, while complicating the command structure by establishing Headquarters Land Forces between himself and General Alphonse Georges, who was in charge of the Armies Northeast.

In addition to muddling command and control, Gamelin dominated the operational planning to meet the invasion. French plans envisioned a move by Anglo-French forces into Belgium to help their neighbors; the question was how far forward they should move. By November, Gamelin had decided to move to the Dyle River, which was farther than Georges proposed, but his plan possessed considerable political and military merit. It defended rather than abandoned Brussels; it would support Belgian forces in the first days of fighting; and it would shorten defensive lines by some 70 kilometers. What made Gamelin's planning a disaster was the "Breda" variant. Gamelin took the French central reserve, the Seventh Army, which was ideally positioned to meet a German Ardennes thrust, and moved it out on the far left wing to link up with the Dutch. With that decision he wiped out his central reserve. In every respect, Gamelin would be a major factor in the Allied catastrophe.

Georges at least had some inkling that the Germans had operational alternatives. On 5 December he warned: "There is no doubt that our offensive manoeuvre in Belgium and Holland should be conducted with the caution of not allowing ourselves to commit the major part of our reserves in this part of the theater, in face of a German action which could be nothing more than a diversion. For example, in the event of an attack in force breaking out in the center, on our front between the Meuse and Moselle, we could be deprived of the necessary means for a counterattack."[10]

French intelligence did suggest such a possibility, while the Belgians also had fears that the Germans might move through the Ardennes. Even the French high command never excluded the possibility of a German attack through the region. After all, had not the French Plan XVII of 1914 thrown a portion of the French Army into the Ardennes? What the French did not expect was the speed with which Germans would move. Like some senior German generals, they believed an offensive through the Ardennes would need infantry support to cross the Meuse and therefore would not cross until the tenth day.

The greatest French error lay in the creation of an army whose doctrine lacked flexibility and the capacity to respond quickly. In effect, the French expected the Germans to fight within a framework entirely similar to their

own. Equally important was the fact that the French Army, unlike the
Wehrmacht, failed to train hard for the coming battle. For much of the
Phoney War, French troops labored on constructing fortifications rather
than in hard training for the coming battle.

Conclusion

Thus, while the Germans were planning an attack on the west through the
Ardennes, the French were completing a redeployment that placed the
Allied center of gravity on the Belgian frontier. The best of the French
Army and the highly mobile British Army were set to rush into Belgium—
away from the point where the main thrust of the German offensive would
occur. Moreover, the French Army's weakest troops, mostly reserve divi-
sions formed from older classes, defended the crucial joint between the
Allied left wing and the Maginot Line along the Meuse River in front of the
Ardennes, while there were few reserves to repair or counterattack a German breakthrough.

On the strategic level, an Allied study of April 1940 summed up the impact of the Phoney War on the balance between contending forces: "Hence
the Reich appears to have suffered little wear and tear during the first six
months of the war, and that mainly as the result of the Allied blockade.
Meanwhile it has profited from the interval to perfect the degree of equipment of its land and air forces, to increase the officer strength and complete
the training of its troops, and to add further divisions to those already in
the field."[11] The Germans had survived their severe economic difficulties;
their army had repaired its tactical weaknesses; the OKH had recast its
plans for a western offensive into a risky but brilliant maneuver; the Luftwaffe had re-equipped a number of its squadrons. Allied inactivity simply
stimulated German confidence. In every category, the Allies were worse off
than they had been six months earlier.

4

GERMANY TRIUMPHANT

1940

In April 1940, Neville Chamberlain announced that "Hitler had missed the bus."[1] The prime minister's confidence reflected a hope that the Allied blockade was strangling Germany's economy and winning the war without the terrible blood-letting of World War I. As Chamberlain wrote to his sister that month: "The accumulation of evidence that an attack [in the west] is imminent is formidable . . . and yet I cannot convince myself that it is coming."[2] But Chamberlain had missed all of Hitler's signs. The leader of the Third Reich *would* risk all on a great offensive, and he had tanks, not busses.

On 9 April 1940, the Germans struck at Denmark and Norway. A common frontier with the Reich rendered Denmark defenseless. After a few shots, Danish resistance collapsed; Germany now possessed a stranglehold over the entrance to the Baltic, while Danish air bases brought the Luftwaffe 200 miles closer to Norway. In the Norwegian campaign (Weserübung), air fields and ports were the crucial centers of gravity. Under the general direction of the OKW, the Germans launched their forces against the Norwegian ports of Oslo, Bergen, Trondheim, and Narvik. The German Navy moved the troops, while supposedly empty freighters carried equipment and supplies. The attack forces were to arrive simultaneously at 0500, 9 April, along a coast nearly a thousand miles long; such coordination demanded meticulous planning and considerable luck. The Germans had to seize the ports before the Royal Navy could intervene, as well as capture the Norwegian air fields to provide the Luftwaffe with bases.

Enough went wrong to suggest Weserübung's narrow margin of success. Even before the attack started, the Germans ran into difficulties. On 8 April, the British destroyer *Glowworm* spotted one of the German task forces on its way to Norway; attacked by the heavy cruiser *Hipper,* the *Glow-*

worm not only got off a warning signal but rammed the cruiser and caused substantial damage. The Polish submarine *Orzel* then sank the German transport *Rio de Janeiro*, which was carrying horses, supplies, and support troops to Bergen. Norwegian fishing boats in the area picked up survivors, most still in uniform, who claimed they were on their way to defend Norway from the British. Thus, two vital clues were available: the Germans were in the North Sea, and their target was Norway.

But the British responded by moving to intercept a breakout of the German fleet into the Atlantic. British intelligence based their estimate on a series of flawed assumptions. The Admiralty ordered its ships to disembark troops that were already on board and to move to block the Icelandic passages. The Norwegians, meanwhile, hardly responded at all to the looming invasion. The cabinet met but dithered, while the army's commander had a nervous breakdown. Some forts guarding major harbors were warned, but air fields were not. Mobilization orders went out by post.

Over the night of 8–9 April, German fleet units began arriving at Norwegian ports. At Oslo, a major force led by the heavy cruiser *Blücher* moved up the fiord. Norwegian reservists at the forts guarding the narrows refused, however, to let the ships pass and fired heavy shells and torpedoes, which started massive fires on the *Blücher*. At 0730 the cruiser turned turtle and then sank, carrying with it much of the Gestapo's files on anti-Nazi Norwegians. Because of their uncertainty about their orders, however, these same forts failed to fire on the remaining ships. The convoy withdrew to land its troops lower down the fiord for an advance on Oslo. Continued paralysis in the Norwegian government and quick thinking by an advance party from the German embassy saved the strike against the capital. Informed the navy was in trouble, the Luftwaffe moved up its airborne assault on Oslo's air field. After paratroopers seized the field, the Germans rushed in infantry; by early afternoon they had enough troops to move into Oslo. But the government managed to escape and eventually initiate a movement of national resistance.

At Bergen, the Norwegians damaged the light cruiser *Königsberg*, but the Luftwaffe silenced the coastal defenses. After completing its mission at Kristiansand, the light cruiser *Karlsruhe* was torpedoed and lost. Elsewhere, the Germans ran into little resistance. Near Stravanger, paratroopers seized the most important air field in southern Norway, while at Trondheim and Narvik German forces landed without difficulty. However, at Narvik only one oiler was available, thus doubling the refueling time for the ten destroyers that had carried the invasion force. That delay played a major role in creating the battle in Narvik fiord. Only here did the Royal Navy move directly. Early the next morning Captain B. A. W. Warburton-Lee, following a German picket destroyer up the fiord, led his five destroyers into the harbor. The British surprised five German destroyers in the main harbor, and in the ensuing attack sank the oiler and two destroyers, while damaging another severely and two lightly. On departure, the British lost two destroyers and their commander, who received a Victoria Cross—the only senior Allied commander in the campaign to act with initiative.

Three days later the British returned with the battleship *Warspite* to finish the job. When it was over, the Germans had lost ten destroyers, almost 50 percent of their destroyer force. Warburton-Lee's feat suggests what the British might have achieved by attacking other ports early in the campaign; for example, the *Hipper* and two destroyers lay in Trondheim until late on the 10th. However, the British did not choose this course.

Control of ports and air fields allowed the Wehrmacht to dominate the Norwegian countryside, as it quickly built up its forces. The first day's disaster prevented the Norwegians from mobilizing ground forces that could impede the German advance. Only at Narvik, far removed from Luftwaffe bases, did the Western powers mount an effective counteroffensive. But their efforts were so cautious and their tactical training so inadequate that the attack was delayed until the end of May, and by that time defeats in France quickly forced them to abandon their gains.

The Seekriegsleitung (the German naval high command), however, had lost none of its ability to confuse strategy with bureaucratic interest. In late May, worried that German successes in France and Norway might bring the war to an end before his battle cruisers saw action, Raeder committed the battle cruisers *Scharnhorst* and *Gneisenau* to a raid off Norway's North Cape. The naval staff hoped to gain a success to influence postwar budget debates. The battle cruisers caught and sank the British aircraft carrier *Glorious,* whose captain, a quarrelsome individual, had sailed independently of the main naval forces so that he could attend the court-martial of his chief flying officer in Scapa Flow. But the British destroyer *Acasta* torpedoed the *Scharnhorst.* The *Gneisenau* was later torpedoed as well, so that both battle cruisers would remain in repair docks until December 1940. Since Raeder had already discussed with Hitler on 20 May the possibility of invading Britain, such a waste of German naval strength off the North Cape counts as one of the most egregious naval misjudgments of the war.

Weserübung represented another in the run of German successes in the first two years of the war. But the Norwegian campaign was a damaging undertaking in the short run, and the long-term gains were questionable as well. Virtually the entire surface fleet of the German Navy had been sunk or damaged, so that by mid-June Raeder had only one heavy cruiser, two light cruisers, and four destroyers ready for combat. Moreover, for the remainder of the war Norway tied down substantial Nazi forces; as late as June 1944 when Allied forces came ashore in France, there were nearly half a million German soldiers still in Norway; and at war's end the Germans still had over 300,000 soldiers there. Submarine bases in Norway—one of Raeder's major arguments for the campaign—proved less well-placed than those in western France, while conquest of France's Lorraine ore fields significantly lessened the importance of Swedish iron ore. In the end, Weserübung was the navy's child—it reflected the tactical strengths of that service but also its lack of strategic vision.

Norway's most important benefit for the Allies may have accrued in the political realm. Many British politicians quite correctly attributed the Norwegian defeat to the failure of prewar defense policies, and Chamberlain's optimistic remarks immediately before Hitler's move against Scandinavia only deepened their dissatisfaction. In an early May debate in the House of Commons, the Conservative government lost a substantial portion of its strength. Summing up the anger in the House, Leo Amery quoted Cromwell to the prime minister: "You have sat too long for any good you have been doing. Depart, I say, and let us have done with you. In the name of God go!"[3] The ensuing vote resulted in Chamberlain's resignation and brought Churchill to power on 10 May 1940 at the head of a united Labour-Conservative government.

Attack on the West

The next campaign reflected the plans and designs that the Germans and their opponents had honed over the winter. On 10 May 1940 a devastating series of air and ground attacks opened the attack on the West, Fall Gelb (Case Yellow). None of the ensuing events in that attack possessed at the time the order and clarity that the participants, their champions, and their critics would see in the aftermath of 1940. Generals and combat soldiers made their decisions under great pressures with incomplete information about their own forces and uncertain intelligence about the enemy. And the legacy of the past weighed on every decision.

The Germans aimed at nothing less than France's overthrow and the destruction of Britain's continental influence. Holland was an integral objective of the campaign, for the shift in operational emphasis from Army Group B and the Low Countries to Army Group A and the Ardennes made a German success in Holland essential if Germany was to keep the atten-

GERMAN INVASION OF THE WEST
May 1940

→ German advance

━━ German front lines

⋁⋀⋁ Allied main defensive lines

🪂 Paratroop drops

0   50 km
0   50 miles

tion of the Allied high command focused on the northern flank. Under Generaloberst Fedor von Bock's Army Group B, the Eighteenth Army invaded the Netherlands. Its divisions consisted mostly of line infantry, but it did possess one panzer division and one Waffen SS (the armed SS) motorized infantry division. Moreover, the Germans used most of their airborne forces (approximately brigade strength) to seize key bridges leading into "Fortress Holland" (the Dutch fortifications protecting central Holland) and speed the panzers' advance.

The airborne attack had two elements. One force struck the main air fields near The Hague so that the 22nd Airlanding Division could fly in and help seize the capital and government. Paratroopers successfully captured the air fields, and the first waves of Ju-52s flew in reinforcing infantry. But Dutch counterattacks soon drove the Germans off the air fields into nearby villages, where the Luftwaffe paratroopers held out until the surrender. The airborne strike disrupted the Dutch high command and distracted its attention from the dangerous thrust of the 9th Panzer Division. Nonetheless, the cost to the Germans was high; over the course of the campaign, the Luftwaffe lost 213 transports, with a further 240 damaged—over 80 percent of the German air transport force.

The second airborne assault attacked the major bridges leading through the Dutch defensive system. On 10 May paratroopers, supported by infantry, landed by amphibious aircraft and seized the bridges at Rotterdam and over the Maas at Moerdijk and Dordrecht. Over the next two days, 9th Panzer Division linked up with the paratroopers; by 13 May, the Germans had driven through the main Dutch defenses, and panzer units and supporting infantry were across the Maas and approaching Rotterdam. On the evening of the 13th, when the Dutch were close to collapse and Rotterdam was on the brink of surrender, Eighteenth Army demanded that everything be done to break Dutch resistance in the city. In response, the Luftwaffe loosed a major air raid that shattered the city's center, killing over 800 civilians and leaving 80,000 homeless. Threatened by more Luftwaffe attacks, the Dutch surrendered to German forces on 15 May.

The OKH's conception for Fall Gelb depended on the Allies rushing to the defense of Belgium. Thus, Bock's Army Group B in the north was crucial to Army Group A's Ardennes drive in the south. Early on the morning of 10 May, glider-borne infantry captured two of the three bridges across the Albert Canal. In addition, Luftwaffe gliders landed directly on top of Fort Eban Emael, key to Belgium's first-line canal defenses. A state-of-the-art fortification, Eban Emael possessed no defenses against airborne attack. Within hours, 80 German paratroopers, using shaped charges and flame-throwers as well as infantry weapons, had blinded and choked the defenders and knocked the fort out of action. The Belgians counterattacked, but too late. German infantry in assault boats soon consolidated the position.

Eban Emael's swift fall, along with the bridges across the Albert Canal, convinced the French that their assessment of German operational intentions was correct. Generaloberst Walter von Reichenau's Sixth Army, led by Erich Hoepner's XVI Panzer Corps, rolled inexorably toward Allied forces moving into Belgium to take up positions on the Dyle River. Hoepner's move toward the Gembloux Gap in north central Belgium, threatening the Dyle position, also agreed with French preconceptions. Moreover, heavy fighting between XVI Panzer Corps and French mechanized units defending the gap on the 14th cost the French heavy losses (33 percent of the unit's Somua tanks and 66 percent of its Hotchkiss tanks involved in the fight). The battle eliminated these French mechanized units as a possible counterattack force against the growing threat in the south.

Initial attacks by the Luftwaffe aimed at gaining air superiority by attacking Allied bases, depots, and aircraft. Bomber formations, in many cases unescorted, carried much of the burden and paid a heavy price. On 10 May the Germans lost 83 aircraft, including 47 bombers and 25 fighters—the heaviest one-day loss in air action for the Germans in all of 1940. But the Germans created much confusion and considerable damage in Allied rear areas. The Luftwaffe's greatest contribution came in the psychological realm; its attacks furthered the impression that everything and everyone was under attack. The initial Allied air effort was late and overly cautious. Not until 1100 hours did Allied air commanders receive permission to attack German forces moving into Belgium, and then only with the admonition that they were to avoid attacking towns and villages at all costs.

Meanwhile, events farther south along the Meuse unfolded with the seeming inevitability of a Greek tragedy. Yet an analysis of German superiority in doctrine, training, and preparation and of French operational miscalculations in planning and deployment for the campaign does not capture the confusion, fog, and friction of the actual events. The struggle on the banks of the Meuse between 13 and 15 May was a close-run thing. Even Guderian, that eternal booster of German military prowess, as well as his own, characterized the success as "almost a miracle."[4]

The drive to the Meuse consisted of three panzer corps, XV under General Hermann Hoth, XLI under General Georg-Hans Reinhardt, and XIX under Guderian. Panzer Group Kleist, under Generaloberst Ewald von Kleist, controlled the latter two. There were a number of ambiguities involved in the drive. First was the fact that the OKH had remained unconvinced that panzer forces could advance through the Ardennes' heavily wooded terrain with just their organic motorized infantry regiments. Thus, Army Group A allocated only four roads for Guderian's advance; the other four routes in the area were for supporting infantry. The aim was to provide substantial infantry reinforcements should the panzer divisions run into effective French and Belgian resistance in the forests of the Ardennes. Similarly, no one knew whether the panzer divisions would succeed in crossing the Meuse on the fourth or fifth day of the offensive. As did most senior commanders, Halder believed that the panzer force could not make a breakthrough and would have to wait for follow-on infantry to arrive on the Meuse on the ninth or tenth day.

With one small exception, Allied resistance in the Ardennes was uninspired. The fact that two companies of the Belgian Chasseurs Ardennais at Bodange held up 1st Panzer Division for a day (from 0745 to 2015) suggests what Allied delaying forces might have achieved with resolute leadership. A greater potential danger to the Germans was the fact that traffic discipline almost entirely broke down in the Ardennes on 12 May; infantry formations moving southwest crossed the line of advance of the panzers and caused a monumental traffic jam. Thus, Halder was not entirely wrong in expecting that the Ardennes drive might take more than a week to reach the Meuse.

But the French sent their horse cavalry into the Ardennes with no clear mission except to delay what they thought to be insignificant forces. The cavalry then failed to inform higher commanders of the actual strength of German forces in the Ardennes. To compound their failure, they came out of the Ardennes badly shaken on the 12th, and this had a deflating effect on the morale of the infantry and artillery awaiting the German assault. Allied air made some efforts to interfere with the German advance, but an umbrella of Luftwaffe Bf 109 fighters inflicted heavy casualties on unescorted bomber formations. On 10 May, 32 British Fairey Battle light bombers attacked targets in the Ardennes; German fighters shot down 13 and damaged the rest; on the next day, the British could manage only eight sorties into the region and only one bomber limped home. Yet, sporadic air attacks led Guderian to change his headquarters on the 12th and to demand greater Luftwaffe support for his corps. By the evening of 12 May, the three panzer corps were coming up on the Meuse from Sedan to Dinant.

Early in the morning of 13 May, the motorized infantry of Major General Erwin Rommel's 7th Panzer Division attacked across the Meuse. They received no air support and relied on divisional artillery and tanks on the right bank of the Meuse for support. The attacking infantry were immediately in trouble. French machine gun and rifle fire slaughtered the infantry, who were crossing in rubber assault rafts. But Rommel provided the drive to keep the attack going in the face of heavy losses—he was across with the first battalion. By early afternoon his infantry had gained a large enough foothold so that engineers could construct bridges for the tanks to follow. For a short period French armor threatened the bridgehead; but German infantrymen, led by the intrepid Rommel, drove the enemy off with light machine guns. That evening, Rommel would dutifully involve himself in construction of the 7th Panzer Division's bridges across the Meuse. His performance on the banks of the Meuse as engineer, company commander, and division commander all rolled into one was one of the most inspired pieces of generalship of the whole war. By evening, 7th Panzer Division was moving its tanks across the river despite harassing French artillery fire.

Confusion on the other side of the Meuse contributed to Rommel's success. When 7th Panzer struck, the French were replacing the 1st Cavalry Division—which the Germans had chased out of the Ardennes—with the 18th Infantry Division, a unit that had just arrived without anti-tank guns or artillery support. Had the Germans tried to cross later, they might well have failed. Nevertheless, the French had come close to stopping 7th Panzer's crossing. A portion of 5th Panzer Division's infantry had an easier time in crossing. Its troops found a lock across the Meuse that the French had failed either to blow up or to defend, because it fell on the boundary line between two units. Elsewhere, 5th Panzer Division's attempts to cross suffered heavy losses. Once across, its forces came under heavy counterattack from French units on 14 and 15 May, but the battle took much of the pressure off Rommel. Thus, French defenses on the northern flank of the Ardennes fell apart.

By 15 May, Rommel had broken through the French positions and was rolling westward. Over 16 and 17 May, his division drove a thin wedge into French defenses (including 50 miles on the 17th alone) and overwhelmed most of the French 1st Armored Division. Rommel noted about the advance: "A chaos of guns, tanks and military vehicles of all kinds, inextricably entangled with horse-drawn refugee carts, covered the roads and verges . . . The French troops were completely overcome by surprise at our sudden appearance, laid down their arms and marched off to the east beside our column. Nowhere was any resistance attempted. Any enemy tanks we met on the road were put out of action as we drove past. The advance went on without a halt to the west. Hundreds upon hundreds of French troops, with their officers, surrendered at our arrival."[5] In two days, Rommel's division captured 10,000 soldiers, 100 tanks, 30 armored cars, and 27 guns. The divisional war diary ended on 17 May with the entry that its units "had no time to collect large numbers of prisoners and equipment."[6]

Rommel's success entirely disrupted the defensive scheme along the Meuse and enabled Reinhardt's XLI Panzer Corps to cross on the 15th. That corps' lead formation, 6th Panzer Division, had come up on the Meuse at Monthermé but had stuck in the face of determined resistance by the 102nd Fortress Division. On the afternoon of the 13th, its 4th Rifle Regiment pushed a few infantry across despite heavy casualties, but only a trickle of reinforcements followed. Then, on the morning of 14 May, French artillery fire wrecked the footbridge and isolated the small bridgehead. But the collapse to the north and the serious situation in the south led the army commander, the corpulent and slow-witted General André Corap, to order a withdrawal from the Meuse. The 102nd Fortress Division possessed neither the training nor the motorized equipment to execute such a retreat in the face of enemy armor. Once the retreat began, Reinhardt's panzers smashed the 102nd Division and immediately broke out into the open.

The most important breakthrough came at Sedan, where Prussian arms had sealed French defeat in 1870. Guderian's XIX Panzer Corps arrived on the Meuse late on the evening of 12 May and immediately prepared to cross. Guderian is often considered the father of the German armored force, largely through the influence of his postwar memoirs, perhaps the most self-serving by any German general, which is saying a great deal. In fact, he was only one of a number of officers (including Beck) who recognized that mechanized divisions would greatly extend the German Army's ability to exploit a breakthrough. In temperament, Guderian was among the most irascible and truculent of the German generals; in 1943 he would refuse to shake the proffered hand of Field Marshal von Kluge, an unheard-of insult in an army of proud, overweening men. Guderian was also an enthusiastic Nazi whose loyalty to the regime would lead to his appointment as the army's chief of staff in the aftermath of the failed 20 July 1944 coup. As a general, Guderian was a ruthless driver whose willingness to take risks in exploiting a situation was exceeded only by Rommel's.

The French positions defending the Sedan were not held by first-line troops—a situation exacerbated by their lack of training during the winter months. Moreover, the French practice of pulling companies out of the line to work on field fortifications and then returning them to a different sector had created a patchwork defensive scheme in which no regimental or battalion commander had control over a specific sector. No less than 15 different companies from three different regiments were intermixed throughout the Sedan defenses, so that there were no clear lines of authority or responsibility. The defensive scheme was one more example of the extraordinarily poor leadership at the top of the French Army.

The Luftwaffe supported the XIX Corps' attack across the Meuse with a prolonged bombardment of French positions. After the air bombardment, each of XIX's three panzer divisions launched their rifle regiments at 1500 hours (German time) to seize the far bank and high ground beyond; 1st Panzer Division in the center received an additional rifle regiment, Großdeutschland, the army's elite guard unit, while 10th Panzer Division also attacked with two infantry regiments. The traditional arms of artillery, infantry, and engineers, working within German tactical doctrine developed back in spring 1918, executed the penetration and initial exploitation battles.

As with the crossings farther north, Guderian's achievements underscore how slim the German margin of success actually was. West of Sedan, 2nd Panzer Division's assault barely got in the river—only one assault boat out of eight managed the crossing—and there were no prospects of further reinforcement. Not until 1st Panzer's success broke down French defenses did the division move its infantry across at 2200, and it could not complete a bridge for its armor to cross until dawn on the 14th. To the south, 10th Panzer Division had as rough a time. Defensive fire entirely stifled the 69th Infantry Regiment's crossing; the French destroyed 48 of 50 assault rafts with heavy losses. The crossing by 1st Panzer Division's 1st Rifle Regiment at Wadelincourt succeeded only through extraordinary leadership, which not only allowed divisional engineers to begin constructing a bridge but also contributed to Großdeutschland's advance. Thus, the critical success came in the 1st Panzer Division's sector. There, the 1st Rifle Regiment crumbled the entire French defensive system. With added pressure from Großdeutschland, German infantry were on the heights south of the Meuse by early evening, and work on building bridges to bring tanks and artillery across the Meuse accelerated.

French positions along the Meuse need not have collapsed as a result of this success; by evening on the 13th, the Germans had only infantry across. Despite frantic efforts, their engineers did not complete the first bridge until midnight. But the French were already in trouble. Artillery units of the defending 55th Division panicked and ran away almost immediately after the Luftwaffe bombardment. Thus, French infantry facing 1st Panzer Division had no artillery support during the critical fighting, and German engineers working on the bridges in early evening received no harassing fire.

Limited to only infantry battalions, the Germans still kept up relentless pressure. The French responded cautiously and haphazardly, confused by the pace of German attacks. Local commanders planned to launch a counterattack, but the planning process and confusion were such that the attack started late the following morning; by that time it ran into more powerful German forces, and in minutes the French 7th Tank Battalion lost 50 percent of its personnel and 70 percent of its vehicles. The French high command remained largely unaware of the looming threat. Gamelin's headquarters summed up its impression by noting "[overall] impression very good."[7]

Worse was coming. By early morning on 14 May, 1st Panzer Division's tanks were rolling across the pontoon bridges; the lodgment was now three miles wide and four to six miles deep. XIX Panzer Corps had entirely broken through the defenses and stood ready for a deep penetration. Desperate calls went out for Allied air power to attack the bridges across the Meuse, but German fighters and anti-aircraft guns savaged the attackers. The RAF lost 40 of 71 bombers. The attacks did cause some difficulties. XIX Panzer Corps recorded that "completion of the military bridge at Donchery had not yet been carried out owing to heavy flanking artillery fire and long bombing attacks at the bridging point."[8] But Allied losses were so high that their air units could not resume the effort on the 15th.

The 14th of May was clearly the last moment when the French had a chance to slow the breakthrough. Their XXI Corps, consisting of the 3rd Armored and 3rd Motorized Divisions, was available to counterattack; moreover, its commander, General J. A. R. L. Flavigny, had been a leading advocate of armored warfare in the 1930s. But neither he nor his division commanders could prepare the corps for a counterattack on the 14th. Instead, the fighting around Stonne drew some of the 3rd Armored and much of the 3rd Motorized Divisions into a pitched battle, while Flavigny formed a linear defense instead of counterattacking. Flavigny's failure to launch any kind of attack confirmed Guderian's feeling that the French had no substantial reserves available in the area and that he could thus afford to exploit his advantage by turning virtually all of XIX Panzer Corps to the west.

Thus, despite heavy losses, and with the German infantry divisions well back from the Meuse and a possible French counterattack facing him from the southeast, Guderian turned west, creating what soon appeared to be a yawning gap between XIX Panzer Corps and the following infantry divisions. Since the Germans did not have a complete picture of the location of French reserves, the growing gap explains the pressure from senior com-

manders for Guderian to halt and secure his flank before joining Reinhardt's and Hoth's exploitation. In hindsight, Guderian was right, but it
was not obvious at the time. Those German worries underscore the importance of Flavigny's failure to counterattack. Any attack, no matter how unsuccessful, would have forced the Germans to pay attention to their southeastern flank. The French high command lost the one thing it could not
afford to lose: time. But by the evening of 15 May, all three panzer corps
were moving west with nothing to their front, while Flavigny's corps
formed part of the flotsam south of Sedan.

The real explanation for the catastrophe along the Meuse lies in the
quality of German leadership, from generals to NCOs. It has become fash-
ionable these days to believe that battles do not matter, or that isolated historical facts (such as the victories along the Meuse) are of little significance,
a matter of mere facticity, compared to the greater "unseen" social forces
molding our world. The Meuse battlefield between 13 and 15 May would,
however, suggest a different view of the world. A relatively few individuals
wearing field-gray uniforms, in a blood-stained, smashed-up, obscure pro-
vincial town, diverted the flow of history into darker channels. The tired,
weary German infantry who seized the heights behind the Meuse and who
opened the way for the armored thrust to the coast made inevitable the fall
of France, the subsequent invasion of Russia, the Final Solution, and the
collapse of Europe's position in the world. The German victory came peril-
ously close to destroying Western civilization.

Guderian's advance on 16 May reached Marle and Dercy, 55 miles from
Sedan—40 miles that day. Despite his success, he received a second order
to halt; infuriated, he resigned on the spot and reported to Rundstedt. Displaying the German high command's toleration of talented officers, no
matter how truculent their behavior, Guderian's superiors were willing to
work out a compromise that left him in command of his corps but authorized him only to continue a reconnaissance in force. His headquarters remained in place, so that high command could monitor his movements. But
Guderian resumed his drive west; he simply strung signal lines behind to
headquarters, to mislead his superiors about his location.

The problem was that many senior German commanders, including Hitler, were increasingly alarmed by the advance's exposed flanks. Moreover,
the fragile relations between OKW and OKH—never good in the best of
times—were particularly tense. A depressed Halder recorded on 17 May:
"Frightened by his own successes, [Hitler] is afraid to take any chance and
so would rather pull the reins on us."[9]

But events had acquired their own momentum. The three panzer corps sliced through French units desperately scrambling to shore up some kind of front. High over the battlefield, the writer Antoine de Saint Exupéry, serving as an observer and eventually to perish as a fighter pilot in 1944, observed: "In every region through which [the German panzers] have made their lightning sweep, a French Army, even though it seems to be virtually intact, has ceased to be an army. It has been transformed into clotted segments. It has, so to say, coagulated. The armored divisions play the part of a chemical agent precipitating a solution. Where once an organism existed they leave a mere sum of organs whose unity has been destroyed. Between the clots—however combative the clots may have remained—the enemy moves at will. An army, if it is to be effective, must be something other than a numerical sum of its soldiers."[10]

Guderian reached St. Quentin on 18 May, with Reinhardt's and Hoth's corps moving up on his right. Seven armored divisions advanced unopposed toward the Channel. Hoth's corps then turned north to form a flank guard, while the other two corps finished the push to the coast. On 19 May, 1st Panzer Division reached Peronne on the old Somme battlefield. The next day, 2nd Panzer Division claimed it was out of gas. After exchanging pleasantries with its commander, Guderian hustled it down the road to Abbeville. That evening German forces reached the Channel.

Disaster, Reprieve, and Final Collapse

The movement of Anglo-French forces into Belgium proceeded flawlessly. In beautiful spring weather, enthusiastic crowds cheered the troops. Nevertheless, the advance ran into considerable friction with the Belgians, who, afraid to compromise their position of neutrality, had refused staff conversations before 10 May. Even more serious was a cumbersome and ineffective command structure. But above all, the French had completely miscalculated German aims and objectives. On 14 May, General Charles Huntziger, Second Army commander, whose responsibility lay south of Sedan, concluded that the Ardennes thrust represented a German effort to roll up the Maginot Line. He pulled his army back to shield its left flank, a move which took the artillery pressure off the 10th Panzer Division and further expanded the gap through which Guderian's forces were pouring. Gloomy reports flooded in. By 14 May, General Georges, commander of the Armies Northeast, had convinced himself that the front near Sedan had disintegrated. According to a staff officer at a conference that morning, Georges collapsed sobbing.

Corap's Ninth Army was in desperate trouble. In the wreckage, the German tide swamped fresh French units like the 1st and 2nd Armored Divisions, which were still moving to the front. The French First Army commander, General G. H. G. Billotte, took no action despite the collapse on his right; although there were indications that Corap was in trouble on the 14th, Billotte failed to react until the 16th. In Paris, panic spread. Hurrying over to consider the situation, Churchill asked Gamelin where the French reserves were. The generalissimo replied: "Aucune [none]."[11] The French cabinet was still unwilling to fire the dispirited commander-in-chief; Premier Paul Reynaud ordered the army's previous commander, General Maxime Weygand, to return to France from Syria. Not until 19 May did Gamelin act. On 17 May General Charles de Gaulle's Fourth Armored Division had achieved a local success against Guderian's supply columns; that temporary success suggested that counterattacks against the northern and southern flanks of the German advance held possibilities. Gamelin ordered Georges to attempt such a maneuver but underlined his desire not "to intervene in the conduct of the battle now being waged, which is in the hands of the commander-in-chief of the North East Front."[12]

Meanwhile, Reynaud restructured his cabinet and eliminated an old enemy, Daladier, from the Ministry of Defense, while he brought in Clemenceau's ferocious private secretary, Georges Mandel, as minister of the interior. But any stiffening was lost as Marshal Phillipe Pétain returned from Spain to the cabinet. Reynaud finally fired Gamelin. His replacement, Weygand, approved the idea of a counterstroke and, after stating there was not a minute to lose, headed off to take a nap.

The arrival of Guderian at Abbeville sent the Führer into rapture. Nevertheless, OKW and OKH failed to order an advance on the Channel ports until the 21st; thus, they lost a day. Behind the armored wedge, German infantry pounded down the dusty roads of northern France. As German infantry divisions deployed into line on the southern flank, the prospect of an Allied counterstroke faded. Nevertheless, nervousness in the OKW increased in inverse proportion to the danger. Contributing to these fears was the only major counterattack launched by the Allied forces. On 21 May, a patched-together British force of 74 tanks, two territorial infantry battalions, and a motorcycle battalion crashed into 7th Panzer Division and SS Division Totenkopf on the right flank of the German advance. The attack caught the Germans by surprise early in the afternoon and achieved an initial success against supply columns.

But the British advance ran into two pieces of bad luck. Rommel was in the vicinity, and the tanks that struck SS Totenkopf hit that division's anti-tank battalion. By evening the British had stalled, and the surviving tanks retreated. On the battlefield they had achieved little, but their attack had increased German nervousness and would play a major role in the British Army's eventual escape. On the 22nd, a small attack from the French V Corps further reinforced OKW fears.

On 21 May, Weygand arrived in the northern pocket cut off by the German advance to the Channel. He did not talk to Allied commanders together and missed Lord Gort, commander of the British Expeditionary Force (BEF). To add to Allied difficulties, immediately after his discussions with Weygand, General Gaston Billotte, commander of the First Army Group (the Allied left wing), was critically injured in an automobile crash. Weygand does not seem to have grasped the seriousness of the situation, but his failure to meet with Gort led him to suspect that the British were preparing to cut and run.

By now the Germans had moved 10 panzer, 4 motorized infantry, and 2 Waffen SS infantry divisions between Arras and the coast. Guderian's panzer divisions were already moving on the Channel ports, and there was no reason that his tanks could not have pushed on to Dunkirk. Early in the morning of 24 May, both Reinhardt and Guderian had troops across the Aa Canal south of BEF positions. At this point the OKW issued one of the most controversial orders of the war, halting the advance on Dunkirk. In retrospect, it was a serious mistake, but under the circumstances it made sense to many German generals, not just Hitler.

In the campaign thus far, the panzer units had borne the brunt of the fighting, as well as the losses. On 23 May, Kleist, commander of Guderian's and Reinhardt's panzer corps, reported that his divisions were exhausted and could not stand up to a powerful enemy counterattack. Rundstedt was equally worried. In conference with Hitler, he agreed that the push by Army Group A's panzer divisions up the coast should stop and that Bock's infantry should assume responsibility for destroying Allied forces in the pocket. Many German commanders also worried that the campaign had gone too well and that their luck was bound to change. Was there another "miracle of the Marne" waiting? Better then to save the armor and allow the infantry to finish the battle. Moreover, Göring suggested to Hitler that destruction of Allied forces be left to his "Nazi" Luftwaffe. Only Halder and Brauchitsch opposed the halt order. On 26 May, Halder fumed: "In one area they [the OKW] call for a head-on attack against a front retiring in orderly fashion and still possessing its staying power, and elsewhere they freeze the troops . . . when the enemy could be cut into any time."[13]

In one of those rare moments when individuals of little apparent capacity for greatness rise to the occasion in a crisis and affect history's course,

Lord Gort, commander of the BEF, saved the British Army. A guardsman with impeccable social connections, Gort had won a Victoria Cross in World War I and then had risen through the ranks of the officer corps without displaying any special qualifications. Appointed CIGS in December 1937 after the sacking of his predecessor, Gort had proven a disappointment to those who believed he might reform the hidebound army.

When the war broke out, Gort moved over to take command of the British Expeditionary Force. As early as 19 May, Gort warned London that the BEF might have to withdraw from the Continent and that Dunkirk was the most sensible port of embarkation. The War Cabinet was not happy but warned Admiral Bertram Ramsey at Dover to gather vessels for a possible evacuation from ports on the French coast. The breaking point between the British and French came over the night of 23–24 May. With the 5th and 50th British Divisions in untenable positions near Arras, Gort ordered a retreat but neglected to inform General Georges Blanchard, the new commander of the Allied First Army Group. Reynaud and Weygand exploded. French anger at Gort's withdrawal suggests that they were already seeking a scapegoat. Major General Edward Spears, Churchill's liaison to the French, heard one of Blanchard's officers on 25 May blurt out in the French Cabinet that France needed to capitulate. At the same meeting Weygand claimed that it was all madness. France had gone to war with an obsolete army against a modern German Army. That evening the French Cabinet discussed the possibility of an armistice.

Gort was well removed from such discussions. Even though he had pulled the 5th and 50th Divisions back from Arras, he had not yet abandoned participation in the proposed counteroffensive. However, as it became clear that day that the Belgians, covering the BEF's northern flank, had reached the end of their ability to resist, he ordered his forces to abandon preparations for a counterattack and to cover a possible Belgian capitulation to the Germans without asking permission of the French. Little was clear on the 26th. Some French leaders seized on Gort's decisions as a sign that the British were running; on the 27th, Weygand was talking about Gort's refusal to fight and the English defection. Nevertheless, by the 26th prospects for a successful evacuation looked better. The stop order allowed the Allies to move covering forces to their southern flank, while the British took precautions against a Belgian collapse. The Royal Navy had already evacuated 28,000 noncombatants, and as troops streamed into the Dunkirk perimeter, the British officially began Operation Dynamo, designed to withdraw their forces from the Continent.

But the French still insisted that evacuations were unnecessary.

Blanchard refused to permit a withdrawal, while Weygand continued to harp on his plans for an attack from the north. Thus, the Germans enveloped most of the French First Army; although the III Corps escaped, the rest surrendered on the 29th. The garrison at Lille followed two days later, but at least its resistance was sufficiently tenacious for the Germans to grant the defenders the honors of war.

Distrust between the French and British swelled. By the afternoon of 29 May, the British had evacuated 70,000 troops, but the French still refused to participate in the withdrawal from Dunkirk. At least the Belgians provided a scapegoat. Early on the 28th, King Leopold agreed to terminate hostilities, but the British had already taken precautions. Nevertheless, the French seized on the surrender to excuse the disaster that was enveloping Allied forces. But even as French leaders excoriated the Belgians, Weygand could not resist the opportunity to blame Leopold's surrender on the British. As he remarked to Pétain, "If only Gort had counter-attacked with more vigor . . . the Belgians, feeling themselves better supported, might have resisted longer."[14]

As the Allies withdrew, German difficulties multiplied. Allied resistance was tenacious, while there was no overall German coordination for attacks on the shrinking perimeter. As late as 27 May, 2 army groups, 4 armies, and 16 corps controlled operations against Dunkirk. Only on 30 May did the Germans finally rationalize the command structure and place operations against the perimeter under Eighteenth Army. As Halder noted, "Countless thousands of the enemy are getting away to England right under our noses."[15] The Germans had failed to grasp that the ocean was a highway rather than the terminal point for an advance. Day and night the evacuation continued. On 31 May, Dynamo reached its high point; 68,000 Allied soldiers escaped, to raise the total evacuated to 194,000. A gloomy Halder noted that Eighteenth Army was not yet in control of all formations attacking the pocket. On 1 June, a further 64,000 troops escaped; by then nearly all the BEF was out. Over the night of 2–3 June, Allied ships pulled the British rearguard and 60,000 more French troops out; by then the total had reached 350,000 troops evacuated.

The German failure at Dunkirk was also a Luftwaffe failure. In swirling air battles over the beaches, German aircraft ran into considerable opposition from the Royal Air Force; these air battles should have warned the Luftwaffe's leaders of their service's weaknesses. Admittedly, the Germans fought at a disadvantage. Bf 109s were at the outer limits of range from their bases in Germany, while German bombers had to fly even greater distances. Consequently, the Luftwaffe found it difficult to coordinate air attacks over the evacuation. As German bombers hammered evacuation beaches, British Fighter Command inflicted heavy losses on the attackers. During the course of Operation Dynamo, the RAF lost 177 aircraft, the Luftwaffe 240. Fliegerkorps II (Second Air Corps) reported that it lost more aircraft on 27 May in attacking the perimeter than in the previous ten days.

The Royal Navy's contribution hardly needs emphasis. Admiral Ramsey, who would play a crucial role in the return to the Continent four years later, organized the navy's efforts, as well as those of civilian mariners, fishermen, and sportsmen. As it became increasingly difficult to use Dunkirk, the small boats made a considerable contribution to evacuations from the beaches. Nevertheless, the Allies paid a price. The British lost 6 destroyers (the French 3), with 19 damaged; 9 other major vessels were lost. But Dunkirk had saved the priceless veterans of the British Army.

Destruction of the Allied left wing rendered France defenseless. On 4 June, Churchill warned the House of Commons: "Wars are not won by evacuations."[16] The French stood alone. Holland and Belgium had surrendered; the BEF had lost its equipment; and most distressingly for the French, the British refused to employ Fighter Command in defense of France. The Luftwaffe had savaged the French Air Force; France's best divisions lay wrecked in Flanders; and a long, exposed front ran from the Meuse along the Somme to the ocean. On that front the French deployed 47 infantry divisions and 6 weak motorized formations. The British still had 2 divisions on the Continent (with 2 more in the United Kingdom); those divisions represented the last fully equipped formations available to Britain. The remaining forces either had just escaped from Dunkirk or were forming up.

Even as the Battle of Dunkirk burned out, the Germans rolled into jump-off positions north of the Somme. The panzers had over a week to refit and redeploy. The OKH appointed Guderian to command a panzer group; his task was to drive to the Swiss frontier and entrap French forces still in the Maginot Line along the Franco-German frontier, where as yet little fighting had occurred. Kleist's panzer group had Paris as its target, while Hoth's V Panzer Corps was to strike south to isolate the French coast. Three German army groups, controlling 119 divisions, attacked slightly over 50 French divisions; the OKH held 23 divisions in reserve. Thus, the Germans possessed nearly a three-to-one superiority. In addition, 10 panzer and 7 motorized infantry divisions gave the Germans overwhelming superiority in mechanized forces. Weygand deployed his forces in depth behind the Somme. Given French weaknesses, that depth was insufficient to stem the German offensive. The French leaders conceived of the battle primarily in terms of restoring the army's tarnished reputation.

Army Group B attacked on 5 June, and Bock's forces encountered stiff resistance. South of the Somme, the French had had two weeks to organize their defenses; French gunners remained in their positions until overrun. So tough was resistance in front of Kleist that the OKH pulled his panzer group back and switched it to a breakthrough farther east. West of Kleist, along the lower Seine, Rommel's 7th Panzer Division captured two rail bridges intact. The first day was slow going, but on the next day 7th Panzer Division was through and rolling toward the Seine. By the end of the campaign, it had swept to Rouen, sidestepped to the coast to put the French IX Corps (including the British 51st Highland Division) in the bag, and then driven on to Cherbourg with an advance of 150 miles on 7 June. In six weeks 7th Panzer Division had captured 97,648 prisoners, 277 guns, 458 armored vehicles, and 4,000 trucks. Rundstedt's Army Group A attacked on 9 June. French defenses on its front rapidly collapsed.

Within the French government, defeatism spiraled upward as the collapse widened. Pétain offered nothing but pessimism, reinforced by Weygand's pleas to save the army. The Anglo-French alliance, patched together in spring 1939, collapsed under the pressure of defeat. Late on 16 June, Reynaud resigned, and Pétain assumed power. Two hours later he asked the Spanish ambassador to arrange an armistice. On Saturday, 22 June, in the Forest of Compiègne, French representatives ended hostilities. Savoring the humiliation, Hitler had German engineers drag out the rail car in which the delegates of the German republic had capitulated in November 1918. It was now the site of a second humbling, this time of the French.

In every respect, German victory represented one of the great military triumphs of history. There were two causes. On one side lay the excellence of the Germans at the tactical and operational levels of war. In no sense did German success represent a revolution in military affairs; rather, an evolutionary process of developing a combined-arms doctrine for mobile warfare and committing their forces to hard training provided the German advantage. Nevertheless, it is interesting to note the explanation that one of the most well-regarded general staff officers had for the German success. General Erich Marcks noted in his diary shortly after the armistice that "the change in men weighs more heavily than that in technology. The French were no longer those of 14/18. The relationship was like that between the Revolutionary Armies of 1796 and those of the [First] Coalition—only this time we were the revolutionaries and *Sans-Culottes*."[17] In other words, ideology had been the key component in the German victory, from Marcks's point of view. The willingness of German infantry units to absorb heavy losses and keep going certainly suggests he was right.

Almost immediately after their defeat, the French began to search for scapegoats. There were, of course, substantial problems with the doctrine and training of the French Army. Yet, it is also clear that French soldiers, for the most part, stood and fought. Over 123,000 died in slightly more than five weeks of fighting. But their sacrifice was in vain, because their leaders throughout the higher levels of command had utterly failed to meet the German challenge. The culprits were Gamelin, Weygand, and hundreds of other generals who served between 1919 and 1940.

The Battle of Britain

The magnitude of their victory deceived the Germans. It seemed impossible that the British would consider further resistance. In fact, the change from Chamberlain to Churchill had created a very different atmosphere in London. But there remained significant opposition in the Cabinet to prolonging the war. In a bitter debate on 27 May, the foreign minister, Lord Halifax, urged his colleagues that Britain should entertain an offer from the Germans "which would save the country from avoidable disaster."[18] But Hitler never made a firm offer, while Churchill assumed an increasingly powerful position against those who urged further appeasement.

In June, Rab Butler, under secretary of state for foreign affairs, approached the Swedish minister about a possible deal with the Germans. A furious Churchill warned Halifax off. Churchill's main problem now was not whether resistance should continue but whether Britain could secure financial and economic support from the United States to continue the war. By the end of the month he had sufficient informal support from President Franklin Delano Roosevelt to order the Royal Navy to disarm Vichy France's fleet. That was executed with minimum bloodshed in Alexandria, Egypt, and in British ports, but the main French fleet units in North Africa were another matter. On 5 July at the great naval base of Mers-el-Kebir, the Royal Navy's Force H from Gibraltar destroyed the battleship *Bretagne* and heavily damaged the battleships *Dunkerque* and *Provence*. Nearly 1,300 French sailors died. The raison d'état of Britain's action against its recent ally was best summed up by Admiral Dudley Pound's comment to the French naval attaché: "The one object we had in view was winning the war and . . . it was as essential for them [the French] as for us that we should do so . . . All trivialities, such as questions of friendship . . . must be swept away."[19] The attack underscored that there was more than rhetoric behind Churchill's speeches.

The Germans misjudged the British resolve entirely and believed the war to be virtually over. As Alfred Jodl, the OKW's operations officer, suggested at the end of June, "The final victory of Germany over England is only a question of time."[20] Basking in a mood of preening self-adulation, Hitler went on vacation. During a visit to Paris, tours of World War I battlefields, and picnics along the Rhine, war was the last matter on the Führer's mind. The German high command's structure was such that when Hitler's attention wandered, there was no one with either the drive or vision to pick up the reins. Consequently, the Germans spent the rest of June and much of July awaiting British overtures for peace.

Such military planning as took place in Germany was negligible. Jodl's memorandum of 30 June suggested two strategic possibilities: a) "a direct attack on the English motherland; b) an extension of the war to peripheral areas" such as the Mediterranean. The first approach offered three options: (1) an air and naval offensive against British trade routes; (2) terror air attacks against British population centers; and (3) an amphibious operation against the British Isles. By extending an air campaign to the interdiction of imports and to terror attacks against the British population, Jodl believed that the Luftwaffe could break British morale. Finally, he noted that German strategy required a landing on the British coast only as a "final blow" (Todesstoß).[21]

Jodl's mix of approaches was symptomatic of the German inability to understand complex strategic problems beyond Central Europe. Eventually, Raeder would come up with a Mediterranean strategy, but that would not be until early 1941, and one suspects his proposal had more to do with interservice rivalry than with any strategic conception. Ironically, Francisco Franco, the Spanish dictator, was making clear at this time his eagerness to join the Axis as quickly as possible. Spanish bases in the Canaries and the seizure of Gibraltar would have significantly improved the Reich's position at a time when there was little the British could have done in response. But convinced the war was over and with little desire to share the spoils with Franco as well as Mussolini, the Germans remained unresponsive.

An amphibious landing on the British Isles was never a serious option. Few senior German military leaders had a clue as to the complexities of such an operation. Both Keitel and Halder referred to the problem in terms of a river crossing. The army itself drew up a plan for Operation Sealion that one can only charitably call ill-informed of naval requirements. With only one heavy cruiser and two light cruisers left after Norway, the navy was in no position to offer serious help. Given the fact that the British had stationed four destroyer flotillas (approximately 36 destroyers) along the south coast, while the home fleet stood ready to intervene, a German amphibious force stood no chance. Even with air superiority, the Luftwaffe could not have prevented the British destroyers from attacking the landing forces, with disastrous consequences for those on board. Finally, the proposed landing craft for Sealion, namely Rhine River barges with no sea-keeping capabilities, suggests the haphazard nature of the undertaking and the complete lack of preparations for amphibious war by the Wehrmacht.

Thus, the possibility of knocking Britain out of the war came down to the Luftwaffe. The German Air Force was the best prepared of any air force in 1940 to execute a strategic bombing campaign. It was the only air force that had developed blind-bombing devices for strategic bombing; moreover, the Luftwaffe possessed pathfinder units and had even developed a long-range escort fighter, inadequate though it proved. But the Germans had substantial problems. No one had yet executed such an air campaign, and therefore they were treading on unknown territory. Where should the emphasis of their attack lie? On British industry? On population centers? On military installations? And how could an air campaign prepare the way for Sealion, should it become necessary? Equally important was the fact that Luftwaffe intelligence failed to enlighten German operational commanders on the complexities of the tasks confronting them.

The gap between British and German intelligence was already wide and growing. The former was enjoying its first successes in breaking the German Enigma encoding system, and poor signal discipline by the Germans was to provide the British with access throughout the war to what should have been a technologically unbreakable system. How much impact Ultra (codename for intelligence provided by intercepting and decoding German messages) had on the Battle of Britain is not clear. What is clear is that Ultra, in combination with radio traffic analysis, gave the British an increasingly accurate picture of the German order of battle as air operations continued into September. Moreover, the Battle of Britain brought British scientists directly into intelligence work.

On the other side, a cavalier disregard for intelligence about enemy capabilities marked Luftwaffe operations throughout the war. In a study dated 16 July 1940, the chief of Luftwaffe intelligence, General "Beppo" Schmid, minimized RAF capabilities in almost every category. He did estimate the numbers of aircraft in Fighter Command correctly but then pegged the capacity of British industry for fighter production at 180 to 200 fighters per month, when in fact British industry produced nearly 500 fighters in July alone. He rated the Bf 109 as superior to both the Spitfire and Hurricane, with the Bf 110 equal to the Spitfire and superior to the Hurricane, which it was not. Schmid also suggested that Fighter Command would deploy all of its strength forward, and thus it would have no significant reserves.

His study made no mention of Britain's radar-based air defense system, although the Germans had known of British experiments with radar as early as 1938. Three weeks later, despite the experience of heavy fighting, Schmid reported that British fighters were controlled by their home stations. Finally, he ended on the optimistic note that "the Luftwaffe, unlike the RAF, will be in a position in every respect to achieve a decisive effect this year."[22] The greatest miscalculation the Germans made, above all, lay in their complete failure to understand the complex adaptive system that Fighter Command had become—one where radar directed all of Fighter Command's interceptions rather than serving as a technological tool to guide a few fighters in intercepting German aircraft.

The long preparatory period between the end of the French campaign and the launching of the air campaign reflected more than just German overconfidence. The Luftwaffe had suffered heavy losses in the French campaign: 30 percent of its bombers, 30 percent of twin-engine fighters, 40 percent of transports, 19 percent of single-engine fighters, and over 15 percent of its fighter pilots. The scale of those losses required time for reconstitution and recuperation as well as the integration of new crews into combat units. Moreover, the execution of an air campaign required a major redeployment of not only combat units but the Luftwaffe's entire logistical infrastructure.

On 30 June 1940, Göring signed an initiating directive for the air campaign. The Luftwaffe would first attack the RAF, its ground support structure, and the British aircraft industry. "As long as the enemy air force is not destroyed, it is the basic principle of the conduct of air war to attack enemy air units at every possible favorable opportunity—by day and night, in the air, and on the ground—without regard for other missions."[23] The RAF, including Bomber Command, would be the main target. But air superiority itself represented a most difficult task, given Luftwaffe strength and capabilities. Because of the Bf 109's limited range, Luftwaffe fighter squadrons could cover the bombers only as far as London, which allowed the RAF to use the rest of the country as a sanctuary. Should the pressure on Fighter Command become too great, the British could always pull back north of London. The Luftwaffe was never in a position to attack the RAF over the whole of the British Isles, and the Germans could only impose on Fighter Command a level of attrition that its commanders would accept.

The Luftwaffe's initial estimate on the duration of the campaign was wildly optimistic: four days to defeat Fighter Command, followed by four weeks for German bombers and long-range fighters to destroy the rest of the RAF and Britain's aircraft industry. But the Germans were up against a resolute and effective opponent, led by a first-class airman, Air Marshal Sir

Hugh Dowding. Dowding had played a major role in developing radar as well as the Spitfire and Hurricane when serving as the head of the RAF's research and development command. He had taken over Fighter Command in 1937 and smoothly integrated the technology into an effective air defense system. During the Battle of France, he had stood up to Churchill and opposed sending more fighters into a hopeless situation—a stand Churchill admired. Dowding's goal was not to win but to prevent the Luftwaffe from gaining air superiority until fall weather made a cross-Channel operation impossible. He deployed approximately one-third of his fighters on air fields in southern England. Fighter Command would defend all the British Isles, but the squadrons in the north represented a reserve that he could feed into the air battle as combat burned out fighter squadrons in the south.

The first, exploratory phase of the battle lasted from the beginning of July until early August, as the Germans sought to draw Fighter Command out over the Channel. The initial battle was a serious error by the Germans, for it provided Fighter Command considerable experience with German procedures and tactics and allowed the British to improve the skill of their radar operators and the system as a whole. Early mistakes, such as that of 11 July when British controllers scrambled six Hurricanes to meet one raider and the fighters then ran into a raid of over 40 aircraft, occurred with decreasing frequency.

The second phase began on 13 August with Eagle Day *(Adlertag)*, when the Luftwaffe was supposed to launch wide-ranging strikes at RAF bases across southern England. Bad weather forced the Luftwaffe's high command to cancel the morning strikes, but some bombers never received the message. The result was a ragged beginning to what was supposed to be a decisive strike. Because of bad intelligence, many German attacks hit RAF fields that were of little importance to the defenses.

Over the course of the succeeding month the opponents filled the sky in a massive battle of attrition. The initial attacks severely damaged a number of air bases and knocked several radar stations off the air. But the Luftwaffe failed to persist in such attacks, since its intelligence never understood the complex interlocking British air defense system. In air-to-air combat, the Spitfires and Hurricanes proved superior to the twin-engine Bf 110s, while the Spitfire more than held its own against the Bf 109. Thus, German single-engine fighters had to provide support even for the Bf 110s. The Stuka Ju-87 dive bombers proved so vulnerable that after a major air battle on 18 August, when British fighters shot down 18, Göring ordered them out of the battle.

The air battles in mid-August dramatized the Luftwaffe's lack of an effective long-range fighter. On 15 August, RAF fighters inflicted 20 percent losses on German bombers and Bf 110s flying out of Norway and proved conclusively that the British Isles were defended in depth. As bomber losses mounted, the Luftwaffe fighter force came under sharp criticism from Göring. The losses of bombers to enemy fighters led the newly promoted Reichsmarschall to accuse his fighter pilots of excessive caution. He ordered them to fly close escort on the bombers, with little latitude to engage British fighters.

The pressure on the opposing fighter communities was intense. In July the British lost 10 percent of their fighter pilots, the Germans 11 percent. In August British losses among Fighter Command pilots climbed to 26 percent, 15 percent for the Germans. In September British losses reached 28 percent, while the Germans lost over 23 percent. Both sides were losing experienced fighter pilots and having to rush untrained crews out of operational training units.

Despite the damage to Fighter Command's base structure, the losses over southern England persuaded the Germans to alter their strategy in early September. Hitler and Göring, fully supported by Field Marshal Albert Kesselring, commander of Luftflotte 2 (Second Air Force), turned to an all-out attack on London. A great daylight raid on 7 September continued into the night and inflicted massive damage on the east end of London and its dockyards. Over the night of 7–8 September, London firemen fought nine fires that rated more than 100 pumps and one fire on the Surrey Docks that rated 300.

But the change granted Fighter Command a much needed rest, particularly for its pilots and ground support units in southern England. The night bombing and daylight probes of the next week put heavy pressure on both London's inhabitants and the German bomber crews. However, not until 15 September did the Luftwaffe launch another major daylight raid against London. By then the lull had allowed Dowding to replace all his fighter squadrons with relatively fresh ones from the north. The great air battles on this day represented the climactic moment in the Battle of Britain.

In the morning, 100 Do-17 bombers, accompanied by heavy fighter cover, fought their way to London, only to be struck over the capital head-on by Douglas Bader's Duxford wing of five fighter squadrons. In the afternoon, 150 Dorniers and Heinkels, again accompanied by heavy fighter escort, attacked London. Over Kent, 175 Hurricanes and Spitfires from 11 Group met the Germans; when the enemy reached east London, Bader's squadrons piled into the German formations. The bombers ran for the coast, while scattering their bombs over the landscape of southern England. The daylight offensive had failed. Hitler postponed Sealion indefinitely.

But Britain was not yet secure. The Germans now turned to a night offensive, designed to inflict substantial damage on British industry and break civilian morale. The Germans expected great accuracy from their blind-bombing devices, Knickebein and X-Gerät, which used radio beams to provide navigational guidance. But in early summer 1940 the British—on the basis of a few scraps of information drawn from crashed aircraft, the interrogation of captured crews, and several Ultra messages—had worked out Knickebein's purpose and technological weaknesses. British scientists then developed countermeasures to distort the accuracy of the German guide beams. The scientific success of the British in the Battle of Britain was the result particularly of a young scientist, R. V. Jones, one of the brightest and kindest men to be involved in the highest levels of decision-making in World War II. By winter, as British countermeasures worked, German bomber crews came to distrust the technology of their bombing aids. Thus, British cities took a heavy pounding over the winter, but German attacks never achieved sufficient accuracy or concentration to break the will of the British people.

Conclusion

The consequences of the collapse of Western Europe were immense. For the Germans, the victory over France suggested that everything was possible for the Third Reich. Seldom in European military history had one nation achieved such a decisive success over another power. Yet the Wehrmacht had not possessed superiority in manpower or materiel except perhaps in the air. German success did not rest on an operational doctrine developed because of its defeat in the last war. Victory resulted from intelligent, thoughtful maturation of battle doctrine from 1917 through to the lessons of the Polish campaign. The development of Germany's combat capability was evolutionary, not revolutionary; the victory in the Battle of France in 1940 rested as much on the performance of infantrymen like Erwin Rommel as it did on tank pioneers like Heinz Guderian. The unifying glue was a coherent, combined-arms approach to modern war. Armor, infantry, and artillery spoke the same language—one of exploitation, decentralized authority, and aggressive leadership.

Yet whatever the army's operational success, victory in France did not solve the strategic problems raised by Hitler's vision. It merely satisfied the immediate economic and strategic requirements created by the outbreak of

war in September 1939. Germany now had control of the economic resources of Western and Central Europe as well as the Balkans, but those resources represented potential rather than immediate productive capacity.

The postwar literature has generally placed the war in the west within a
different framework than that in the east. In fact, *both* wars represented
portions of the same ideological struggle. In 1940, quaint aristocratic customs, such as the rendering of honors upon surrender to the French garrison at Lille by their besiegers, still occurred. But the war in the west was
not always a battle between noble warriors. On 27 May 1940, a company
of the SS Totenkopf Division captured 100 prisoners of the Second Royal
Norfolk Regiment. The company commander, Obersturmführer Fritz
Knochlein, lined the prisoners up against a barn wall and machinegunned
the lot. Any survivors were bayoneted and shot. German military authorities brought no charges against Knochlein, nor did his division regard his
actions as anything out of the ordinary.

From surface appearances, France would seem to have lost the most in
the 1940 campaign. But in fact, the biggest loser was the Soviet Union. On
18 June the Soviet foreign minister, Molotov, expressed to the German ambassador "the warmest congratulations of the Soviet Government on the
splendid successes of the German Wehrmacht."[24] More than mere words
lay behind Molotov's statement. A report of the Reich's Economics Ministry noted a month later the enthusiastic efforts of the Soviet government to
accomplish the delivery of raw materials urgently needed by the German
war economy. Of course, Stalin took cold comfort in the fall of France; his
policy had rested on the belief that another war of attrition would occur in
the west, one that would exhaust both sides and allow the Soviet Union to
take advantage of the collapse of European capitalism. But if the fall of
France upset Soviet calculations, Stalin refused to see that his regime was
in mortal peril. Yet, the direct result of the French defeat was that the Soviets would fight alone on the Continent for three long years. The second
front that Stalin would so desperately demand from the Allies in the years
leading up to June 1944 had disappeared in France in May 1940.

Finally, Churchill brought extraordinary leadership to the struggle. He
would later claim that he had only given voice to the feelings of the British
people in 1940. But, in fact, he recognized that there could be no compromise with the evil of Nazism and that the United States would recognize
that fact in time. He also understood that the dynamics of conflicting ideologies would bring a violent end to the Nazi-Soviet Non-Aggression Pact.
And so he nobly gambled the last resources of a fading empire in the belief
that the struggle was not yet lost. He was right.

5

DIVERSIONS IN THE
MEDITERRANEAN AND BALKANS

1940–1941

On 10 June 1940, from the balcony of the Palazzo Venezia in Rome, Benito Mussolini announced to the bellowing multitudes below that Italy had declared war on France and Britain. In effect, Mussolini's declaration of war reflected his deep commitment to the Rome-Berlin Axis, born in the aftermath of the Abyssinian War of 1936. It also reflected the megalomaniacal aims of Mussolini and his followers to turn the Mediterranean into an Italian *mare nostrum* (our sea).

Italy's entrance into the war could not have come at a worse time for the Allies. Mussolini's decision embodied his lusts, the ideology of his regime, and the overweening expectations of the Italian upper and middle classes. There had never been a "good" Mussolini; his relatively pacific behavior in the 1920s was simply an adaptation to an international environment that left little room for his evil schemes. Hitler's ascent to power in the next decade fed Mussolini's growing ambitions, which blossomed in the shade of the darker and more dangerous flower to the north.

Italy's entrance into the war was anything but smooth. The inchoate decision-making processes of the Fascist regime rested on the Duce's will. Of planning there was none. The services were not ready for war. The army had carried out an expansion program far beyond its means and operational good sense. The navy had good ships but neither the leadership nor industrial support required to operate them effectively in wartime, while the air force possessed nothing but obsolete aircraft. No one thought to recall Italy's merchant shipping before declaring war; consequently, nearly a million tons eventually wound up in Allied hands. The bravery of the Italian people had no hope of making up such deficiencies.

Not surprisingly, the Italian military believed that Italy would not have to fight; Mussolini, on the other hand, wished to conquer a Mediterranean

91

empire that would transform Italy into a great power and concurrently allow his regime to settle accounts with the monarchy, the Church, and the middle class. This misunderstanding between leader and military bedeviled strategic planning throughout summer 1940, when France's collapse and Britain's weakness offered Italy substantial opportunities to strike in the Mediterranean. But both the regime and its military leadership decided that Italy would fight a "parallel war" in the Mediterranean, one that remained entirely independent of German influence and support.

In the last days of France's resistance, the Italians launched a muddled attack on the few French forces in the Alps. Order and counterorder flew back and forth between Mussolini, Field Marshal Pietro Badoglio, chief of Commando Supremo, and the field commanders. The result was wholly negative—no gains with heavy casualties.

France's defeat opened up fleeting possibilities in the Mediterranean. Britain's strategic position was vulnerable. The Royal Navy was split between Alexandria and Gibraltar. Malta, which was a British possession, was unusable except by raiders and submarines; it possessed a garrison of only five infantry battalions, local reservists, and three obsolete aircraft left by mistake on the island and soon named *Faith, Hope,* and *Charity.* Egypt's defenses were in little better shape. General Sir Archibald Wavell commanded 36,000 men, not yet fully organized. The 7th Armored Division lacked an armored regiment in each brigade and part of its artillery. A further 27,500 soldiers in Palestine were even less prepared. The Egyptian Army was of little military value and represented a distinct threat to internal security.

Faced with this favorable situation, the Italian high command could decide on nothing. Badoglio pleaded insurmountable obstacles as an excuse for declining every one of the Duce's suggestions. Yet at the heart of Italian difficulties lay Mussolini's own inability to enunciate a coherent strategy. Consequently, his shifting interests moved from dreams of expanding into the Balkans at the expense of Yugoslavia and Greece, to conquering the French Empire, to dominating the eastern Mediterranean, and even to partitioning Switzerland. In early July, Badoglio suggested an offensive against Egypt; the army staff admitted that "currently, given the present situation, and with arrival of the materiel presently being readied or awaiting embarkation for Libya, our land forces in North Africa are sufficiently strong for the initiation in the near future of a decisive offensive with as objective, the Anglo-Egyptian forces presently in Egypt."[1]

Crucial to a successful offensive against Egypt was the security of Italy's lines of communications across the Mediterranean. Malta, which the Brit-

AXIS GAINS IN THE MEDITERRANEAN
1940 – 1941

- Axis states and territories in June 1940
- Axis satellites
- Axis occupied
- → Main direction of Axis advance
- ⇒ Main direction of Allied advance

1. Italian advance into Egypt September 1940
2. British counteroffensive December 1940 – February 1941
3. British troops to Greece March 1941
4. Axis invasion of Yugoslavia and Greece April 1941
5. Axis airborne invasion of Crete May 1941
6. Allied evacuation of Greece and Crete by June 1941
7. Arrival of German Afrika Korps February 1941
8. Axis advances in North Africa to May 1941
9. Allied counterattacks Brevity in May and Battleaxe in June 1941

ish possessed, represented an obvious threat to those lines; nevertheless, the Italian Navy's commander dismissed the island as something the air force could neutralize. The Italian Navy, however, soon found itself engaged by the Royal Navy directly. In early July the Battle of Calabria occurred as the opposing fleets provided cover for major convoy movements, the Italians to Libya, the British to and from Malta. The Italian Navy possessed every advantage. It knew of the British movement through decrypts; night favored the Italian Navy's small unit tactics; the Italians could have concentrated a superior battle fleet; the action took place close to Italy; and two of the British battleships were slow, vulnerable World War I veterans. But before the battle, Admiral Domenico Cavagnari reduced the odds favoring his forces by ordering the two new Italian battleships to remain in harbor. With its movements tightly controlled by Rome, the Italian fleet fled on contact. Nevertheless, the British holed the battleship *Cesare*, while the Regia Aeronautica showed up late and then proceeded to bomb both fleets impartially.

When Mussolini pushed for action, the Italian generals replied with their typical stubbornness. In Libya, Graziani bemoaned his military inferiority. An RAF raid in August on his headquarters sent the marshal scurrying back to Cyrene, far from the Libyan-Egyptian frontier, while claiming that the accuracy of the attack reflected the work of traitors and spies. Yet even as Mussolini pressed Graziani in Africa, Greece and Yugoslavia were emerging in discussions as possible targets for expansion into the Balkans. By mid-August Berlin had picked up some of the threads of Mussolini's thinking. On the 16th, Ribbentrop summoned the Italian ambassador and warned him that any Italian move against Yugoslavia would displease the Reich, which desired to maintain the status quo in the Balkans in order to prevent Soviet intervention. The crestfallen Italian Foreign Minister Galeazzo Ciano recorded in his diary: "It is a complete order to halt all along the line."[2] Three days later the Germans repeated the warning about any Italian action against Greece.

With his plans for the Balkans halted by German fiat, Mussolini increased the pressure on Graziani. Losing patience with the general's prevarications, Mussolini ordered an immediate offensive and announced to the Council of Ministers that if Graziani failed to attack he would be sacked. Confronted with this ultimatum, Graziani ordered an advance, while complaining in his diary about the unfairness of it all. The ensuing performance of Graziani's subordinates speaks volumes about his military leadership. General Maletti, the "wolf of the desert" in Graziani's memoirs, failed to pick up his Arab guides or the requisite maps, lost his way, and had to be found by the Regia Aeronautica just before his column exhausted its water. The advance to Sidi el Barrani on the northwestern Egyptian coast pushed the British back without doing any damage. Motorized Italian formations, accompanied by a few tanks, came to rest in static positions, none mutually supporting, at the end of tenuous lines of communications, and with their southern flank up in the air in the desert. Graziani's bombast that the British soldier would soon "learn to recognize the valor of the Italian soldier" could not cover his lack of resolution.[3]

Meanwhile, the British assembled their strength. The dispatch of tanks from Britain in September promised that Britain's desert army would not remain permanently inferior.

Catastrophe for Italian Arms

Through September 1940, Mussolini had waged a parallel war in the Mediterranean with the Germans watching. Internecine quarrels within the Balkans now precipitated Italian action, and that action turned indecision into an avalanche of disasters. At the end of World War I, the Treaty of St. Germaine had given most of Transylvania to Romania despite its large Hungarian population. Not surprisingly, the Hungarians were enthusiastic revisionists, but their lack of resources held their political ambitions in check. Now in the chaos of summer 1940 they saw an opportunity to settle with Romania, especially as the latter had just ceded Bessarabia and Bukovina to the Soviets. By the end of August, Hungary and Romania were close to war.

Given the importance of Romanian oil, the Germans found this state of affairs intolerable. With the Italians, they stepped between the prospective combatants. At the end of August, Ribbentrop and Ciano summoned Hungarian and Romanian negotiators to Vienna; the Axis foreign ministers imposed a settlement that severely truncated Romania, but the agreement hardly satisfied Hungarian appetites. The settlement induced an immediate political convulsion in Romania. King Carol abdicated, and General Ion Antonescu seized the post of prime minister, then quickly established himself as dictator. The country teetered on collapse, offering inviting possibilities to the Soviets.

But Hitler was not about to allow Soviet intervention in Romania. After bilateral discussions between the Germans and Romanians, Hitler sent a military "mission," ostensibly to strengthen the ties between the Reich and Romania by bringing Romanian troops up to German standards. By December 1940 this German advisory force had grown into the 13th Motorized Infantry Division (reinforced), the 16th Panzer Division, two fighter *Staffeln* (squadrons), one reconnaissance *Staffel,* and two flak regiments. The advisers' "real tasks," as Keitel made clear, were "to protect the oil districts . . . prepare the Romanian armed forces . . . in accordance with German interests [and] . . . prepare . . . for the employment of German and Romanian forces in case the Soviets force a conflict [on the Reich]."[4]

Hitler's cavalier disregard of Italian interests in Romania outraged Mussolini. According to Ciano, the Duce told him immediately after the German move: "Hitler always confronts me with a fait accompli. This time I am going to pay him back in his own coin. He will find out that I have occupied Greece."[5] Right away, the Italians began planning for an attack on Greece. But they did so without halting the demobilization of their army that had begun in October and had already reduced ground forces from 1,000,000 to 600,000 men. The reasons for the demobilization had been economic as well as political: the harvest and industry needed manpower, and the public needed some reassurance that events were returning to normal. Incredibly, the army executed the demobilization by age group, so that every division in Italy lost a substantial portion of its manpower. Consequently, in October, when Mussolini, egged on by Ciano, pushed his military toward an operation against Greece, Italian forces were undermanned and unprepared for war, though their generals were all too willing.

The Italians foresaw a two-stage campaign. First, their forces in Albania (a country that Mussolini had seized in April 1939) would drive south and occupy northern Greece, as their navy seized the most important Aegean islands. Then the troops would continue the march south to Athens for a final assault. Heavy bombing to terrorize Greek civilians would help precipitate the fall of the regime. These plans revealed an unhealthy contempt for the Greeks' ability to defend themselves, along with a disregard for the most obvious operational problems. To begin with, Italian forces in Albania could claim a bare one-to-one ratio with Greek defenders. Moreover, Albania had only enough logistic infrastructure to support forces already in that country. Once the attack on Greece began, Italy would have no capacity for sending new formations into the theater or for a rapid buildup, given the demands for ammunition, food, and fuel from the battlefront. The Italians also assumed that, given Bulgarian-Greek hostility, the mere existence of the Bulgarian Army would freeze much of the Greek Army in Thrace.

Meanwhile, the Greeks had picked up indications that an invasion was coming, and on 23 October the Greek ambassador in Rome warned his government to expect an invasion between the 25th and 26th. Thus alerted, the Greeks mobilized. Their forces along the frontier were quite similar in size and composition to the Italians', but Greek artillery was better. The Italians were superior in tanks and aircraft, but their tanks were lightly armored, while the Regia Aeronautica had neither the training nor the navigational equipment to fly in bad weather. Launched into northern Greece with no logistic buildup, in some cases even without winter clothing, and no clear superiority in either weapons or manpower, the Italians marched straight into defeat. Initially, they drove the Greeks back along the Central Front and advanced 60 kilometers down the valleys on the southwestern border. But bad weather kept the Regia Aeronautica at bay. Italian aircraft confined themselves to attacks on Greek cities like Salonika rather than supporting their hard-pressed ground forces. The Bulgarians failed to move, while the Greeks shifted reserves to the Albanian front and soon gained local superiority. Heavy casualties bled Italian units white, and the supply system failed in about every respect.

The Italian commander, General Visconti Prasca, exacerbated the chaos by panicking. By 7 November, the Italian left flank near Kroce was on the verge of collapse. As hopes of a *Blitzkrieg* faded, the Italians moved to a strategy of attrition to wear the Greeks down. Prasca was replaced by General Uboldo Soddu, who was hardly an improvement; as army group commander, he whiled away his evenings writing musical scores for movies. By the end of November the Greeks had driven the Italians back into Albania.

Meanwhile, the Royal Navy added to Mussolini's woes. Using one aircraft carrier and twelve torpedo planes, Admiral Andrew B. Cunningham struck the Italian fleet at Taranto, on the instep of the Italian boot. The night torpedo attack came as a complete surprise; by the morning of 12 November, three Italian battleships were resting in the mud, one irreparably damaged. Accompanying the air strike was a British cruiser raid into the Strait of Otranto. Attacking forces sank four merchant vessels and temporarily broke the supply lines between Albania and Italy.

Hard on the heels of Taranto came real catastrophe in Greece. As reinforcements merely dribbled into Albania from Italy, the Greeks, now fully mobilized, launched a major counterattack on 14 November. The campaign rapidly turned into a rout; the Greeks surged into Albania in early December, and by the 4th Soddu lost control and suggested a retreat to Valona and Durazzo. By now Mussolini had fired Badoglio; his replacement, General Ugo Cavallero, hastened to Albania to buck up Soddu. The Italians held, but barely, and Soddu's days were numbered, especially after Mussolini discovered that he was still composing film scores. For the next month and a half the Italians hung on in a precarious position. The regime declared total mobilization, but it could not undo the damage of October's demobilization. Hastily cobbled-together units crossed over to Albania, where they were immediately committed to battle.

By the end of January the Italians had succeeded in stemming the Greek advance. By February they were strong enough to counterattack, though with disappointing results; the Greeks hardly budged despite attacks that led to extraordinarily high casualties among Italian units. The failure of Italian counterattacks in February represented the last gasp of Mussolini's parallel war in the Mediterranean. Italy was well on the way to becoming a German satellite.

The British Attack

Britain's Mediterranean position in July 1940 was dark indeed. With the fleet split between Alexandria and Gibraltar, and barely two divisions in Egypt, the British still decided that the Italians would have to fight for their *mare nostrum*. By fall 1940 the British mood was shifting to one of confidence, a mood bolstered by Italian inactivity. In the desert, British raiding parties had established ascendancy over their Italian opponents. In September as the Italians advanced into Egypt, General Sir Archibald Wavell, commander in the Middle East, determined to counterattack, if the Italians moved past Sidi el Barrani. But Wavell's strategic problems extended beyond Egypt, since Abyssinia and Greece were also within his area of responsibility. He seems to have regarded Abyssinia as a serious threat to the Red Sea and an opportunity for an easy victory—a view that Churchill shared. In fact, Abyssinia was an irrelevancy; Italian forces there possessed neither the logistical infrastructure and support nor the military range to threaten anyone except the Ethiopians, who, with British help, had launched a major insurgency throughout the country.

Wavell decided that one of his two counterattacking divisions, the 4th Indian, would pull out after the first move against Italian forces in Egypt and redeploy to Abyssinia, to be replaced by an Australian division. Wavell's decision reflected his belief that the blow against Graziani would be no more than a short, sharp raid to knock the Italians out of Egypt; he did not anticipate a major victory. The available British troops were excellent. Before the war Percy Hobart, Britain's foremost expert in armored war, had trained many of the units in the 7th Armored Division into first-class formations; the 4th Indian Division was also excellent, while the 6th Australian Division made up for its training deficiencies with enthusiasm and courage. On the Italian side, Graziani's Tenth Army had deployed in unsupporting fortified positions scattered around the desert, with mobile formations supposedly covering the gaps. However, the British already ruled the open desert.

The British skillfully veiled their preparations; they pushed supply dumps out in front of their main positions, while planting rumors in Egypt about preparations for a retreat. The Italians fell for the deception. General Richard O'Conner, the desert army commander, moved his forces through the gap in the Italian dispositions between the coastal camps of Nibeiwa, Maktila, and Sidi el Barrani and the camps farther inland, a space of nearly 14 miles. The 7th Armored Division formed a mobile covering shield, while the 4th Indian Division chewed up the Italian camps in the coastal grouping. Not only did the British penetrate through the gap, but the coordinated attack on the Nibeiwa camp lasted only three hours and bagged 2,000 prisoners. Without hesitating, the British moved on to attack the next camp, which fell by early afternoon.

Over the next two days O'Conner's forces destroyed the Italian forces around Sidi el Barrani. Of the seven divisions in the Italian Tenth Army, only the Cyrene Division got away, although it abandoned most of its equipment and supplies. Graziani collapsed. Exposed Italian units at Sollena retreated to Bardia, while Graziani, with Mussolini's support, determined to hold Bardia *and* Tobruk.

The British took the remainder of December to sort out their logistics on the Egyptian frontier. Wavell had neglected to inform O'Conner of the replacement of the 4th Indian Division by the 6th Australian, and this compounded other problems caused by the exchange. The two-week hiatus in switching the divisions may have been decisive in preventing the British from reaching Tripoli before Rommel arrived with German reinforcements. The Australians were not in a position to attack Bardia until early January. Spearheaded by engineers and artillery, they punched into the fortress, and then the infantry, supported by tanks, mopped up over the next three days. At a cost of 454 casualties, the Australians managed to kill, wound, or capture 40,000 Italians. Several hundred motor vehicles, 13 medium and 117 light tanks, and 400 guns fell into Australian hands.

O'Conner's forces then drove rapidly up the coast to attack Tobruk with the same results. On 21 January, supported by armor, Australian infantry bashed their way into the badly laid-out Italian defensive system. Once inside Tobruk, they picked off the Italian units one at a time; 25,000 Italians, with 208 guns and 87 tanks, surrendered. Commonwealth casualties were barely 400.

Turning command over to his chief of staff, Graziani fled to Tripoli after ordering his forces to abandon Cyrenaica. Using decrypts, British intelligence picked up the Italian retreat on the coastal bulge along the Gulf of Sirte. The Australians hustled the Italians up the coast, while in one of the more daring moves of the war O'Conner launched the 7th Armored Division across the desert to cut the Italians off. Under the temporary command of Brigadier John Caunter, British armor reached Beda Fomm before the Italians and thus blocked their retreat. In a confusing series of skirmishes, in which the Italians displayed little coordination, the British held. They reinforced their light units steadily, while Caunter commanded British tank units in outstanding fashion. As a result, Caunter's force destroyed the remains of Tenth Army, and the Italian resistance in eastern Libya collapsed.

Caunter's fate, however, suggests why the British Army rarely reached this high level of battlefield success. He had commanded 7th Armored Division during two crucial engagements (the initial attack on Barrani and then Beda Fomm) because of the divisional commander's illness. Shortly after the second operation, 2nd Armored Division arrived in Egypt; its commander died almost immediately. With his battle experience, Caunter should have been the ideal candidate for the post, but instead he was shipped out to become the Indian Army's expert on armored warfare.

O'Conner urged a continuation of the drive, but this suggestion met a tepid response in Cairo. Wavell's cables to London indicate his belief that substantial difficulties stood in the way of such a drive; throughout O'Conner's advance, Wavell had displayed little understanding of the speed and tempo of mechanized warfare. London, which might have responded to encouraging reports from the Middle East, was already turning its sights to the Balkans. Thus, the British advance halted in front of El Agheila in Libya; the 7th Armored Division returned to Egypt, to be replaced by an unprepared 2nd Armored Division whose new commander knew nothing about desert conditions. At the same time, Wavell broke up O'Conner's XIII Corps Headquarters.

In September 1940 the Germans had dabbled with the idea of sending a panzer corps to help the Italian drive on Suez, but Mussolini had not been receptive. The collapse of Italian forces changed the situation and forced the Germans to intervene. Rommel received the command and arrived in Libya on 12 February. Without question, he was the most outstanding battlefield commander of the war. Like virtually the entire German officer corps, he was a convinced Nazi. After the war a number of general staff officers attacked him as being merely a competent division commander who possessed little understanding of strategy or logistics. In fact, Rommel was less unrealistic about logistics than those general staff officers who planned the invasion of the Soviet Union. As to the charge that Rommel was merely a competent tactician, it should be noted that although he had minimal control over Germany's Mediterranean strategy from 1941 to 1943, he saw earlier than most—in 1942—that the balance had shifted against Germany.

For now, though, as a newly promoted corps commander, Rommel had a simple mission. He was to prevent a complete collapse of the Axis position in North Africa. Given the momentous preparations already under way in Eastern Europe, Halder saw this task as entirely defensive, to protect Tripoli. Rommel, however, had no intention of remaining immobile. His sixth sense suggested the British were not prepared, and he struck. Wavell had ripped XIII Corps apart, O'Conner had left the desert, and inexperienced British commanders and units lay at the end of long lines of communications. Neither the new corps commander, Lieutenant General Sir Philip Neame, nor the 2nd Armored Division's commander, Major General M. D. Gambier-Parry, had experience in mobile, combined-arms warfare. On 31 March, Rommel's 5th Light Division slammed into the British at Mersa Breza. Coordination between the British corps and subordinate units fell apart; Wavell rushed O'Conner back, but it was too late. To compound the defeat, the Germans captured O'Conner and most of his staff in the confusion.

Rommel's advancing forces drove the British out of Libya, with the exception of the garrison at Tobruk. The British decision to hold that position complicated the German logistic situation considerably and forced Rommel to split his command. Nevertheless, the daring offensive of Rommel's Afrika Korps had transformed the situation in North Africa, while horrifying Rommel's superiors in Berlin and terrifying the Italians. Ever the careful Bavarian schoolmaster, Halder thought that Rommel had gone mad. But Rommel's offensive had prevented the British from solidifying their hold on Cyrenaica. His success also ensured that British air attacks from Malta and the fields around Benghazi would not strangle Axis forces in Libya by cutting off the supply lines to North Africa from Italy.

German Intervention in the Balkans

By the time Rommel arrived in North Africa, the Germans were well on the way to preparing their intervention in the Balkans. The German leadership had already made up its mind to invade the Soviet Union in summer 1941, so German interest in the Mediterranean lay in protecting the southern flank of the coming campaign against the Soviet Union. But the Italian disaster in Libya loomed as a serious threat to the stability of the region. The Germans thus had to secure Greece and Romania in order to protect the flank of their forces invading the Soviet Union.

The decision to intervene in the Balkans confronted the Germans with the logistic and diplomatic difficulties of committing major forces to southern Europe. Winter weather exacerbated the difficulties. Any deployment against Greece would have to use bases in Bulgaria, which the Germans did not secure until January 1941 because of Bulgarian fears about the Turks. Yugoslavia might have provided an easier route, but the Serbs proved recalcitrant, especially in view of Italian difficulties in Albania. Atrocious weather delayed the German buildup in Romania. Not until February, a month and a half behind schedule, did they cross the Danube into Bulgaria. Thereafter the buildup proceeded with the usual German efficiency.

Hitler ordered the Wehrmacht to occupy the whole of Greece and drive the British into the sea. Nevertheless, planning for the invasion of the Soviet Union, known as Operation Barbarossa, added to the difficulties of a Balkan campaign by complicating the logistical buildup. By the end of March, Field Marshal Wilhelm List's Twelfth Army, supported by the Luftwaffe's Fliegerkorps VIII, had deployed on the Greek-Bulgarian frontier.

The British agreed to send ground forces to Greece in February, and they began arriving in early March on the Greek mainland. The decision to aid the Greeks against the Axis had come after anguished debates within the cabinet. Churchill, for his part, was torn between the prospects of further successes in Libya and aiding the Greeks; but, as he made clear to Wavell, he favored the former until the drive in Libya should run out of steam. Moreover, he did temper his enthusiasm for aiding the Greeks on a number of occasions. In February 1941 he cabled his Middle East commanders: "Do not consider yourselves obligated to a Greek enterprise if in your hearts you feel it will be another Norway fiasco. If no good plan can be made please say so. But of course you know how valuable success would be."[6] However, Anthony Eden, Sir John Dill (the CIGS), and Wavell found it impossible to resist the pull of Greece despite the fact that such aid flew in the face of strategic sense. The Greeks had fully committed themselves to the fighting in Albania. To the east of that front they held two major positions which could block a German advance from Bulgaria, but both were open to possible flanking moves through Yugoslavia. Moreover, the Greeks were defending forward in Macedonia up toward the Bulgarian frontier. Nevertheless, despite the hazards, the British agreed to the Greek defensive scheme. The Allies determined to hold the Aliakmon line with 23 instead of the required 35 battalions.

Meanwhile, German forces assembled in Bulgaria. By 9 March the 5th and 11th Panzer Divisions were covering the Turkish frontier. Within slightly more than a week, four corps headquarters and eight divisions had reached the Greek frontier. German diplomats were also active; Nazi pressure forced the Yugoslavs to join the Axis on 25 March. The Germans did make one important concession that could have helped the Greeks considerably: Yugoslavia would not have to allow transit of Axis troops across its territory. This would have forced the Germans to assault the Greek defenses directly.

On the evening that Yugoslav negotiators returned to Belgrade from Berlin, a coup d'état led by Yugoslav air force officers toppled the government in an open rejection of its pro-Axis foreign policy. Wildly cheering crowds in Belgrade bedecked the city with French and British flags. The Serbian officers refused, however, to go beyond the coup for fear of provoking German retaliation, although they did hold conversations with Dill. While they promised to resist any German invasion, they refused to take any overt preparations, such as mobilization that would have provided a more effective defense.

Hitler had no illusions on the reliability of those responsible for the coup. Within hours, he communicated to the OKW his desire to "smash Yugoslavia." By evening, after conferences with Brauchitsch and Göring, Hitler had signed Directive No. 25. Besides military objectives, Hitler directed the Luftwaffe to destroy "the city of Belgrade . . . from the air by continual day and night attacks."[7] German military planning displayed its usual adaptability. As Halder admitted later, the OKH had already begun theoretical planning for a possible invasion of Yugoslavia; all it needed to do was to solve the practical difficulties. Within a week, the OKH had altered Twelfth Army's preparations in Bulgaria to include Yugoslavia and had established Second Army under Generaloberst Freiherr von Weichs in southern Austria and Hungary to execute the main attack on Yugoslavia.

Panzer forces from these armies, one advancing from the north, the other from the south, were to strike at Belgrade. In addition, the inclusion of Yugoslavia in the campaign allowed Twelfth Army to swing through Macedonia and take the Greeks in the rear. Finally, independent of the OKH, Hitler ordered the 2nd SS Motorized Division under XLI Panzer Corps to strike from Timisoara in Romania against Belgrade. Halder and Brauchitsch protested and finally managed to get operational control over the thrust.

Along with army redeployments went an extensive movement of Luftwaffe units. Nearly 600 aircraft from bases as far away as southern France redeployed to the Balkans, where German air strength rose to over 1,000 aircraft. The reason for this massive shift is apparent from the orders directing air attacks on Yugoslavia. Those orders excluded attacks on industrial plants or transportation, since the Germans planned to make use of the Yugoslav economy and infrastructure. *The* major task, concurrent with winning air superiority, was "the destruction of Belgrade through a great air attack." The air attack was to begin on the morning of the first day and continue into the night. The day attacks were to use a heavy load of incendiaries "to ease the problem of marking the city for the night attack."[8] Further bombings of Belgrade would occur on D + 1 (the day after the first attack). The codename Punishment accurately reflected Hitler's fury. By the time that the Luftwaffe had completed its attacks on Belgrade, 17,000 civilians had died.

The Balkan campaign split almost immediately into two separate theaters. Since the Yugoslavs had failed to mobilize, the German attack fell on a badly prepared opponent. The destruction of Belgrade, the center of Yugoslav communications, exacerbated the situation further. The Yugoslav high command had spread its forces along the entire length of its frontier; it even entertained illusions of attacking the Italians in Albania. However, the only chance for a sustained resistance lay in abandoning the entire northern half of the country, including territories gained at great cost in World War I.

The opening of hostilities with Yugoslavia, however, depended on the start time for the invasion of Greece. German air attacks on Belgrade commenced on 6 April; the main ground attacks followed on the 8th. The gap reflected the difficulties the German Second Army had had in its deployment. On 6 April, XL Panzer Corps struck at Skopje in southern Yugoslavia and across the southern flank of the Yugoslav Army; its objective was to outflank Greek positions. Led by 9th Panzer Division and SS Regiment Leibstandarte Adolf Hitler, the Germans broke the Greek Third Army after fierce fighting and flanked Greek defenses. The advance of XL Panzer Corps covered the flank of First Panzer Group, which jumped off against Belgrade on 8 April. First Panzer Group's strike from Bulgaria consequently had its path prepared by the collapse of Yugoslav defenses to the south. After heavy fighting, Kleist's units achieved operational freedom on the 9th and were on their way to the town of Nis and beyond. Their success led the OKH, which had scheduled XLI Panzer Corps to attack on 12 April, to move up the attack to the 11th. The other corps of Weichs's army moved two days early, even though troop deployments were not complete. As Kleist drove from the southeast, XLI Panzer Corps struck from the east, while 8th Panzer Division sliced to the rear of Belgrade from the northeast. The capital fell on 12 April; soldiers from Das Reich hoisted the swastika over the German embassy and the smoking city.

With Belgrade's fall, the Yugoslav Army collapsed into complete disarray.

Fighting had already broken out between Croat and Serb units; the campaign turned into a complete rout. Mountain and infantry units led by the 14th Panzer Division took Zagreb with little resistance. Meanwhile, the 8th Panzer Division swung southwest to reach Sarajevo and meet up with the 14th Panzer Division (also under XLI Panzer Corps) driving southeast from Zagreb. Yugoslavia's conventional military forces ceased to exist. On 17 April, with their high command already in German hands, representatives of the Yugoslav government capitulated to Weichs in Belgrade. The Wehrmacht had destroyed Yugoslavia in barely a week.

The Germans now hurriedly recalled units committed to Yugoslavia so as not to disturb time tables for Operation Barbarossa. That rapid redeployment left thousands of undefeated Yugoslav troops in the mountain areas. The government may have ceased to exist, but partisan resistance began almost immediately. The seeming completeness of German victory only masked the smoldering fires of violent Balkan nationalism.

The Greek campaign replicated Yugoslavia's subjugation, except that in this case the British were also humiliated. By striking at Skopje, XL Panzer Corps had outflanked Greek lines, but initial attacks on the Nestos line in northern Greece by the XVIII Mountain Corps only achieved limited success. However, the German drive through Yugoslavia forced the British and Greeks to retreat. The German advance engulfed the Greek rear areas in Albania. As the Germans rapidly pursued fleeing Allied forces toward Thermopylae, Greek generals in Albania deposed their commander and sought terms—terms that did not include the Italians.

Given the Greek collapse, the British could not hold Thermopylae. Nevertheless, the defense of the pass slowed the German advance. As the Germans pushed past Thermopylae, List launched a paratrooper drop on the Corinth Canal to cut off the retreating British forces as well as to capture the canal intact to protect the Italian-Romanian oil link. However, the British crossed the canal before the attack and destroyed its bridges. Meanwhile, despite almost total Axis air superiority, the Royal Navy evacuated 50,732 out of the 62,000 British soldiers in Greece.

With Greece and Yugoslavia eliminated, the Germans attacked one last objective: Crete, the southernmost island in the Aegean. Hitler ordered an airborne attack to finish the campaign and secure the Romanian oil fields from the threat of bombing attacks. General Kurt Student, the paratrooper pioneer, had already proposed an airborne assault on Crete; at the same time, the OKW proposed an assault on Malta. Hitler decided on Crete. Given that Malta would have required considerable redeployments, Crete was the correct choice. But such an attack would have to rely almost exclusively on airborne forces; the German Navy scratched together some transport, but movement across the Aegean would need Italian naval support. Given the March disaster at Cape Matapan, where the Royal Navy had sunk three Italian heavy cruisers, chances of an Italian sortie were minimal.

In the air, the Luftwaffe enjoyed complete superiority. Almost 500 transport aircraft and 100 gliders were available for the air assault; still, the number of transports available placed considerable limitations on planning. Moreover, deployment of so many transports, plus 280 bombers, 150 dive bombers, 180 fighters, and 40 reconnaissance aircraft, created a logistic nightmare on the air fields of Greece. Shortages of transport aircraft forced the Germans to plan a two-wave attack for Operation Merkur. The morning assault would strike Maleme air field and Canea on Crete's western side; transport aircraft would return with a second wave in the afternoon to attack air fields at Retimo and Heraklion in the center. The Germans had two divisions available: the Luftwaffe's 7th Airborne and the army's 5th Mountain. As in Holland, the Germans hoped that by seizing the air fields they would create a bridgehead they could expand by aerial reinforcement.

If the Germans had possessed an accurate intelligence picture, they might never have launched the attack. German intelligence reports severely underestimated the number of Commonwealth troops on Crete and assumed that the local population would be friendly. In fact, General Bernard Freyberg, commander of the Allied forces, deployed about 28,000 British, Australian, and New Zealand troops, plus a number of ill-equipped Greek formations. Many of Freyberg's forces had fled from mainland Greece and the German onslaught without their heavy equipment, but they were first-class soldiers, and their morale remained high. The British also enjoyed the advantage of Ultra, which delivered the German plans in considerable detail, including the fact that the island's air fields would be the main target. Other sources complemented Ultra intelligence.

On the day before the attack, the Greeks shot down a Bf 110 and recovered the operational order for the 3rd Parachute Regiment from the wreckage. Freyberg, then, had solid evidence of what to expect. However, he ignored the intelligence and emphasized a defense against a seaborne attack. He reported to Churchill immediately before the attack that he had other worries besides an airborne attack. Thus, throughout the crucial first days of the Battle of Crete the defenders focused on the seaborne threat rather than the actual airborne assault. Consequently, the bulk of Commonwealth forces defended the beaches while most anti-aircraft guns covered the Suda Bay–Canea sector. Only one infantry battalion held the crucial Maleme air field; the remainder of the 5th New Zealand Brigade covered the coastal road.

Initially, the German attack hovered on the brink of military catastrophe. On the way to Crete, the glider carrying the commander of the 7th Airborne Division parted its tow rope, lost a wing, and crashed onto the island of Aegina. On Crete, German paratroopers jumped into a hornet's nest of resistance. Anti-aircraft fire blasted transports and gliders alike; the German command structure dissolved on the ground. The Maleme drop found itself without any workable radios to warn Athens of its desperate plight. Thus, the afternoon drop on Heraklion went in on schedule and deposited its paratroopers on the other side of the island and into the same predicament as those who had landed on Maleme and Canea. To add to German troubles, the Royal Navy intercepted two convoys of troop reinforcements on their way to Crete; after chasing off protecting Italian torpedo boats, the British sank ten caïques filled with German troops and equipment. No further reinforcements followed by sea.

Nevertheless, the turning point in the battle came during the first night at Maleme. Lieutenant Colonel L. W. Andrew, commander of the 22nd New Zealand Battalion, had won a Victoria Cross in the last war. But now, tired and under terrible strain from the fighting, Andrew pulled his men off the hill overlooking the Maleme air field. The Germans were equally exhausted; their casualties had been disastrous. But with the New Zealanders off the heights, the Luftwaffe could begin air landing the 5th Mountain Division on the next day. While subsequent counterattacks battered the invaders, the Germans did not lose their hold on Maleme. Moreover, throughout the second day, Freyberg's attention remained on the threat from the sea. He held his reserves around Suda, while the New Zealanders received only one more battalion, and that arrived late because the coastal defense of Suda Bay received priority.

Once the German buildup was under way, the British position deteriorated. For the third time in a year, the Royal Navy undertook a major evacuation under heavy air attack. In the teeth of total German air superiority, it achieved that task. But the cost was heavy: 3 cruisers and 6 destroyers sunk; 2 battleships, 1 carrier, 6 cruisers, and 7 destroyers damaged.

In the end, Crete represented a severe strategic blow to the Allies. Possession of the island would have provided the British a base to intercept Romanian oil through the Aegean and then an air base to launch direct attacks on Romanian air fields. It would also have provided an ideal position to supply arms to resistance forces throughout Greece. On the German side, Crete was hardly a great success, considering that the 7th Airborne Division suffered heavier casualties than the invasions of Greece and Yugoslavia combined.

Conclusion

For Hitler, the Mediterranean campaign of 1940–41 represented a diversion. In summer 1940 he had assigned the region entirely to Mussolini, while he himself dreamed of *Lebensraum* at the expense of the Soviet Union. German approaches to Marshal Phillipe Pétain, the head of the collaborationist regime in Vichy France, and to Franco in October 1940 represented an effort to distract the British by keeping them so busy in the west that they could not interfere in the coming eastern campaign.

Hitler was right, for from the strategic point of view the Middle East offered few possibilities. The entrance of Italy into the war had closed the Mediterranean to the Allies; consequently British shipping moved around the Cape. The journey was significantly longer but did not place an intolerable burden on British resources. Moreover, there were few resources and raw materials in the Mediterranean basin essential to Britain's conduct of the war.

Britain's strategic hopes rested in the mobilization and participation of the United States and perhaps the Soviet Union in the war. All of this Hitler anticipated. Therefore, his approach to the Mediterranean represented an expedient strategy until he could deal with Germany's eastern problem. Hitler, of course, had hoped that the Italians could handle the Mediterranean by themselves; in addition, he hoped that there would be some degree of effectiveness in Italian policy. But he underestimated the extent of Italian incompetence and irresponsibility. From October 1940, the Germans had to engage in damage limitation. That led to the reinforcement of North Africa by the Afrika Korps and to the sledgehammer assault on Greece and Yugoslavia, which reduced both to harsh occupation.

Initially, the Mediterranean proved a most surprising and welcome success for the British. But Wavell thought small and failed to see the vulnerabilities of the Italian position in Libya. Thus, the British wasted the opportunity to advance on Tripoli for the sake of clearing Abyssinia. Moreover, the failure to pursue the Italians in Libya to the full extent eventually led to the disastrous involvement in Greece. And finally, failure at Crete robbed the British of a valuable base and allowed the Germans to protect their southern flank for the invasion of the Soviet Union.

But the conquest of Greece and Yugoslavia opened a darker chapter in

European history. The Germans extracted so much foodstuffs and raw materials from Greece that widespread famine broke out the following winter.
That famine fueled the growth of resistance forces, since the Germans
failed to complete the conquest in their rush to deal with the Soviet Union.
From the beginning, the German reply to partisan war was a policy of ruthlessness that led to hundreds of bloodstained Serbian and Greek villages; it
also resulted in the immediate shooting of thousands of Serbian and Austrian Jews by the German Army. Without instructions from Berlin, military
authorities in the Balkans in summer 1941 embarked on the mass slaughter of Jewish hostages that mirrored what their colleagues were doing so
enthusiastically in the Soviet Union.

There was thus a full congruence of the officer corps with the Nazi regime in the identification of Jews as partisans and therefore subject to an
immediate sentence of death. Not surprisingly, civil, class, and tribal conflict among the Balkan peoples soon fanned the flames of revolution
against the Axis occupiers. The timeless description by Thucydides of the
Civil War on Corcyra in the 5th century BC suggests the horror that Mussolini and Hitler had unleashed: "But war is a stern teacher; in depriving
them of the power of easily satisfying their daily wants, it brings most people's minds down to the level of their actual circumstances . . . In their
struggles for ascendancy nothing was barred; terrible indeed were the actions to which they committed themselves, and in taking revenge they
went farther still. Here they were deterred neither by claims of justice nor
by the interests of the state."[9]

6

BARBAROSSA

1941

Stalin's toast at the celebratory banquet in August 1939 caught the moral parameters of the Nazi-Soviet Non-Aggression Pact: "To Heinrich Himmler, the man who has brought order to Germany." At the time, it appeared that the Soviets had gained the best of the bargain: they could remain out of the war, pick up their territorial booty in Eastern Europe, and await the collapse of the capitalist West from another blood-letting. About all the Germans had gained was a secure eastern front, while they settled matters in the west—if they could. In late September 1939 the Germans even surrendered their claims to Lithuania in return for control over all Polish-speaking territory—a move of some strategic consequence to the Soviets, since it pushed Leningrad 200 miles farther away from Nazi territory. Relations between the two powers warmed considerably. In December, Stalin telegraphed Ribbentrop that the blood of Nazi and Soviet soldiers had "cemented" the two peoples. Ribbentrop himself recorded that the cordiality with which Stalin and Vyacheslav Molotov, the Soviet foreign minister, had received him in the Kremlin made him feel as if he were at a gathering of old National Socialist Party comrades.

Hitler hoped that if and when the Western powers declared war, the Soviets would help to break the blockade. They did, but not in any substantial fashion until February 1940, when the flow of raw materials and foodstuffs to the Reich significantly picked up. In return for finished goods such as machine tools, the Soviets exchanged oil, raw materials, and rubber supplies across the Trans-Siberian Railroad. According to the Reich's Four Year Plan office, Soviet aid was of "decisive military importance" in supporting the offensive against the West. In 1940 Soviet exports to Germany made up 66 percent of all phosphorous imports, 63 percent of chrome imports, 55 percent of manganese imports, and 33 percent of oil imports to the war economy.

The French collapse in May 1940 encouraged Stalin to seize the rest of the territories promised by the Nazi-Soviet Non-Aggression Pact. Lithuania, Latvia, and Estonia begged for inclusion in the workers' and peasants' paradise. The Soviets also demanded that Romania surrender the provinces of Bessarabia and Bukovina (the latter not covered by the pact). Yet Stalin failed to divine the danger in this path. On 1 July 1940 he noted to the new British ambassador, Sir Stafford Cripps, that Germany did not intend to dominate Europe.

But Hitler's guarantee of Romania's independence in August infuriated the Soviets, while the movement of German troops across Finland to Norway in September annoyed them even more. Their complaints were sharp, but their actions spoke weakness. In November, Molotov traveled to Berlin to open negotiations for an alliance at a time when the Germans were already deep into planning an invasion of the Soviet Union. Molotov spent much of the trip to Berlin looking for listening devices in his rail car. The visit was not a success. Molotov heard out Hitler's and Ribbentrop's monologues with barely concealed suspicion. He suggested that Soviet participation in the Tripartite Pact—the alliance of Germany, Italy, and Japan—was acceptable in principle, provided the Soviet Union became a full partner. The Germans were not interested.

Within several weeks of Molotov's return, the Soviets reiterated their desire to join the Tripartite Pact. Berlin remained silent. In early January 1941, shortly after the signing of a renewed economic agreement, Molotov plaintively asked the German ambassador why he had received no response. At the same time he notified the Germans that the Soviet Union considered Bulgaria as lying within its security zone. Yet within a month and a half the Wehrmacht had bridged the Danube and rolled into Bulgaria, as it deployed its troops toward the Greek frontier. Again, Soviet protests received no response.

In early April the Soviets reacted to spreading German influence in the Balkans by signing a treaty of alliance with the Yugoslav colonels who had undertaken the coup in Belgrade. The Nazis then launched a massive invasion of Yugoslavia. Seriously worried, the Soviets continued to meet their side of the economic agreements with over-fulfillment of raw material shipments, even as the Germans fell further and further behind in deliveries of finished goods. By 22 June 1941, the Soviets had delivered 2.2 million tons of grain, 1 million tons of oil, and 100,000 tons of cotton. These deliveries (particularly of oil) proved essential for the Wehrmacht's conduct of the coming invasion.

Stalin displayed little awareness of the gathering storm. He completely ignored warnings from the West as well as his own intelligence services. Certainly German disinformation contributed to Stalin's disbelief, but stubbornness was also a factor. On 13 April in a farewell ceremony for the Japanese foreign minister, he embraced the German ambassador and exclaimed: "We must remain friends and you must do everything to that end!"[1] On 14 June the Soviet news agency Tass reported that rumors of Germany's intention "to launch an attack on the Soviet Union" were completely unfounded.[2] Not until midnight on the evening of 21–22 June 1941 did the Kremlin issue a warning order to its commanders, while in the early morning the last train carrying goods from the east rumbled onto German territory. At 0330 hours on 22 June 1941 German forces opened their offensive from East Prussia to the Black Sea. The next morning Molotov plaintively complained to the German ambassador, "Surely we have not deserved that."[3]

Preparations for War

The Soviet Union's economic preparations for war had begun in the late 1920s with the first Five Year Plan. Stalin feared that the capitalist powers were preparing an invasion; not surprisingly, much of the economic buildup took place east of Moscow in the Urals and Siberia. By the late 1930s these efforts had created a military-industrial complex of enormous potential. In 1939 Soviet industry raised defense production by 46.5 percent. From January 1939 through June 1941, 105,000 machine guns, 100,000 submachine guns, 82,000 artillery tubes and mortars, over 1,800 tanks, 15,000 anti-tank guns, and over 2,700 aircraft rolled off the production lines. This economic capacity explains much about the Soviet Union's survival after the grim defeats of 1941.

The dark side of Soviet preparations lay in the nature of the tyranny that Stalin and Lenin established. For Stalin, the logic of politics demanded the liquidation of potential as well as overt enemies. Consequently, he brutally purged the Soviet bureaucracy beginning in 1934. The military's turn came in 1937. Destruction of the Red Army's officer corps ended efforts to improve the military weaknesses apparent in maneuvers throughout the mid-1930s; the purge also removed most forward-thinking officers. Particularly tragic was the elimination of M. N. Tukhachevsky, who along with V. K. Triandafillov had pioneered the radical ideas of deep battle and deep operations in the Red Army—concepts that involved mechanized forces penetrating the heart of enemy country.

The result was the reorganization of the Red Army and breakup of ar-

1. Set afire by a Dutch Communist, the Reichstag burns over the night of 27-28 February 1933. This act of political arson provided Hitler with the excuse he needed to destroy his enemies and establish his dictatorship.

2. Hitler and his henchmen at a Nazi Party rally in the early years of the Thousand Year Reich. To the right of the Führer are Hermann Göring, Joseph Goebbels, and Rudolf Hess.

3. A solemn Adolf Hitler accepts the ovation of the Reichstag deputies after the successful annexation of Austria. Göring, resplendent in his Luftwaffe uniform, stands on the podium. To the Führer's left are Hess and his new foreign minister, Joachim von Ribbentrop.

4. Waving a piece of paper he and Hitler had signed that morning, Neville Chamberlain returns in triumph from the Munich Conference. An appreciative crowd greets the prime minister.

5. Furious that Chamberlain and Daladier had robbed him of the chance to attack the hated Czechs, Hitler takes the salute of a German Army unit occupying the Sudetenland in early October 1938.

6. Vyacheslav Molotov, Soviet Foreign Minister, puts his signature to the Nazi-Soviet Non-Aggression Pact on 22 August 1939. Ribbentrop appears to be somewhat nonplussed at being among his racial enemies, but Stalin is obviously delighted at the outcome. A photo of Lenin looks down benignly on the proceedings.

7. The German Army's commander, Walter von Brauchitsch (left), and chief of staff, Franz Halder (right), confer with the commander of the 31st Infantry Division (middle) during the course of the Polish campaign.

8. The not-so-modern German Army: an infantry regiment led by two officers marches down a Polish road near Dobromil-Przemysi in September
1939.

9. The modern German military: staff cars and motorcycle dispatch riders
of the Waffen SS regiment Leibstandarte Adolf Hitler confer on a Polish
road in early September 1939.

10. German assault troops attack a Polish defensive position with grenades in September 1939.

11. German soldiers supervise a party of Poles digging graves for those already shot. After completion of their grim task, these men, too, were shot. Over 3,000,000 Poles were killed by their Nazi masters over the course of the war.

12. Goose-stepping soldiers lead the German Army's victory parade in Warsaw in early October 1939. Senior generals take the salute.

13. The epitome of the general staff tradition, Field Marshal Gerd von Rundstedt (left) served Hitler's Thousand Year Reich from the beginning of the war to the bitter end.

14. The epitome of the muddy boots soldier, Erwin Rommel (above) not only avidly read books but wrote them as well. A loyal supporter of the regime at the beginning of the war, Rommel began to have doubts by summer 1944.

15. Waffen SS troops come under heavy fire during the initial hours of the invasion of Holland. Their camouflage smocks and helmet covers identify them as members of the Waffen SS rather than the army.

16. German assault troops prepare to cross the Meuse in their inflatable rubber rafts. French artillery is falling nearby.

17. The Germans lead British and French prisoners of war away from the wreckage of the Dunkirk beaches. But enough soldiers of the British Army escaped to make continued resistance possible.

18. A Frenchman weeps in frustration and sorrow as German troops move into Paris in mid-June 1940.

19. With the surrender of France already an accomplished fact, Hitler and Mussolini meet in Munich to discuss the further division of the world. Hundreds of thousands of Bavarian Nazis greet the delighted victors.

20. Although inferior to the Spitfire and Bf 109, the British Hurricane, with a good fighter pilot at its controls, could give an excellent account of itself. In summer 1940 Hurricanes carried the burden of attacking the German bombers, while Spitfires held off the Bf 109s.

21. Behind Tower Bridge, much of east London and its great docks go up in flames after savage Luftwaffe air attacks on 7 September. But the change in German tactics afforded Fighter Command precious time to recover its equilibrium.

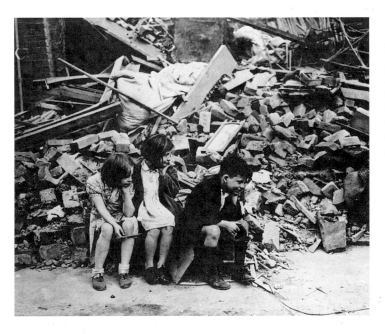

22. Homeless children in London's East End survey the wreckage of their home and belongings as a result of a night attack by the Luftwaffe in September 1940.

23. The great dome of St. Paul's stands silhouetted in a sea of flames during the massive Luftwaffe attack on London over the night of 29 December. Much of the surrounding area was wrecked, but the cathedral remained largely undamaged.

24. Heinrich Himmler, commander of the SS and architect of the Holocaust, visits a POW camp filled with Soviet prisoners during the early weeks of Operation Barbarossa. An army officer, most probably the camp commandant, accompanies Himmler, while a Luftwaffe NCO looks on from the background.

25. The commander of Panzer Group Three, Generaloberst Hermann Hoth (middle), confers with staff officers during the initial stages of the invasion of the Soviet Union.

26. A member of one of Himmler's Einsatzgruppen prepares to execute a Ukrainian Jew. In the background, besides soldiers and SS men, there is a teenage member of the German Reichs Arbeitsdienst (work service) performing his labor service before induction into the army.

27. Finnish soldiers press home an attack on Soviet positions in summer 1941, in retaliation for Soviet aggression in November 1939. Both sides paid a heavy price for these wars.

28. Aside from bayonets, bullets, and enthusiasm, the Red Army did not have much to fight with during the long dark summer of 1941.

29. As German artillery falls in the background, the Soviet cavalry attacks near the Yelnya salient in late summer 1941.

30. The Soviets launch a counteroffensive at the Folkshov Front during winter 1941-42. Whether on the offensive or defensive, the Soviets always suffered heavy casualties.

mored formations, which Tukhachevsky had sponsored. Even as late as winter 1939–1940 the NKVD was shooting operational commanders and logistics experts tainted by their connection to Tukhachevsky's experiments or contacts with the Germans. By 1941 the Red Army's leadership consisted of new and untried officers with a mere crust of senior commanders attuned to the moods of the dictator but not much else.

In the minds of most planners in the Soviet military, France's rapid collapse lay in its capitalist political and economic system. Such thinking did not bode well for Soviet assessments of German capabilities. The weaknesses in the Red Army were clear enough: a lack of initiative among junior officers and NCOs, a lack of coordination between combat arms, sloppy staff work, and a supply system that functioned sporadically. The Soviet high command gave considerable attention in 1940 to correcting these deficiencies, but at the same time it was grappling with the problem of putting back together the armored formations that Stalin had dissolved in 1939.

Stalin's greatest fear was not insurrection among the military, however, but the political unreliability of the Soviet peoples. Could he trust his citizens to resist a foreign invasion? From the dictator's perspective, the regime could not surrender any territory, including the newly occupied districts of Poland and the Baltic republics, lest such losses undermine the Soviet Union's political stability. Consequently, the Red Army rolled forward to positions on the newly acquired frontier, while engineer troops demobilized the Stalin Line on the old frontier. However, construction of these new defensive positions began only in early 1941. How then to defend Soviet territory?

A series of war games from December 1940 to January 1941 suggested vulnerabilities to a German invasion. But this conclusion only buttressed Stalin's intuition: Soviet forces must reinforce the frontier so that the Germans could not break through. Then the mobilization of reserves would allow a counterattack—no territory lost, no political problems. Throughout the spring, the Soviets steadily enlarged their frontier forces to nearly wartime strength. In early June after hearing there were 149 divisions in the west, Stalin still asked Zhukov whether that was enough.

Two additional factors exacerbated Soviet difficulties. The first was Stalin's misjudgment of where the Germans would strike. Because of Germany's economic difficulties, Stalin calculated that the Germans would deliver their main blow in the south. Of the approximately 130 Soviet divisions on the frontier, 60 defended the Ukraine, 40 held the center, and 30 the Baltic states. The northern and central fronts were the most weakly defended, and these turned out to be where the main brunt of the German offensive would fall.

Adding to the Red Army's difficulties was a failure to reequip the Soviet front line. Many of the army's units in the west were undergoing a major reorganization and retraining to correct the weaknesses exhibited in the war on Finland. In some ways the Red Army was in worse shape when the campaign began than the French Army had been in May 1940. Moreover, Stalin's tyranny demanded that the NKVD root out all signs of defeatism. Consequently, few within the military bureaucracy dared to voice their fears. Even the idea that the Red Army might have to fight a defensive war suggested an unacceptably defeatist attitude. Consequently, many units involved in the June fighting discovered they had maps only of German territory, where they would presumably advance, and not of the home territory they were defending and through which they might have to retreat. However clever the Germans were at deception, it was Stalin who ensured that the German attack would catch the Red Army completely by surprise.

As Hitler picnicked along the Rhine in June 1940, German pride in the Wehrmacht's victories reached new heights. That July the Sicherheitsdienst (the SD, the SS security service) reported that the majority of Germans hoped Britain would refuse the Führer's peace offer so that the Wehrmacht could smash the British. Yet, Hitler turned against the Soviet Union, rather than Britain, almost immediately after the fall of France. He remarked to Brauchitsch and Halder on 22 July that the British had stayed in the war only because of their "1) hope for change in America . . . [and] 2) hope in Russia."[4] By the end of the month Hitler had firmly decided to invade the Soviet Union. Besides the strategic reasons, his own ideological predilections pushed him toward conquest in the east. As he suggested to his generals in January 1941, "German victory incompatible with Russian ideology. Decision: Russia must be smashed as soon as possible."[5]

Hitler emphasized to his commanders that the war in the east marked a different struggle. In March 1941 the Führer described the coming campaign to the generals in the following terms: "*Clash of two ideologies:* Crushing denunciation of Bolshevism . . . Communism is an enormous danger for our future . . . This is a war of extermination . . . *War against Russia:* Extermination of Bolshevist Commissars and of the Communist intelligentsia . . . We must fight against the poison of disintegration. This is no job for military courts . . . Commissars and GPU men are criminals and must be dealt with as such."[6] Hitler's comments directly influenced the OKW and OKH planning that shaped the war in the east. The general guidelines for the war (dated 13 May 1941) and the Commissar Order, which decreed the shooting of all Red Army commissars upon capture, dispensed with Germany's international and legal obligations even before the war started. The vision of an ideological crusade spread throughout the Wehrmacht's entire structure. Even a future participant in the 20 July plot against Hitler, General Erich Hoepner, issued the following directive to his Fourth Panzer Group: "The objective of this battle must be the demolition of present-day Russia and must therefore be conducted with *unprecedented severity* . . . In particular, *no adherents of the contemporary Russian Bolshevik system are to be spared.*"[7]

As a result of this ideological framework, the Germans never paid the slightest attention to the deep-seated hostility to Stalin's tyranny that much of the Russian population felt. Instead of enlisting the Soviet peoples in the effort to overthrow the Communist regime, the Nazis drove them into the arms of their rulers. Moreover, because of their contempt for Slavs, the German military, not just Hitler, consistently underestimated the staying power and sophistication of their opponents. Hitler commented before the invasion began that once the Germans kicked in the door, the whole structure, ruled by Jewish subhumans, would collapse. Similarly, General Günther Blumentritt, a sophisticated general staff officer, claimed in 1941 that "Russian military history shows that the Russian combat soldier, illiterate and half-Asiatic, thinks and feels differently [than the German]."[8]

Two weeks after the signing of the armistice with France on 17 June 1940, Brauchitsch ordered Halder to begin thinking about an invasion of the Soviet Union. Planning proceeded fitfully for the rest of the month because it was not entirely clear what the goals might be. As Halder noted on 22 July 1940: "What operational objective could be obtained? What strength have we available? Timing and area of assembly?"[9] Hitler had commented to General Alfred Jodl, chief of the operations section of the OKW, that the campaign to destroy the Soviet Union would begin in May 1941. Two days later a conference further clarified German strategy. Hitler informed Halder and Brauchitsch that the coming offensive "achieves its purpose only if the Russian state can be shattered to its roots in one blow." In chaotic fashion he sketched his conception for the campaign: "Operation will be divided into three actions: *First Thrust:* Kiev and securing flank protection on Dnepr . . . *Second Thrust:* Baltic States and drive on Moscow. *Finally:* link up of northern and southern prongs."[10]

As planning began, the general staff's geographic department suggested that occupation of Leningrad, Moscow, the Ukraine, and the Caucasus would not exhaust Soviet economic potential. The Five Year Plans had created substantial economic strength along and east of the Urals that would

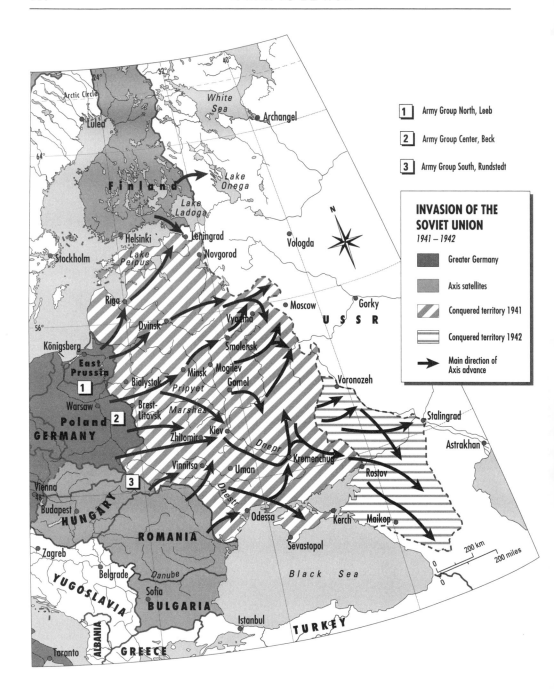

1   Army Group North, Leeb

2   Army Group Center, Beck

3   Army Group South, Rundstedt

**INVASION OF THE
SOVIET UNION**
1941 – 1942

Greater Germany

Axis satellites

Conquered territory 1941

Conquered territory 1942

Main direction of
Axis advance

allow the Soviets to continue resistance, even should most of European Russia fall. Astonishingly, planning for Operation Barbarossa ignored that factor. By late July Halder had formed his own conception of the campaign: a drive on Moscow that would compel "Russian concentrations in the Ukraine and at the Black Sea to accept battle with inverted front."[11] Yet even before differences between Hitler and the army emerged, the Germans had accepted the assumption that the Wehrmacht could defeat the bulk of Soviet forces before winter's onset. A number of fundamental errors flowed from that assumption.

On 5 August 1940, Major General Erich Marcks presented his draft conception to Halder. Marcks posited the main strategic aim as destroying Soviet forces, with the main drive heading north of the Pripyet marshes toward Moscow; subsidiary drives would protect the flanks. Invading troops would then advance as far as the Archangel-Gorky-Rostov line to eliminate the air threat. Marcks argued that the decisive battles would occur in the first weeks and that panzer forces would play the crucial role; their penetrations would destroy the Red Army in the border areas. Once German forces had broken through, Soviet command and control would collapse, allowing piecemeal destruction of the remaining armies. Marcks estimated that German ground forces would require somewhere between nine and seventeen weeks to achieve their strategic objectives.

Marcks's estimate raises a number of interesting questions, especially considering the enormous distances involved. His diary suggests a belief in the ideological superiority of the Wehrmacht over its potential opponent. That superiority, inherent in Hitler's thinking as well, explains the extraordinary optimism about the possible length of the campaign. A study by the OKW in September and the OKH's operations branch in October reinforced Marcks's preliminary estimate that German forces could achieve the defeat of the Soviet Union before winter. These studies also indicated that the projected theater's funnel-shaped geography would not favor German forces. If the Red Army escaped defeat on the border, space, time, and distance would favor the Soviets. However, instead of leading the Germans to question the assumption of a quick victory, these studies reinforced their inclination to regard the frontier battles as decisive.

Hitler, of course, subscribed to the OKH's intentions of destroying the Red Army along the border. In early December he commented to Brauchitsch and Halder that "what matters most is to prevent the enemy from falling back before our onslaught . . . Aim of the campaign: crushing of Russian manpower; no group capable of recuperation must be allowed to escape." But Hitler also emphasized that the drive into the Ukraine was key; controlling the Baltic was almost as significant, in order to protect the iron ore trade with Sweden, while "Moscow [was] of no importance."[12] His conceptions informed Directive No. 21, the basic guideline for Barbarossa. The directive emphasized the destruction of the Red Army along the frontier but emphasized that these preliminary battles were to set the stage "for a pivoting movement performed by strong motorized elements that will drive northward in order to annihilate the enemy forces in the Baltic area in conjunction with the northern army group which will be driving from East Prussia in the general direction of Leningrad." Similarly, after destruction of Soviet forces in the center, the Germans would pursue the beaten enemy into the Donets basin. Directive No. 21 did suggest "that Moscow be reached as soon as possible. The political and economic significance of capturing this city is tremendous."[13] What the directive represented was an agreement among the German high command, including Hitler himself, not to agree. The basic premise of German planning now was that operations should strive to destroy the Red Army on the frontier; after that nothing was clear.

In summer 1940, while planning for Barbarossa was already under way, the first movements of German forces to the east began. Eighteenth Army redeployed to the east, followed in September by Army Group B and Fourth and Twelfth Armies, accompanied by ten infantry and one panzer division. In addition, three panzer and two motorized infantry divisions returned to eastern Germany to retrain for combat in the east and prepare deployment areas and communications networks required by the coming flood of German forces. Masking the buildup was essential to German plans. The initial movements could be explained as a covering force. Thereafter the problem became more complex as the tempo of deployment picked up. But it was not until late May and June 1941 that the Germans flooded the border areas in occupied Poland and East Prussia with nearly two divisions per day. By then it was too late for Soviet intelligence to digest the extent of German deployments, at least before the invasion. The final deployment included 28 panzer and motorized infantry divisions, the backbone of German offensive strength. Logistical support and stockpiles were already in place, while the Soviets still failed to appreciate the German movements.

Barbarossa depended on creating a logistical system capable of supplying the Wehrmacht over the Soviet Union's immense distances. But this requirement lingered at the bottom of German priorities throughout the planning period. On 31 July 1940 Hitler had ordered the army to expand to 180 divisions from approximately 100. Moreover, the number of panzer divisions doubled, while motorized infantry divisions increased to ten. To achieve this goal his planners had to decrease the tank regiments in each panzer division from two to one, while each new panzer division required a new motorized infantry regiment and a new motorized artillery regiment, plus signal engineers and supply troops. This reorganization caused a supply nightmare in patching together new motorized and mechanized formations. The extent of the reequipment of mobile formations would probably have forced a postponement of the start date, even without the Balkan campaign.

To equip the new formations, the Germans assembled a hodgepodge of weapons and vehicles. Army trucks came from the peacetime economies of Western Europe, from captured Allied equipment, and even from Switzerland. None of these trucks had been designed for use on anything other than Western Europe's well-constructed roads; the conditions of Soviet roads would lead to innumerable breakdowns. The weapons that equipped German combat formations came from an even wider assortment of suppliers. Czech tanks still made up a substantial portion of armored strength; the diverse weapons and supply vehicles were distributed throughout the army with little rationale. Among the infantry divisions, the logistical situation was even worse: French, Czech, and even Norwegian artillery, vehicles from virtually every European nation, and small arms from non-German sources (often Czech) were all present. Thus, supply and maintenance units confronted the impossible task of supplying units that often were equipped with entirely dissimilar weapons and support vehicles.

Barbarossa's logistical complexities were clear by November 1940. That month, the OKH's chief logistics officer, Major General Eduard Wagner, warned that the distances and the time factor would exacerbate the already-critical problem of equipping German forces. Wagner calculated that the Wehrmacht's logistic system could support the forces at a depth of 500 kilometers east of the frontier—a distance short of Leningrad, Moscow, and the Donets basin. His warning made little impression. Moreover, German logisticians warned that advances of 300 to 400 kilometers would demand a pause for resupply and restocking of forward units. But then the supply authorities themselves made a number of overly optimistic assumptions; for example, they calculated that ammunition expenditures for the campaign would not exceed those of the battle in France. Consequently, the invading troops crossed into enemy territory with only two to three basic units of fire (a day's estimated ammunition) in the hope that the supply system would cough up enough shells until the collapse of Soviet resistance. Since the supply system could barely transport sufficient fuel and ammunition to frontline units, foodstuffs for the troops and fodder for the horses had to come from foraging—and this encouraged further mistreatment of civilians. Finally, the railroad repair troops, whose support was essential to the success of the campaign, were inexplicably assigned the lowest priority in the move forward.

And so 22 June came. At the operational level the Germans expected to destroy the Red Army in the frontier zones. But beyond that the German high command had not decided on the campaign's next objectives—largely because Halder and Brauchitsch feared that a decision by Hitler would force them to focus on Leningrad and the Ukraine, which they did not want to do. The support structure was anything but secure. Should the Soviets survive the first blow, the logistical system would be hard pressed to support the Wehrmacht in the depths of Russia. To worsen their prospects, the Germans were not coming as liberators but as destroyers of European Jewry and enslavers of the Slavs. As Hitler commented, "Naturally this great area would have to be pacified. The best solution was to shoot anyone who looked askance."[14] Such attitudes condoned terrible crimes and underestimated Germany's opponent.

Yet, despite those extraordinary weaknesses, Stalin came close to giving the game away. By stationing the Red Army's best units in the border areas, he ensured their destruction at the campaign's outset, while his fears about the Soviet Union's political stability would lead him to throw away most of the Red Army's reserves of men and equipment before winter. Only after many costly lessons did the Red Army master the art of war against its opponents.

The First Phase

Early in the morning of 22 June 1941, a German signal unit intercepted the following Soviet radio messages: "Front line unit: 'We are being fired upon. What shall we do?' Army headquarters: 'You must be insane and why is not your signal in code?'"[15] That same morning Halder recorded laconically in his diary: "Tactical *surprise* of the enemy has apparently been achieved along the entire line."[16] Before dawn German bombers crossed the frontier at high altitude to avoid alerting Soviet defenses. They then attacked air fields where Soviet aircraft were parked in neat rows. The few Soviet aircraft that struggled aloft soon fell victim to German fighters. Fliegerkorps IV reported that in its first strikes it destroyed 142 aircraft on the ground and 16 in the air. By noon the Soviets had lost 528 aircraft on the ground and 210 in the air in the western military districts alone; over the entire

Eastern Front they lost more than 1,200 combat aircraft in the first 8.5 hours. Ill-trained Soviet pilots floundered in impossible tactical formations, while Luftwaffe attacks resulted in the collapse of Soviet command and control. Field Marshal Erhard Milch recorded the destruction of 1,800 aircraft on 22 June, 800 on the 23rd, 557 on the 24th, 351 on the 25th, and 300 on the 26th.

The ground war was an even greater disaster. In some areas border guards offered heavy resistance; but where it counted the Germans broke through and the panzers moved rapidly to exploit the ensuing collapse. The STAVKA (the Soviet high command) played into German hands. For the most part it ordered counterattacks in all directions. At the end of the day it issued a reassuring, but false, communiqué indicating that the Germans had made only insignificant gains that morning, and that in the afternoon "attacks by German troops along most of the length of our frontiers were beaten off and losses inflicted on the enemy."[17] In fact, across the entire breadth of the front, the Germans had achieved surprise. Already their panzer and motorized divisions had left behind Soviet frontline positions and were advancing deep into the Red Army's rear.

With two infantry armies and one panzer group, Army Group North jumped off from a small wedge of territory in East Prussia. Fourth Panzer Group's tanks quickly achieved operational freedom and raced for the Dvina River in Latvia. Manstein's LXVI Panzer Corps reached that river in four days and captured the bridges at Dvinsk, 200 miles from its starting point on the East Prussian frontier. Along the way, German armor smashed Soviet reserves moving toward a front that the troops still believed to be in the distance. Manstein then urged Hoepner, commander of Fourth Panzer Group, to push the other panzer corps up behind Manstein's forces and allow LXVI Panzer Corps to continue its drive beyond the Dvina. But neither Hoepner nor the army group commander, Field Marshal Ritter von Leeb, knew whether their mission was to drive on to Leningrad to the north or to guard the flank of Army Group Center's advance toward Smolensk to the east. In the coming weeks they attempted both, and in the end failed at both. Leeb's tentative leadership further increased the problems of an army group confronting too much space with too few resources.

Manstein remained at Dvinsk, while XLI Panzer Corps arrived on his flank at Jacobstadt. The ensuing pause to allow XLI Panzer Corps to catch up gave the Soviets time to recover their balance, pull back from Lithuania and Latvia, and move reinforcements in from the east. In early July, Fourth Panzer Group resumed its advance on an axis running from Dvinsk toward the southern tip of Lake Peipus on the way to Leningrad. While XLI Panzer

Corps advanced directly on Ostov, Manstein's panzer corps swung east through the Stalin line into the impenetrable forests of northern Russia. By 9 July, Manstein was stuck in the woods; once extracted from its difficult position, his corps followed XLI Panzer Corps and then swung to the northeast and Lake Ilman. The rest of Fourth Panzer Group headed toward the Baltic at Narva. By the end of July Leeb was three-quarters of the way to Leningrad; his troops had smashed most of the Soviet defenders to their front. Nevertheless, Army Group North had mishandled its mechanized drive by advancing on two axes, while its forces were dispersed at the end of long, tenuous lines of communication. The German infantry remained far behind, and ammunition and food were in short supply for the panzers.

The Soviets confronted a nightmare. Unclear as to their responsibilities, since the Red Army's leaders had forbidden flexible preparations for defensive warfare, Soviet forces in the Baltic dissolved before the onslaught. Infantry divisions on the Northwestern Front dropped to one-third of authorized strength. By early July, tens of thousands of Soviet civilians were desperately building a defensive line near Luga 60 miles southwest of Leningrad, while Soviet forces barely patched together defenses to block a German rush on the city. Moreover, a new threat loomed; the Finns mobilized and attacked. While they did not advance beyond their old 1939 frontier, their offensive isolated Leningrad from the north.

The worst disasters, however, occurred in the center. There, the Red Army had deployed its troops well forward in Soviet-occupied Poland. The commander, Lieutenant General D. G. Pavlov, who on return from Spain had urged the dissolution of the mechanized corps, lost his nerve. North and south of Brest-Litovsk, Army Group Center's panzer groups expanded their breakthroughs and rolled deep into the Soviet rear. Slavishly following Moscow's orders, Pavlov ordered counterattacks, but his orders had little relevance to forces already dissolving or in hopeless positions. Communications collapsed as German commandos cut wires and destroyed radio stations. Heavy Luftwaffe bombing further wrecked the Red Army's cohesion. Within the first 16 hours, the German advance had unhinged the Northwestern Front from the Western Front. While Pavlov shoveled units into the jaws of the encirclement, Second and Third Panzer Groups swung in to meet near Minsk on 28 June. The German Fourth and Ninth Armies, consisting of infantry divisions, accomplished a smaller encirclement at Bialystok.

By the evening of 25 June, The Soviet Tenth and Third Armies were desperately trying to withdraw from Minsk. Division and corps staffs lost contact with subordinate units. Pavlov irrevocably lost control. But to the astonishment of the Germans, many Soviet troops resisted despite their hopeless position. Approximately 324,000 prisoners fell into German hands, and an equal number were dead or wounded. But the real catastrophe was that the Red Army lost many of its best officers and NCOs, men who would have been of inestimable value when the reserve armies assembled.

In addition to Soviet casualties, the Germans counted 3,300 Soviet tanks and 1,800 artillery pieces on the battlefield. They had destroyed Third and Tenth Armies and had inflicted heavy losses on the Fourth, Eleventh, and Thirteenth Armies. Stalin had Pavlov shot. The initial successes of their troops led to euphoria in the German high command—a confirmation of the assumption that the Wehrmacht could win the war by defeating the Red Army in the border areas. Halder noted on 3 July: "One can already say that the task of destroying the mass of the Red Army in front of the Dvina and Dnepr has been fulfilled . . . We can calculate on meeting [further] east . . . only disjointed forces which alone do not possess the strength to hinder [our] operations . . . It is therefore not claiming too much when I assert that the campaign against Russia has been won in fourteen days."[18]

The German novelist Theodor Plievier best caught the nature of the German armored advance: "The stream of tanks thundered over the bridge. The infantry lying at the side of the road were covered with dust. When there was a halt the men . . . could have a good look at the tanks. Only the driver sat inside, the crew sat on top—the commander on the edge of the turret with his headphones on, the others behind him . . . The column went on, there was a halt, and then it started again, rolling ahead at ten miles per hour . . . There was no sign of the sun, which must be sinking, for all this rattling and roaring and whining and screeching that crept by blotted out the day. The long stream of armor and the long wake of thick dust it stirred up stretched as far back as the Bug far into the heart of Poland . . . So it rolled along the road through Brest Litovsk, Minsk, and Smolensk, rolled along the military highway to Moscow."[19]

Yet troubles still confronted the Germans. Soon after the panzer spearheads closed at Minsk, Halder hoped that Guderian would continue his advance beyond Mogilev to the Dnepr, although the OKH could not give an order to that effect due to Hitler's interference. Nevertheless, the OKW fell in with Halder's wishes; on 3 July it allowed the advance to resume to execute an encirclement of Smolensk. Third Panzer Group moved first. Guderian's forces still held the southern line of the Minsk cauldron awaiting supporting infantry. The push immediately ran into heavy resistance, for the Red Army had hastily thrown together a new defensive line. Under the general direction of Fourth Army the two panzer groups moved on the

Dnepr. As the panzers enclosed a new pocket around Smolensk, the infantry divisions fell further behind.

By mid-July the Red Army had lost the battle for the Dnepr-Dvina line. On 16 July, Guderian's 29th Panzer Division captured Smolensk. Yet, despite Hoth's urgings, the gap between the two panzer groups in Army Group Center could not be closed; Guderian's panzer group defended too much territory to the south and lay under heavy counterattack from Marshal S. K. Timoshenko's forces. Not until 24 July could Hoth close the Smolensk encirclement with the 27th Motorized Division. Only on 5 August did the Germans complete their destruction of Soviet units within the pocket; another 300,000 prisoners, 3,205 tanks, and 3,000 guns swelled the German totals. But Red Army resistance even in hopeless situations continued unabated; the commander of the 18th Panzer Division remarked that the Germans must reduce their casualties "if we do not intend to win ourselves to death."[20] Army Group Center had advanced 500 miles, two-thirds of the way to Moscow.

The situation in the south was quite different. There, the Soviet commander, Colonel General M. P. Kirponos, had undertaken elementary precautions in the last days of peace by mobilizing and redeploying his forces to more defensible positions. In the first days of Operation Barbarossa, he assembled six mechanized corps to attack the flank of Generaloberst Ewald von Kleist's First Panzer Group. From the beginning, Kleist's tanks found the going tough. The fact that many of his mechanized units had participated in the Balkan campaign added to his difficulties. A series of fierce frontier battles occurred as First Panzer Group struggled to achieve a breakthrough; its advance eventually threatened to encircle three Soviet armies (Sixth, Twenty-Sixth, and Twelfth). The Soviets, however, successfully retreated to the old frontier, although they lost much equipment as they fell back. On 8 July, Zhitomir fell and the Germans stood only 90 miles from Kiev. But pressure from Soviet armies in the Pripyet marshes forced Rundstedt to divert Sixth Army to the northeast instead of using it to support First Panzer Group. As Sixth Army fought off Soviet attacks, First Panzer Group swung away from Kiev in response to Hitler's order that Army Group South not launch a direct attack on the city by armored units. Sixth Army could not move its infantry up until the end of July; consequently, Rundstedt and Kleist opted for an armored drive southward to trap Soviet units retreating from the Dnestr River. Thus, First Panzer Group scored an impressive success in early August at Uman when it encircled 20 Soviet divisions and three armies. It reported 103,054 prisoners, 858 artillery pieces, 317 tanks, and 5,286 trucks captured.

By early August the Germans had advanced deep into Russia; where they had not destroyed, killed, or captured the enemy, they had driven the Red Army back in disarray. The Wehrmacht was almost to Leningrad, Smolensk had fallen, and the Ukraine west of the Dnepr was within the grasp of German forces. Yet, the German position was much weaker than it seemed. The high command had no clear sense of the next objective for the German offensive. Hitler still clung to the idea of the great resources in the south. For his part, Halder postponed discussions with the Führer in the hope that he would come around to the OKH's view. Finally, the purged, ill-prepared, and ineffectively led Red Army had already proven adept at prolonged, tenacious resistance, long after logic dictated that its units would surrender or collapse.

The August Pause

In planning Barbarossa the Germans had assumed that after the initial onslaught and the destruction of the Red Army along the frontier, the Soviets would not be able to field substantial reserve forces—certainly not in any coherent fashion. In late July and August the Germans learned the folly of such ill-founded optimism. By the end of June the Soviets had called up 5.3 million reservists; 13 field armies (a Soviet army was approximate to a German corps) deployed in July, 14 in August, 1 in September, and 4 in October. Units from Siberia and the Far East allowed the Soviets to move 8 additional armies forward in the defense of Moscow, with 10 more arriving in spring 1942. All told, the Soviets deployed 97 existing divisions to the west over summer 1941 and created no less than 194 new divisions and 84 separate brigades.

The sheer weight of numbers began to wreck German plans. On 11 August Halder noted, "The whole situation shows more and more clearly that we have underestimated the colossus of Russia . . . This conclusion is shown both on the organizational as well as the economic levels, in the transportation, and above all in infantry divisions. We have already identified 360. The divisions are admittedly not armed and equipped in our sense, and tactically they are badly led. But there they are; and when we destroy a dozen the Russians simply establish another dozen."[21] Reinforcing Halder's pessimism were the heavy casualties that panzer divisions suffered in July. For example, 20th Panzer Division had lost 35 percent of its officers, 19 percent of NCOs, and 11 percent of its men by 26 July. Equally disturbing was the higher-than-expected quality of some Soviet military equipment, particularly the T-34 tank, which proved to be extremely effective in combat.

The Germans' operational pause between the end of July and the end of

August did not result from Hitler's and the OKH's arguments as to whether the next offensive should target Moscow or Leningrad and Kiev. Rather, the Germans halted because of their inability to transport sufficient supplies of ammunition and fuel forward, coupled with the impact of the Soviet Union's mobilization. As Halder pointed out, Soviet reserves were desperately short of equipment, lacked experienced officers and NCOs, and possessed the barest tactical knowledge, but they provided the manpower for a series of counterattacks that now broke on German spearheads. In early August, Timoshenko, commanding Soviet forces in the center, launched four of these reserve armies (approximately 37 divisions) in a series of attacks that slashed at Guderian's southern flank. These offensives were uncoordinated and lacked the sophistication to cause anything more than local difficulties. But they forced the Germans to fight, and they drained the ammunition and fuel reserves required for a resumption of the German advance.

The farther the German advance attempted to go, the greater became the supply difficulties. Civilian trucks, stolen from Western Europe, disintegrated on the primitive Soviet roads. Within 19 days of the start of the campaign, the Wehrmacht had lost 25 percent of these vehicles with little chance of replacement. The Germans hoped to ease the supply situation by rapidly repairing and converting Soviet railroads to standard European gauge. But there were two significant problems with this plan. First, mechanized units had moved along Soviet roads rather than rails, often leaving the tracks in the hands of Soviet forces. Moreover, the repair and conversion work itself proved more difficult than expected. As early as 29 June, the Luftwaffe had to fly fuel to Fourth Panzer Group. Supply trains to Army Group North, which were scheduled to unload in three hours at the transfer point from German to Soviet gauge, were taking 80 hours. Observers described the resulting traffic jam as catastrophic. Exacerbating difficulties for Army Group North's spearheads was the fact that its lines of communications (over 400 miles) remained exposed to attacks. By the end of July, ammunition stocks in the divisions and corps had sunk to 50 percent of normal levels and were still dropping.

Army Group South's situation was hardly better. Rundstedt's troops faced terrible weather conditions—periods of blazing heat and dust followed by torrential downpours. By 19 July, half of Army Group South's trucks were out of commission. Bitter arguments broke out between units over the hijacking of trains and supplies. On 1 August, within a week of the scheduled push down the Dnepr, Rundstedt's forward units had between one-sixth and one-seventh of their basic ammunition load. Army Group

Center fared equally poorly. By early July Bock's panzer divisions were losing tanks because the supply system could not provide parts. Combat demands during the closure and destruction of the Smolensk pocket resulted in high ammunition expenditures, while heavy counterattacks by Soviet reserve armies exacerbated ammunition shortages. Fuel supplies had to be curtailed in order to bring up more ammunition. Consequently, Army Group Center could build up only a few supply dumps for a renewed offensive; frontline units fired off ammunition as fast as it arrived; and the troops lived off the land. By the end of July all trains moving supplies forward in Army Group South were turned over to Third Panzer Group for its drive into the Ukraine (still well below its expectations), while trucks from Ninth Army had to drive 300 miles to frontier depots. Stockpiling of fuel for a renewed drive on Moscow never began.

Supply problems bedeviled the Luftwaffe as well. By mid-July, its units were seriously short of fuel and ammunition. On 5 July Fliegerkorps VIII reported that fuel had run short, even though it had already scaled back operations. Its commander, Generaloberst Wolfram von Richthofen, noted that "supply is for us the greatest difficulty in this [campaign]."[22] As ground forces spread out in the theater, demands for close air support grew; that in turn resulted in a shuttling of Luftwaffe units from one army group to another. Such shifts strained the supply system even more and almost caused a complete breakdown by late fall 1941. By that time operational ready rates for bomber squadrons in the entire Luftwaffe had fallen below 50 percent, plummeting to 32 percent in December.

In the face of such difficulties, the Germans argued the various options among themselves at great length. At the end of July Hitler made clear that his strategic goals remained intact. The Wehrmacht must remove Leningrad and the Soviet forces in the Baltic as military factors, while the Ukraine and the Donets basin with their reserves of coal must be conquered as well. Hitler could not make up his mind between these two fundamental goals for the campaign. His fixation on Leningrad and the Ukraine suggests that he was uncertain whether the Wehrmacht would achieve victory before winter. At the same time, the OKH and frontline commanders were still urging an advance on Moscow, which they believed would win the war, although their claims then and after the war were not backed with any concrete evidence.

In early August Hitler flew to Army Group Center to confer with Bock, Guderian, and Hoth. He expressed wonderment at how well operations had gone, considering the Red Army's surprising strength, and he admitted that Army Group North might not need support from the center. Nevertheless, he again emphasized that the Ukraine and Donets basin were essential to the Soviet Union's economy. Interestingly, he foresaw a termination of major operations in the south by mid-September due to rainy weather and in front of Army Group Center by October. Despite the Führer's lack of interest in Moscow, Bock stressed that only the capital offered the possibility for a decisive victory but emphasized that such a victory would require increased logistical support. Such arguments were academic because the logistical situation remained troublesome; only Guderian's panzer group had some margin for offensive operations.

In the end, however, Hitler decided to strike at the Ukraine despite the fact that the OKH and OKW agreed (for one of the few times in the war) that German forces should concentrate on Moscow. He did concede that Army Group Center could launch an offensive against Moscow before winter, but only after Nazi forces had sealed the Ukraine and established the preconditions for capturing Leningrad.

Not surprisingly, the German advance in August was minimal. In the north, Leeb's forces slowed to a snail's pace; where they had averaged nearly 17 miles per day before 10 July, they now were averaging one mile. Hoepner argued that Fourth Panzer Group should withdraw from the unsuitable terrain in front of Leningrad (barely 70 miles away) and leave the city's capture to the infantry divisions.

The heaviest fighting occurred in front of Army Group Center. In mid-July Guderian had seized the high ground around Yelnaya as a jumping-off point for Moscow. In late July and August no less than six Soviet armies counterattacked the Yelnaya and Smolensk positions, while eleven Soviet armies attacked Army Group Center's forces from Velkie Luki in the north to Gomel in the south. Despite Hitler's interest in the Ukraine, Guderian and his superiors argued that German troops should hold Yelnaya for reasons of prestige. Soviet attacks, often poorly executed, broke with ferocity on troops in the Yelnaya salient; motorized and Waffen SS units of Guderian's panzer group held the ground until early August, when Fourth Army's infantry divisions caught up.

The conditions of this battle were something the Germans had yet to experience in the war. For example, with no depth to its defenses, the 78th Division held a front of 18 kilometers with no reserves and with Soviet positions right on top of its troops. The result was heavy casualties. Within a four-day period, the division lost 400 men in an effort simply to hold its line; throughout its time in the salient, it was under constant artillery bombardment. By the time the Germans abandoned Yelnaya in early September, the battle had wrecked five infantry divisions. After the war, Marshal

Georgi Zhukov claimed German casualties at 45,000 to 47,000 men, an accurate estimate.

By 1 September the Germans had suffered 409,998 casualties on the Eastern Front, out of 3,780,000 soldiers available at the beginning of the campaign. Even with replacements, combat units were short 200,000 men. More alarming was the fact that the OKH had already distributed 21 out of its initial reserve of 24 divisions to reinforce the army groups; virtually no reserves remained. The status of vehicles and mechanized units was equally alarming. Only 47 percent of the panzers were in commission; the rest were destroyed, disabled, or deadlined for repair and maintenance.

In August Kleist drove First Panzer Group down the right bank of the Dnepr east of Kiev. For the Soviet Southwestern Front, this created a dangerous situation that grew in seriousness as German forces advanced into the Dnepr bend and as Guderian's panzer group shifted its weight against Gomel. Kiev itself held, but farther east the Germans pushed on both sides of the growing salient. As early as the end of July, Zhukov had urged Stalin to pull back; the dictator refused and relieved Zhukov as chief of staff. Stalin's hand remained firmly on the helm. Soviet troops in the south would stand and fight where they were.

The uncertainties, if not despair, of the last days of June disappeared into a ruthless drive for survival. In mid-July Stalin had reimposed the commissar system on the officer corps. Nevertheless, the same inadequacies that had contributed to the early Soviet defeats still permeated the system. In the far north, tens of thousands of Leningraders dug anti-tank ditches to protect the city, but Soviet authorities refused to evacuate the old and young or to stock provisions for a siege. To do so would have suggested that the front might not hold and could lead directly to the firing squad. Neither soldiers nor citizens of any age could escape the draconian threats of the Soviet system.

Kiev and Moscow

In late August Guderian cleared out Soviet forces near Gomel and moved on the Ukraine. By early September the Germans had improved the railroad to Gomel, which provided a logistical line of crucial importance for Guderian's drive. As Second Panzer Group swung south, it exposed its left flank to a Soviet counterattack. However, anticipating that the Germans would attack toward Moscow, the Soviets refused their southern flank and thereby eased Guderian's advance. Second Panzer Group now churned its way southward. On 26 August, 3rd Panzer Division seized a bridgehead over the Desna at Novgorod Severskie; the Germans had broken through the Southwestern and Bryansk fronts. Guderian's forces ran at Romny, while Kleist crossed the Dnepr at Kremenchug. The STAVKA froze. It ordered General A. I. Eremenko to attack Guderian's forces from the flank; it still hoped that counterattacks on Kremenchug would drive the Germans back across the Dnepr, while Kirponos held Kiev. Despite warnings from commanders on the scene as well as from the Ukraine's commissar, Nikita Khrushchev, Stalin refused to authorize a retreat.

On 15 September the spearheads of First and Second Panzer Groups met near Lochvica, 100 miles east of Kiev. Inside the encompassing panzer arms, four Soviet armies (Fifth, Twenty-First, Twenty-Sixth, and Thirty-Seventh) were all destroyed. By the end of September the Germans could claim 665,000 prisoners since the capture of Gomel. Furthermore, the Germans found 824 tanks, 3,018 artillery pieces, and 418 anti-tank guns among the wreckage.

Astonishingly, the Germans had not yet abandoned the idea of capturing Moscow. Victory at Kiev had met one of the preconditions for a resumption of Army Group Center's advance. Meanwhile, in the north, Leeb's forces fulfilled the other precondition. By early September the Germans had cleared the Soviets from Estonia, while Eighteenth Army fought its way forward toward Tikhvin, and panzer and motorized units battled their way into Leningrad's suburbs. The capture of Schlüsselberg on the shore of Lake Ladoga cut rail and road links between Leningrad and the rest of the Soviet Union. Hitler ordered Army Group North to surround the city, starve its population out, and destroy every building by a massive artillery and air bombardment. But by the Führer's order, German troops were not to fight their way into the city. The siege of Leningrad had begun.

As the Kiev cauldron seethed, the OKH and the OKW refocused on Moscow and resumed the offensive in the center. The major drive behind planning and execution was Halder, who persuaded Hitler to embark on this decisive effort to break the Red Army. The chief of the general staff believed that once German troops captured Moscow, the Soviet Union would collapse, removing the strategic, operational, and logistic problems confronting the Wehrmacht. As with Schlieffen's search for a decisive victory over France before 1914, Halder sought a battle of annihilation in front of Moscow, another Cannae that would knock the Soviet Union out of the war permanently and end the threat of a two-front conflict.

While Army Group South was destroying Soviet forces in the Ukraine, Army Group North was closing in on Leningrad. Zhukov had arrived in the city on 13 September to restore order to a collapsing situation, but he was not able to prevent Leeb's infantry from encircling Leningrad on land. By the end of September, Eighteenth Army had reached Lake Ladoga and virtually isolated Leningrad from the rest of the Soviet Union. Still, by this point Hitler had pulled Fourth Panzer Group and most of its units away from the north to reinforce the coming attack on Moscow. Moreover, the Führer decided that a direct attack on the city would be too costly, so he ordered the advance to halt and German artillery and the Luftwaffe to destroy the city by bombardment.

The situation in the city was desperate. Fearing that they might be accused of defeatism, the local authorities had stockpiled neither food nor fuel for a siege. Nor had they bothered to evacuate the elderly and the young from the city. There still remained a water route across Lake Ladoga, but the loss of Tikhvin on 8 November cut even the Lake Ladoga route off from supplies. Thus, Leningrad would remain completely isolated for a full month until the Soviets managed to regain Tikhvin in early December. That success allowed the Soviets to establish a tenuous supply route across Ladoga and move a minimum of supplies into the starving city. Over a million citizens of Leningrad would die during the course of the siege from German bombs and shells, starvation, disease, and the cold—victims of Nazi aggression and Soviet incompetence.

On 6 September, Hitler and the OKW issued a new directive that agreed with Halder's emphasis on Moscow. Upon successful completion of operations on the flanks, parts of Second and Sixth Armies would come under the control of Army Group Center, while all of Second Panzer Group would return to Bock. The shift to the center was marked: not only did Second Panzer Group return, but one army corps of four infantry divisions and a panzer corps of two panzer divisions and two motorized infantry divisions shifted north to support Guderian. For its part, Army Group North lost Fourth Panzer Group with five panzer and two motorized infantry divisions. Altogether the offensive would launch three panzer groups against Moscow at the beginning of October. They represented the bulk of the Wehrmacht's mechanized forces.

Three substantial problems should have called into question the wisdom of launching another great offensive: the lateness of the season; the pervasive lack of supplies; and the serious losses that mechanized and motorized divisions had suffered since June. Supply difficulties had improved little since July. As Fourteenth Army's commander reported in mid-September: "At the moment [the supply system meets] current consumption only. The transportation system [has] not so far allow[ed] the establishment of depots sufficiently large to enable the troops to receive what they need in accordance with the tactical situation. The army lives from hand to mouth, especially as regards the fuel situation."[23] But the most alarming situation lay in the readiness of the armor. Panzer divisions had already written off 30 percent of their tanks; a further 23 percent were in repair shops. Over half the panzer divisions committed to Army Group Center's offensive possessed less than 35 percent of their fighting vehicles. Herculean efforts by Halder and the supply services only raised that total by another 10 percent before the offensive commenced.

Setting the tone for the advance on Moscow (known as Operation Typhoon), Hitler issued a proclamation demanding that the attacking troops end 25 years of Bolshevism in Russia—a system of rule, he claimed, equaled only by capitalistic plutocracy. "The support of these systems is also the same in both cases: the Jew and only the Jew."[24]

The German halt in August and the attacks on the flanks in September had lulled the STAVKA. Given the lateness of the year and the approach of bad weather, it seemed inconceivable that the Germans would launch another offensive. Distracted by the Kiev disaster and the isolation of Leningrad, the Soviets missed the shift of German forces to the center. Moreover, the Red Army had been attacking in the center since the end of July, and it had undertaken few defensive preparations. Finally, the Soviets had deployed their forces across the breadth of the front and possessed few reserves.

Returning from Army Group South, Guderian started his drive two days early to reach the Orel-Bryansk road. Given the wide-open situation in the south, Second Panzer Group's attack was completely unexpected. On 1 October, XXIV Panzer Corps took Sevsk. Despite fuel difficulties the panzers pursued their advantage; overall, the panzer corps advanced 85 miles on that day. On 3 October, 4th Panzer Division arrived at Orel and there caught the Soviets so much by surprise that trams were still running as the German tanks rolled in. On 2 October, the other two panzer groups blasted their way into the open. By 6 October, Bryansk had fallen and Soviet control over the entire Central Front had collapsed.

The German advance struck so swiftly and unexpectedly that Moscow's initial intimation of disaster came from a speech Hitler delivered in Berlin announcing the beginning of the final offensive. The STAVKA received no intelligence indicating that anything had gone wrong except for the fact that communications between Moscow and the fronts confronting the German Army Group Center had ceased. On 5 October, Soviet reconnaissance pilots reported a German armored column 25 kilometers long advancing on the great highway from Smolensk to Moscow. Despite NKVD efforts to arrest the pilots as panic mongers, their reports alerted the authorities to the extent of the danger.

Operation Typhoon ripped open the front line from Bryansk to Vyazma and encircled two enormous groups of Soviet armies. In the north around Vyazma, Nineteenth, Twenty-Fourth, and Thirty-Second Armies were in the bag; in the south, Third, Thirteenth, and Fiftieth also disappeared into German POW camps. The Germans claimed another 600,000 prisoners. Thousands of others escaped; some joined the partisans, but tens of thousands died in the cauldrons of surrounded German troops. The total number of prisoners claimed suggests the immensity of the defeat. For the second time in a month, a catastrophe had overtaken the Red Army. So great was the booty in materiel that Goebbels's Propaganda Ministry announced the end of the war in the east. Yet in spite of the catastrophes, the situation was not yet hopeless for the Soviets. The Germans had begun Typhoon with a bare minimum of supplies; their advance slowed to a crawl with the arrival of the fall rains in mid-October, and Luftwaffe support ceased almost entirely.

The question as to whether the advance should continue in the face of logistic difficulties and the approaching Russian winter rarely surfaced in top-level discussions among German leaders. Of senior commanders in Army Group Center, only Field Marshal Günther von Kluge, commander of Fourth Army, appears to have recognized the danger. His war diary noted that operations in Russia had reached a critical point "since the troops on one hand with no winter clothing and on the other facing impossible and tenacious opponents defending the roads found the advance extraordinarily difficult."[25] The exhaustion of armored forces after the battles of Bryansk and Vyazma provided additional emphasis to Kluge's words. The 10th Panzer Division, which had possessed 200 tanks on 10 October, was down to 60 by the 16th; the 4th Panzer Division possessed only 38. At this point the fall rains arrived, and the period of *rasputitsa* turned the Russian roads into seas of glutinous mud.

As the German drive stalled, the Soviets struggled to rebuild the defenses in front of Moscow. STAVKA rushed Zhukov back from Leningrad to handle the defense. Zhukov may have been the greatest operational commander of the war. He was certainly one of the bright lights for the Red Army in the dismal year of 1941. An NCO in the Tsarist army and then an officer in the Red Army during the Russian Civil War, Zhukov had risen rapidly through the ranks in the interwar period. He did not serve in the general staff, which may have saved his life during the purges. His success against the Japanese at Khalkin-Gol in September 1939 had further burnished his reputation, as had his performance during the crucial war games in January 1941 that Stalin had carefully watched.

At the outset of war, Zhukov was the head of the STAVKA, a position he was temperamentally unsuited for. His clear-headed advice earned him a return to the front in July, a sure indication of how highly Stalin thought of him, given the dictator's normal treatment of those with whom he disagreed. Zhukov was ruthless and harsh with his subordinates and earned the deep enmity of most of his colleagues. But he was enormously competent, brave, and sophisticated in understanding what was possible. He could make mistakes, but he spoke his mind on military matters freely and clearly. By the time of his return to Moscow in mid-October, Zhukov had restored the situation in Leningrad so that there was some hope of holding the city. The situation he now confronted with Typhoon in full swing appeared even more desperate. Few reserves remained after the profligacy of the summer. Still, something was left—infantry scraped from other frontiers, the last call-ups of 1941, the workers' militia of Moscow, and the first arrivals from Siberia. Zhukov now husbanded these units to build up reserves for a counterattack, after the Germans had exhausted themselves.

German preparations for winter remained almost nonexistent. Planners still assumed that most divisions would return to the Reich before bitter cold weather set in. Only 58 divisions were to remain to administer the conquered land. But the supply system, barely able to stockpile supplies for Typhoon, was incapable in the muddy season of bringing up sufficient fuel and munitions for the advance. Even more dangerous, winter fuels and winter clothing could not reach the 58 divisions that were to remain in European Russia, much less the other divisions, should the Soviets not collapse. Moreover, the Germans could not accumulate stockpiles behind the front to negate the inevitable difficulties the Russian winter would cause the transportation system. Nevertheless, the advance on Moscow continued. The generals believed that it would be better to spend the winter in Moscow than in the countryside. Intelligence again underestimated the Soviets by suggesting that recent victories had finally exhausted enemy reserves. Bock drew the conclusion that "the Germans could now afford to take risks."[26]

In discussions with the chiefs of staff of the various army groups in mid-November, Halder hoped that it might not snow for another six weeks, which would allow the troops to reach Vologda, Stalingrad, and Maikop. The staff officers, more in tune with conditions on the Eastern Front, were not so optimistic. Guderian's representative even suggested to Halder that Second Panzer Army was "neither in the month of May nor in France."[27]

Moscow hypnotized both Halder and Bock, although the latter did not subscribe to the idea of wide-ranging operations beyond Moscow, which both the OKH and OKW were planning. The senior generals consistently referred back to the failure on the Marne in 1914 to justify fighting it out to the last battalion.

With November's frosts, the German advance could resume over frozen ground. Second Panzer Army (recently renamed) found surprisingly weak resistance on its front, and one of its panzer corps advanced 25 miles in one day. However, Kluge's Fourth Army ran into such heavy Soviet resistance that its commander suggested pulling back to a better defensive line. Elsewhere the advance inched forward. Third and Fourth Panzer Groups shoved passed Klin and opened up a 27-mile gap in Soviet defenses. But there was not enough strength to create another success on the order of Bryansk or Vyazma.

While Bock confronted an increasingly dangerous situation as his troops struggled forward in worsening weather, the OKH and OKW argued that Moscow represented only a preliminary step in an advance on Voronezeh and Yaroslavi farther east. On 3 December, Bock told Jodl that his troops were exhausted and supplies nonexistent, but he was continuing to attack "'tooth and claw' . . . because keeping the initiative was preferable to going over to the defensive with weakened forces in exposed positions."[28] By now the temperature had fallen to below zero Fahrenheit, while heavy snowfalls accompanied the bitter cold. Over the night of 4 December, the temperature fell to $-25°$ F; one German regiment suffered 300 frostbite casualties, and a number of the wounded froze to death. A withdrawal might have saved something. Certainly, the Germans could have retreated to more defensible lines. But neither Bock nor Brauchitsch nor Halder dared suggest a retreat to Hitler. Rundstedt showed more character. His troops captured Rostov on 29 November, but they were exposed, low on supplies, and heavily outnumbered. Consequently, he ordered Kleist to fall back on the Mius River. Hitler immediately fired Rundstedt and replaced him with Reichenau, who reissued the same orders. Army Group South, as a result, escaped some of the difficulties that were to plague Army Group Center in the coming months.

As the Nazi and Soviet forces fought themselves to exhaustion in the closing weeks of 1941, the Pacific boiled over. Japanese aircraft attacked Pearl Harbor on 7 December. Within three days Hitler had taken the decision that ultimately would seal the fate of the Third Reich: he declared war on the United States. His decision resulted from a number of misperceptions. On one hand, he saw the United States as a mongrelized mixture of races. Nevertheless, over summer 1941 Hitler had displayed some reluctance to respond to U.S. naval provocations in the North Atlantic and its support for Britain with Lend Lease—a program of massive U.S. aid for Britain and eventually the Soviet Union. Nevertheless, the Kriegsmarine attempted to persuade the Führer to declare war on the United States, and on 9 July went so far as to suggest that the American occupation of Iceland demanded an "immediate armed assault on all USA ships within publicly proclaimed war zone."[29]

But the decision hinged more on military events in early December 1941 than on any strategic calculation. German fortunes were unraveling in Russia—Rostov abandoned, Rundstedt fired, the fate of Army Group Center trembling in the balance, and Army Group North under great pressure. Even in North Africa the war was not going well. Into the gloom came the news that the Japanese had gained a stunning military success against the Americans. And America represented a target against which Nazi Germany could strike with some prospect of success; at least that was what the Kriegsmarine promised with its U-boats. Hitler's calculation also rested on the Nazi explanation for Germany's defeat in 1918: the German Army had supposedly stood unbeaten and unbroken on the battlefield but had been betrayed by the Jews and the Communists. The arrival of two million American troops and America's economic support of the Allies in 1918 had not figured in the German explanation of their defeat, and this stubborn underestimation of American strength by the Germans would be Hitler's undoing.

As to strategic assessment, there was none. The Kriegsmarine thought that a declaration of war was a good idea; the army and Luftwaffe could not have cared less. As his staff celebrated the news of Pearl Harbor, Hitler casually asked where Pearl Harbor was. No one knew. The declaration of war on the United States was one of the worst mistakes Hitler made. By that action he allowed Roosevelt to portray the Germans and the Japanese as a united enemy. At a minimum it permitted the United States to pursue a "Germany first" strategy, one that within a year would bring U.S. ground and air forces to Europe in substantial numbers.

The Winter Campaign

On 5 December, Soviet forces went on the offensive in front of Moscow under appalling conditions: snow, high winds, and sub-zero temperatures. Zhukov's counterattack struck the Germans immediately after they had exhausted themselves. The attackers were stronger than they had been in front of Bryansk and Vyazma in early October, while both their air and ground forces were close to their supply dumps.

But there were weaknesses. Soviet command and control was still primitive. Consequently, Zhukov recommended limited objectives that for the short term would cripple Army Group Center and perhaps destroy a portion of that army group by spring. But Stalin believed that as in 1812, total victory—the destruction of an invading European field army—was at hand. Therefore, early in the offensive, when the Germans were most vulnerable, he withheld reserves and committed Soviet forces to every front from the Crimea to Leningrad, rather than concentrating the effort against Army Group Center's exposed forces. In the south, Soviet landings on the Kerch peninsula relieved pressure on Sevastopol, but the Germans maintained their hold on the Crimea and throughout Army Group South's domain. In the north, Soviet attacks forced the Germans out of Tikhvin, which then allowed supplies to move across the ice of Lake Ladoga to Leningrad. But the city had exhausted its supplies, and starvation stalked its streets. And while support for Leningrad was a political necessity, the attacks on Army Group South were wasteful and underscored Stalin's mistaken overestimation of the Red Army's capabilities.

Nevertheless, the Soviets came close to overwhelming Army Group Center and destroying at least one, if not several, German armies. The most dangerous breaks came on the flanks. By 10 December the Russians had cut the road past Klin, Panzer Group Three's main escape route. Its war diary describes the situation in the following terms: "Discipline is breaking down. More and more soldiers are heading west on foot without weapons, leading a calf on a rope or pulling a sled loaded with potatoes. The road is under constant air attack. Those killed by bombs are no longer being buried. All the hangers-on (cargo troops, Luftwaffe, supply trains) are pouring to the rear in full flight. Without rations, freezing, they are pushing back. Vehicle crews that do not want to wait out the traffic jams in the open are drifting off the roads and into the villages. Ice, inclines, and bridges create horrendous blockages."[30] Exposed to temperatures well below zero and blinded by blowing snow, German troops found the task of survival a nightmare. The cold was so intense that weapons often did not work and engines would not start.

Panzer Groups Three and Four actually broke contact and fell back on the Lama and Ruga Rivers, where they enjoyed a respite. But Hitler decided that the German armies must stand and fight where they were. Moreover, since in his view the generals had failed, Hitler fired the army's senior leaders in the midst of a vast and complex military conflict and replaced virtually the entire leadership in the east. Brauchitsch went, replaced as the army's commander-in-chief by the Führer himself. Hitler also fired the remaining army group commanders, Bock and Leeb, along with Guderian, Hoepner, and a number of other senior generals. The OKH assumed control of operations on the Eastern Front, while it lost its responsibilities for controlling the army's units in other theaters. Instead, the OKW assumed control of ground operations in the Mediterranean and Western European theaters. The army no longer had a commander for its war, while the navy and Luftwaffe waged independent wars. Only in the Führer's mind did the pieces of some grand strategy fit together. And there was still no strategic decision-making body within the Third Reich, not that the service chiefs had ever argued for one.

Meanwhile, Army Group Center's difficulties went from bad to worse. On 19 December, LVI Panzer Corps reported a combat strength of 900 men, while XLI Corps had only 1,821 men combat-ready. Panzer Group Three had 63 light and 21 heavy howitzers at its disposal. Persistent cold reduced the already inadequate supply capacity of the system by 50 percent; frequent heavy snows brought train movements to a complete halt. For a time it seemed as if the German Army in the east would suffer the fate of Napoleon's Grand Army in 1812. Halder's diary caught the grim progress of events: "20 December: Still very tense . . . 29 December: *A Very bad day!* . . . 30 December: *Again a hard day!* . . . Very serious crisis in Ninth Army . . . 31 December: *Again an arduous day* . . . 2 January: A day of wild fighting . . . 3 January: Another dramatic scene with the Führer, who calls in question the generals' courage to make hard decisions . . . 8 January: *Very grave day.* The westward advance of the Sukhinichi breakthrough is becoming threatening for Kluge . . . 11 January: *The whole day with Field Marshal von Kluge at Führer hq* . . . The situation now is becoming really critical."[31] The commander of the 26th Infantry Division noted about one of his regiments: "Infantry Regiment 78 can no longer be considered a regiment. It has only 200 men. The Russians have cut its communications. Its radios . . . and machine guns are frozen . . . machine gun crews are dead alongside their weapons."[32]

By early January Zhukov's forces had driven in both flanks of Army Group Center. The situation was particularly dangerous where the Soviets advanced past Rzhev and headed toward Vyazma and the rear areas of Third Panzer Army, but as Soviet spearheads lapped around German flanks, Soviet frontal attacks pushed the Germans back from the growing bulge. Sounding much like Hitler, Halder urged Kluge that "there must be a man who can put things right there, if not a divisional commander then some colonel, and if not then a major who has the necessary energy and determination."[33] By the end of January, Soviet forces were attacking Vyazma from three different directions, and on 26 January they cut Fourth Army's supply lines, which the Germans were not able to reopen until the end of the month. But the Germans held the roads and supply centers, and slowly they regained their equilibrium. The great sweeping movements the Red Army was attempting were well beyond its capabilities. By early March the Germans had established some stability to their rear areas and along the front lines.

Elsewhere on the Eastern Front the Soviets came no closer to major success. Attacks on Kerch threatened Manstein's Eleventh Army but were contained. A major attack broke contact between Army Group South's Sixth and Seventeenth Armies and for a time appeared on the brink of isolating Seventeenth and First Panzer Armies. But the Soviets never reached the Dnepr. German pressure contained the breakthrough and eventually strangled the precariously placed spearheads. In the north the Soviets gained a few local successes. Attacks in January allowed the Soviets to isolate two German corps at Demyansk and a smaller pocket at Cholm. Despite heavy losses, the Luftwaffe supplied both encirclements from the air. Its losses were exorbitantly high in these relief operations. By May when the Germans broke the encirclement, the Luftwaffe had lost 265 transport aircraft, 30 percent of their fleet of Ju-52s.

A dangerous Soviet breakthrough to the north of Novgorod in January gained even less. It stalled behind German lines, because the attackers could not drive the Nazis out of the crucial roads required for resupply. Instead of cutting its losses, STAVKA reinforced failure and lost the entire Second Shock Army and its commander, Lieutenant General A. A. Vlasov, as spring rains turned the ground to mud. The Soviet failures were a direct result of Stalin's interference, just as the terrible defeats of summer and fall 1941 had resulted from his incompetence as a military leader. By pursuing victory everywhere, he robbed his armies of their chance to defeat Army Group Center.

Thus, the Germans escaped general defeat, but the responsibility for the military failure in front of Moscow rested as much on the German generals as on Hitler. Admittedly, the Führer had set impossible goals, but with hardly a murmur the generals had pursued a decisive victory that had eluded their predecessors on the Marne. However, when disaster threatened during the winter, Hitler provided the blind determination that prevented defeat from turning into collapse. His triumph of the will guaranteed that the Third Reich would drag much of Europe into the abyss of three more long years of war.

The Moral Parameters

After the war, German generals argued that they had resolutely refused to issue the infamous commissar order, which decreed the immediate execution of all commissars on capture. And to explain other atrocities against Soviet prisoners of war, the generals claimed that the maiming of German wounded in the early days of the invasion by Soviet soldiers induced German soldiers, certainly without the approval of their commanders, to step beyond the bounds of international law. The fate of Soviet POWs paints a much different picture. A report of March 1942 on the possible use of Soviet POWs for the war economy indicates that out of 3.6 million Soviet soldiers captured by the Germans in the war to that point, only 100,000 were still capable of working in German industry. Most of the rest were already dead or dying. Göring laughingly commented to the Italian foreign minister, Ciano, in November 1941 that "hunger among the Russian prisoners had reached such an extreme that in order to start them toward the interior it [was] no longer necessary to send them under guard; it is enough to put at the head of the column . . . a camp kitchen, which emits the fragrant odor of food."[34]

Ironically, at a moment when the German war economy was starved for workers, Hitler refused to employ Soviet prisoners in any capacity. It was the army that held responsibility for the care of Soviet POWs. The callous treatment the Germans meted out to Soviet prisoners directly reflected the regime's ideological program, as well as the army's acceptance of that program. While one can account for some of the deaths by the extraordinary numbers who surrendered, the huge percentage of soldiers who died in captivity underscores the convergence of the army's ideology with that of the Third Reich.

If the army let disease and starvation seal the fate of the POWs, the acceptance by most army authorities of the commissar order was direct and immediate. From 22 June to 19 July 1941, Panzer Group Four reported 172 commissars liquidated; up to 24 July, Second Army claimed 177; up to the beginning of August, Panzer Group Three had shot 170. The OKW provided the driving force behind much of the criminal behavior. Its decree of 17 July stated: "The special situation of the Eastern campaign therefore demands *special measures* which are to be executed free from bureaucratic . . .

influence and with a willingness to accept responsibility. While so far the . . . orders concerning POWs were based solely on *military* considerations, now the *political* objective must be obtained which is to protect the German nation from Bolshevik invaders and forthwith take the occupied territory in hand."[35]

Hitler's goals pleased most of the army's senior leadership. Both Reichenau and Manstein issued orders of the day to their troops about the proper political attitudes toward the war in the east. Reichenau's order noted: "The soldier must have understanding for the necessity of the harsh yet just punishment of the Jewish sub humans . . . [He] is called upon to achieve two goals: 1) The extermination of the Bolshevik heresy . . . 2) The merciless extermination of foreign treachery and cruelty to safeguard . . . the German Wehrmacht in Russia."[36] A delighted Hitler termed Reichenau's order outstanding. Manstein commented that "behind the front, too, the fighting continues . . . Jewry acts as the middle man between the enemy in the rear . . . [and] the remaining Red Army forces and the Red leadership. More than in Europe, it . . . forms the center for all unrest and uprising."[37]

A slogan about partisan war linked the treatment of both Russians and Jews in the great atrocities of 1941: "Where the partisan is, the Jew is, and where the Jew is, is the partisan."[38] Across the breadth of European Russia, the invading Germans took matters into their own hands, as Hitler intended. Einsatzgruppen were responsible for the great bulk of the killing, but they received full cooperation from the army. At Babi Yar outside of Kiev, SS-Sonderkommando 4a murdered 33,771 Jews and other Soviet citizens in a two-day orgy of violence in revenge for Soviet destruction in Kiev. The local army commander, Major General Kurt Eberhard, cooperated enthusiastically, even providing the SS with an army propaganda company to persuade Kiev's Jews that they were moving for resettlement. On numerous occasions troop commanders ordered their men to participate in "special actions" against Jews and Communists. The repetitive nature of such orders suggests the level of cooperation between SS and army that occurred throughout the German advance. Everywhere the Germans advanced, the tide of murder, violence, and destruction followed, on the Jews above all, but on the Soviet population in general.

Conclusion

The Wehrmacht's victories over the summer and fall of 1941 obscured how high the odds were against Operation Barbarossa. By defining the war as a

Vernichtungskrieg (war of destruction), Hitler and the Wehrmacht ensured that the Soviet peoples would rally to Stalin's tyranny instead of enlisting in an effort to overthrow the Soviet regime. It was not that Russia was unconquerable; surely the collapse of 1917 indicates the opposite. But the campaign rested on the mistaken beliefs that the Wehrmacht could defeat the Red Army within five months and that once the Germans challenged Stalin, the apparently rotten political edifice of the Soviet Union would collapse. The conditions of the racial war, the commissar order, the extermination of the Jews, and the looting of the local population inevitably led to a strengthening of Soviet resistance to the invader.

Moreover, German logistical and intelligence weaknesses were extraordinary. They too define the "German way of war." The German military leadership was incapable of addressing the harsh realities that began affecting its operations as early as late July. The generals never considered alternative courses of action; the campaign had to be won by winter, and so Brauchitsch, Halder, and Bock drove the exhausted, weary, fought-out German troops to the gates of Moscow and defeat.

Stalin also deserves a full share of the blame for the German successes. His great purge of the military in the period from 1937 to 1939, his mendacious and dishonest foreign policy, his obdurate overconfidence, and his dismissal of all the warning signs of invasion magnified the extent of the catastrophe that engulfed the Red Army after 22 June 1941. Even with winter's arrival and the exhaustion of German forces, Stalin bungled the opportunity to turn the tide. The price of the nation's survival in 1941—anywhere from 5 million to 8 million Soviet citizens dead—suggests not just the cost of war but the wages of tyranny. But the killing had not ended. It had only begun.

7

THE ORIGINS OF THE
ASIA-PACIFIC WAR

1919–1941

As his train pulled into Berlin in March 1941, Foreign Minister Matsuoka Yōsuke wondered if Japan could steer its perilous course between Germany, the Soviet Union, and the United States and finally establish itself as the master of Asia and the first modern nonwhite Great Power. He had taken over responsibility for Japan's foreign relations in July 1940. Now, nine months later, he faced his greatest challenge: to use the Tripartite Pact of September 1940 with Germany and Italy to keep the United States at peace and break off its assistance to China and the British Empire. Largely Matsuoka's own work, the Tripartite Pact pledged the three major Axis powers to come to one another's assistance if a nation currently a non-belligerent attacked one of its signatories. Since Germany and the Soviet Union were still bound by their neutrality pact of 1939—a horrid surprise to Japan—only the United States fit the treaty's description.

If anyone could end the China Incident—Japan's euphemism for the vengeful slaughter of hundreds of thousands of Chinese during the invasion of China in 1937—and expand the Japanese Empire without war (only a fifty-fifty chance, Matsuoka told his staff when he left Tokyo), Matsuoka Yōsuke was the man. With no advantages other than his own energy and intelligence, he had risen to the top of Japanese politics and business as a relentless administrator, brilliant planner, and tireless talker. Even his admirers called him the "talking machine" and wondered if he was truly brilliant or just mad. The devoted father of seven, he treated most people as children, and his abruptness, arrogance, and quixotic views on Japan's future confused many of his contemporaries. With big glasses, a small mustache, and a short, stout body, Matsuoka appeared to Europeans as a stereotypical Japanese functionary. Such an impression could not have been more misleading. Matsuoka was driven and dangerous, dedicated to using the European war to fulfill Japan's destiny to rule all of Asia. And he believed he understood that America's weakness and fear of a European war could be exploited—the sooner the better.

Matsuoka Yōsuke could claim special expertise in American life: he had grown up in Oregon. After running away from home to be an apprentice seaman, he had been deserted by his shipmates in Portland at the age of thirteen. For the next ten years (1893–1903) he survived through the generosity and sympathy of an American family that housed and fed him while he attended school and worked as a laborer and law clerk. His desperate energy and intelligence carried him past sheer survival, and his English improved rapidly. He attended a Protestant church. When he returned to Japan to begin his climb to power and wealth in Manchuria, he did so as a graduate of the University of Oregon. His knowledge of Western business eventually made him president of the South Manchurian Railroad and a trusted friend of the Kwantung Army—the near-autonomous Japanese army defending Manchuria—and its most prominent officers, including General Tojo Hideki.

As army influence grew in Tokyo, Matsuoka's influence grew with it. By the early 1930s he served as ambassador to the League of Nations, and he walked out of the League debates over Japan's seizure of Manchuria in 1931. He announced Japan's departure from the League with pride. After becoming foreign minister, he showed his talent for coercive diplomacy by wringing an agreement from Vichy France to put Japanese troops in northern Indochina. He then threatened to blockade Hong Kong if the British did not close the Burma Road, the major route of military supplies to the Chinese Nationalists. Riding these successes like a samurai on a quest of vengeance, Matsuoka then negotiated the Tripartite Pact and announced in early 1941 that he would visit Berlin, Moscow, and Washington and produce an arrangement that would end any American threat to Japanese imperialism. He announced with equal certainty that Germany would soon defeat Britain, and that the Soviet Union would be so intimidated by the German-Japanese threat of a two-front war that Stalin might even join the Tripartite Pact.

By May 1941, Foreign Minister Matsuoka returned to Tokyo with his grand scheme in tatters and his reputation damaged beyond repair. He had become so obsessed with reaching an "understanding" with the United States that he had misjudged the shifting power alignment in Europe. Britain had not been defeated, and in Berlin the Germans confided that they might invade Russia. Matsuoka did not believe them. When he arrived in Moscow in April, he immediately initiated a nonaggression pact with the

Soviet Union, which enraged both the Germans and the militarists in Tokyo. In the meantime, his indirect overtures to the United States went nowhere and stiffened American resolve to aid Britain and China.

Assaulted by his critics in Tokyo for making a deal with Stalin, Matsuoka
argued that his strategic aims had not changed, only his tactics. Japan was
still an Axis ally and would use its power to keep the United States out of
the European war. In May 1941, the foreign minister now thought that the
chances of a negotiated settlement of the China Incident with the United
States were no better than three-in-ten. A month later he announced that
he could see no purpose in continuing his negotiations in Washington:
"Even if I am told to carry on with diplomacy, I think that diplomatic maneuvering with the United States is over and done with at this point."[1]

The Making of Modern Japan

Isolated from the traffic of Chiyoda-ku, Tokyo, Yasukuni Shrine is one of
the hundreds of major Shinto *jinja* that provide islands of greenery and
quiet in one of the world's most frantic cities. Built in 1869 during the reign
of the Emperor Meiji (1867–1912), it was a *shokonsha* or a Shrine for Inviting Spirits, in this case the spirits of all who died in the civil war to reestablish imperial rule in Japan. After ten years the shrine was retitled Yasukuni
Jinja or the Shrine of Establishing Peace in the Empire, and it received special imperial support since it would be the official shrine immortalizing all
the Japanese who died in military service after 1853. Yasukuni is the Japanese equivalent of the Tomb of the Unknown Soldier in Arlington National
Cemetery.

Yasukuni Jinja now specializes in World War II memories. Until 1937 the
spirits of the departed warriors of the Emperor numbered in the range of
200,000, roughly the same number as the American servicemen who have
perished in Asian wars from 1898 to the present day. After 1945, however,
Yasukuni memorialized over two million military dead whose ashes or
bones rested in distant jungles and beneath a vast ocean. The old men who
visit Yasukuni still see themselves as loyal soldiers of the Emperor who
only did their duty like their dead comrades.

At the beginning of the Meiji Restoration in 1867–68, the Emperor, re-
empowered by the four clans that toppled the Tokugawa Shogunate,
pledged himself to restore Japanese self-respect. Two recent experiences
created the Japanese sense of military inferiority: the entry of a U.S. Navy
squadron into Tokyo Bay in 1854 and the Royal Navy's bombardment of
Kagoshima and Shimonoseki in 1862–63 in retaliation for the mistreat-

ment of Western nationals. By the end of the century, the modernized Japanese Army and Navy looked Europeanized in matters of uniforms and weapons, but the soul of the armed forces remained rooted in the samurai tradition of Japanese feudalism. In 1894–95, Japan defeated its only Asian rival, China of the Ch'ing Dynasty, in a naval campaign marked by surprise and the full exploitation of modern warships. A land campaign in Korea and Manchuria proved that German-made weapons and the Japanese warrior spirit could produce impressive victories. The same formula worked in 1904–5, this time with Imperial Russia as the stunned loser. The twin victories brought Taiwan and Korea under Japanese rule and opened Manchuria to economic exploitation under the protection of resident Japanese soldiers. Participation in the suppression of the Boxer Uprising (1900) also produced concessions and privileges for Japan within China.

If the Japanese armed forces, supported by the elite of the court and bureaucracy and admired by the people, thought they would somehow stretch two victories into a third greater and more magnificent conquest, just as their German teachers had in 1870–71, their experience in World War I proved disappointing. In part because of an alliance with Britain signed in 1902, Japan in 1914 attacked and captured the German leaseholds of Kiaochow and Shantung* in China. Some Japanese officials and part of the public supported Sun Yat-sen's revolutionary movement in China, but Japan assumed that its interests required a new policy toward its giant neighbor, a policy of anti-European hegemony that challenged the Open Door policy of the United States, which argued against special concessions to *all* nations. With Japanese sensitivities already rubbed raw by the discriminatory treatment of Asian immigrants in the United States, Tokyo wanted no more instruction on its moral duty to respect the territorial integrity and political sovereignty of China.

Without heeding European cautions and the prudent counsel of some of its own political elite, the Japanese government rejected an Allied proposal that Germany's China concessions now revert to China, then governed by Yuan Shih-k'ai and, after his death in 1916, by a coalition of warlords. Instead, Japan presented its Twenty-One Demands, a manifesto of acquisitiveness. Basically, the demands would have made China a protectorate and ceded direct control of the German concessions and much of Manchuria to Japanese domination. Bolstered by American support, the Chinese refused the demands for much of 1915, but finally agreed to enlarge Japa-

---

*Chinese names are romanized according to the Wade-Giles system in use in the 1940s, not Pinyin used today.

nese privileges in Manchuria in exchange for protection in China proper. The settlement for Manchuria, however, led to acute Japanese interest in the Russian Revolution of 1917 and the fate of Siberia and Russia's Maritime Province, anchored at Vladivostok on the Sea of Japan. Under cover of an Allied military expedition to Siberia to save the Russian war effort, the Japanese sent 72,000 soldiers deep into Asian Russia, principally to ensure that neither the Allies nor the Bolsheviks restored Russian military power. By 1920 the Japanese also occupied the southern half of Sakhalin Island. Once again, however, Western political pressure during the World War I peace negotiations in 1919 forced the Japanese to leave Siberia in 1922, but not South Sakhalin.

Like the citizens of the United States and Western Europe, the Japanese people themselves sought "normalcy" in the 1920s, which meant reductions in military spending, an abatement of hostility to the West, and an improvement of economic conditions through trade and internal agricultural and industrial production. Despite the influence of Shintoism (a state religion of ancestor and emperor worship), Confucianism, and Germanized corporations and universities, the urban Japanese population showed serious interest in life, liberty, and the pursuit of family happiness. The Japanese Diet, a pale copy of Western assemblies, suddenly showed new courage in the 1920s and backed the appointed courtiers in the cabinet against the militarist-expansionists. Military officers still enjoyed inordinate prestige, but for a moment the cautious conservatives—an alliance of court nobility and Westernized technocrats—persuaded the successive cabinets to pursue an international policy of cooperation rather than confrontation. The "peace party" profited by the death in 1922 of Prince and Field Marshal Yamagata Aritomo, whose power in the army and in the court made him a cabinet maker and breaker.

In late 1921, Japanese diplomats journeyed to Washington, D.C., to demonstrate their nation's new-found sense of international responsibility by agreeing to three treaties designed to stabilize the status quo in Asia. Signed in Washington in February 1922, the Five Power Treaty (Japan, Britain, France, Italy, and the United States) put a ceiling on the building and modernization of large warships. With respect to Britain and the United States, Japan accepted a one-third inferiority in numbers (15:15:10 battleships) and 40 percent in tonnage in return for restrictions on building and fortifying all non-homeland naval bases in the Pacific. The Four Power Treaty pledged the signatories (Japan, Britain, France, and the United States) not to attack one another's colonies. The Nine Power Treaty (including Japan) placed China off-limits for further imperialism. Struggling through another experiment in weak, decentralized government, China needed every advantage it could find, and the Nine Power Treaty gave it a small measure of protection. Manchuria's status, however, underwent no major change, which meant that several nations and international business consortiums retained special privileges. Another important aspect of the Washington treaties was that they freed Britain from its 1902 treaty with Japan.

Although the international treaties signed in Washington slowed Japanese expansionism in the 1920s, the countervailing winds of domestic politics created conditions for a resurgence of Japanese "manifest destiny" in the 1930s. Instead of a government dominated by clan representatives, formally recognized as the Privy Council of aged statesmen, the cabinets of the 1920s represented an uneasy and inherently unstable coalition of conservative courtiers, senior military officers, moguls of the burgeoning industrial conglomerates or *zaibatsu,* and a new group of party politicians and bureaucratic technocrats. The political parties, except for the socialists, were weak and riven by corruption and personal feuds and enjoyed no special public appeal. Ironically, the liberalization of political participation in the 1920s also created a politicized urban middle class that proved easy to agitate and manipulate through the schools, media, and government bureaucracy. Alarmed by the prospect of democratic reform, the Diet passed the Peace Preservation Act of 1925, which imposed ten years' imprisonment on those who joined societies seeking to alter the government or challenging private property rights. With little imagination, such an act could be extended to any dissident political group. What made the law even more menacing was the fact that the police who enforced it fell under the indirect control of the minister of war.

Even with reduced budgets, the Imperial Japanese Army (IJA) and Imperial Japanese Navy (IJN) retained a hard grip on the lives of the Japanese. Conscription continued after World War I, and the school system required reverence for the Emperor and the armed forces. As the army and navy modernized some of their weapons, especially aircraft, they developed strong working ties with the *zaibatsu.* The army, as the principal administrative arm of the government in Manchuria and Korea, developed not just autonomy abroad but the political power that could bring down cabinets in Tokyo. So great became the influence of the Kwantung Army in Manchuria that a clique of its officers could shape Japanese policy.

The Cherry Society of dissident officers, founded in 1930, sought to change Japan through military revolution; their status in the army effectively protected them from the Peace Preservation Act. Somewhere on the

murky side streets where military intelligence agents and right-wing terrorists roamed, the Cherry Society cultivated political violence and probably influenced the murders of Prime Ministers Hamaguchi Yuko in 1930
and Inukai Ki in 1932. Even if some senior officers tried to operate within
the norms of civilian control, their subordinates and the public regarded
the protection of Japan from modern corruptions like democracy and materialism as the army's sacred duty.

A mature, forceful Emperor might have rallied the peace party coalition
and controlled the military, but the slight, bespectacled Hirohito, who became Emperor in 1926 at the age of twenty-five, accepted his traditional
nonactivist role. He entitled his reign *showa* or "enlightened peace," but his
first twenty years of rule proved neither enlightened nor peaceful. Much
influenced by British culture, Hirohito most valued his role as reigning
monarch. Although his power was theoretically absolute, his real power
remained limited, but real enough. When the army and navy in 1936
sought his approval for planning wars against China and Russia (the "continental strategy") and against the Europeans in Southeast Asia (the "move
south strategy"), he approved both. Perhaps the Emperor supposed that
interservice rivalry and internal factionalism within both the army and
navy officers' corps would produce stalemate. If so, he badly misjudged his
generals and admirals.

The Collapse of the Asian Order

After subduing Japanese imperialism through the Washington treaties, the
governments of the United States, Britain, and the European states with
Asian interests regarded Japan as a full-fledged member of the international community, as a signatory of the League of Nations agreement, and
as a global trading partner. The United States, for example, welcomed Japanese investment in American-owned industries and exported scrap iron
and petroleum to Japan for the *zaibatsu*'s factories. Of course, Japanese immigrants were not welcome in the States, except in Hawaii, where they
and the Koreans (nominally Japanese citizens) proved to be industrious
agricultural stoop-laborers. British and American attitudes toward the Japanese still reflected traditional anti-Asian racism. Foreigners perceived industrial progress in Japan as merely copying European practices—reverse-
engineering of the grandest sort to which the Japanese added no original-
ity. Westerners often overlooked the Japanese research and development
strategy, which was to catch up with the West as fast as possible and then
innovate where opportunities arose for real product improvements, such

as the Zero fighter aircraft. With an overabundance of traditional rice farmers, a new industrial work force of limited skills, and a managerial elite that did not really understand Western entrepreneurship, however, Japan could not be taken seriously as an economic competitor. Moreover, its lack of natural resources except coal meant that it had to remain a supplicant in the international trading order of the 1920s, still only a protégé of Britain and the United States. Japan's role seemed to be confined to making silk garments and producing cheap textiles from imported cotton.

Westerners, especially the British and Americans, tended to exaggerate their influence on Japanese culture and to underestimate the latent hostility in Japan toward Western civilization. For example, Westerners accused Japanese visual arts of effeminacy and mistook the delicate presentation of Japanese food for forced dieting. Western attitudes toward Japan shaped the operetta *The Mikado* and the opera *Madame Butterfly*, which portrayed the Japanese as tragicomic figures. Few Westerners could appreciate the cultural undertow of despair, persistence, and violence unless they had sampled the theater of *kabuki, bunraku,* and *noh.* Wearing sailor and soldier suits to grammar school did not turn Japanese children into little Englishmen and Germans; their language and scholarship took them back to the great days of Hideyoshi, the sixteenth-century Japanese imperialist, not to the eighteenth-century European Enlightenment.

Christian missionaries in particular almost always exaggerated the impact of Western religion in Japan. Fewer than one percent of the population showed even passing interest in Christianity except for access to the YMCA. Some Japanese did become serious converts to Christianity—and a few Allied POWs eventually owed their lives to these gallant co-religionists. But often "interested" Japanese simply were looking for a good way to learn English and to gain entry into prestigious universities in the United States and England. Western, popular culture—music, sports, and films—on the other hand, fascinated the Japanese, but it did not transform them. Yamamoto Isoroku, the admiral who eventually led the Combined Fleet to its initial victories against the Americans, saw a great deal of the United States during his two tours in North America to learn English and serve as a naval attaché (1919–1921 and 1926–1928). Although he marveled at America's size and economic vitality, he regarded the U.S. Navy as incompetent and Americans as self-indulgent weaklings. Like another visitor to the United States in the same era—a gaunt, small Vietnamese named Ho Chi Minh—Yamamoto concluded that America offered his nation little of spiritual value.

The only Western export that the Japanese truly respected was industrial technology, particularly the rate at which Western factories spewed forth durable goods. More for reasons of national power than private consumption, Japan plunged into the interdependent world of commerce and resource competition with the ardor of a new convert. Like Britain, its Western model, Japan moved quickly toward industrialization; by 1937 a majority of its people lived in cities—37 million out of a population of 70 million. Also like Britain, Japan could not be a manufacturing giant without a wide variety of imports: oil, iron, minerals, rubber, cotton, wool, and wood. Some foodstuffs, especially protein-rich meat, were difficult to produce in the confined spaces of the islands and had to be imported. Only in coal production might Japan be self-sufficient, thanks to mines in northern Korea and Manchuria. Unlike Britain, Japan had no empire from which to draw cheap raw materials. Formosa and Korea hardly gave Japan autarky, and its special privileges in Manchuria did not suffice. By the 1930s Japanese politicians—their weak attachment to the concepts of international markets and free trade severed by the Great Depression—saw the economic exploitation of China as Japan's only salvation from economic retreat.

When its economy swooned in the 1930s, Japan chafed under the economic barriers it faced in Asia. The colonial status of Indochina, Burma, Malaya, the Philippines, and the Dutch East Indies limited Japanese access to these markets, while the hostility of Britain, the United States, and the Soviet Union toward Japanese economic penetration in Manchuria and China seemed to embody imperialist discrimination, if not outright hypocrisy. The American position was the most incomprehensible to the Japanese. The Americans had never shown the same exploitative ardor in China as the Europeans had; their attachment appeared to be more a matter of sentiment and cultural imperialism. China had received only one percent of America's overseas investment, and the United States sent only four percent of its exports to China. American investment and trade with Japan was at least five or six times greater than that, and it was expanding, despite America's racist immigration policies. In the end, Japanese officials thought, American economic sanity would prevail, and the United States would accept Japan's need to dominate China's economy.

The Russian problem was different. The Soviet Union had replaced Germany as the patron of Chiang Kai-shek's Nationalist government, based at Nanking, even though the Nationalists had driven the Chinese Communists into northwestern China in 1931. The Japanese looked on with alarm as the Soviet-Chinese relationship warmed in the 1930s, and the prospect of greater military collaboration between the two powers grew.

If the United States and the Soviet Union made strange bedfellows in China, they also seemed to work in concert—in result if not intent—to weaken the European colonial regimes in Asia. The Soviet approach was straightforward and consistent: Western imperialism in Asia should fall to the revolt of the oppressed masses. The Japanese, who had supported Asian revolutionaries before the rise of Communism in the 1920s, watched the growth of subversive undergrounds in Indochina and the Dutch East Indies, convinced that they could exploit the coming collapse of European imperialism. The Americans and their interests were harder to understand than the Europeans, who seemed ready to police their colonies with a hard hand, as the British had demonstrated in India and the French in Indochina. The American Congress, by contrast, passed legislation in 1934 that promised Philippine independence a decade later; the Roosevelt administration allowed a retired army chief of staff, Douglas MacArthur, to go to Manila to start a Filipino national army—to recreate the very army that an American army had crushed 35 years before. The United States maintained regular forces around Manila Bay that could not by themselves defeat a determined invasion, but Congress was unlikely to invest military money in a nonwhite colony that it yearned to detach from the American flag. In China, the United States maintained troops in Shanghai, Tientsin, and Peiping to pressure the Europeans to surrender their special privileges and trading rights.

Before any other foreign powers or their own leaders in Tokyo could intervene, the officers of the Kwantung Army pushed forward with their own plans to establish complete Japanese control of Manchuria. Some saw it as the essential first step toward a larger plan to conquer China, for a secure base in Manchuria would provide industrial raw materials and food and check Soviet military assistance to either the Chinese Nationalists or Communists. Building on the anxiety caused by antiforeign riots throughout China proper in 1925–1927, the Japanese staged terrorist incidents throughout Manchuria and called for harsh measures against the insurgent Chinese. In 1928 an officer clique at Kwantung headquarters blew up a train carrying General Chang Tso-lin, the warlord of north China and Manchuria and a rival of Chiang Kai-shek. This bit of *kabuki* backfired, since Chang Tso-lin's warlord son, Chang Hsueh-liang, "the Young Marshal," uncovered the plot and allied himself with Chiang Kai-shek. Other warlords followed his example, including an American favorite, Feng Yuhsiang, a nominal Christian who baptized his troops with fire hoses. The Japanese had made Chinese belligerency a nightmare come true.

In September 1931 Japanese Army conspirators tried again to create a wave of fabricated terrorism that would justify a military takeover of Manchuria and the elimination of residual European influence and Chang Hsueh-liang's army. This time, staged demolitions in Mukden and elsewhere preceded a rapid Japanese occupation of key political and economic sites, the disarming or routing of Chinese soldiers and police, and a rush of reinforcements from the Japanese Army in Korea and its Korean auxiliaries. Key conspirators in Tokyo blocked ministerial action until the occupation neared completion; army officers at the Imperial General Headquarters blessed the "incident" after the fact and helped bring down the cabinet in December. The army kidnapped Henry Pu Yi, the last Ch'ing emperor, from Tientsin and installed him as the emperor of Manchukuo, a puppet state. To preempt Chinese intervention, the Kwantung Army actually attacked Chinese garrisons in north China and Mongolia between 1931 and 1935, despite a League of Nations resolution (without sanctions) disapproving Japanese aggression. Neither the United States nor Britain took action, while the Soviets sold their railroad interests in Manchuria and retreated to the north.

During this march to glory, the Japanese waged a harsh, bloody, punitive campaign in Shanghai in 1932 in retaliation for anti-Japanese terrorism and riots in that port. The Chinese Army fought with considerable effectiveness, and the Japanese found themselves hard-pressed to drive the Chinese from the city. Only by using a marine brigade and three army divisions were they able to defeat the Nineteenth Route Army, which was trained and armed by German and Soviet advisers. In the meantime, the Japanese withdrew from the League of Nations and renounced the three Washington treaties it signed in 1921.

The growing tumult in China encouraged the division and radicalization of the Japanese Army's officer corps, where one group of senior officers, labeled by their opponents as Toseiha or the Control Clique, committed themselves to the cause of expansionism in China and preparation for an inevitable war with the Soviet Union. The other faction, which had begun in the 1920s as the Young Officers Movement, urged caution abroad and revolution at home, a rejection of Western materialism and capitalism, the leveling of social classes, and a return to a dictatorial emperorship that would exalt traditional Japanese values. One part of this movement, named Kodoha or the Imperial Way Group, became the shooting edge of political extremism in Japan. It played a role in six army mutinies and acts of political terrorism in Japan between 1931 and 1935. The Control faction, led by General Nagata Tetzusan, started a purge of the army's key billets that would eliminate 3,500 Kodoha oppositionists, including the Kodoha

JAPANESE EXPANSION

1920 – 1941

Japanese empire
and mandate 1920

Territory added by 1931

Territory added by 1933

Territory added by 1937

Territory added by 1941

U S S R

Irkutsk

Trans-Siberian railway

MANCHURIA

Harbin ○

Vladivo

Ulan Bator ●

M O N G O L I A

Peking ●

Se

Jap

Seoul ●

Pu

C H I N A

Nanking ●

Shanghai ●

Nagasaki

TIBET

Lhasa ●

Chungking ●

East
China
Sea

Delhi ●

NEPAL

BHUTAN

Okinawa

Taihoku

K'un-ming ●

Canton ●

Formosa
(Taiwan)

Calcutta ●

Burma

Hanoi ●

Haiphong ●

Hong Kong ●

I n d i a

Mandalay ●

20°

Bombay ●

Bay of
Bengal

Rangoon ●

SIAM

Bangkok ●

French Indo-China

1940 Japanese
established bases
in the northern part
of French Indochina

Manila ●

Philippine Islands

Madras ●

Saigon ●

South
China
Sea

Colombo ●

Ceylon

N. Borneo

Sarawak

Malaya

Kuala Lumpur ●

0°

Singapore ●

Borneo

D u t c h   E a s t   I n d i e

Celebes

INDIAN OCEAN

Palembang ●

Java Sea

Batavia ●

Java

Timor

N

20°

90°

110°

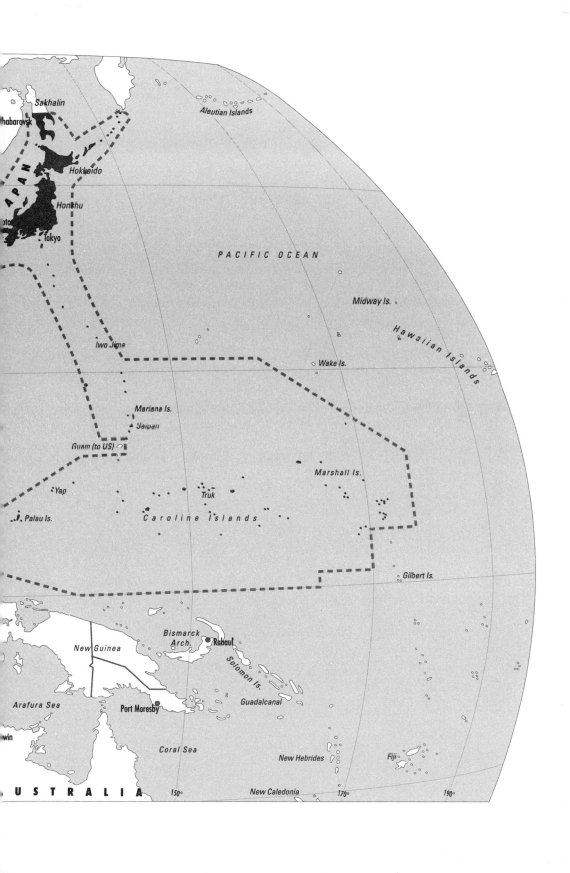

Sakhalin

Aleutian Islands

habarovsk

JAPAN

Hokkaido

Honshu

otoa

Tokyo

PACIFIC OCEAN

Midway Is.

H a w a i i a n   I s l a n d s

Iwo Jima

Wake Is.

Mariana Is.

Saipan

Guam (to US)

Marshall Is.

Yap

Truk

C a r o l i n e   I s l a n d s

Palau Is.

Gilbert Is.

Bismarck
Arch.   Rabaul

New Guinea

Solomon Is.

Arafura Sea

Port Moresby

Guadalcanal

win

Coral Sea

New Hebrides

Fiji

U S T R A L I A   150°   New Caledonia   170°   190°

hero General Araki Sadao, who was removed from his post as minister of war. Enraged, a Kodoha officer assassinated Nagata in August 1935; Hirohito demanded the murderer's court-martial and execution—novel assertions of discipline that the Japanese Army usually avoided. The firebrands of Kodoha now concluded that they could save the throne only by removing Hirohito.

In an act of *gekokujo* (principled indiscipline) staged 26–29 February 1936 (the so-called Two-Twenty-Six Incident), 1,400 Kodoha officers and soldiers attempted to kill three key Court officials, two senior cabinet ministers, and Nagata's successor as inspector-general of training. They did indeed kill five men, but only two were on the death list. Their plans to seize government and army buildings failed, and the mutineer officers soon saw their troops abandon them. The eventual result was the execution of nine ringleaders and the imprisonment, discharge, and retirement of Kodoha's surviving leaders. In crushing the coup, Control officers, including such expansionist missionaries as Major General Ishiwara Kanji and Major General Doihara Kenji, known for his special operations as Lawrence of Manchuria, moved into key planning billets.

Continental imperialists now held sway throughout the Japanese Army, not just in Manchuria. The military stressed the threat of international Communism, dramatized by the declaration of the Seventh Cominterm Congress in 1935 that all revolutionary socialists and liberals should form a common front against Fascism. To the Japanese generals, such pronouncements looked suspiciously like a growing alliance between the Soviet Union and Nationalist China, with even Mao Tse-tung's Communists welcomed into the anti-Japanese forces. As director of army war planning, Ishiwara urged his contemporaries to ensure Japanese control of northern China for economic reasons and to give the army geographic depth in the coming war with the Soviet Union. The government should start a dramatic program of industrial modernization, which required continued support from Britain and the United States.

Although the general staff in Tokyo wanted to avoid war if possible, the Kwantung Army in Manchuria had its own vision of Japan's future. As explained by General Tojo, the dour military policeman whose control of the Kwantung Army during the Two-Twenty-Six Incident had made him its chief of staff, that plan included moving against the north Chinese warlords before they joined the Nationalists. Kwantung Army leaders also warned Tokyo about another alliance between the Nationalists and Communists. In December 1936 Chang Hsueh-liang held Chiang Kai-shek a virtual prisoner in Sian until the Generalissimo agreed to call off his anti-

Communist crusade. Chiang Kai-shek and Mao Tse-tung then pledged unity against the Japanese.

Only a month before, the Japanese saw another omen: improved efficiency in the Chinese Army. Following the policy of using Japanese-sponsored Chinese forces to start the subversion of the warlord regimes, Tojo sent a small army of Japanese-led Mongols into northwestern China, where they met a Chinese army under General Fu Tso-yi. The Chinese actually won a battle at Suiyuan and forced the Mongols to retreat. The Japanese saw the Soviets' fine hand in this battle, which provided additional justification for signing the Anti-Comintern Pact with Germany in November 1936. This treaty made broad statements about the war against Communism, but it basically pledged that neither Germany nor Japan would assist the Soviet Union if one of the signatories went to war with the Soviets.

These limited Japanese military operations in northern China brought no serious European intervention, not even from the Soviet Union. The diplomats dithered, but the consensus from Europe, alarmed by Hitler's annexation of Austria, was that the United States should assume principal responsibility for policing Japan. Congressional and public isolationism made it difficult for Roosevelt to assist China, even by halting the flow of oil, scrap iron, and strategic metals to Japan. The Department of State had an articulate faction of Sinophiles, but they could not overcome Secretary of State Cordell Hull's fear of war with Japan or the arguments of the Europeanists that a confrontation in the Pacific would only deepen the growing political crisis in Europe. Japan did little to mask its intention to revise the international system, but its recurring political upheaval at home and growing military pressure against the warlords of north China brought no American response except the "moral protest" of not recognizing the puppet regimes in Manchuria and the contested Mongol provinces. The United States had no taste for a confrontation over distant Asian lands.

The Sino-Japanese War

As confused messages poured into his headquarters in Nanking, Chiang Kai-shek, still smarting from his embarrassment in the Sian Incident, could see no alternative to war as a result of the most recent Chinese-Japanese clash near Peiping. All the Generalissimo knew was that Japanese and Chinese soldiers had shot at one another in the dark. Chiang ordered local commanders to stand firm against the Japanese. "If we allow one more inch of our territory to be lost or sovereign rights to be encroached upon, then we shall be guilty of committing an unpardonable crime against the Chinese race . . . even at the expense of war, and once war has begun there is no looking back."[2]

The mood in Tokyo was equally belligerent, although elements of the army general staff, led by General Ishiwara, feared that expanded operations in north China would weaken preparations for war with the Soviet Union. The commander of the North China Garrison Army in the Peiping-Tientsin area harbored no such reservations, nor did the Kwantung Army in Manchuria. Outraged by Chinese efforts during the sporadic fighting of July, which included several revolts of Chinese collaborationist troops and the massacre of disarmed Japanese, the government of Prince Konoe Fuminaro saw no alternative but to crush Chinese military power in all of north China. After the war ministry had dispatched five divisions to China to join the division already there, the Japanese believed they would now end the so-called North China Incident. Instead, they found themselves mired in the Resistance War Against Japan, as the Chinese named the conflict.

The Japanese enjoyed relatively easy successes in the first months of the Sino-Japanese war. With its supply lines back into Manchuria secure and Peiping and Tientsin under control in August, the Japanese Twenty-Ninth Army followed the railroads and roads west and south to complete the occupation of China's five northern provinces by October 1937. On paper, the Chinese armies overwhelmed the Japanese; Chinese generals claimed to command 176 divisions, numbering two million soldiers. Most of these forces, however, were little more than bandits or light infantry, armed with rifles, light machine guns, and mortars. Only the 33 German-trained divisions directly under Chiang Kai-shek's control approached Western standards of effectiveness; they had artillery, support services, communications units, and air support.

Everywhere except in these few crack Nationalist divisions and the three surviving divisions of the Communist Eighth Route Army, Chinese morale was low. Most of the Chinese armies lived off the land, received booty for pay, and had no desire to campaign away from their home regions. To fight them meant that they had to be attacked, and their dispersion gave the Japanese the luxury of defeating them one at a time. Colonel Joseph W. Stilwell, the American military attaché, called the Chinese Boy Scouts serving as medical volunteers the most courageous and disciplined Chinese in the field. Early in the war, only one Chinese formation, the Communist 115th Division, commanded by an ambitious young general named Lin Piao, defeated a Japanese brigade in a battle at Pingsingkuan in September 1937.

In contrast to the Chinese soldiers, the Japanese Army went to war with a heritage of victory, a balanced force of combat arms and support services, a German-type staff system, artillery and tanks appropriate for a campaign in China, and the spirit of *bushido,* the warriors' code of victory or death and no mercy to the enemy. The Japanese Army benefited from the fact that it had begun a weapons modernization program in the 1930s that brought it up to Western standards, at least those of World War I. The major check on Japanese aggression was simply the size of their army and the slow process of regimenting their civilian population and economy to war. At the beginning of the Sino-Japanese conflict, the army could field only 17 divisions and the Kwantung Army, five. Even four years later, with mobilization in full swing, the army had grown to only 31 divisions (each 20,000) and the Kwantung Army to 13. Acutely aware of its human and economic vulnerabilities, the Konoe government in 1937 adopted parallel courses of coercion and persuasion. It conducted negotiations directly with the Nationalists and demanded the right to dominate northern China through its puppet regimes. The Japanese also sought Chinese collaborators who would overturn Chiang Kai-shek, such as a Kuomintang notable who defected named Wang Ching-wei. And with German help they tried to isolate China from foreign intervention. Finally, they kept up the military pressure, moving south to cities on the Yellow River along the Tsingtao-Sian line in early 1938. This prudent strategy might have had some chance of success but for one fact: the Japanese themselves had already ruined it by opening a second front in Shanghai.

Chiang Kai-shek chose to make Shanghai the place he would defeat the Japanese, and he committed his best Nationalist troops under the watchful eye of the Western press and the Shanghai foreign community, still protected by an Anglo-American garrison. When local troops joined anti-Japanese rioting and murders in August, Chiang supported his local commander with four German-trained divisions and eventually committed approximately 50 divisions (700,000 soldiers) to contain and then destroy a 10-division Japanese army (300,000 soldiers and marines). With this buildup under way, Chiang ordered his air force on 14 August to bomb Japanese aviation units, shipping, and installations within Shanghai; some of the bombs fell into the International Settlement, killing some 2,000 people, most of them Chinese. Some observers concluded that the Nationalists had demonstrated their own reckless disregard for life in order to encourage European intervention. Instead, the Japanese armed forces (including naval units and naval aviation) opened a campaign of vengeance and extermination that drove the Chinese from Shanghai by the end of November. The Chinese fought valiantly and lost half their numbers; neither side gave safe haven to the wounded and captured. In terms of its impact on Western observers, the Battle of Shanghai did not shift the balance of sentiment either way except to stun people with the ferocity of what the Japanese now called the China Incident.

Having ruined the best Nationalist divisions, the Japanese Central China Expeditionary Force drove west along the Yangtze toward Nanking and Chiang Kai-shek's government. The remnants of the Chinese army mounted some resistance, but the Japanese entered the city on 13 December in the wake of a devastating air and artillery bombardment. The Japanese Army then abandoned its disciplinary restraint, which had been imposed to maintain the authority of the officer corps rather than demonstrate humanitarian values. Almost anyone became fair game to the enraged Japanese. Their aircraft attacked foreign warships evacuating Nanking's panic-stricken Europeans; the U.S. Navy gunboat *Panay* had two sailors killed and 50 sailors and passengers wounded in one air attack. The Japanese government showed its sensitivity to American opinion by apologizing to the United States and arranging indemnity payments in only two weeks. The Chinese population, however, felt the harsh hand of genocide; in eight weeks of mayhem witnessed by thousands of Westerners and surviving Chinese, Japanese soldiers of all ranks tortured, raped, mutilated, and murdered tens of thousands of Chinese of all ages and both sexes. The Nationalist government estimated the death toll at 100,000 victims, but several postwar investigations put the figure closer to 200,000. The defense of Shanghai had stirred Chinese nationalism, and the "rape of Nanking" gave the Chinese a common cause they had not shared for centuries against a foreign invader. Moreover, Western media coverage of the war intensified—and not to the benefit of Japan.

The Japanese field armies south and north of the Yellow River valley marched toward each other in what its commanders hoped would be the end of the war. In the meantime, Japanese diplomats, often through German intermediaries, sought some sort of settlement with the Nationalists that would ratify the military victory without further campaigning or a harsh pacification program. Retreating to another new capital far up the Yangtze at Chungking, but still under the threat of air attack, the Nationalist government now called for total national resistance and prolonged partisan warfare.

Chiang Kai-shek's situation was desperate. Soviet military assistance was uncertain, while the Germans saw no profit in continuing their military mission to Chiang. The Führer realized that switching his support to Japan would weaken the Soviet Union and the British Empire—a siren song skillfully sung in Berlin by Ambassador (General) Oshima Hiroshi. The Japanese made sure the Germans understood that the war in China was also a war on Communism; the growing power of the Chinese Communist partisan forces in northwest China provided the evidence. The Konoe government demonstrated its self-confidence in January 1938 by announcing that it would no longer recognize Chiang Kai-shek's government and would deal only with alternative political movements—except, of course, the Communists.

The possibility that the war in China might later include conflict with the Soviet Union and an Anglo-American coalition justified increased regimentation and repression within Japan itself. Now echoing calls for "moral and cultural revitalization" that sounded like the radical authoritarianism of the army's crushed Kodoha faction, the Konoe government pressed the Diet to pass the National General Mobilization Law of February 1938, which allowed the cabinet to rule without reference to the Diet. Liberals, socialists, and Christian pacifists found themselves driven to the margins of Japanese society, often removed from their jobs and sometimes jailed. The Japanese public began to feel the economic pressure of the war; rationing gradually included some types of food, clothes, consumer goods, and imports. Financed largely by borrowing and monetary expansion, military spending consumed 75 percent of public funding. Inflation increased, as did Japan's dependence on the imported raw materials that fueled the *zaibatsu*'s expanding war production; except for iron ore and coal, strategic materials (especially oil) had to come from abroad. Even with new agricultural land brought into production, Japan had to import food staples, including rice.

Japanese military successes in 1938 reinforced a policy of conquest and occupation. Despite another rare Nationalist military victory at Taierhchuang in March–April 1938, the Chinese defense of the Yellow River valley collapsed with the loss of the key railroad city of Hsuchow in May 1938 and the destruction of the Chinese Second Group Army of 600,000 soldiers by a Japanese Army of 400,000, well-supplied with artillery and tanks. Again the Chinese lost more than half their men. In the meantime, another Japanese force, commanded by General Doihara, captured Wuhan, which placed the Japanese astride the last north-south rail line out of China and a key site on the Yangtze River. Additional expeditionary forces leap-frogged down the coast from Shanghai to Canton in October 1938, finally seizing Hainan Island in the Gulf of Tonkin in February of the next year. These coastal enclaves strengthened the Japanese maritime blockade on China and placed forces where they could menace French Indochina and the Philippines.

After the military successes of 1938 were assessed, the Japanese prime minister announced with satisfaction that Japan had embarked on a crusade to end European imperialism in Asia. Japan would become the bulwark of a "New Order" for Asia, the Dai To-A Kyoeiken or Greater East Asia Co-prosperity Sphere. The New Order would end imperialism, stop Communism, and unite Asians in a great cultural and spiritual alliance free of Western taint. Articulating anti-Western grievances he had been nursing since his service at Versailles in 1919, Prince Konoe announced the closing of the Open Door.

Prince Konoe's victory declaration in November 1938 proved premature, and he himself resigned barely two months later, at the beginning of a fateful year for Japan—a year so full of evil auguries that even the military wondered about the wisdom of war on China. The more the Japanese pushed into China, the farther they seemed from peace. In addition, other enemies appeared ready to challenge them, and the Germans proved as perfidious as the British. For the first time, the United States edged toward official measures to aid Nationalist China when Congress approved a modest request of $25 million in credits from the Roosevelt administration. Designed to shore up Chungking's international credit, the loan represented a shift toward interventionism, despite Hull's continued resistance. An alliance of pro-China officials in the State Department, the Treasury, and the White House emerged. Several media moguls with pro-Chinese sympathies, especially Henry Luce of *Time* and *Life* magazines, encouraged them. Missionaries and businessmen, who often shared true admiration for ordinary Chinese if not the Kuomintang, urged the government to more aggressive action. Chiang Kai-shek had the good sense to use his wife, the luminous Madame Chiang (Soong Mei-ling) and her gifted siblings by birth and marriage as his personal representatives. The Soongs spoke English, had years of experience in the Shanghai foreign community, practiced Christianity, and knew American politics from their school days in the United States and from many subsequent visits.

Roosevelt, whose family fortune had started with the China trade in the early nineteenth century, came to the conclusion in late 1938 that Japan must pay some price for its cupidity and blood-lust. He began to think about economic sanctions and to gauge public acceptance of such measures. Public reaction to the *Panay* attack suggested that he had a soft mandate for action, a judgment shared by the congressional leadership. Although the practical problems of getting military supplies to China made direct assistance as yet impossible, the first step in punishing Japan and weakening its industrial mobilization would be the abrogation of the 1911 Treaty of Commerce and Navigation, which had given Japan generous access to American suppliers and financial institutions. In July 1939 Congress abrogated the treaty. Still, the Japanese had six months to repent before the act went into effect.

The Europeans dealt the Japanese more telling blows. Except for Britain, whose appeasement extended to Tokyo as well as Berlin, the Western European nations backed the United States, while Germany and the Soviet Union went their separate ways. The Nazi-Soviet Non-Aggression Pact in August 1939 stunned the Japanese, and they wondered what had happened to the grand alliance against Communism. The Kwantung Army received an even bigger surprise when it clashed with Soviet forces along the Manchurian-Soviet-Mongolian border in August 1938 and May 1939. In the second battle, the Nomonhan Incident, the Soviets destroyed a reinforced Japanese division, which fled as well as died. The Soviets enjoyed firepower and mobility the Japanese could not match, and the army general staff wondered if it could continue to spread its divisions over the vastness of China while it confronted the Red Army along the Manchurian border. In China itself, the Nationalist armies had dwindled to nuisance status, but partisan forces, many led by dedicated Communists, now attacked the detachments guarding the thin system of railways and roads upon which the Japanese Army in the interior depended. In conventional terms, the Japanese Army had won the war in China, but it could not end it.

In a conversation with an American officer who visited his Yenan headquarters, Mao Tse-tung scoffed at the claim that Japan had conquered China: "China is like a gallon jug which Japan is trying to fill with a half-pint of liquid."[3] Mao's assessment was not far wrong if one focused simply on people-in-arms. Despite the fact that Chinese armies had lost more than a million men, there were still two million soldiers in regular or partisan units, even if they were poorly armed, trained, and officered. Half of China's population of 450 million, living on 60 percent of China's rice lands, still remained outside the Japanese occupation zone. Mao Tse-tung reminded the Chinese that time worked for them: "The Japanese militarists are gradually losing the initiative because of their shortage of troops . . . because of the fact that they are fighting on foreign soil . . . and because of their stupidities in command."[4]

China, however, remained isolated from the outside world except by air and two primitive roads from Burma and French Indochina. Moreover, most of its limited industry had fallen into Japanese hands. Even if the Chinese government could purchase arms in Western Europe, it still depended upon British and French-controlled ports and roads to deliver these weapons to the Nationalist Army in western China. The Japanese did not let this traffic go unnoticed; they pressured the British into closing the Burma Road in 1940. In July 1940 Japanese forces landed in the Hanoi-Haiphong area in northern Indochina and, with the resigned cooperation (after two days of battle) of a Vichyite French colonial administration, closed the last road to Nationalist China.

The outbreak of war in Europe in September 1939 did nothing to change the strategic stalemate in China, which had its own "phoney war" through winter 1939–40. Not that the opponents failed to seek regional advantages. The Japanese attempted twice to take Changsha in the Hunan province (April–October 1939 and April–June 1940) and twice decided the casualties did not justify a continued advance into this southern inland city. The Japanese started to call their periodic moves "punitive expeditions," and in north China the senior Japanese general characterized the war as a guerrilla suppression campaign that justified "the Three Alls" policy of total killing, burning, and destruction. The Chinese Nationalists showed some signs of military revival, but in January 1941, instead of concentrating on the Japanese, Chiang Kai-shek used one of his better armies to crush the Communist New Fourth Army, an effective force operating behind Japanese lines in north China. Chiang's latest exercise in political suicide also eliminated Wang Ming, the New Fourth Army's patron within the Communist ruling elite. He was Mao Tse-tung's leading rival and leader of the pro-Soviet clique in the Chinese Communist Party. With Wang removed, no one was left to obstruct Mao's path to power.

The United States Moves

For both Japan and the United States, the fall of France and the beleaguered stand of the British Empire brought the first of two great changes in the global strategic situation. In another change of government, Prince Konoe returned to head a more aggressive cabinet in July 1940 and appointed two stalwarts of Japanese rule in Manchuria, General Tojo and Matsuoka Yōsuke, as war minister and foreign minister. To complete the dissolution of Japan's political parties, the Konoe government announced the formation of the Imperial Rule Assistance Association, a coalition of extreme nationalist groups that resembled the Nazi Party. Konoe's focus, however, settled on the need to find a *modus vivendi* with the Chinese. He even tried to open negotiations with Chiang, at the cost of demoralizing his various Chinese puppets, but the initiatives went nowhere. He decided to try to restore Japan's relations with Germany, and in September 1940

Matsuoka completed the complex negotiations that produced the Tripartite Pact alliance of Germany, Japan, and Italy against the United States. The Germans thought that such a threat would limit the assistance the United States might give Britain; the Japanese thought the pact would give the United States and the Soviet Union pause before extending aid to China or the European colonies of Southeast Asia. The pact also provided for German economic and military assistance to Japan.

Contrary to expectations, the German conquest of Western Europe dramatically stiffened American resolve to aid Britain and confront Japan, not just over China but over the future of colonial empires throughout Asia. In January 1940 Roosevelt had already instructed the U.S. Navy to shift the battle fleet to the undeveloped base at Pearl Harbor, Hawaii, in an act of deterrent diplomacy that actually reduced the fleet's readiness. The fall of France, however, indicated that more drastic measures might be necessary to lend direct assistance to Britain and to keep Southeast Asia's resources out of Japanese hands. Roosevelt persuaded Congress to start the revision of the Neutrality Acts, if only because the administration might strengthen its hemispheric defenses by cooperating with the Allies. The China lobby also took heart when Chiang's request for another loan of $100 million won approval in November 1940. The Japanese embassy, on the other hand, could not stop the imposition of a partial embargo on exports to Japan of American scrap iron and steel, other strategic metals, and oil in July and September 1940. These acts only whetted the Japanese appetite for leadership in the Tripartite Alliance.

Although passed principally to assist the British, the Lend-Lease Act of March 1941 allowed the Roosevelt administration to consider direct military assistance to Chiang Kai-shek, whose continued resistance was helping to pin down the Japanese Army in China and away from Southeast Asia. The Nationalists, represented by T. V. Soong in Washington, submitted a request for three major programs: (1) creation of a 1,000-aircraft air force to be commanded by a retired U.S. Army officer, Claire Chennault, in Chinese employ; (2) construction equipment to improve China's roads and railways; and (3) arms and equipment for 30 modern divisions. The U.S. Army and the Office of Lend-Lease Administration approved a more realistic program of $145 million, divided between aircraft and army weapons, since much of the heavy equipment China requested could not reach the country. The administration also approved the army's proposal to send a permanent military mission to China to train the Nationalist Army. The difficulties of shipping materiel to China allowed the United States to tell Japan that it still had time to negotiate a settlement.

Before serious American-Japanese discussions could begin, however, the strategic sea-state shifted dramatically again: Germany invaded the Soviet Union. Through the lengthy and accurate messages sent by Ambassador Oshima from Berlin, Konoe knew about Operation Barbarossa early in 1941 and allowed Matsuoka to negotiate a Neutrality Pact with the Russians in April 1941. The pact and Barbarossa ended the Soviet threat to Manchuria and the Home Islands. The Japanese could now think about committing their one great unused asset, the Imperial Navy's Combined Fleet, commanded by Admiral Yamamoto. The most aggressive members of the Konoe cabinet argued that a decision for war could not wait; oil and food reserves had started to fall in 1941. In addition, the Japanese military insisted that the United States must be stopped before its assistance to the Nationalists produced a real Chinese air force, a small modern army, and larger paramilitary forces, already nipping at the Japanese Army's overextended divisions. Still hopeful that the United States would abandon its support of China and the Allied colonies, Konoe dissolved his second cabinet to get rid of Matsuoka.

Watching growing American support for Britain and a reeling Soviet Union, the Japanese military believed the United States would not fight a major war with Japan because to do so would allow Nazism to succeed in Europe. Now was the time to make the strategy of 1936 work: *hokushu nanshin* or "hold north, go south." As a first step, the Japanese occupied the rest of French Indochina in July 1941, which allowed them to create a new operating base at Cam Ranh Bay. The United States immediately retaliated by freezing Japanese funds and assets in the United States and putting a complete embargo on oil and strategic metals.

Throughout the summer and early autumn of 1941, Japanese and American officials considered the immediate prospect of war, and neither set of diplomats and officers found much comfort in their calculations. American planners had worked on a variety of contingency plans since the fall of France, and Roosevelt had pushed them to accept the principle of Germany First if the United States was forced to declare war on the Axis nations at the same time. The defense of the Philippines and Allied colonies would have to be a holding action, conducted by scratch forces contributed by the British, Dutch, Australians, and Americans; land-based aircraft, a combined Allied fleet without carriers, and the colonial armies, stiffened with a few Europeans and American divisions, would have to do the best they could. The U.S. Army, for example, provided only one regular division and an air force of 250 planes to the defense of the Philippines; all the other divisions were made of raw Filipino volunteers and draftees. The war plan that appeared most likely to be used in autumn 1941 was Rainbow Five, which assumed little hope of stopping the Japanese. In the broadest terms, the only serious threat the United States could mount was a sortie into the Central Pacific by the Pacific Fleet, already weakened by redeployments to the Atlantic and the shuttling of reinforcements to bastions such as Guam, Wake Island, Midway Island, and the Philippines via Australia.

Faced with the prospect of war, Prince Konoe in July 1941 tried to slow the firebrands in his own cabinet. He argued that Roosevelt would see reason and abandon Asia as the crisis mounted. Konoe thought he could at least buy time before the confrontation with the United States. He found support in the navy's planning staffs in Tokyo and with the Combined Fleet, based now in Hokkaido, away from the prying eyes and distractions of Honshu. The planners went over the plans and war games time and time again. The army confidently reported that it could make the "go south" strategy work in a lightning campaign requiring no more than 15 of the 51 divisions available. There would be only five divisions left in the Home Islands.

The real issue was the navy, which had a well-trained and superbly equipped aviation force of 2,000 carrier and land-based aircraft and a battle force built around ten battleships and ten carriers. The army, however, questioned the navy's ardor for war, especially that of Admiral Yamamoto. Japanese strategy became a matter of interservice rivalry. Yamamoto expressed little doubt that the navy would make the "go south" plan work in the operational sense, but he wondered whether the United States would hold to its Germany First strategy in the face of defeat in the Pacific. Rather, he expected that racial embarrassment and national pride would drive the United States into an anti-Japanese crusade, not to a gracious acceptance of Japan's natural right to dominate Asia. Yamamoto did not question the wisdom of attacking the Philippines, which was sure to bring America into the war, because the Japanese forces could not operate farther south with such a threat in their rear. He could not, however, assume responsibility for the navy's success if he was not allowed to attack the Pacific Fleet at its moorings in Pearl Harbor.

Prince Konoe participated in the deliberations about war with the Europeans and the United States, but he could not hide his doubts of a quick victory, encouraged by Yamamoto's assessment. His cabinet ministers thought otherwise, arguing in July 1941 that the "go south" plan should begin as soon as possible. Another major examination of the international situation in early September produced the same result: war with the United States was inevitable, and victory would come from striking first *now.* Konoe held on to his post until October, but he resigned under pressure, in October 1941. General Tojo became prime minister. On 5 November he and the other key ministers again reviewed the plans, which now included Yamamoto's Pearl Harbor option as the price for navy participation in "go south." Tojo ruled that unless the United States met Japan's demands for hegemony in Asia by 25 November, the war plans would go into effect.

Conclusion

The days of peace for the United States dwindled to a precious few; but for Japan, December 1941 brought a chance to end four years of war in China and free Japan from racial humiliation and economic interdependence. Blinded by their own sense of cultural superiority and distorted notions of industrial progress and economic determinism, the Japanese could not fathom why the United States should care about the Chinese, who exhibited an irrational traditionalism and pathetic social disorganization. Having convinced themselves that the United States had no real gods but profit and consumption, the Japanese could not imagine that the flames which consumed the U.S. Pacific Fleet's battleships on 7 December 1941 would ignite a deadly firestorm of revenge, racism, embarrassment, and idealism in the heart of the American people.

8

THE JAPANESE WAR
OF CONQUEST

1941–1942

The planes roared over the U.S. naval base at Pearl Harbor at 7:55 A.M. Hawaiian time with the bright rays of the rising sun behind them. Aboard the American warships anchored throughout Middle Loch, East Loch, and "Battleship Row" next to Ford Island, the color parties at the fantails of their ships paused before hoisting the American flag to stare at the oncoming aircraft. Some guessed that they must come from the carrier *Enterprise*, already a day overdue from taking reinforcements to Wake Island. Then the bombs began to fall.

At nearby Hickam Field where the aircraft of the U.S. Army Air Forces (USAAF) sat in neat rows along the runways, Private Earl Schaeffer ran to the sound of the bombs: "Well, I saw many fires, aircraft burning, building afire, much smoke coming from the Pearl Harbor area. It was too much! I just couldn't comprehend just what was going on." He stared in disbelief at the huge red rondelles on the fighters sweeping up and down Hickam's runways, blasting at the parked aircraft with 20mm cannon and machine guns. He realized "the awful truth" and felt sick as he watched the Mitsubishi A6M2 Zero fighters make pass after pass above the flaming wreckage of the bombers along the flightline.[1]

The Road to War

Although the requirements for an attack on Pearl Harbor had been well known to planners in both the Imperial Japanese Navy and the U.S. Navy for a decade, only the staff of Admiral Yamamoto Isoroku, commander of the Combined Fleet, could turn the studies and war games into blazing reality, creating a naval *jujitsu* throw that floored the Pacific Fleet at a moment of unanticipated weakness. After he concluded in early 1941 that

169

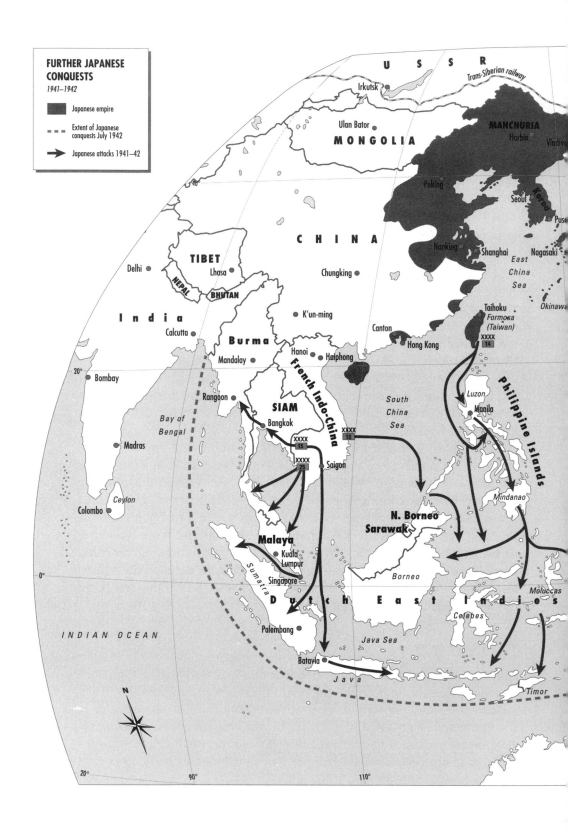

FURTHER JAPANESE CONQUESTS
1941–1942

Japanese empire

Extent of Japanese conquests July 1942

Japanese attacks 1941–42

U S S R

Trans-Siberian railway

Irkutsk

Ulan Bator

MONGOLIA

MANCHURIA

Harbin

Vladiv...

Peking

Seoul

Korea

Pus...

CHINA

Nanking

Shanghai

Nagasaki

East China Sea

Okinawa

Delhi

TIBET

Lhasa

NEPAL

BHUTAN

Chungking

K'un-ming

Canton

Taihoku
Formosa
(Taiwan)

XXXX
14

India

Calcutta

Burma

Hanoi

Haiphong

Hong Kong

Mandalay

Bombay

20°

Rangoon

SIAM

Bangkok

French Indo-China

South China Sea

Luzon

Manila

Philippine Islands

XXXX
15

XXXX
16

Bay of Bengal

Madras

XXXX
25

Saigon

Mindanao

Colombo

Ceylon

N. Borneo
Sarawak

Malaya

Kuala Lumpur

Singapore

Borneo

Moluccas

0°

Sumatra

Dutch East Indies

Celebes

Palembang

Java Sea

INDIAN OCEAN

Batavia

Java

Timor

N

20°

90°

110°

40°

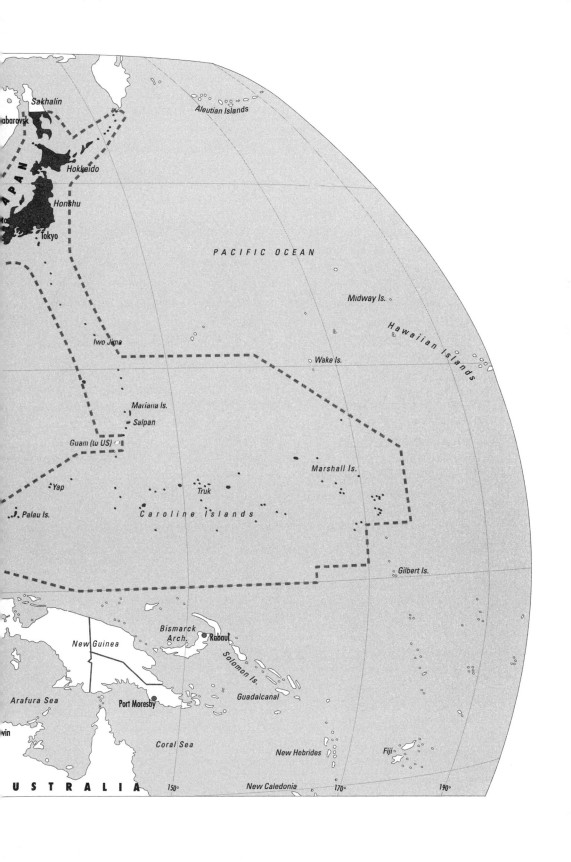

Sakhalin
Aleutian Islands
abarovsk
Hokkaido
Honshu
JAPAN
Tokyo
PACIFIC OCEAN
Midway Is.
Iwo Jima
Hawaiian Islands
Wake Is.
Mariana Is.
Saipan
Guam (to US)
Marshall Is.
Yap
Truk
Palau Is.
Caroline Islands
Gilbert Is.
Bismarck
Arch.
Rabaul
New Guinea
Solomon Is.
Arafura Sea
Guadalcanal
Port Moresby
win
Coral Sea
New Hebrides
Fiji
AUSTRALIA
150°
New Caledonia
170°
190°

war had become inevitable, Yamamoto used his charisma, technical mastery of naval operations, and indomitable will upon the IJA and IJN general staffs to convince them that the Pearl Harbor attack was essential for an "American-British-Dutch War." Since July 1941 the army and navy staffs in Tokyo had studied and discussed with considerable passion the various options for such a war, galvanized by the judgment that oil starvation would make an attack essential within the next 18 months unless the United States reversed its economic sanctions.

The key economic objectives were Malaya and the Dutch East Indies, but the first question was whether these objectives could be attacked and secured without a simultaneous attack on the Philippines. For once the Japanese generals showed more political sophistication than their naval opposites. Even if American land-based bombers (the B-17s of the Far East Air Force) and the Asiatic Fleet of cruisers, destroyers, and submarines posed a threat to the invasion fleets, the issue of American participation should be left to the erratic Americans. The generals proposed to bypass Luzon.

The IJN planners, however, judged the risk too high and insisted that the American bases on Luzon be made primary objectives, even if an attack ensured war with the United States. The argument then shifted to the elimination of the U.S. Pacific Fleet, based in Hawaii with its forward operating bases at Guam and Wake Island for reconnaissance aircraft and submarines. A staff exercise on 10–13 September proved the feasibility of the Pearl Harbor operation, but the arguments about its wisdom continued into October. When even the IJN general staff questioned the risks of the Hawaiian operation, Yamamoto threatened to retire, an act viewed by his peers as a potential disaster to the morale and effectiveness of the Combined Fleet.

By the end of October, war plans identified the Philippines, Pearl Harbor, and Malaya as the first objectives of the "move south" campaign, with subsidiary operations against Hong Kong, Wake Island, and Guam. The Dutch East Indies would await later conquest, but all these objectives should be secure within 150 days. By then the Allies would no longer have air, naval, and ground forces capable of blocking the seizure of all the South Seas Resource Area. Yamamoto and the leaders of the invasion task forces now turned to massing their units, determining their local requirements, and honing their eager soldiers and sailors for the final solution to European influence in Asia.

As the Japanese order-of-battle took shape in the autumn of 1941, Yamamoto's strategic assertiveness reflected the disproportionate role of the Imperial Japanese Navy in the forthcoming war. The Japanese Army could provide 12 divisions and 4 independent brigades and 2 air groups of 700 aircraft for the southern campaign. One division from the Twenty-Third Army (Canton)* would take Hong Kong. Four divisions of the Twenty-Fifth Army, commanded by Lieutenant General Yamashita Tomoyuki and based on Hainan Island and Indochina, would conduct the invasion of Malaya. The two divisions and two separate brigades of the Fourteenth Army, based on Formosa and the Ryukyus under the command of Lieutenant General Homma Masaharu, had the mission of invading Luzon and taking Manila Bay and thus destroying the forces and bases critical to Filipino-American resistance. The three divisions of the Sixteenth Army, commanded by Lieutenant General Imamura Hitoshi and drawn from the forces in the Home Islands and Indochina, provided some strategic reserve, since they would invade the Dutch East Indies only when the operations in the Philippines and Malaya were judged successful. Reinforced regiments of the IJN's Special Landing Forces (Japanese "marines") assumed the responsibility for assaulting Guam and Wake Island. The army's commitment represented about one-fifth of the 1941 fighting power of the Japanese Army.

The only reassuring factor was that the Allied ground forces were even less numerous, less well-trained, and less enthusiastic. The British had garrisoned Hong Kong with a British-Canadian brigade group of six infantry battalions and supporting arms (10,000 officers and other ranks). The forces defending Malaya, including the island bastion of Singapore, numbered nearly 90,000, more than the Japanese attack force of 60,000. This Commonwealth army, hurriedly assembled in late 1941, had little Royal Air Force support (158 aircraft inferior to the Japanese), no tanks, and insufficient field artillery. Moreover, the Indian Army provided the majority of the forces (two divisions and one brigade group), and the Indians were not the cream of their own army, which had already deployed to the Middle East and Africa to fight the Italians and Germans. A newly raised Australian division (the 8th Division, Australian Imperial Force) defended southern Malaya; Singapore itself was defended by two Malay-British brigades, with another posted across the straits of Johore. The Royal Netherlands East Indies Army (KNIL) numbered about 40,000 officers and men, one-third of them Dutch or Eurasian and the rest Javanese and other Indonesians; the only real reserve was the colonial police, which shared internal peace-keeping duties with the KNIL. Its peacetime constabulary function meant that the KNIL was a light infantry force, deployed at potential

*A Japanese army was a corps in U.S. usage, that is, two or more divisions, reinforced.

economic targets (oil fields) and population centers throughout the major islands of Java, Sumatra, Dutch Borneo, Celebes, and the Moluccas.

The Dutch Navy stationed 3 cruisers, 7 destroyers, and 15 submarines to cover over 2,000 miles of littoral. The British assembled a more considerable naval task force at Singapore, built around the battleship *Prince of Wales* and the battle cruiser *Repulse,* screened by 23 cruisers and destroyers. This surface force, however, had no real air cover, since the carrier hastily dispatched from the Mediterranean broke down en route.

The Filipino-American land forces on Luzon posed no greater threat, with the exception perhaps of the army fighter and bomber squadrons gathered at Clark Field and capable of missions as far as Formosa. The U.S. Navy's Asiatic Fleet, under Admiral Thomas C. Hart, numbered 3 cruisers, 13 destroyers, and 29 submarines, the latter a potential threat but armed (unknowingly) with defective torpedoes. Like the 100,000-man ground force, the air forces fell under the command of Douglas MacArthur, restored to active duty as the Commanding General, U.S. Army Forces Far East. MacArthur, former army chief of staff and a Philippine field marshal, took over in July 1941. If noble words could kill, MacArthur would rank with Genghis Khan as the slayer of millions, but the Japanese soon proved that words could never hurt them. In seasoned troops and modern weapons MacArthur stood nearly defenseless. His ground forces formed around one regular U.S. Army division (the Philippine Division) and one trained Philippine army division. Both divisions were based upon five infantry regiments of Philippine Scouts, one Scout cavalry regiment (the 26th Cavalry), and five U.S. Army artillery battalions. The other American contribution was one infantry regiment, but the War Department had reinforced MacArthur with two National Guard tank battalions and three National Guard and regular coast artillery and anti-aircraft artillery regiments. The rest of MacArthur's ground forces were 11 divisions of about 80,000 Filipino militiamen, called to duty (most without prior training) throughout autumn 1941. Even when officered by American reservists and Filipino Reserve Officers Training Corps (ROTC) graduates, these divisions had about the same armament and state of training as the average Nationalist Chinese division.

In sum, the three Allied defense groupments of 1941—British Commonwealth, Dutch-Indonesian, and Filipino-American—had little but raw numbers on their side. The only real hope they had was that Allied aviation and naval forces might upset the delicate timetable and deployment plans of the Japanese. The Japanese—well-informed by their agents on the lack of Allied preparedness—concentrated on neutralizing air and naval opposition. Their plans allocated roughly half of the Combined Fleet to the invasion forces in the Western Pacific and half to the Pearl Harbor Striking Force, directed personally by Admiral Yamamoto through his senior air admiral, Nagumo Chuichi. Nagumo sailed with 6 of the IJN's 8 large carriers, but with only 2 battleships, 2 cruisers, and 11 destroyers. Most of the IJN's surface combatants remained in the Western Pacific, where 8 battleships, 2 carriers, and more than 100 crack IJN cruisers and destroyers remained to confound the Allied fleets. Land-based Japanese naval aviation squadrons ensured air cover. Even if the Pearl Harbor raid had failed or been aborted, the IJN fleet in the Western Pacific would have overwhelmed the Allied fleet sent against them.

As the forces for conquest gathered, the Japanese government attempted to revive negotiations with the American government on the faint chance that the threat of imminent defeat would drive the Roosevelt administration to capitulate. The Chinese and British governments, equally alarmed, urged Roosevelt to stand firm. Official and unofficial diplomats, obsessed by their fear of war, scurried about with all sorts of proposals, but essentially both sides stood firm after July 1941. The Japanese offered several schemes to withdraw from Indochina and China proper if the rest of the world would recognize that Japan should have special economic rights in China and absolute control of Manchuria and other border lands beyond the Great Wall. Although China would remain an independent nation, it would be a de facto protectorate of Japan, the Japanese argued, much as Cuba and Panama remained wards of the United States.

Secretary of State Cordell Hull responded with definitive language in October 1941: the United States might soften its economic boycott if Japan would agree to leave Indochina and China within two years and return to the principles of the Nine Power Treaty, which guaranteed sovereignty for China. As these negotiations continued, the United States took the initiative in sponsoring military conferences on the defense of the Western Pacific and Southeast Asia, which stimulated some marginal reinforcements. The Tojo government thought the talks would prove fruitless and ordered war planning to accelerate in September, but the more conservative members of the Planning Board (an agency to coordinate industrial mobilization) and the military and naval staffs urged a more indirect march toward war that would extend into December. The essential preparations had been completed in early November, and the Japanese government decided on November 5 that unless the United States met its conditions later in the month, it would initiate operations against the United States, Great Britain, and the Netherlands.

With no progress divined by the diplomats in the continued negotiations, the Tojo government and the military staffs—collectively identified as the Imperial High Command Headquarters—ordered the Pearl Harbor Striking Force to sail from its anchorages in the northern Kurile Islands on 26 November. Similar movements began from Japanese bases on Formosa, the Marianas, China, and Indochina. With some access to Japanese diplomatic and military coded message traffic, the American government saw the deployments, but it missed the eastward sortie of the Pearl Harbor Striking Force, which moved under radio silence behind a harsh early-winter storm front. Imperfectly deployed, the 14th Naval District reconnaissance planes and ships missed the oncoming Japanese carriers, which also avoided any merchantmen in transit in the empty Northern Pacific. All the intelligence indicators clearly suggested a Japanese offensive in the Western Pacific, but the hints of the Pearl Harbor attack remained indistinct. The sense of the American military commanders in Washington and Hawaii was that a Japanese attack on Pearl Harbor (or the Panama Canal) would harvest nothing but outrage, regardless of what physical damage might occur. Although more astute analysis of the intelligence indicators might have produced greater readiness in Hawaii, the Roosevelt administration and the senior military commanders believed that war was inevitable but an attack on Pearl Harbor incredible.

In Washington, Secretary Hull, the Wilsonian senator from Tennessee who stopped short of peace at any price, agreed to meet with his two Japanese negotiating opposites, the Emperor's special representative, Kurusu Saburo, and the ambassador to the United States, Admiral Nomura Kochisaburo, at the odd time they requested, 1 P.M. on Sunday, 7 December 1941. Before his afternoon meeting, Hull already knew that the Japanese embassy had received a long and complicated message from Tokyo. American cryptologists were hard at work deciphering the message. The military and diplomatic watch officers found the contents of the message and its timing ominous and communicated their anxiety to Hull. The secretary learned about the attack on Pearl Harbor while Kurusu and Nomura awaited their audience.

When Hull finally saw them at about 2:30 P.M., he immediately accused them of duplicity, treachery, and mendacity for bringing him an ultimatum full of "infamous falsehoods and distortions on a scale so huge I never imagined until today that any Government on this planet was capable of uttering them." After they fled from his enraged presence, Hull called the Japanese "pissants and scoundrels."[2] They did not know of the Pearl Harbor attack. The Tojo government's scheme to present the United States with a bill of grievances and a call for capitulation at the very time bombs rained on the Pacific Fleet had not worked. It was the first time, but not the last, that Japanese plans proved too clever by half.

Defeat in the Pacific

Within minutes after the first bombs fell on its battleships, the Pacific Fleet headquarters and its aviation headquarters sent radio messages to its units, other stations in the Pacific, and (via San Francisco) to the Navy Department in Washington: "Air Raid, Pearl Harbor—This Is No Drill." Secretary of the Navy Frank Knox recoiled in amazement, thinking the message must mean the Philippines. Lunching with trusted aid Harry Hopkins in the Oval Office, Franklin Roosevelt heard the news from Knox and had the same reaction. The Japanese had made a political error of the first order by striking American territory. He told Hopkins he could no longer control events, since Congress would no doubt declare war on Japan immediately. He hoped he could keep his agreement with Churchill to fight Germany first, but he had already bowed to political pressure to reinforce the Philippines, against the counsel of his military advisers. He called the Chinese ambassador with the news but warned him not to encourage too much rejoicing in Chungking. By midafternoon Roosevelt had an early report from Pearl Harbor about the extent of the damage, which was serious but not irreparable; he did not release the losses to the press. He then authorized unrestricted air and submarine warfare against the Japanese Empire. He was already at work crafting his message to Congress about the "day that will live in infamy."

Leaving towers of smoke behind them, the Sea Eagles of the Japanese naval aviation corps roared away from the destruction they had wrought throughout Oahu. They had attacked in two waves, separated by about an hour in take-off time, and within seven hours the last aircraft had landed on its home carrier. The first wave of 183 torpedo planes, dive bombers, level bombers, and fighters had done most of the damage in about 30 minutes of attack; when the second wave of 170 level bombers, dive bombers, and fighters arrived, they found their targets obscured by smoke, and they encountered intense and very angry anti-aircraft fire. The first wave split into four subgroups and went for their primary targets: the army's Hickam, Wheeler, Bellows, and Mokuleia fields, the Marine Corps air stations at Ewa and Kaneohe Bay, and the Naval Air Station, Ford Island. Of the almost 400 military aircraft on Oahu, 188 were destroyed and 159 damaged.

The other primary target set was the 8 battleships anchored along Battleship Row at Ford Island, and any other warships at anchor. Although more than 200 ships and craft were inside the harbor on 7 December, only 46 were warships, and none of them was a carrier. The battleships drew the most attention; all were hit hard, and two (*Arizona* and *Oklahoma*) sank beyond repair and carried with them most of the 2,100 sailors and marines who died that day. Of the 38 cruisers and destroyers, only 8 received damage, and all survived to sail and fight again. Total deaths on Oahu numbered 2,400 and the wounded 1,200.

Except to the hardened professionals around Admiral Nagumo who knew the raid's shortcomings, Pearl Harbor ranked with the greatest of Japanese military victories, made all the sweeter since it came at the expense of the feared and despised U.S. Navy. At a cost of 29 aircraft (19 lost in the second wave), the Sea Eagles had eliminated the Pacific Fleet as an immediate threat to all forces deploying to seize Malaya, the Philippines, and several lesser objectives. When Commander Fuchida Mitsuo, who led the first strike, urged a third strike, Nagumo rejected the plan. The Americans had two carrier task forces (*Enterprise* and *Lexington*) somewhere to the south, and the surviving cruisers and destroyers at Pearl might sortie to join them. Nagumo had no cause to worry on this score since the senior American admirals at Oahu had decided that they now faced an invasion, a threat largely imagined by traumatized senior army officers, who had lost most of their aircraft. Nagumo also had no confidence that the Japanese submarine force would assist him; indeed, his assessment proved accurate, since the Americans had already sunk one large submarine and five midget subs that were supposed to penetrate Pearl Harbor. Nagumo's critics within his own ranks thought he should have sent a third attack against the fuel farms and installations that supported the Pacific Fleet, but these targets (with the exception of the large dry docks) could easily be replaced and refilled. The immediate goal—to shock the U.S. Navy into temporary inaction—had been accomplished.

Within hours of the Pearl Harbor strike, the Japanese armed forces began six months of conquest that brought them to the gates of India and the sea approaches to Australia and Hawaii. The smaller objectives (measured by both geography and the size of the defense forces) fell quickly: Hong Kong, Guam, New Britain Island with its natural harbor of Rabaul, Bougainville and Buka with coastal plains for air fields in the northern Solomons, and the Gilbert Islands. Hong Kong provided the staunchest defense of the British possessions during the week of 9–15 December, when almost half the Commonwealth troops became casualties; the fighting enraged the Japanese, who raped, murdered, and pillaged their way through the European and Chinese population of the colony. Elsewhere, the defenders usually fought just long enough to destroy critical facilities and attempt some sort of evacuation.

The exception was Wake Island, the U.S. naval aviation outpost 2,000 miles west of Hawaii and defended by a marine fighter squadron and part of a defense battalion. The military garrison also received some assistance from a civilian work force of 1,200. The first Japanese attempt to take Wake, after a devastating air attack on 8 December, collapsed when marine pilots and artillerymen sank or damaged six ships. The Japanese returned in much greater strength two weeks later—before the Pacific Fleet could mount a determined relief expedition—and took the island at the cost of 1,000 more casualties. Unlike its obfuscation of the Pearl Harbor defeat, the Roosevelt administration stirred public opinion with tales of marine gallantry (mostly true); "Remember Wake Island" joined "Remember Pearl Harbor" as a rallying cry.

No one except the Japanese Army found much to remember fondly about the major campaigns that conquered Malaya and the Philippines, both hopelessly isolated by Japanese air and naval supremacy. In planning the Malayan campaign, General Yamashita and his staff counted on air and naval superiority to compensate for the Twenty-Fifth Army's numerical inferiority, which was exacerbated by a lack of transport shipping and a failure to bring army units to full wartime strength. With his initial assault force reduced to the equivalent of half his four-division army, Yamashita chose to give the Commonwealth forces a death of a thousand cuts, staging multiple landings in northern Malaya, then working his way down the peninsula to Singapore while his army strength increased. Army and naval aviation squadrons, supplemented by the two IJN task forces that included carriers and battleships, would isolate Singapore from reinforcements. Yamashita had confidence that his infantrymen, supported by light tanks and artillery, would demonstrate their physical fitness and training against any sort of Commonwealth force, especially the Indians.

With a special lack of operational insight, much like that of the French in 1940, the British senior commanders, Air Chief Marshal Sir H. R. Brooke-Popham of the Royal Air Force and Lieutenant General Arthur Percival, decided to defend everywhere. Their critical weakness was a lack of combat aircraft that could match the Japanese; their only real striking power was Force Z, the naval task force built around the *Prince of Wales* and *Repulse*, commanded by Vice Admiral Tom Phillips. Instead of holding only Johore and Singapore, the British tried to provide some protection for all of Malaya's Europeans and their economic assets and, with less commitment, the Malayan and Chinese population.

The Japanese Twenty-Fifth Army, which also had to divert troops to secure objectives in "neutral" Thailand, found its initial operations against
two Indian divisions and an Indian brigade surprisingly easy. The IJN made
its greatest contribution by sinking *Prince of Wales* and *Repulse* with land-
based bombers on 10 December, two days after the first landings. Admiral
Phillips and more than 800 sailors went to the bottom with their ships, the
first capital ships under way and fighting to be sunk by aircraft alone. The
debacle was the first of many for the British. Two Japanese battalions, reinforced with tanks, scattered one Indian division; and less than two Japanese divisions, moving by foot, bicycle, and landing craft, turned every Indian position by land and sea until the remnants of the Indian III Corps fell
back to Johore, taking with them in confusion and panic that part of the
Australian 8th Division that had tried to halt the Japanese parade down
Malaya's east coast. Many Malays welcomed the Japanese as liberators and
proved avid guides.

Thus, Percival found himself defending Johore after all but with only
about half the force he originally commanded and that part already demoralized, with the exception of the uncommitted regular British battalions
held in Singapore. The defense of Johore lasted only a week despite the aggressive direction of operations by Brooke-Popham's successor, General Sir
Archibald Wavell. After an unbroken series of defeats, the survivors of the
Indo-Australian force crossed the causeway to Singapore on 31 January.
They found the island ill-prepared for a serious defense, even though the
Royal Navy, Royal Air Force, and an entire British division had been at war
for two months and could employ plenty of Indian and Chinese laborers.
The dreamlike campaign continued to a nightmarish end.

The siege of Singapore between 31 January and 15 February fell somewhere between a reenactment of the Thirty Years' War and a Gilbert and
Sullivan operetta. Yamashita still had no more than three worn infantry divisions for an amphibious attack across the Straits of Johore, but Percival
had even fewer first-class troops to defend the north coast and hold the defenses of the city itself on the island's southern face. The Japanese tried to
give the British a massive civil affairs problem by bombing the city as well
as military targets; the civil administrators dealt with the growing disorder
and flight from Singapore harbor with no more competence than they supported the British Army.

At this point in the campaign, both the British and Japanese had run
short of ammunition and food, with the British still holding a slight edge in
logistical sustainment. Yamashita wanted his enemy to have no time to regain his balance, so he pushed assault forces from all three of his divisions

across the straits during the night of 8–9 February. The weight of the attack fell on the Indo-Australian battalions in the island's western sector; the third force of the Imperial Guards Division fought with high casualties to pin the British regulars in their eastern sector, while the veteran 5th and 18th Divisions enveloped Percival's defense line and captured the city's critical water reservoirs. Two days of serious fighting sealed the outcome. Singapore fell into catastrophic disorder, with violence, arson, drunkenness, and looting widespread before the Japanese arrived. After Percival's surrender, the Twenty-Fifth Army restored order—and then turned the city over to the Japanese military police (the dreaded *kempetai*), who promptly began the systematic execution of the Chinese and Eurasian middle class in order to halt any resistance movement.

After the fall of Singapore, the myth of the British moral right to rule disappeared forever in Asia and Africa. Australia thereafter assumed that only the United States could be counted on to defeat Japan or any other Asian enemy. For the Japanese, it was the most thrilling of many exciting victories in 1942, for Britain had always been the hated and feared father of Japanese modernity. General Yamashita and his army had produced a military miracle; in only 70 days, at the cost of 10,000 casualties, they had captured an economic jewel and opened the way to the Dutch East Indies. They had inflicted over 38,000 casualties upon a more numerous foe and taken more than 130,000 prisoners and internees. The Malayan campaign was for the Japanese Army what Pearl Harbor was for the IJN: a celebration of Japanese superiority of the spirit against centuries of Western cultural arrogance and racism. It also produced a very bad case of "victory disease."

Conquest of the Philippines

If the disaster in Malaya discredited the British Empire, the doomed defense of the Philippines turned an American general, Douglas MacArthur, into an international hero and ensured that the future war with Japan would be fought under his influence. It was one of the most bizarre twists of World War II, for MacArthur made a defeat look like a victory of sorts, largely because of the dogged resistance of his common soldiers against what appeared to be overwhelming odds.

A pioneer in army public relations even before World War I, MacArthur had already established his credentials as a hero of the Republican Party, an opponent of American subversives from the Right and Left (mostly Left), a champion of the Chinese and Filipinos, and an outspoken critic of British influence on American foreign policy. One of his contemporaries characterized him as the greatest actor ever to serve in the U.S. Army, and another observed that MacArthur did not have a staff but a court. His behavior under stress—including combat—confounded worshipers and detractors alike; he could be absolutely insensitive to danger, yet he also shrank from direct contact with combat troops, especially the sick and wounded. He had a habit of becoming ill at times of crisis, and his behavior even when he was young (and in 1941 he was sixty) suggested chemical depression and a tendency to hyperventilate and vomit. He always kept a physician in close attendance, and he observed his meal and rest schedule with the precision of a Swiss watchmaker. Without doubt, he understood American politics and the role of media manipulation in shaping policy. FDR once characterized MacArthur as one of the two most dangerous demagogues in American politics, the other being Huey Long.

MacArthur always knew he was at the center of the world stage, and he had no intention of allowing the Philippines to fall without a struggle of legendary proportions. The very real difficulties he faced were daunting enough, and it is doubtful that he or any other American general could have saved the islands, but his own and others' errors put his forces at grave risk from the very first day of war. MacArthur's first hope was that his Army Air Forces' first line squadrons—107 P-40 fighters and 35 B-17s—could provide an effective air defense for Luzon and foil any invasion force. They faced the IJA's 5th Air Group (500 aircraft) and the IJN's 11th Air Fleet (200 aircraft), both based on Formosa. Even before the war began, MacArthur, Brigadier General Richard K. Sutherland (his chief of staff), and Major General Lewis H. Brereton, commander of the Far East Air Force, had disagreed about the use of the B-17s. The ground generals wanted the bombers to displace to safer airfields to the south, where they could attack invasion fleets. But Brereton doubted that his bombers could play this role; rather, they should attack the Japanese air fields on Formosa. At various times in early December MacArthur appears to have approved both options, but Sutherland still thought the B-17s should go south, and Brereton thought they should fly north.

With nine hours' warning that the war had begun, the B-17s and P-40s (which could not be used for escorts anyway) were still parked along the runways at Clark and Iba air fields, where the bombers and fighters of the Japanese 11th Air Fleet found them. In a slaughter of parked aircraft that duplicated the disaster at Pearl Harbor—with much less excuse—the Far East Air Force lost more than half of its aircraft and almost all of its B-17s and P-40s. The Clark-Iba massacre, which included many pilots and skilled technicians, ensured that the Japanese would not face any significant air threat when the Fourteenth Army began landing operations. Similar air attacks the same day ravaged the naval bases at Subic Bay and Cavite.

Following a prewar agreement to create an Allied fleet, Admiral Hart's warships were already on their way to the Dutch East Indies when Japan struck Luzon. MacArthur thus faced General Homma's two reinforced divisions and army support troops (46,000) with only a ground force, even though his Filipino-American army held a numerical advantage. MacArthur assumed, correctly, that the Japanese wanted Manila and the military and naval bases around Manila Bay. The remaining navy harbor defense forces and his own coast artillery made a direct attack unlikely, so he assumed, also correctly, that the Japanese would land at Lingayen Gulf and march south down the Rio Grande valley on Manila; he also thought the Japanese would land somewhere in the south and surround the city.

To defend Luzon, MacArthur formed three regional forces (corps) that divided his nine Luzon divisions, four to the north, three to the south, and two to Manila. He added Philippine Scout infantry, artillery, and cavalry regiments to the northern and southern forces. He held the bulk of the Philippine Division, the newly arrived 4th Marine Regiment evacuated from Shanghai, the Philippine 91st Division, and all other regular U.S. Army units and National Guard tank battalions under his control near Manila. He also rejected the precautionary moves of his army-approved war plan, Orange 3, which directed his force to retreat to the Bataan peninsula and thus conduct a prolonged defense while it guarded Manila Bay and awaited rescue. MacArthur considered the plan defeatist and canceled the buildup of ammunition, food, and medical supplies from the depots around Manila. The month of December passed without any measures to prepare Bataan for protracted resistance.

Ignoring the distraction of small Japanese landings in southern Luzon, MacArthur's army faced the main invasion in Lingayen Gulf, which began on 22 December in two-division strength. Despite MacArthur's brave rhetoric about fighting the Japanese on the beaches, Major General Jonathan Wainwright's two Philippine divisions could not contain the landing force. Four days later, after using the valiant 26th Cavalry from the Philippine Division to stem the rout, MacArthur suddenly ordered both of his Luzon corps to execute War Plan Orange 3, the withdrawal to Bataan. Although 80,000 soldiers of the Filipino-American army reached Bataan, accompanied by 26,000 civilians from the Manila area, this host would have to survive in a malaria-ridden, mountainous jungle without adequate food, medical supplies, and ammunition.

The IJA Headquarters in Tokyo judged the American situation so hopeless that it withdrew the veteran 48th Division for operations in the Dutch East Indies, replacing it with a brigade of reservists. Homma's army remained at around 40,000—half the size of MacArthur's force—and its reorganization allowed the Filipino-American force to escape and prepare its first defense line. MacArthur's force also went on half-rations, less than 2,000 calories a day. On 9 January 1942, Homma struck the eastern part of the American defense with the reserve 65th Brigade and exploited a gap in the center of Wainwright's position created by Mount Natib and its "impassable" jungles. (Wainwright now commanded a two-corps army of seven Philippine divisions, reinforced with two Scout regiments.) Only the commitment of the entire Philippine Division in a battle around Abucay allowed the army to fall back to a second defense line on 22 January.

In the meantime, scratch forces of American regulars (aviators without planes, coast artillerymen without guns, cooks without stoves) wiped out a regimental-size Japanese amphibious force that had landed on the peninsula's west coast. Although its relative combat effectiveness improved—the Japanese were now losing men to battle and disease by the thousands—Wainwright's army further reduced its rations, conserved its ammunition, and looked in vain for replacements. The hard-fighting Scout regiments had already shrunk to less than half-strength, and the American regiments, whether regulars like the Thirty-First Infantry or ad hoc like the air force regiment, began to suffer the same attrition.

Despite its weakness, the Filipino-American force held its second line from 26 January until 8 February, when Homma called off his second offensive, having suffered 7,000 casualties. Although Wainwright's forces had held their position and even eliminated several penetrations with fierce counterattacks, it had taken the best units to hold the front. It was the high point of the defense of Bataan, a clear tactical defeat for the Japanese. But the cost had been prohibitive. Wainwright reported that only one-quarter of his army, which still numbered over 70,000, had the energy and resources for another fight. The Japanese Twenty-Fourth Army was in almost as pitiable condition, but it could draw supplies and replacements from Formosa and Japan, and while it did so, Homma satisfied himself with a desultory siege of the Americans throughout most of March. The fate for Wainwright's army was written by one of its officers:

> saved for another day
> Saved for hunger and wounds and heat
> For slow exhaustion and grim retreat
> For a wasted hope and sure defeat.[3]

MacArthur's own role in the Battle of Bataan demonstrated his unique leadership style: when he was good, he was very, very good, and when he was bad, he was horrid. Once he ordered Orange 3 into effect, he entered a world of his own, living after 24 December in his headquarters in Malinta Tunnel underneath the island bastion of Corregidor. He made only one trip to Bataan, and on that trip he avoided any personal contact with his army; he communicated with Wainwright by phone and radio or called him to Corregidor for meetings. His principal goal was to galvanize Washington into sending him reinforcements; his pleas, which soon brought him into direct communication with FDR himself, contained all sorts of threats and charges of duplicity in Washington. In fact, the War Department had started a pipeline of troops, aircraft, and supplies to Australia, but no one could see much chance that convoys could reach Mindanao, let alone Manila Bay. MacArthur also bombarded the world with press communiqués that misrepresented his own role and hid the dire condition of his army and exaggerated the plight of the Japanese. Through the ordeal on Bataan, he allowed his overzealous supply officers to transfer scarce food and supplies from Wainwright to his own 12,000-man garrison in quantities double those needed for a siege that lasted until July. As Wainwright's army wasted away, MacArthur told Roosevelt that he planned to win or die on Corregidor.

The schemer in the White House had no intention of allowing the schemer of Malinta Tunnel to become a martyr. FDR ordered MacArthur off the island, an order the general obeyed on 11–12 March with the help of the navy's surviving PT boats. Left with little more than MacArthur's spare cigars and shaving cream, Wainwright took command of U.S. Army Forces Far East.

Yet FDR's decision to save MacArthur carried opportunities and risks. Roosevelt saw that MacArthur might rally a disheartened Australia, which now faced direct Japanese attack, and might provide the leadership time to organize the American forces gathering in Australia to defend the Malay barrier. FDR's decision also created a political challenge. The "Asia First" media—a coalition of powerful Republican senators and many voting Republicans—had made MacArthur their favorite general. Consequently, the Joint Chiefs of Staff, no strangers to the MacArthurian way of war, agreed with reluctance to create a new theater for him, the Southwest Pacific, based in Australia, where he could prepare for some as yet ill-defined counteroffensive.

But MacArthur's own goals were not ill-defined: "I shall return!" he said. He didn't plan to return to Washington. Having enjoyed unbroken success on the battlefield in World War I, he had now tasted defeat, and at the hand of despised Asians. He knew about the Germany First strategy, but he had no intention of letting it go unchallenged, even if it meant forming an alliance with the U.S. Navy. Roosevelt, in fact, advanced MacArthur's deification by awarding him the Medal of Honor, an award MacArthur's general-father had won in the Civil War.

Back in the Philippines, there were no psychic rewards and precious little future for Wainwright's army, surviving on 1,000 calories a day by the end of March. It was an army as skinny as its commander that tried to halt a new Japanese offensive on 3 April. Massing his best regiments against the shadow of the Philippine II Corps on the eastern sector, Homma pressed the attacks home with ample fresh troops until the front collapsed on 5 April. With no maneuver room and no reserves, Major General Edward P. King, the senior officer on Bataan, surrendered the feeble survivors on 9 April.

Their ordeal did not end, however, because the Japanese, not inclined to be gentle with POWs anyway, had not planned for such numbers of prisoners. Instead of an estimated 25,000 captives—they thought more Americans would escape to Corregidor—the Japanese took custody of 12,000 Americans and 60,000 Filipino soldiers, as well as 26,000 civilians. Helterskelter, the Japanese Army marched the POWs off to an assembly camp in central Luzon without provision for food, water, medical care, and motor transportation. Before the end of the Bataan Death March weeks later, 600 Americans had died of disease and exhaustion or had been murdered by their guards; the numbers of Filipino deaths reached 6,000–7,000. Filipino nationalists later claimed that American rations had saved the whites at the expense of Asians. What is more clear is that the Japanese again showed that they were not just anti-European racists but that they enjoyed the murder and oppression of other Asians, too. Although there was plenty of anti-American resentment in the Philippines, the Japanese Army ensured that it too would be a target of guerrilla resistance as early as May 1942.

After another month of futile but inspiring defense, the Filipino-American forces on Corregidor and in the southern islands finally surrendered, but not before they had again inflicted more casualties and operational frustration on the Japanese. On Corregidor, a siege alone could not force capitulation; it took a full amphibious assault to persuade General Wainwright to seek terms on 6 May. On Mindanao, on Jolo, and in the Visayans, other Filipino-American units fought the Japanese from December until June 1942; some of these forces refused to surrender and disappeared into the mountains to become guerrillas. In the meantime, President Manuel Quezon formed a Philippine government in exile, fueled with evacuated money and tied with agents to the survivalist-collaborationist regime of José Laurel, Manuel Roxas, and the elite Aquino family. If and when Mac-Arthur returned, the welcoming party was already intact and excluded only a small clique of true collaborationists and the deeply anti-American and Marxist People's Anti-Japanese Army or *hukbalahap*.

The dogged defense of the Philippines did not slow the Japanese conquest of the Netherlands East Indies (NEI), since the Sixteenth Army did not detach forces to aid Homma; in fact, Homma sent two divisions south while still engaged on Bataan. The initial Allied war effort, directed by Wavell as the head of combined American-British-Dutch-Australian (ABDA) Command, could not stop the Japanese landings or parachute assaults in the NEI's northern tier of islands in December and January. Flanked both east and west by additional landings, ABDA gathered its scarce air and naval forces in an attempt to hold Java and thus keep the lines to Australia open and to support the defense of Singapore. This defense failed also when Japanese naval aircraft destroyed most of the Allied air forces in late February; on 27 February the ABDA fleet of five cruisers and nine destroyers met a similar force from the Imperial Japanese Navy and learned a costly lesson in naval gunnery, the use of long-range torpedoes, and the importance of reconnaissance and coordination. In a battle in which naval air played no role, the IJN ruined the ABDA fleet, eventually sinking all five cruisers (including the very durable USS *Houston*) and all but four destroyers. The battles of the Java Sea and Sunda Strait sealed the doom of Java, which capitulated on 9–12 March. Among the 93,000 Allied troops (mostly Indonesians) entering captivity were 650 American soldiers and sailors who had been stranded in defeat. The Japanese seized the oil fields they sought and rejoiced that the native population seemed enthusiastic that fellow Asians had run off the Dutch.

The Japanese conquest of Burma completed the complex and hazardous set of operations put into action with the attack upon Pearl Harbor, but the Japanese Fifteenth Army, under Lieutenant General Iida Shojiro, had only two divisions to commit against a Commonwealth force built around two weak divisions of Indian and Burmese infantry, supported by British infantry, artillery, and aviation units of limited size. The Japanese had every reason to occupy southern Burma and the key port city of Rangoon in December 1941 and January 1942, if only to eliminate Rangoon as a way station for British reinforcements to Singapore and American assistance to the Chinese Nationalists. The Americans, for example, had deployed two P-40 squadrons of the Flying Tigers of the American Volunteer Group (AVG) to Kunming by November 1941 but had left another squadron in Burma for air defense. Commanded by Claire Chennault, officially a retired army captain and colonel in the Chinese air force, the pilots of the AVG, who numbered around 100, were regular and reserve military pilots masquerading as mercenaries. The mission of the AVG was to provide some air defense for the Nationalist bases in western China and the Burma Road, which began in Kunming and ended at the rail terminus of Lashio inside Burma.

Enjoying air superiority, however, and the assistance of Burmese collaborators, the Fifteenth Army, reinforced to four divisions, again proved that Japanese tactics, especially flanking movements at night through difficult terrain, could not be halted by roadbound Allied troops, whatever their potential firepower. Recognizing the dire threat to his supply lines, Chiang Kai-shek committed nine Chinese Nationalist divisions to Burma, more or less under the direction of his American chief of staff, Lieutenant General Joseph W. Stilwell, an "Old China Hand" who did not fancy the Generalissimo or the assignment or the British. By May 1942 the Japanese had added Burma to their list of conquests at a cost of only 2,000 battlefield dead, and even fewer deaths (1,400) among the Commonwealth forces. Led by the one successful British general of the campaign, William Slim, the Anglo-Indian forces retreated into India while the Chinese, with less than 5,000 dead, fell back to China, leaving Stilwell (by his choice) to march into India with his small, disheartened staff. He joined MacArthur as a general with a "return" promise. The Burma Road closed for good.

The American Response

From the ashes of Pacific defeat, a phoenix of eventual victory, hatched by Roosevelt and fed by public outrage, started to test its wings in Washington and Honolulu. A strategy for continued war with Japan depended on air power. From his new nest in Australia, Douglas MacArthur added his own strident calls for an aerial onslaught against the perimeter of the new Japanese Empire—in his case the seizure of air bases in New Guinea—to begin his march of revenge to the Philippines. At the level of political direction, Roosevelt simply announced to Churchill that although he understood the British requirement to defend India, he regarded the war with Japan as essentially an American task, supported by his two new wartime clients, Nationalist China and Australia. FDR simply stated the obvious: that only American air-naval power could eventually roll back the Japanese from their Pacific outposts and liberate the conquered states of Southeast Asia and China.

Although FDR's most trusted military adviser, Army Chief of Staff

George C. Marshall, worried about the diversion of army resources from Europe to the Pacific war, he also understood that the Pacific Fleet retained much of its combat power, which would surge in 1943 with the arrival of battleships, carriers, and cruisers already being built, ships that would not be needed in the campaign against the German submarines. Air assets were another matter, but Marshall admitted that the army had tactical aviation forces that could be used to good purpose in the Pacific. For the U.S. Navy, the only enemy that mattered was Japan, the enemy of choice since World War I. Moreover, Admiral Ernest J. King, the chief of naval operations, nursed such a severe case of Anglophobia that British admirals and generals sometimes wondered whether *they* were the navy's enemy. They were not, but their European theater and imperial interests were, and King held their military competence in contempt. He himself proved inept enough in directing the 1942 anti-U-boat campaign in the Atlantic, and that unpleasant experience probably inclined him to fight a war he liked much better.

King's protégé for the war against Japan, Admiral Chester W. Nimitz, lacked King's burning hatred of Japan, but he at least wanted to keep the old navy in the war while it awaited the new navy of 1943. Nimitz's first disappointment was the poor performance of his submarine force, whose timid commanders and flawed torpedoes produced few successes until aggressive skippers, experienced crews, and dependable torpedoes could exploit the excellence of the navy's most modern submarines. Though himself a submariner by experience, Nimitz appreciated the potential striking power of carrier task forces, his most potent remaining offensive weapon. With cruisers and destroyers to protect it from air attack and submarines, a carrier task force (consisting of one or two carriers) could strike and escape any IJN heavy surface force. If it operated away from Japanese land-based aircraft, its chances of survival appeared excellent.

The U.S. Navy, aided and abetted by MacArthur's Allied intelligence agency in Australia, also enjoyed a substantial advantage over the Japanese because of its growing skill in collecting and analyzing enemy radio traffic. Known generically as "signals intelligence," the navy's staff communications security and intelligence unit in Washington (Op 20-G) vied with its partner in Nimitz's headquarters, Station Hypo of the Fleet Radio Unit Pacific (FRUPAC), directed by the navy's unconventional codebreaking genius, Commander Joseph R. Rochefort. The navy had more than 20 years' experience in intercepting Japanese diplomatic and military communications; the challenge lay in making any sense of the intercepts, sent in code and protected by the rapid shift of codes and call signs. Once at war, the Japanese had increased the number of operational messages but slowed the pace of changing codes and call signs because of the wide dispersion of its forces. Although navy intelligence analysts had gained some access to the IJN's principal code, JN-25, they had gained greater skill in identifying the call signs of transmitting stations as well as the location of the transmissions. Their educated guesswork had recorded only one major failure—Pearl Harbor—because Nagumo's strike force had sailed in radio silence. Supplemented by submarine and aerial reconnaissance, the signals intelligence effort now gave the navy the information it needed for successful operations.

As Japanese expeditionary forces seized the South Seas Resource Area and its Pacific defense perimeter, the Combined Fleet and the Pacific Fleet avoided each other, as if content to steel themselves against lesser opponents until they met again. The Japanese carriers sailed as far as the Indian Ocean, and their confident air groups raided ports in eastern India and Ceylon, sinking two British cruisers and a carrier 6–9 April 1942. The Indian Ocean raid had one fortunate outcome, however: it delayed a change in the Japanese naval code by two months. American intelligence analysts collected an unprecedented amount of readable message traffic, including Yamamoto's strategic plans.

Thousands of miles away, carrier task forces of the Pacific Fleet tested themselves with raids on Japanese outposts in the Marshall Islands in January 1942 and then attacked Wake Island, Rabaul on New Britain Island, and some targets along the north coast of New Guinea, all with four carriers. American naval aviators began to work out the tactics of air combat with the Zero, a faster and more agile fighter than the F4F Wildcat, and to coordinate dive-bombing and torpedo strikes against warships. The raids created a new media hero, Vice Admiral William F. Halsey, a carrier admiral with a gruff sea-dog style and a fountain of anti-Japanese quotes for an adoring media. More importantly for real operations, the task force staffs and air groups got priceless experience at precious little cost.

Halsey's task force of *Enterprise* and *Hornet* pulled off the first American naval coup of the war, a bombing strike by army B-25 bombers on Tokyo. Dreamed up by FDR and King, the raid, led by Lieutenant Colonel James H. Doolittle, put twelve bombers over Tokyo on 18 April and three others (straying in transit) over other Honshu cities. The deaths and damage of the raid were negligible but shocking. Not one bomber fell to Japanese air defenses, although the Japanese later captured 9 aircrewmen (out of a total of 80) who had flown on to Chinese air fields or crash landed on the Asian mainland. (The Japanese later tried and executed three aircrewmen for killing civilians, but five survived the war.) That the Doolittle raiders could fly B-25s off a carrier (Roosevelt said they came from "Shangri-la") and land in China dramatized the fact that the Japanese Army and the Combined Fleet had unfinished business with the United States.

The Doolittle raid galvanized the Japanese forces in China to give the Chinese Nationalist army and its American aviators an overdue object lesson. In addition to fighting several respectable actions in central Burma, the Nationalists beat back another three-division sortie toward Changsha in January 1942. Western reporters made the battle sound like a minor Stalingrad. Chennault's American Volunteer Group also demonstrated its proficiency in shooting down careless Japanese bombers, destroying 286 aircraft at the cost of 50 planes and 9 pilots before the group dissolved in July 1942. In May 1942 a Japanese expeditionary force of 100,000 marched into the north China provinces of Chekiang and Kiangsi and conducted a four-month retaliatory reign of terror, including the use of poison gas and epidemic disease germs, upon the Chinese irregulars and peasants who had welcomed Doolittle's squadron. The punitive expedition may have killed as many as 250,000 Chinese as well as closing the rough air fields the Americans had used. The concept of using China as a base for offensive air war against Japan did not, however, perish in Washington or in Chennault, now an American general.

In Japan, the major responsibility for stopping the new aggressiveness of the U.S. Navy rested with Admiral Yamamoto's Combined Fleet, whose battleships and carriers had thus far escaped serious damage. One task awaited in the South Pacific, where the Australians and Americans had patched together a string of naval way stations and air bases to defend the underbelly of the eastern Malay barrier (New Guinea and the southern Solomons) and the island groups (mostly French, but including American Samoa) that protected the convoy routes from California and the Panama Canal to Australia and New Zealand, MacArthur's "Final Redoubt." Naval intelligence officers listened to the Combined Fleet reorganize and redeploy after its return from the Indian Ocean. In April 1942 they predicted another major Japanese naval campaign all the way from the Aleutians to Australia. King and Nimitz massed their own forces (four carriers and their escorts) in Hawaii for a showdown with the Japanese. Two months later they had managed to fight and win two sea battles—not quite a Trafalgar but far from an indecisive Jutland.

Relatively certain that the forthcoming Japanese operation would strike Port Moresby, New Guinea, and probably other Allied outposts along the Malay barrier, Nimitz sent a two-carrier task force (*Lexington* and *Yorktown*) to meet a five-unit IJN task force, organized to execute Operation MO (take Port Moresby) and to inflict damage on any intervening Allied naval force. Two of the Japanese task groups contained carriers: the light *Shoho* in one, and two Pearl Harbor veterans, *Shokaku* and *Zuikaku*, in the other. The Australian and American navies deployed 21 cruisers and destroyers, the IJN 24. Although the Allies could deploy more than 400 land-based aircraft and the Japanese only 161, the carrier air groups were nearly equal in operational strength, at around 150 each. These aircraft decided the battle, since the land-based bombers did virtually no damage and the surface warships never made contact. In what became the normal confused minuet of Pacific war naval engagements between carriers, the Japanese and American carrier groups advanced and retreated, veered away or closed the distance in deference to weather, the available light, and very confused and incomplete information about each other. Both sides made wild claims about the damage they inflicted, but the results proved decisive for the Allies.

The Battle of the Coral Sea proved that American naval aviators, despite inferior aircraft, could fight the Sea Eagles on equal terms. In the one day of great combat, 8 May, American dive-bombers and torpedo planes badly damaged *Shokaku*, having sunk *Shoho* the day before. In air attacks and aerial combat, the Americans lost 33 aircraft. The Japanese lost twice that number to American fighters and anti-aircraft fire but sank *Lexington* and damaged *Yorktown*'s deck. *Zuikaku*, untouched, had nevertheless lost almost all of its air group. The U.S. Navy lost a fleet oiler and a destroyer, while seven Japanese ships in the invasion convoys went down. In sum, the senior Japanese admiral decided not to continue Operation MO because his fleet had lost absolute air superiority.

A greater disaster awaited the Combined Fleet, this time under Admiral Yamamoto's direct command. In a battle to be fought on and above the seas north of Midway Island, the bait in the trap, Yamamoto planned to ambush Nimitz's remaining two carriers, *Enterprise* and *Hornet*. With four large carriers under Admiral Nagumo in his task force, Yamamoto saw little chance for defeat. Nevertheless, he also brought 11 battleships and 16 cruisers with him, as well as 53 destroyers, a surface force for which the Americans had no answer since they needed their 24 cruisers and destroyers to protect their carriers from submarines and air attacks. Nimitz could commit 121 land-based aircraft for varied duties, including offensive action, the Japanese none, but once again this American capability proved virtually useless. The Japanese would enjoy a three-to-two aircraft advantage, which would have been even worse had not Pearl Harbor's repair crews put *Yorktown* back into minimal working order. Japanese Navy commanders

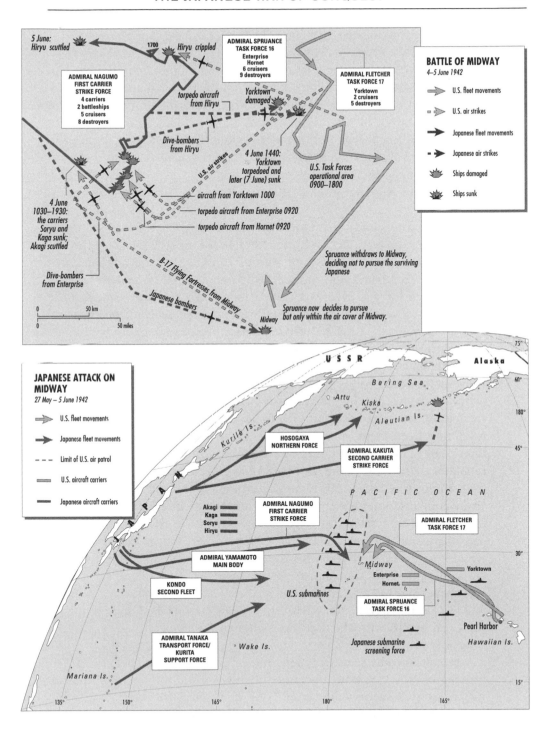

5 June:
Hiryu scuttled

1700 Hiryu crippled

ADMIRAL SPRUANCE
TASK FORCE 16
Enterprise
Hornet
6 cruisers
9 destroyers

ADMIRAL FLETCHER
TASK FORCE 17
Yorktown
2 cruisers
5 destroyers

BATTLE OF MIDWAY
4–5 June 1942

U.S. fleet movements

U.S. air strikes

Japanese fleet movements

Japanese air strikes

Ships damaged

Ships sunk

ADMIRAL NAGUMO
FIRST CARRIER
STRIKE FORCE
4 carriers
2 battleships
5 cruisers
8 destroyers

torpedo aircraft
from Hiryu

Yorktown
damaged

Dive-bombers
from Hiryu

4 June 1440:
Yorktown
torpedoed and
later (7 June) sunk

U.S. air strikes

U.S. Task Forces
operational area
0900–1800

4 June
1030–1930:
the carriers
Soryu and
Kaga sunk;
Akagi scuttled

aircraft from Yorktown 1000

torpedo aircraft from Enterprise 0920

torpedo aircraft from Hornet 0920

Dive-bombers
from Enterprise

B-17 Flying Fortresses from Midway

Japanese bombers

Spruance withdraws to Midway,
deciding not to pursue the surviving
Japanese

Midway

Spruance now decides to pursue
but only within the air cover of Midway.

0   50 km
0   50 miles

JAPANESE ATTACK ON
MIDWAY
27 May – 5 June 1942

U.S. fleet movements

Japanese fleet movements

Limit of U.S. air patrol

U.S. aircraft carriers

Japanese aircraft carriers

U S S R   **Alaska**

Bering Sea   60°

Attu   Kiska   180°

Aleutian Is.   45°

Kurile Is.

HOSOGAYA
NORTHERN FORCE

ADMIRAL KAKUTA
SECOND CARRIER
STRIKE FORCE

P A C I F I C   O C E A N

J A P A N

Akagi
Kaga
Soryu
Hiryu

ADMIRAL NAGUMO
FIRST CARRIER
STRIKE FORCE

ADMIRAL FLETCHER
TASK FORCE 17

Midway   Yorktown   30°

Enterprise
Hornet

ADMIRAL YAMAMOTO
MAIN BODY

KONDO
SECOND FLEET

U.S. submarines

ADMIRAL SPRUANCE
TASK FORCE 16

Pearl Harbor

Hawaiian Is.

ADMIRAL TANAKA
TRANSPORT FORCE/
KURITA
SUPPORT FORCE

Wake Is.

Japanese submarine
screening force

Mariana Is.   15°

135°   150°   165°   180°   165°

75°

had every reason to believe they would finish the destruction of the Pacific Fleet that they had begun on 7 December 1941.

Armed with good intelligence about his enemy's ultimate intentions and considerable capabilities, Nimitz did not fall for a strategic ruse (an invasion in the Aleutians) nor for an operational ruse (the air attacks on and potential invasion of Midway). Instead, he directed his commanders at sea, Admirals Frank Jack Fletcher and Raymond A. Spruance, to seek out Nagumo's carriers and dodge Yamamoto's big guns. Even though some uncertainty remained about the exact location of the Japanese carriers, Spruance and Fletcher ordered all their air groups into the attack on 4 June.

Japanese scouts had not yet located the American carriers, but the direction of American air attack would make their location obvious. All the calculations were over, the risks mounting. Thinking that he had adequate time for a second strike on Midway, Nagumo ordered his reserve aircraft rearmed and the returned first wave planes refueled at an inopportune moment—just as the first American strike aircraft arrived. In an aerial Charge of the Light Brigade, three American torpedo squadrons plunged toward the Japanese carriers to no avail and no hits; of the 41 aircraft that bored in on the carriers, only 6 returned. As the Japanese task forces weaved under the clouds of anti-aircraft fire and Zeros splashed one American aircraft after another, the navy dive bombers and accompanying Wildcats easily penetrated the thin Sea Eagle combat air patrol and fell upon Nagumo's fleet. In ten minutes, three Japanese carriers became flaming wrecks, beyond saving or salvaging. The fourth, *Hiryu*, survived to launch a retaliatory strike the same day that redamaged *Yorktown*, which finally sank three days later. Late in the afternoon of 4 June more American scout-bombers found *Hiryu* and damaged it so badly that its crew scuttled it the next day, completing the sweep of the Japanese carrier force. In a third day of pursuit, the navy pilots sank one cruiser and damaged another, while Spruance maneuvered his two carriers and Fletcher's surviving escorts out of range of Yamamoto's surface force. At a cost of one carrier and a destroyer and 147 aircraft, the Pacific Fleet had "scratched" 4 cruisers and 322 IJN carrier aircraft, along with their pilots, many perishing in onboard fires and explosions. The Japanese suffered 3,057 deaths in battle, the Americans but 362.

It remained to be seen whether the Sea Eagles could be defeated in air combat, but the U.S. Navy had a new fighter on the way, the F6F Hellcat, which it tested successfully against one captured Zero, pried intact from the Aleutian tundra where it had crashed in June 1942. Not only would new carriers soon arrive in the Pacific, but they would carry new-model fighters, scout dive-bombers, and torpedo planes that would match the best Japanese aircraft. In the meantime, pilot experience and prudent tactics would have to suffice.

Conclusion

The Battle of Midway represented the highwater mark of Japan's geographic expansion, but not a major change in the strategy of seize-and-hold. Shaken by the loss of four carriers and 100 invaluable pilots, the Japanese admirals still controlled a balanced fleet with excellence in gunnery, night fighting, and ordnance that surpassed the U.S. Navy. The four carriers could be replaced—as they were in 1944—but the temporary material and psychological setback for the IJN offered the Allies an opportunity to take the strategic initiative. In a sense, the Japanese high command could simply hold the Combined Fleet, which still had four large carriers, at the central bases of Rabaul and Truk and dare the Pacific Fleet to take the offensive. The original Japanese plan, however, had been gravely wrong about the war's duration. The short war had become a long war—the road to Japanese ritual suicide, *seppuku*.

9

THE

ASIA-PACIFIC WAR

1942–1944

After the Japanese naval defeats in May and June 1942, the Asia-Pacific war drifted toward a limited, extemporized conflict of opportunism and attrition. Like a Pacific typhoon, the war swirled in upon itself with increasing violence, sucking in men and machines. The Anglo-American strategy of Germany First and the Soviet strategy of Germany Only prevailed, but the temptation to take limited offensives against Japan reflected political pressures that even Eurocentric statesmen could not ignore. The Allies emerged from this 18-month trial in better shape than Japan, but not by much.

For Japanese Army and Navy planners in Tokyo, the setbacks at the Coral Sea and Midway only accelerated plans to assume a strategic defense along the frontier of the 1942 conquests. Japanese intelligence estimated that the Allies would not undertake offensive operations until 1943, a date determined by the arrival of new carriers and battleships for the U.S. Pacific Fleet. On the Asian mainland, the Soviets would remain neutral as they struggled with the Wehrmacht, and the British-Indian army and the Chinese, with their large but poorly trained and equipped armies and inadequate air support, could not mount a serious challenge.

Moreover, the Indian Army faced the prospect of continued upheaval on the home front; in the middle of defeat in Burma, the Congress Party, led by Mohandas K. Gandhi and Jawaharlal Nehru, declared India free of the British *raj*—an announcement which set off widespread urban rioting and communal violence. The other surviving Commonwealth bastions, Australia and New Zealand, had sent their expeditionary forces to the Middle East. With only one battle-worthy division (the 7th) in Australia, Prime Minister John Curtin asked Churchill to return the 9th Division to Australia. When Churchill argued that the British could not spare the 9th Division, and the Australians heard that it might be sent to Burma instead, they felt, once again, that they could not entrust their safety to the Commonwealth alone.

The Coming Campaigns

The Japanese did indeed have designs on Australia since it provided the Allies with a base from which to attack the Netherlands East Indies and Malaya, essential components of the Greater East Asia Co-prosperity Sphere. Fearing they faced a protracted war and the prospect that Germany might not defeat the Soviet Union, the Japanese planned to continue the slow advance against New Guinea, the southern Solomons, and the Franco-American islands to the east that protected the lifeline from Australia to North America and Hawaii. Although the Japanese shelved plans for expeditions against Samoa and New Caledonia, they established strong army and navy headquarters (the Seventeenth Army and Ninth Fleet) at Rabaul to direct operations against Port Moresby, develop new bases in the southern Solomons, interdict Allied shipping in the South Pacific, and bomb Darwin, the only developed base on Australia's north coast.

Far to the north, they planned to use the newly seized islands of Attu and Kiska to blunt any American movement along the western Aleutians. These offensive plans, however, did not change the overall conviction that the Southern Army had served its purpose and could release half its divisions for service in China or a strategic reserve in Japan. Army and navy aviation as well as the surface and submarine fleets would guard the approaches to the Western Pacific from the new island bases—"unsinkable carriers" to the optimistic planners.

Disturbed by the Japanese punitive campaign in north China that followed the Doolittle raid, Chiang Kai-shek feared that the loss of the Burma Road and the demands of other theaters would cut Lend-Lease programs for China. His short-term concern was the expansion of the Japanese occupation into western China; his strategic goal was to strengthen the Kuomintang and Nationalist Army against the Communists. Chiang's special problem was the senior American officer organizationally at his side but physically in India, Lieutenant General Joseph W. Stilwell. As early as 1942 Stilwell found himself at odds with Chiang over the reform and employment of the Chinese Army. Stilwell had 2 divisions with him at Ramgarh, India (X Force), and he believed he controlled 12 more divisions in Yunnan province, China (Y Force). After the Burma campaign, none of these divisions had more than half their manpower, and they lacked weapons and training. Chiang did not view either force as adequate for his needs.

Instead, he presented an ambitious plan to Roosevelt in June 1942. The Three Demands, drafted by Brigadier General Claire L. Chennault, argued that China held the key to defeating Japan with land-based air power. Chiang could not wait for Stilwell to reopen the Burma Road with a new extension from Ledo in northern India. Instead, the United States should send three divisions to undertake this mission while Chennault built an American air force of over 500 aircraft in China. This force would employ heavy bombers that would attack Japanese supply lines and bases along China's coast. Until the Burma Road reopened, air transports from India would supply the air force in China. Chiang demanded an airlift capacity of 5,000 tons a month, an incredible figure, since the designated transport, the twin-engine C-46, had only a four-ton load capacity. At the time of the Three Demands, Chennault's 130 aircraft required 2,000 tons of supplies per month, which meant a 500-aircraft force would probably need 10,000 tons a month, not 5,000. Moreover, who would guard the air bases? The Chiang-Chennault plan said that an elite, American-armed Nationalist Army (Z Force) would perform this mission, which sent the logistical requirements even higher.

Roosevelt and the Joint Chiefs of Staff knew they could not meet the Three Demands, but they could not ignore the fact that the Nationalists might tie down much of the Japanese Army. A military renaissance in China, built around 30 elite Nationalist divisions, would protect the air force Chennault wanted. Despite British skepticism about China, Roosevelt promised to do something about getting money and Lend-Lease supplies to Chungking. He did so for several reasons: a sincere conviction that China might become a regional power; his optimistic expediency in military affairs; and his sensitivity to the China lobby, which included influential members of his own cabinet as well as Republican senators and media moguls.

When Roosevelt concluded in June 1942 that the Allies could not open a second front in Europe that year, he provided his military chiefs with an opportunity to argue that offensive action against Japan would be possible, if it did not endanger the invasion of North Africa. Admiral Ernest J. King, chief of naval operations, had consistently argued for an immediate naval campaign in the Pacific; the army now advocated a similar plan. From Australia, MacArthur demanded reinforcements, especially air and naval forces, while submitting a plan for a lightning campaign against the Japanese air and naval bastion of Rabaul. The strategic arguments bounced from Washington and Honolulu to Melbourne and back; it soon became clear that King would not give an army theater commander (namely, Mac-Arthur) control of his carriers. He agreed only to a slow, steady campaign northward, not a charge toward Rabaul. On 2 July the Joint Chiefs of Staff issued a definitive directive that the isolation of Rabaul would begin with the capture of Santa Cruz and Tulagi, then spread from the Solomons to New Guinea. Finally, an air-ground expeditionary force directed by Mac-Arthur would besiege Rabaul itself.

Two problems plagued the coming campaigns. The first was the indefinite nature of the command relationships, which reflected differences in national objectives. In the China-Burma-India theater the British aimed at maintaining control of India and using amphibious operations to outflank the Japanese forces in southern Burma; they saw no reason to use scarce forces to support a moribund Chinese Nationalist government that wanted to end British influence in Asia. The American position, however, was that northern Burma had importance as an overland route to China. The fact that Stilwell held complementary positions as both a Chinese and American commander and was arbiter of U.S. Lend-Lease supplies in the theater complicated Anglo-American differences. His personal distaste for both Chiang and Chennault made his position even more difficult—at least for others—and he showed little respect for the British. Roosevelt had made Chiang believe that he was a critical leader in the Allied coalition, even ensuring that Madame Chiang and her brother, T. V. Soong, received the royal treatment in Washington, where Soong at one time held the dual posts of foreign minister and ambassador to the United States. The question of how to deal with China strained Anglo-American planning.

In the South Pacific, the command relations were just as tortuous, although they turned on service issues. As American commander in the Southwest Pacific theater, MacArthur was answerable to the Joint Chiefs of Staff and only through them to the Combined Chiefs of Staff. In reality, however, MacArthur made himself de facto field marshal of the Australian armed forces through his personal influence with Prime Minister Curtin. Although MacArthur appointed a genuine war hero, General Thomas Blamey, as the Allied ground force commander, MacArthur's theater staff remained largely American, and he routinely formed task forces of American troops outside Blamey's command. As the campaign developed, the Australian Army wondered why it consistently received unpleasant assignments with virtually no recognition or American support. The reason was that Curtin valued MacArthur's political connections.

MacArthur had his eye on other matters, particularly blackmailing the

U.S. Navy into greater reinforcements in the South Pacific. If Marshall sometimes wearied of dealing with MacArthur, King did not, and he made sure that Nimitz, who was commander of Pacific Ocean Areas as well as commander-in-chief of the Pacific Fleet, made the critical decisions on the allocation and employment of American naval forces. With King's approval, Nimitz created a subordinate command, the South Pacific theater, outside MacArthur's direct command but geographically a neighbor and responsible for the southern Solomons. Vice Admiral Robert L. Ghormley and then Vice Admiral William F. Halsey held this command.

With "Germany First" as the coalition strategy and with forces gathering for an invasion of North Africa, the Pacific commanders cried poor. Their litany of woe overlooked several factors which indicated that they could not have used greater forces than they already had—forces which, in any event, approximately equaled the number of men (roughly 300,000), ships, and planes (except bombers) that went to Europe through mid-1943.

The first factor the Pacific commanders overlooked was the primitive transportation infrastructure in the South Pacific and the burden of weather and terrain. In rough terms, one American soldier required 4.5 *tons* of material to deploy abroad and one ton a month to maintain; the gasoline demands of combat vehicles and aircraft measured from 50 to several hundred pounds a day, and battleships and carriers consumed oil at a rate of 6–9 tons per hour. Yet the South Pacific had no ports and air fields to support this kind of supply effort outside of Australia and New Zealand. The war in the Pacific required more engineers, port management units, aviation service troops, stevedores, and truck drivers than infantrymen and pilots.

In addition, a second factor—the dampness, heat, and abundance of disease-carrying insects—made the South Pacific the worst medical risk of the war for Americans. Burma was no different, and in both locations non-battle casualties outstripped combat casualties. The medical situation only compounded the third factor overlooked by the American commanders: operational problems. Planners could predict the supply constraints, even if operational commanders sometimes pretended they did not exist. The Allies could also expect that in some classes of weapons, mostly aircraft and naval ordnance, they would face some technological inferiority. What they did not admit—and the generals and admirals were the most at fault—was that they did not know how to fight at the operational level. The battles of the Coral Sea and Midway underlined for naval aviators how much they had to learn; their army peers, especially bombardment squadrons, still believed they could bomb enemy warships. Army and Marine Corps divisions shared a similar lack of experience in infantry-artillery-armor coordination in jungle operations. Much of the combat leadership in all the services had to learn on the job; even World War I veterans (and there were precious few) had to learn how to command divisions through staffs, not battalions through personal charisma.

Some officers proved incompetent and cowardly, as they do in all armies, but the more serious problem was simply moving from a peacetime mindset to the harsh realities of war. Reflecting the operational inexperience of U.S. and Commonwealth forces, naval surface units, for example, did not fight their Japanese counterparts with reasonable effectiveness until late 1942 and suffered avoidable losses well into 1943. Night actions sorely tested the competence of the Allied navies, although never their courage. The same conditions applied to aerial combat and night ground defensive actions. The Asia-Pacific war of 1942–1944 gave the Japanese plenty of opportunity to see whether the Allies had the seriousness of purpose that the Japanese called *makoto*.

New Guinea

With little to show for their commitments in Asia, U.S. military leaders chose to fight Japan where they saw some chance of offensive action. The initiation of South Pacific offensive operations rested on a level of Allied military strength that encouraged caution. In the Southwest Pacific, MacArthur had only two untested American divisions, two Australian divisions, and an Allied air force of 500 aircraft. The Australian-American naval forces had no greater power than the ground and air forces until reinforced by the Pacific Fleet, based in Hawaii and California. The South Pacific theater had one marine division available, with another and the equivalent of three infantry divisions potentially available, if they could be spared from guarding the logistics lifeline.

Of course, the Japanese had not yet strengthened their South Pacific bases either, but by mid-1942 they had established an area army headquarters (the Eighth) with two subordinate armies (the Seventeenth and Eighteenth) that at one time or another controlled eight divisions and assorted naval garrison troops. The strength of the Japanese position was landbased air power, the Japanese Army's Sixth and Seventh Air Divisions, and the IJN's Eleventh Air Fleet. Eighth Fleet, later designated the Southeast Area Fleet, controlled naval operations from Rabaul.

The location of the Solomons—a double string of islands that stretched

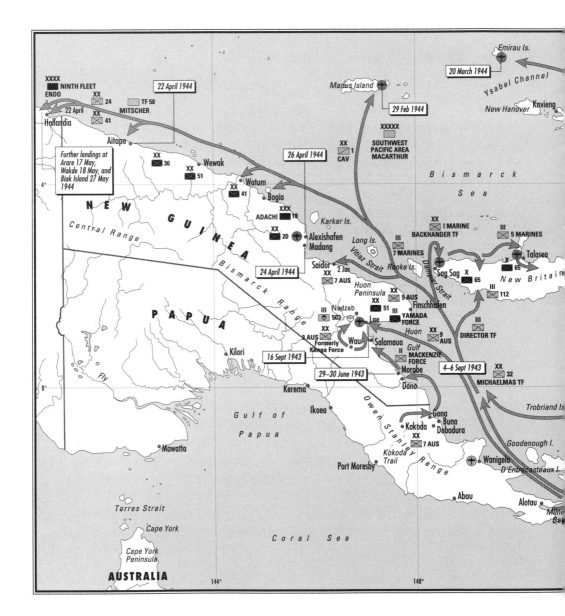

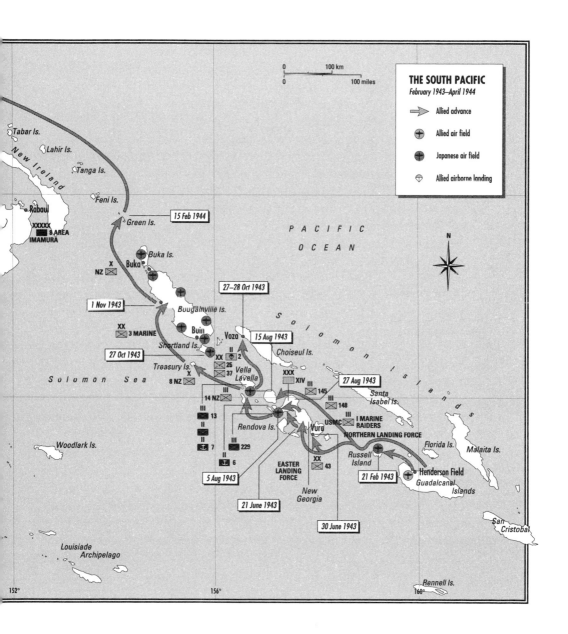

THE SOUTH PACIFIC
February 1943–April 1944

Allied advance

Allied air field

Japanese air field

Allied airborne landing

Tabar Is.

Lahir Is.

Tanga Is.

New Ireland

Feni Is.

Rabaul

XXXXX
8 AREA
IMAMURA

Green Is.

15 Feb 1944

PACIFIC

OCEAN

Buka Is.

Buka

X
NZ

N

1 Nov 1943

Bougainville Is.

27–28 Oct 1943

XX
3 MARINE

Buin

Voza

15 Aug 1943

Choiseul Is.

Solomon

Shortland Is.

27 Oct 1943

Treasury Is.

XX
II   2
25
37

Vella
Lavella

XXX
XIV

III   145

27 Aug 1943

Santa
Isabel Is.

Solomon   Sea

X
8 NZ

III
14 NZ

III   148

Islands

III
13

II

Rendova Is.

Yuru

USMC

III
I MARINE
RAIDERS

NORTHERN LANDING FORCE

Woodlark Is.

II

III
229

II   7

II   6

EASTER
LANDING
FORCE

XX
43

Russell
Island

21 Feb 1943

Florida Is.

Malaita Is.

Henderson Field

5 Aug 1943

21 June 1943

New
Georgia

Guadalcanal
Islands

San
Cristobal

30 June 1943

Louisiade
Archipelago

Rennell Is.

152°   156°   160°

0   100 km
0   100 miles

600 miles from Bougainville-Buka to San Cristobal—does not alone explain why this became the most-embattled sector of the Pacific War in 1942–43. In purely military terms, the islands' value rested in their usefulness as air base sites. As part of the Midway operations in summer 1942, the Japanese, who had started work on a base structure in the northern Solomons early in 1942, jumped all the way to Guadalcanal and Tulagi in the south to establish forward operating bases. They ultimately planned air and naval raids against the maritime lifeline to the south, guarded by Allied air bases and naval stations at New Caledonia, New Hebrides, the Fijis, and the Samoan islands. Yet, once the campaign was joined, Japanese senior leaders (General Imamura Hitoshi and Vice Admiral Mikawa Gunichi) should have husbanded their forces for the defense of the Vitiaz-Huon peninsula on New Guinea and New Britain Island, which Imamura did, and Rabaul and Bougainville-Buka, which Mikawa did not.

The critical element in the Pacific War remained the opposing fleets, especially the battleships and carriers. In 1942 the Japanese held the edge in carriers (7 to 4) despite the loss of 5 carriers at Coral Sea and Midway. The United States had more battleships than Japan (15 to 11). Yet, the rough equality of 1942 would shift to the Americans as new vessels authorized in 1938–1940 took station. Already the Japanese had fewer warships than the naval general staff thought adequate to defeat the United States in a protracted war. The Japanese Navy's own building program would not produce additional major warships until 1944, when five new fleet carriers would become operational in that year alone. The IJN had commissioned its last battleship in 1942.

The condition of Japanese naval aviation also reflected the navy's fragility. Although the aviation industry could build new planes, the commanders of the elite Sea Eagles did not liberalize their demanding and lengthy training process, which meant that the Japanese Navy could not replace pilot losses as rapidly as the U.S. Navy could. The Americans developed a larger and more rapid pipeline of aviators serving the fleet, a system that allowed them to rotate squadrons in the combat zones and thus preserve veterans to form the cadre of new squadrons. The U.S. Navy started the war with twice as many pilots as the IJN, and the American training system produced qualified pilots in 18 months, as compared with 50 months in Japan. Trapped by their rigid training program, Japanese veteran pilots received little relief from operational squadrons.

The campaign in the South Pacific ultimately depended on how closely the opposing forces could integrate air, land, and naval operations, since no element of military power by itself could prove decisive. The Japanese problem remained the difficulty of interservice cooperation, which meant that the army and navy (and their separate air arms) fought different wars and blamed any failures on their service counterparts. The Americans, of course, could do the same and did, but assertive theater commanders (in this case MacArthur and Halsey) enforced cooperation, with the backing of the service chains of command and the Joint Chiefs. The factors that made the Allied campaign complex was Australia's participation and the role of MacArthur.

MacArthur recognized that Australia was the Pacific War's England, an island bastion from which to mount expeditions against the Malay barrier islands all the way to the Philippines. He needed Australian air and ground units to supplement his own forces, and he depended on the enthusiastic commitment of home-front civilians for logistical support. Although he gave its generals no special role, MacArthur valued Australia's ability to keep a substantial part of the Commonwealth war effort focused on the Pacific. He also often used Australian diplomatic channels to evade the U.S. military chain of command.

Early in the New Guinea campaign, MacArthur revealed some unique leadership characteristics. MacArthur's staff, dominated by the so-called Corregidor Gang, tried to convince themselves and others that MacArthur was a military genius. Some people believed it, but many did not. MacArthur's paranoia, lust for personal publicity, political ambition, structured and comfortable life-style, and hypochondria were well known in the army. One of his intimates said that MacArthur hated funerals and hospitals and avoided them at all cost. In World War I, he had refused to wear a gas mask (and was gassed twice) because of claustrophobic panic, not bravado. His emotional balance was precarious. These personal foibles, which made George Patton look normal, diverted attention from what should have been the real issue: MacArthur's professional military competence. His erratic performance in the Philippines should have led to his relief and retirement, but, instead, the Medal of Honor and a flood of media attention, encouraged by Roosevelt, diverted attention from America's military disasters. Then, having created a monster, FDR and the Joint Chiefs had to live with MacArthur and his powerful friends.

Of the senior commanders in the Pacific, MacArthur was the least qualified, on strict military criteria, to play a major role. He had spent his first 14 years in the army as an engineer. In World War I he had served as a division chief of staff, as commander of an infantry brigade, and, for two weeks with no combat, as an acting division commander. After five months of battle in France, MacArthur saw no field service again, and his premature generalship and assignments cut him off from the rigorous professional military education of the interwar years. He was a general-impresario, a man most given to geopolitical lecturing, not generalship.

Part of the function of MacArthur's staff was to keep his morale up. But another important piece of their mission was to protect the general from people (including newspaper reporters) who might discover his superficial grasp of operational and technical details. His subordinate generals and admirals received only broad guidance—a leadership technique which worked at times and not at others, especially if operations soured. Army aviation flourished in this uncertainty, but the navy, the army, and the Australians found their supreme commander a heavy burden. Fortunately, the Japanese decided to contest the Solomons offensive with more determination than they defended New Guinea and New Britain (Rabaul).

After the Australians repulsed multiple advances on Port Moresby (from July through September 1942) and the Combined Chiefs of Staff approved a limited offensive in New Guinea, MacArthur started operations to isolate Rabaul with an advance on the Japanese base system on northern Papua New Guinea, the Gona-Buna-Sanananda enclave. With most of Japan's naval and air power focused on the Solomons, the two-division expeditionary force faced only weather, terrain, and the stubborn remnants of a one-division force the Japanese had on the narrow peninsula of Papua. Still, it took two months of the grimmest sort of jungle combat to kill the Japanese defenders. Ernest Gerber, a squad leader in the 32d Infantry Division, found that the utter darkness of the jungle matched his ignorance: "We didn't understand jungle warfare . . . we didn't understand the Japanese. We thought the war would be fought by gentlemen. When a guy had had enough, he'd give up and that was that. That's not how it was. We found that out very quickly."[1] Eventually, almost 3,000 Allied soldiers fell to bullets and another 18,000 to disease against 10,000 Japanese, most of whom died in battle or from starvation-induced diseases. MacArthur could not accept the slowness and the butcher's bill; he relieved Major General Edwin F. Harding, commander of the one embattled American division. Harding's sin was his unwillingness to accept MacArthur's unrealistic timetable and his excuses for the lack of reinforcements (from Harding's own division), firepower, and logistical support. MacArthur blamed the navy for not providing shipping. He accused his own soldiers of shirking.

The campaign, however, suggested to MacArthur that he must exploit his superiority in tactical aviation and the growing amphibious capability of his theater naval forces, now designated the Seventh Fleet. His unwillingness to create a joint staff doomed MacArthur to fight his war without fast carrier task forces. He could and did, however, request timely support from Nimitz's Pacific Fleet when an operation allowed adequate preparation and the objectives had real targets for air attacks. MacArthur decided in early 1943 to bypass some Japanese strong points and attack others (usually those defending air fields) under the cover of Lieutenant General George C. Kenney's Fifth Air Force. A brilliant aircraft developer, trainer, organizer, and combat pilot in World War I, Kenney cajoled more planes and men from his friend General "Hap" Arnold, chief of the army air forces, largely because he accepted aircraft types that did not appeal to air commanders in Europe: P-39s, P-38s, P-40s, A-20s, and B-24s. Kenney made do with sound tactics and exceptional pilots; navy amphibious task forces sailed without severe setback, protected by the army's air umbrella.

Kenney's offensive operations against Japanese bases and shipping made leap-frogging possible. One of his greatest victories came in March 1943, when his airmen sank 4 destroyers and 8 large transports in the Bismarck and Solomon seas. Another operation in August, staged from hidden advanced bases, allowed Fifth Air Force to destroy 4 air fields at Wewak on New Guinea's north coast. Neither of these operations proved costly to Kenney, who lost only 8 aircraft and approximately 40 airmen, while destroying more than 200 enemy planes and 1,000 aircrewmen and ground crews.

Under a growing and destructive Allied air component, consisting of the Far East Air Forces of the U.S. Fifth and Thirteenth Air Forces and the Royal Australian Air Force, all under Kenney's operational control, MacArthur started up the coast of New Guinea in June 1943. Allied forces landed by sea and parachute drop near Lae and bypassed several Japanese bases in the jump up the coast. With five Australian and two American divisions, MacArthur occupied the Huon peninsula by January 1944, but two of the three Japanese divisions he faced escaped entrapment, although they could no longer count on maritime resupply. The coastal hopping continued through Wewak, Hollandia, and Wakde and Biak Islands, while the 1st Marine Division and an army regiment crossed the Vitiaz Straits and landed at Cape Gloucester and Arawe, New Britain, to start overland toward Rabaul in December 1943. Other American amphibious forces attacked the Admiralty Islands the following February. Rabaul was encircled and its garrison of 135,000 awaited its doom.

By the time Operation Cartwheel staggered to a close, MacArthur, the Combined Chiefs of Staff, and the Japanese had lost interest in the campaign. In September 1943 Imperial General Headquarters adopted a new strategic concept that largely conceded New Guinea and the Solomons as well as the Marshall and Gilbert island groups in the Central Pacific in order to husband air and naval forces for defense of the Western Pacific and Southeast Asia. Exceptionally well served by Ultra radio intelligence and his Australian-Dutch-American intelligence community, MacArthur knew much more about the Japanese than they knew about him. Air superiority and aerial reconnaissance (as well as an expert mapping agency) provided essential topographical information. He shared the knowledge with the Joint Chiefs that he faced a dogged but abandoned Japanese Eighteenth Army. Thus he stepped up the pace of operations to rush his forces so far toward the Philippines that they could not be stopped.

Ill-served by his intelligence officer (or G-2) Charles Willoughby, MacArthur sent forces against numerically superior Japanese garrisons on several occasions and exposed his naval forces with objectives beyond land-based air cover. The navy rushed light and escort carriers to Vice Admiral Thomas C. Kinkaid's Seventh Fleet, but the Japanese produced only one major aerial counterattack, Operation I-GO in April 1943. The damage from this air offensive proved bearable, but it demonstrated that air superiority is almost never absolute—a lesson Allied airmen, but not their army commanders, understood.

Reflecting an unhealthy degree of contempt for the Japanese Army, MacArthur committed his ground forces to high-risk operations in the name of surprise. The landing at Lae in September 1943 required the coordination of a 7,800-man Australian force, an American parachute regiment dropped 20 miles inland, and the timely arrival of more Australians marching overland or ferried in by transports to an airstrip seized by U.S. paratroopers. The 10,000 Japanese defenders surprised everyone by not counterattacking the isolated groups as they fought their way through the entrapment and fled into the mountains.

MacArthur raised the risks when he attempted to exploit the Lae victory. At Arawe, the 112th Cavalry Regiment met a more numerous Japanese force and had to fight hard for over a month to hold its beachhead. The 1st Marine Division spent four weeks mired in a New Britain swamp teeming with Japanese before it could conduct even limited offensive operations. MacArthur paid no attention to either force except to abandon his idea of an overland campaign on New Britain. In September the Australian 9th Division found Japanese defenders at Finschhafen to be twice as numerous and more determined than predicted, and the Australians had to fight for three months to take a position MacArthur had called a week's work. The 158th Regimental Combat Team landed at Sarmi only to find itself outnumbered two to one; it required rescue by the U.S. 6th Infantry Division.

A regimental attack on Los Negros faced even worse odds (4:1); the whole 1st Cavalry Division had to come in to prevent a repeat of the Little Big Horn.

Such events added to the Oz-like character of the war in the Southwest Pacific. MacArthur often announced the successful completion of operations long before the fighting had actually ended. In a sense, the Japanese stay-behind, fight-to-the-death tactics made such announcements correct as soon as the Allies stormed ashore, but it did not inspire infantrymen facing the dangerous task of killing the Japanese defenders bunker by bunker.

MacArthur also had a way with casualty figures. He convinced himself and others that his way of war—that is, bypassing some Japanese enclaves—minimized Allied losses and hence showed greater effectiveness than operations mounted by commanders (usually admirals and marine generals) in other parts of the Pacific. Even though he exaggerated Japanese losses, MacArthur spoke the truth about the ratio of combat deaths suffered between the opposing sides, but the differences were attributable to artillery density, air superiority, medical care, and logistical support, not the simple act of bypassing Japanese positions—though the press releases might lead one to think otherwise.

For one thing, MacArthur never acknowledged that operational conditions in his theater exacted a heavy toll. The army division that took Biak, for example, killed 4,700 Japanese at a cost of 400 dead and 2,000 wounded but sent another 7,000 soldiers to the hospital with diseases and accidental injuries. At Wadke, the 187th Regimental Combat Team lost fewer than 200 soldiers while killing almost 800 Japanese, but it emerged from the battle unfit for further combat because of exhaustion and disease. Moreover, MacArthur failed to acknowledge the severity of losses in his Australian divisions. In the 1942 Buna campaign, the Australians lost 2,017 dead, 3,533 wounded, and 9,250 stricken with malaria. Of the 24,000 casualties among MacArthur's ground troops in 1943, 17,000 were Australians. Jungle warfare exacted special costs. Wounds from gunfire struck down infantrymen at a rate twice that of European combat and proved more difficult to repair; the Southwest Pacific theater had the worst return-to-duty rates in the U.S. Army. It also had the highest rate (44 per 1,000) of neuropsychological breakdowns in the American armed forces.

MacArthur minimized the toll in the Southwest Pacific, but the Joint Chiefs noticed. Despite MacArthur's rhetoric about his life-saving operations, the Chiefs did not relish allowing MacArthur to liberate the Philippines. Such a decision did not, however, rest on professional military analysis.

The Solomons

Of the five sectors in the defense perimeter of the new Japanese empire, three lay on the line of the Malay barrier (Burma, New Guinea, and the Solomons) and one placed Japanese troops on Attu and Kiska Islands, part of the Aleutian chain extending westward from Alaska. The fifth was the Marshall and Gilbert atolls in the Central Pacific. The northern army outposts did not last long; an American army division retook Kiska in August 1943, and the Japanese abandoned Attu. Neither foe had any taste for a serious campaign near the Arctic Circle among bleak islands useful only as weather stations and communications sites for air and naval operations. Like New Guinea, the Solomons represented the other end of the discomfort spectrum: volcanic mountains wreathed with tropical rain forests; septic, tepid rivers whose steep, muddy banks made them nature's moats; rainy coastal jungles with hot, rotting vegetation, home to hostile insects and voracious microbes that feasted on Europeans and Asians alike. The Melanesians in the southern Solomons tended to support the Allies, while those in the northern Solomons did not, but fear and a desire to survive neutralized the behavior of all but a dedicated pro-British few.

The Pacific War remained essentially a maritime struggle, and the Solomons campaign represented the third confrontation of two great navies. Admiral Mikawa was an aggressive, talented commander, and he believed that his surface forces could carry the burden that the carrier forces could no longer bear, provided the land-based Sea Eagles won air superiority. Behind Mikawa stood the great Yamamoto himself, working from the Combined Fleet's advanced base at Truk. Stung by the defeat at Midway, Yamamoto looked for every opportunity to draw the Pacific Fleet into the range of his aircraft and battleship guns. The U.S. Navy had yet to best his surface force of battleships and cruisers, which had suffered no major losses. Yamamoto could interpret the Battle of Midway as a result of sheer bad luck that would not happen again, especially if he and Mikawa waged a campaign that exploited the U.S. Navy's relative lack of experience. Although he did not know it, Yamamoto faced two very cautious adversaries, Vice Admirals Robert L. Ghormley and Frank Jack Fletcher, both of whom lacked the character to lead hard-pressed American forces.

Despite known weaknesses in training and logistical sustainability, Ghormley executed the order from King and Nimitz to land the 1st Marine Division on Guadalcanal and Tulagi-Gavutu on 7 August 1942. The move caught the Japanese by surprise. The key objective, identified by Rear Admiral Richmond K. Turner and Major General A. A. Vandegrift, was the

Japanese air field near Lunga Point, a coastal plain almost in the middle of Guadalcanal's north coast. Control of the air field (named Henderson Field by the Americans) became the focus of the campaign until its end in January 1943. Landing on Guadalcanal against slight opposition, the marines soon learned that ground defense was only part of the equation of victory; they had no illusions about Japanese fighting ability since their comrades on Tulagi and Gavutu had had a stiff fight in taking those small islands. The key issue became air-sea control, without which the landing force could not sustain a ground defense of Henderson Field. Land-based air would have to provide continuous air cover for ships bringing in reinforcements and supplies. The issue was clearly drawn within three days of the landing. Mikawa reacted to the landing with massive air strikes on the amphibious force. In two days his Sea Eagles attacked Turner's force with 70 bombers and lost 28 of them and their escorting Zeros; Admiral Fletcher's fighters lost 21 aircraft in the interception effort, a loss severe enough for Fletcher to cut short his carrier-based air support by 12 hours.

Covered by the air assault, Mikawa himself took seven cruisers and one destroyer south and engaged Turner's cruiser-destroyer screen on the night of 8–9 August. Mikawa caught the Australian and American warships completely unaware. Without the loss of a single ship in the battle (they lost a cruiser to a U.S. submarine on the way out), the Japanese sank four cruisers and a destroyer and badly damaged another cruiser and two destroyers. In the mayhem of close-quarters naval gunfire, 1,534 Allied sailors died, a heavier loss than Pearl Harbor. Mikawa, however, broke off the action before reaching the transports because he feared that daylight would bring a U.S. air attack. He did not know that Fletcher had already withdrawn, soon to be followed by Turner's amphibious task force.

One of Admiral Mikawa's staff officers recalled the missed opportunities: "With the benefit of hindsight I can see two grievous mistakes of the Japanese navy at the time of the Guadalcanal campaign: the attempt to conduct major operations simultaneously at Milne Bay [New Guinea] and in the Solomons, and the premature retirement from the Battle of Savo Island. I played a significant part in each of these errors. Both were a product of undue reliance on the unfounded assurances of our army and of a general contempt for the capabilities of the enemy. Thus lay open the road to Tokyo."[2] Despite Ghormley's defeatism—five weeks later he advised Vandegrift to consider surrendering his division or abandoning his position for guerrilla warfare in the mountains—Turner started shuttling planes and supplies to Guadalcanal as soon as Henderson Field became operational on 20 August. Marine and navy fighters from the field would cover the naval resupply. Turner's stubborn commitment gained critical support when Halsey replaced Ghormley on 18 October, and Thomas C. Kinkaid and other naval warriors replaced Fletcher.

The contest for Guadalcanal took on a deadly rhythm that did not change until November 1942, an unbroken cycle of air-sea-land actions that finally brought American victory. This was "make see" war, full of fatal learning. The existence of Henderson Field started the ever-widening gyre of operational requirements. As long as American aircraft—squadrons from all the services—could use the field and another constructed nearby, they could attack Japanese reinforcements and protect their own convoys, but only in daylight operations. The Japanese brought ground troops south at night by fast transports and barges to encircle the air field. They made three major attacks on the air field in regimental, brigade, and division strength from 21 August until 26 October. Each attack failed in the face of stubborn marine defenders, aided in October by the staunch U.S. 164th Infantry Regiment. The Japanese, however, kept matching American ground reinforcements until November; they also landed long-range artillery that menaced the air field until the Americans drove them westward with their own heavy artillery and a ground offensive. In the last two months of the campaign, the opposing ground forces, which ultimately included two infantry divisions and a second marine division, attacked the Japanese field force and finally persuaded its commander, Lieutenant General Hyakutake Haruyoshi, to rescue the survivors, some 13,000 men of the 36,000 sent to Guadalcanal. American ground forces lost approximately 2,500 combat dead, but their wounded (4,183) were only half the losses to disease and other forms of breakdown.

In the battle for air superiority, the Americans ultimately emerged victorious, in part because the marines kept the field safe from ground attack. Nevertheless, the 1st Marine Division, which included two battalions of anti-aircraft and coastal artillery, could not stop the air or naval bombardments. The marines could also not stop the "Tokyo Express" of warships and transports from delivering men and supplies. That mission depended on the airmen and sailors. The Japanese bombed the Lunga Point perimeter as often and as furiously as they could, usually coordinating air attacks with other operations, but never quite closely enough. Based in Rabaul and the northern Solomons, Japanese bombers, mostly naval Mitsubishi Type 1 "Bettys" with a two-ton bomb load, had a five-hour trek south. The coastwatchers of Operation Ferdinand—a network of observers and support parties organized by the Allied Intelligence Bureau and manned by British and Australian islanders—often observed and reported Japanese air raiders from start to finish. The timing of these air attacks became predictable, driven by time-space factors. The marines even ate by the Japanese air attack clock; their two-meals-a-day regime was driven more by the threat of lunchtime bombings than a shortage of rations; still, the skipped meals and stress brought disabling fatigue and reduced resistance to tropical diseases.

Living and flying in primitive conditions, marine and naval aviators met the Japanese attacks with determination and growing skill. They focused on the bombers and accepted the danger of the escorting Zeros. The Americans, however, like their RAF counterparts in the Battle of Britain, knew they could fight longer than their foes, and if they could avoid death in the cockpit, an aggressive air-sea rescue service would pull them from the water. A wounded Japanese pilot, such as ace Sakai Suburo of the Sea Eagles, had to survive a six-hour return trip to the north. Using the weaving tactics of four-aircraft sections, U.S. pilots found they could fight the Zeros on equal terms, provided they did not engage the Zeros in aerobatics. Marine aces began to multiply at Henderson Field, making John Smith, Marion Carl, and Joe Foss household words in the United States. Able to shuttle squadrons in and out of Guadalcanal from safe bases to the south, Rear Admiral John S. McCain and his successors as Solomons senior air commander not only protected Guadalcanal but stationed ground-attack aircraft and scout-bombers there to attack Japanese infantry and transports, if located during the daylight hours.

The critical question became who would control the night and the surface waters around Guadalcanal, and the answer from Savo Island until 12–15 November was the Imperial Japanese Navy. Even in daylight actions the U.S. Navy paid a high price to remain on the ocean. Covering reinforcing operations during 23–30 August, the carriers *Enterprise* and *Saratoga* suffered serious damage. Japanese reinforcements got through to the island, even though one light carrier was sunk and a heavy cruiser was damaged. Japanese aircraft losses, however, outnumbered American losses three to one. In a similar engagement over the night of 11–12 September the two navies again took each other's measure. The Americans lost the carrier *Wasp*, while the new fast battleship *North Carolina* and a destroyer suffered incapacitating damage. Only one carrier and one battleship remained as the core of the operating forces in the South Pacific.

Turner got his supply convoys through, but so did the Japanese. The struggle continued. Another nighttime melee between opposing cruiser-destroyer task forces near Savo Island occurred on 11–12 October. When the two forces staggered apart, the Japanese had lost a cruiser, and two other warships were damaged; the American force had a cruiser and two destroyers damaged but only one destroyer sunk, which was a victory of sorts. The Japanese, however, followed the engagement by sending battleships to bombard Henderson Field, destroying almost 50 aircraft, and continued these nighttime attacks for three more days. More Japanese reinforcements reached the island.

Under Halsey's prodding, the admirals afloat decided to challenge the Japanese in night fighting. The next engagement on 26 October, however, again involved the carrier task forces that hovered beyond the narrow waters around Guadalcanal. In the battle of Santa Cruz, American aircraft damaged two Japanese carriers and a cruiser and shot down 100 aircraft or caught them on the carrier decks. American losses were almost catastrophic: the carrier *Hornet* sank and the *Enterprise,* a battleship, a cruiser, and a destroyer were heavily damaged. Seventy-four naval aircraft completed the casualty list.

The climax of the campaign came over four days, 12–15 November, and ended in an American victory—barely. As Turner shepherded another convoy of reinforcements toward Guadalcanal, Halsey sent three task forces to engage the Japanese: 13 cruisers and destroyers to escort the convoy, a carrier task force with one barely operable carrier, *Enterprise,* and a task force built around the damaged *South Dakota* and a new battleship, *Washington.* The Japanese destroyed Rear Admiral Daniel J. Callaghan's cruiser-destroyer force, sinking six ships and damaging all of the rest but one. Even though Callaghan and Rear Admiral Norman Scott died on their bridges, this was no Savo Island. The Americans left one Japanese battleship and two destroyers damaged enough to be easy targets in daylight for American aircraft. Admiral Kinkaid's *Enterprise* carrier air group could not work from its own deck, but it could and did reinforce the marines at Henderson Field, and these forces pummeled the Japanese transports. They could not stop Japanese warships, which shelled Guadalcanal with impunity, but the Japanese still lost seven transports.

The battle continued when Rear Admiral Willis Lee brought his two battleships and four destroyers forward for another night action on 14–15 November. The Japanese sank or damaged all of Lee's ships except *Washington,* which ruled the wreckage surrounding it, including a Japanese battleship and a destroyer. A much superior Japanese force (two more battleships and a heavy cruiser) broke off the action and retreated north. It left behind 13 destroyed transports and some 6,000 dead Japanese soldiers, most victims of subsequent air strikes.

The Guadalcanal campaign persuaded Yamamoto to cut his losses and hold the Combined Fleet for some later and more favorable fleet engagement, but the Japanese Navy faced an unhappy future. It had inflicted severe losses on the U.S. Navy: 2 carriers, 7 cruisers, and 15 other warships. It had killed almost 5,000 American sailors (a loss so traumatic that for years afterward the navy refused to reveal its casualties) and had destroyed 134 aircraft. But Japanese losses had also been grievous: 2 battleships, 1 light carrier, 4 cruisers, 17 other warships, and about 1,200 naval aviators and 3,500 sailors. The Japanese had lost 500 aircraft, mostly those of the Eleventh Air Fleet and the carrier air groups, and 14 transports. Although the Japanese might replace planes and ships, they could not replace skilled pilots and seamen.

What was also impossible to replace was the psychological advantage the Japanese had lost. On a level sea where they did not yet command overwhelming advantages in numbers, skill, and technology, Americans of all the services had demonstrated they could defeat the best of the Japanese armed forces. Veterans of the Solomons campaign did not lose their respect for the tenacity and skill of the Japanese, but they no longer regarded them with fear and awe—their state of mind in early 1942. With more resources pouring into the South Pacific theater in early 1943, the Allies' prospects of victory soared.

The shift in advantage to the Pacific Fleet in November 1942 was not absolute, even though Yamamoto now withheld his battleships and carriers. His cruisers and destroyers, skilled in night actions and armed with the lethal Long Lance torpedo, kept caution alive among American captains. In the year that followed the great battles of November 1942 off Guadalcanal, the Japanese Navy and U.S. Navy fought each other seven more times. In two night actions (Tassafaronga, 30 November–1 December 1942) and Kolambangara (12–13 July 1943) the Pacific Fleet lost two cruisers and a destroyer, but in these and other actions the Japanese Navy lost two cruisers and ten destroyers, although some of the latter had been converted to transports. Tassafaronga in particular showed what became of task forces that did not respect the Imperial Japanese Navy and use its radar wisely; a squadron of Japanese destroyers sank one cruiser and badly damaged three others with Long Lance torpedoes at no cost to themselves. In fact, they convinced the Americans that they were being shelled by battleships. Such embarrassments could not stop the inexorable American climb up the Solomons chain toward Rabaul.

Smarting from the loss of Guadalcanal, Yamamoto gathered his naval air armada in the South Pacific for Operation GO, ordered from Imperial General Headquarters, an air strike at the American air bases and harbors in

New Guinea. Under the supervision of Vice Admiral Koga Mineichi, the tall, dapper, calm professional who commanded the Third (Carrier) Fleet at Truk, the Sea Eagles from two carriers joined their land-based comrades at Rabaul and Bougainville. On 11–14 April 1943 the combined force of 340 aircraft of all types swept over New Guinea as far as Milne Bay with a ferocity unmatched since Pearl Harbor. The exuberant pilots reported catastrophic losses to Allied shipping and aircraft, which proved highly exaggerated but pleased Yamamoto. His loss of 40 aircraft and aircrew seemed worth the cost. In the glow of imagined victory, the admiral went to Bougainville for an inspection and fell into an aerial ambush set up by long-range American P-38s, whose pilots knew Yamamoto's route from compromised radio messages. On 18 April the Japanese Navy's greatest leader perished when his bomber crashed in Bougainville's jungle. Yamamoto's death removed Japan's only admiral whose stature equaled the army generals in strategic leadership.

His successor, Admiral Koga, mounted an even more massive aerial counteroffensive, Operation RO, in early November 1943. Again, carrier air and land-based bombers gathered in the northern Solomons; the operation against the Allied invasion fleets off Bougainville and New Britain islands and air bases eventually involved as many as 500 aircraft. Alerted by superior radio intelligence, the Americans launched their own air strikes, especially from Halsey's carriers. In three great air battles, 2–9 November, the Japanese may have lost as many as 200 more precious naval aircraft and pilots. This time the Americans wildly exaggerated their air success, but the actual Japanese losses were bad enough and cost Koga command of the Combined Fleet. His successor, Admiral Ozawa Jisaburo, immediately advised Imperial General Headquarters that Truk should be abandoned like Rabaul, while he formed new carrier air groups.

With Guadalcanal secure, Halsey seized the initiative and started an exploitation campaign to seize the air bases and anchorages developed by the Japanese during the southern Solomons campaign. He could now depend primarily on land-based marine and army fighter-bomber squadrons and even army bombers. However, he had learned that land-based bombers could not put Rabaul out of action or provide decisive support, so he needed forward operating bases for more effective aircraft. Although his naval forces would be adequate—provided the Combined Fleet remained passive—Halsey did not have a seasoned landing force since the 1st and 2nd Marine Divisions had gone off to other missions and the Americal and 25th Infantry Divisions needed reconstitution. He therefore had to patch together a landing force of the army's XIV Corps (three new divisions), reinforced by marine defense and raider battalions, along with two New Zealand brigade groups.

At New Georgia in the central Solomons the operations did not go well, repeating many errors of the army's debut in offensive jungle warfare at Buna, but by early autumn 1943 the Allies had the central Solomons in hand and ready to serve as advanced air and embarkation bases. On 1 November 1943 the fresh 3rd Marine Division assaulted Bougainville, followed by the U.S. 37th Infantry Division. After another hard fight in the jungles, conducted in a web of vines and mud, the combined force swelled to include three more Australian and American divisions. No matter how bitter and difficult the fighting on Bougainville, the Allies no longer faced a concerted Japanese effort to hold the Solomons—or Rabaul—only a dedication to make the Allies win at the highest possible cost. Bougainville remained unconquered until the end of the war.

As it entered its final phase in late 1943, the campaign to isolate Rabaul had shown what the Allies might accomplish when they exploited their growing ability to dominate the air-sea war. Pummeled by constant air attacks, Japanese high commanders extracted what ground troops they could from their isolated garrisons, but Allied air superiority made that difficult. On Bougainville, for example, the Australian II Corps killed approximately 8,500 Japanese soldiers in what amounted to a medieval siege in the jungle, losing only 516 dead and 1,572 wounded. Nearly 10,000 Japanese perished of disease and starvation before war's end, when 13,000 survivors surrendered.

Rabaul suffered the same fate. While the Allies dropped more than 20,000 tons of bombs on the port, its defenders dug deeply enough to make an assault unattractive, which meant that an Australian division had to besiege it for almost a year before the war ended. It accepted the surrender of almost 90,000 Japanese military and civilian personnel in 1945. In the meantime, probably another 10,000 Japanese died from all causes. The Allied campaign in the South Pacific, having reduced Japanese air and naval power, dragged on to the funereal laments of the victors and vanquished alike.

The Asians at War

Winston Churchill knew history. Indeed, he wrote history, and he understood that war meant far more than the clash of armies and navies. The wars that influenced Churchill most were ones which he had not fought or written about: the wars with the French between 1792 and 1815.

Churchill's strategic challenge had striking similarities with that faced by William Pitt the Younger, one of his predecessors as a wartime prime minister. Churchill knew the weaknesses of the British Empire he had sworn to preserve. Now that Japan had created its own overseas dominion, Churchill thought the Greater East Asia Co-prosperity Sphere might be assaulted by subversion and economic warfare as well as military attack. Playing on FDR's natural anti-imperialism, the prime minister had no difficulty applauding Roosevelt's announcement at Casablanca in January 1943 that the Axis powers could not negotiate a settlement that preserved any of their new conquests. In Cairo the following November, Churchill, Roosevelt, and Chiang Kai-shek announced that Japan could not hold any of its conquests since 1895.

Except for China, Roosevelt saw the political realities of Asia more clearly than Churchill. European imperialism in Asia and the Pacific had been moribund in 1941, and the Japanese had only delivered the coup de grâce. The Allies faced a special problem in Asia that they did not in Europe: the Asians in Japanese-occupied territories might not welcome them as liberators and might not regard the Japanese as conquerors. The Japanese had advertised themselves as the *real* anti-imperialists, the saviors of their fellow Asians from Anglo-American exploitation. The Japanese, in fact, held a well-publicized Pan-Asian conference in 1943. They pointed to their collaboration with the Thais and the anti-Kuomintang Chinese as an example of their seriousness in forming an anti-European commonwealth. The only Asians excluded from Japanese beneficence were the Communists. Another group of Asian oppositionists drew their inspirations not from their service to Marxism but from their commitment to Christian values. Resisters and collaborators did not divide on class lines; economic royalists could be found in both camps. The real faultlines among the occupied Asians developed around issues of anti-imperialist ideology, ethnicity, religion, and regional rivalries.

The likelihood that the Allies could create an anti-Japanese resistance seemed bleak, even in 1943. Instead, it appeared that the Japanese had found willing allies in almost every former European colony as well as in China and Thailand. India even seemed on the verge of Japanese subversion, when the riots of 1942 almost paralyzed the telecommunications system and railroads in that country. The Japanese approached their Indian POWs and offered them an alternative to slave labor and death: join the Indian National Army and go to Burma to preserve order and prepare for the invasion of India. The Indian National Army, perhaps 20,000 at peak strength, found its most powerful voice in Subdas Chandra Bose, a former Congress president in exile in Germany. Its military commanders were a handful of former Indian officers. The Japanese, however, did not really want to use Indian soldiers, so the INA fielded only one token division that collapsed in the debacle of 1944–45.

The effort to exploit the Burmese proved even more hopeless. At first Burma looked like a model New Asia nation. From the wreckage of British rule, a charismatic Burmese nationalist, Ba Maw, formed a government and won nominal independence in August 1943. One of his Thakin (Master) party peers, the even more charismatic Aung San, formed a Burma Nationalist Army to preserve order and keep the hill minorities in line. Aung San, however, disliked the Japanese and his Burmese rivals almost as much as the British, and he formed another group, the Anti-Fascist People's Freedom League, under cover of the BNA in 1944. This shadow army defected to the British in March 1945 in time to kill some Japanese and win forgiveness. The Kachins, Karens, and Chins, who had been persecuted by the Japanese and Burmese, already had integrated some 20,000 soldiers into the British Fourteenth Army by 1943, which gave them better credentials for resistance than the Burmese but did not protect them from postwar battles with Aung San's army.

The Japanese enjoyed their greatest success at consensual collaboration in the Netherlands East Indies, but even there the Allies exploited pockets of resistance. The Japanese benefited initially from a conquest that did not kill many Indonesians, followed by an enlightened administration under General Imamura Hitoshi. The Japanese and the Javanese became willing partners in establishing an independent Indonesian government in 1944 and in establishing economic organizations that would extract and ship Indonesian oil and minerals to Japan. Achmed Sukarno provided the Japanese with an authentic Javanese anti-imperialist to support. The Japanese allowed the creation of a paramilitary force, Pembala Tanah Air (PETA) or "Volunteer Army of the Defense of the Fatherland," for internal security duties, a force that reached 70,000 and worked closely with the *kempeitai*, the dreaded Japanese military police. The emergence of the Javanese as the political elite of Indonesia, however, made it possible for Allied agents (most of them Dutch and Australian) to organize partisan groups on Sumatra, Borneo, and Timor, supplied and supported by General MacArthur through his Allied Intelligence Bureau, the only combined agency he allowed in his theater, largely to exclude the Office of Strategic Services (OSS), which was responsible for subversive operations. The partisans annoyed the Japanese on the remote islands but found it impossible to dent the Japanese-Javanese security system, and PETA ended the war largely intact and ready to resist Dutch reoccupation.

Elsewhere in Asia, the Communists took the initiative in forming resistance movements, and only in the Philippines did an alternative resistance structure emerge. Largely on the basis of their experience in north China, where the Communist partisan forces numbered probably a million in 1943, the Japanese assumed that being a Chinese guerrilla meant being Communist, an assumption they helped make a self-fulfilling prophecy. Yet nationality did not define Communism, since Filipino, Korean, and Vietnamese Communists also bedeviled the Japanese and captured the mantle of authentic nationalism.

In Malaya, at least, the Japanese read the tea leaves correctly. They started their own troubles by executing at least 5,000 leading Chinese and their families after the fall of Singapore. The Japanese occupiers faced a serious challenge in Malaya, since the Chinese population there (two million) was almost as large as the Malay population (2.5 million) and had strong ties to both the Communist and Kuomintang parties in China. Although the Malays and Indians (750,000) did not organize major resistance groups, the Chinese, correctly anticipating that they would suffer most from a Japanese occupation, created a resistance network as soon as the war began.

Sponsored, funded, and trained by the Special Branch, Malaya Police, the driving force in the underground was Lai Tek, secretary-general of the Malaya Communist Party, also in British pay as an informer. After the Japanese victory, Lai Tek set up his network of commissars and military leaders—and then betrayed them to the Japanese in two separate incidents that cost the resistance over a hundred key leaders. His own power and security assured, Lai Tek contacted Force 136 (the SOE, or Special Operations Executive, in India) and asked for more support for his guerrilla army. A British liaison mission arrived in Malaya in 1943, including the charismatic Lim Bo Seng, a young, wealthy member of the Kuomintang and an English speaker. Already suspecting Lai Tek, the British warned Lim Bo Seng not to remain in Malaya, but he stayed and organized his own partisan unit. Also betrayed by Lai Tek, Lim Bo Seng died in 1944 after months of Japanese torture and became a heroic martyr to the Singaporean Chinese.

Although the 8,000-man Malayan People's Anti-Japanese Army (MPAJA) conducted 340 attacks (its figure) on enemy outposts, the Communists mostly fought to survive. As suspicion grew about Lai Tek's loyalty, power in the resistance gravitated toward his 23-year-old deputy, Chin Peng, whose ability to speak English qualified him as the Force 136 liaison officer. Chin Peng used his power to organize the MPAJA for a postwar struggle for control of Malaya. He directed only enough operations to keep his force qualified for British assistance, but the MPAJA remained focused on its internal rivals. Of the 7,000 victims it killed during the war, the majority were fellow Chinese, including around 2,500 members of the MPAJA. Force 136 received some useful intelligence and other assistance from the MPAJA, but the Malayan resistance did little to weaken the Japanese occupation.

In Indochina, the colonial government pledged its loyalty to Vichy France, and in Cambodia and Laos, where the French ruled indirectly through traditional royal families, the Japanese found little resistance. In Vietnam, however, the Japanese learned that at least two major anti-colonial movements threatened their control. The most influential, the Viet Nam Quac Dan Dong, had survived the French repression of the 1930s and infiltrated the Franco-Vietnamese security forces in the 1940s, where it gradually built a shadow government. In March 1945, the Japanese Army launched a preemptive strike against the Franco-Vietnamese army and police force that it believed would soon attack it. It killed or executed 1,700 potential resisters and imprisoned the rest. In the wake of this disaster, the Allies had no choice but to open relations with the small remnant of the Vietnamese Communist Party, which had established base camps along the Chinese border at the headwaters of the Red River. The leader of this group was an emaciated intellectual of iron will and much European travel who went by the nom de guerre of Ho Chi Minh. In 1945, both Force 136 and the OSS had missions with the Viet Nam Doc Lap Dong Minh (Viet Minh), largely to gather intelligence and support air operations.

In the Philippines, the Japanese also found their initial victory a source of domestic political strength, which they then squandered. The American defeat destroyed any myth of Western omnipotence, but the Japanese missed the point: the Filipinos already knew the Americans were poor imperialists. No doubt survivalism helped the Japanese establish a certain amount of authority; nationalist political leaders, the Catholic high clergy, and wealthy native landholders seemed content to accept Japanese occupation. The Japanese found the Philippine Constabulary willing to enforce local order. However, the Japanese soon learned (and their intelligence was quite good) that they faced a substantial resistance movement, divided roughly along ideological lines. The Filipino Communists created the Hukbong Bayan laban Sa Hapon (Hukbalahap) or People's Anti-Japanese Army, whose strength came from the traditional anti-imperialist and anti-landlord peasantry of central Luzon. Led by Luis Taruc, the Huks knew who the enemy was, and it was not necessarily the Japanese; before the end of the war they may have killed as many as 15,000 Filipinos, collaborators and *americanistas*, compared with 5,000 Japanese.

The Huks had plenty of local competition. The surrenders of 1942 had not accounted for every American or Filipino who wanted to kill Japanese in the name of American patriotism and Filipino independence. Resistance groups appeared in late 1942–43 on every major island; by 1943 probably half the active guerrillas (estimated at 60,000 in all) were not Huks but *americanistas* under the joint command of American and Filipino army officers like Ramon Magsaysay, later president of the Republic. By 1943 most of these groups had opened communications with MacArthur's headquarters, which supplied them with arms, radios, and medical supplies.

The Japanese Army, especially its intelligence officers and military policemen, had already gained rich experience in Korea, Manchuria, and China on how to stop incipient insurgencies with the clever manipulation of rewards and punishments. They contained the partisans in north China and Manchuria with their own forces as well as collaborationist Chinese and Koreans. Japanese counterpartisan forces almost totally eliminated a Sino-Korean guerrilla army in Manchuria (which included an obscure Korean officer named Kim Il Sung) in 1941. The Japanese at least held the Chinese Communist Eighth Route and New Fourth Armies at bay, even if they could not eliminate them. The very demands of the war, however, doomed the Japanese efforts to control the people of their new economic empire. Like England, Japan could not survive and wage war without massive imports to its island empire.

During 1942 Japanese economic administrators organized the extraction and shipment of all sorts of essential goods from China, Korea, and Southeast Asia. Oil, iron ore, tin, rubber, magnesium, quinine, manganese, nickel, bauxite, salt, coal, sugar, rice, tea, and other raw materials flowed to Japan. None of this economic activity, however, enriched the providers, since it had no anchor in international trade and the Japanese had no incentive to reward their economic satraps. In Korea, for example, the production of rice doubled, but the amount of rice available to Koreans dropped by half. Japanese exploitation, driven by wartime demands, soon proved more onerous than European peacetime economic colonialism had been. This source of alienation might have been bearable, but the Japanese also needed to export labor. Aping their German allies, the Japanese exploited non-Japanese laborers to fill the void created by drafting Japanese workers into the armed forces. Without any choice, the number of non-Japanese "economic soldiers" sent to the Home Islands or elsewhere soared between 1943 and 1945: 800,000 Koreans, 300,000 Indonesians, 1,000,000 Chinese, and 100,000 Malays. Such a policy could hardly strengthen the affective bonds within the Greater East Asian Co-prosperity Sphere.

Given the limitations of the resistance movements, the Allies could not use guerrillas as a substitute for regular forces in Asia at any time during the war, much to the frustration of the Pittian-Churchillian romantics in SOE and OSS. The first barrier was simply the heritage of European colonialism, especially in the Dutch, British, and French colonies. The Japanese were not sensitive liberators, but at least they were not Europeans. Another limitation was the immediacy of Allied support. With the prospect of assistance and liberation far away, why should resistance movements take special risks against the Japanese Army?

The Allied guerrilla managers faced a difficult problem, too. If they kept the partisan bands small, they improved their chances of survival and enhanced their usefulness in terms of providing intelligence for conventional operations. A small guerrilla force also could rescue downed airmen and perform other tasks without attacking Japanese positions, blowing up critical installations and transportation centers, and ambushing Japanese units. Such dramatic attacks were likely to galvanize the Japanese to execute civilian hostages, destroy villages, and mount serious counterguerrilla operations. Partisans could not really create "second fronts" within each occupied Asian country, although their threat had to be taken seriously by the Japanese. If subversion could not rewrite the strategic landscape, then some other attack on the Japanese war economy would have to fill the void.

The Submarine War

The U.S. Navy believed it could weaken Japan's grip on Asia's resources without depending on strategic bombardment or guerrillas. It proposed the destruction of the Japanese merchant marine by unrestricted submarine warfare, since Japan's war industry and the fabric of its society, like Britain's, depended upon the uninterrupted flow of raw materials and food to the Home Islands. Although the navy had developed its own submarine force to support fleet operations, newer classes of American submarines (principally the *Tambor* and *Gato* classes, also known as fleet boats) had the range to reach the trade routes of the Western Pacific, even the waters of the Home Islands. Moreover, like the U.S. Navy, the Japanese Navy had paid little attention to anti-submarine warfare or the organization of convoys. Within a week of Pearl Harbor, three American submarines were on their way to Japanese waters; other boats stationed at Cavite, the Philippines, looked for targets. Yet for almost two years the submarine forces of the Pacific Fleet, divided between Australia and Hawaii, proved no more effective than bombers from China. The limitations of American commerce raiding early in the war provided one more reason why the Allies had no choice but to fight the Japanese Army and Navy somewhere in the Pacific.

The U.S. Navy's submarine service had developed a prewar reputation for excellence that rivaled naval aviation or the German submarine force. The navy carefully selected crew members for their intelligence, technical skill, and emotional stability; faced with stressful living conditions and dangerous duty, submariners received extra pay and special comforts while ashore. Officers enjoyed the prospect of challenging assignments and command at ranks lower than their more comfortable peers on battleships and cruisers. The safety concerns and expenses of peacetime training, however, did not test submarine commanders, and in the war's first year one-third of them lost their assignments because of ineffectiveness. Nevertheless, the human material of the force remained outstanding from first to last. It had to be, for the U.S. submarine force endured the highest risks of any American combatants in World War II. Almost 22 percent of its deployed crews were killed on wartime patrols (3,500 of 16,000 sailors), the highest percentage of deaths in any American combat arm.

The navy built quality submarines to match its superior submarine crews. Breaking away from the practice of building ships in government shipyards, navy submariners developed a close working relationship with German and American makers of diesel and electric engines and steel pressure hulls; the most influential of the companies were the Electric Boat Company (Groton, Connecticut), Maschinenfabrik-Augsburg-Nürnberg (Germany), Allis-Chalmers, General Electric, and General Motors. Submarine commanders worked closely and persuasively with their counterparts in the Bureau of Engineering, the navy's department for submarine construction. The course of submarine development was not straight or smooth, but by 1941 the American submarine force believed correctly that it had boats with superior diesel engines for rapid surface movement (maximum 20 knots), superior electric engines of sufficient safety and durability for underwater attacks, and welded hulls and machinery that met the challenges of the unforgiving ocean and enemy. This assessment proved correct.

Given the navy's expectations, the combat performance of submarines in 1942 and 1943 was just another example of blighted hopes. In 1942 the Japanese merchant marine lost only 180 ships (including two oil tankers) of 800,000 tons; the next year American submarines improved the score to 335 ships (23 tankers) of 1.5 million tons, still not crippling losses. The Japanese replaced the lost tonnage with relative ease in 1942; their annual loss represented only one-sixth of Allied losses to German submarines. Japanese merchant tonnage remained close to 5 million tons until mid-1943. Since Japanese anti-submarine warfare efforts cannot explain this pallid record—the U.S. Navy lost only 7 boats in 1942 and 17 in 1943—the disappointment had to be self-inflicted.

It was. As with every military force in World War II, American submariners had to make tactical adjustments, but their principal problem was defective torpedoes. American boats went to war bristling with torpedoes and launch tubes; they carried a normal load of 24 "fish" fired from six launching-tubes forward and four aft. The Bureau of Ordnance had outdone itself in developing the Mark XIV torpedo, almost 15 feet in length, capable of speeds up to 46 knots over a range of 4,500 yards. The Mark XIV carried 500 pounds of TNT, soon replaced by almost 700 pounds of Torpex, an even more devastating explosive—provided the warhead actually exploded.

Therein lay the problem, for the Mark XIV carried two types of detonators, magnetic field and contact, and neither worked correctly. Moreover, the Bureau of Ordnance's engineers had calibrated the torpedoes' depth settings 10–15 feet in error due to tests without a full explosive load. Through hard experience, submarine commanders determined that the complex firing pin for the magnetic exploder had a design flaw that made it explode prematurely or not at all; since the exploder was so highly classified, few knew what the problem might be until one courageous captain pulled a warhead apart and tested it. Convinced the magnetic exploders would not work, he and others disarmed them and went to the contact exploder. This detonator also failed to work every time, again because of a design problem in the firing pin that could, happily, be reengineered and compensated for by changing tactics. In the course of coping with the Mark XIV warhead problems, the submariners discovered the depth setting problem as well. Commander Tyrell Jacobs, who had discovered the exploder problem, actually conducted tests in combat, and another captain maneuvered under fire to launch four Mark XIVs at an anchored freighter. Launched with varied depth settings, none damaged the ship, and one exploded on the beach. The skipper then sank the freighter with two older models.

Outraged at the torpedo problem, Rear Admiral Charles A. Lockwood, Hawaiian force commander, conducted his own unauthorized tests and finally won admission from the Bureau of Ordnance that its engineers had erred. By the end of 1943—a year in which they had fired ten "fish" for every ship sunk—American submarines finally had dependable warheads. Combined with new search radars to detect enemy aircraft and surface vessels and active and passive sonar for underwater detection, the submarines enjoyed substantial technical advantages over the Japanese. They also received better guidance for intercepting targets, provided by the Ultra codebreaking system, which had been denied U.S. submarines for much of 1942–43 for fear of capture and compromise. The Japanese merchant fleet did not have long to live.

The early performance of the Japanese submarine force was not much better, despite its elite sailors, its well-built, modern boats armed with a variant of the Model 95 Long Lance torpedo, and an adequate sonar and radar capability. The force was not large, but the Japanese Navy could draw on 56 I-Class boats comparable with the U.S. Navy's fleet boats. Nevertheless, the Japanese submarine force mounted no real campaign against Allied shipping in the Pacific. Although the force increased to almost 200 boats before the war's end, Japanese submarines sank only 171 warships, naval auxiliary vessels, and merchant ships of approximately one million tons. To be sure, Allied vessels carrying raw materials to North America traveled routes at the limits of Japanese range, but the Allied war effort required the massive shipping of troops, weapons, and supplies to the South Pacific and Australia well into 1944 and then north to the Philippines. Similar convoys followed the Pacific Fleet westward in late 1943. The Japanese did little to impede the flow of materiel. From December 1941 to July 1942 their submarines and aircraft sank 21 merchantmen, most along the Malay barrier and in the Indian Ocean. Over the next 18 months the Japanese sank only 10 merchantmen, 9 in the Southwest Pacific or Indian Ocean.

Allied losses soared with the introduction of the *kamikaze* suicide aircraft, which simply crashed into their victims; but the 14 ships sunk and 53 damaged in Philippine waters and northward owed nothing to the I-boats. With little to show for their sacrifice, the Japanese Navy lost 128 submarines in World War II (112 to the Americans), and the percentage of Japanese submariners lost exceeded even that of the U-boat force.

The Japanese submarine failure did not lie in technology but rather in faulty operational doctrine and poor communications security. The Japanese Navy expected its boats to attack enemy warships. Thus, Japanese submarine captains displayed much more aggressiveness in attacking U.S. warships than merchant ships. Yet, battleships and carriers had destroyers and destroyer-escorts to protect them. American anti-submarine operations improved with more escort vessels, aircraft, radar and sonar, and experience. In addition, served with Ultra information on Japanese submarine deployments, anti-submarine task forces consistently found Japanese submarines in predictable cordons in front of the Pacific Fleet. In one memorable twelve-day period in 1944, three U.S. destroyer-escorts sank six I-boats. Japanese submarines did not even specialize in operations against U.S. submarines until late in the war, when the Home Waters had become a pond for American boats. During the entire war, Japanese submarines sank only one American submarine, whereas U.S. submarines accounted for 17 Japanese submarines lost. The Japanese Navy's commitment to heroic naval battles produced one of the larger missed opportunities of the war—the chance to destroy the troop transports, oilers, and ammunition ships on which the Allies depended in the South Pacific.

The China-Burma-India Theater

The strategy for the defeat of Japan could not have been simpler: Allied air, land, and sea forces would advance on three broad axes to roll back the new Japanese empire to the Home Islands, which Allied forces would then invade and occupy, if necessary. British Commonwealth forces would advance from India through Burma to Malaya and Hong Kong; Australian-American forces would drive north and west from Australia into the Netherlands East Indies and the Philippines; and the United States, rich in naval air and surface units, would attack across the Central Pacific toward the Philippines and Formosa. Destruction of the Japanese armed forces (especially air and naval units) would proceed simultaneously with the ruination of Japan's economy, dependent upon seaborne oil, minerals, coal, rubber, and foodstuffs. Any amateur who could read a map could design such a grand strategy. Making it happen proved quite a different matter.

The Allied military experience in the China-Burma-India (CBI) theater demonstrated how difficult it would be to mount a cohesive offensive effort from nations with conflicting interests and asymmetrical capabilities. Not until 1943 did British commanders in India believe that their principal field force, the Fourteenth Army, could conduct even limited offensive operations. They tested their forces with a one-division advance along the Arakan coast and found the Japanese and terrain unconquerable. The Arakan offensive demonstrated what the Fourteenth Army commander, General William Slim, feared. Only wide-ranging amphibious operations could take his army past the rugged Chin Hills guarding Burma from the west and blocking access to the river valleys leading to Mandalay and Rangoon. A hardened field soldier who had learned his trade on the Western Front and in the Indian Army, Slim combined troop-leading and training skills with personal and moral courage as well as charm, a sound grasp of soldiering, and a solid appreciation of Asian warfare and the excellence of the Japanese Army. He had experienced the catastrophe of the 1942 retreat from Burma and the abortive attack in the Arakan. His honesty and character made him the obvious choice to reshape the Fourteenth Army, a force built on the Indian Army but including the ever-dependable Gurkha Rifles of Nepal, unproven infantry battalions from East and West Africa, and infantry battalions and supporting arms from the British Army.

In theory, the concept of amphibious envelopments reaching to Singapore made sense to everyone except the other Allies and much of the Royal Navy. With the demands of other theaters, the Allies could not find adequate amphibious shipping for even a modest operation aimed at Rangoon and scheduled for late 1943 or 1944. Slim now saw no alternative but an overland advance by his army, gradually reinforced from the Middle East and India proper, where the internal security mission required fewer British battalions by 1944. The Japanese Fifteenth Army, under Lieutenant General Mutaguchi Renya, also grew in the same months from four to eight divisions, thus raising the prospective cost to Slim of an overland battle through the mountains of western Burma. If Slim could find no reasonable alternative to a conventional offensive, others offered shining promises of easy victory. Churchill and Roosevelt, politicians and opportunists to the core, grasped these false options with enthusiasm.

Already tied to Nationalist China by sentiment and prior commitment, Roosevelt never abandoned his hope that Chiang Kai-shek's armies would go on the offensive and that Chiang himself could actually play the role of regional leader. From mid-1942 until mid-1943 Roosevelt struggled to keep China in the war, aided in his quest by Marshall and Stilwell. In October 1942 Roosevelt answered Chiang's Three Demands with limited promises of an air buildup in India and a serious effort to bring Lend-Lease supplies to Kunming by air. The Allies could complete the Ledo extension of the Burma Road only by driving at least one Japanese division from northern Burma with some sort of Sino-American army. Roosevelt did not promise to send ground combat forces, even though Stilwell favored this option. Encouraged by Hap Arnold's staff and Chennault (now commanding the Tenth Air Force in China) to think more about offensive air operations from China, Roosevelt in May 1943 chose (much to Stilwell's dismay and Chiang's delight) Chennault's concept of a major bomber offensive against China's coastal cities and Japanese sea lanes. Chennault, the air defense expert, suddenly promised victory through bombing, probably influenced by his nominal theater air commander, Major General Clayton D. Bissell, and Bissell's patron, Hap Arnold. The air plan, however, offered Stilwell some solace, since such a commitment required an open Ledo-Burma Road and a reformed Chinese Army to protect the bomber bases in

China. At the Quebec conference of August 1943, Churchill, Roosevelt, and the Combined Chiefs of Staff approved an offensive in north Burma.

With his schemes for amphibious operations frustrated by shipping shortages, Churchill supported American plans for the China-Burma-India theater, even though he had little faith in Nationalist China. Moreover, Churchill fell under the spell of one of the war's most eccentric and charismatic commanders, Brigadier Orde Wingate. A Middle Eastern expert with guerrilla successes in the Sudan, Ethiopia, and Palestine, Wingate argued for unconventional warfare in Burma. Slim doubted Wingate would find the Japanese as impressionable as his Middle Eastern foes, and he resented Wingate's influence with Churchill, who allowed Wingate to strip Fourteenth Army of some of its best British, Gurkha, and African troops.

Bursting with energy, Wingate formed the 3,300-man 77th Brigade in 1943, the Long Range Penetration Group (LRPG) or "Chindits," a nickname drawn from the ferocious winged lions of stone guarding Burma's temples. Wings had much to do with the Chindits, since Wingate expected his force to land by glider or parachute behind Japanese lines and then be resupplied by air. Fighter-bombers would provide fire support instead of artillery. The first experiment in February–June 1943 was no great success, proving only that Chindits got tired and sick like everyone else and could not live by airdrops alone. The Chindits killed three times as many Japanese as they themselves lost (68 to 28), but almost the entire force ended the operation unfit for future duty. Slim certainly did not see the Chindit operations as a substitute for his campaign.

Wingate's quixotic schemes then grew into a larger and more optimistic plan for a return to Burma in 1944 on the same model. Churchill liked the concept, while Stilwell saw Wingate's force as a useful instrument in his own plan to lead a Sino-American ground force against Myitkyina, a crucial road junction on the way to Lashio, terminus of the Burma Road. With the approval of Admiral Lord Louis Mountbatten, appointed the theater commander in September 1943, Wingate wrested control of troops in India that were outside Slim's command and formed a six-brigade LRPG of 20,000 officers and men. Stilwell had no comparable ground force. He had two small Chinese divisions under his direct control, and Marshall had provided only a makeshift infantry regimental combat team drawn from "volunteers" from the U.S. Army. Designated the 5307th Composite Unit Provisional, the unit preferred the name Merrill's Marauders, thus identifying themselves with Brigadier General Frank D. Merrill, one of Stilwell's favorite staff officers but an inexperienced commander with a serious heart condition.

Stilwell, however, had some other assets to entice Wingate into the north Burma campaign. First, he had the full cooperation of the American air forces (if not Chennault), since an open Ledo-Burma Road would dramatically reduce the airlift requirements over "the Hump," the dangerous southeastern extension of the Himalayas. Moreover, the prospect of Chinese bases attracted American bomber generals, who were not having great success yet over Germany and who had made huge investments in a new long-range bomber, the B-29 Superfortress. Arnold and Bissell organized their own special operations wing, the 5138th Air Force Unit or the 1st Air Commando Group, commanded by Colonel Philip "Flip" Cochran, who proved one of the most able officers in the China-Burma-India theater. Stilwell promised Wingate that Cochran's 200-aircraft group, which included fighter-bombers and transports as well as gliders and reconnaissance aircraft, would provide the Chindits the aerial support the RAF could not, if Wingate coordinated his operations with the Myitkyina expedition.

Both Stilwell and Wingate assumed they would enjoy the services of the pro-Allied Burma hill tribes. The major mountain tribal groups—Nagas, Kachins, Karens, Chans, and Shins—numbered a minority of about 7 million of Burma's 17 million people. The Nagas, Kachins, and Karens had served happily in the colonial security forces, had fought the Japanese in 1942, and now wanted weapons to fight Burmese collaborators and the Japanese. Many Karens had become Christians, and the Kachins rivaled the Gurkhas in their warriorlike qualities. In 1943 the hill tribes welcomed new guerrilla leaders from the United States and the Commonwealth, Detachment 101 of the OSS and Force 136 of the British Special Operations Directorate. Generously supplied with arms, money, supplies, and radios, these partisan teams rallied thousands of Kachin and Karen tribesmen. They, too, depended on the 1st Air Commando Group for support.

While Slim's Indian divisions conducted cautious offensive operations in central and south Burma in 1943–44, the Chindits, Marauders, and Chinese marched or flew into north-central and northern Burma in February and March 1944. Wingate did not intend to support Stilwell, but he died in an air crash in March, and his successor then coordinated the movement of the six LRPG brigades with Stilwell's force. Unfortunately, Stilwell underestimated the fighting skill and tenacity of the Japanese 18th Division, under Lieutenant General Tanaka Shinchi, and he used his forces (including air support) with such profligacy that the Chindits and 1st Air Commando were combat-ineffective before Myitkyina fell. The Marauders and three Chinese divisions fought their way to the headwaters of the Irrawaddy by April 1944 but exhausted themselves in the process. In the battles of Walawbum and Shadzup, only the timely arrival of the Chinese saved the

Marauders from disaster. Merrill himself collapsed with another heart attack.

Stilwell then ordered the remnants of his expeditionary force on a 65-mile trek to Myitkyina, which it besieged in June and finally captured in August with the help of more Chinese and the Burmese partisans. The campaign destroyed the Marauders and crippled the Chinese X Force. The campaign did not end, however, since Chiang had finally ordered Y Force into Burma from the east, while Marshall sent two more U.S. infantry regiments (Mars Force) to the CBI to replace the Marauders, who mustered barely 200 effectives from an original 3,000-man force. Chiang's price of cooperation was Stilwell's relief, since he viewed "Vinegar Joe" as pro-Communist. Stilwell did know which Chinese regime would seize the Mandate of Heaven. The Kuomintang, he noted, was characterized by "corruption, neglect, chaos, economy [bad], taxes . . . hoarding, black market, trading with the enemy." The Communists "reduce taxes, rents, interest . . . raise production, and standard of living, participate in government. Practice what they preach."[3] Vinegar Joe, sick and bitter, left the CBI before the north Burma force finally met Y Force at the Chinese border south of Lashio and allowed U.S. Army engineers to link the Ledo Road with the highway to Kunming.

By the time the land route to China had been reopened, the Chennault air plan had already come a cropper. Even Roosevelt finally accepted the conclusion his military chiefs had reached long before: the Chinese Nationalists would do little to defeat Japan. Within China, signs of shirking were only too clear. Inflation and corruption, fueled by American supplies and money, became rampant. Chinese military casualties fell below 300,000 for the first time since 1937. The American military mission in Chungking, now directed by Major General Albert C. Wedemeyer, believed that only the Communist Eighth Route Army and the OSS-supported Chinese-Mongolian partisans were real fighters.

The decline of the Nationalist Army did not reflect any lack of effort by Tenth Air Force's air transports in flying "the Hump." By August 1943, C-46s were delivering 5,000 tons of supplies a month to China, an unthinkable figure when Chiang had demanded that support a year earlier. By January 1944, Tenth Air Force effort reached 15,000 tons a month. The commitment took a heavy toll. The transport force lost at least one aircraft for every one of the 500 air miles between India and China; more than 1,000 aircrewmen perished along the route. At its peak strength, Tenth Air Force had 650 aircraft in the air every day, around the clock. This effort made it possible for Chennault to mount Operation Matterhorn, the strategic bombardment of Chinese and Formosan targets with B-24s and B-29s based in China.

The opportunity cost to the Chinese Nationalists was high, too, since 90 percent of the cargo tonnage in 1943–44 was aviation gasoline and ordnance, not Lend-Lease arms for the Chinese Army. This imbalance exacted its toll all too soon. As the airlift over "the Hump" provided more logistical support, Arnold sent more operational wings to China and created a new command for Chennault, the Fourteenth Air Force, which included one B-29 bombardment wing. When Churchill and Roosevelt met Chiang Kai-shek on their way to Teheran in November 1943, they promised Chiang, awash in self-importance, a great air war from China against Japan. Their meeting coincided with the first American bombardment of Formosa. They also promised to push operations in Burma to open the Ledo-Burma Road and increase Lend-Lease aid. In return for recognition of his role as Allied Generalissimo in Asia, Chiang promised to use his army to the best of its limited ability to support the American and British offensive.

The Japanese did not look kindly on the growing U.S. Army Air Forces presence in China, however, and ordered the China expeditionary army to begin ICHI-GO (Operation One) in January 1944. For the next ten months the Japanese Army pushed the Nationalists back and overran base after base, forcing the forward-based Fourteenth Air Force fighters and bombers deeper into China, more than half of which remained unconquered. The Chinese Army's resistance was erratic and ultimately futile, but Japanese casualties and the lengthening logistical tail of the Japanese divisions brought operations to a halt in January 1945. The Japanese generals in China cautioned Tokyo that they could not advance far enough to capture the bases of the new B-29s, which had a range of 4,000 miles.

The strategic bombing champions, however, had already concluded that an enlarged Matterhorn was too tall a challenge. With the decline of Fourteenth Air Force and military support of Chiang Kai-shek, operations in the China-Burma-India theater, divided into the Southeast Asia and Chinese theaters in 1944, reverted to a British Commonwealth effort to restore the British Empire, a goal the United States failed to support with any enthusiasm. The war with Japan would be won elsewhere.

Conclusion

Campaign by campaign, theater by theater, the Allies had mounted limited offensives against the Japanese armed forces and economy, but not one had paid any large dividends by early 1944. In their accumulated effect, however, especially the attrition of Japanese naval aviation and the fixing of scarce divisions of the Japanese Army in Asia, the Allied war along the Equator and the Malay barrier had stretched the Japanese defense lines almost to the breaking point and had even forced the virtual abandonment of the base system in the northern Solomons. Although the American and Commonwealth ground forces that were engaged in tropical combat suffered crippling losses, they represented only a fraction of the divisions that became available in 1944; for example, of the 21 U.S Army divisions that eventually fought the Japanese, only 8 fought in New Guinea and the Solomons. For all the beatings the U.S. Navy had to absorb in some 15 battles with the Imperial Japanese Navy in the South Pacific, battles in which it lost 31 warships, the navy could count on its losses being replaced and its damaged warships hastily repaired. The Japanese had no such assurances. Moreover, even if Nationalist China did not fulfill FDR's expectations, the United States had gained a determined ally in Australia. The Commonwealth's campaign had forced Japan to keep a substantial part of its army in Southeast Asia as well as in China. Somewhere, somehow, the Allies would find a way to break through Japan's thinning perimeter defenses.

10

THE BATTLE
OF THE ATLANTIC

1939–1943

In mid-March 1943, the Battle of the Atlantic reached its climax. Three great convoys, two fast and one slow, crossed the Central Atlantic on their way to Britain. Altogether, 28 escort vessels would be involved at one time or another in protecting these convoys. The slow convoy (SC 122, with 60 merchant ships) successfully maneuvered past a patrol line of U-boats. But the two fast convoys (HX 229, with 40 merchant vessels, and HX 229A, with 38 merchant ships), because of their escorts' inability to refuel in heavy weather, sailed up directly behind SC 122. Then, having avoided the U-boat line due to special intelligence, by chance HX 229 ran into a single U-boat (U-653), returning home with a damaged engine. Informed of the fast convoys' location, the U-boat high command concentrated ten boats on what it believed was the slow-moving convoy, SC 122.

In a terrifying night of torpedo explosions, star shells, lifeboats strewn across the sea, and sinking ships, the harried escorts desperately sought to master a deteriorating situation. They failed. Almost at will, U-boats sailed in and out of the convoy and fired at ships and escorts alike. They sank seven merchant vessels. Moreover, the proximity of SC 122, only 150 miles ahead of HX 229, brought the U-boats down on it as well. As U-338 was rushing to join the attack on HX 229, it ran into SC 122 and in less than ten minutes fired five torpedoes and sank four ships. Only the arrival of long-range aircraft from Northern Ireland prevented complete catastrophe.

In a three-day running battle, U-boats sank 21 of the 90 merchant vessels in the three convoys. By 20 March they had already put more than half a million tons of Allied shipping out of service. The biting smell of fuel oil, the sound of exploding torpedoes and ships breaking up, and the fear in the eyes of rescued merchant sailors underlined the catastrophe. If the U-boats had continued their success, they might have broken the will of the merchant sailors and stopped the North Atlantic convoys. But they did not, and their failure carried with it the most important victory the Allies won in World War II; for without that victory at sea, the Combined Bomber Offensive, the invasion of Europe, and the flow of Lend-Lease to the Eastern Front would have been in jeopardy.

Under bleak North Atlantic skies, as sailors stood for interminable hours on pitching decks pelted by rain, snow, and sleet, watching and waiting for attacks that all prayed would never come, Allied convoys sailed against a determined foe. Upon the success or failure of their efforts depended the Anglo-American attempt to project their industrial and military power back onto the European Continent. The Battle of the Atlantic lasted from 3 September 1939 through the end of the war in Europe. It involved massive industrial resources, the exploitation of modern technology, and the decisive intercession of intelligence during critical periods of the battle. In the end, victory in the Battle of the Atlantic repaid the Allies for their efforts and extracted from the Germans a heavy price they could ill afford.

The Early War

At the outbreak of hostilities in September 1939, the weakness of the German battle fleet (consisting of just two battle cruisers) dictated a return to the war on British commerce that the U-boats had waged in World War I. But here too the Germans were not prepared. German submariners had not thought through many of the larger operational problems involved in a campaign against Allied commerce. They possessed a small but elite force of submarines and a new tactical approach that aimed to mass the U-boats in groups ("wolfpacks") to attack Allied convoys. But the small size of their U-boats (750 tons), the lack of an effective naval intelligence service, and a general technological backwardness placed the U-boat effort in a doubtful position for the conduct of a long-term campaign.

In late August 1939, the Kriegsmarine deployed its submarines into the Atlantic and unleashed its surface raiders and warships on British trade. The sinking of the pocket battleship *Graf Spee* (a glorified heavy cruiser slightly over 10,000 tons armed with 11″ guns) near Montevideo in December 1939 indicated considerable problems with Admiral Erich Raeder's strategy of using his large warships as commerce raiders. Raeder was the ultimate battleship admiral. In the prewar period he had dismissed carriers as useless, underestimated the U-boat's possibility, and aimed the Kriegsmarine to fight a surface war against British commerce. But World War II broke out well before *his* navy was ready. On 3 September he noted inconsolably: "Today the war against England and France broke out . . . It is self-evident that the navy is in no manner sufficiently equipped in the fall of 1939 to embark on a great struggle with England . . . Surface forces . . . are still so few in numbers and strength compared to the English fleet that they . . . can only show that they know how to die with honor."[1] Displaying a ruthless discipline that rivaled that of the army, Raeder and his successor ensured that the German Navy lived up to this hope. There would be no naval mutiny as had occurred in 1918.

The U-boats, however, achieved considerable success in the first two months of the war; but when they had to return to harbor to refit and resupply, Allied losses to enemy submarines dropped below 100,000 tons per month. Through April 1940 the U-boats proved a deadly nuisance but nothing more. There were some spectacular exploits, such as Günther Prein's sinking of the battleship *Royal Oak* after a hair-raising journey into the well-defended anchorage at Scapa Flow in the Orkney Islands. But the experiences of the first months of the war confirmed the last war's lessons: convoys, even with minimal escorts, were essential to the survival of merchant shipping. By the end of 1939, out of 5,756 vessels sailing in convoys, U-boats had sunk only five.

The long-term problems confronting the Royal Navy, however, were considerable. It possessed too few escorts, air support was minimal, and the escorts had yet to face the wolfpacks. Moreover, because it had woefully underestimated the U-boat menace, the navy had not developed tactics and operational concepts adequate to protect large convoys. As for the Royal Air Force, it offered little help. Not until late 1942 did the RAF Coastal Command begin to receive the resources it needed to play its part in the battle. In many respects, then, the British response to the U-boat campaign represented a series of desperate measures to keep Allied commerce flowing at the levels required to support the war effort, to enhance Britain's war production, and to sustain the British people through it all.

The fall of France in June 1940 altered the geographic framework of the Battle of the Atlantic. In early July, U-30 entered Lorient from its Atlantic patrol—the first submarine in what would become a massive basing of U-boats on the French coast. From French bases, U-boats had easy access to the terminus of Britain's sea lines of communications, while the Luftwaffe could conduct its reconnaissance missions and air attacks on shipping with greater ease. Nevertheless, because Raeder devoted much of the German Navy's construction to the surface fleet of battleships and cruisers in the early war years the number of new boats entering operational service in 1940 barely matched U-boat losses. In July 1940, Vice Admiral Karl Dönitz, commander of U-boats, controlled only 29 boats.

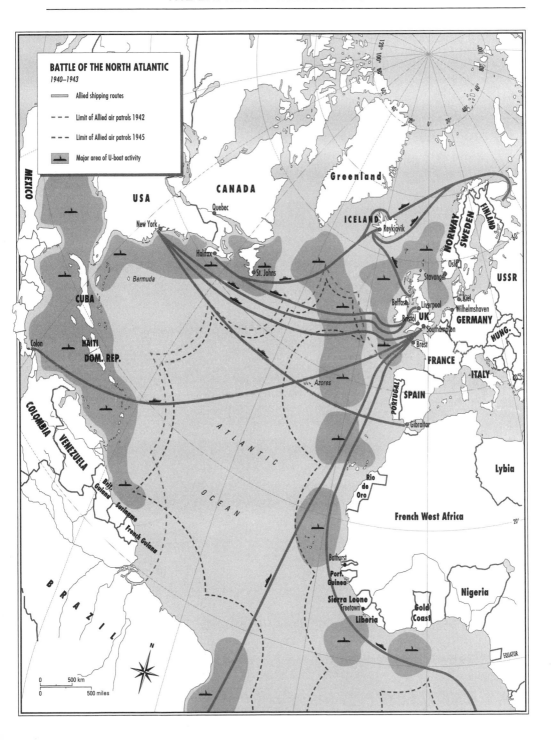

BATTLE OF THE NORTH ATLANTIC
1940–1943

	Allied shipping routes
– – –	Limit of Allied air patrols 1942
– – –	Limit of Allied air patrols 1945
	Major area of U-boat activity

Greenland

CANADA

USA

Quebec

New York

Halifax

St. Johns

Bermuda

CUBA

HAITI
DOM. REP.

Colon

COLOMBIA

VENEZUELA

Brit. Guiana

Suriname

French Guiana

B R A Z I L

A T L A N T I C

O C E A N

Azores

ICELAND

Reykjavik

NORWAY

SWEDEN

FINLAND

Oslo

Stavanger

Kiel

Belfast

Liverpool

Bristol

UK

Southampton

Brest

FRANCE

SPAIN

PORTUGAL

Gibraltar

Wilhelmshaven

GERMANY

HUNG.

ITALY

USSR

Lybia

Rio
de
Oro

French West Africa

Bathurst

Port.
Guinea

Sierra Leone

Freetown

Liberia

Gold
Coast

Nigeria

EQUATOR

MEXICO

N

0   500 km

0   500 miles

Dönitz had been a highly decorated U-boat commander in World War I until captured by the British in 1918. After a successful career in surface vessels that lasted into the mid-1930s he took over the effort to rebuild the U-boat force. Dönitz was a confirmed Nazi who believed that submarines offered the best avenue to defeat the British. He was also a micromanager, and his obsessive control of U-boats at sea and the concomitant reliance on massive numbers of Enigma messages to and from the U-boats played a major role in the ability of the British to break into the highest levels of German radio traffic. Dönitz also displayed little interest in technology until it was too late; as a result, his boats would confront vastly more sophisticated opponents in the climactic battles of 1943 with the technological capabilities they had possessed at the war's outset.

Dönitz's operational aim for his offensive was simple: to sink the maximum number of Allied ships possible, without regard to their cargoes, their destination, or even whether they had any cargo on board at all. Yet the number of U-boats on station in the Atlantic rarely reached ten over the rest of 1940. This was because at any given time one-third of the U-boat fleet was in harbor refurbishing and repairing, while another third of the fleet was in transit either to or from areas of operations.

Still, British production of escort vessels was hardly more effective in bridging the gap between requirements and availability. From September 1939 through May 1940, British shipyards launched only 14 destroyers and, through the end of 1940, a bare 6 anti-submarine sloops. Because of the Royal Navy's desperate need for anti-submarine vessels, it opted for a stop-gap measure, the corvette, a ship based on whale-catchers that British dockyards had built for the Norwegians. Weighing less than a thousand tons, corvettes were barely faster than U-boats on the surface. As for their handling characteristics, a veteran of corvettes in the North Atlantic once suggested that they rolled on wet grass.

Exacerbating British problems was the high cost of the Norwegian campaign in spring 1940 and the Dunkirk evacuation in May and early June; then in summer the threat of a possible German amphibious invasion tied up many British destroyers through the end of October in defense of the Channel. Consequently, a small number of U-boats were able to inflict heavy casualties on the lightly protected convoys that reached the British Isles in summer and fall. From July to September, U-boats averaged nearly a quarter of a million tons sunk per month, at a cost of less than two boats per month. In October, British losses rose to 352,407 tons, virtually all within 250 miles of Ireland's northwest corner.

The fate of convoys SC 7, HX 79, and HX 79a in mid-October 1940 demonstrates the destruction U-boats could inflict when concentrated. The Germans picked up SC 7, a slow convoy, and deployed five boats, including Otto Kretschmer's deadly U-99, on the unlucky ships. Despite a reinforcement of four escorts, many of the captains of the merchant vessels panicked and the convoy scattered, making the job easier for the Germans. Kretschmer, who sank 6 of the 18 ships lost by the convoy, reported the explosions of torpedoes all over the convoy. His war diary recorded: "2358: Bow shot at large freighter approx 6,000 tons. Range 750 yards. Hit below foremast. The explosion of the torpedo was immediately followed by a high sheet of flame and an explosion which ripped the ship open as far as the bridge and left a cloud of smoke 600 feet high. Ship's forepart apparently shattered. Ship still burning fiercely, with green flames."[2]

Having barely recovered from the first night's battle, the U-boats ran into HX 79 the next evening. That convoy had no less than nine escorts, but they were not well-trained, and the U-boats ran down the convoy columns, firing torpedoes to port and starboard, while the escorts chased fruitlessly around the perimeter. Over a three-day period the Germans sank 38 ships while losing only a single boat. From their point of view, this was indeed "a happy time." Yet for all the losses the British suffered in these battles, one figure stands out: of 217 merchant ships lost to U-boats in the last half of 1940, only 73 (roughly a third) occurred in convoys. Clearly, all too many British merchant vessels were still sailing independently, without the protection of escort vessels. Churchill noted after the war: "How willingly would I have exchanged a full-scale attempt at invasion for this shapeless, measureless peril expressed in charts, curves, and statistics!"[3]

October was the worst month of 1940. When the threat of a German invasion of Britain ended, the number of destroyers available for escort service increased, and the Royal Navy could devote greater resources to the battle in the Atlantic. From a high of 352,407 tons in October, losses dropped to 146,613 in November and 212,590 in December. Confronting stronger convoy escorts in British waters, the U-boats moved out into the broad expanses of the Central Atlantic. There, the Germans found it more difficult to locate convoys and to concentrate U-boats. The Germans were also paying for their failure to increase submarine construction significantly in the first year of the war. Despite the successes of his U-boat aces, Dönitz had not succeeded in cutting off the British Isles from their vital sources of supply.

In the early days of the war, the U-boat command had struck with minimal resources in a favorable tactical situation. But the Germans had failed to think through the long-range implications of what they were doing; their early successes afforded the British fair warning as well as time to adapt. Thus, in the long run, the U-boat campaign of 1940 was counterproductive. It was incapable of striking a decisive blow, and yet it alerted the British to the fact that U-boats posed a threat to their national existence. In the end, the Germans set in motion a host of frantic research and development programs within the Royal Navy and Air Force that eventually led to improved radar and sonar for anti-submarine vessels, better depth charges, the hedgehog (a forward-firing anti-submarine weapon that did not interfere with a ship's sonar), anti-submarine torpedoes that aircraft could drop, and direction-finding equipment (D/F) that provided escort vessels with accurate bearings on the radio transmissions of U-boats that were stalking their convoys. The British also initiated operational research to improve anti-submarine tactics and alter the size of convoys to maximize the effectiveness of escorts.

In 1940 the United States, which barely produced a million tons of merchant vessels that year, recognized that the German assault on world shipping posed a significant threat to its own strategic position. The Roosevelt administration initiated planning for a massive merchant shipbuilding program, and by summer 1941 Henry J. Kaiser's yards in the United States launched their first vessels. Soon they would also develop the Liberty ship, which was constructed in sections and then welded together—a mass-production concept that revolutionized shipbuilding. The availability of hundreds of Liberty ships entirely undermined the strategic assumptions of Dönitz's U-boat campaign. Ironically, if the Germans' fall 1940 U-boat campaign had not proved so destructive to British shipping, the American program might well have begun later and reached lower levels of production in the ensuing years.

In fall 1940 the U.S. government made a direct commitment to the Battle of the Atlantic in response to a growing recognition by Americans that the war in Europe was relevant to U.S. interests and that the United States needed to support the Allied effort. In September the British and U.S. governments signed an agreement that provided Britain with substantial war materiel, including 50 "surplus" U.S. destroyers that had been mothballed at the end of World War I. In exchange, the United States received leasing rights to bases in Newfoundland, Bermuda, Nova Scotia, and British possessions in the Caribbean. This agreement would prove crucial to Britain's ability to conduct the war in Europe. Although the aged destroyers were miserable ships in terms of their handling characteristics, they provided an

31. Japanese soldiers guard Chinese prisoners captured during the Shanghai Incident in 1932. Antiforeign destruction and violence gave the Japanese a rationale for a major military campaign, a prelude to war in 1937.

32. Vice Admiral Yamamoto Isoroku (left), vice minister of the Navy, and Admiral Osumi Mineo (right), minister of the Navy, led the purge of Treaty of Washington sympathizers from the Japanese Navy in 1936-1938 and prepared the fleet for war with the United States. Admiral Yamamoto later commanded the Combined Fleet in the operations against Pearl Harbor (1941) and Midway (1942).

33. An abandoned child wails among the wreck-
age of a Shanghai railroad station after a
Japanese bombing attack in 1937. The Japanese
campaign on Shanghai destroyed the best
Chinese Nationalist divisions but slowed the
Japanese advance up the Yangtze River valley.

34. Chinese civilian dead clog
the stairways to Chungking's
underground air-raid shelters.
Victims of a panic-stricken mob,
4,000 innocents perished in the
struggle to reach safety.

35. Chinese civilians bear the brunt of Japanese firepower in 1937, as the Axis
powers try to destroy enemy governments by direct attack on noncombatants.

36. A section of the Ledo Road, built in 1942-1944, reflects the engineering challenges of maintaining overland contact between the Allied bases in India and the Nationalist Chinese armies and American air-bases in China. Allied supplies had to be flown over "the Hump" of the Himalayas by transport planes until the Ledo Road was completed.

37. Australian infantrymen of the 8th Division cross a Malayan river in 1941. A numerically inferior Japanese army outmaneuvered and outfought a British-Indian-Australian defense force and captured Singapore in February 1942.

38. The flight deck crew of the Japanese carrier *Akagi* raises a rousing *banzai* as the first wave of dive-bombers and torpedo planes launch for the attack on Pearl Harbor, 7 December 1941.

39. On the ramp of the Ford Island naval air station at Pearl Harbor, U.S. Navy PBY amphibian scout aircraft and reconnaissance-gunfire spotter SOC-4 float planes burn after the first Japanese attack. The principal Japanese targets, the carriers *Enterprise* and *Lexington*, were at sea and escaped the attack.

40. The battleship *Arizona* rests on the bottom at its anchorage off Ford Island, Pearl Harbor. A heavy Japanese bomb penetrated the deck and set off an explosion of the forward magazine, killing 1,103 officers and men of the Navy and Marine Corps, most of whom were trapped below decks, where they remain today in the *Arizona* memorial.

41. The Japanese killed 2,335 American servicemen and 68 civilians in the raid, while losing only 55 aircrewmen and 29 aircraft, as well as 12 submarines. These Hawaiian civilians perished under the guns of a strafing Zero.

42. An Army Air Forces B-25 medium bomber leaves the carrier *Hornet* for a raid on Tokyo and three other Japanese cities on 18 April 1942. The bombers, commanded by Lieutenant Colonel James H. Doolittle, did little damage but raised American morale and angered the Japanese enough to cause them to mount a raid on Midway Island.

43. In a rare moment of shared pleasure, Generalissimo Chiang Kai-shek, Mrs. Chiang (Soong Mei Ling), and Lieutenant General Joseph W. Stilwell of the U.S. Army pose for photographers at Stilwell's headquarters in Burma, where a Chinese Nationalist army had gone to aid Britain in 1942. The Japanese drove Stilwell's expeditionary force back to China.

44. The American defenders of the fortress island of Corregidor in Manila Bay, the Philippines, emerge from Malinta Tunnel, head-quarters for General Douglas MacArthur and his successor, Lieutenant General Jonathan M. Wainwright. Corregidor's capitulation on 6 May 1942 ended organized resistance to the Japanese in the Philippines.

45. U.S. Navy Douglas SBD-3 scout-bombers attack Japanese warships off Midway in June 1942. In two days the scout-bomber squadrons of three U.S. carriers sank four Japanese heavy carriers and one cruiser, the first defeat for the Japanese Combined Fleet and a turning point in the war.

46. Chinese Nationalist infantrymen, directed by Stilwell, engage the Japanese in northern Burma in order to open an overland route for Allied supplies to China. Two divisions from the American-trained and supplied Yunnan Force played a decisive role in the capture of the transportation center of Mytikyina in May-June 1944.

47. American infantrymen from the 43rd Infantry Division land on Rendova Island, central Solomons, during the South Pacific campaign of 1942-1944. The purpose of the campaign was to capture the major Japanese base of Rabaul.

48. Greek troops deep in the mountains of Albania near Mt. Eyuzati in early winter 1941 drive the Italians back. The Italian invasion of Greece from Albania unleashed a catastrophe for the peoples of the Balkans.

49. Rommel visits the 15th Panzer Division between Tobruk and Sidi Omar during the swirling Crusader battle. Caught by surprise for one of the few times in the war, Rommel nevertheless came close to defeating the British effort to relieve Tobruk.

50. British armored forces moving past Tobruk in spring 1942. Obviously no Germans are nearby, as the crews are exposed.

51. In El Alamein, Egypt, the Germans have soldiers of the Australian 2/3rd Pioneer Battalion pinned down from three sides near a railroad embankment, 31 October 1942.

52. In late winter 1942 Soviet troops, supported by armor, attack a village held by German troops.

53. The Soviets counterattack during heavy fighting at Stalingrad in late fall 1942. The condition of the urban terrain speaks for itself after two months of ferocious combat.

54. German troops begin their retreat from the Caucasus in winter 1942-43. While they did not confront fighting as heavy as that in Stalingrad, the winter conditions and the foreboding landscape suggest the travails German troops confronted on the Eastern Front.

55. Long columns of German POWs make their way out of Stalingrad after Paulus's surrender. Of the 90,000 who fell into Soviet hands, barely 5,000 survived the war to return to Germany in the 1950s.

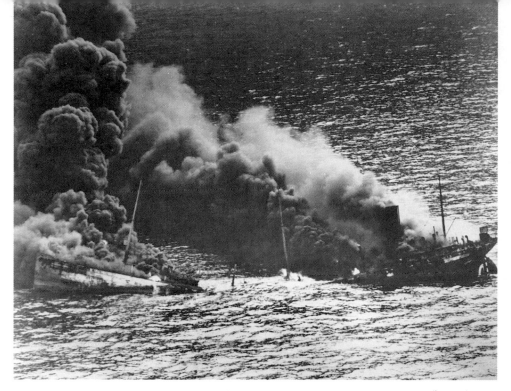

56. In clouds of smoke and burning petroleum, another Allied tanker goes to the bottom, a victim of U-boats. There was little chance that the crew escaped.

57. On 17 April 1943 the U.S. Coast Guard cutter *Spencer* attacks and sinks the U-175. Crewmen watch as depth charges explode. The convoy continues on its way.

58. German sailors watch as a pattern of aerial-dropped depth charges begins to work its way directly toward the U-boat. The first explosion is already visible.

59. Three members of a submarine crew sit on board a U.S. Coast Guard cutter after their capture.

60. Workmen finish the hull of a submarine at the Electric Boat Company in Groton, Connecticut. Another sub is silhouetted in the background.

61. Mass-produced Liberty ships await their final fitting out before they are loaded with supplies and move into the vast Pacific.

62. This Ford assembly plant in Willow Run, Michigan, which produced B-24s, and others like it led a British historian to write that by 1943 U.S. factories were turning out bombers like candy bars.

63. Nancy Harkness Love, director of the U.S. Woman's Auxiliary Ferry Squadron, prepares to pilot an aircraft from the factory to its overseas departure base. As the war continued, women came to play an increasingly important role in the support structure.

invaluable reinforcement to the British and Canadian navies in a time of dire need.

By early January 1941, the Battle of the Atlantic had reached an impasse. The Germans awaited the arrival of their new boats, while the British searched for reinforcements for their escort forces. Neither side could interest their air staffs in contributing significant assets to the battle. The Luftwaffe made a half-hearted effort by adapting its four-engine transport, the Focke-Wulf 200C Condor, to service in the Atlantic. Flying from Brittany, the Condors circled far into the Atlantic and then back to land in Norway. They proved invaluable for reconnaissance as well as attacks on convoys; one of their number even played a major role in sinking the large liner *Empress of Britain* in October 1940 by bombing the liner and starting major fires on board. But Göring refused to provide further resources to the navy, while the Condor found it difficult to stand up to the strains of combat.

The RAF proved just as reluctant as the Luftwaffe to devote air power to the Atlantic war. Its senior leaders argued that bombers could make a greater contribution by attacking Germany and disrupting the naval war production effort there than in fighting U-boats that were already in operation. In retrospect, the air staff's position represented nothing more than its ideological faith in strategic bombing. In fact, until 1943 Bomber Command's attacks on the Third Reich had little effect on German industry and morale, while the gap in air cover in the Central Atlantic remained unclosed until spring 1943. All the while, statistics were proving again and again that convoys with air cover suffered substantially fewer casualties than convoys that had to fight their defensive battles with only surface forces.

Besides aircraft and submarines, the Royal Navy confronted another danger in the Atlantic in the first half of 1941. Not only did the Germans send out well-equipped raiders disguised as merchant ships, but the Kriegsmarine's surface fleet displayed an aggressiveness that it would not show for the rest of the war. By the end of 1940, German dockyards had completed refits of the battle cruisers *Scharnhorst* and *Gneisenau* from damage suffered off Norway's North Cape in early June. After a short workup, the battle cruisers embarked on a raid on North Atlantic convoys in late January 1941. Slipping past British air and sea patrols, they broke out into the Central Atlantic. Refueling from tankers and supply ships sent ahead, the battle cruisers attacked only those convoys or ships without heavy escort. Over a two-month period they sank 115,622 tons of merchant shipping and thoroughly disrupted North Atlantic convoy routes; and then, at the end of March, they slipped safely into the French port of Brest.

By April the *Bismarck,* the newest and most powerful German battleship, had completed its sea trials and the training of its crew. Since the *Scharnhorst* was due for a major refit, Raeder planned to send the *Gneisenau* out to meet the *Bismarck* in the Central Atlantic, the two ships to be accompanied by the heavy cruisers *Prinz Eugen* and *Hipper.* But an extraordinarily brave attack on *Gneisenau* by RAF Coastal Command aircraft hit the battle cruiser with a single torpedo that put it in dry-dock. Then, over the night of 10–11 April, British bombers hit the *Gneisenau* still in dry-dock and caused further damage. That attack removed the heavy ships available in Brest from service, at least temporarily.

Nevertheless, Raeder decided to send *Bismarck* and *Prinz Eugen* out into the Atlantic against the convoy routes despite the protests of the surface fleet commander, Vice Admiral Günther Lütjens, that an attack on the North Atlantic convoy system by a single battleship was too risky. Raeder overruled Lütjens, who now commanded an operation about which he had considerable doubts. Raeder's decision most probably rested on the hope that the navy could gain a major success before Operation Barbarossa began on the Eastern Front, since that war would certainly not highlight his service or its contributions to the Third Reich.

The *Bismarck* sortie began badly. The Swedes picked up the battleship's movement past their shores and relayed the intelligence to the Royal Navy. British photo reconnaissance aircraft then monitored the arrival and departure of the German ships from Norway. As the Germans slipped through the Denmark Straits, two Royal Navy cruisers picked up the *Bismarck* and *Prinz Eugen* with their radar in the early evening of 23 May. The cruisers shadowed the Germans out toward the open Atlantic. The following morning the Royal Navy's battle cruiser *Hood* and the new battleship *Prince of Wales* intercepted the German ships. But instead of attacking on a head-on course that would have limited the lightly armored *Hood's* exposure to plunging fire, the British intercepted on an almost parallel course— one, moreover, that masked their aft turrets, allowing them to fire only from their forward turrets. Thus ensued a long-range gun duel that favored the Germans. Just after 0600 on 24 May, a 15″ shell from the *Bismarck* hit one of the *Hood's* magazines; the resulting explosion blew up the battle cruiser. There were only three survivors. The *Prince of Wales,* still unprepared for combat with civilian workmen on board, was in no condition to match the *Bismarck* and withdrew, leaving the shadowing to the cruisers.

The *Bismarck* and *Prinz Eugen* eventually escaped their shadowers, and for a while it appeared that both would reach Brest. But a Catalina long-range patrol aircraft, provided by American Lend-Lease, spotted the *Bismarck*, now alone, in the Central Atlantic. At extreme range, Swordfish torpedo aircraft from the *Ark Royal* carried out attacks despite scudding clouds and rain. Out of 13 torpedoes, only two found their mark, but one jammed the *Bismarck*'s rudders, so that the battleship lost steering headway and resulted in the great ship moving in endless circles. That lucky hit allowed pursuing British forces to catch the German battleship the following morning.

A sustained gun duel took place in which the superior British forces pounded the *Bismarck*. The damage the German battleship absorbed indicated the wonderful workmanship of German industry, but the episode again underscored the bankruptcy of Germany's naval strategy. While the sortie had destroyed the *Hood*, the destruction of the *Bismarck* more than compensated for the British loss. Raeder's strategy of surface raiders had largely failed. *Scharnhorst* and *Gneisenau* lay in French ports, where they remained a threat to the convoy routes but where they themselves were under constant threat of attack from the RAF's Bomber Command.

As the U-boat battle moved into the Central Atlantic at the end of 1940, the problem for both sides was intelligence. The Germans had to find the convoys; the British needed a way to avoid the U-boat lines that Dönitz placed across likely convoy routes. Signals intelligence—the use of enemy signals to determine the location of units and decryption of those messages—became critical to both sides. Initially, the Germans enjoyed an advantage, but one balanced by the fact that early in the war there was less radio traffic to catch than there was later. Consequently, the two sides played a game of blindman's bluff in the dismal midwinter Atlantic gales—conditions almost as trying for submariners as for corvette crews. To add to German woes, in December 1940 the British Admiralty began evasive routing of convoys away from concentrations of U-boats, which the British identified with intelligence obtained from radio D/F stations.

Nevertheless, by March 1941 Dönitz could deploy increasing numbers of U-boats to the Central Atlantic, virtually all of which remained beyond the range of British long-range bombers. Through decrypts of British radio communications as well as U-boat sightings, the Germans were able to concentrate wolfpacks on convoys that were sailing through this gap in British air cover. The U-boats were clearly gaining the upper hand, but they were not completely successful. In March alone, four U-boat aces either went down with their boats or were captured. Captain Donald MacIntyre's well-trained escort group sank Joachim Schepke's and Kretschmer's boats with the help of the deadly new Type 271 radar. A British destroyer caught Schepke on the surface and rammed his boat. These were critical losses for the Germans, considering that in the course of the war no more than 30 U-boat skippers, or 2 percent, would account for 30 percent of the ships lost by the Allies. Over 75 percent of the U-boats launched never sank a single Allied vessel.

Still, the U-boat menace was growing steadily. In March and April 1941 German submarines sank nearly half a million tons of shipping; in May, 324,550 tons; and in June, 318,740 tons. By July Dönitz would possess 65 U-boats, and by January 1942 the count would reach 91. There seemed little the British could do in the face of these swelling numbers; the German U-boat force's increasing strength did not augur well for British prospects for the last six months of 1941.

Intelligence Enters the Battle

The appearance of radio transmitting and receiving devices early in the twentieth century allowed modern states to wage war over ever greater distances and with ever more dispersed forces. Navies in particular, with their ships scattered over thousands of miles of oceans, depended on these instruments for precise coordination. But radio message traffic was easily intercepted—thus the need to encode operational messages. In the 1920s a German business firm had developed a machine, the Enigma, which seemingly offered an unbreakable means to encode and decode messages. The person sending the message typed it out on a standard keyboard; then, through a complex system of rotors and connectors, Enigma encrypted the material, which was sent to a receiving unit. By using the same settings, the receiving unit was able to transcribe the message back into plain text. The German Navy and Army (and later the Luftwaffe) quickly adopted the Enigma system to protect their communications.

But unbeknownst to the Germans, the Poles obtained an Enigma machine in the early 1930s, and their mathematicians broke into the German message traffic. In 1939 the Germans stopped the Poles from reading Enigma messages by making their military encoding machines more complex. But in August of that year, by presenting the British with both a machine and a full briefing on their work just before their country went down in flames, Polish intelligence provided the British with a theoretical and actual depiction of how the Enigma system worked.

Since those using the Enigma system changed the position of rotors each day, British codebreakers had to determine the new rotor settings every 24 hours. To do this, they could either rely on the capture of the German schedule for the daily settings—an unreliable means—or discover mistakes (cribs) made by German operators or stations (such as transmitting the same message heading at the same time each day). The Luftwaffe's radio operators were notoriously careless with their procedures, and as a result the British had begun reading the Luftwaffe's message traffic in summer 1940 with increasing accuracy and speed. The resulting intelligence was codenamed "very special intelligence," or Ultra.

The operators in the German Navy were more careful. Thus, through spring 1941 British cryptologists enjoyed little success in breaking into the naval message traffic. But all that was about to change. In March 1941 the British captured the German armed trawler *Krebs* during a raid on the Lofoten Islands north of Norway. Along with the vessel they seized the enciphering tables for its Enigma machine. That in turn allowed Bletchley Park—the location of the British decryption effort—to begin breaking into the German Navy's message traffic.

From that success and the resulting decryption of communications, the British learned that the Germans were operating a weather ship off the coast of Iceland. In early May the Royal Navy mounted a well-planned cutting-out operation that captured the ship along with the Enigma keys for June. Two days later the Royal Navy seized an even bigger prize when convoy escorts captured U-110, commanded by the ace Julius Lemp, and stripped the boat of all Enigma materials, including the keys for the highly secret "officers only" traffic.

The Germans had anticipated that the British might achieve such a coup but confidently believed that their enemies would be able to break into Enigma transmissions only during the immediate months for which they possessed the list of Enigma settings. German signals experts had not calculated on the scale of the British codebreaking effort, which drew on the experiences of the Poles and the French as well as their own in cracking other Enigma codes. Once Bletchley Park had a chance to analyze the German Navy's radio traffic over May and June, British codebreakers began reading German transmissions to and from U-boats with great regularity. Consequently, even after the captured keys had run their course, the British had established enough cribs to read the traffic for the remainder of 1941. Moreover, access to messages between U-boat Headquarters and its boats allowed Bletchley Park to gain an almost complete operational picture of its opponents: how Dönitz deployed his boats; how he concentrated the wolfpacks; how long U-boats operated at sea; and what Dönitz's operational intentions were at any given time.

The results were immediate and perceptible. The first successes came when Royal Navy task groups destroyed the supply ships the Germans had sent into the Atlantic to resupply the surface raiders and U-boats. Those ships had played a crucial role in the battle cruiser raid in the winter and had refueled the *Prinz Eugen,* allowing that ship to make Brest. Learning their locations through decrypts of messages that ordered them to meet with U-boats or other ships, the Royal Navy had destroyed all the German supply ships by early June. Ironically, two of these ships were not supposed to be attacked for fear of compromising Ultra, but were run down in chance sightings. The Germans conducted two investigations of this sudden logistical massacre, one in summer 1941 and the second in 1942, but investigations failed because they started from the premise that Enigma was unbreakable.

The elimination of the supply ships, followed by attacks on German raiders, eased the strain on the Royal Navy. Ultra's contribution to the antisubmarine battle now became the most significant intelligence victory of the war, and the only episode in which intelligence alone had a decisive impact on military operations. British codebreaking successes allowed the convoy planners at Headquarters Western Approaches (the headquarters responsible for protecting the great convoys in the Atlantic) to determine where the Germans were establishing patrol lines in the Central Atlantic to intercept convoys; for the rest of 1941 they were then able to alter the courses of convoys to avoid such danger spots. To the U-boats, the Atlantic seemed suddenly empty, as one convoy after another sailed out of harm's way. The British had few new weapons, no additional resources, and no new tactics; yet the drop in losses was remarkable. They had recently increased the speed of ships that sailed independently, but that does not seem to have been decisive.

Convoy HX 13 suggests what the new intelligence contributed. U-203 had sighted and reported the convoy's course in late June 1941. Immediately, the tracking room at Headquarters Western Approaches changed the convoy's course and redeployed escorts from two other convoys that were not under threat of attack. Coastal Command aircraft also came to the defense of HX 13, which forced the gathering U-boats to submerge and made it difficult for them to track the convoy's course. After five days Dönitz gave up; he had lost two of his boats and several others sustained damage, while the convoy had lost only five merchant vessels.

Ultra's greatest contribution lay in the number of convoys that escaped U-boat attention altogether. In July 1941, the first month that the British had the full benefit of Ultra, the losses due to U-boats dropped to 94,209 tons, the lowest since May 1940. But July was no fluke. In August the British lost only 80,310 tons to U-boats. In September and October the numbers rose to 202,820 tons and 156,554 tons respectively, only to drop again to the astonishingly low levels of 62,196 and 124,070 tons in November and December. Increased losses in September and October were almost entirely due to German reconnaissance aircraft that picked up and monitored the progress of convoys moving between Gibraltar and the British Isles. Ultra intelligence could do nothing about diverting convoys away from the danger posed by aerial reconnaissance. If anything, the strains on British escort resources were increasing throughout the period. The serious situation in the Mediterranean, the threatening storm in the Far East, and, at the end of September, the departure of the first British convoy to Murmansk with help for the Soviet Union all stretched British resources to the breaking point. Moreover, the number of U-boats available to the Germans was growing steadily in the last half of 1941.

The losses on the Gibraltar run reached such a grave point by October 1941 that the Admiralty suspended these convoys until it could assemble sufficient escort forces to challenge the large number of U-boats working in the area. By mid-December the British were ready to send out convoy HG 76 from Gibraltar with no less than 16 escorts, including their first escort carrier, to protect a large convoy of 32 merchant vessels. However, the surface force and the escort carrier were under separate commanders, which was to have an unfortunate result late in the battle. The surface escort group was directed by Commander Johnny Walker, the most effective antisubmarine officer of the war—a ferocious naval warrior with enormous technical knowledge. In the interwar navy, Walker had focused on antisubmarine warfare; the navy passed him over for promotion to captain. But in the desperate struggle in the Atlantic, Walker's competence proved of inestimable value.

It took the Germans two days to find convoy HG 76, despite reports of its departure by Spanish agents. Alerted by special intelligence, Walker had taken HG 76 on a route well to the south of those normally traveled by Gibraltar convoys. On the third day the escort carrier *Audacity*'s aircraft caught U-131 on the surface and, with the help of destroyers, sank the submarine. After preventing the Germans from penetrating the convoy screen, Walker's escorts caught U-434 the next morning and sank it, too. That night the Germans attacked the escort screen and sank the destroyer *Stanley*, but Walker's *Stork* blasted U-574 to the surface with depth charges and then rammed it. The next night the escorts got U-567. Meanwhile, the *Audacity*'s aircraft drove off the Condors and forced the U-boats that were shadowing the convoy to submerge, thus making their task almost impossible.

Unfortunately, the escort carrier's commander refused Walker's advice to keep his ship within the convoy screen at night. The result was that U-751 torpedoed and sank the *Audacity* on the evening of the 21st. But shortly thereafter the Germans broke off the action, having lost four boats in return for sinking only two merchant vessels, an escort carrier, and a destroyer. The experience of HG 76 proved that a combination of air power with an effective, well-trained escort force could present Dönitz's U-boats with a serious threat. The lesson was clear: Ultra might help, but the defeat of the U-boat menace would require well-trained and technologically sophisticated escort forces in sufficient numbers.

In summer 1941 the Roosevelt administration took a more assertive naval position in the North Atlantic. On 20 June, U-203 had shadowed and attempted to attack the U.S. battleship *Texas* in the waters immediately off Iceland. On 7 July a U.S. Marine brigade officially took over the defense of Iceland, and in less than two weeks Roosevelt ordered the navy to escort the shipping of all nationalities to Iceland. U.S. escorts also assumed some of the burden of escorting Allied shipping in the Western Atlantic. The American occupation of Iceland drew an immediate response from the highest levels of the German military: Raeder scurried to Rastenburg, where Hitler was directing Barbarossa, to suggest that the American move constituted a declaration of war. The Führer, however, made clear his desire not to involve the United States in the war at present.

Nevertheless, German naval leaders continued to press for a declaration of war, or at least permission to wage a full-scale war on American commerce, solely on the basis of immediate operational advantages. What makes this particularly astonishing is that the German Navy's high command (the Seekriegsleitung) undertook no studies on the strategic implications of war with the United States. The German naval leadership was nothing if not persistent, however, and in mid-September 1941 Raeder, accompanied by Dönitz, again visited Rastenburg and urged Hitler to allow the U-boats to undertake a full-scale offensive against American warships and merchant vessels. The Americans certainly provided provocation, as Roosevelt responded to a torpedo attack on the destroyer *Greer* by denouncing the "piracy" of the attack, an attack which the *Greer* had in fact provoked. But Hitler still refused to declare war on the United States.

The same day that German naval leaders were conferring with the Führer, the U.S. Navy assumed responsibility for the Newfoundland-Iceland leg of the North Atlantic convoy system. An undeclared war was in full swing in the North Atlantic, and it was unavoidable that, despite the Führer's wishes, U-boats would attack American naval vessels. In mid-October the confrontation came with the attacks on convoy SC 48. U-568 spotted the destroyer USS *Kearny* highlighted by a burning Norwegian tanker and fired a spread of three torpedoes. One hit, and the resulting explosion almost broke the *Kearny*'s keel, killing 11 American sailors. Roosevelt was incensed enough to announce that a shooting war had started and that history would record who had fired the first shot. Within 72 hours another U-boat quite literally blew the destroyer USS *Reuben James* out of the water and killed 115 American sailors. But neither Hitler nor Roosevelt proved willing to declare war—yet.

The Dark Months, January 1942–March 1943

At the beginning of 1942 three crucial events influenced the course of the Battle of the Atlantic. First, on 11 December 1941 Hitler, emboldened by the Japanese attack on Pearl Harbor, declared war on the United States. Second, the U-boat high command launched its boats against coastal traffic off the eastern shores of the United States. And third, the Germans introduced a fourth rotor into the Enigma machines used by the U-boats—an action that completely closed down Bletchley Park's ability to read German naval signals for the next year. Hitler's declaration of war reflected his desire to strike at someone, given the desperate situation on the Eastern Front, where military catastrophe threatened German forces in front of Moscow. At least for the Seekriegsleitung, the United States offered an easy target.

Ironically, given the navy's eagerness to attack U.S. shipping back in 1941, Dönitz had only a handful of boats available for the initial effort off the eastern seaboard of the United States when Hitler finally declared war. The serious situation in North Africa in late 1941 with the British success against Rommel and the first convoys to the Soviet Union led the OKW to divert a significant number of U-boats to those theaters. Moreover, Hitler worried about Norway's security. Consequently, of 91 operational U-boats in January 1942, Dönitz had to deploy 23 to the Mediterranean and 16 to Norway. Instead of waiting and concentrating sizeable forces against the Americans, the Germans attacked in early January with barely a half-dozen boats.

From its onset, the U-boat offensive against U.S. Western Hemisphere shipping, dubbed Operation Drumbeat, met a completely unprepared opponent. Despite having the benefit of British experiences, the U.S. Navy acted as if the Battle of the Atlantic had no relevance to the protection of shipping in the Caribbean and along the Atlantic coast of the United States. Consequently, there were few means to incorporate British intelligence into operations; there were no convoys because U.S. commanders believed weakly escorted convoys were worse than no convoys at all; air and naval cooperation was minimal; anti-submarine vessels patrolled on rigid timetables so that U-boats could predict their appearance; and anti-submarine tactics drew virtually no lessons from British experiences. It was Admiral King at his worst; he was simply not going to learn anything from the British, whatever the costs.

Furthermore, despite the outcry over Pearl Harbor, the peacetime atmosphere in the United States contributed to American difficulties. The cities and towns of the eastern seaboard maintained no blackout, so that their glow highlighted ships against the western sky even on the blackest nights. The U.S. Navy's Tenth Fleet, directly commanded by King, remained in the dark on how to conduct anti-submarine operations. For the U-boats, Operation Drumbeat became a second "happy time." While Dönitz's boats slaughtered merchant ship after ship, the U.S. Navy failed to sink a single U-boat until April 1942.

U-boats sank more U.S. vessels off the eastern seaboard of the United States in 1942 than they had sunk off Britain's western approaches in fall 1940. In January, U-boats destroyed 48 ships of 276,795 tons; by February Dönitz had concentrated a larger number of U-boats off U.S. shores and moved some boats into the Caribbean. Merchant ship losses in North American waters for February were 73 ships of 429,891 tons; in March the total rose to 95 ships of 534,064 tons. With 834,164 tons of Allied shipping lost around the world, March 1942 was one of the war's three worst months. Yet Tenth Fleet obdurately refused to introduce convoys because it believed that it did not possess sufficient escort vessels and that no convoy was preferable to a weakly escorted one. All the British experience of the previous two years had exposed how unfounded in reality this belief was, but U.S. admirals were not about to learn from the Royal Navy.

The British were appalled. They sent Commander Roger Winn, head of the operational intelligence center, to Washington. When King's chief of staff, Rear Admiral R. E. Edwards, told Winn that "the Americans wished to learn their own lessons and that they had plenty of ships with which to do so," the latter exploded: "The trouble is, admiral, it's not only your bloody ships you're losing: a lot of them are ours!"[4] The result of Winn's forthright criticism was that the U.S. Navy established its own tracking room to integrate intelligence into the conduct of convoy and anti-submarine operations. Improved cooperation among British, American, and Canadian operational centers eventually helped win the battle, but it took time to develop the necessary level of expertise on the western side of the Atlantic, and that time was paid for in lost ships and seamen.

The U.S. Navy was unprepared to handle the U-boat onslaught for many of the same reasons that had confounded the Royal Navy in 1939. There were too few escorts, little practical experience, faulty ideas, and a general lack of cooperation between army and naval aviation. But the largest weakness lay in the inability of the Americans to incorporate intelligence into anti-submarine operations. As a result, they had difficulty gaining an understanding of the overall situation—one, moreover, that was changing month by month. By spring, with an assault on oil tanker traffic in the Caribbean, U-boat attacks had spread from Newfoundland to Trinidad, a distance of nearly 2,500 miles.

The Americans addressed the problem in part through their legendary productivity. In April the United States embarked on a program to produce 60 escort vessels in 60 days, and when it achieved that goal, it announced another such program. The Royal Navy contributed 10 corvettes and 22 anti-submarine trawlers to the American effort to defend the merchant ships carrying the great cargoes of Lend-Lease materials to Europe. But the real difficulty was to bring the training of officers and men who manned the escort vessels up to a standard that would allow them to find, attack, and sink U-boats—a tactical task that demanded great skill as well as patience.

Initially, the situation was little better in the air. By the end of March 1942 the Americans had 167 aircraft to patrol the east coast from Maine to Florida. By July these numbers had nearly doubled, but it was the introduction of convoys in April that allowed the new air power to be effective. By mid-May the convoy system, including air cover, was firmly in place along the Atlantic seaboard, and U-boats disappeared to easier hunting grounds in the Gulf of Mexico and Caribbean. There, the U.S. Navy had yet to undertake any measures to convoy crucial shipping, particularly tankers, out of those harbors. In May the Germans sank more tonnage in the Gulf and Caribbean than they had in any month of 1940—a total of nearly half a million tons. And this success came at an astonishingly low cost; in the first half of 1942, U.S. air and surface anti-submarine forces managed to sink only eight U-boats. Allied losses in tankers were particularly heavy. In 1942 they lost 1,667,505 tons of tankers in addition to the 936,000 tons they had lost in the first two years and three months of the war; during the entire period from 1 September 1939 through 31 December 1942, the Allies managed to produce only 1,754,000 tanker tons.

In May Dönitz indicated to Hitler that, were the Americans to establish more effective defenses in the Caribbean and the Gulf of Mexico, he would shift the U-boat war back to the North Atlantic. But for the time being, he believed he could concentrate more boats and continue the "happy times" against the Americans. He was wrong. By the end of June the Americans had implemented defensive measures for most of the merchant shipping in the Caribbean and Gulf. If they did not have sufficient air power, escorts, or training to sink U-boats, they could at least deny the enemy the easy task of attacking independent sailings. In July, sinkings by U-boats dropped by one-third, while the number of boats lost increased to ten (six in American waters), compared to only four in May and three in June.

The first half of 1942 had been nothing short of a catastrophe for Allied shipping. Despite the advantage the British had gained in the last half of 1941, the battle had shifted back to the disastrous situation of fall 1940, except this time on the opposite side of the Atlantic. All told, the Allies lost three million tons of shipping in American waters during the first half of 1942. By shifting to a new theater where their opponents had not learned all the harsh lessons of 1940, the Germans had achieved a significant success. Moreover, the war waged by U-boats had spread from the Mediterranean and Arctic all the way across the North Atlantic into the Caribbean— an expansion of the watery battleground that stretched Allied resources to the breaking point. To add to these difficulties, simultaneous pressures in the Pacific extended both Allied commitments and losses. Only the Japanese refusal to use submarines against merchant shipping kept losses in the Pacific within reasonable bounds.

Yet, there were positive results in the campaign, for the string of U-boat victories so distracted the Germans that they failed to notice Britain's success at cracking Enigma during the last half of 1941. By the time the Germans introduced a fourth wheel to Enigma in February 1942 that ended Bletchley Park's ability to decipher U-boat messages for the rest of the year, the British had already learned much about U-boat operations, and new D/F equipment was providing considerable intelligence about the location and focus of the U-boat effort. But the British could no longer manipulate the convoy routes in the North Atlantic to their advantage in the way they had for the previous six months. This factor would have been glaring except that Dönitz's change in the U-boats' deployment to the east coast of the United States masked the impact of changes in the Enigma system.

Inexplicably, over the first half of 1942 Dönitz had forbidden U-boats to attack North Atlantic convoys as the submarines sailed to their destinations along the eastern seaboard of the United States and in the Caribbean. But in mid-summer the attention of the U-boat high command shifted back to the North Atlantic, where the contest now favored the Germans. The lack of signals intelligence in the last half of 1942 and the increased numbers of boats in the Atlantic made it difficult to direct convoys around the patrol lines that Dönitz established. The Germans had cracked a number of British codes, particularly the Admiralty's merchant shipping code, which gave the U-boat high command excellent intelligence on the timing and direction of major convoys. Nevertheless, with all these advantages, the Germans still confronted the considerable problem of finding and attacking convoys in the vast, heaving Atlantic. Over the coming 11-month battle in the North Atlantic, 105 out of 174 scheduled convoys (over 60 percent) crossed the Atlantic without suffering a U-boat attack.

On the other hand, the technological aids the British were developing to attack U-boats were only slowly reaching the escort forces. Few vessels had yet received either new D/F equipment or the 271M radar. The new direction-finding equipment allowed escort vessels to pinpoint the location of U-boats at sea, while the new radar gave escorts better resolution at greater distances and with more reliability.

Moreover, the sailors brought to the battle by the U.S. and Canadian navies were new and mostly untrained. Hence, it took time for the new ships and their crews to bring as many merchant ships safely to harbor as possible; and that, rather than sinking U-boats, was their primary mission. The crews' biggest worry was the large gap in the Central Atlantic where Allied air cover could not reach. This lack of air support resulted directly from the refusal of Allied air forces to divert any of their long-range bombers to the battle against the U-boats. The lack of a sufficient number of escort carriers made the problem of no air support that much worse. The long-range B-24 Liberator bomber offered the only means to close the gap, but the air forces on both sides of the Atlantic remained stubbornly opposed to assigning first-line bombers to the Central Atlantic. Meanwhile, owing to Germany's accelerated U-boat construction program, 30 new boats per month were reaching Dönitz's command as of July 1942, while he had lost only 26 boats in the first half of the year.

Even the surface situation seemed to turn against the Allies early in 1942. In February the Germans slipped *Gneisenau, Scharnhorst,* and *Prinz Eugen* up the Channel, where they met a minimal British response. Nevertheless, both battle cruisers ran into mines and had to go into dry-dock for repairs, and only the *Scharnhorst* eventually returned to active service. Meanwhile, the Germans concentrated their remaining surface forces, including the *Bismarck*'s sister ship, the *Tirpitz*, in northern Norway, where those ships posed a direct threat to the convoys running to Murmansk— one of the nastiest stretches of water in the world with raging gales and Arctic temperatures. To a considerable extent, the Murmansk convoys represented a propaganda gesture to the Soviets, since only approximately one-quarter of the Lend-Lease sent by the Western powers to support the Soviet effort passed by this route. Nearly half of Lend-Lease sent to the Soviet Union transited by way of Siberia, after crossing the Northern Pacific and the Sea of Japan on its way to Vladivostok. The remaining quarter reached the Soviets via Iran and the Persian Gulf. Yet the British and Americans felt compelled to commit their naval forces and merchant vessels to the Murmansk run because of the military burden the Soviets were carrying.

The threat of a German battle fleet hiding in the Norwegian fiords, the unrelenting air assault by the Luftwaffe, the omnipresent submarines, and the horrendous weather all made the Murmansk run a nightmare. In May 1942, convoy PQ 16 ran into no less than 108 successive waves of attacking Luftwaffe bombers and lost 8 out of 25 merchant vessels. In July, the First Sea Lord, Admiral Sir Dudley Pound, believing that the *Tirpitz* had sailed against convoy PQ 17, ordered the convoy to disperse. The German heavy ships were not out, but Luftwaffe bombers and U-boats were, and after they had finished pouncing on the dispersed vessels, only 11 of 34 survived to limp into Murmansk harbor.

For a short period the Western powers discontinued the Murmansk run, but in September, with longer nights and worsening weather, they resumed again with PQ 18. In the face of the triple German threat in the air, on the surface, and under water, PQ 18 required an escort that included 1 carrier, 2 battleships, 7 cruisers, 30 destroyers, 2 anti-aircraft ships, 4 corvettes, 3 minesweepers, 4 trawlers, 2 submarines, and 2 fleet oilers to protect a convoy totaling 40 merchant ships. All these escort vessels had to be withdrawn from supporting Atlantic convoys whose cargoes and crews represented a considerable contribution to the war effort, and had to fight their way through fierce Luftwaffe attacks, which sank 10 of the 40 ships. The Germans lost 41 aircraft during the battle, mostly to anti-aircraft fire. The U-boats sank another 3 merchant vessels, while losing 3 of their own to destroyers, so that in the end 27 ships got through to Murmansk.

The Battle of the North Atlantic went against the Allies throughout the rest of 1942. German decrypts of Allied message traffic and the extended patrol lines of U-boats—a reflection of their vastly increased numbers—ensnared many convoys. Without air support to force U-boats to submerge, where they could not keep pace with the convoys, the escorts confronted attacks night after night. October and November were particularly bad months, the ravages of the U-boats perhaps exacerbated by the diversion of escorts to support Operation Torch—the Anglo-American invasion of French North Africa—as well as supplying the ground forces in Tunisia. In October U-boats sank 101 ships of 637,833 tons, while the following month they destroyed 134 ships of 807,754 tons—their highest total for the war. The German success in November might have been even greater but for the fact that the OKW ordered Dönitz to move a substantial number of boats against the Allied landings in North Africa. Overall, U-boats sank over 6 million tons of Allied merchant shipping in 1942, a total that came close to matching the tonnage that American shipping yards turned out over the course of the year.

Yet, not everything favored the Germans. U-boat losses were climbing. In the last six months of 1942 the number of boats lost reached 65, as compared with only 21 in the first half of the year. Although U-boat command was still receiving more new boats than it was losing, this tripling of losses underlined the increased effectiveness of Allied countermeasures. Even more disturbing to the Germans was the fact that the U-boats achieved little against the well-protected convoys supporting the North African invasion.

Three key pieces were coming together for the Allies: long-range air cover was shrinking the gap over the Central Atlantic; research and development was equipping Allied aircraft and escorts with more efficient radars, D/F equipment, weapons, and communications gear; and the number of escort vessels was climbing. The Germans had no comparable technological improvements to support their U-boats. For example, U-boats were still not equipped with radar. All they had was raw numbers, and even that factor had a negative as well as a positive side: the need to man the new boats led to a decline in the level of training and experience of U-boat skippers. Increasingly, U-boat successes, when they occurred, were the work of a handful of bold and experienced commanders.

Thus the Germans' opportunity to crush the Allied convoy system in 1942 was indeed real, but it was fleeting. While Dönitz focused on numbers, his only hope was that the tide of sunken ships would break the morale of the merchant sailors who manned the ships. But the winter of 1942–43 was one of the harshest on record; from December through March one storm after another blew across the Atlantic. Conditions on even the largest vessels were terrible, and crews on smaller ships like corvettes had to work in monstrous seas that could be called hellish were they not so bitterly cold. But for much of December 1942 and January 1943 U-boats could not operate, and so Allied losses fell to 345,902 tons and then to 261,359 for those months. And in December Bletchley Park broke back into the four-rotor Enigma system that encoded the U-boat message traffic.

Historians often suggest that the Battle of the Atlantic reached a climax in February and March 1943. But that period might be more accurately described as the swan song of the U-boat campaign. In the remaining portion of the air gap, the U-boats inflicted serious losses on the convoys they found. But with Bletchley Park's aid, Western Approaches Command guided many other convoys around U-boat patrol lines. The German interception services were reading the British convoy codes, so both sides played a chess game of move and countermove. March was the last bad month of the U-boat war for the Allies; it was so bad that some planners in the Admiralty actually suggested abandoning convoys. But the Allied leadership refused to contemplate a capitulation. Quite simply, there was no other way to move the mass of ships on which the Allied war effort depended across the great ocean spaces.

In April and May 1943 the tables turned irrevocably against the U-boats. Escort carriers arrived to provide some convoys with their own air cover; long-range aircraft closed the air gap in the Central Atlantic; escorts were sufficiently well-equipped to allow group commanders to sink many of the U-boats they encountered, while the training and experience of escort groups began to pay big dividends. In February and March, Allied escorts sank 49 U-boats, and in May alone they sank 41. The crushing losses in May forced Dönitz to concede defeat and pull his boats out of the North Atlantic. The 135 U-boats sunk between May and October 1943 dramatize how much the tactical balance shifted in favor of the Allies' anti-submarine forces. In the three years and three months before 1943, they had managed to sink only 153 U-boats. For Dönitz, the war was over.

With the battle already lost, the U-boat high command suddenly began to interest itself in technological support for its offensive. The *Schnorchel* gave the U-boats some new advantages that allowed them to travel underwater and use their air-breathing diesel engines at the same time. The Germans also introduced devices to combat British radar and acoustic torpedoes that homed on the sounds made by the propellers. But all of this was a case of too little, too late.

In January 1943, before the tide turned against the U-boats in the Atlantic, Hitler promoted Dönitz to the position of commander-in-chief of the

German Navy. That promotion had resulted from the failure of the heavy cruiser *Hipper* and the pocket battleship *Lützow* in late December 1942 to inflict any serious damage on a Murmansk convoy guarded by destroyers. Furious, Hitler had fired Raeder and demanded that the entire surface fleet be paid off. But Dönitz eventually changed the Führer's mind. As it turned out, he might well have accepted the Führer's decision and discharged not only the surface fleet but the entire submarine force, for all the good either group would do during the remainder of the war. British battleships would catch and sink the *Scharnhorst* off Norway's North Cape at the end of 1943, while the *Tirpitz* would be ignominiously sunk in a Norwegian fiord as a result of an RAF raid in fall 1944. As for the U-boat fleet, its boats became the hunted rather than the hunters for the rest of the war. German sailors would have contributed more to the defense of the Fatherland by fighting in Normandy or on the Eastern Front than by waiting for Bomber Command to blow up the *Tirpitz* or going to their doom in U-boats.

The Battle of the Atlantic in Retrospect

The Germans might have improved their chances of winning the war if they had never prosecuted the Battle of the Atlantic but had expended all their resources on the air and ground campaigns. The Third Reich lacked the resources to fight a world war on so many fronts, and war demands hard choices. But Hitler's method of decision-making, coupled with the inability of the German military to think at the strategic level, made it impossible for leaders of the Third Reich to make the choices that might have brought them victory.

It was not so much the successes and failures of the U-boats themselves as the indirect effects of the U-boat offensive that helped turn the war against Germany. Without the terrible losses inflicted by the U-boats in summer and fall 1940, the United States might never have embarked on its massive program to construct merchant shipping. The German successes off the east coast of the United States in early 1942 added even greater impetus to Roosevelt's support for the program. By 1945, 99 new shipbuilding yards owed their existence to the federal government's sponsorship. Over the course of the war, the results spoke clearly in the advantage the Allies gained in new production versus losses (see Table 1).

But it took more than new shipyards to tip the balance; American businessmen brought the processes of mass production to the construction of merchant shipping. Standardized design of components allowed not only assembly-line techniques but prefabricated assembly. The most famous of

Table 1. Merchant Shipping Losses/Shipping Gains, 1940–1945

July–September	1940	−1,150,000
October–December	1940	−1,000,000
January–March	1941	−900,000
April–June	1941	−1,100,000
July–September	1941	−150,000
October–December	1941	−200,000
January–March	1942	−1,300,000
April–June	1942	−500,000
July–September	1942	+250,000
October–December	1942	+500,000
January–March	1943	+1,250,000
April–June	1943	+2,900,000
July–September	1943	+3,250,000
October–December	1943	+3,540,000
January–March	1944	+2,580,000
April–June	1944	+3,190,000

such ships were, of course, the Liberty cargo ships, the first of which was launched in Baltimore in September 1941. By the end of the war, American shipyards were producing over 2,700 sister ships to the same design. Throughout the dark year of 1942, U.S. production kept pace with the huge losses that the Allies suffered. But the defeat of the U-boats in May 1943 and the consequent drop in losses resulted in an enormous expansion of the merchant ship fleet in 1943 and 1944. In 1943 alone, Allied production almost made up for the combined losses of the first three years of the war. It was barely enough: the projection of American military power in the Pacific and in Europe, as well as U.S. economic support of America's British and Soviet allies, stretched the shipping pool to the breaking point. Without Dönitz's jump-start of U.S. industry, America's production of merchant shipping might not have reached sufficient levels early enough in the war to support these diverse efforts.

As was so often the case with their strategic assessments, the Germans had underestimated their opponents. The efforts of Bletchley Park played a crucial role in deflecting the U-boat offensive, particularly in the last half of 1941, when the British were most vulnerable. In spite of great circumstantial evidence that the British had broken into their codes, the Germans refused to believe the evidence because of their confidence in the superiority of their technology. As a result of this arrogance, the British were able to tip the playing field against the U-boats for virtually the entire last half of the war. The Germans found it impossible to believe that they could be out-fought and out-thought.

But cryptoanalysis alone cannot account for the failure of the German naval effort. At the start of the war Dönitz tapped a relatively small staff to control the U-boat battle against British commerce. For a battle that con-fined itself to the coasts of the United Kingdom, a highly centralized, small staff might have sufficed. But as the campaign against British commerce expanded and became ever more complex, the German staff at U-boat Headquarters remained at the same small staffing levels; if anything, it con-tracted, as Dönitz attempted to close off what the Germans regarded as hu-man leaks in their security systems. A number of important consequences flowed from this decision. Most obvious was the general exhaustion of all the officers involved in running the U-boat campaign. But more disabling than the mistakes that flowed from this general weariness was the inability of U-boat Headquarters to step back and take a longer look at the war, both to assess its intelligence situation and to implement technological improve-ments. Like the RAF's Bomber Command, U-boat command interested it-self in technology only when the war turned against it, and by then it was too late for a technological fix.

The Germans also failed to recognize how effectively their opponents were using technology to counteract the U-boat attacks. Part of this was due to inadequate staffing and analysis, but part was the result of Dönitz's decision to move his submarines from one theater to another as Allied es-corts and tactics adapted. By consistently seeking the weak link in the Allied system of shipping, the Germans eventually came up against an Allied defense system that used the same effective defensive responses ev-erywhere. Then without any real changes in their own technological and tactical effectiveness, the U-boats were quite literally sunk.

Equally open to criticism is Dönitz's handling of the campaign's opera-tional parameters. The tight leash on which he held his U-boats for much of the war robbed them of their flexibility; it also played a major role in providing the vast set of messages that Bletchley Park required to break into Enigma. As was so typical of the German approach to war, Dönitz fully seconded Raeder's efforts to get Hitler to declare war on the United States in the second half of 1941. Yet, when that declaration of war came, instead of concentrating his submarines for a deadly strike against the east coast of the United States, the Gulf of Mexico, and the Caribbean, Dönitz committed his boats in small numbers. The damage they wrought was considerable, but in the end it merely forced the United States to devote sufficient naval forces and resources to the problem without delivering irreparable damage to the Allied cause. Operation Drumbeat reflected the German habit of taking the easiest tactical and operational path without the slightest thought to the strategic or long-range consequences.

Conclusion

The Allies eventually won the Battle of the Atlantic, but at a needlessly high cost. The figures for casualties among those who served in the British Merchant Navy underscores this point: out of 185,000 who served, 32,952 or 17 percent lost their lives—a higher casualty rate than that suffered by any of the three British military services. The armed forces' lack of interest in anti-submarine warfare before the outbreak of the war was inexcusable, especially in light of their experiences in World War I. When the threat emerged again early in World War II, anti-submarine forces received the attention they deserved, but by then it took the most desperate measures, including putting the entire British nation on a near starvation diet, to overcome the challenge.

What is even more astonishing, half a century after the war, was the obdurate unwillingness of the Allied air forces to devote the resources necessary to close the gap in the air cover over the Central Atlantic. Except for Coastal Command, the RAF leadership opposed the commitment of long-range aircraft to protecting convoys with a fervor that bordered on fanaticism. And the airmen maintained this position throughout 1942 and into 1943, when finally their political masters forced their hand. The result was the unnecessary loss of hundreds of ships and many, many lives.

But with the exception of the RAF bomber barons, the effort to thwart the U-boats was one of the high points of war for the British armed forces. When its leaders recognized the threat, the Royal Navy developed the tactics, the technology, and the leadership to handle the grim business of anti-submarine warfare. The integration of technology into effective tactical systems was crucial to mastering the U-boats in 1943; similarly, the integration of intelligence into the conduct of anti-submarine and convoy operations substantially boosted the chance of victory. The mental flexibility of those responsible for the anti-submarine campaign, in particular Admirals Percy Noble and Max Horton, allowed the British to get maximum utility out of civilian scientists, reserve intelligence officers, and operations research analysts. At the same time that Dönitz was enclosing his staff in a tighter and tighter grip, the British were expanding and adapting theirs.

In the end, though, it was the courageous willingness of Allied merchant sailors to go down to the sea despite the appalling conditions of the North Atlantic and the terrifying losses on some convoy runs that won the day. As the solemn service of celebration at Liverpool Cathedral noted in August 1945: "These were the men / who were her salvation / who conquered the waters and the underwaters / who / in storm and calm / taught England to live anew, / and fed her children."

YEAR OF DECISION
FOR GERMANY

1942

German strategy had staked all on Barbarossa, and the defeat in front of Moscow in early December 1941 proclaimed the scale of this misjudgment. At the beginning of the war's third year, the Germans confronted a great worldwide coalition, formidably strengthened by Hitler's declaration of war on the United States on 11 December 1941. The conflict had truly become a world war unimaginable to the combatants of World War I. As battles raged in the Pacific and the British and Americans attempted to stem the Japanese flood, the Germans still remained the great threat. Europe would remain the place where the war's outcome would be determined.

Barbarossa's terrible losses had dulled the Wehrmacht's edge. The fundamental question confronting the combatants in 1942 was whether the Reich could patch together sufficient military forces to finish the war, or whether the United States and Britain, desperately arming to make up for the "locust years," and the Soviet Union, grievously wounded in 1941, could hold on long enough for their economic strength to prevail. When told of Pearl Harbor, Churchill had exclaimed that the Allies had won. To most observers in early 1942, however, Germany's certain defeat was not so obvious. Nor were Germany's responses to its mounting opposition inevitable. In fact, the Germans could have pursued alternative paths that might well have prolonged the war in Europe. It was the strategic decisions and the outcome of the battles of 1942 that set the final course of the war.

By 1942 the British system for making strategy and military policy was well in place. In the 1930s, without coherent leadership at the top, the British bureaucracy had tended to choke on the weight of the paperwork produced by its many committees. But under Churchill's inspiring leadership, as both prime minister and minister of defense, a carefully articulated hierarchy of committees produced coherent and intelligent policy that translated into effective strategy. Directly under Churchill were the War Cabinet and the Chiefs of Staff Committee, which together controlled the larger political and strategic questions raised by the war. Under them, a whole host of committees analyzed significant problems; and if they came up with the wrong answer, which at times they did, it was not for lack of trying.

Churchill hectored, badgered, and drove his colleagues ceaselessly in his pursuit of victory. He was not an easy man to get along with in the best of times, and under the pressures of war he was at times insufferable. His relationship with his chief military adviser, the CIGS, Field Marshal Sir Alan Brooke, was frequently on the brink of complete breakdown. And yet Brooke in his often acerbic diary caught glimpses of the Churchillian genius; in a late night encounter with the prime minister he recorded: "He [Churchill] had the gramophone turned on and in his many colored dressing gown, with a sandwich in one hand and watercress in the other, he trotted round and round the hall giving little skips to the time of the gramophone. On each lap near the fireplace, he stopped to release some priceless quotation or thought. For instance he quoted a saying that a man's life is similar to a walk down a long passage with closed windows on each side. As you reach each window an unknown hand opens it and the light it lets in only increases by contrast the darkness at the end of the passage."[1]

One of Churchill's military assistants characterized the changeover from Chamberlain in this way: "The days of mere 'coordination' were out for good and all . . . We were now going to get direction, leadership, action with a snap in it."[2] Hastings Ismay, one of Churchill's senior advisers during the war, commented to Claude Auchinleck in 1941 that "the idea that [Churchill] was rude, arrogant, and self-seeking was entirely wrong. He was none of those things. He was certainly frank in speech and writing, but he expected others to be equally frank with him."[3]

Churchill's immediate problem was the army. As Brooke confided in his diary in 1942: "Furthermore [the military performance of the army] is made worse by the lack of good military commanders. Half our Corps and Division Commanders are totally unfit for their appointments, and yet if I were to sack them, I could find no better! They lack character, imagination, drive, and power of leadership."[4] These defects were now becoming glaringly apparent on the battlefields of North Africa.

North Africa

When Erwin Rommel arrived in Libya in February 1941 with his Afrika Korps, he had immediately attacked British forces and driven them back to

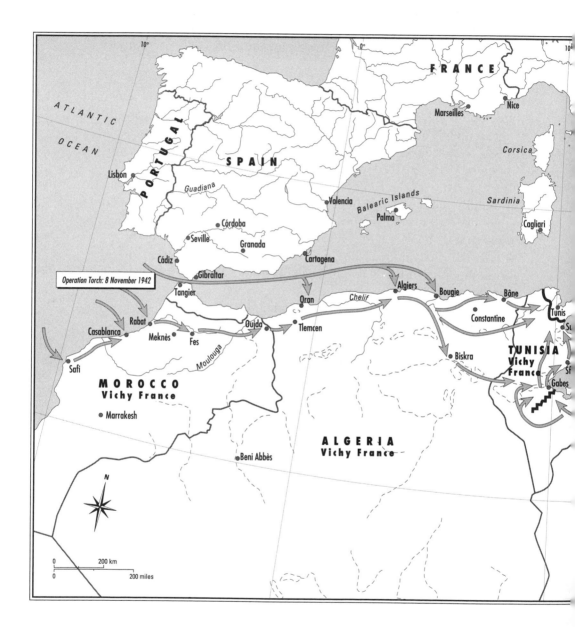

ATLANTIC
OCEAN

PORTUGAL

SPAIN

FRANCE

Marseilles   Nice

Corsica

Sardinia

Lisbon

Guadiana

Valencia
Balearic Islands   Cagliari
Palma

Córdoba

Seville

Granada

Cádiz
Cartagena

Gibraltar

Operation Torch: 8 November 1942

Tangier

Oran   Chelif   Algiers   Bougie   Bône
Tunis
Rabat   Sı
Casablanca
Meknès   Fes   Oujda   Tlemcen   Constantine
Moulouga   TUNISIA
Safi   Vichy
Biskra   France
MOROCCO   Sf
Vichy France   Gabes

Marrakesh

ALGERIA
Beni Abbès   Vichy France

N

0   200 km
0   200 miles

ALLIED ADVANCE IN THE MEDITERRANEAN
1942–1943

➡ Allied advance

▨ Allied front line, 23 October 1942

▬ Axis front line, 3 May 1943

⋀⋁⋀ Axis defensive line

Venice
ROMANIA
YUGOSLAVIA
Sofia
BULGARIA
Rome
ITALY
ALBANIA
Istanbul
Taranto
Salerno
GREECE
TURKEY
Palermo Messina
Sicily Regio
Catania
Izmir
Athens
Adalia
Malta
(British)
Operation Husky: 10 July 1943
Canea Candia
Crete
Nicosia
Cyprus

M e d i t e r r a n e a n   S e a

Operation Lightfoot: 23 October 1942
Supercharge: 2 November 1942

Tripoli
Derna
Port Said
Misurata
Benghazi
Tobruk
Suez
Canal
Sirte
Bardia
Matruh Alexandria
El Alamein
Suez
El Agheila
Cairo

Nile

LIBYA
EGYPT

Egypt. But his Achilles heel turned out to be his supply lines; rarely did he receive sufficient supplies across the Mediterranean. The Germans were quick to heap scorn on Italian incompetence in protecting the sea lanes, but in fact this particular logistical problem was caused by the incompetence of German signals intelligence in not recognizing that the Allies had compromised Enigma. Through Ultra—intelligence based on the breaking of the most sophisticated German and Italian ciphers—British air and naval power, operating out of Malta, attacked the supply convoys escorted by the Italians and consistently interrupted Rommel's supply lines.

The British hold on Tobruk, a port on the Libyan coast, added greatly to the Afrika Korps' logistic burden. Tobruk placed Rommel on the horns of a dilemma: he could not advance on Egypt until he captured this port; yet a major offensive against Tobruk would expose his forces in Egypt to a British attack. Halder, the OKH chief of staff, regarded Rommel's dilemma with grim satisfaction. Still, it must be said that Rommel was never responsible for German strategy in the Mediterranean. His mission was straightforward: to protect Libya, maintain Mussolini's prestige, and keep the British occupied, and until October 1942 the Afrika Korps achieved these goals at relatively low cost.

In accomplishing these goals Rommel proved himself the premier battlefield commander of the war. While he had not passed the examinations for entrance to the Kriegsakademie—the preparatory step to becoming a general staff officer—he was a devoted student of military history and his profession, as well as the author of one of the most thoughtful combat memoirs of World War I. He was also a leader of men, with a profound ability to inspire his troops to do their utmost in the face of enormous difficulties. His energy, combined with a sixth sense for the battlefield, led to a boldness in combat that at times bordered on rashness. But Rommel rarely missed the opportunities that his opponents all too often provided. He was undoubtedly a firm supporter of the Nazi regime; yet on a number of occasions he disobeyed some of its more odious orders, such as the commando order. In 1941 he was clearly at the height of his powers of command, and those powers now magnified all the advantages the Germans possessed in doctrine, training, and battlefield effectiveness. Operation Battleaxe—a major British offensive in June 1941 against German defensive positions on the Halfaya Pass on the Egyptian-Libyan frontier—exposed the depth of British weaknesses. Field Marshal Archibald Wavell, commander of British forces in the Middle East, under pressure from Churchill, launched a two-pronged attack, first to capture the pass and then to advance to Tobruk. Well-sited German 88mm anti-aircraft guns, used as anti-tank weapons, wiped out the first offensive move. British forces, in three disjointed columns, failed to support one another, but such disarray was only the beginning.

Rommel arrived the next day from German positions in front of Tobruk. The British, having no coherent doctrine, much less one for mechanized warfare, fought isolated battles, while German armor, infantry, and artillery fought as highly coordinated teams. By morning of the third day, the Afrika Korps threatened to envelop much of Britain's Eighth Army. Only a precipitous retreat saved the British from complete defeat. Tank losses suggest the extent of the debacle: the Germans lost 12, many repairable, while the British lost 91. The defeat, combined with Wavell's mishandling of troubles in Iraq and Syria, led Churchill to replace him with General Claude Auchinleck. Yet Eighth Army learned little from their experiences. While British commanders recognized the effectiveness of 88s as anti-tank weapons, they underestimated the mobility with which the Germans used the weapon. Even more seriously, they lacked any comprehension of the enemy's combined-arms doctrine.

In November 1941, with Operation Crusader, the British tried again. This time they caught Rommel by surprise, and in a swirling, confusing battle, Commonwealth forces enjoyed considerable superiority over their opponents—four to one in tanks (710 to 174 with an additional 500 in supply channels to replace losses). But the British wasted the advantage of surprise by divergent, unsupported brigade-sized efforts. In one action the inexperienced 22nd Brigade charged well-sited Italian anti-tank positions and lost 25 percent of its tanks. Eighth Army units consistently failed to support one another, while the Germans attacked with the full weight of the Afrika Korps' two panzer divisions.

But the Germans had their own problems. Blinded by British air superiority, they never gained a clear idea of British intentions. A badly organized attack, delivered late near Sidi Rezegh, cost the Germans half their tanks. Rommel followed that strike with a thrust which carried the Afrika Korps to the Egyptian frontier and for a short time threatened to unhinge Eighth Army. Its commander, General Alan Cunningham, ordered the offensive abandoned, but Auchinleck personally took command and ordered the battle continued. The British now stood firm in the rear and resumed the advance on Tobruk to break through to the garrison. The Germans, on the other hand, fumbled their strike at the Egyptian frontier and, confronted with increasing danger around Tobruk as well as a worsening supply situation, broke off the battle.

The retreat took the Germans all the way back to El Agheila, where they had started in April 1941. British numbers on the battlefield had told, while British air and naval attacks from Malta on Axis supply lines had destroyed a significant percentage of the shipping crossing to Libya. But help was on the way for the hard-pressed Afrika Korps. Hitler ordered Luftflotte 2 (Second Air Force) and its commander, Field Marshal Albert Kesselring, from Russia to the Mediterranean. In addition, the OKW ordered a number of U-boats transferred to the theater. Thus, the effort from Malta had an impact not only on the Battle in North Africa but on the Eastern Front and the Battle of the Atlantic as well.

Luftflotte 2 made an immediate difference. The flow of supplies to Rommel improved, and in January 1942 he counterattacked and drove the British back to Gazala. There the front stabilized for the next four months, as the exhausted armies settled down in the winter rains to prepare for a resumption of heavy fighting in the spring. The British established a defensive line of fortified infantry positions that reached deep into the desert; like the Italian positions in front of Mersa Matruh in fall 1940, these positions were not mutually supporting. Behind the front line the British deployed their armor in brigade-sized formations. The intention was to avoid fighting a defensive battle; with their superiority in numbers British commanders believed they would be on the offensive. Yet, looking at Ultra reports, Churchill could not fathom why Eighth Army was waiting to attack. But Churchill never understood the British Army's weaknesses in doctrine, training, and combined-arms capabilities; unfortunately, neither did his commanders, who had done little to repair Eighth Army's tactical and operational deficiencies.

Rommel struck first. Over the night of 26–27 May the Afrika Korps' mobile force moved south around the Gazala line and the fortress defensive position of Bir Hacheim, manned by the 1st Free French Brigade. For reasons that remain inexplicable to this day, British commanders believed that a German attack, if it came at all, would come against their center. Consequently, they deployed their armor to counterattack there and not to guard against a major flank attack. Despite the fact that armored car patrols picked up Rommel's move over the course of the night, British commanders refused to believe the warnings. As a result, powerful German forces first overran the 3rd Indian Motor Brigade, then the 7th British Motor Brigade, and then the 4th Armored Brigade in succession, none of which paid the slightest attention to what was happening to their neighbors. The Germans also overran 7th Armored Division's command post and captured its commander, General F. W. Messervy, who had commanded 1st Armored Division four months earlier when the Germans had wrecked that unit.

Nevertheless, Rommel soon ran into difficulties. He had hoped to drive to the coast and encircle the entire Gazala line, but the Afrika Korps slammed into British armor in the center of the Gazala position and took heavy losses from new Grant tanks, provided by U.S. Lend-Lease. After a second day of fruitless attempts to break through to the coast, Rommel halted the Afrika Korps behind the Gazala line and attempted to break through British minefields and defensive positions to open up a supply channel. The balance in armor still favored the British by nearly three to one. Trapped with his back to British minefields, Rommel threw out a screen of 88s. Here, British generalship came to his rescue. General Neil Ritchie, Eighth Army commander, persisted in launching a series of ill-coordinated and unsupported armored attacks. Heavy air attacks, tank attacks, and artillery bombardments fell on German forces in the "cauldron," but none in a coordinated fashion.

As the Germans beat off British attacks, they captured the defensive position at Sidi Muftah in the Gazala line on 1 June. They thus opened up a path for supplies to reach the panzers. A major British attack on 5 June again ran into Rommel's anti-tank screen and suffered heavy losses—230 tanks. On 10 June, the Germans finally took the French positions at Bir Hacheim, although many of the French escaped in the night. By this point the British, though still enjoying an advantage in armor, were badly shaken. With his supplies in hand, Rommel struck out from his defensive position. Again the British failed to coordinate their operations. Rommel trapped two British armored brigades on 12 June between his panzer divisions; a third British armored brigade, rushing to the rescue, ran into the usual screen of anti-tank guns. To add to the disaster, the hapless Messervy found himself cut off from his troops for the third time in as many weeks. This battle finally tipped both the armored equation and the battle's initiative firmly into Rommel's hands. The British scrambled to escape.

Most of the infantry in the Gazala positions withdrew unharmed, but only because Rommel was focusing on more distant objectives. As the British debacle gathered momentum, Churchill demanded that Auchinleck hold Tobruk. Rommel's forces swept by the fortress on 19 June and captured the air fields east of the port; the Afrika Korps was apparently headed toward the Egyptian frontier. Tobruk's garrison was reasonably large, consisting of the 2nd South African Division, the Guards Brigade, and the 32nd Tank Brigade with 70 tanks. But none were ready for a siege. Confident that the Germans had headed east, the defenders settled down to await events. But at dawn on 20 June a massive bombardment hit Tobruk's southeastern perimeter; the Germans had returned. Within three hours

German infantry were through the defenses. On the following morning, the South African commander surrendered, and Tobruk was finally in German hands.

At this point, Rommel, newly promoted to field marshal, argued for an advance into Egypt, while Kesselring pushed for an airborne assault on Malta. Hitler, undoubtedly recalling the heavy losses on Crete and not trusting the Italian Navy, opted for a continued advance. In fact, the Afrika Korps had taken heavy losses and was in no condition to take Egypt; only a complete collapse by the British could have allowed it to reach Alexandria. Auchinleck had already intervened and relieved Ritchie. He established the Eighth Army in defensive positions near El Alamein, 60 miles from Alexandria. Lying directly south of British positions was the Qattara depression, a great dry salt sea, impassable to heavy vehicles. There would be no open flank. In that position, Auchinleck's successful defense halted a series of Afrika Korps attacks in early July. For a short period, the British had the chance to gain a major victory, but the Eighth Army possessed neither the confidence nor initiative required to launch a counterattack.

In early August, immediately after Auchinleck's successful defense at El Alamein, Churchill and the CIGS Brooke arrived in Cairo. Quite correctly, because of Auchinleck's failures over the past year, they decided to replace him with General Sir Harold Alexander. The new Eighth Army commander was to be the XXXth Corps Commander, Lieutenant General W. H. E. "Strafer" Gott. But Gott was killed in an air raid, and the new Eighth Army commander turned out to be a relatively unknown corps commander from Britain, General Bernard Law Montgomery.

Montgomery proved to be one of the great field commanders of World War II. He was not a nice person; dogged, conceited, vain, completely sure of his own abilities, and incapable of understanding other human beings, Montgomery also possessed the attributes of a great general. He was rigorous and enthusiastic, and exhibited considerable flexibility; he was a first-class trainer; and he understood the mind and stomach of the common soldier. He understood that he must fight his battles within the limitations imposed by the weaknesses of the forces under his command. Thus, he refused to fight the Germans in a war of mobility but instead forced them to fight on his terms—with firepower and sheer numbers.

Montgomery had barely three months to get the Eighth Army ready for its offensive; yet, he restored the army's morale, made clear at every level that it had a new commander, and established large supply dumps. He told the troops on the Alam Halfa Ridge at El Alamein that they would stay there alive, or they would stay there dead. At the end of August, Rommel launched another offensive to drive the British out of the Alamein position. After administering a serious rebuff to the Afrika Korps, Montgomery refused to exploit his success; instead, he continued the buildup for his own offensive in late October. By October Montgomery possessed advantages of nearly four to one in troop strength (230,000 to 80,000), three to one in tanks (1,500 to 500, only 260 of which were German), and nearly four to one in aircraft (1,200 to 350). Once again the island fortress of Malta, recovered from the aerial pounding it had suffered in spring 1942, was playing its role with Ultra's assistance in interdicting the supplies being sent across the Mediterranean.

Montgomery's plan was straightforward. A series of diversionary attacks would draw German attention to the south, while the carefully prepared main thrust, in which artillery and engineers would cut paths through the minefields, would create a breakout. In late October when Montgomery's attack began, Rommel was back home in Germany recovering from jaundice. His temporary replacement, General Georg Stumme, died of a heart attack as the battle began, while the Germans failed to respond quickly. When they did react, they lost nearly half the Afrika Korps' tanks in ill-planned counterattacks. The 15th Panzer Division had already lost three-quarters of its tanks in savage fighting. Rommel did not arrive back in North Africa for nearly forty-eight hours. Meanwhile, the British had their own troubles. Gaps through the minefields proved too narrow, while attacking infantry often failed to secure the far ends of the lanes. As a result, many British tanks were trapped in the minefields, where they took heavy losses from Axis anti-tank guns.

Then and thereafter, Montgomery insisted that his offensives had worked according to plan. In fact, he adapted to actual conditions. By the evening of the second day he recognized that his initial plans were not working. On the 28th after a one-day redeployment, the British struck an even heavier blow in the north; that thrust also failed, but the fighting wore Rommel's armored strength down to 90 tanks, while the British still possessed 800. On 2 November the British struck again, and again their armor crawled through the German minefields, where the tanks ran into the inevitable screen of anti-tank guns. The attackers suffered heavy losses—over 200 tanks—but the Afrika Korps was now down to 30 tanks. On the 3rd of November Rommel ordered a retreat, but at mid-day Hitler issued a stop order, a decision adding to German losses and making it impossible for the Afrika Korps to make a stand in Libya. On the 4th, the Germans finally slipped away, but in the confusion the British captured General Wilhelm Ritter von Thoma, one of Germany's leading tank pioneers.

On 8 November the strategic situation in North Africa changed fundamentally with the landing in Morocco and Algeria of Anglo-American ground forces under the command of Lieutenant General Dwight David Eisenhower. Eisenhower had rocketed to the top of the American command structure over the past two years. In 1940 as a junior colonel he had begged Patton for a job. But his performance in staff positions and maneuvers brought him to General George Marshall's attention, and Marshall—chief of staff of the U.S. Army and almost always an extraordinarily good judge of talent—had recognized Eisenhower's gifts. Ike's enthusiastic and jovial personality led far too many to underestimate a will of iron and an extraordinary intelligence. Not an intellectual, Eisenhower nevertheless had prepared himself for the coming test as thoroughly as any American senior army officer with the possible exception of Patton. But unlike so many of his contemporaries, Eisenhower was a man willing to subordinate his ego for the greater good. And his personality was such that he was able to get a group of diverse officers from different services and different nations to pull together as a team. Finally, Eisenhower was able to recognize what was possible in a political sense, given the complexities of coalition warfare—again a unique ability in an arena of raging national egos.

Operation Torch reflected the triumph of British strategic arguments over those of the Americans, who had pushed for an invasion of northern France as early as possible. But the reality in 1942 was that the U.S. Army was still only putting together its combat forces. Hence any invasion of the Continent would have to rely almost entirely on the British, who with their experience in fighting the Germans and the strain of two years of war had little desire to invade the Continent just yet.

Nevertheless, Marshall, strongly opposed a landing in North Africa for fear that the commitment of Allied forces to the Mediterranean would prevent a landing in northern France until 1944. Marshall was one of the great figures in the war. A graduate of Virginia Military Institute, he correctly believed that he had received a terrible education—a state of affairs he spent the rest of his life repairing. As he told a contemporary, one could not understand strategy unless one had read Thucydides. On his way to the top of the army, Marshall had impressed virtually everyone he came in contact with except Douglas MacArthur, who was always hostile to those who were his equal. Marshall possessed an austere personality, so austere that a mere glance was enough to suggest to Franklin Roosevelt that even the Commander-in-Chief should not call him George. He had an exceptionally good eye for talent, and over the course of the war he would make few mistakes in the selection and promotion of senior army officers. Above all, Marshall lived by the motto of another military institution, "Duty, Honor, Country," and he would set a standard of behavior that few West Point alumni could match.

Nevertheless, it took a direct order from Roosevelt, overruling Marshall and his military advisers (something Churchill never did), to commit American troops to the landings in North Africa. The rationale for the president's decision stemmed from domestic politics. The United States had to involve its forces in combat with the Germans in 1942 or else the political pressures for a "Japan First" strategy might become intolerable.

The Vichy French military in North Africa, burdened by the Armistice's restrictions, had no chance of prolonged resistance against the Allied invasion. But French troops with antiquated weapons fought hard against Allied landings, particularly in Algeria. The difficulties U.S. forces encountered against an underequipped opponent underlined how unprepared they were to handle the Wehrmacht. The plans had called for a rapid advance to Tunis once Allied forces had consolidated the position in Algeria, but the Germans arrived first. The Vichy French governor in Tunisia willingly opened the gates for the Germans (in marked contrast to the vigorous response of Vichy soldiers in Algeria to the Torch landings).

Luckily for the Allies, in November 1942 the German high command was in its usual state of disarray. The Führer was on the way to Munich by train to give his annual speech on the anniversary of the 1923 Beerhall Putsch. Hurried consultations by teletype from Thuringia could not cobble together an effective strategic response to Torch. The OKW staff remaining in East Prussia suggested that North Africa could not be held, but, as one staff officer noted, this assessment "passed unnoticed in the general jumble of vague political and strategic ideas based primarily on considerations of prestige."[5] There was certainly no overall strategic or operational assessment of additional commitments in North Africa. Hitler rushed paratroopers to Tunisia, and armored and infantry units followed by sea. Shortly thereafter, he ordered the Wehrmacht to occupy the rest of France, ending the last shreds of independence that Marshal Pétain's collaborationist regime still enjoyed. The French fleet scuttled itself in Toulon rather than join the Allies. The OKW had now committed much of the Luftwaffe's transport fleet and the German Army's reserves to operations on the far side of the Mediterranean, where only tenuous supply links with the Italian mainland existed.

Preliminary Moves in the East

By March 1942, operations on the Eastern Front had finally slithered to a halt in the spring *rasputitsa* (mud period). The opposing armies were exhausted. Yet both continued to overestimate their own strength while underestimating that of their opponents. In the short run the Soviets paid for that miscalculation; in the long run the Germans paid even more. In assess-

THE EASTERN FRONT
November 1942 – June 1943

Major Soviet attacks
November–February

Major German counterattacks
February–March

German withdrawal

Front line fall 1942

Front line 1 July 1943

ing the strategic situation, Hitler estimated that Germany must eliminate the Soviet Union in 1942 before the Western powers could mobilize their economic and military resources for an invasion of the Continent. But the battering the Wehrmacht suffered over the winter limited his options. The German Army could no longer support offensive operations across the breadth of European Russia as it had in 1941. Since Hitler had coveted the Ukraine and the Soviet Union's raw materials from his earliest writings, it is not surprising he again focused on the potential economic gains in southern Russia.

In the midst of the winter's desperate fighting, the Führer had informed Field Marshal Bock, who was assuming command of Army Group South after Reichenau's heart attack and subsequent death in an aircraft crash on being returned to Germany, that his army group would attack in the spring. From February 1942 on, Bock received top priority in replacements, new divisions, and equipment, while Fourth Panzer Army moved south from Army Group Center with some of its best divisions. By April, Hitler's military plans had coalesced sufficiently to issue a directive for Operation Blau (Blue). The target of the upcoming offensive would be the Caucasus oil fields, in order to cripple the Soviets and relieve the petroleum shortages that had plagued the Reich's war effort. Stalingrad was also an objective, but even for Hitler it was less important than the Caucasus, at least in the planning stages of Blau. Implicit in German planning was the belief that Stalingrad's capture would cut the Soviets off from their oil. Thus, there was a divergence in Blau's objectives (Stalingrad to the east, the Caucasus to the south), as well as a contradiction between the desire to capture the oil for German use as opposed to cutting the Soviets off from their own petroleum.

Yet the Germans mounted the coming offensive on a shoestring. Any advance would substantially extend the German front, particularly along the Don River. Because of troop shortages in the east, the Germans would have to rely on the armies of their allies to defend the lengthening front. Thus, Hitler called on Romania, Italy, and Hungary to supply the divisions necessary to protect the Don River flank, with the Italians sandwiched between the Hungarians and Romanians to keep the two Balkan armies from fighting each other instead of the Soviets. The fact that only 15 infantry and 6 motorized infantry and panzer divisions of Army Group South's 65 divisions were at full strength suggests the seriousness of the German Army's manpower and materiel shortages despite desperate efforts to build up Bock's forces. A further 17 infantry and 10 motorized infantry and panzer divisions were rebuilt on the front lines to something approaching full strength. The remaining 17 infantry divisions—over 25 percent of Army Group South's strength—were not rebuilt and remained short of officers, soldiers, and equipment. Clearly, the Germans expected that Soviet losses since June 1941 had exhausted the Red Army. Not surprisingly, German intelligence provided little warning of the rapid recovery made by Soviet armament production in the Urals during the winter.

Before Blau started, Manstein's Eleventh Army was to clean up the Crimea by driving Soviet forces off the Kerch peninsula and capturing Sevastopol. By this point in the war, Manstein was well on his way to becoming the premier German general of the war. A brilliant staff officer, he had been one of Beck's protégés and had played a major role in the army's buildup. As a result of the Fritsch-Blomberg purge, he had moved from the OKH to command a division and, with the outbreak of war, to become Rundstedt's chief of staff. His obdurate support for Army Group A's interests over the winter of 1939–40 led to his being replaced in spring 1940 and assigned to an infantry corps command. His performance in this role was sufficiently noteworthy to lead to the command of a panzer corps in 1941. His outstanding success in Barbarossa's opening moves soon led to another promotion: this time to command of Eleventh Army. Besides his acknowledged brilliance as an operational commander, Manstein was inordinately ambitious even among his peers. He indicated his support for the Nazi regime by his pronouncements to his troops and his support for special actions in his area of command.

Manstein kicked off German operations in the Crimea with an attack on Kerch on 8 May. The offensive caught Soviet defenders by surprise; and by striking the strongest point in their line, Manstein unbalanced their defensive scheme. Stalin's political commissar, L. Z. Mekhlis, led an inept defensive team. With effective support from Wolfram von Richthofen's Fliegerkorps VIII, Manstein's troops outmaneuvered the defenders and completed the conquest of the peninsula by 19 May. The Soviets lost 175,000 men along with 4,646 artillery pieces, 496 tanks, and 417 aircraft. When these losses were coupled with the 225,000 casualties the Soviets had suffered since February, it is not surprising that even Stalin found the defeat too much. He fired Mekhlis, who never received another important military post.

While Manstein was attacking Kerch, the Soviets had launched a major offensive against Kharkov. At the end of the winter battles, the Soviets possessed two small bridgeheads over the Donets—one northeast, the other southwest of Kharkov. From the Soviet point of view, a limited offensive to encircle this important logistic center appeared attractive, given what they knew about the German dispositions. The Soviets believed that the strain of the winter battles had left the Germans close to collapse; but in fact, Soviet intelligence had failed to pick up the flow of reinforcements into Army Group South. By striking Kharkov, the Soviets were attacking one of the few places where the Germans possessed strong reserves.

On 12 May, Marshal S. K. Timoshenko's forces attacked. Instead of the battered 12 infantry divisions and 1 panzer division they expected, they hit 16 infantry divisions, 2 refurbished panzer divisions, and 3 infantry battle groups. The northern pincer succeeded in pulverizing the German 294th Infantry Division but then ran into Sixth Army's well-prepared forces. Not only did the attackers find themselves under a major counterattack, but they were mercilessly pounded by the Luftwaffe. Initially the southern pincer did better, achieving a clear breakthrough. For a short time the German line west of the Donets bend teetered near collapse. But the German high command made the daring decision to wait for reinforcements to arrive at Seventeenth Army from Kleist's First Panzer Army to the south. The Germans thus allowed the Soviets to make major gains before their counterattack started.

Seventeenth Army had already prepared for a limited offensive on the Izium bulge, whence the southern pincer of the Soviet offensive had started. The German counteroffensive now came on the back side of that salient. At the last moment, Bock got cold feet, but Hitler, Kleist, General Friedrich Paulus, the new Sixth Army commander, and the staff at Army Group South maintained the view that a massive, well-prepared counterattack from the south represented a better, though riskier, solution than attempting to patch together a defensive front.

On 17 May, the Germans attacked the unsuspecting Soviets, who remained focused on their own offensive. Kleist's eight reconstituted infantry divisions, two panzer divisions, and one motorized infantry division piled into the Soviet southern flank. By the 18th, with Operation Fridericus close to success, Soviet commanders as well as the STAVKA were still concentrating on their offensive against Kharkov. Over the next three days Kleist's attack narrowed the corridor running through to the attacking Soviet forces; by the 22nd the Germans had sealed off the encirclement, thereby entrapping the Soviet Fifty-Seventh Army and the Bobkin Group of mechanized units. Soviet casualties were 170,958 killed, missing, or taken prisoner, with a further 106,232 wounded. The Germans counted 1,200 Soviet tanks and 2,600 artillery pieces in the wreckage. In effect, the Soviets had wasted virtually all their reserves on the southern front.

Still, the catalogue of Soviet woes was not complete; on 2 June a massive

German artillery and air bombardment of Sevastopol began. Fliegerkorps VIII and Eleventh Army's artillery prepped the defenders for the next four days, while air and naval forces cut Sevastopol off from the outside world. The ground attack started on the morning of 7 June; intense fighting followed, during which German infantry made relatively small gains. But as the battle proceeded, the German drive picked up speed. By mid-month the Germans had taken Forts Stalin and Maxim Gorky. On 29 June, taking a major risk, Manstein launched LIV Army Corps across Severnaya Bay in an amphibious assault that caught Soviet defenders by surprise. Sevastopol's defenses collapsed, but the resistance of individual groups made the mopping-up process costly. By 4 July the battle was over, and the Germans counted over 90,000 POWs. Hitler promoted Manstein to field marshal for his victories but refused to listen to his advice that the Eleventh Army remain in the south to provide a strategic reserve for the coming summer offensive. Instead, the Führer decided to transfer its units directly to Blau or other projects such as the capture of Leningrad.

In the space of two months, the Germans had delivered three severe setbacks to Soviet forces. Ironically, those defeats prepared the stage for major Soviet victories within the next six months, because they forced the STAVKA to face up to the weaknesses of Soviet troops and commanders and to forge a stronger connection between means and ends. As Stalin suggested to Marshal Timoshenko and Nikita Khrushchev: "Battles must be won not with numbers but by skill. If you do not learn to direct your troops better, all the armaments the country can produce will not be enough for you."[6] The Germans, on the other hand, learned the wrong lessons; the victories in May and June deluded the Führer and many of his principal advisers into believing that the defeats in winter 1942 were almost exclusively due to weather, not ineptitude. Moreover, Rommel's successes in North Africa added to this euphoria in the OKW. The Germans' sense of racial and, by extension, military superiority remained intact. Hitler's risky decision to overrule Bock and go for the counterblow at Kharkov had paid off, and this was one more indication to the Führer that his judgment was superior to that of the military professionals.

Operation Blau

The German command structure by now was thoroughly muddled. Hitler, as commander-in-chief of the army, was clearly going to meddle in the conduct of Blau to an even greater extent than he had in Barbarossa the year before. Thus, the OKW would also have its say in supporting the Führer's inclinations at the expense of Halder and the OKH. Bock's position as the overall field commander for Blau was weak for several reasons: he had been fired from Army Group Center in December; his handling of the Soviet offensive against Kharkov had been none too adept; and German plans already called for splitting off a substantial portion of German forces on the southern front to form another army group. Of the other commanders, Hoth, as commander of Fourth Panzer Army, already had a justified reputation as one of the most skilled professionals in the army. Though somewhat colorless, Hoth was a consummate professional.

But the new commander of Sixth Army, Paulus, was a question mark. Up to this point in the war, he had been a successful staff officer: chief of staff to Reichenau's Sixth Army and then the chief operations officer in the OKH, where he had proven an able and trusted support for Halder. However, Paulus had yet to hold a field command, and some senior officers doubted whether he had the disposition for a major independent command, especially one that would be under the Führer's thumb.

On 28 June 1942, the German summer offensive began at last. Operation Blau was to involve three distinct phases. The first would be an advance to Voronezh to establish a blocking position that would protect the flank of the advance as it turned south. Then German forces would drive southward toward the Donets and lower Don; formations from Romania, Hungary, and Italy would follow to mop up and man a lengthening flank. Finally, the First and Fourth Panzer Armies would attack across the Don into the Caucasus, while Sixth Army advanced across the steppe toward Stalingrad. In late June a plane carrying the plans for Blau crashed behind Soviet lines. The German high command argued bitterly about who was responsible for the loss, but the Soviets, partly by inclination and partly through German deception, remained convinced the Germans were preparing for an attack on Moscow.

Thus, Blau's opening moves caught the Soviets by surprise. On the first day, the XLVIII Panzer Corps advanced 30 miles toward Voronezh against spotty resistance. Two days later, despite heavy rain, Sixth Army achieved a clean breakthrough that took its troops over the Korocha River. In the north, the mud was so bad that the Großdeutschland and 16th Motorized Infantry Division had to place their lead units on foot. The Germans pressed across the Olym River on the way to Voronezh. But as a pocket formed with Fourth Panzer Army's advance in the north and Sixth Army's in the south, the STAVKA, instead of ordering the defenders to hold, ordered the Soviet Fortieth and Twenty-First Armies to retreat eastward. Bock focused on capturing Voronezh, much to Hitler's and Halder's dismay, since they were already planning the drive south.

A series of badly coordinated counterattacks by the Soviets resulted in

9th Panzer Division's destroying two enemy tank brigades on 6 July. Voronezh fell the same day, but aside from capturing territory, the Germans had little to show for their efforts. The escape of Soviet units from the pocket as well as a major pullback in front of Sixth Army by the Soviets' Southwest Front caught German commanders by surprise. In effect, the Soviets were finally trading space for time and refusing to put forces at risk by holding positions that German operations had already compromised. The Soviet assumption that Moscow was still the main German objective helps explain Stalin's willingness to yield territory. With their reserves concentrated to protect Moscow, the Soviets could not think in terms of grand offensive designs in the south; rather they had to save what they could.

However, the Germans had their problems as well. Bock had virtually all the armor in the north by Voronezh, while Paulus had only one panzer division and one motorized infantry division to pursue the Soviets down the Don. On 9 July the OKH executed the long-planned division of Army Group South into Army Group B (under Bock) and Army Group A (under Field Marshal Wilhelm List), the latter to drive across the lower Don into the Caucasus. But there was already inordinate squabbling in the German high command. Bock and Halder quibbled over past mistakes; Keitel added nothing except sycophantic comments, and the Führer urged all of them that time was of vital importance. Hitler summarily relieved Bock on 13 July and replaced him with Generaloberst Maximilian von Weichs. Not surprisingly, Bock's latest warning that German armies were only conquering empty territory went unheeded.

On 16 July, Hitler moved the OKW's and the OKH's command elements to Vinnitsa in the Ukraine, so that he could run both army groups directly. By now Blau was little more than a race to occupy Soviet territory. The willingness with which the Soviets retreated presented the Germans with entirely new conditions. Army Group A's advance allowed it to sweep forward to Rostov. In three weeks Army Group A took only 54,000 prisoners, while the advance was already damaging the Wehrmacht's overstretched logistical support. The supply system confronted the same difficulties it had faced the year before—great distances, poor weather, and inadequate roads—while the extent of the expanding front required ever more troops to guard the Don flank.

In mid-July Hitler was still focusing on encircling Soviet forces near Rostov and capturing that city. To do so, he provided a three- to four-day hiatus to the Soviets, who escaped across the Don in droves, as the German Sixth Army remained immobilized for lack of supplies north of the Don bend. Paulus's logistical situation depended on a single low-capacity rail line from which trucks had to haul supplies over ever-lengthening distances. The movement of Hoth's Fourth Panzer Army across Paulus's rear, at Hitler's direction, to accomplish the Rostov operation served only to exacerbate logistic difficulties. Hitler was not yet concentrating on Stalingrad, but the crossing of the Chir River west of the city by Paulus's troops certainly alerted the Soviets to the danger. The capture of Rostov yielded virtually nothing in the way of prisoners, while First Panzer Army had only 80,000 prisoners to show for its advance of over 200 miles.

Suddenly, on 19 July, Hitler reoriented the offensive from the Caucasus to Stalingrad. The OKH ordered Hoth to give up LI Corps (three infantry divisions) and XIV Panzer Corps (two motorized infantry divisions and one panzer division) to Sixth Army. Nevertheless, the Führer abandoned none of his goals in the Caucasus. In pursuit of the impossible, his Directive 45, issued 19 July, maintained that operations thus far had accomplished the "deep" objectives of the offensive, including the "conclusive destruction of Soviet defensive strength." The reality was not so conclusive. In the north, Paulus had relatively weak forces advancing on Stalingrad, while the Soviets had already undertaken extensive measures to prepare the city's defenses. The divergence of the German drives to the east and to the south was already exercising a malignant influence over German operations. First Panzer Army and Seventeenth Army flowed into a vacuum in the Caucasus as Soviet forces retreated. The distances between objectives in this area worked against German ambitions, while Hitler's refusal to focus on any specific objective made matters worse.

The Caucasus mountains served to protect Soviet forces along the Black Sea; although the Seventeenth Army captured Maikop, the Soviets had so thoroughly destroyed its oil wells that the German war economy received not a drop of oil from that source. First Panzer Army almost reached Grozny in the central Caucasus, but a steadily weakening logistic system and the bleeding away of Luftwaffe support to Stalingrad provided little prospect for strategic success. The stalemate in the Caucasus was sufficient for Hitler to fire List. Halder also found himself relieved as the army's chief of staff, while much of the OKW's operations staff felt the Führer's wrath. Jodl almost got the sack, and Hitler would probably have replaced him with Paulus in late fall had not other events intervened.

The firing of these senior generals in summer 1942 was not the result of events on the Eastern Front alone. It reflected a larger effort being undertaken by Hitler and the army's personnel office to alter radically the officer corps' ethos and bring it more closely in line with Nazi ideology, at least from the Führer's perspective. These reforms aimed at turning the army into a true instrument of National Socialism by removing what Hitler regarded as the general staff's baleful influence on the army's *mentalität*. The new National Socialist army henceforth would reward battlefield performance and ideological commitment rather than technical and educational accomplishments. It would rest on performance rather than on class. And it would provide none of the carping criticism and questioning of the Führer's "genius" that Hitler believed had led to the failure of Barbarossa.

Meanwhile, Sixth Army advanced on Stalingrad at a snail's pace. In late July Paulus lost half his supply quota to units in Army Group A with higher priorities. But the Soviets also confronted difficulties. On 28 July, Stalin signed Order 227 that soon took its name from the sentence: "Not a Step Back!" It ordered ferocious measures, such as the immediate execution of anyone who failed in the line of duty. At the same time, Paulus's advance was now to be supported from the south, as Hitler ordered Fourth Panzer Army to turn back toward the northeast and Stalingrad. On 7 August, Sixth Army attacked the Kalach bridgehead on the Don's western bank and trapped the Soviets' Sixty-Second Army. Four days later the Germans had finished cleaning out the pocket, and another 50,000 Soviet prisoners were on their way to the merciless POW camps in the Reich. Yet the logistic support Sixth Army received barely sufficed to supply troops with current expenditures of ammunition and fuel, much less to build up reserves. The Luftwaffe attempted to help, but at best its efforts could only alleviate the most desperate shortages. On the 21st, Paulus, ignoring Soviet bridgeheads on the west bank of the Don, launched LI Corps across the river toward Vertyachiy. The move surprised the Soviets again. By the next day Sixth Army had an extensive bridgehead across the Don, pointing at the Volga.

German plans called for Sixth Army to drive straight through to the Volga above Stalingrad, from whence it could drive south to take the city. Meanwhile, follow-up units would drive south to link up with Hoth's Fourth Panzer Army and encircle Soviet forces on the Don. But the link-up failed to catch the Soviets; Sixty-Fourth Army and what was left of Sixty-Second Army had already slipped into Stalingrad, where civilians had been hard at work constructing defenses. Hitler now firmly determined to take Stalingrad—a sharp break with his attitude the year before when he held Rundstedt back from Kiev and ordered Leningrad besieged but not attacked for fear of another Verdun. In keeping with his ideological aims, he ordered his commanders to wipe out Stalingrad's male inhabitants and deport the female population to slave labor in the Reich.

The Luftwaffe caught the spirit of the Führer's directive. On 3 September, Richthofen launched a massive 24-hour aerial assault that left much of

Stalingrad in flames. In the long run the attack was counterproductive because the wrecked buildings and factories made excellent fortified defensive positions for the Soviets. By early September the campaign to take Stalingrad had stretched the Luftwaffe to the breaking point. The Germans had begun Blau with 1,610 aircraft, but by the end of July they were down to 1,359, while operationally ready rates had dropped from 71 to 56 percent. Between Blau's inception and 10 October, bomber strength declined from 480 to 232 because of losses, supply difficulties, and the wear and tear on aircraft. At the same time, calls on the Luftwaffe for interdiction, close air support, logistical support, and even the strategic bombing of Stalingrad were skyrocketing, while the Luftwaffe's logistic system was becoming as strained as the army's.

As with Barbarossa, Blau represented an enormous overreach by the Germans in logistic as well as strategic terms. The objective of obtaining Caucasus oil was not attainable given the distances; Grozny was over 600 miles from where the summer offensive had kicked off. And the objective of taking Stalingrad made even less strategic (or operational) sense than Kiev or Leningrad did; the only justification was the prestige of taking Stalin's city. Moreover, the willingness of the Soviets to trade space for time robbed the Germans of the chance to destroy large Soviet forces. Thus, Blau failed to repeat the great victories of 1941. In part the German failure could be attributed to missed opportunities. For example, on 10 October Richthofen launched his bombers against the refineries around Grozny and inflicted substantial damage. But, as the Americans discovered in 1943, single strikes against petroleum targets, no matter how spectacular, do not achieve long-term effects and Richthofen's forces did not repeat the raid. Had the Germans taken a larger view, they might have used captured air bases in the Don bend as a means to execute a sustained air campaign against the Soviet petroleum industry. Such a balanced assessment of strategic and operational objectives was not part of the German repertoire. Instead, under the Führer's command, German troops struck out across the vast expanse of southern Russia with no coherent goals except the idle hope that the Soviets would collapse.

Stalingrad: Verdun in the East

A grim, street-by-street struggle over Stalingrad's smashed-up houses and factories flamed along the west bank of the Volga River throughout September, October, and into November. The Soviets had brought in a new team to conduct the city's defense. General A. I. Eremenko, recently recovered from wounds suffered earlier in the war, was in overall command, with General V. I. Chuikov directing the ground battle in the city. As attacks by Sixth Army and Fourth Panzer Army, preceded by massive artillery and air bombardments, slowly ground forward into the city, the Soviets fed in sufficient forces to maintain a tenacious hold on the ruins. Where German operations in the first stages of Blau had proceeded in rapid advances across great swaths of territory, the Wehrmacht now crawled slowly from one geographic objective to the next. Sixth Army reported in late September that it had taken Height 107.5 and the blocks of houses to the northwest as well as a gully. On 28 September, LI Corps reported that it had occupied approximately half the Barrikady settlement and two-thirds of a block of houses near Mamai Hill as well as the western part of the Krasny October works. Throughout the rest of September, all of October, and into November the Germans battered their way across a landscape of rubble and building shells. The cost was horrendous. Despite a constant flow of reinforcements, German infantry strength steadily dropped. By early October, frontline battalions possessed an average of 3 officers, 11 NCOs, and 62 soldiers. Soviet defenders were no better off. Under heavy bombardments and constant attacks, Soviet strength, despite nightly reinforcements across the Volga, also ebbed. By mid-November the Germans had battered the defenders back onto a thin strip along the cliffs overlooking the Volga.

The fighting was at such close quarters that even Richthofen admitted the Luftwaffe's helplessness in distinguishing friend from foe. By November, virtually all of the German reserves had been sucked into the city. To the immediate north the Third Romanian Army, backed up by a weak panzer corps, protected Sixth Army's left flank. Moreover, Army Group B's flank along the entire northern bend of the Don depended on a Hungarian, a Romanian, and an Italian army, none of which possessed the military effectiveness to resist a major Soviet offensive. South of Stalingrad, Fourth Panzer Army, partially committed to the fighting in the city, maintained its flank with the help of the Romanian VI and VII Corps, neither of which was prepared for combat conditions on the Eastern Front. German intelligence, however, failed to pick up signs that anything unusual was afoot on Sixth Army's flanks. On 8 November Hitler, undoubtedly frustrated by unfolding events in North Africa, announced to the party comrades celebrating the 1923 Beerhall Putsch that Sixth Army had conquered Stalingrad. The German soldier now stood on the Volga, and there, the Führer pronounced, he would remain.

In September the Soviets had begun planning for two major military operations to take place in late fall. The first, Operation Uranus, was to encircle the German forces fighting on the Volga; weak Romanian forces on the flanks of Stalingrad offered a tempting target. Colonel Generals Aleksandr Vasilevsky, in overall command, and N. K. Vatutin, commander of the Southwestern Front, played the key roles in planning, which involved extensive use of deception *(maskirovka)* to shield Soviet deployments into the area. At the same time, Zhukov was also planning a major offensive, Operation Mars, to take out the exposed Rzhev salient in Army Group Center. The Mars operation appears to have been the larger and more ambitious. Uranus was to be the subsidiary offensive to draw off German reserves from Army Group Center, so that Zhukov's offensive would have the possibility of gaining a major victory to the west of Moscow. The contrast between the fate of these two offensives reveals what the Germans might have achieved with a more cautious operational approach in summer 1942.

Mars followed within a week of the attack on Stalingrad and aimed to inflict the same fate on the German Ninth Army as Uranus was to inflict on Sixth Army. Like Uranus, Mars was to be followed by an even larger offensive to destroy Army Group Center. The fact that Zhukov took the lead in planning and executing the offensive suggests the importance STAVKA gave to his operation. But Mars was to be Zhukov's biggest failure. Unlike the situation around Stalingrad, the German Ninth Army (under General Walter Model), which protected the Rzhev salient, possessed relatively fresh units, including the 1st, 5th, and 9th Panzer Divisions and the 14th and Großdeutschland Motorized Infantry Divisions. Moreover, substantial reserves, including the 12th, 19th, and 20th Panzer Divisions, were available from Army Group Center. And Model was a master of defensive warfare, as events the previous winter had already proved.

The Soviets deployed 11 combined-arms armies (each the equivalent to a German corps) and some of the best units in the Red Army. On 25 November the Twenty-Second and Forty-First Soviet Armies struck the western side of the Rzhev salient, while General Ivan Konev's Twentieth and Thirty-First Armies attacked the eastern side. After ferocious fighting, the Soviets managed only to encircle the town of Belyi. Moreover, they almost immediately came under heavy counterattacks by Field Marshal Kluge's reserves. With reinforcements from Army Group Center, Model had six panzer divisions and two motorized infantry divisions available to drive the attacking Soviet formations back.

At times Ninth Army approached defeat, but the extraordinary performance of the troops inflicted heavy casualties on the Soviets. A German account of one action reported that "Feldwebel [Sergeant Major] Schafer, who had already destroyed five tanks the day before, rolled forward from combat base Hubert . . . [in a Mark IV tank] with a 7.5 cm anti-tank gun under his command . . . and immediately attacked the enemy tanks. These were mostly T-34s, with three KV-1s among them, all with infantry mounted aboard. Schafer, who still had a few [anti-tank rounds] at his disposal, at first fired at and destroyed one KV-1 and five T-34s. After his ammunition ran out, he wheeled his tank and assault gun into the nearest shelter [to pick up an ammunition reload]. He then rolled back to the north through the driving snow and wheeled into the rear of the enemy tanks. Here, he destroyed nine additional T-34s and one KV-1 [before himself being knocked out of action]."[7]

The result of the battle was an unmitigated disaster for Soviet arms—almost as big a defeat for the Soviets as Stalingrad was to be a victory. When Zhukov finally shut Mars down with only very minor gains, the Soviets had suffered approximately 100,000 dead and over 235,000 wounded—close to three-quarters of the losses suffered in the November, December, and January fighting around Stalingrad and along the Don. The only positive result from Mars was that it prevented Army Group Center from transferring reinforcements to the south, where crucial events were unfolding.

Uranus was another matter. The heavy fighting since May had burned out much of Sixth Army, while the only reserves the Germans possessed were a few Luftwaffe field divisions and the 22nd Panzer Division. Against the Romanian forces and these scanty reserves, the Soviets marshaled powerful forces. The lead four armored corps possessed 660 first-class tanks. Meanwhile, intelligence was assuring German commanders that the Soviets lacked the potential to launch a major offensive. At the highest command level, the Germans were in even more confusion than usual. After his annual speech in Munich, Hitler headed off for Berchtesgaden, taking Keitel and Jodl with him. The OKW operations staff remained in Salzburg for talks with the Italians about the Mediterranean situation, while in East Prussia the OKH staff under the army's new chief of staff, General Kurt Zeitzler, remained isolated and irrelevant.

On 19 November the storm broke. After a night of heavy snow and falling temperatures, over 3,500 Soviet artillery pieces opened up on the Romanian Third Army's positions north of Stalingrad. By noon Fifth Tank and Twenty-First Armies had broken through Romanian defenses entirely; two tank corps moved through the breach and into the open and advanced nearly 70 kilometers before the day was over. Equally bad news came the next morning in the south, as Fifty-First Army wrecked the Romanian VI Corps; the Soviets now had two major breakthroughs on each side of Stalingrad. The German response was entirely at the local level. Late on the 19th, Army Group B ordered Sixth Army to suspend offensive operations and move three panzer divisions and an infantry division out of the city to protect a left flank that no longer existed. Paulus merely waited on events.

The response at higher levels was even less decisive. Zeitzler called Hitler with "alarming news," but the Führer apparently believed that XLVIII Panzer Corps could patch the front back together in the north. In fact, it was already being destroyed by overwhelming Soviet strength. Hitler's response was to strip the commander of the 22nd Panzer Division of his rank and imprison him. As the situation deteriorated, the Führer decided to return to his East Prussian headquarters in Rastenburg by rail and aircraft and was out of contact with the OKH for much of the 21st and 22nd. Without guidance from the OKH, those on the scene allowed matters to take their course. Richthofen warned Sixth Army that the Luftwaffe could not supply its forces in Stalingrad by airlift. Paulus's chief of staff replied that there was no other choice but to resupply by air.

To a certain extent, he may have been right. The fighting for Stalingrad had so eroded Sixth Army's strength and its reserves of fuel and ammunition that even if it had pulled out, it was in no condition to fight a major winter battle on the steppes. Zeitzler argued furiously with Hitler that he should allow Sixth Army to retreat, but assurances from Göring that the Luftwaffe could supply the city persuaded the Führer to stand fast on the Volga. Keitel did his usual best to encourage the Führer's worst instincts. The frustrations of the past several weeks, especially the reversal of fortunes in North Africa, contributed to Hitler's decision. In retrospect, Göring's intervention was catastrophic, for the Luftwaffe had no chance, even under the best of conditions, of supplying Sixth Army with its requirements. Winter was already closing in and the Soviet offensive had captured the air fields the Germans had prepared for winter operations. Thus, the Luftwaffe would have to operate from fields with only the most primitive infrastructures. On the 24th, the day after the Soviet pincers encircled Sixth Army, Richthofen and other Luftwaffe commanders again warned that an airlift, given the conditions, would be impossible. It was too late, for Hitler had made up his mind.

Late on the 23rd, IV Tank Corps from the north closed the ring around Stalingrad, when it met units of the IV Mechanized Corps at Sovetskiy. The Soviet offensive had encircled over a quarter of a million German and Romanian soldiers and ripped an enormous hole in German lines. By limiting their objectives and focusing on Sixth Army's destruction, the Soviets were well on the way to achieving a major victory. They displayed considerable discipline in comparison to their conduct of operations the previous year. Instead of continuing operations to exploit the gaping hole they had made, the Soviets established two strong defensive rings around Stalingrad, the first to keep the garrison in, the second to prevent a breakthrough from the outside.

On the other side of the lines, Hitler selected Manstein to handle Stalingrad's relief, with command over the German Sixth and Fourth Panzer Armies as well as Third and Fourth Romanian Armies, while Paulus flew back into the pocket. He was certainly not the man to take decisive or independent action. The suddenness as well as the ferocity of the offensive had caught the Germans entirely off guard. As one commentator has noted: "An encirclement of a modern army is a cataclysmic event. On the map it often takes on a surgically precise appearance. On the battlefield it is a rending operation that leaves the victim to struggle in a state of shock with the least favorable of all military situations: his lines of communications are cut; his headquarters are often separated from the troops; support elements are shattered; and his front is open to attack from all directions. The moment the ring closes every single individual in the pocket is a prisoner. Death is in front of him and behind him; home is a distant dream. Fear and panic hang in the air."[8]

On the 24th Manstein arrived at the headquarters of Army Group B. There he was warned that Sixth Army's position was untenable, but the field marshal sent a more optimistic report to the OKH suggesting a breakout was not immediately necessary. That message, along with Göring's promises, sealed the fate of Sixth Army. Manstein, now commander of Army Group Don, confronted two orders of business. The first was to build up Luftwaffe strength sufficiently to provide an effective airlift; the second was to organize a relief force to break through to the Volga. The former turned into a nightmare. Between mid-August and mid-November, the OKL had withdrawn a considerable part of the air strength in the east for operations in the Mediterranean.

Moreover, the Luftwaffe's transport fleet was already heavily committed to the Tunisian operation, where it had suffered heavy losses. Only by stripping training units could the Germans concentrate a respectable number of aircraft. An assortment of transports—Ju 52s, Ju 86s, He 111s (now assigned to transport units)—flew from the Reich to primitive operating bases in the Don bend. In addition to the transport squadrons, Richthofen received Fw 200 Condors, Ju 290s, and even some He 177 bombers (whose welded engines still had a distressing tendency to decouple in flight). Transport aircraft dribbled out to the airlift. Not until 2 December did

Richthofen possess 200 transports, and the airlift failed to reach 300 aircraft until a week later.

The main operating air fields would be Tatsinskaia and Morozovsk, neither possessing permanent hangars. Thus, maintenance crews, few of whom were familiar with conditions on the Eastern Front, worked in the open in freezing temperatures and howling winds that made essential maintenance a nightmare. Operationally ready rates plummeted to 20 percent; these low in-commission rates had the positive effect of limiting the flying time of inexperienced crews but they did nothing to improve the airlift. The OKH and OKL's attempts to direct the airlift from Berlin and Rastenburg prompted Richthofen to complain that he was little more than "a highly paid noncommissioned officer."[9]

The airlift began on 25 November with 30 Ju 52s. They carried in only 75 tons of supplies. Over the remaining five days of November the transports barely matched what Göring had promised for a single day. Only on three days in December did the Luftwaffe reach 300 tons, and on some days during periods of bad weather the airlift got hardly anything to the beleaguered garrison inside Stalingrad. Even the arrival of the Luftwaffe's supply genius, Field Marshal Erich Milch, did little to improve the situation. Göring's incessant interference led an exasperated Richthofen to suggest that Hitler send the Reichsmarschall to command the entire relief effort: "The optimistic leader at the place, over which he is optimistic."[10]

The losses suffered at Stalingrad (and North Africa) did irreparable harm to both the Luftwaffe's transport and its bomber forces. The airlift cost the Luftwaffe 269 Ju 52s, 169 He 111s, 42 Ju 86s, 9 Fw 190s, 1 Ju 290, and 5 He 177s—the equivalent of an entire Fliegerkorps—to weather, fighters, and anti-aircraft guns. And in the end, the small quantities of supplies German transports flew in served only to prolong the battle to no purpose.

While the Luftwaffe struggled to supply Stalingrad, Manstein assembled a relief force. Reinforcements began arriving at Army Group Don in early December, and Manstein prepared to drive a corridor through Soviet lines to the garrison within. But the Soviets were preparing a major offensive aimed at Axis armies positioned along the Don. Nevertheless, LVII Panzer Corps drove deeply into the ring around Stalingrad, its lead units reaching within 35 miles of the city. Manstein urged both Hitler and Paulus to order Sixth Army to break out, but Hitler refused, and Paulus was unwilling to disobey Hitler's instructions.

On 16 December the Soviets launched Operation Little Saturn against the Italian Eighth Army and Third Romanian Army along the Don. Neither force had the strength to resist a Soviet offensive, and both collapsed. German troops, buttressing their allied formations, were too weak to seal off enemy penetrations, and the Soviets tore a hole over 100 miles in length along the Don front northwest of Stalingrad. Manstein immediately abandoned his effort to reach Sixth Army, which remained in its positions. Soviet forces poured through the gaps in the north and drove straight toward the air fields on which the airlift depended; moreover, they held the operational potential to drive on Rostov and put Army Group A, still deep in the Caucasus, in the bag.

Göring refused to sanction withdrawals from the Tatsinskaia and Morozovsk air fields until Soviet ground forces were in sight. On Christmas eve, as Luftwaffe transports desperately attempted to get airborne, the Soviets captured Tatsinskaia; the supply dumps and many aircraft fell into Soviet hands before the Germans could destroy them. That same evening, Soviet artillery fired on Morozovsk. Surviving German transports had to pull back to the air field at Novocherkassk—350 kilometers from Stalingrad. The greater distance required more fuel on board, and consequently payload had to decrease.

Manstein had now become desperately worried by the threat to Rostov. A lengthy series of arguments ensued between those on the scene, supported by Zeitzler and the Führer, about whether Seventeenth and First Panzer Armies should pull out of the Caucasus. Finally, Hitler grudgingly agreed to a withdrawal. However, even then he gutted the order's impact. Instead of pulling Army Group A back through Rostov, he permitted only First Panzer Army to retreat across the Don, while Seventeenth Army retreated to the Kuban area across from the Crimea. There it would supposedly be positioned for an offensive into the Caucasus in 1943.

These momentous events sealed Stalingrad's fate. Ineffectual at the beginning of the month, the airlift only provided the barest of essentials. For their part, the Soviets determined to finish off the pocket and release the forces surrounding the city for operations elsewhere on the Eastern Front. On 7 January the Soviets sent three emissaries into the city to demand Sixth Army's surrender. Paulus passed the terms along to Hitler, who demanded a fight to the finish. Manstein concurred, for the German high command had no choice but to demand that Sixth Army resist as long as possible and thus prevent the Soviets from redeploying forces from the Volga to battles farther west. On 10 January the Soviet offensive opened with a preliminary bombardment by 7,000 artillery tubes. Nevertheless, the Soviets considerably underestimated the forces encircled in Stalingrad. For the first five days they made limited progress, but on 15 January the

German front along the Rossoshka River cracked. As a result, Soviet forces were soon on Pitomnik, the main German air field in the pocket. There was a subsidiary air field on the city's outskirts, but Sixth Army had done little to prepare it for use. From this point the Luftwaffe could only parachute supplies into the garrison, further lowering the minimal support Sixth Army was receiving.

By the 17th the Soviets had captured two-thirds of the pocket. On the 22nd, Fifty-Seventh Army broke through German lines near Voroponovo Station and surged into the city. The half-starved garrison was almost completely out of fuel and low on ammunition. Paulus requested permission to surrender, but again the Führer ordered a fight to the bitter end. Under unspeakable conditions, in a city already wrecked from end to end by the battles of the previous autumn, the Germans contested every street and building. The wounded froze to death, morale collapsed, and order began to break down. Brick by brick, wall by wall the Soviets retook the city, to the shrieks of exploding artillery and dying soldiers. On the 25th, the defenders raised the Reich's battle flag to encourage the survivors to make a last-ditch stand. On the 28th, Sixth Army stopped issuing rations to the wounded. On the 31st, the southern part of the city surrendered; the newly promoted Field Marshal Paulus led the way into captivity. In the northern pocket around the Tractor Works, XI Corps fought on for another two days. On 2 February, it transmitted the last message from inside the pocket.

The cost to both sides was terrible. Approximately 147,000 Germans and Romanians died and 91,000 became prisoners—of these, only 5,000 survived captivity in Soviet POW camps. The Germans had also flown approximately 30,000 wounded out during the siege. Casualties on the Soviet side were much worse—as many as half a million. The expenditure of 911,000 artillery shells, 990,000 mortar shells, and 24,000,000 rifle and machine gun rounds by the Soviets in January and early February gives some indication of the ferocity of the battle. In every respect Stalingrad was a catastrophic defeat for the Germans—one that turned the balance in the east in favor of the Soviets.

Crisis, Recovery, and Defeat

As Stalingrad died, Manstein confronted a seriously deteriorating situation. Four Soviet armies, supported by a cavalry and a tank corps, approached Rostov, while Army Group A's retreat from the Caucasus had only just begun. Army detachments Fretter-Pico and Hollidt held the Chir line behind the Don for a short period but soon had to fall back on the Donets despite

Hitler's objections. On 7 January, only the commitment of a newly organized battalion of Tiger tanks prevented the Soviets from breaking through to Rostov and cutting the rail and road lines on which First Panzer Army's retreat depended. However, winter weather hindered the Soviets more than the Germans. Alternating between periods of thaw and below-zero temperatures, the Russian winter made offensive operations extraordinarily difficult, even for the hardiest Soviet troops.

Hitler's interference continued. While the headquarters of First Panzer Army retreated through Rostov, Hitler allowed only one panzer division, one infantry, and two security divisions to move to support Army Group Don. The remainder fell back with Seventeenth Army into the Kuban bridgehead. But as Manstein desperately struggled to patch together a collapsing front along the Don, the Soviets intended nothing less than the destruction of German forces in the south. Nevertheless, as they had done the previous year, Soviet ambitions exceeded the available resources and the skill of their commanders. In the last half of January, three massive attacks hit the Germans and their allies. The first, conducted by three armies, struck German and Hungarian forces along the middle Don. Eleven days later a major attack drove the Second Army back across the upper Don at Voronezh and enveloped two of its three corps. At the same time Voronezh Front and Southwestern Front threw six armies at the patched-together line north of Rostov. But these attacks lacked the operational focus that had marked the Stalingrad offensive, and the Soviet advance flowed into areas that were not of critical importance to the Germans. Moreover, the attackers themselves had suffered heavy losses in the fighting and faced serious equipment shortages. Finally, the Soviets had outrun their logistic support; they did not yet have the massive truck fleets that Lend-Lease would provide in 1943 and 1944, while winter conditions made resupply difficult.

The Southwestern Front's advance was the most dangerous. By mid-February Soviet forces had pressed on to Kharkov, which fell as the SS Corps defending the city disobeyed its orders and retreated. But the Germans were concentrating their forces. In early February three reconditioned Waffen SS divisions—Totenkopf, Das Reich, and Leibstandarte Adolf Hitler—were available, while Hitler allowed Manstein considerable freedom to use the seven understrength but veteran panzer and panzer grenadier (retitled motorized infantry) divisions then in Army Group Don's area of responsibility. The Führer flew out to visit Manstein on 17 February—possibly to relieve the field marshal, certainly to blast him for Army Group Don's defensive attitude. But Manstein had a surprise for the Führer; his forces were ready to launch a major counterattack. Moreover, by this point Luftwaffe squadrons had recovered much of their punch as they fell back on their supply depots and received new aircraft and pilots from the Reich. They were also operating from semipermanent air fields possessing at least rudimentary maintenance facilities, while Richthofen had rationalized the command structure. In addition, Soviet advances had carried the Red Army well beyond the reach of its own air support.

While German strength was gathering, the Soviets set in motion ever more ambitious operations. Two major attacks hit Army Group Center in an attempt to take out the Orel salient and then clear the Briansk region. Both depended on continuing success in the south. However, Soviet forces from Stalingrad never properly deployed, while Army Group Center's defenses, prepared for the past year and a half, proved formidable. The Soviets made considerable gains against Second Army, but as the situation in the south worsened, the Germans restored their front lines and even regained some of the territory lost. In the south, Soviet spearheads advanced into the trap Manstein had set.

The German counterattack began on 20 February with a stunning success. The XL Panzer Corps caught Group Popov northwest of Stalino and encircled the Soviet armored force. After heavy fighting, Lieutenant General A. F. Popov extricated some of his units, but only after serious losses in manpower and equipment. First Panzer Army then supported the flank of Fourth Panzer Army's attack toward Kharkov and cleared the Donets basin.

Fourth Panzer Army jumped off from the Dnepropetrovsk bridgehead. Its initial moves, spearheaded by SS Totenkopf, trapped sizeable Soviet forces south of the Samara River. Hoth's forces picked up speed as they drove toward the northeast and Kharkov. So sudden and unexpected was the German offensive that the Soviets failed to react. By the 26th, lead German units had reached Lozovaya. Despite the spring thaw, Fourth Panzer Army made good progress against confused Soviet resistance. Over the first five days of March, Hoth's troops advanced 50 miles. By the 9th, II SS Panzer Corps was approaching Kharkov from the west with explicit instructions to bypass the city and drive toward the northeast. Then, it was to drop an encircling force behind the city.

But the II SS Corps commander, General Paul Hausser, disobeyed his orders and launched two of his divisions directly into the city. After three days of vicious house-to-house fighting, SS troopers had retaken the city, though with heavy casualties. What probably saved Hausser from court-martial was the fact that his corps then advanced along the railroad line and took Belgorod—30 miles down the line—in four hours. On the 21st, with the spring mud season in full flood, Manstein closed down the counteroffensive. It proved to be the last offensive operational success the Germans could claim on the Eastern Front.

In the heavy fighting that accompanied the advance, Richthofen's Luftflotte 4 provided significant support. Not only did the German airmen clear the skies of Soviet aircraft—for the last time in the war—but Stukas and medium bombers pounded Soviet units mercilessly. Where the Luftwaffe had barely averaged 350 sorties per day in January, it now provided over 1,000 interdiction and close air support sorties daily. On 23 February, as First Panzer Army's units attacked, Richthofen's pilots provided 1,200 sorties. But these efforts to support the army did not come lightly. Over the course of February and March the Luftwaffe lost 56 dive-bombers, 217 bombers, and 163 fighters.

The spring thaw had finally brought an end to operations that had begun in May 1942. Ironically, with the exception of the Kursk salient, which the Soviet attack on Army Group Center's Second Army had fashioned in February 1943, the front followed almost exactly the same positions of the previous year. The Wehrmacht had gained practically nothing by its immense exertions. The question confronting the Germans was whether they had any strategic options that would allow them to avoid defeat. Conceivably, Germany might have to face a second front in France before the year was out, and at a minimum it would have to deal with major military operations launched by the Western powers in the Mediterranean. Moreover, the Allies' Combined Bomber Offensive was severely disabling the German war effort—so much so that at this point the army groups in the east began to assess the state of morale back home.

Some OKW planners prudently urged a defensive posture in the east; moreover, Heinz Guderian, brought back from retirement as the chief of the armored forces, also cautioned against major attacks against the Soviets. But by the end of winter 1943, Hitler and most senior army leaders could conceive of no operational option other than a resumption of the offensive on the Eastern Front in the summer. The question then was where? In early spring Manstein suggested that the Germans encourage the Soviets to launch a major operation against Army Group South and even allow them to make gains before launching a counterblow. Hitler, however, was not in the least interested in an operational approach that might result in the loss of ground. Consequently, Manstein suggested to the Führer and OKH that the Kursk salient offered the possibility for an encirclement, the northern arm coming from Orel, the southern driving northeast from

Kharkov. Hitler was intrigued, and planning for the operation immediately went forward.

What was soon called Operation Zitadelle initially had some prospect for success. The Soviet salient at Kursk was vulnerable to thrusts from Kharkov and Orel, particularly since both cities were major German logistic centers. But much was riding on the operation, for the Germans were depending on its success to blunt further Soviet offensives in 1943. Thus, Hitler was looking for a rapid and decisive victory. His operations order, issued on 15 April, stated that the coming Battle of Kursk must serve as a beacon. Therein lay the rub, because the earlier the Germans launched Zitadelle, the riskier the operation would be but the greater the prospect for a major success. Hitler, however, was no longer in the mood to take risks. Over the coming months he delayed the start so that the Wehrmacht could deploy maximum forces, allow time for more Panther and Tiger tank production, and prepare every aspect of the offensive in meticulous detail.

The problem was that the Soviets, unlike the year before, knew about German plans. After Soviet military leaders persuaded Stalin to allow the Germans to make the opening move—again unlike the previous year—the Soviets undertook a massive program to prepare Kursk's defenses, while at the same time deploying substantial reserves to intervene in the battle at the decisive moment. The Soviets kept most of these defensive measures, as well as the redeployment of their mobile reserves, hidden from the Germans. Soviet *maskirovka* was now so skillful that the Germans would fail to pick up the preparations for virtually every major Soviet offensive for the remainder of the war—such was the intellectual superiority of Soviet operational art and the effect of German attitudes toward the Slavic "subhumans."

Both sides marshaled massive forces for this climactic battle of World War II—the largest battle in human history. The Ninth Army under General Model was to strike south from the Orel salient, while Fourth Panzer Army, its eastern flank protected by Army Detachment Kempf, struck north from Kharkov. Model had two panzer corps with six panzer divisions and one panzer grenadier division. Hoth's Fourth Panzer Army possessed the most powerful striking forces with the II SS Panzer Corps of three SS armored divisions, along with the XLVIII Panzer Corps of two panzer divisions and panzer grenadier division Großdeutschland. On its flank Kempf would deploy three panzer divisions. In total, Army Group South possessed six panzer and five panzer grenadier divisions. In addition to new Mark III and Mark IV tanks, produced by Albert Speer's mobilization of the European economy, the attacking force possessed the heavy Tiger with its

88mm gun and a new medium tank, the Panther. Hitler had deliberately postponed Zitadelle to increase the numbers of these new super tanks. But the Panther did not have an impressive debut, while the Tiger remained underpowered for its size. Altogether, the attacking German forces numbered 435,000 soldiers, 9,960 artillery pieces and mortars, and 3,155 tanks.

On the other side of the hill, the Soviet high command was finally beginning to jell. Stalin's harsh education in military affairs, achieved at a cost of millions of Soviet soldiers, had reached the point where he was reasonably confident in the judgments of his military subordinates. Despite the defeat of Operation Mars, Zhukov had already shown himself to be an exceptional commander; his relationship with Stalin had strengthened after a rocky spell at the beginning of the war. As Zhukov recalled after the war ended, on at least two occasions he had gone to a meeting with the dictator unsure whether he would literally survive. But by now a whole generation of younger commanders had begun to emerge—combat-hardened officers who had tested themselves in the terrible battles of the Eastern Front and were beginning to prove themselves the equal in every respect of their German counterparts.

The Soviets undertook a massive construction program to blunt the coming attack. Two of the most impressive young commanders in the Red Army fought the battle for the Soviets. Marshal K. K. Rokossovsky commanded the Central Front and assumed responsibility for the northern shoulder of the Kursk salient; under him were three armies. Rokossovsky had been an inmate in the Gulag in 1940, from whence his jailers had dispatched him with the grim warning that he could always return. In the south, N. A. F. Vatutin commanded the Voronezh Front, where the main German attack came. His first-line defense held no less than four armies, with a fifth immediately available. Konev's Steppe Front, with five armies, stood in reserve for the Kursk defenders. Altogether the first-line Soviet defenses marshaled one million soldiers, 13,013 artillery pieces and mortars, and 3,275 tanks; and in reserve were an additional 449,133 soldiers, 6,536 artillery pieces and mortars, and 1,506 armored fighting vehicles. Aside from the sheer magnitude of their forces, the Soviets constructed a massive set of field fortifications. In the south were three separate lines varying in depth between 6 and 18 miles, and Soviet engineers sowed over half a million mines. In an unusual admission of foreboding, Hitler told Guderian shortly before Zitadelle began that every time he thought of the operation he felt sick to his stomach.

Zitadelle began on 5 July. From the start the operation ran into intense Soviet resistance. So well-informed were the Soviets that they began bombarding German frontline positions 30 minutes before Zitadelle was to start; they thus caught the first echelon of storm troops in their jump-off positions. In the north, Model struck along a frontage of 50 kilometers. By the second day, Ninth Army's lead elements had advanced at most 12 kilometers into Soviet defenses, where they stalled well short of Rokossovsky's third line. Model characterized the struggle as a battle of attrition—precisely the kind of battle the Germans had wished to avoid.

Manstein's forces did marginally better in the south, perhaps because they were the stronger pincer arm. Attacking along a front of over 50 kilometers, Fourth Panzer Army penetrated the Soviet frontline positions in the first several hours. But by early afternoon they were entangled in the second-line Soviet defenses, of whose existence the Germans had not known. Ferocious fighting brought the advance to a halt in the midst of heavy thunderstorms that turned the battlefield into a sea of mud. Moreover, Detachment Kempf, which was supposed to protect Hoth's flank, made little progress. For the next five days, Manstein's forces pushed their way through the Soviet defenses at heavy cost, with Großdeutschland losing 230 out of its 300 tanks.

German tactics were thoroughly unimaginative—great wedges of armor led by Tigers and Panthers sheltering the less effective Mark IIIs and IVs. But finally, on 11 July, Manstein gained some operational room. The II SS Panzer Corps and Kempf's panzer divisions encircled and destroyed a substantial number of Soviet troops. On the following day, approximately 400 tanks of the II SS Panzer Corps broke through to Prokhorovka Station. The Soviets immediately counterattacked. Zhukov, the STAVKA representative, approved Vatutin's request for the release of forces from the Steppe Front to conduct a counterattack. An all-day tank battle involving 1,200 armored vehicles ensued—the world's largest tank battle until the Gulf War. In losses, the conflict was a draw, with the Soviets losing 400 tanks and the Germans 320. But the Soviets held their ground and could repair a substantial number of their damaged vehicles.

While the battle raged across the scarred, burned, and churned grasslands of European Russia, the Luftwaffe and the Red Air Force waged a desperate struggle for air superiority. A Soviet surprise air raid early on the morning of 5 July failed because the Germans received warning from their ground radar stations. But from that point, the battle went against the German airmen. On Zitadelle's first day, Luftwaffe crews flew 3,000 sorties, with Stuka crews flying as many as six missions in 24 hours. The 37mm anti-tank gun mounted on that aircraft proved particularly effective against Soviet tanks. But Soviet fighters and heavy concentrations of anti-aircraft guns produced heavy casualties for the Luftwaffe, and the Germans never gained air superiority over the battlefield. Meanwhile, significant improvements since the winter in the skill of Soviet airmen, as well as increases in the sheer numbers of aircraft, allowed the Red Air Force to inflict substantial damage on German ground forces.

By 12 July, only Manstein wished to continue the battle. With two relatively fresh panzer divisions in hand, he argued that he could break through to Kursk. However, Manstein's claim was wishful thinking in the face of the depth of Soviet reserves. In fact, he recognized that continuation of the offensive was the only way to prevent the siphoning off of German strength to meet the Allied invasion of Sicily on 8 July. He was right; Hitler ordered Zitadelle to cease, so that major reinforcements could be sent to the Mediterranean theater. In the end, the defeat at Kursk underlined how much things had changed by summer 1943. The Soviets had taken everything the Wehrmacht could throw at them and had entirely blunted the German offensive.

The period between summer 1942 and summer 1943 saw a drastic decline in the German strategic position on the Eastern Front. The summer 1942 offensive had seized indefensible territory at considerable cost. Hitler's decision to hold fast at Stalingrad only exacerbated a bad situation. The destruction of Sixth Army then threatened Germany's position along the entire southern portion of the front. Only Manstein's brilliant counteroffensive at Kharkov restored the balance briefly. Nevertheless, the Germans continued to underestimate their opponents, while the Battle of Kursk destroyed much of the German Army's mobile forces in the east. The time of reckoning was at hand.

Defeat in the Mediterranean

The Anglo-American landings on the Algerian and Moroccan coasts in November 1942 had upset the balance in the Mediterranean theater. Hitler's seizure of Tunisia provided the Axis a breathing space, but the decision rested on no coherent operational or strategic analysis. The Germans proceeded to rush large forces to consolidate their hold on Tunisia and preserve their control of the mid-sea passage. Those forces were sufficient to stop the Allied advance out of Algeria. As a result, the Axis powers poured nearly a quarter of a million troops into the enclave. Again, no one in the German military hierarchy stopped to consider how they might be supplied, given the threat posed by British aircraft on Malta.

Moreover, instead of appointing an overall commander for the North African theater, Hitler divided even the ground command. Rommel would remain in command of the Afrika Korps, now retreating across Libya toward Tunisia, but Generaloberst Jürgen von Arnim would command the divisions rushed to Tunisia. Arnim was the worst sort of general staff officer—arrogant, hard to work with, and contemptuous of those not wearing the claret stripe of the general staff. Kesselring held overall command of German forces in the Mediterranean. "Smiling Albert," as he was nicknamed, provided considerable charm and a Nazi ideological bent to his command. As the situation in North Africa deteriorated, Kesselring issued an endless series of optimistic and soothing reports to the OKW, while suggesting to his pilots that Japanese fanaticism provided an excellent example of how they should conduct themselves. The great German fighter pilot, Johannes Steinhoff, recalled attending a Kesselring conference in March 1943: "Never in my life will I forget the Air Fleet situation conference which I was permitted to attend. There was I, a combatant officer, witnessing the prognostication and synthetic portrayal of the future course of the battle in North Africa . . . I found the foppish affectation and general superciliousness [of the staff officers] insufferable."[11]

While the Germans organized the defenses of Tunisia, the British and Americans held a momentous conference at Casablanca. Starting on January 14, in chill, damp villas, Roosevelt, Churchill, and their respective military advisers conducted ten days of discussions on Allied strategy. The Americans were still committed to the concept of a landing in Northwest Europe in 1943; they had no interest in further operations in the Mediterranean after the defeat of Axis forces in Tunisia. But the British had no intention of supporting such a strategic approach, and with far superior staff work they won nearly every major argument with the Americans. There would be no major landing on the French coast in 1943, and Allied forces would invade Sicily in the summer.

In retrospect, the British were entirely right. None of the preconditions for a successful landing on the coast of France yet existed. The Battle of the Atlantic was not over; the Luftwaffe had yet to be defeated; the logistical infrastructure for the immediate support of the invasion did not exist; and Allied air forces were not capable of interdicting the landing area and preventing the Germans from moving rapidly against the invasion. About the only argument the Americans won was a symbolic agreement to coordinate the efforts of the Allied strategic bombing forces.

While the senior Allied staffs were arguing about strategy at Casablanca, the Afrika Korps arrived in Tunisia. Rommel received only minimal cooperation from Arnim. The field marshal proposed a major operation with their combined panzer forces to strike at the supply dumps and air fields the Allies had constructed in Algeria; the operation would take place before the British Eighth Army had closed on Tunisia. Arnim, however, had no intention of cooperating with Rommel, and so the attack occurred under two separate and suspicious command structures. Nevertheless, the Germans achieved a considerable local success. Major General Lloyd Fredendall, one of the few bad appointments Marshall made in the war, commanded the American II Corps defending the central Tunisian front. Quartered in a deep cave far from the battlefield, Fredendall deployed his forces badly and then failed to provide leadership in the crisis that occurred when Rommel attacked. The result was a tactical setback at Kasserine Pass, one that should not have been entirely unexpected, given how little time the Americans had had to train.

The Americans, however, proved fast learners, while Fredendall's replacement, George Patton, aroused the fighting spirit of U.S. troops, even if at times he churned up more hatred for himself than for the Germans. George Patton was one of the more bizarre characters produced by the United States Military Academy and the United States Army. He was also a great general. Field Marshal Douglas Haig, commander of British forces on the Western Front in World War I, met Captain Patton in 1917 when he was aide to Pershing and pronounced that Patton had big things in store for him. Badly wounded as the commander of a tank unit in 1918, he returned to the dull, peacetime life of the interwar U.S. Army, where he slowly rose in the officer corps. Warned that his advocacy of the tank might put his career in jeopardy, Patton returned to the cavalry. But behind Patton's demeanor of the swash-buckling, polo-playing cavalryman was a serious soldier who prepared himself intellectually for the coming war. Independently wealthy, Patton was able to accumulate an impressive library and travel extensively. Patton's professional weakness was his lack of a technical background that would have enabled him to influence the inept decisions the army made in procuring tanks. His personal weakness lay in an inability to control either his emotions or his mouth.

In the long run Kasserine Pass was of importance in setting the U.S. Army on the path to becoming a truly effective military organization. Unfortunately, many British senior officers failed to recognize that Kasserine Pass represented the teething problems of a U.S. Army only beginning rearmament. Thus, for the remainder of the war they would consistently underestimate the increasingly impressive capabilities of U.S. ground forces.

Meanwhile, General Dwight Eisenhower, initially the commander of Operation Torch, reorganized the air, naval, and ground relationships among the Allied forces. Thus, he created the first truly combined (inter-Allied) headquarters. Eisenhower's gifts as a conciliator and strategist were exceptional; he was also willing to learn from experience. And his usually patient personality allowed him to mold a group of disputatious and quarrelsome generals from different countries into a winning team. That nearly everyone underestimated him was a major factor in his effectiveness. He was now to display those talents in marshaling and organizing Allied forces attacking the Axis positions in Tunisia.

In early March 1943, fully alerted by Ultra, Montgomery administered a severe beating to Rommel's forces on the Tunisian-Libyan frontier. The failure to stop Eighth Army was Rommel's swan song in Africa; he returned to Germany for further medical treatment. By now the situation of Axis forces in Tunisia was rapidly deteriorating. Allied fighter aircraft had gained the upper hand, so that the Stukas could no longer operate without suffering heavy casualties. On the ground, Allied pressure placed Axis troops in an impossible situation.

But it was the unceasing Allied air campaign against Axis shipping and ports that bit most deeply. Informed by Ultra of virtually every Axis air and naval movement, Allied air attacks devastated the convoys crossing to North Africa. In mid-March Fliegerkorps Tunis concluded that the courses of its convoys across to Tunisia from Sicily were being betrayed to the Allies, but the Germans found it impossible to believe that their own communications might be the problem. By the end of March the Germans had to shut the convoys down entirely and move to airlift. In April and early May, Allied fighters—fully alerted to the German flight schedules by Ultra—wrecked the aerial bridge from Sicily to Tunis. In a five-week period the Germans lost over 200 transport aircraft.

A series of Allied attacks drove German forces in Tunisia into an ever-shrinking pocket. In late April, led by the British First Army and the U.S. II Corps, the Allies broke the Axis bridgehead into two separate positions, which they then reduced in short order. With relatively little ammunition, virtually no fuel, and their backs to the Mediterranean, the Axis forces collapsed, although the Italians resisted longer than their German allies. Over the last week of April and the first week of May, Germans and Italians flowed into Allied POW camps; in all, the Allies captured 275,000 soldiers in what was almost as critical a defeat as Stalingrad, for it eliminated virtually all the German reserves in the Mediterranean.

The Anglo-American forces were in a position similar to that of the Soviets immediately after Stalingrad. But where the latter had displayed too little caution in their moves across the Don, the Anglo-Americans would display too much caution. With hardly any German troops in Sicily, Corsica, or Sardinia, Allied senior leaders refused to assume any serious risks. Instead, they waited for over two months while they prepared the invasion of the Mediterranean in meticulous detail. Not until 10 July 1943 did they finally launch Operation Husky against Sicily. In that two-month period they lost the possibility of seizing Corsica and Sardinia and confronting the Germans with the threat of Allied landings from southern France to Sicily.

But caution was the order of the day—on the British part because of fear of German capabilities, on the American part by a desire to minimize commitments in the Mediterranean. At the Trident Conference in Washington that May, the Americans at least agreed to continue Allied efforts in the Mediterranean beyond Sicily in order to knock the Italians out of the war. But at the same time they forced the British to agree that the invasion of northern France would take place in May 1944. The result of this horse trading, however, was an unimaginative direct attack on Sicily that failed to take advantage of Allied naval, amphibious, and air superiority as well as Axis weaknesses in the air and on the ground.

Husky's success was helped considerably by skilled Allied deception plans that persuaded substantial elements of the OKW and most importantly Hitler that the Allies would not, after all, attack Sicily or the Italian mainland but rather the Balkans and Greece. In June and July 1943 the OKW deployed substantial reinforcements to Greece, including the 11th Luftwaffe Field Division, the 104th and 117th Jäger Divisions, the 1st Panzer Division, and the 1st Mountain Division. So worried were Hitler and the OKW that they even dispatched Rommel to Salonika to meet the expected invasion. Instead, these German forces guarded Greek beaches—not bad duty for early summer 1943.

The invasion of Sicily was the largest amphibious operation of the war, at least on the first day. Montgomery drew up the plan and not surprisingly gave pride of place to Eighth Army, which he still commanded. The British would land on the southeastern corner of Sicily and drive north to Messina to cut off the German and Italian garrison. To the west, the American Seventh Army under Patton would provide a flank guard.

In early June a massive air campaign fell upon Italian and German air bases throughout Sicily. Battered Luftwaffe squadrons no longer could hold their own. The experienced pilots had been steadily killed off, to be replaced by fresh-faced boys who had little chance of surviving. The amphibious landings in early July went well, although there was some stiff opposition over the course of the first day. But the campaign did not turn out as Montgomery had hoped. Almost immediately the British drive to the north ran into difficulties; Montgomery then took over roads assigned to Seventh Army. But by that time Patton, who had no intention of acting in a supporting role to Montgomery, had launched American forces west to capture Palermo and then back across the northern coast to reach Messina before the British.

The invasion of Sicily did lead to Mussolini's overthrow and it forced the Germans to terminate Zitadelle in the east—the first direct major combat contribution the Allies made to the Soviets. But on the operational level its results were less than satisfactory. The Allies gained little more than the island of Sicily, and for the first time, but not the last, Anglo-American commanders allowed sizeable numbers of Germans to escape to fight another day. In this case, the Germans established massive flak (anti-aircraft gun) positions on both sides of the straits of Messina and then ferried virtually all the surviving troops across to the mainland. Neither Allied air nor naval power intervened effectively. On a more personal but distressing note, George Patton, displaying a characteristic lack of self-control, slapped two GIs suffering from shell shock and malaria. The incidents almost terminated his military career, and they resulted in his replacement by the dour, unimaginative, and deeply jealous Omar Bradley as the top commander of U.S. ground forces.

There was, however, one major strategic gain in the Mediterranean campaign of 1942–43: it opened the sea to Allied merchant shipping, and by thus shortening the route to the Middle and Far East it freed somewhere between three and four million tons of merchant vessels for other purposes.

Conclusion

The period between May 1942 and July 1943 witnessed a major shift in the fortunes of war. German victories in summer 1942 represented the last moment when the Wehrmacht's skill and force structure were still sufficient to gain and hold the initiative. But these victories in the Mediterranean and on the Eastern Front entailed an enormous miscalculation of the Third Reich's ability to coordinate, command, and supply its forces on two fronts. By exhausting themselves in pursuit of unachievable goals, the Germans created opportunities for Allied counterattacks which proved devastating. From this point on, the initiative would rest with Germany's opponents. The Germans would have to await each blow with grim determination and the dark hope that they could fight long and hard enough to split the Allied coalition apart, short of total victory.

12

THE COMBINED
BOMBER OFFENSIVE

1941–1945

Traditional military history, particularly operational history, is in many respects easy to write. The ebb and flow of active campaigns provide ready patterns on which to construct a narrative. Key events announce themselves, victors and vanquished are obvious, and, above all, one can trace the outcome to specific battles and incidents that gave rise to larger results. In tracing the genesis and conduct of the Anglo-American Combined Bomber Offensive, such simplicity is seldom evident. A number of features work against a tidy narrative. The campaign itself involved a shifting pattern of expectations and purposes as Allied air commanders determined, mostly by trial and error, how best to employ their forces. There was, moreover, a numbing sameness to the campaign: a continuous series of missions in which thousands of young men, week after week, left their bases to battle Arctic temperatures, enemy fighters, and anti-aircraft fire to drop their bombs on targets that largely remained obscure.

Early Lessons

The origins of strategic bombing can be traced back to the doctrines and expectations of the interwar period, particularly the belief that bombers could evade enemy defenses and attack population centers and industries. Air power advocates confidently predicted the disruption of enemy society, the elimination of its industrial potential, and the collapse of civilian morale. This vision, far from striking its partisans as barbaric, on the contrary offered the prospect of escaping the slaughter of World War I. Steeped in the potential of strategic bombing and socialized to regard that mode of warfare as the cornerstone of their independence, airmen brought a dedication to their vocation that was almost messianic. Their belief in the bomber's invincibility rested on a couple of key assumptions. First, they believed that bombers would enjoy the initiative because of their invisibility in the great spaces of the sky. Second, because bombers in the late 1930s bristled with defensive armament, airmen believed that any losses which might occur would remain within "acceptable limits."

When war came, things turned out differently. In September 1939 as Germany invaded Poland and Britain declared war on the Third Reich, the RAF's Bomber Command found itself without plans, trained manpower, or equipment to undertake an aerial offensive. In the "Phoney War" period of 1939 and early 1940 as the Allies waited for the Germans to strike, the British bent over backward not to harm civilians, choosing instead to confine their efforts to dropping propaganda leaflets and attacking naval targets in daytime. But even these limited operations highlighted the RAF's shortcomings. Leaflet-dropping missions suggested the difficulties of finding targets in bad weather and at night. And daylight attacks on naval targets, such as the ill-fated attack on Wilhelmshaven in December 1939, led to heavy losses at the hands of enemy fighters. Defense against aerial attack was indeed possible, and if the bombers "always got through," few returned.

Despite these vulnerabilities, after the collapse of France in June 1940 and the expulsion of British forces from the Continent, strategic bombing represented the only means Britain had to strike back at Nazi Germany. As Churchill suggested, "There is one thing that will . . . bring [Germany] down, and that is an absolutely devastating, exterminating attack by very heavy bombers from this country upon the Nazi homeland."[1] And so the great effort began. The first raids attacked specific target sets within the Nazi economy, such as oil. The results were not good. For example, in December 1940 the RAF attacked the oil refinery at Gelsenkirchen with 262 tons of bombs, and the crew reported success. When reconnaissance photos showed no damage—the raid had failed to put even a single bomb on the refinery—the air staff disregarded the aerial reconnaissance photographs entirely and continued to emphasize precision night attacks. Yet for all of its talk about precision, air staff studies began to speak increasingly of "collateral damage" to structures in the vicinity of the target, and before long Bomber Command was selecting targets with the explicit intention of exploiting the possibilities of such damage. Moreover, prewar conceptions of bombing as a means to destroy civilian morale now explicitly entered into the RAF's practical calculations. In fall 1940 Sir Charles Portal, still commander-in-chief of Bomber Command, suggested: "We have the one directly offensive weapon in the whole of our armory, the one means by which we can undermine the morale of a large part of the enemy people, shake their faith in the Nazi regime, and at the same time and with the same bombs dislocate the major part of their heavy industry and a good part of their oil production."[2]

The emphasis shifted from oil refineries to morale as limitations on accuracy became ever clearer. Ironically, this shift came almost concurrently with the Luftwaffe's *Blitz* on London, which demonstrated the ability of the British to endure heavy bombing *without* a collapse in morale. Churchill's remark that "bombers alone provide the means of victory" was all too true in 1940–41, but not in the way it might have seemed. The bomber offensive had to fulfill a political more than a military function—namely, proving to foreign and domestic observers alike that Britain remained firmly in the war. As Harry Hopkins, Roosevelt's closest adviser, remarked to Churchill: "You have no idea of the thrill and encouragement which the [RAF] bombing has given to all of us."[3]

August 1941 brought an end to the imagined efficacy of night precision bombing. That month, Churchill's scientific adviser, Lord Cherwell, ordered an investigation of bombing accuracy through an examination of bomber photos. The resulting Butt Report yielded many depressing insights. It concluded with the observation that of all aircraft claiming to have attacked the target, only one-third actually hit within five miles of the aiming point (a target area of 75 square miles). Bomber Command immediately cried foul, but the report's independent status gave it credibility. Churchill noted to Portal, now chief of air staff, that the report required the most serious attention. The Butt Report's pessimism reinforced similar, privately held opinions emerging within the air staff itself. By underlining the RAF's difficulties with navigation and bombing accuracy, it reinforced those who supported development of technological aids. The report had other implications as well. Only a city-busting campaign seemed within the RAF's potential, and even that would require no less than 4,000 bombers to achieve. There was, of course, the possibility of returning to daylight bombing, but that would necessitate developing an effective long-range escort fighter to attack enemy fighters and protect the bombers. As an article of faith rather than technological knowledge, the air staff believed that one could not combine the speed, maneuverability, and firepower of a fighter with the range of a bomber. When Portal indicated to Churchill the RAF's belief that a long-range escort fighter was technologically infeasible, the prime minister replied that the air staff's position "closed many doors."[4]

In February 1942, Arthur Harris assumed control of Bomber Command as the campaign's promise of decisive results was rapidly fading. A dispirited Churchill noted that the most Britain could hope for was that the bombing campaign would become increasingly annoying to the Third Reich. Under such circumstances, only Harris's leadership and commitment could have sustained the demand on Britain's resources that the campaign demanded. Harris was a true believer. A native of Rhodesia by birth, he had joined up in 1914 and become a pilot during World War I. Always picturesque in his language, he had emerged as one of the most outspoken young airmen in Trenchard's RAF. While attending the army's staff college at Camberley, Harris had almost been expelled for writing a paper which suggested that the army would not buy a tank until it found a model that whinnied, ate hay, and thereafter defecated. Like all great commanders, he had the ability to inspire subordinates, but he displayed little interest in technology—even to the point of entirely discounting the Luftwaffe's use of radio beams to improve its bombing aim in 1940. Harris detested anything that diverted heavy bombers from their true role, the bludgeoning of German cities. He disliked the idea of attacks on economic choke points, such as ball-bearing factories or oil plants—"panacea" targets, he called them. He was even suspicious of attacking German morale, although he tolerated the idea. "Area" bombing, in his view, depended for its effect on sheer destruction. Blow up enough cities, and the Germans would crack.

Harris's appointment coincided with two developments that gave the night bomber offensive a new lease. The first was the navigational aid Gee, which used radio signals from Britain to enable the navigator to determine the aircraft's position and find the target. Gee significantly improved the accuracy of blind bombing within its range, which barely reached over the Rhine. But as British scientists correctly estimated, its operational life did not last more than six months before the Germans developed countermeasures. During that period, however, Harris sought maximum tactical advantage from the new system. A major raid on Lübeck destroyed almost half of the city, and bombs dropped on Rostock inflicted even greater damage. Success against these targets—chosen because they were easy to find and highly flammable—resuscitated Bomber Command's prestige and ensured that the RAF would continue to receive a considerable portion of Britain's industrial production.

The second development was the appearance of the true heavy bomber, four-engine monsters capable of carrying far larger bomb loads. With the Halifax and particularly the Lancaster, Bomber Command possessed aircraft that could deal out terrible punishment. The first "Thousand Bomber" raids in May 1942 clinched the matter. To demonstrate strategic bombing's

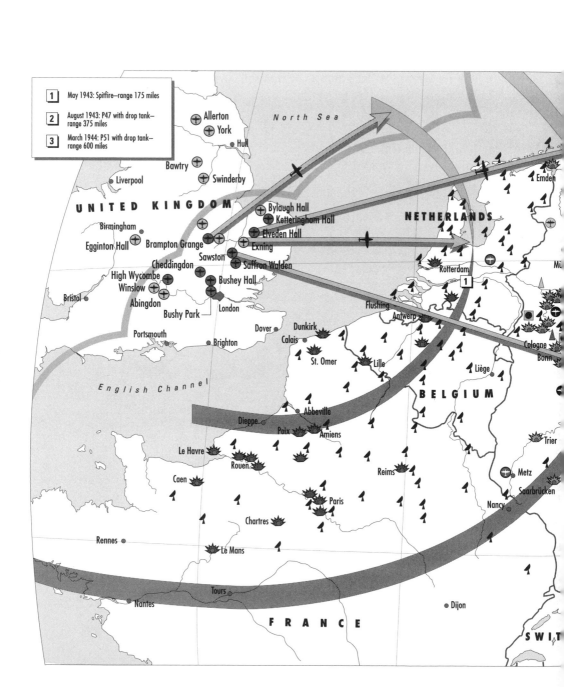

1 May 1943: Spitfire—range 175 miles

2 August 1943: P47 with drop tank—range 375 miles

3 March 1944: P51 with drop tank—range 600 miles

North Sea

Emden

Allerton
York
Hull

Bawtry
Swinderby

Liverpool

UNITED KINGDOM

NETHERLANDS

Bylaugh Hall
Ketteringham Hall
Elveden Hall

Birmingham

Egginton Hall   Brampton Grange   Exning

Rotterdam   Mü

Cheddingdon
Sawston   Saffron Walden

High Wycombe
Winslow   Bushey Hall

Bristol

Abingdon   Flushing

Bushy Park   London   Antwerp

Portsmouth   Dover   Dunkirk

Brighton   Calais

St. Omer   Lille   Liège

Cologne
Bonn

BELGIUM

English Channel

Abbeville

Dieppe   Poix   Amiens

Le Havre   Reims   Trier

Rouen

Caen   Metz

Paris   Saarbrücken

Chartres   Nancy

Rennes

Le Mans

Tours

Nantes   Dijon

FRANCE

SWIT

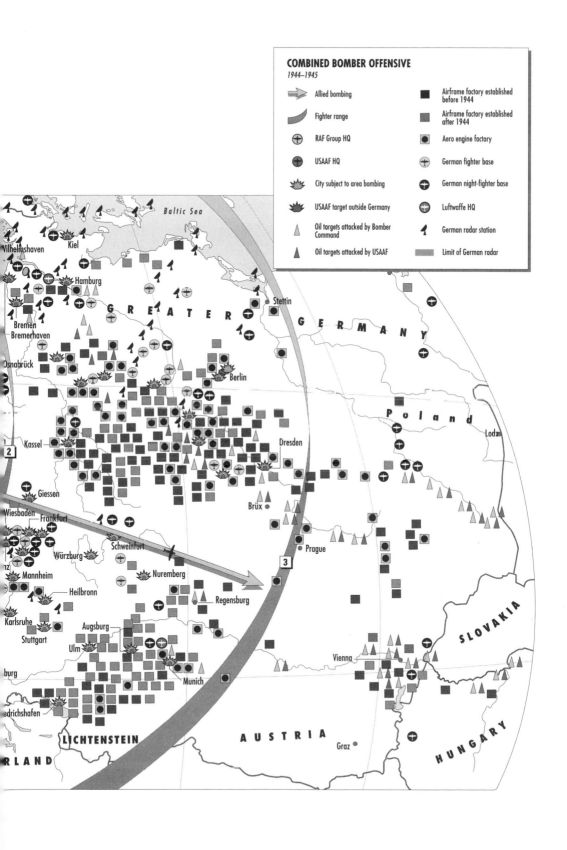

COMBINED BOMBER OFFENSIVE
1944–1945

➤ Allied bombing		■	Airframe factory established before 1944
Fighter range		■	Airframe factory established after 1944
⊕ RAF Group HQ		◉	Aero engine factory
⊕ USAAF HQ		⊕	German fighter base
☀ City subject to area bombing		⊕	German night-fighter base
☀ USAAF target outside Germany		⊕	Luftwaffe HQ
△ Oil targets attacked by Bomber Command		➤	German radar station
△ Oil targets attacked by USAAF		▨	Limit of German radar

Baltic Sea

Vilhelmshaven
Kiel
Hamburg
Bremen
Bremerhaven
Osnabrück
Stettin
G R E A T E R   G E R M A N Y
Berlin
P o l a n d
Lodz
Kassel
2
Dresden
Giessen
Brüx
Wiesbaden
Frankfurt
Prague
Würzburg
Schweinfurt
3
Mannheim
Nuremberg
Heilbronn
Karlsruhe
Regensburg
Augsburg
Stuttgart
Ulm
Munich
Vienna
SLOVAKIA
burg
drichshafen
LICHTENSTEIN
A U S T R I A
Graz
H U N G A R Y
RLAND

potential, Harris concentrated 1,043 bombers for a single night attack on Cologne. On the night of 30–31 May the Rhineland city suffered more damage than in the previous 70 attacks, as Bomber Command dropped 1,455 tons of bombs on the target. The attack burned out 600 acres of the city, 300 in the city center. The loss rate for the attacking bombers, 5.94 percent, was high but within acceptable limits. While damage to the city proved temporary, the political reaction in Britain to the first "Thousand Bomber" attack was enthusiastic. And while this was the only time in 1942 that Bomber Command could marshal this level of effort, its capabilities steadily grew, while the German leadership persisted in underestimating the danger in the skies.

By early 1943 the new four-engine bombers were available in increasing numbers, and technological aids, such as Oboe (a radio navigational device) and H2S (a radar target locator), along with the new Pathfinder force of elite crews to locate and mark the targets, allowed Bomber Command to deliver a series of devastating blows against the Ruhr Valley. The attacks of spring 1943 represented a turning point in the bombing campaign. Harris's forces were now able to deal out crushing punishment on nearly all major raids. However, the cost remained high: Bomber Command flirted with defeat as loss rates headed toward unacceptable levels—no less than 872 bombers over spring 1943. Then in July Harris introduced "Window"— strips of aluminum which when dropped reflected back to German radars the image of a bomber. With their screens filled with these images, German radar operators were helpless.

At the end of July, Bomber Command turned against Hamburg in a series of raids aptly codenamed Gomorrah, after the evil Biblical city that was destroyed by God. With Hamburg's defenses blinded and its location on an estuary easily identified through navigational aids, British bombers achieved devastating accuracy, beginning with the first attack over the night of 24–25 July. But it was the second attack that caused the catastrophe. Much of Hamburg's fire-fighting force was on the city's north side responding to earlier raids. The weather conditions were perfect: hot, dry, and clear. And defenses were helpless. Within 20 minutes from the time the first Pathfinder markers illuminated the target area in the center of the city, downtown Hamburg exploded in flames. The growing pyre was fed by some of the Reich's largest lumberyards, and succeeding bombers had no difficulty finding their target and unloading their bombs. The inferno reached temperatures as high as 1,000° F, while superheated air rushed through the city at speeds close to 300 mph. One German remembered the firestorm this way: "Many people started burning and jumped into the canal. Horrible scenes took place at the quay. People burned to death with horrible suffering; some became insane. Many dead bodies were all around us."[5] In some areas rescuers found only ashes as the remains of those who had sought shelter from the bombing: the heat had entirely incinerated the bodies. At least 40,000 Germans died. More than half of the city's living space, 75 percent of its electric works, 60 percent of its water system, and 90 percent of its gas works were destroyed. Following the raids, industrial production fell 40 percent for large firms and 80 percent for medium and small concerns.

Accounts of the devastation at Hamburg spread throughout the Reich, and this fearsome disaster worried the Nazi leadership even more than the physical damage. Albert Speer, Hitler's chief of armaments production, warned Hitler that six more raids with similar levels of destruction could halt the Reich's armament production. The Führer replied that Speer would somehow straighten things out. In retrospect, Hitler was right, but largely because even in 1943 Bomber Command found it difficult to repeat this level of success in future raids. Nevertheless, in August, Bomber Command destroyed much of the experimental rocket station at Penemünde. But as fall approached, German defenses recovered, and Bomber Command's losses started rising once again.

The Americans Arrive

Unlike the RAF or the Luftwaffe, the U.S. Army Air Forces enjoyed the luxury of observing the first two years of the air war from the sidelines. But the Americans learned little from the experience of their Allies. There is no evidence that the additional time had any impact on American airmen's conceptions of the campaign they aimed to wage; in their minds, only a large precision-bombing force could destroy the Nazi war economy by attacking the electric grid, transportation network, and key industries such as oil. The U.S. Army Air Forces based this operational approach on a planning document drawn up by the war plans division in August 1941 entitled AWPD/1 (Air War Plan D/1). It envisioned a large precision-bombing force that would destroy the Nazi war economy by attacks on key industries. Objectives included the electric grid, transportation network, and oil industry. On the basis of this document, the Americans devised an elaborate, detailed, and complex precision-bombing scheme which they proposed to follow unswervingly. It took considerable time, however, to prepare U.S. forces. The first American raid on the Continent did not occur until August 1942, when Boeing B-17 bombers, escorted by British fighters, attacked

Rouen's railroad marshaling yards. For the rest of 1942 most American attacks stayed within range of fighter cover, and therefore loss rates remained low.

The Allied landings in North Africa in November 1942 diverted much of U.S. Eighth Air Force's bomber command to the Mediterranean. Consequently, not until spring 1943 did its bomber strength reach the levels required to launch unescorted air attacks into German air space. When these raids began, German air defenses of fighters and anti-aircraft guns (flak) proved more formidable than the Americans had expected. On 17 April, B-17s attacked the Folke Wulf factory near Bremen, which manufactured fighter aircraft; 16 U.S. bombers were lost and 40 damaged, representing 40 percent of the attacking aircraft. Over the summer, target selection combined prewar doctrine with wartime realities. The primary objectives were factories producing fighter engines and airframes, followed by submarine yards, ball-bearing factories, and oil refineries. The emphasis on reducing fighter production reflected the Allies' respect for the Luftwaffe. Destruction of Germany's ball-bearing factories would, the airmen hoped, have cascading effects on all industrial production.

In June Eighth Air Force struck two targets beyond the range of escort fighters. Both raids suffered heavy losses. The first, an attack on the synthetic rubber complex at Hüls, proved one of the most successful of the war. But the Americans failed to return for a second raid for over a year, and after extensive repairs, the plant reached peak production in March 1944. In July the daylight air war reached a new level of intensity when, over the course of a couple of weeks, American bombers struck Hamburg, Hanover, Kassel, Kiel, and Warnemünde. They ran into ferocious opposition from enemy fighters and lost 87 bombers. Then on 27 July, P-47 fighters, for the first time using drop tanks, which allowed them to carry extra fuel and thus extend their range, caught enemy fighters above the Rhine—attacking B-17 stragglers returning from a bombing mission.

Eighth Air Force launched its most ambitious attack on 17 August—a double raid on the ball-bearing factory at Schweinfurt and the Messerschmidt assembly complex at Regensburg. The attacks went in separately, despite plans for the two formations to support each other. After savaging Brigadier General Curtis LeMay's B-17 formation of the 3rd Bombardment Division, Luftwaffe fighters had time to recover, replenish, and rearm before the second raid arrived. The total number of B-17s shot down over the course of the day was 60, or over 15 percent of the attacking force; in one day's action Eighth Air Force had lost 10.3 percent of its aircraft and 17 percent of its crews.

Although the bombers did substantial damage to the ball-bearing factories, production did not grind to a halt. The factories, which accounted for 45 percent of Germany's ball-bearing production, were essential to German war production, just as the planners of the air raid had estimated, but a number of incalculables prevented the Eighth from doing effective damage to the Reich's war economy. First, the bombs that Eighth used were not heavy enough to destroy machine tools on factory floors. And second, any equipment losses that did occur were quickly replenished by the ever-helpful Swedes and Swiss, while German industry itself possessed significant reserves.

The double raids on Schweinfurt and Regensburg in mid-August represented a serious defeat for American daylight bombers. Nevertheless, increased B-17 production and the arrival of more crews from the States allowed Eighth Air Force to continue its attacks. After a pause in September due to August's heavy losses, October saw a series of violent air battles.

The month's operations began with heavy attacks on Bremen and Vegesack on the 8th. The attackers suffered severely—30 aircraft lost and 26 heavily damaged. The raid initiated a week of intense operations. On 9 October the Americans attacked the Arado factory at Anklam and the Focke Wulf plant at Marienburg deep in Germany, both of which were important aircraft production sites; the depth and extent of the raid caught enemy defenses by surprise, and destruction was significant. The next major raid on 10 October ran into heavy opposition. Relays of German fighters attacked the first group on the way in and out from the target and blasted the lead formation, flown by the 100th Bombardment Group, out of the sky. Not one of the group's 12 aircraft returned. Out of 119 bombers in the first wave, the Germans shot down 29, representing a 24.4 percent loss.

Four days later—"Black Thursday" to the crews who flew the mission—the American bombers revisited Schweinfurt and took an even worse mauling. Enemy fighters and flak shot down 59 B-17s over Germany or German-occupied territory; 1 crashed in the Channel; 3 were abandoned by their crews while over England; 2 crashed on landing; and 17 of the 139 planes that managed to land were scrapped due to battle damage, while the remaining 122 suffered damage to a greater or lesser degree. As for personnel, at the end of Black Thursday 5 men on returning aircraft were dead and 43 were wounded, while 594 men were missing over German-held territory.

One person on the ground described the returning crews in the following terms: "As the crews come in their faces [are] drawn and wan, not just from weariness, but because too many friends have gone down in flames in front of their eyes. Too many. Jerry had thrown so many planes at them they were bewildered. And for another reason. There was still tomorrow, and the tomorrow after that." Virtually every surviving aircraft returned with damage and casualties. As one survivor commented to those waiting on the ground: "Jesus Christ, give us fighters!"[6]

The losses on the second Schweinfurt raid underlined what the first attack on the city should have made clear: unescorted bomber formations could not fight their way through skies where significant enemy fighter defenses existed. The attack did do heavy damage to ball-bearing production facilities, and Speer worried that the Americans would return before production facilities could be dispersed. But with heavy losses and serious morale problems, Eighth Air Force could not reattack Schweinfurt for the foreseeable future, while Bomber Harris, with his contempt for panacea targets, *would* not attack Schweinfurt.

The Luftwaffe's Response

With the start of Barbarossa, the Luftwaffe found itself engaged on three fronts: Western Europe, the Mediterranean, and Eastern Europe. Nevertheless, through late 1942, much of the Luftwaffe's strength was focused on fighting the Soviets; approximately 50 percent of its forces were tied up in that theater, where 60 percent of its losses would occur. Germany had entered World War II with an air defense system considerably inferior to Britain's, despite superior technology. The burden of defending the cities of the Third Reich fell to anti-aircraft artillery forces, since the fighters were committed to the air battle over enemy territory. The Germans continued to emphasize flak throughout the war, despite their understanding that even radar-guided fire was ineffective, especially against aircraft at high altitudes. Nevertheless, Hitler, with his love of guns, was a major supporter of the Luftwaffe's flak forces. Equally important was the fact that anti-aircraft guns blasting into the skies of the Reich provided the German population with a psychological crutch. As late as 1943 Joseph Goebbels, the Nazi propaganda minister, with the support of the Gauleiters (the Nazi Party district leaders), was berating the Luftwaffe because it had insufficient flak batteries defending the cities of the Fatherland.

In July 1940 the Luftwaffe established the 1st Night Fighter Division in Brussels under General Joseph Kammhuber, with a number of day fighters that possessed no radar. The first defensive measures involved extensive use of searchlight belts in western Germany to illuminate British bombers, which single-engine Bf 109 fighters would then attempt to destroy; such efforts achieved few successes. In October 1940 the Germans introduced the Würzburg radar and by 1941 had established a defensive belt of radar stations reaching from Denmark to Holland and then south through Belgium to northern France. The system provided early warning as well as ground control intercept (GCI) capability to support a force of night fighters equipped with airborne radar sets. By early 1942 the Kammhuber Line, as the system came to be known, showed considerable depth and sophistication, but it also possessed a major weakness. With one GCI center and one fighter defending a given area, Bomber Command could swamp the defenses by sending in a compact stream of bombers.

The growing threat did not awaken the German high command. Through 1942 the OKW remained fixed on the Eastern Front, even after the nasty shock of the Thousand Bomber raid on Cologne at the end of May. The attack on Cologne made Hitler furious. In a tirade aimed at Hans Jeschonnek, the Luftwaffe's chief of staff, he ridiculed the Luftwaffe's attempts to portray the defense of Cologne as a victory. For Hitler, the only reply to such terror raids was retaliation in kind. As he saw it, the attack represented an attempt by the British to open a second front in the skies. But Bomber Command's efforts for the rest of the year failed to achieve successes similar to the Cologne raid, and as the OKW reported widely dispersed raids over summer and fall 1942, the threat slipped from Hitler's mind. Consequently, the Luftwaffe's night forces received minimal support. From 116 aircraft in September 1940, Kammhuber's forces grew to 250 by September 1941, but to only 345 by September 1942. Rather than expend resources on night defenses, the Germans attempted to force the British to end strategic bombing attacks with retaliatory raids, such as the so-called Baedeker raids on England, a thoroughly Douhetian approach.

By early 1943 the RAF was swamping the Kammhuber Line. But the Nazi leadership was still thinking in terms of retaliating rather than mounting an effective defense. The destruction of much of the Ruhr valley was bad enough, but the Hamburg raid gave the threat new urgency. On 30 July 1943 Field Marshal Erhard Milch, the Luftwaffe's chief of production, warned that Germany was facing an intensification of enemy air attacks. If it could not master the threat, Germany would be in desperate straits. Milch then announced that Hitler had put top priority on fighter production, which was to increase to 2,000 aircraft per month by summer 1944. The Eastern Front would have to make do until the Luftwaffe had reduced the bomber threat on the Home Front. In fact, even as much of the Luftwaffe's fighter strength returned to the Reich, Hitler remained uninterested in a shift to a defensive strategy. Shortly after the destruction of Hamburg, he warned his advisers that "terror can only be broken with terror." Attacks on German air fields made no impression on him, but the smashing of cities was another matter. And the enemy would feel the same way when German raids destroyed their cities. Moreover, "the German people demand reprisals."[7] Already, by this point in the war, the Germans were pouring immense resources into the V-1 and V-2 rocket programs, in the hopes that these new weapons would deliver the retaliatory assault Hitler promised.

Meanwhile, the rising intensity of American attacks represented a new threat to the Reich. The great air battles of summer 1943 placed a terrible strain on the Luftwaffe, enough to cause Jeschonnek's suicide on the morning after the American attack on Schweinfurt and the RAF attack on Penemünde. Yet the Germans survived the American onslaught and won a respite from the daylight air offensive, owing to two strategic decisions they made: to concentrate single-engine fighters in the Reich by transferring almost all their fighters back to Germany, and to use new weapons and tactics against the daylight attackers. The first decision meant that the Germans were yielding control of the air over their hard-pressed ground forces on the Eastern Front as well as in the Mediterranean and North Africa. The second decision meant that, by fall 1943, new tactics and weapons would allow German fighter commanders to significantly impair the American daylight offensive. By September the Germans had refined their defensive system against daylight raids. First, German Bf 110 twin-engine fighters flew along the edge of U.S. B-17 formations, just out of range of the bombers' defensive armament, and fired rockets into the bomber groups. Then Bf 109 and Fw 190 fighter aircraft launched head-on and stern attacks to break up the formations. With stocks of ammunition and fuel dispersed throughout the Reich, Luftwaffe fighters could fly multiple sorties against bomber raids without returning to their home stations.

Nevertheless, no matter how successful the German air defenses, there were warning signs of impending defeat. Though bomber formations suffered heavy losses, they also inflicted serious casualties on their tormentors. In September the Luftwaffe lost 276 single-engine fighters in the west (17.4 percent of its fighters) and another 284 in October. Even more dangerous for the long run were losses of fighter pilots. In July, August, and September 1943, approximately 16 percent of German fighter pilots were killed, maimed, or missing in combat each month; and in November and December the figure was close to 10 percent each month. The average monthly strength of pilots in operational fighter squadrons in the Luftwaffe for 1943 was 2,105, while losses of fighter pilots over the year were

2,967 pilots killed, maimed, or missing—a turnover of 141 percent. Such losses were less than the crew losses suffered by the U.S. Eighth Air Force (approximately 38 percent in May and June, 35 percent in July, 31 percent in August, 20 percent in September, and 37 percent in October). To put the comparative risk in statistical terms, a young German in 1942 had a better chance of surviving the war by joining the Waffen SS and fighting on the Eastern Front than by becoming a fighter pilot, while a young American that same year had a better chance of surviving by joining the marines and fighting in the Pacific than by flying with Eighth Air Force in 1943. But over the long haul the Americans, with their large numbers of pilots and planes in reserve, could absorb such losses. The Luftwaffe could not, and the collapse of its fighter defenses in 1944 reflected the cumulative impact of this attrition.

Not surprisingly, the persistence of daylight air attacks outraged Hitler. Since he refused to alter production priorities, he and Göring searched for other answers. One solution was greater National Socialist enthusiasm for the defense of the Fatherland. As Göring argued to his pilots and staff on numerous occasions, the requirement of the hour was for a more fanatical approach to air defense; he also issued a string of rebukes that the Reich's troubles were a direct result of the cowardice of the fighter pilots. Göring and Hitler were not the only ones to make such claims. Much admired by postwar Anglo-American commentators (but less so by those who served under him), Field Marshal Kesselring displayed an unswerving enthusiasm for the fanaticism of others in combat. As early as March 1943, he was urging his hard-pressed fighter pilots to model their approach on that of the Japanese and sprinkling his messages with threats of courts-martial for those whose fanaticism was insufficient.

But the insurmountable obstacle in defending German airspace was Hitler's own lack of interest in the air war at home. It was more of an embarrassment to him than anything else. At one point the Nazi leader even argued that destruction of Germany's cities "actually works in our favor, because it is creating a body of people with nothing to lose—people who will therefore fight on with utter fanaticism."[8] A conversation between Göring and Milch in November further amplifies this point. Milch suggested that alongside the life-and-death questions of the Eastern Front, he was equally worried about what the homeland would do when American bombers returned in 1944. Göring replied that "when every city in Germany has been smashed to the ground, the German people would still live. It would certainly be awful, but the nation had lived before there were cities." Milch then suggested that such an occurrence might affect arms production, but Göring was not listening. He asked his production chief which was the greater danger to the war effort: Berlin's destruction or the arrival of the Soviets on German soil? The latter, Göring noted, was the "number one danger."[9]

In actuality, the Germans had lost the air war as early as 1941, when they chose to ignore the lessons of the Battle of Britain and failed to put their aircraft industry on a wartime footing. The Germans had prepared to fight a war in Central Europe, but the numbers of planes and pilots that sufficed within the Reich's prewar frontiers could not meet air force commitments from the Bay of Biscay to Moscow and from the North Cape to Libya. The most dangerous trend in 1941 was a production program inadequate for both the short and long run.

The Luftwaffe had entered the war with surprisingly low production levels, though these levels reflected the economic reality of the prewar years. The victories of 1940, however, fundamentally improved the Reich's economic and strategic situation; now the Germans could draw on Europe's resources. With that potential, they could have organized the new conquests in concert with their own economy to increase armaments production. Displaying a shortsightedness that is hard to fathom in retrospect, they did no such thing. Göring summed up Nazi economic policy in the early war: "As for myself, I think of pillage comprehensively."[10] Nazi exploitation of conquered economies largely involved looting expeditions in which competing military and civilian authorities divvied up the booty. Captured raw materials along with considerable amounts of machine tools went straight back to the Reich. These transfers made little economic sense, since factories in the homeland, particularly in the aircraft industry, were already underutilized.

The appointment of Milch to control aircraft production in summer 1941 was a major improvement. In a speech to the Reich's chief industrialists, Milch outlined new production targets and demanded that they judge what was and was not possible. Furthermore, he refused to allow industry to proceed with serial production of aircraft but insisted, rather, that it move to mass production, at least of older types of aircraft. The change in leadership came too late, however. By 1941, the Western powers were already outproducing Germany in aircraft by a wide margin. In the last quarter, Anglo-American production was nearly four times greater in fighters than Germany's; in twin-engine aircraft, the lead was nearly double; and in four-engine aircraft, it was a whopping 40 times greater. The 1941 totals were only a part of the story. The British and Americans were also making basic investments for far greater increases in production in coming years;

given the potential of the American economy, such preparations were on a much larger scale than anything the Germans imagined.

As German aircraft and crew losses mounted from the end of 1941, the Luftwaffe squeezed out of its industry and flying schools what it could and shoved inexperienced crews and poorly made aircraft into frontline units. Meanwhile, the Nazi leadership ignored the danger. With great glee, Goebbels recorded every Allied disaster in 1942, while dismissing as idle boasting American production figures. The reality emerged clearly enough in 1943. In that year, German industry produced 64 percent more aircraft than in 1942, with a dramatic rise of 125 percent in fighter production. In May, German industry produced 1,000 fighters for the first time; by July, production had reached 1,263. It was not enough. The increasing aircraft and aircrew superiority of Allied air forces caused such a heavy rate of attrition in the Luftwaffe that, despite greatly increased production, German frontline units grew in strength by only a small amount.

Milch made a sustained effort to apprise Hitler and Göring of the threat. Hitler remained unconvinced. In early July 1943, Kammhuber presented a proposal to the Führer for a radical restructuring of the air defenses to meet the bombers. Hitler responded by demanding the origin of "these crazy numbers" and added that "if the numbers of Allied production were correct, then he would have to stop the offensive in the east and concentrate everything on air defense."[11] Since he had no intention of doing any such thing, the figures, he assured Kammhuber, must be false.

The Night Defense of the Reich

Jeschonnek's suicide in August 1943 resulted in the appointment of General Günther Korten as the Luftwaffe's chief of staff. Korten understood Germany's desperate situation and aimed at two strategic objectives: building up the domestic air defenses and establishing a strategic bombing force to attack the Soviet war economy. He confronted an impossible task, however, for the Luftwaffe had already lost its chance to defend the Reich. Hitler refused to give priority to fighters over bombers, owing to an unwillingness, even at this late date, to recognize the major reason behind Germany's desperate plight: the overwhelming superiority of Allied production. Both he and Göring dredged up many excuses as to why Allied bombers were flying deep within the Reich's airspaces, but a recurring theme was the cowardice of the fighter pilots. Given the astonishingly high losses among these young men, such charges dramatize the hypocrisy of Germany's leaders.

In September and October 1943, Bomber Command's assault continued with a series of devastating attacks against German cities. On 5 September Harris's forces concentrated heavy bombing on the Mannheim-Ludwigshafen area and destroyed both towns. On 4 October they pulverized Frankfurt am Main and on 8 October destroyed most of Hanover's center. The most damaging attack came on 22 October against Kassel; Pathfinder marking aircraft were so accurate that 86 percent of attacking crews dropped their loads within three miles of the aim point. The concentration created a second firestorm; the ruins still smoldered seven days later.

In November Harris committed his command to destroying Berlin. In a note to Churchill, he suggested: "We can wreck Berlin from end to end if the USAAF will come in on it. It will cost us between 400–500 aircraft. It will cost Germany the war."[12] Harris hoped to win the war over the winter by area bombing alone. He now crossed the line between realistic perseverance and stubborn adherence to preconceived ideas. He could not have selected a more difficult target. Berlin lay deep in Germany, so that the attacking forces had to fly long distances into the teeth of enemy air defenses. The capital's size exacerbated the problem. It was relatively easy for British bombers to drop their loads within city limits; it was another matter to achieve the concentration required by area bombing. Moreover, Berlin lay beyond the range of navigational devices, while the city possessed too few terrain features for radar to obtain a clear picture for bomb aimers. Finally, Europe's oncoming winter weather proved to be a nightmare.

The Germans also confronted difficulties. They too had to fly in appalling weather. But by fall 1943 their night fighter defenses had improved significantly in both equipment and tactics after the summer's defeats. German scientists had developed a new airborne radar, SN2, that operated on a longer wavelength; consequently Window no longer worked. On the tactical side, German night fighters abandoned the approach that had tied fighters to individual radar sites. Now, guided by a running commentary and radio beacons, they could scramble to intercept the bomber stream. This looser arrangement had some drawbacks; the RAF could lure the fighters toward diversionary raids, thus protecting the main attack. But on the whole the new defensive scheme allowed for greater fighter concentrations against the bombers.

The offensive against Berlin began in November 1943 with four major raids. Initial losses were surprisingly low, but the loss rates were misleading. On several nights, conditions were so bad that night fighters never got airborne. Such conditions provided a protective cloak for the British attacks, but they also prevented the attackers from achieving any significant bombing concentrations. Nevertheless, damage was heavy as large numbers of bombs cascaded down all over Berlin. A gloomy Goebbels recorded: "The situation has become more alarming in that one industrial plant after another has been set on fire . . . The sky above Berlin is bloody deep red, and of an awesome beauty. I just can't stand looking at it." Nevertheless, the propaganda minister comforted himself with British overstatements of the damage and forbade denials in the hope that the "sooner London is convinced that there is nothing left of Berlin, the sooner will they stop their offensive against the Reich's capital."[13]

In December, British bomber losses began to increase dramatically; by January, they were unacceptable. Missing rates on six Berlin raids that month averaged 6.1 percent, and Bomber Command's attacks on other cities equally deep in Germany averaged 7.2 percent. The British lost 316 bombers over the course of the month, a loss rate that no air force could endure. The technological and tactical balance had now swung in favor of the defense. By January 1944, German night fighters were flying out over the North Sea to intercept bombers. Their increasing successes forced the British to take drastic action. The planning and conduct of raids became more complicated, with spoof attacks, interference with German communications, and abandonment of route markers to guide the bomber stream. Nevertheless, Harris persisted in his campaign to the end of March and came close to wrecking his command.

In early March, Bomber Command attacked targets in southern Germany; at month's end the British again mounted deep penetration raids into the Reich. On 24 March, Harris's forces struck Berlin one last time and lost 77 bombers (9.1 percent). On the 26th, the Command struck Essen a devastating blow; and since it was close to Germany's western border, the British suffered a minimal loss of nine bombers. The accuracy at Essen, however, underlined how dependent Bomber Command was on navigational devices, and the radio beams on which the bombers navigated could reach only western sections of the Reich. Over the night of 30–31 March, Bomber Command launched the last deep penetration raid of the Berlin offensive. It occurred in weather conditions that were perfect for enemy interceptors. Not only did the track of the bomber stream provide little deception, but it passed directly over one of the main radio beacons for enemy fighters. The Germans shot down 108 bombers, with the Halifax bombers suffering an appalling loss of 20.6 percent.

In five months, Bomber Command had lost 1,128 aircraft, nearly all of them four-engine bombers. Moreover, while loss rates were substantially greater than those suffered in earlier battles, the benefits to the Allies were palpably less. As Air Marshal D. C. Bennett, commander of the Pathfinders, commented after the war, the Battle of Berlin "had been the worst thing that could have happened to the command."[14] By the end of March, Harris had arrived at the same point the Americans reached the previous October. Night bombers, unprotected by long-range escort fighters, were suffering prohibitive losses.

The Day Battle

Faced with tremendous losses on the Schweinfurt raid due to a lack of fighter escorts, the Americans set in motion a desperate attempt to extend the range of their fighters by adding drop tanks. This scheme was only marginally successful, but concurrently the P-51 Mustang long-range fighter appeared on the scene. The P-51 was an orphan at birth. North American Aircraft developed the ground attack aircraft early in the war to land a contract with the British. The initial model possessed good low-altitude capabilities, but its original Allison engine lacked the power to operate effectively at higher altitudes. In summer 1942, British engineers upgraded its power plant to a Rolls-Royce Merlin engine; by October 1942, they had transformed a turkey into an eagle. The road to production, however, proved difficult. Both Britain and the United States were reluctant to push for production, since the plane was the product of neither air establishment. But by summer 1943 the P-51's potential was obvious, especially considering the aircraft's range. The second Schweinfurt disaster provided a final incentive to get P-51s into large-scale production without delay.

From late October through early January, American forces concentrated their attacks in western Germany, which was within the range limits of current Allied escort fighters. Nevertheless, the raids took a heavy toll of aircraft on both sides—an attrition that the Luftwaffe was less able to sustain. Owing to periods of bad weather, the swelling forces that American production was making available could not be immediately employed, and at the end of the year major changes occurred in the U.S. command structure. A new air force, the Ninth, assumed control of tactical air units supporting the invasion. Moreover, Fifteenth Air Force was beginning to build up its heavy bomber formations in southern Italy, which allowed it to strike at targets in Austria, Bavaria, and the Balkans. Generals Carl "Tooey" Spaatz and James Doolittle moved from the Mediterranean to assume control of U.S. air forces in Britain. Their boss, General "Hap" Arnold, made clear in a Christmas message that their mission was to "destroy the enemy air force wherever you find them, in the air, on the ground, and in the factories."[15]

Doolittle was one of the most interesting and innovative airmen of the war. He had joined up and learned to fly during World War I but had not made it to the war. In the interwar period, he pursued a dashing career as a fighter pilot, a role that cast him in the lead of technological innovation. In a tour of South America, he fell out of a Chilean officer club's window while drinking and broke both ankles but continued his flying tour of South America until his return to the United States. But Doolittle was far more than a wild fighter pilot. He earned a Ph.D. from Massachusetts Institute of Technology in aeronautical engineering, and he pioneered the development of blind landing devices in the mid-1930s. He left the Army Air Corps in 1930 to work for Shell Corporation, where he was a pioneer in the development of higher octane fuels—a major advantage for Allied air forces early in the war.

Doolittle returned to active duty as a reserve officer as the war clouds gathered in 1940. At Arnold's behest, he put together the 1942 Tokyo raid and then rose rapidly to the command of heavy bombers in the Mediterranean. From that theater, he was warning his superiors in Washington in May 1943, well before anyone else in Europe, that they had better develop long-range escort fighters or the strategic bombing effort was going to run into serious difficulties. Eventually rising to the rank of lieutenant general, Doolittle was the highest-ranking U.S. reserve officer in the war. In the 1980s President Ronald Reagan promoted him to four-star rank.

In mid-January Eighth Air Force again launched a deep-penetration raid into Germany. Demonstrating the growth of the bombing force, 663 bombers struck several targets. However, out of 174 attacking the aircraft factories at Oschersleben, the Germans shot down 34, while the total force lost 60 bombers. Heavy losses resulted from the weak support that escort fighters could provide; only one group of P-51s was yet available. Eighth Air Force finally got a break in the weather in mid-February. Spaatz and Doolittle threw everything they had against the Luftwaffe and its support structure. By this point, Eighth Fighter Command possessed 539 P-38J Lightnings, 416 P-47D Thunderbolts, and 329 P-51B Mustangs. For a week, good weather prevailed; the result was a massive, extended air battle, termed "Big Week" by the victors. Relays of fighters accompanied the bombers to the targets and back, although the shortage of P-51s still made coverage less than perfect. The major target was the aircraft industry, particularly factories producing fighters. In the long run, the Germans overcame the extensive damage and achieved a 50 percent increase in fighter production, but the success came at the cost of shutting down production of virtually every other type of aircraft; the increase by weight in German aircraft production over 1944 was only 20 percent.

Big Week began on 20 February with a multitarget attack on the German aircraft industry—the major objective of the raids. Escorted by 885 fighters, over 1,000 bombers sortied from American air bases in Britain. The first day's attack met relatively light opposition, but for the rest of the week swirling air battles criss-crossed Central Europe; they culminated in attacks on the 24th and 25th. On the 24th, American units lost 66 bombers but only 10 fighters, a reflection of desperate Luftwaffe attempts to get at the bombers. On the following day, Eighth lost only 17 bombers out of 820 dispatched. But Fifteenth Air Force (the strategic bombing force in Italy) lost 41 bombers out of 116 in its attack on Regensburg. Thus, the Americans lost 124 bombers in two days, double the loss of the Schweinfurt raids of 1943.

The capacity of the U.S. strategic bombing forces to bear such losses was a mark of how much they had grown since fall 1943. The Eighth and Fifteenth Air Forces could absorb an attrition rate close to 20 percent over February, while the Germans could not. In February and the following months Luftwaffe pilot and aircraft losses ended the Luftwaffe's ability to mount an effective air defense *anywhere*. The defensive tactics that had worked when bomber formations were unaccompanied no longer worked for the Germans. P-51s savaged the Bf 110 twin-engine fighter force, while Luftwaffe Bf 109s and Fw 190s had a desperate fight for survival against the escorts. The sustained combat of Big Week devastated the Luftwaffe's single-engine fighters. U.S. losses for the next three months suggest that the process of defeat was prolonged rather than short, one that finally cracked the Luftwaffe in May. But February's returns were dismal enough: 33 percent of single-engine fighters written off. Even more damaging was the loss of 17.9 percent of the Luftwaffe's fighter pilots.

Attrition in March was even heavier, as Eighth Air Force extended operations all the way to Berlin. On 4 March, American bombers attacked the capital for the first time. Two days later a second raid encountered tenacious opposition and lost 69 bombers. The third raid within six days occurred on the 8th. Goebbels and his Propaganda Ministry could only lamely explain that "if occasionally [American bombers] fly in clear sky without at the moment being pursued by the dreaded German fighters, only the layman is fooled, and then only for a few moments . . . In their case, the closed drill formations are not a sign of strength."[16]

Attrition of German fighter pilots reached a new high in March, nearly 22 percent. The rise reflected several factors. The most obvious was the high tempo of operations. Although persistent periods of bad weather prevented another "big week," the Americans kept up unremitting pressure. Raids, particularly on fighter production facilities, forced the Luftwaffe to come up and fight. Another factor was the growing strength of U.S. long-range escorts. Moreover, Doolittle authorized his fighters, after having accomplished their major mission in escorting bombers, to attack German aircraft anywhere in the Reich and savage German air fields with low-level attacks. A final factor was pilot expertise: the heaviest losses in the Luftwaffe occurred among the inexperienced pilots; the fact that American and British aviators were receiving nearly twice the number of flight-training hours put new Luftwaffe pilots at a great disadvantage, and pilot error began to tell. But the law of averages was also catching up with even the most experienced German pilots. In March the Luftwaffe lost two Geschwader commanders, one with 102 kills, the other with 161.

April witnessed unremitting pressure on the defenses. That month Eighth Air Force lost more bombers than in any other month of the war. In May the Luftwaffe cracked. From this point, American bomber losses declined significantly, both in raw numbers and as a percentage of aircraft lost in each raid. From May on, German fighters inflicted only sporadic damage on daylight raiders, while their own losses remained at insupportable levels. In May alone the Luftwaffe lost 25 percent of its fighter pilots, and in the first five months of 1944 its fighter force had lost 2,262 pilots out of the 2,395 fighter pilots on duty on 1 January.

Such unsustainable attrition caused a ripple effect throughout the force. In order to keep up with the demand for new pilots as experienced ones were killed, the Luftwaffe training command kept shortening the syllabus and lowering the number of required flying hours for new trainees. German fighter pilots spent less than 80 hours flying operational aircraft before being sent on their first combat mission, while RAF and USAAF pilots received 225 hours in operational aircraft. A Luftwaffe study could only suggest that its young pilots compensate for this obvious disadvantage with greater enthusiasm and valor. They could not, but they died by the thousands trying.

Normandy and Oil

On 1 April 1944, all air assets of the Western powers, including Eighth Air Force and Bomber Command, came under the operational control of the Supreme Commander Allied Expeditionary Forces Europe, General Dwight D. Eisenhower. Eisenhower's deputy, Air Marshal Sir Arthur Tedder, with considerable help from Solly Zuckerman, his chief scientist, had designed an air campaign plan to destroy the Wehrmacht's ability to build up and supply its forces in the future invasion area. Tedder was an anomaly among RAF senior leaders during the course of the war. He was consistently willing to take a joint service perspective rather than follow the narrow prejudices of his own service. As the commander of RAF forces in the Middle East, Tedder had recognized immediately that strategic bombing had little relevance to the needs of his theater. Thus, he concentrated on developing a balanced force that could succeed at a number of missions: air superiority to allow the British Army to accomplish its tasks without harassment by Luftwaffe aircraft; close air support to aid hard-pressed ground forces against the Afrika Korps; interdiction strikes against the Axis infrastructure in North Africa; and strike missions against Rommel's supply lines crossing the Mediterranean. After the successful Torch landings and the hook-up of Allied forces in Tunisia, Eisenhower and Tedder formed a partnership that endured for the rest of the war. Tedder and Zuckerman's plan would seek to destroy the railroad network in western and central France and cripple road traffic by destroying bridges on main arteries.

Not surprisingly, Harris waged a furious effort to prevent Bomber Command's participation in Tedder's proposal. His first line of argument—that his command was winning the war by itself—lay in tatters with defeat in the Battle of Berlin. But Churchill feared that raids against French marshaling yards, most of which lay in populated areas, would cause heavy casualties among French civilians and irreparable damage to postwar relations with France. Harris reinforced these fears with less than candid arguments that his bombers could not accurately hit targets in France. But his pilots proved him wrong, and Bomber Command executed much of the effort against French railroads with greater accuracy than American precision attacks.

The argument between Tedder and the Americans was less clear. Spaatz introduced a new element into the equation with the proposal that his bombers should attack Germany's petroleum infrastructure, the destruction of which would help Allied ground forces more than destruction of the French transportation system. Given his authority, Eisenhower won the argument, but he compromised around the edges. Thus, the Eighth Air Force's strategic bombers rendered significant support to the interdiction campaign. Out of 80 crucial transportation targets in France, Bomber Command attacked 39, Eighth Air Force 23, and Allied tactical air forces 18. In mid-April, as Allied air attacks bit, French railroad traffic began a precipitous decline. Initially, the Germans cut civilian traffic to support military needs, but sustained air attacks soon affected military traffic as well. During May, fighter-bomber attacks on the Seine bridges and trains accelerated the decline. By late May, French railroad traffic was barely half of what it had been in January, and thereafter it declined to 10 percent. Attacks on the rail system in western France were particularly effective, and by mid-June it had ceased to operate.

A German report in early June noted: "In [France and Belgium], the systematic destruction . . . since March of all important junctions of the entire network—not only on the main lines—has most seriously crippled the whole transport system (railway installations, including rolling stock). Similarly Paris has been cut off from long-distance traffic; and the most important bridges over the lower Seine have been destroyed one after the other . . . The rail network is to be completely wrecked . . . This aim has so successfully been achieved—locally at any rate—that the Reichsbahn [is] . . . considering whether it is not useless to attempt further repair work."[17]

The transportation plan's success was a major contributor to the Allied victory in Normandy. Since much of the Wehrmacht consisted of infantry whose equipment was horse-drawn, the Germans depended on railroads to move reserves and supplies. Destruction of that logistical support made it difficult to redeploy and supply German reserves once the invasion began. Thus, the Germans lost the race to reinforce in Normandy even before the invasion began. Destruction of the transport system forced German infantry to fight without adequate artillery, while even infantry ammunition remained in short supply. Moreover, the motorized and mechanized units encountered great difficulty in driving forward into Normandy because of damage to the road network. The Germans did maintain a sustained defense in Normandy, but that was largely because there remained one hole in the interdiction campaign: the barge traffic down the Seine. On that line the Germans moved enough supplies forward to keep the front from collapsing.

In mid-May, Eisenhower allowed Spaatz to launch his bombers against the German petroleum industry. The Americans at last had found the weak spot in the German war economy. Since the early days of the war, the Germans had worried about oil. In September 1940, Hitler remarked that British efforts to sabotage Romania's oil fields brought him considerable anxiety. He added that there were two vital raw materials Nazi Germany needed: Swedish iron ore and Romanian petroleum. From 1940, fuel shortages plagued Germany's conduct of the war, and many of Hitler's decisions involved either protecting or gaining access to petroleum. Yet with the exception of the Ploesti raid of 1943 against the Romanian petroleum industry, the Allies failed to strike at the Reich's petroleum sources, and the Germans found this inexplicable. Writing in March 1944, Speer's staff warned that enemy air forces might attack the oil industry in order to end the war quickly. In April a Luftwaffe staff officer was more direct. Considering that the major refineries and fuel plants in Germany lay within the area threatened by air attack, he found it extraordinary that the Allies had not yet struck at oil, a target that would jeopardize the Reich's war effort.

But now in May 1944 all that changed. Eighth Air Force's attacks against the synthetic oil industry in the Reich complemented raids by Fifteenth Air Force out of Foggia in Italy against Romanian refineries and production facilities. The first strike from Britain came on 12 May; 935 bombers sortied against the synthetic oil plants at Zwickau, Merseburg-Leuna, Brüx, Lutzkendorf, Bohlen, Zeitz, and Chemnitz. Allied bombers and escorting fighters encountered severe resistance. The results, while encouraging, were not decisive. The great Leuna plant, though damaged, lost only 18 percent of its capacity. Speer was, nevertheless, enormously worried.

What Speer did not know, and what emerged only among Ultra revelations in the early 1980s, was the role that special intelligence played in keeping U.S. strategic bombing focused on the petroleum industry. As the officer handling Ultra noted in his after-action report, intercepted communications indicating that petroleum shortages were general and not just local played a crucial role in persuading "all concerned that the air offensive had uncovered a weak spot in the German economy and led to exploitation of this weakness to the fullest extent."[18] On 16 May, Bletchley Park forwarded a German message canceling an order that Luftflotten 1 and 6 (First and Sixth Air Forces) surrender to Luftflotte 3 (Third Air Force) five heavy and three light flak batteries each. These batteries were instead to move to Luftflotte Reich (Air Force Reich) to protect the hydrogenation plant at Troglitz. In addition, a number of other flak units were moved to protect other major fuel plants. On the 21st, another intercepted message warned its addressees that they could expect major shortfalls in June's allocations of fuel in view of the attacks on petroleum facilities in Romania and Germany. After feverish efforts, production had come close to regaining preattack levels by the end of May. On the 28th, Eighth returned to attack oil targets throughout Germany. Over a two-day period, it lost 84 bombers, but this time it badly damaged the petroleum industry. Combined with Fifteenth Air Force's raids on Ploesti, American attacks cut petroleum production in half.

The impact of the raids was apparent almost immediately. On 6 June, Bletchley Park provided the following decrypt: "As a result of renewed interference with the production of aircraft fuel by Allied action, most essential requirements for training and carrying out production plans can scarcely be covered by quantities of aircraft fuel available . . . To assure defense of Reich and to prevent gradual collapse of readiness for defense of German air force in east, it has been necessary to break into OKW reserves . . . In no circumstances can greater allocations be made."[19]

May's attacks were a prelude to punishing raids over the succeeding months. After a two-week pause, during which Allied bombers supported the invasion, the Americans staged a series of new attacks that knocked out 90 percent of aviation fuel production, so that by the end of the month total production had sunk to a minuscule 632 tons. By mid-July the Germans had repaired facilities sufficiently to quadruple production. More U.S. raids with Bomber Command's support then lowered production to 120 tons per day. By the end of July these air attacks had knocked out 98 percent of the production capacity for aircraft fuel. For the remainder of the war, American strategic bombing concentrated on fuel plants and refineries. In July, Leuna reached only 70 percent of normal production, while other main production facilities had dropped to between 43 and 58 percent. Only Ludwigshafen remained in full production. Continuing attacks kept a lid on oil production throughout the rest of the war.

The implication of these attacks was not hard to see. In June, Speer warned Hitler that he needed six to eight weeks to restore production. Should the Führer not provide defensive support to the oil industry, the enemy would recognize recovery efforts and destroy the repairs. By midsummer 1944, as fighter production reached new highs, the Luftwaffe possessed neither fuel nor pilots to employ all the new fighters German industry was producing. In the final analysis, Tedder's transportation plan and Spaatz's fuel plan were complementary. Together, they starved the German troops in Normandy of the supplies and fuel to defeat the invasion. Then, after the collapse in late July, the Germans could not make a fighting withdrawal because they lacked the fuel required for mobile warfare, thus sparing France even greater destruction than Allied air power had already wrought in the spring and summer.

At the beginning of September, the strategic bombers reverted to the control of the air commanders. Not surprisingly, the bomber barons returned their forces to attacking what they believed to be the crucial targets.

Bomber Command resumed area bombing with a vengeance; since the Germans had lost their early warning stations in France, British bombers could fly deep into the Reich without suffering heavy losses. Moreover, the arrival of Allied forces on the German frontier allowed the British to set up radio beacons for accurate navigation deep into the Reich. At the same time, the Americans reinvigorated their campaign to destroy the synthetic fuel industry as well as other industrial targets.

Meanwhile, Tedder brought forward a plan to destroy the Reich's transportation system. He argued that the campaign against the French system provided a model on which to base a new campaign to bring Nazi industry to a halt. The air commanders strongly resisted the proposal; only after considerable argument and pressure did they agree to provide provisional support. The Americans would attack transportation targets when the weather was not suitable for precision raids against oil targets, while Bomber Command would use marshaling yards and the railroad stations in city centers as the primary aim points for its area attacks.

The final plan divided Germany into nine specific districts, five of which lay to the west of Kassel. In central and eastern Germany, the plan identified transportation districts in Silesia, around Vienna, to the west of Berlin, and in Bavaria. The aim was to break the rail network, so that raw materials, finished goods, and parts could not move. Crucial to success would be the disruption of not only the German railways (Reichsbahn) but also the canal and waterway systems.

The attacks began in September and almost immediately had an impact. For the week ending 19 August, the Reichsbahn loaded and dispatched 899,091 cars; by the week ending 28 October, that figure had fallen to 703,580; and by the week ending 23 December, it had fallen to 547,309 despite heavy demands from the Ardennes offensive. By December 1944, the capacity of marshaling yards had declined to 40 percent of operating capacity; by February 1945, it was down to 20 percent. The Ardennes offensive indicates that by late fall, transportation attacks could not yet prevent the Wehrmacht from preparing and launching major ground operations. But these attacks were already damaging the ability of the German war economy to function.

The accelerating collapse of the transportation system was soon strangling the war effort and economy by disorganizing the flow of weapons, ammunition, and parts to the front. Under such conditions, neither planning nor production could take place in an orderly fashion. The collapse of the coal industry suggests the extent of the problem. In January 1944, the Essen division of the Reichsbahn had loaded a daily average of 21,400 cars. By September, that total dropped to 12,000, of which only 3,000–4,000 were long-haul commitments. By February, Allied transportation attacks had cut the Ruhr off from the rest of Germany. The Reichsbahn often had to confiscate what little coal was loaded just to keep its locomotives running. Underlining the impact of the attacks was the state of coal production and stocks in the Ruhr between August 1944 and February 1945. Although coal production fell dramatically during this period, stocks in the Ruhr rose from 415,000 tons to 2,217,000 tons; stocks of coke similarly rose from 630,000 tons to 3,069,000 tons. The Ruhr was swimming in coal that the railroads could no longer transport even to industries within the region, much less to the rest of Germany.

Nevertheless, the Allies failed to use their full capabilities to shut down the Reich's transportation system. Harris's commitment to area bombing meant that Bomber Command never threw its full weight behind attacks on "panacea" targets. And the Americans remained heavily committed to the oil plan. Still, a general collapse of the war economy during the winter occurred. It was not a sudden, cataclysmic collapse, and for that reason it has remained difficult to identify except through the accumulated evidence of shortages and substitutions—for example, ethanol for gasoline in trucks.

In summer 1944 German armies in both the east and west had lost massive amounts of equipment. Nevertheless, because armament production remained largely unimpeded, the Wehrmacht reequipped the surviving divisions and new recruits to defend the frontiers. That, however, was the army's last shot. Beginning in January 1945, the collapse began in the east, followed a month and a half later in the west. On neither the Rhine nor the Oder could German troops regroup for an effective last-ditch stand on the ruins of the Reich. It was not that German soldiers were unwilling to continue the fight. The cause of the collapse had to do with the fact that the transportation offensive had successfully destroyed the war economy, and the Wehrmacht no longer had the weapons, the ammunition, and particularly the fuel to sustain the struggle. Even blind fanaticism could not maintain an effective defense in such circumstances.

The Air War in Retrospect

In the air war over Europe, virtually nothing happened the way prewar air champions had predicted. What widened the gap between expectations and realities was the airmen's assumption that their operational approach guaranteed victory—a victory they could achieve without the terrible cost in blood and treasure that had marked World War I. So it came as a major surprise that ambiguity and uncertainty governed this war as any other.

Enemy air forces consistently interposed themselves between attacking bombers and their targets, and consistently inflicted unacceptable levels of attrition on the attackers. Western air propagandists later claimed that, once dispatched, bomber formations never failed to attack their target, but such arguments miss the real issue. When Eighth Air Force attacked Schweinfurt in August and October 1943, its B-17s could not return to the target to complete the destruction for substantial periods of time because German fighters had so severely mauled the attacking force.

The second major surprise had to do with the modern industrialized state's ability to absorb punishment and still function. It was not that bombing had a psychological effect that turned German citizens into more effective workers; rather, modern industrialized states, whether democratic or totalitarian, could mobilize manpower and resources in almost endless quantities. And when popular morale faltered, the modern state possessed the police powers required to keep the population in line and on the job.

The received postwar wisdom suggests that strategic bombing played a relatively unimportant part in winning World War II. The thrust of the argument is that the opportunity costs of bombing were excessive in comparison to its gains. Yet, the evidence points in a different direction. The effectiveness of Bomber Command's area campaign is difficult to measure in quantitative terms. One can surmise that within areas devastated by attacks, substantial slowdowns in production occurred. How much the Reich's war production might have increased without the retardant effects of such attacks is impossible to calculate. What one can suggest is that a German economy unburdened by air attacks and drawing on all of Central and Western Europe might have reached far higher levels of productivity.

It is easier to estimate Bomber Command's indirect effects. British attacks on cities and civilian morale led the Nazi regime to make two crucial errors in its response to the threat. On one hand, British raids caused a substantial distortion in the production and use of ammunition and artillery. The German population drew considerable confidence from large numbers of anti-aircraft batteries blasting away at the attackers. By summer 1943, 89 flak batteries defended Berlin, and the growth in flak forces during the war was considerable. From 791 batteries in 1940 defending the Reich, the numbers grew to 967 in 1941, 1,148 in 1942, and 2,132 in 1943; such increases represented an enormous investment in resources and manpower. The presence of well over 10,000 anti-aircraft guns (all of which could have been highly effective as anti-tank weapons)—not to mention the half million men and women manning them, who could have been contributing to industrial output or fighting on other fronts—would have had a significant impact on the ground war in the east or west in 1943 or 1944.

The second indirect effect of area bombing came in the strategic and operational reactions of the Nazi leadership. The bombing did hurt morale severely, and the leadership, drawing on its belief that Germany had lost the last war because of a collapse of civilian morale, cast its response in accordance with a popular mood that demanded retaliation. In their enthusiasm for offensive strikes against Britain, the Germans consistently refused to provide sufficient resources for air defense.

Moreover, the emphasis on retaliation resulted in an even greater strategic error, which was overinvestment in exotic weapons of revenge. By the end of 1943 the army was close to production of its V-2 ballistic missile, and the Luftwaffe was in the final stages of developing its V-1 cruise missile. The V-1 caused considerable diversion of Allied defensive forces at a cost that was not excessive to the Germans, and so its development was not necessarily a bad strategy. But the V-2, while a triumph of engineering, was not a monument to good sense. It demanded complex technological support; it was inordinately expensive; it used up scarce raw materials; and its production overloaded the instrument and electrical component industries. In summer 1943, German leaders had to choose between restructuring the aircraft industry to ensure sufficient day and night fighters to meet the bomber offensive or laying the production base for V-1s and V-2s. In a decision crucial to the outcome of the war, Hitler chose the latter; he refused to meet strategic bombing with a military response. As Göring commented in October 1943, the German people did not care whether the Luftwaffe attacked British air fields: "All they wished to hear when a hospital or children's home in Germany is destroyed is that we have destroyed the same in England; then they are satisfied."[20]

The result was an emphasis on V weapons that distorted air defense programs. It prevented the Germans from developing effective anti-aircraft rockets and drained off significant resources from fighter production. The U.S. Strategic Bombing Survey estimated that the industrial effort and resources devoted to these revenge weapons equaled production of 24,000 fighter aircraft. A more recent analysis suggests that the V-2 affected the German war economy to an extent equivalent to the burden the Manhattan Project placed on the United States. But as was so often the case, the United States could afford the cost, while the Reich could not. Measured against its return on investment, the V-2 was undoubtedly the most cost-ineffective weapon of the war.

The impact of American strategic bombing is easier to assess because it did have specific target sets. In 1943, U.S. bombers attacked two target sets: the ball-bearing and aircraft industries. The attacks on the former failed because the Eighth Air Force could not deliver a sustained and consistent effort against the industry; consequently, the Germans were able to rebuild the facilities at Schweinfurt, disperse production, increase imports, and turn to alternatives such as roller bearings. U.S. attacks on aircraft production were more successful. The raids did not defeat the Luftwaffe, but they created the preconditions for Allied air superiority in 1944. They caused a significant drop in new fighter production as early as the last half of 1943 and, while costly, also imposed a high rate of attrition on the Luftwaffe.

In 1944, the American air campaign shifted its focus first to the Luftwaffe and its industrial base and then, in May, to petroleum facilities, which remained the major U.S. objective to the end of the war. The effects of the raids on aircraft factories were indirect. First, increases in German fighter production came almost entirely at the expense of bomber production. Second, and more important, the Luftwaffe was forced to come up to protect its industrial base, and in the skies over the Reich, U.S. long-range fighters broke the back of German air power. As a result, the Allies gained air superiority over the Continent, including the beaches of Normandy, and daylight bombing continued unimpeded for the rest of the war.

Attacks on the petroleum industry placed considerable impediments in the way of German military operations. Fuel shortages forced the Luftwaffe to reduce the number of flying hours. And without sufficient petroleum, ground units could not maneuver. For example, there were 1,800 tanks present in Silesia in January 1945, but nearly all were immobilized for lack of fuel. Consequently, German ground forces were incapable of defending that crucial industrial base.

Strategic bombing's greatest contribution came in the last months of the war, with Tedder's second transportation campaign. That effort did not prevent the Germans from making a last stand on their frontier, one that lasted into winter 1945. Nor could it prevent them from assembling the forces for the desperate Ardennes offensive of December 1944. But by that month Allied air attacks were well on the way to shutting down the war economy. German industry was collapsing, and the few weapons and ammunition being produced could not get through to the troops. Movement on the railways and waterways almost ceased, and German armies, starved of fuel and munitions, could not handle the rapidly moving enemy ground forces. Thus, there was no final *Götterdämmerung* to prolong the war into summer 1945.

Conclusion

Strategic bombing was crucial to the Allied victory. Unfortunately, by claiming too much for air power, airmen created false perceptions. The

Combined Bomber Offensive contributed to victory because it supported, and was supported by, the efforts of Allied ground and naval forces. The cost was high, and with hindsight one can argue that strategic bombing was often waged unimaginatively, that air forces failed to adapt to the real conditions of war, and that airmen often restricted the potential of air power. But are not these misconceptions and failures of imagination the conditions under which all wars are fought? In the end, what is certain is that the Combined Bomber Offensive was essential to the defeat of Nazi Germany. It was not elegant, it was not humane, but it was effective.

13

THE DESTRUCTION OF
JAPANESE NAVAL POWER

1943–1944

For Admiral Ernest J. King, Jr., the only war that would ruin Japan was not being fought. This war had raged in his imagination since he became an ensign in 1901, fourth in his Naval Academy class. In 1943, already past the mandatory retirement age of 64, King reigned as the foremost champion of the war with Japan within the Roosevelt administration. His influence stemmed completely from his professional expertise and force of mind, not his character. The kindest thing one of his admirers and closest associates, Rear Admiral Charles M. "Savvy" Cooke, Jr., could say was that King was "a man of action," while another intimate simply called King "meaner than I can describe."[1] Twice passed over for chief of naval operations in peacetime, King returned to Washington from command of the Atlantic Fleet to be chief of naval operations and commander-in-chief of the U.S. Fleet in December 1941. He had one mission: crush Japan.

King was just the man to ruin the Japanese, since he had a lifetime of practice in crushing rivals and embarrassing associates. His valedictory speech from high school had been entitled "Values of Adversity," and he spent his naval career learning from adversity, usually of his own making. Starting his career as an ensign on destroyers, he went on to engineering assignments. After more service in destroyers and command of a refrigerator ship, he commanded a submarine flotilla. Believing his career frozen, King accepted the challenge of qualifying as a naval aviator at 47, finishing the shortened flying syllabus for senior officers so that he could command a naval air station, a seaplane tender, and the carrier *Lexington*. Having reached flag rank in 1932, he even served as chief of the Bureau of Aviation.

Becoming an admiral improved King's behavior not a whit. He raged at subordinates in public, ruled his bridge with fear, and railed at incompetents and officers he thought too charming. He made life miserable for any-one around him, including a wife and seven children, by chain-smoking, binge-drinking, and flagrant philandering. Yet his sheer mastery of every aspect of naval warfare and administration kept him moving from one challenging assignment to another, despite his personality.

From the beginning of his service as chief of naval operations and fleet commander—a fusion of responsibilities unknown in the navy's history—King proved he would fight his war his way, which meant an institutional focus on the Pacific War, a focus so intense that King himself botched the war on the German U-boats in 1942. He simply ignored this failure and pushed for more offensive action in the Pacific. He disagreed with cau-tious colleagues or superiors more often than not. He said no with routine abruptness to FDR, Secretary of the Navy Frank Knox, George C. Marshall, Douglas MacArthur, and the British representatives on the Combined Chiefs of Staff. He had an overriding strategic goal: to destroy Japanese mil-itary might and to detach the U.S. Navy from the thrall of the British and MacArthur. Unlike MacArthur, King had no roots in Congress, the media, or any political party. Instead, he depended entirely on his absolute sense of purpose and strategic correctness to insist that the Allies could not defeat the Japanese along the Malay barrier at an acceptable cost in time and lives.

Among King's many intellectual qualifications was the ability to count. All the shipbuilding numbers of 1943 showed that the U.S. Navy would enjoy overwhelming numerical superiority in ships and naval aircraft in 1944. By the end of 1943, King's navy had a 10:4 advantage over the Impe-rial Navy in heavy fleet carriers, a 9:5 advantage in light carriers, and a 35:3 advantage in small escort carriers. The ratios in naval aircrewmen and air-craft were even better for the Americans. The IJN had 9 battleships (two commissioned since Pearl Harbor) to the U.S. Navy's 19, of which 7 were new, fast battleships that could keep pace with the carriers. The Japanese had 34 cruisers of all types, the Americans 48. Even with its losses in 1942, the U.S. "Treaty Navy"—that portion of the fleet commissioned before 1940—had not disappeared; 12 of 18 heavy cruisers were still in action, and only one more (Indianapolis) would go to the bottom before war's end. Between April 1943 and April 1945, 12 new heavy cruisers would join the fleet, and not one of them would be destroyed.

Moreover, King knew that his warships could range across the Central Pacific, supported by a growing fleet train of logistical vessels. More than 200 ships in this service force could perform logistical missions without an-choring. These fleet oilers, ammunition ships, and stores ships made up the underway replenishment groups that remained constantly at sea until empty, meeting the various carrier and surface groups to pass on everything from black oil to beans to wardroom movies. Before the war ended, the navy had a service force of over 1,000 ships.

King's greatest political-strategic victory of the war came over the British and U.S. armies in 1943 when he won formal recognition from Roosevelt and Churchill that the war with Japan could be won only by an American naval campaign across the Central Pacific, a campaign directed by him and his principal field subordinate, Chester W. Nimitz. The first phase of the debate occurred before, during, and after two Roosevelt-Churchill conferences in early 1943: "Trident" in Washington, D.C., and "Quadrant" in Quebec. Aided by his best strategist, Admiral Cooke, King fought for his version of JCS 287, an American-drafted "Strategic Plan for the Defeat of Japan." In its earliest drafts, this plan simply reflected the current reality that there were campaigns under way in Burma, China, and the South Pacific. Although army planners, dedicated to a second front in Europe, showed little interest in the war with Japan, the army still endorsed MacArthur's "I Shall Return" campaign. King insisted that any campaign should focus on the destruction of Japan's overseas resources, which meant an offensive directed only toward the Western Pacific sea lanes. He played on FDR's declining confidence that the British and Chinese would ever contribute much to a war of economic strangulation against Japan. When the British chiefs finally admitted that they would not release forces from the Mediterranean for Asia, King pressed for the endorsement of CCS 242/6, "Agreed Essentials in the Conduct of the War," which basically made the war with Japan an American responsibility. Roosevelt and Churchill approved this document on 25 May 1943.

The operations they authorized, however, offered little promise of a new campaign in the Central Pacific; it was a rebirth of War Plan Orange, with its focus on a Trafalgar-like naval victory over the Japanese fleet. The only operation thus far approved was Nimitz's plan to capture some Japanese atoll air bases in the Gilbert and eastern Marshall island groups. This operation found its justification as part of the last phase of Cartwheel, the continuing isolation of Rabaul. Yet it could also be useful as the opening phase of a campaign to capture the Imperial Navy's major operating base at Truk in the eastern Carolines. The debates within the JCS strategic planning committees continued, fueled by protests from MacArthur that a Central Pacific drive would divert scarce resources (especially tactical aviation) from his magnificent New Guinea campaign. The Joint Chiefs did not pay much attention to MacArthur's analysis, but they did nothing to make him think that he would not be supported. In July 1943, additional strategic guidance identified Truk and Palau, another major Japanese base in the western Carolines, as crucial objectives for a naval campaign in 1944. This axis of advance was pure War Plan Orange, since it led directly westward to Mindanao, also an objective much on MacArthur's map.

King remained unconvinced that the Philippines should be the principal focus of a Central Pacific campaign. He, in fact, agreed with MacArthur that the original War Plan Orange now made little sense, since there was no beleaguered American force in Manila Bay to rescue. The only thing in need of rescue was MacArthur's beleaguered reputation, and King saw no point in doing that either, since liberating Luzon would simply kill thousands of Japanese and Filipinos, not to mention American soldiers, without any important impact on Japan's air and naval power or industrial activity. King expressed his doubts by challenging the selection of Palau as an objective and pointing instead to Formosa as a better place than the Philippines to interdict Japanese overseas trade.

King found support in his position from General Hap Arnold, air forces commander, and Nimitz, both of whom argued that the Marianas (Saipan, Tinian, and Guam) should be taken. Their capture would defer any forced choice between the Philippines and Taiwan, and these islands had great potential as forward operating bases for submarines and long-range bombers. Saddled with a very costly and risk-ridden program to develop a heavy, long-range bomber—the B-29 Superfortress—Arnold wanted this bomber based in a safe place (not in China!) from which it could reach the flammable cities of Japan. Nimitz had another agenda (as did King), and that was to force Japan's Combined Fleet into a decisive fleet action. Knowing that the Japanese military staffs had made the Marianas an essential part of the defensive perimeter, King liked the idea of pointing the Fifth Fleet (Nimitz's Central Pacific force) slightly north of the straight route to the Philippines.

By the end of 1943, King had largely succeeded not only in making the United States the principal arbiter of Pacific strategy but in making American strategy synonymous with navy strategy. In the flurry of activity set off by the meetings with Chiang Kai-shek in Cairo and with Stalin in Teheran, the American strategic planners made it clear in CCS 417 (issued in December 1943) that the war with Japan would be won by American forces advancing upon the Home Islands from the east, not by an American-Chinese-Commonwealth coalition force based in Asia. The British chiefs, who had never shown much enthusiasm for the Churchill-Mountbatten schemes to recover Burma and Malaya, agreed. Among the many objectives now identified as important to a Pacific campaign were the Marianas.

The plans approved in 1943 did not exclude Luzon but only endorsed MacArthur's return to Mindanao, not a complete Philippines liberation. MacArthur still did not support a Central Pacific campaign, but he liked the idea of closing the South Pacific theater and terminating Operation Cartwheel without the capture of Rabaul. The army's South Pacific ground forces (six infantry divisions and supporting corps troops) and the Thirteenth Air Force would transfer to MacArthur's command, while most of the navy's warships would return to the Fifth Fleet. Nevertheless, some new warships (especially cruisers, escort carriers, and beaching amphibious ships) would join MacArthur's Seventh Fleet.

In January 1944, Admiral King, representing the Joint Chiefs, flew to Honolulu to meet with the principal strategic planners from all the Pacific forces. He found, to his dismay, that many of them did not share his conviction about the importance of the Marianas. The two loudest critics were Lieutenant General George C. Kenney and Lieutenant General Richard K. Sutherland, MacArthur's chief of staff and a person as unpleasant as King. King found Nimitz weak in forcing his will on the army, a trait Nimitz's navy and marine officers already had observed. Back and forth, the planners argued about the location of the key objectives and the timing of future operations. The Marianas remained on the list of preferred targets, but Palau remained as well, now joined by Luzon. There was no consensus on timing or even on just which of the dual axes of advance should receive the most emphasis. At some phases of the argument, King could do little more than stress that the Joint Chiefs would make the final decisions, not the theater commanders. When he returned to Washington, King—still enraged by the resistance to his strategic vision—saw no alternative but to pressure Nimitz to get on with the war, to drive the Fifth Fleet deep into the heart of the Japanese defenses of the Central Pacific, and to adopt Admiral William F. Halsey's simple South Pacific guidance: "Kill Japs! Then kill more Japs!"

The Central Pacific Drive

Once King had made the Central Pacific campaign the navy's final solution to the Japanese problem, the details of campaign planning fell to Nimitz, his staff, and his component commanders. Nimitz tended to operate as the chairman of the board, requiring that his own staff and those of subordinates from all the services submit plans and counterplans for his consideration. King, predictably, allowed his own operational brain trust to make "suggestions," which had a way of turning into orders. For example, some planners wanted Nimitz and his principal operational commander, Vice Admiral Raymond A. Spruance, to bypass the Gilberts and strike directly into the eastern Marshalls. The objectives should be the atolls of Jaluit, Mille, Majuro, Maloelap, Wotje, and Kwajalein. Each objective was the same: an irregular ring of small, coral islands topping a great reef system, which included smaller reefs around each island. Even the biggest island was seldom larger than five to seven square miles, but if the islands ran from northwest to southeast to conform with wind patterns, they could be made into airstrips. Moreover, the large lagoon inside the great reef could serve as an anchorage. The island air fields were Japan's "unsinkable carriers."

Nimitz and Spruance, both cautious commanders, doubted that their existing naval, air, and landing forces could take all these objectives in the Marshalls more or less simultaneously. Instead, they preferred some less-demanding objective (an ironic judgment) in the northern Gilberts, preferably Tarawa atoll, also the site of a small Japanese air base. Among their concerns was the limited size of their amphibious landing force, which consisted of the veteran 2nd Marine Division and the unproven 27th Infantry Division, made up of New York National Guardsmen who had been stationed on the Hawaiian Islands for over a year. MacArthur kept the 1st Marine Division for the Cape Gloucester landing, and Halsey had command of the 3rd Marine Division for Bougainville. All three landings would occur within six weeks of one another, which certainly presented the Japanese with problems but also endangered the Gilberts operations. King and the other Joint Chiefs decided that Nimitz's force was too large to use against only one atoll. Nimitz received an order to capture another island air field, Nauru, 400 miles west of the Gilberts. Nimitz countered with a substitute objective for the 27th Division: Makin atoll at the northern edge of the Gilberts. The 2nd Marine Division would make the main effort at Tarawa, while the New Yorkers made the lesser landing at Makin, which had been attacked in 1942 by a marine raider battalion and found relatively undefended.

Although the Americans kept a wary eye on the location and activities of the Combined Fleet, they did not believe that the Japanese would risk their battleships and carriers to save the Gilberts, perhaps not yet even the Marshalls, whose seizure would put Truk at risk. Air strikes, submarine patrols, and all sorts of electronic intelligence programs confirmed that the

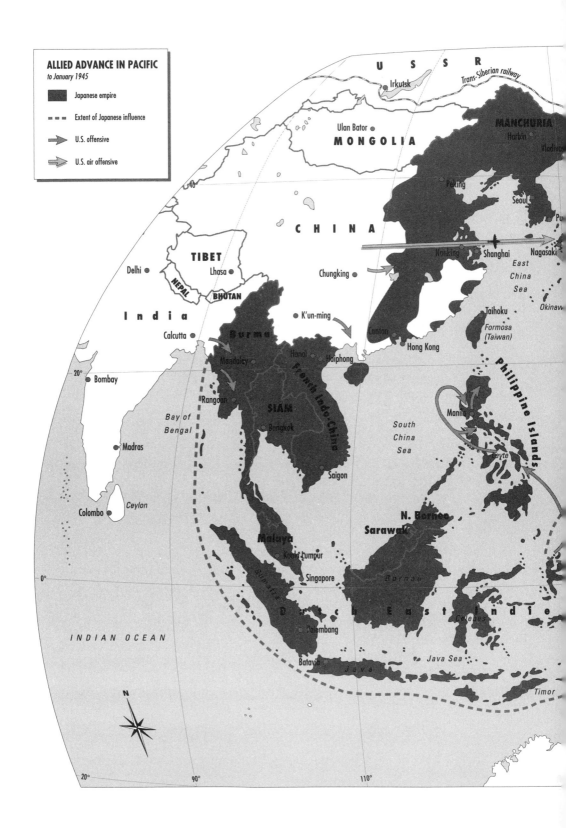

ALLIED ADVANCE IN PACIFIC
to January 1945

Japanese empire

- - - Extent of Japanese influence

→ U.S. offensive

→ U.S. air offensive

U S S R

Irkutsk

Trans-Siberian railway

Ulan Bator

MONGOLIA

MANCHURIA

Harbin

Vladivostok

Peking

Seoul

Pu

CHINA

Nanking

Shanghai

Nagasaki

East
China
Sea

TIBET

Lhasa

Chungking

Delhi

NEPAL

BHUTAN

Taihoku

Okinawa

India

K'un-ming

Canton

Formosa
(Taiwan)

Calcutta

Burma

Hanoi

Haiphong

Hong Kong

20°

Bombay

Mandalay

French Indo-China

Philippine Islands

Rangoon

SIAM

Bangkok

Manila

Bay of
Bengal

South
China
Sea

Madras

Saigon

Leyte

Colombo

Ceylon

N. Borneo

Sarawak

Malaya

Kuala Lumpur

Singapore

Borneo

0°

Sumatra

Dutch East Indies

Celebes

Palembang

INDIAN OCEAN

Batavia

Java

Java Sea

Timor

N

20°

90°

110°

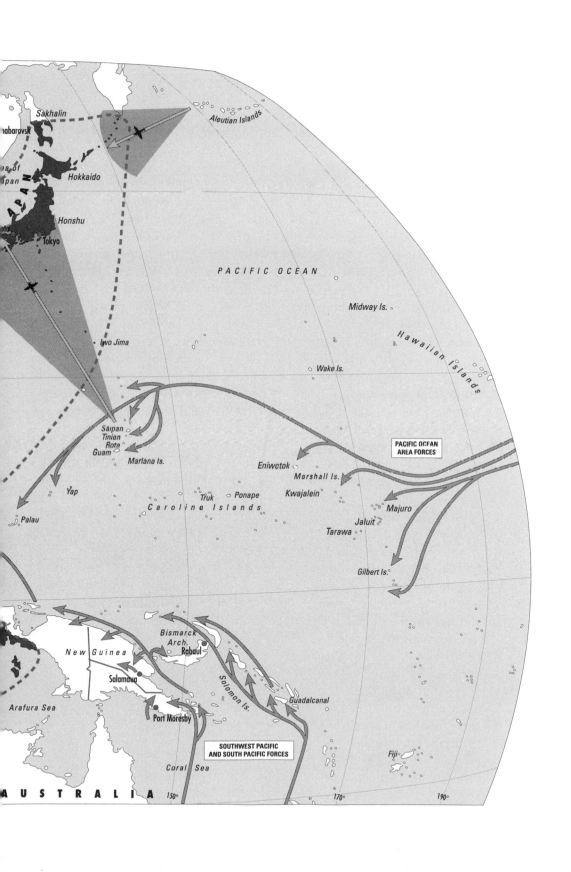

Sakhalin

abarovsk

ea of
pan

Hokkaido

JAPAN

Honshu

Tokyo

Aleutian Islands

PACIFIC OCEAN

Midway Is.

Hawaiian Islands

Iwo Jima

Wake Is.

Saipan
Tinian
Rota
Guam

Mariana Is.

Yap

Eniwetok

Marshall Is.

Kwajalein

PACIFIC OCEAN
AREA FORCES

Palau

Truk   Ponape

C a r o l i n e   I s l a n d s

Majuro

Jaluit

Tarawa

Gilbert Is.

Bismarck
Arch.

New Guinea   Rabaul

Salamaua

Solomon Is.

Guadalcanal

Port Moresby

Arafura Sea

SOUTHWEST PACIFIC
AND SOUTH PACIFIC FORCES

Fiji

Coral Sea

A U S T R A L I A   150°   170°   190°

Japanese command for the threatened islands—the Fourth Fleet of Vice Admiral Kobayashi Masashi—had only one naval air flotilla, three light cruisers, and about 28,000 troops and construction laborers to defend the Marshalls, with another 5,500 troops (principally crack Japanese naval infantry and base defense forces) guarding the Gilberts. As the intelligence picture became clearer in late 1943, the naval staffs felt more and more confident that Operation Galvanic would be easy enough, while the landing force commanders, especially Major General Holland M. Smith of the Marine Corps, felt their reservations mount. The problem was Betio island, the main objective at Tarawa, which bristled with almost 200 cannon and hundreds of machine guns, all emplaced in bunkers of concrete, palm logs, matting, and thick layers of sand. The heaviest defenses faced out to sea, which made an assault from inside the lagoon an attractive option.

The landings at Tarawa and Makin islands proved a victorious but costly lesson in the conduct of amphibious operations for all the American services. Some people and services learned better than others. The issue was the type of operations that had to precede a landing. Spruance and his amphibious force commander, the pugnacious Richmond Kelly Turner of Solomons fame, understood the value of isolating the northern Gilberts from Japanese air and naval attack; early in October, carrier aircraft and air force bombers attacked most of the Japanese air fields and anchorages in the Marshalls and Gilberts. Except for some unseen submarines, Japanese naval and air reinforcements disappeared. The defenders would have to fight without hope of help. To reduce the Japanese defense system, Turner's slow battleships, old cruisers, and destroyers would have to combine with naval aviation from escort carriers (squadrons untrained in ground attack) to shell and bomb the Japanese into death or stupefied submission. The fire support concepts dated to World War I: if one delivered a certain tonnage of explosives upon a calculated area, the enemy would at least be "neutralized," a worrisome usage since a neutralized force might very well unneutralize itself. Nervous about concentrating warships and transports around a small island, the admirals wanted landings characterized by speed and tactical aggressiveness, supported by a preparatory bombardment measured in hours (three or four in this case), not days.

The 2nd Marine Division (under Major General Julian C. Smith) had seen combat, but it had not made an amphibious assault. Yet a decade of exercises and study prepared the marine planners to recognize almost all of their potential problems—though not their solution. A major part of the problem was simply the inexperience and arrogance of their senior naval counterparts. Any attempt to alter the navy's gunfire support plan met a stone wall. There would not be a longer preparatory period, which meant that there could be no careful damage assessment, redirection of fires, or precise placement of heavy shells on specific targets like major bunkers. The ship-to-shore movement would have to emphasize putting as many marines from three infantry battalions (with supporting artillery and tanks) ashore as fast as possible, but over a reef 600–1,000 yards from the Betio seawall. The trick would be to get across the interior reef to the island, which was two miles long and less than a mile wide. The marines had an answer: the tactical use of the new landing vehicle tracked (LVT) or amphibian tractor (amtrac). But the division had to share the available amtracs with the 1st and 3rd Marine Divisions in the South Pacific. Nevertheless, the division added some 50 tractors to its allotment of 75; it later argued that 300 would have been a better number.

Even if the assault battalions got ashore with acceptable losses—and no one knew what that figure was—the Generals Smith (Holland and Julian) worried about reinforcing the assault regiment across the reef, especially if the estimates on tidal states proved too optimistic. They also took no comfort when Turner designated one of their three marine infantry regiments the Gilbert islands joint landing force reserve, which put it out of their reach without his approval. Turner, who had tried to manage the land campaign in the Solomons, had not reformed. If the standard landing craft could not get over the reef, which required three to four feet of draft, the reinforcements would have to transfer to the amtracs at the reef or wade ashore under fire. Bringing machine guns and mortars ashore would be difficult, and pack howitzers and tanks could easily wind up as just another part of the barrier reef. Julian Smith thought that placing artillery on a nearby island might help, but the navy would not take the time or allocate the boats for a pre-landing landing. More than one navy officer assured Holland Smith that Betio would be easy to take, even though the American marines' inexperience would undoubtedly cause some problems. Smith thought the real problems were the inexperience of the navy commanders and the fanaticism of the Japanese, and that many marines would die because of a failure to make this distinction.

The Battle of Betio raged 20–23 November, and the furious blood-letting of those days shocked even the marines and positively traumatized Admirals Nimitz, Spruance, and Turner. Killing the Japanese garrison cost the 2nd Marine Division more than 1,000 dead and another 2,300 wounded; the better part of two marine infantry regiments fell in action. The first three assault battalions had to overcome undestroyed bunkers one at a time at high cost; the next three battalions waded across the lagoon when the "dodging tide" stopped their boats at the reef, and only remnants got ashore. Japanese cannon wrecked too many amtracs to fetch the reinforcements. Only when part of two battalions attacked along the island's long axis, across the face of four wrecked battalions, did Japanese resistance collapse.

The marines themselves admitted that they needed more work in coordinating demolitions and flame-throwers with tanks and artillery, but everyone agreed that naval gunfire and the amtrac force would have to improve in quality and quantity. The marines, given to brutal candor, shocked the Home Front, too, by showing photographs and film of the Tarawa slaughter to awaken the public to the challenges ahead. The public and politicians (some in uniform) reeled with dismay, since they had not yet seen the horrors that war was inflicting on American troops. On a visit to Betio, Nimitz himself was sickened by the sight of bloating corpses and rotting body parts. Clearly, the Fifth Fleet's amphibious assault techniques needed work.

Senior army commanders in the Central Pacific theater, primarily Lieutenant General Robert C. Richardson, argued that Holland Smith's operational assumptions and World War I tactics would ruin any landing force, but the performance of the 27th Infantry Division in taking Makin did not make the army's case. Landing a regimental task force of 6,500 soldiers of all arms, the division took three days to defeat a mere 400 defenders, albeit at a light cost of 200-plus casualties. Smith was on hand to watch four infantry battalions endanger almost everybody within range, and he made no friends with his heated commentary on army tactics. The soldiers' sloth became more than an irritant when a Japanese submarine sank the escort carrier *Liscome Bay* and killed 642 sailors. Since the *Liscome Bay* had a Makin mission that kept it in local waters, the army's critics did not admit that the carrier went down more than a month after the island fell. The entire affair produced a bad odor around the 27th Infantry Division from which it never recovered, and the performance of this one inept army division went on to poison marine-army relations throughout the rest of the war.

Nimitz urged Spruance to keep the campaign going, whatever the shocks of Operation Galvanic. He made a bold decision to bypass most of the Marshalls and take only one of the atolls, Kwajalein, an original objective in the island group. All the other atolls would be besieged by land-based air and warships or simply would be ignored. Nimitz showed that his grasp of the importance of isolating Japanese islands was as good, if not better, than MacArthur's. Moreover, all elements of Turner's amphibious force and

Smith's landing force, as well as the carriers whose squadrons had the task of attacking the island objectives, improved their operational performance. Naval gunners and airmen practiced in Hawaii on attacking specific ground targets with the help of aerial and ground spotters, linked to them by radio. For the ship-to-shore movement, the new 4th Marine Division (led by veterans) deployed 370 amtracs to take the linked islands of Roi-Namur (3,500 defenders), while the veteran 7th Infantry Division went ashore at Kwajalein island with 174 amtracs. Both the marines and soldiers enjoyed the direct fire support of armored amtracs bristling with cannon and machine guns; from nearby small islands, five battalions of artillery supported each division's assault regiment.

The objectives of Operation Flintlock came under heavy bombing and naval shelling three days before the landings, with much-improved effect. Special teams of navy engineer-swimmers (the frogmen of the Underwater Demolitions Teams) and army amphibious engineers deployed to blow holes in the reefs and destroy any obstacles. In less than three months, the Fifth Fleet had put together all the essential elements for an amphibious assault and took all the objectives in four days, with fewer than 2,000 casualties.

Since the Fifth Fleet had proven its effectiveness in amphibious operations so convincingly in the eastern Marshalls, Nimitz, with King's enthusiastic support, advanced his timetable for taking all of the eastern Mandated Islands. Only one real objective, Eniwetok atoll (consisting of three defended islands), remained in front of the major Japanese fleet base of Truk, one of the Carolines. Under continuing aerial bombardment and surrounded by U.S. submarines, Truk itself showed little sign of Japanese air and naval activity, so Nimitz and Spruance saw minimal risk in moving the anticipated date of invading Eniwetok to 17 February rather than 1 May. Without much of a clean-up campaign in the eastern Marshalls, Spruance assembled the varied task forces of the Fifth Fleet and sailed 1,000 miles closer to Japan to prove that Operation Flintlock was no fluke.

His landing force, consisting of two reinforced regiments of marines and soldiers, numbered more than 8,000, while the defending Japanese, an elite Imperial Army amphibious brigade, mustered but 2,000 fighters. In five days (17–22 February 1944) the landing forces destroyed the Japanese garrison at a cost of about 300 dead and missing and 700 wounded. The Japanese defenders proved tenacious, even stopping the army assault battalions on Eniwetok, because of a careless and hasty naval gunfire bombardment. The real news, however, was that the Japanese fleet and air arm remained inactive. Truk lost its importance, joining Rabaul as another former Gibraltar of the Pacific. Nimitz's confrontation with the Combined Fleet was once again postponed.

The Japanese Respond

The American naval campaign across the Central Pacific sent shock waves through Imperial General Headquarters. The news of Tarawa had heartened the military leadership in Tokyo, since similar defenses in the Marshalls would gain more time to repair Japanese naval aviation, retrain the fleet, and transfer elite army troops from China and the Home Islands to defend the Marianas and the Philippines. Yet in only four months the Americans had penetrated 1,300 miles through the Mandates and had eliminated Truk, just as they had ruined Rabaul, as a forward operating base for air and naval forces. In February 1944, the senior officers of both Japanese services locked in mortal combat over an appropriate response for the dual-axis American advance. Prime Minister Tojo raged at the other generals and admirals, who blamed one another for the empire's disarray and vied for preferential production quotas of aircraft and weapons. As Tojo understood, future plans were irrelevant for the moment. How and where could the Japanese stop the Americans? His advisers thought that the war must be prolonged with the hope that something might happen somewhere that would buy the Japanese more time to strengthen their inner defenses and preserve access to the raw materials of Southeast Asia. One key adviser, General Sato Kenryo, proposed that they abandon the Marianas, that the natural defense line should be the Philippines. Tojo assumed command of the Ministry of War himself, replaced the navy's obdurate chief of staff, and then rejected Sato's advice. The decisive battle against the Americans would come at the Marianas.

Even though Tojo hardly dared share his inner doubts, he had already considered whether Japan should sue for peace, perhaps through the Russians, who were still neutral. Although his own informers within the military did not have the full picture, Tojo knew that the late Yamamoto's disciples in the navy believed that the war was lost and that the only goal was to minimize the damage to Japan. Given the officer corps' habit of assassinating dissidents, any senior officer who harbored such "peace thoughts" did so in seclusion. Tojo never shared his own doubts but rather ordered a full-scale return to the strategic offensive for 1944, with the hope that if the Allies could be defeated just once more, they might seek a compromise peace.

Tojo envisioned three major offensive efforts: a campaign against the Commonwealth army in India, a campaign against the Chinese Army and the American air bases in western China, and a joint army-navy effort to inflict a defeat on the Fifth Fleet. MacArthur's drive up and past the New Guinea coast could be ignored; the desperate holding actions would continue there on the assumption that MacArthur would head for the southern Philippines rather than the more valuable Netherlands East Indies.

Although Tojo tried to ignore much of the evidence of Home Front strangulation, he understood Japan's vulnerability to economic collapse. The effect of maritime losses to American submarines had already reached worrisome proportions, and the Japanese understood American bomber mania, which had led to the costly effort to build and maintain bomber bases in China. If and when the Americans found a place to station the new B-29 Superfortress, the Home Islands would be subjected to horrific bombardment, which would only compound the shortages forced by American submarines. The concern over strategic bombardment linked the three theaters that Imperial General Headquarters selected for offensive campaigns in 1944. Some success in all three theaters would reduce the stress upon Japanese air defenses of the Home Islands, which were not well-developed except for organizing the civilian population to seek shelter and fight fires as well as dispersing some of the population away from the cities. Although the IJA's air force developed an air defense system of some technical and operational sophistication, it could not reproduce the massive Luftwaffe defenses of Germany for lack of time and resources. In addition, the Japanese services wanted to husband their air forces for offensive action.

No one great strategic master plan emerged from Japanese headquarters, but the many sequential and parallel decisions of early 1944 took Japan's armed forces to catastrophe. Only the China campaign went more or less as planned, since the series of operations in April–October 1944 did indeed drive the Nationalist Army and the American Fourteenth Air Force deeper into western China. Although the B-29s could still reach the Home Islands from China, the air force soon abandoned China as its principal base for bombing Japan. What raids it staged would instead be sent against targets in China and Formosa, none of which were decisive.

The Japanese strategic initiative in the Burma-India theater began with promise and ended in disaster. The Burma Area Army (under Lieutenant General Kawabe Masakazu) had two armies of eight-plus ground divisions and one air division (over 100 aircraft) to confront the British Fourteenth Army and the odd lot of Wingate's Chindits, the American Air Commando-Marauder task force, and several Chinese divisions. Even with better access to the primitive transportation system of the Burma-Chinese frontier, the Burma Area Army could commit only three divisions to its offensive; it also had to block the Chinese Army in Yunnan, fight off the Chindit-Marauder campaign in north Burma, and confront General William Slim's African and Indian divisions deployed along the southern Chin hills. Nevertheless, the Japanese Fifteenth Army nearly accomplished the impossible, disrupting the offensive plans of a numerically superior Allied army and air force.

The Kohima-Imphal offensive did not take Slim by surprise, though he had little choice but to meet it with the forces on hand—the IV Corps of three Anglo-Indian divisions—or surrender his own plans to take the general offensive in Burma in 1944. In theory, the Japanese preemptive offensive gave Slim an unparalleled opportunity to weaken the Burma Area Army before he ordered an advance toward Mandalay and Rangoon without any amphibious operations. Slim chose to surrender the initiative to the Japanese, a decision he made in the face of much adverse advice, because he believed that his army could now fight the Japanese on equal terms or better, given his superiority in air forces, armor, and logistical support. As the campaign developed from March through July 1944, however, the Japanese divisions advanced more rapidly and ferociously than Slim anticipated. But their assaults never quite broke the IV Corps, which rallied on the Imphal plain and fell back into fortified positions around Imphal.

In late March the campaign built to a crisis. With only one division available to reinforce or counterattack, Slim and the IV Corps commander, Lieutenant General Geoffrey Scoones, decided to commit it toward Imphal and hope that the division defending Kohima would win alone. If Kohima fell, the Japanese might break the Assam railroad system at Dimapur, a major setback for Fourteenth Army. The Indo-British 5th Division, reduced by one brigade to defend Dimapur, held Kohima long enough for Slim to muster additional reinforcements. Nowhere in World War II—even on the Eastern Front—did the combatants fight with more mindless savagery. In April, however, the Japanese infantry, unsupported and starved for supplies, lapsed into a numb defensive, and Slim put a fresh division into the mission of destroying the Japanese 31st Division.

As the British IV Corps slipped around the Japanese through the hills of the upper Irrawadday, it met the Japanese 15th Division, and the slugfest for the Chin ridges continued with cascading losses. In a campaign of attrition fought in the rainy season, Slim's army pushed the Japanese Fifteenth Army back to the east, until Commonwealth forces advancing from the north met another corps counterattacking from the south on 22 June. With almost 60,000 casualties (13,376 dead), the Burma Area Army had lost its offensive capability and became vulnerable to Slim's postponed offensive. His own losses (almost 16,000) were hardly inconsequential, but Slim correctly assessed Fourteenth Army's renaissance. His Commonwealth troops had lost their fear of the jungle and the Japanese. All that air support, artillery, and armor could do to support the infantry battalions would be done, and the Allied forces would enjoy a level of logistical support about which the Japanese could only dream. Tactical risks could be taken because air support and resupply drops could eventually reach even the most isolated units. The care and evacuation of casualties had reached artful proportions, and preventive medicine and good discipline had reduced disease losses to a minimum. Lacking these battlefield advantages, the Japanese Army had no future in Southeast Asia.

The ultimate fate of Japan's war effort in 1944 depended, however, on the naval campaign under way in the Pacific. The surface fleets and carrier task forces had avoided one another for much of 1943 and the first six months of 1944. But with the Seventh Fleet escorting MacArthur's land forces westward and the Fifth Fleet charting a new course across the Central Pacific, the U.S. Navy now held the strategic initiative—except that it had not yet brought the Imperial Japanese Navy to bay.

The submarine force of the Pacific Fleet, however, had no trouble closing with the enemy, and its operations weakened the defenses of the Philippines and the Marianas as well as accelerating Japan's economic decline. In part, the success of the American submarine service was a matter of numbers and experience; as of January 1944 the number of submarines had doubled since the war's beginning, and it increased again by 50 percent to 156 boats by year's end. Incremental modification of the submarines' hulls, engines, deck guns, and radar-sonar systems gave them technical advantages, and the torpedo problem had been largely solved by modifying the Mark XIV or using the Mark XVIII, which had its own technical drawbacks, but exploding the warhead was not one of them. In sum, the American submarines could operate in groups, attack and retreat with more success, and inflict almost certain destruction upon all but the largest Japanese warships. Moreover, the submarine crews became just the right mix of veterans and ardent newcomers. The force might draw inspiration from its heroic skippers of 1943, but it did not depend on them.

Focusing its attacks on military convoys and merchantmen, the submarine force made it difficult for the Japanese Army to redeploy to the Marianas and the Philippines. In the three and a half months before the invasion of Saipan, the Japanese lost the equivalent of two divisions and their fortification materials to submarine attacks. A convoy carrying two divisions to New Guinea lost seven of nine transports en route. The Japanese generals charged with the defense of the Philippines in 1944 complained to Tokyo that they could not execute Tokyo's plans because of shipping losses. Guided by navy codebreakers and intelligence analysts, who could decipher most of the Japanese shipping codes, the submarines pounced on any convoy attempting to run the blockade to the Central Pacific. Although the anti-submarine forces of the Japanese increased and improved, they could not contest any of the high seas beyond the immediate approaches to the Home Islands, which meant north of Formosa and the Ryukyus. The escort forces also had orders to protect incoming oil tankers, not outward-bound army transports. This cruel choice simply reflected the perilous condition of the Japanese war effort.

In one of those rare cases in which statistical analysis tells the true story, the numbers of 1944 provide a clear picture of Japan's impending economic collapse. Oil dependency spelled Japan's defeat, because its industry and armed forces moved on fossil fuels. Coal might compensate for oil in running factories, but not ships and planes. Producing oil in Southeast Asia posed no problem, but getting it to Japan did; Japanese tankers delivered only one-tenth of the oil produced in 1944–45. In 1944 alone, the Japanese brought less than 200,000 tons to the Home Islands. Similar shortages, unexplained by local consumption, developed in all crucial raw materials: cotton, rubber, paper pulp, cement, ferrous metals, iron ore, sugar, coal, lumber, and nitrates for fertilizer and explosives. Of the 3.8 million tons of Japanese shipping of all classes sunk in 1944, U.S. Navy submarines destroyed 2.3 million tons. The Japanese merchant fleet began the year with 5 million tons of shipping and ended the year with half this amount. Despite the fact that Japanese maritime administrators built virtually nothing but oil tankers in 1944, they could not prevent the tanker fleet from falling from around 700,000 tons to less than 300,000 tons in twelve months. Tankers in the service of the Japanese military did not survive, either. Before the end of 1944, American submarine commanders started to complain about how few targets they could find along routes to the Home Islands.

Allied aerial attacks did not contribute to Japan's economic attrition until 1945. While the submarine force reduced the raw materials and food for Japan's industrial society, the U.S. Army Air Forces planned to destroy the cities themselves, not just starve the workers and their families. From Arnold down to the new generation of bomber generals, tested in the skies above Germany, the future of the air war with Japan rested on the development and rapid deployment of the air force's most expensive and risky project, the B-29 Superfortress. Conceived in 1940, the Superfortress depended on advanced, high-risk engineering achievements that made the B-17 look like a Model T Ford. Virtually every challenge in meeting the requirements for a very long-range heavy bomber (4,000 miles round-trip range and a ten-ton bomb load) forced the army air forces into uncertain technological fields in metallurgy, avionics, electrical fire-control systems for aerial defense, engine design, airframe structure, and radar-dependent navigation and bombing systems. The development process alone cost $3 billion by 1942, and the estimated cost of each aircraft in that year was $1.5 million. At the time, a single B-17 cost $240,000. Further design changes to reduce weight and increase range brought the estimated unit cost down to $700,000 by 1943. More engineering delays plagued the program, but in 1943 the army air forces gave production contracts to three aircraft builders for about 1,200 aircraft. Most of the B-29s rolled out of the plants of its principal developer, Boeing Aircraft.

Unlike the secrecy of the Manhattan Project to create the atomic bomb and the advanced research in radar and other electronic-related weapons such as the proximity fuse for artillery and anti-aircraft shells, the B-29 project rolled along with high publicity and high expectations. Thus, Arnold felt a special need to bring the program home by deploying the new bombers against Japan as early in 1944 as possible, while his B-17s and B-24s continued to pulverize Germany and support the combatant forces in the Pacific. During operational testing of the aircraft, however, test pilots discovered a serious design flaw in its engines. Instead of purring along and producing 2,200 horsepower (twice that of a B-17 engine), each of the four air-cooled R-3350 Curtis-Wright engines had a tendency to lock and burn at high revolutions-per-minute—a certainty at high altitudes with maximum bomb loads. Almost every other advanced system had problems, although not so fatal. In 1943 some air forces officers nicknamed the B-29 "the Annihilator," and they weren't talking about annihilating the Japanese. Even when all the necessary modifications had been identified and re-engineered, it required 25,000 skilled man-hours to fix each bomber—at even more cost. By mid-1944 the army air forces had taken delivery of fewer than 100 B-29s, but Arnold wanted even this paltry number in action immediately. His determination to take the Marianas without delay bordered on obsession.

The Marianas Campaign

With the capture of the Marshalls all but certain by March 1944, Admiral Nimitz, still shaken by the losses at Tarawa and worried about the Japanese Navy, decided that he did not want to capture Saipan, Guam, and Tinian.

In an example of group-think, his staff and many of his naval commanders shifted their views on strategy toward General MacArthur's perspective: merge all the American forces on a single axis of advance and head for the Philippines. In the strictest operational sense, this concept had merit. If Truk no longer posed a threat, then the bases at Yap and Palau and the anchorage at Ulithi in the western Carolines should be the next objectives, with potential operating bases in the Philippines to follow. Somewhere in the Western Pacific the Japanese Combined Fleet would have to come out and fight. Such an engagement would occur far enough to the west and south that land-based Japanese naval air in the Marianas, Formosa, and the Bonin and Ryukyu island chains would not be a factor. With MacArthur's encouragement, Nimitz queried King in March 1944 whether the Joint Chiefs really had to have the Marianas.

King responded in terms that Nimitz and MacArthur, who often heard different words in the same message, could not misunderstand. The Joint Chiefs wanted the Marianas taken early in the summer without any further quibbling. The dual-axis advance would continue, with MacArthur's forces scheduled to move on Mindanao in the early autumn—on the assumption that Japanese air and naval forces would pose no major threat. Even if the admirals in Honolulu did not think strategic bombing would hasten victory, they would, nevertheless, ensure that the airmen would get the bases they sought on Guam and Tinian. Moreover, MacArthur would not become the single Allied theater commander in the Pacific War, which even Nimitz agreed would be unthinkable.

King told Nimitz that in fact he was dividing the Fifth Fleet into two fleets: the Fifth and the Third. MacArthur would retain the Seventh Fleet as his theater naval force. Although Spruance would retain command of the Fifth Fleet for the Marianas campaign, the subsequent command of the key carrier task forces and supporting new battleships and cruisers would go to Admiral Halsey as commander of the Third Fleet. The pool of operating forces would not change, but the headquarters directing them would. One would operate while the other planned. Nimitz and Spruance immediately saw new merit in the Marianas campaign and put their staffs to work planning for the climactic campaign of the Pacific War, Operation Reforger; it would be conducted by the Fifth Fleet, with the Third Fleet on hand to exploit its victory.

Spruance could no longer justify his cautiousness by claiming naval weakness. For any forthcoming battle, he would have Task Force 58, commanded by the tough and experienced carrier commander Vice Admiral Marc Mitscher and his equally tested task force commanders. Task Force 58 deployed for the Marianas with 7 fast battleships, 15 carriers with 891 aircraft, 21 cruisers of all types, and 69 destroyers. The Fifth Amphibious Force (under Vice Admiral Turner) would invade Saipan and Guam in the course of three days in mid-June with over 400 warships and amphibious assault vessels. Although Holland Smith held the titular position of commander joint landing forces, he actually assumed command of V Amphibious Corps, while Lieutenant General Roy S. Geiger commanded the III Amphibious Corps. Smith's Northern Troops and Expeditionary Landing Force (an awkward title for the joint ground and land aviation corps) included the veteran 2nd and 4th Marine Divisions and the 27th Infantry Division, which had already earned Smith's disdain for lackluster fighting in the atolls campaign. Smith's force included corps-level amphibian tractor battalions, artillery, tanks, engineers, and logistical units, as well as accompanying marine and army aviation units. Geiger's corps had much the same character: the experienced 3rd Marine Division and 1st Marine Brigade and the untested U.S. 77th Infantry Division.

In the meantime, the Japanese admirals behaved just as their American counterparts thought they would, which was to mass their forces for a decisive battle somewhere in the Philippine Sea—some 1,500 miles of ocean that separated the Marianas from the Philippines. In Tokyo, Imperial Japanese Headquarters appointed a new chief, Admiral Toyoda Soemu, for the Combined Fleet. He replaced Admiral Koga, who had disappeared during an air flight in April 1944. In the subsequent reorganization, command of the First Mobile Fleet, consisting of the surface and carrier battlegroups of the navy, went to Admiral Ozawa Jisaburo, a pugnacious carrier admiral whose reputation for aggressiveness had not yet dimmed. Toyoda and Ozawa drew up concurrent plans that eventually fused as Operation A, a plan for the decisive fleet engagement that they had not fought at Midway. While the admirals planned, the First Mobile Fleet assembled in the Tawitawi anchorage between Mindanao and Borneo; units arrived from Singapore, the Philippines, and the Home Islands, all under the watchful eye of American submarines and the alert ears of naval communications intelligence experts. The First Mobile Fleet grew to impressive proportions: 6 battleships, 9 carriers with about 500 aircraft, 13 cruisers, and 28 destroyers. Important in Japanese plans, the land-based First Air Fleet deployed about 1,000 aircraft to various air fields that would allow its elite torpedo and bomber squadrons to cover the Philippine Sea, protected by escorting Zeros. The Japanese submarine force also redeployed toward the Marianas, but with no real haste.

As the First Mobile Fleet with its supporting force of oilers and submarines assembled, Toyoda and Ozawa drove their staffs to provide more operational integration for the decisive battle. The staffs war-gamed and analyzed every phase of the operation. Even the Emperor himself observed one of Toyoda's exercises—an indication of the navy's level of desperation. The concept of Operation A reflected the weakened state of the Japanese carrier aviation force, with its improved aircraft but inexperienced pilots, most of whom had less than six months' solo time. The remaining veteran pilots went to the First Air Fleet. The Japanese aviators had one advantage: their aircraft had greater ranges than their American counterparts, which meant that the carriers could launch attacking flights beyond the range of U.S. Navy air attack. The land-based bombers could cover even greater distances. With aviation gasoline in short supply, the Japanese naval aviators would have to press home their attacks and hope that they could find air fields on Guam, Saipan, and Tinian for refueling. The planners, in fact, counted on the First Air Fleet to strike the most telling blows on the Americans, then land in the Marianas to refuel and rearm before attacking the Americans on the way home. While the air melee was distracting the Americans, the fast battleships and heavy cruisers would rush eastward for a night surface engagement, exploiting the U.S. Navy's one remaining tactical weakness.

The Imperial Japanese Navy entered the campaign with warships at the edge of technological excellence but with serious operational weaknesses. Ozawa's flagship, the 29,300-ton carrier *Taiho*, represented state-of-the-art engines, anti-aircraft armament, radar, an armored flightdeck, and internal survivability improvements. Commissioned in 1944, *Taiho* had been rushed into service with its engineering officer as commander, since no one else had the training to operate the ship; its limited sea trials quickly revealed that its sailors had not mastered the technology. Other warships were put in service with similar shortages of trained seamen in their crews. Added to these manpower problems was the Japanese Navy's erroneous belief that its communication system remained secure from American codebreakers. Whenever a senior officer suspected that the basic codes hid nothing, someone advanced a new explanation for ambushed convoys and air attacks that materialized from nowhere. On the eve of Operation A, Ozawa finally demanded a full change of the fleet's code books, but this action only made coordination more difficult for the Japanese forces, while coming too late to confuse the Americans, who had already prepared for a great battle in the Philippine Sea.

The Japanese defenders of the Marianas faced the same challenge as their dead comrades in the Marshalls, which was to make the American landing forces pay a high price for their new aggressiveness. In this case, they had a solid mission: keep the island air fields in Japanese hands as long as the First Mobile Fleet and First Air Fleet could use them. Saipan had substantial naval personnel ashore—6,000 officers and men commanded by Vice Admiral Nagumo Chuichi, the naval aviator who attacked Pearl Harbor. Guam had a smaller naval detachment. The Marianas' defenses, air and ground, depended on the Thirty-First Army (under Lieutenant General Obata Hideyoshi) of two divisions, two mixed brigades heavy in artillery and armor, and supporting engineering and service troops—all told, a ground combat force of 59,000 divided among three islands.

The Saipan defense force (under Lieutenant General Saito Yoshitsugu) was the largest and best armed, with 32,000 officers and men, including a regiment of 48 tanks. Saito also inherited responsibility for a civilian population of 20,000 people of all ages and sexes, who had come to Saipan early in the 1920s from Okinawa as agricultural workers. Saito's planned complexes of fortifications, designed for an island rich in caves and steep mountains, had not been completed in June 1944. American air strikes and submarines had slowed the flow of reinforcements and supplies; when the 43rd Division embarked for the island, its first convoy came through intact, but the second lost five of seven transports and cargo ships. In addition, American carrier aircraft had bombed and photographed the island since February, concentrating especially on Aslito air field and an additional strip Japanese engineers had begun nearby.

The air strikes Saito's garrison endured represented Spruance's conviction that Task Force 58 must defeat the First Air Fleet before the landing forces went ashore or the fleets engaged one another. Well-served by all his intelligence sources, including Ultra information, Spruance had a sound grasp of Ozawa's battle plan. Mitscher's pilots, well-trained and equipped with the latest model F6F Grumman Hellcat, started the pre-landing air strikes throughout the Marianas and Bonins on 11 June, engaging the interceptors of the First Air Fleet and scattering the bombers. Before Task Force 58 and the First Mobile Fleet actually met, American pilots—in eight days of fighting—reduced the First Air Fleet by half in aircraft available for combat. Only partially informed of this first setback, Admiral Ozawa waited until he was sure that the Fifth Fleet would indeed invade Saipan and then ordered Operation A to proceed. When Turner's naval gunfire support ships opened up on Saipan on 13 June, Ozawa weighed anchor and sailed the *Taiho* through the San Bernardino Strait between the islands of Samar and Luzon to meet his oilers and the rest of the Mobile Fleet on the afternoon of 16 June. American submarines and, later, scout aircraft tracked his fleet. In the meantime, the Japanese on Saipan faced the full wrath of the V Amphibious Corps.

Despite predictable confusion in reaching the correct beaches, the four marine regiments that landed on Saipan on 15 June showed just how overwhelming the Americans had become in ship-to-shore movement. Six amphibian tractor battalions, half army and half marine, carried the eight assault battalions to the beach in 719 tractors, almost half of them armored and cannon-bearing. In less than 30 minutes 8,000 marines plunged ashore, with a loss of about 20 tractors. Once ashore, however, the marines met a maelstrom of artillery and mortar fire from batteries in the nearby hills, where naval shells could not reach them. No marine or army artillery had landed on undefended islets nearby to provide fire support, and navy close air support still did not meet the demanding requirements of bombing near troops. As the 2nd Marine Division wheeled north into the hills above the air fields, the 4th Marine Division's assault battalions tried to move inland in their amtracs to take Aslito, but Japanese infantry and anti-tank guns stopped the advance. Before the campaign ended, 164 amtracs came to ruin as the marines tried to use them as combat vehicles ashore, where their thin armor and high profile made them vulnerable. Much to Holland Smith's anger, the Japanese had fully grasped Saipan's defensive possibilities. This battle would be a murderous war of attrition between implacable foes.

As the battle on Saipan ripened into another bloodbath, the Fifth Fleet and First Mobile Fleet moved to engage each other, Spruance with characteristic caution and Ozawa with characteristic aggressiveness but less tactical information. Not only would Japan's First Air Fleet offer Ozawa little help, which he did not fully realize until 15 June, but the submarine force had done nothing to upset the Americans, while managing to lose 17 of its 25 deployed boats. Task Force 58 had two carrier groups in position to attack, but Mitscher chose to wait while his remaining two carrier groups returned from their strike on the Bonins. In the meantime, Spruance canceled the invasion of Guam (scheduled for 18 June) and ordered Turner's amphibious force away from the Saipan beaches. Unlike Guadalcanal, the marines assumed the movement would be short-lived, and they had already had three days to unload crucial ammunition and supplies. On the clear morning of 19 June, young Japanese Sea Eagles roared off the flight-decks of their carriers, bound for one of the greatest aerial massacres of World War II.

Known officially as the Battle of the Philippine Sea, the naval aviators of Task Force 58 called the engagement "the Marianas Turkey Shoot," and the veterans marveled at the ineptness of the Japanese pilots they faced. Japanese carrier aviators flew 328 sorties and lost 243 aircraft, while the Japanese First Air Fleet lost another 50. At a cost of only 20 interceptors, the Hellcats, fully exploiting their shipboard radar intercept systems, flew over 400 sorties that ravaged the Sea Eagles. That afternoon, American submarines sank the *Taiho* and another carrier.

Then, much to the dismay of his carrier admirals, Spruance ordered the action broken off with Ozawa's force still in range, and Task Force 58 sailed east to protect the amphibious force from a possible night surface action. This decision—which sent naval aviators into apoplexy years afterward—does seem too cautious, given American superiority in numbers and effectiveness, but Spruance may have thought he had used up his luck at Midway. Thus far, his force had suffered only minor damage from the few Eagles that evaded his combat air patrols, and he wanted to keep it that way.

Spruance, with every intention of returning to the battle the next day, changed course to westward that night, but not soon enough to close with Ozawa, who had also turned westward for home. Not until late in the afternoon of 20 June did American scouts find the First Mobile Fleet, which now had only 35 fighters to protect 6 carriers and 6 battleships. Mitscher sent an attack force of over 200 aircraft after the Japanese fleet, not knowing that the position report he had received had been inaccurate. Even when he learned that his pilots would probably return—if at all—with empty gas tanks, he did not stop the mission. The American aircraft scored hits on 6 warships and sank a light carrier at the loss of 20 aircraft in action (and 11 aircrewmen) before returning to their carriers in the dark. Despite the threat of submarine attack, Spruance ordered the fleet lighted, but 80 aircraft crashed nevertheless during the recovery phase of the strike. The loss of 38 more pilots and crewmen on 20 June, while comparatively low, took away some of the luster from the victory of 19 June. Mitscher himself summed up the two days' toll: "The enemy had escaped. He had been badly hurt by one aggressive carrier strike at the one time he was in range. His fleet was not sunk."[2]

Even though Ozawa's defeat made further resistance futile, General Saito turned the battle for Saipan into a bad memory for the marines and soldiers of the V Amphibious Corps. Exploiting the terrain with great skill, the Japanese sold their 41,000 lives dearly in a battle that lasted almost a month, not the few days that some optimists had predicted. The American ground forces suffered more than 14,000 casualties and might have lost even more men had not Saito's subordinates mounted several dramatic *banzai* charges, including some with tank support. The last *banzai*, on 7

July, ended the lives of some 2,000 Japanese soldiers but also overran two army infantry battalions and three marine artillery battalions. This miserable melee of close slaughter only brought the fighting to new heights of wretchedness.

The 27th Infantry Division again showed sluggishness in combat, an unpardonable sin to Holland Smith, who relieved the division's commander. The following furor did not subside until the Joint Chiefs intervened and the commandant of the Marine Corps agreed to push Smith upstairs to a nonoperational assignment. Smith had correctly evaluated the failings of the 27th Division; new commanders and better-trained troops improved it some, but not much. But he had also proven his own limitations as a corps commander—just as the army charged—by showing little grasp of time-space factors and fire support coordination, a weakness observed by his own staff and his division commanders. The Saipan experience further strained relations between the marines and the army, especially since Nimitz had no stomach for settling confrontations.

Beyond contributing to poor service relations, Saipan also produced a shocking preview of what the war might hold as it moved into the populated islands of the Western Pacific: the death of innocents. As the marines and soldiers fought their way north up the island, they discovered the shattered bodies of elders, women, and children who had fallen to air strikes and artillery fire. They found civilians among the slaughtered of the 7 July *banzai* charge. Worse was to come as they reached Marpi Point, where they trapped perhaps a thousand Japanese soldiers and another thousand civilians of both sexes and all ages. They then watched in horror as the Japanese defiantly shot, beheaded, drowned, and blew up one another, despite the pleas of Japanese linguists, some of them *nisei* soldiers, to surrender. The marines found themselves attempting to kill some Japanese in order to save others, often to no avail. The surf that pounded the rocks of Marpi Point turned red, choked with corpses. Most of the American observers turned away from the scene, sickened by the needless death and horrified by the implications of such fanaticism for the rest of the war. Fighting and killing Japanese soldiers, even in the "no quarter" battlefields of the Pacific, at least fell into the broad expectations of war; the deaths at Marpi Point did not.

Until he could be sure that Japan's First Mobile Fleet would not return and that Saipan had fallen, Nimitz supported Spruance's decision to postpone the landings on Guam and Tinian. For General Geiger's Southern Troops and Landing Force, the postponement meant plowing endless wakes in the ocean, safe from Japanese air and submarines. As one sergeant remembered the scene, when the marine division and brigade finally went ashore on 21 July, they were mad enough at the U.S. Navy that they would have killed their own grandmothers. Instead, they faced another determined Japanese defense force of 18,500 that had used the extra time to build more mountain strongholds. The delay also meant that army air forces strikes began 6 May, carrier strikes on 11 June, and naval gunfire bombardment on 8 July, all on the original schedule. Despite the extended bombardment, General Geiger assessed the still-heavy resistance in the steep hills just behind the beachhead and ordered the 77th Infantry Division ashore the same day as the landing.

Geiger and Major General Andrew D. Bruce proved that marine and army generals could work well together; their troops learned to admire each other's combat skills, and the marines appreciated the solid performance of the army artillery and amtrac battalions that supported III Amphibious Corps. A veteran of Guadalcanal and Bougainville, Geiger showed that at least one marine general knew how to lead a corps with competence. The Japanese tested every element of his command with night *banzais,* clever defense positions, surprise shellings, and stolid last stands. Several friendly-fire incidents marred the battle but did not start another round of interservice hostility. The island finally fell into American hands on 10 August, although some Japanese soldiers—unaware that the war had ended—remained in the hills until 1972.

To the Americans, the battle for Guam became a poignant reminder of the reasons for fighting a war at such terrible cost. Guam had been American territory before the Japanese invaded, and its recapture, including a flag-raising at the site of the old marine barracks, made this an emotional campaign. Geiger's scheme of maneuver ashore ensured not only the early capture of Orote Point air field but the liberation of Guam's populated areas, including 20,000 Chammorro people, who had been imprisoned and abused by the Japanese for two and a half years. The battle cost some Guamanian lives, but the Guamanians welcomed the Americans back with enthusiasm and joined the battle as scouts and carriers. Despite restrictive rules of engagement, naval gunfire and air support were excellent. The fighting itself brought 7,800 casualties to the American corps (about 2,000 dead), and one marine regiment took casualties comparable to those in the later battles for Iwo Jima and Okinawa. Among the American dead were two strong colonels, Sam Puller, the brother of marine legend "Chesty" Puller, and Douglas C. McNair, only son of Lieutenant General Leslie J. McNair, commander of army ground forces, who was killed the same month in France. The American deaths, however, ensured that Guam would quickly become a B-29 base and a forward operating base for the navy's submarines and service forces.

The capture of Tinian between 24 July and 1 August fell to the reconstituted 2nd and 4th Marine Divisions, supported by four first-class army amphibian tractor battalions, 13 artillery battalions, and an engineer battalion. Crossing the four miles of straits between Saipan and Tinian, the marines surprised the Japanese (who numbered 8,000) by landing across some narrow northern beaches, then attacking south, instead of landing mid-island on a broader front. The rapidity of the attack and the deluge of supporting fires allowed the marines to convert a two-battalion front into a two-division enclave in 48 hours and to take some commanding heights without serious loss. With about 2,000 total casualties (and only 328 killed), the marines destroyed the Japanese garrison with methodical daylight advances and stubborn night defenses against the predictable *banzai* charges. The captured air field at Tinian rapidly became the principal base for the B-29s assigned to bomb the Home Islands. As an exercise in tactical skill, the Tinian operation made clear that the Japanese could not inflict worrisome casualties unless they changed their defensive tactics. The American high commanders did not want to give them time to learn new lessons.

The Return to the Philippines

Even as the Marianas campaign continued, General MacArthur pressed his argument that the Philippines, not Formosa, should be the focus of the next great offensive, a position still contested by Admiral King. MacArthur advanced one argument that King himself accepted: the Philippines could be a base from which to break off Japan's trade routes. MacArthur also took the moral-political position that the United States owed the Filipinos their freedom, having abandoned them in 1942. President Roosevelt himself journeyed to Honolulu in July 1944 to hear the arguments from Nimitz and MacArthur. MacArthur also probably divined FDR's desire to be seen with the great Republican general, since FDR had already declared for a fourth term as president. Neither MacArthur nor Nimitz argued that Formosa should be next. In fact, even King's own planners thought an invasion of Formosa would be premature, given the remaining Japanese air and naval forces. After more consideration, the Joint Chiefs in early September rejected MacArthur's plan to sail directly for Luzon and approved instead a more modest proposal to land on Mindanao in November 1944.

Japanese planners harbored no doubts that the Americans would next attack the Philippines. Such considerations had already added some confusion to the sortie against the Fifth Fleet in the Philippine Sea. Even with the Sea Eagles no longer able to fly off carriers in sufficient strength, the Imperial Navy's general staff concluded that the ample surface forces of its Combined Fleet and land-based aircraft might still deliver a staggering blow to the U.S. Navy and thus repulse or slow any Philippine invasion. Working with a new harmony born of desperation, the navy and army staffs drafted a national contingency plan, Sho Go or Operation Victory, that reached the commanders in late July 1944. Admiral Toyoda had already concluded that the Philippines would be the next great battleground, and he alerted his air and naval task force commanders to prepare for action in Philippine waters. In the broadest terms, the Japanese Navy formed two large task forces for Sho Go: the carriers and their escorts of the First Mobile Fleet of Admiral Ozawa, stationed in the Home Islands, and the Second Fleet of battleships and cruisers commanded by Admiral Kurita Takeo, a tough sailor who had the dubious distinction of having more flagships shot out from under him than any other Japanese admiral.

Toyoda's concept for the forthcoming fleet action, to which Ozawa and Kurita registered complaints, counted on the U.S. Navy's continuing fixation with destroying Ozawa's First Mobile Fleet, which had escaped during the Battle of the Philippine Sea. Toyoda considered Ozawa's four-carrier force a sacrificial diversion and rejected his sensible proposal that the First Mobile Fleet revert to fleet air defense, since Ozawa conceded that the Sea Eagles had lost their offensive punch. Toyoda decided instead to depend on land-based air to provide cover for his main effort, a direct thrust by Kurita's Second Fleet at the American invasion armada and at any carriers that did not go hunting for Ozawa. Toyoda directed Kurita to create his own First Diversion Force out of 7 of Japan's slowest battleships and cruisers. Kurita's Central Force, the cream of the navy's gunships, would include the superbattleships *Yamato* and *Musashi,* 3 older battleships, 12 cruisers, and 15 destroyers. Moreover, it would go into action with improved radars and fire control systems as well as special anti-aircraft ammunition.

From the perspective of the senior commanders and the staffs of the gathering Japanese and American forces, the first consideration was air superiority. MacArthur continued to harp on the inadequate number of carriers in his Seventh Fleet, which drew its naval air support from the small groups (40 or so aircraft) embarked on its 16 *Casablanca*-class escort carriers, which were simply 11,000-ton flattops built on the hulls of large merchantmen. MacArthur insisted that Kenney's tactical aviation (except for the B-24s) could not reach Philippine targets from their current bases to the southeast. He hectored the Joint Chiefs to force Nimitz to hold back nothing from Task Force 38, the four task groups of no less than 16 fleet and light carriers, all but two of which were brand new and amply supplied with fresh air groups. (A fleet or *Essex*-class carrier employed around 80 aircraft, while the light *Independence*-class carrier employed between 40 and 50 aircraft.) Nimitz answered MacArthur's concerns in several ways, the most important being an aggressive plan to strike Japanese air bases as far as the Ryukyus and to seize key islands in the Palau island group some 800 miles west of the Philippines. As in the Central Pacific, two of the rugged Palaus—Angaur and Peleliu—had air fields, but the real prize from the navy's perspective was Ulithi atoll, where the Pacific service force could meet the carriers in safety and increase the tempo of air operations.

Always eager to get along with MacArthur, Nimitz spent much of July 1944 showing his co-theater commander how cooperative the navy could be, even incurring King's wrath with his concessions. One of the advantages of reorganizing the highest operational echelon of the Pacific Fleet into two components, Fifth Fleet and Third Fleet, came in assigning Halsey's Third Fleet to MacArthur's preliminary moves toward the Philippines. MacArthur and Halsey were South Pacific comrades and mutual admirers. Nimitz reaffirmed his own promise to take the key islands of the western Carolines. The erosion of Japanese air and naval strength in the Carolines reduced the operation from a four-division landing to a two-division attack on Peleliu and Angaur by the 1st Marine Division (which had no atoll warfare experience) and the 81st Infantry Division (which had no landing experience at all).

As this amphibious force gathered in the Southern Pacific, Halsey roamed the Western Pacific in a series of raids by Task Force 38. Halsey's aviators attacked air fields and harbors on Yap, Mindanao, the Palaus, and Formosa with enthusiasm and reported a huge score, some 500 aircraft of the 1,500 Japanese aircraft deployed or in transit for the emerging decisive battle. Japanese claims of American planes downed and ships sunk were even more fantastic, but the Americans this time proved to be most affected by euphoria. Halsey urged MacArthur and Nimitz to abandon Mindanao as an objective and to go right for Leyte, a recommendation approved by the Joint Chiefs on 13 September, with the target date of mid-October. Two days later the Palau landings went off as scheduled, even though much of the rationale for the operation had disappeared.

The Palau landings became an orphaned operation, characterized by the absence of leadership as the 1st Marine Division fought itself to exhaustion on Peleliu. The adequacy of air and naval gunfire support also declined. At

Angaur the limited support made little difference, since the 81st Division destroyed the Japanese garrison of 1,500 in four days (17–20 September 1944), showing good training and tactical patience appropriate for a division full of late-war draftees in their thirties. Peleliu, defended by 10,500 tough Japanese soldiers, proved to be quite another matter. Assuming that Peleliu would go the way of other Central Pacific atoll attacks, the commander of the 1st Marine Division predicted a victory in a few days and then watched his three infantry regiments shrink in four weeks of arduous warfare fought against Japanese who were emplaced in caves. Two regiments from the 81st Division had to join the battle in order to finish it, and paid for their assistance in much higher casualties than they had suffered on Angaur. From 15 September to 15 October, Peleliu was the marines' worst nightmare, costing the 1st Division 6,400 casualties. Unlike the Marianas campaign in which Japanese soldiers had counterattacked and fought in other conventional ways, the Peleliu defenders fought to the last from their holes, thus minimizing American fire superiority. It was an early lesson that perhaps the Japanese had changed their way of battle, but the Americans had failed to notice.

Even with a flawed intelligence organization, the Japanese divined that the Americans would soon land somewhere in the Philippines, and they doubted that Mindanao would be the objective. The Japanese detected a northern tilt to the American axis of advance, reinforced when Halsey launched another series of massive carrier raids in early October on Okinawa, Formosa, and the Philippines. Although the American claims of Japanese aircraft destroyed were excessive, the real damage was substantial enough to force Toyoda to consider putting one of the Operation Victory variants into effect, which he did in a confused set of instructions on 10–11 October. Instead of allowing another surface force commanded by Vice Admiral Shima Kiyohide to join Ozawa and ambush Task Force 38, he ordered this force of seven warships to abandon the defense of Formosa and join the First Diversion Force, destined to force the Surigao Straits while Kurita's Center Force struck directly at the Seventh Fleet. Shima's force would have certainly added additional guns to either Kurita or Ozawa, but instead it contributed nothing to the greatest sea battle of World War II. Another problem that Toyoda only dimly recognized was that his surface task forces would not have adequate land-based air cover; he also had great difficulty getting any hard intelligence data on the dispersed American task forces. The Americans, on the other hand, with radio intelligence, submarine sightings, and air patrols, found all elements of Sho Go shortly after they began to concentrate their forces.

The series of naval engagements known as the Battle of Leyte Gulf (24–26 October 1944) ended any possibility that the Japanese Navy could influence the course of the Pacific War. The battle showed the high competence and courage of the U.S. Navy at the tactical level, even though a determined enemy could have found surprising opportunities to exploit its operational weaknesses. The problem started at the top. Without a single commanding officer with clear authority to control every aspect of the Leyte campaign, the American forces could and did fight separate battles. MacArthur and Kinkaid had one concern: to land four army divisions on the east coast of Leyte and to capture air fields for Kenney's air squadrons. Nimitz, however, had directed Halsey to look for a decisive fleet engagement while at the same time protecting the invasion force—two missions which might or might not be compatible. The Japanese ensured that this kind of mission ambiguity would plague the Third Fleet. As the four different Japanese naval task forces advanced toward the Philippines, MacArthur's U.S. Sixth Army (under Lieutenant General Walter Krueger) landed on Leyte against light resistance on 20 October. The Japanese finally knew with certainty where they would find the American navy.

The Battle of Leyte Gulf began and ended in confusion, but the Americans emerged victorious, if unhappy and mildly scared. American reconnaissance submarines and aircraft spotted Kurita's Center Force inside the San Bernardino strait on 23–24 October. On the 24th, Halsey ordered Task Force 38 to attack this force. Similar sightings located the two southern task forces of Nishimura and Shima, and Kinkaid detached a task force of his slow battleships, cruisers, and destroyers south to cover the mouth of the Surigao Straits, another passageway to the invasion fleet operating off Leyte. Between submarine attacks and air strikes on 24 October, the Center Force suffered serious losses, exacerbated by the land-based Second Air Fleet's determination to attack Halsey rather than protect Kurita. The day-long attacks sank the *Musashi* (which took 19 torpedo and 17 bomb hits) and damaged four other warships; to avoid further damage, Kurita ordered his force westward from the strait before daylight faded.

At almost the same time, American scout planes sighted Ozawa's carriers sailing south along the eastern coast of Luzon off Cape Engaño. Halsey ordered the Third Fleet north, leaving no task force to cover San Bernardino strait. He did, however, order Rear Admiral Willis Lee, the hero of the last sea battles off Guadalcanal, to prepare to form Task Force 34, a powerful unit of fast battleships and cruisers, for possible redeployment to the south if ordered. Kinkaid thought the message also meant that the act had been done, but it had not. Halsey's staff may have fumbled the order, but Lee

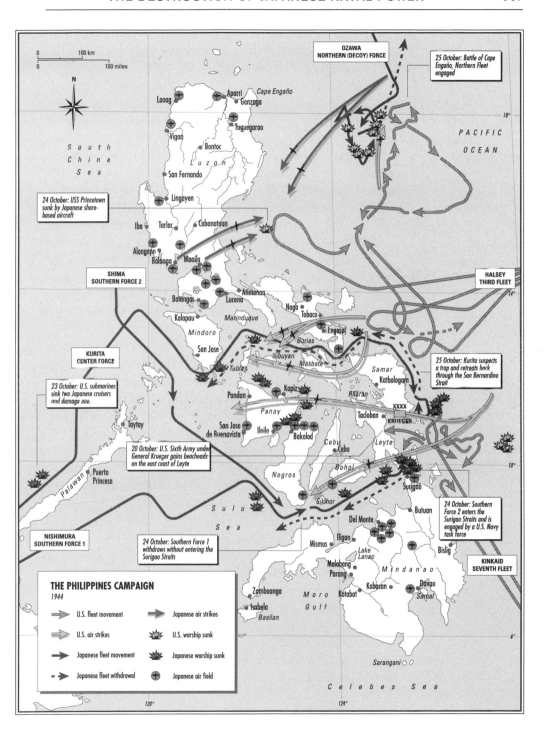

OZAWA
NORTHERN (DECOY) FORCE

25 October: Battle of Cape
Engaño, Northern Fleet
engaged

0 100 km
0 100 miles

N

PACIFIC

OCEAN

18°

Laoag
Aparri
Cape Engaño
Gonzaga

South
China
Sea

Vigan
Tuguegarao
Bontoc
Luzon

San Fernando

24 October: USS Princetown
sunk by Japanese shore-
based aircraft

Lingayen

Iba
Tarlac
Cabanatuan

Alongapo
Balanga
Manila

SHIMA
SOUTHERN FORCE 2

Batangas
Lucena
Alimonan

HALSEY
THIRD FLEET

14°

Kalapau

Naga
Tobaco

Marinduque

Mindoro

San Jose

Tablas

Burias
Sibuyan
Masbate

Legaspi

KURITA
CENTER FORCE

Samar
Katbalogam

25 October: Kurita suspects
a trap and retreats back
through the San Bernardino
Strait

23 October: U.S. submarines
sink two Japanese cruisers
and damage one.

Pandan
Kapiz
Bilaran

Panay
Taytay

San Jose
de Buenavista
Iloilo
Bakolod

Tacloban
XXXX
KRUEGER

20 October: U.S. Sixth Army under
General Krueger gains beachheads
on the east coast of Leyte

Cebu
Cebu

Leyte

10°

Puerto
Princesa

Palawan

Negros

Bohol

Sikihor

Surigao

24 October: Southern
Force 2 enters the
Surigao Straits and is
engaged by a U.S. Navy
task force

NISHIMURA
SOUTHERN FORCE 1

Sulu

Sea

Butuan

24 October: Southern Force 1
withdraws without entering the
Surigao Straits

Del Monte

Mismus
Iligan

Malabang
Parang
Lake
Lanao

Mindanao

Bislig

KINKAID
SEVENTH FLEET

Zamboanga
Isabela
Basilan

Kabacan
Kotabat

Davao
Samal

6°

Moro
Gulf

THE PHILIPPINES CAMPAIGN
1944

Sarangani

U.S. fleet movement — Japanese air strikes
U.S. air strikes — U.S. warship sunk
Japanese fleet movement — Japanese warship sunk
Japanese fleet withdrawal — Japanese air field

Celebes Sea

120°
124°

certainly understood that he did not have a new mission. Lee thought he should have remained near Kinkaid, since he had no confidence that the air attacks had really driven off Kurita's force.

In the meantime, Kinkaid had to cope with the twin columns of Nishimura and Shima, and he took decisive action that produced a dramatic victory in the Surigao Straits in the dark night of 24–25 October. Under the command of Rear Admiral Jesse A. Oldendorf, Kinkaid's 6 battleships, relegated to shore bombardment duty, and 8 cruisers sank all but one of Nishimura's 12 warships and chased Shima's force away. It was an especially sweet victory for the battleships, 5 of which had been almost destroyed at Pearl Harbor. In a classic action that began with the bravura of PT boat and destroyer torpedo attacks and ended with devastating radar-controlled gunfire from big battleship guns, Oldendorf's force won the battle without loss; the only American warship seriously damaged was a destroyer caught in friendly fire. The same sort of uneven battle developed during the daylight hours of 25 October off Cape Engaño. Believing that they had stopped Center Force, Halsey's aviators turned on Ozawa's sacrificial fleet with gusto and sank all four carriers and three destroyers.

Hidden by this fog of American victories, Kurita turned his task force around and returned to hunt for the Seventh Fleet or random incautious carriers. He commanded four battleships and eight cruisers. Early in the morning of 25 October, Kurita's force met six escort carriers and seven destroyers and destroyer-escorts, codenamed Taffy 3, off the coast of Samar. Commanded by Rear Admiral Clifton Sprague, Taffy 3—outgunned in everything but courage—spent four hours fighting off Kurita with little help. It lost one carrier and three escorts in the process. Suicidal attacks by U.S. naval aircraft and the escorts swung the action toward the Americans, even though they sank not one Japanese ship. Desperate messages for rescue flooded the navy's airwaves but produced nothing. Lee's Task Force 34, still north with Halsey, could not reach the battle after it received definite orders to go there, four hours after the fight began. Oldendorf's force was equally indisposed to the south.

Kurita thought the American battleships were charging to the rescue, however, and he also believed he had engaged large carriers rather than escort carriers—two miscalculations that distracted him from pressing into the invasion fleet. Rear Admiral Koyanagi Tomiji, Kurita's chief of staff, thought that Center Force had two missions which could not be reconciled: attack the Seventh Fleet and try to catch Halsey's carriers from the rear as they sailed north after Ozawa's decoys. As Koyanagi recorded in his memoirs: "Kurita and his staff intended to take the enemy task force as the primary objective if a choice of targets developed. Naturally, our encounter with the enemy off Leyte on 25 October was judged to be the occasion for such choice. On the other hand, there was considerable risk in changing our primary objective when we did not know the location of the other enemy forces or how effective our land-based air forces would be. We should have chosen the single, definite objective, stuck to it, and pushed on. Leyte Gulf lay close at hand and [the Seventh Fleet] could not run away."[3]

Before anyone could trap him, Kurita ordered his force back through the San Bernardino straits, where it had to endure more submarine and air attacks that ultimately sank three cruisers. Lee's Task Force 34 never closed with the enemy, missing one last chance to demonstrate that battleships still had a role in great sea battles. As the last of the remnants of the Combined Fleet scattered for safe haven, Toyoda counted his losses: 4 carriers, 3 battleships, 10 cruisers, and 9 destroyers. Another 10,000 Japanese sailors had perished in less than a week. The Imperial Japanese Navy, having enjoyed 50 years of success on the high seas, could no longer challenge the U.S. Navy in fleet actions.

Awash in post-action recrimination over Halsey's failure to detach Task Force 34, the senior American admirals in Philippine waters and back in Honolulu might have pondered some other losses. Between 10–16 October on their way to Leyte, three cruisers and three escort carriers of the Seventh Fleet were so badly damaged by air attacks that they had to withdraw. On 24 October Japanese airplanes attacked the light carrier *Princeton*, part of Task Force 38, and set it afire with only one bomb; when the carrier blew up during the rescue, the explosion ruined the cruiser *Birmingham*. The next day a flight of Japanese naval aviators pledged to one another to press their attacks to the point of crashing into American ships. They then took off from a Luzon air field and hurtled into another of Kinkaid's escort carrier groups, sinking one escort carrier and damaging four warships. On 4 November, suicide aircraft hit two transports, killing more than 100 soldiers and sailors. Of the 3,000 or so American sailors who died in Philippine waters on 24–26 October, more than half had not been engaged in the Battle of Leyte Gulf at all.

As the navies steamed through their voyage of destruction in waters off the Philippines, MacArthur's landing force, initially four infantry divisions, also found Leyte full of unpleasant surprises. Although MacArthur proved too shrewd a commander to predict a quick victory, his planning for the invasion of Luzon kept slipping from its initial target date in December to some indefinite time early in 1945. MacArthur's planning hit an immovable object: the Japanese Army and army aviation. Unlike prior operations in the Southwest Pacific, the Japanese showed no hesitancy in moving re-inforcements against the Leyte landing force. They also threw army avia-tion squadrons into the battle in both conventional and suicide attacks, and they even conducted commando raids upon American air fields. The dog-ged nature of the Leyte defense stemmed from the decision of the South-ern Army theater commander, Field Marshal Terauchi Hisaichi, to commit forces planned for the defense of Luzon. His senior Philippine commander, General Yamashita Tomoyuki, wanted to hold his Fourteenth Area Army for a long delaying action on Luzon, but Terauchi ordered him to send reinforcements south while he had some aviation support. Army head-quarters in Tokyo agreed to transfer troops from Manchuria to Luzon, so Yamashita's total force in the Philippines remained around 200,000, with the garrison of Leyte growing from 23,000 to almost 70,000 during the course of the campaign. Part of this force included the Fourth Air Army, which committed 1,500 aircraft to Philippine operations in the last three months of 1944.

Still demonstrating some bad operational habits, MacArthur's staff un-derestimated the size of the initial Leyte garrison and accepted a level of risk that proved dangerous to the Sixth Army, a force that expanded from four to eight divisions, or about 200,000 officers and men. The risk in-volved the assumption that the Fifth Air Force would open two to five air fields early in the campaign, replacing the navy's carrier aviation, which would continue to raid Formosa and Luzon. The Seventh Fleet's escort car-riers, pummeled by the sea battles of October, sought other waters. MacAr-thur did not make too large a fuss over this issue once Sixth Army was safely ashore and held at least two air fields, accomplished soon after the landings of 20 October.

The difficulty arose because the Japanese chose to raise the ante in the air battle, and the weather did not cooperate with the army engineers in making the Leyte airstrips operable. MacArthur and the Fifth Air Force commander, Major General Ennis C. Whitehead, thought they would have at least ten air groups of all kinds operating from Leyte within two weeks of the landing. Instead, they had only one field, at Tacloban, operational for one P-38 group on 27 October. A second field, at Dulag, opened in Novem-ber. A heavy autumn monsoon, aided by a nasty typhoon, turned Leyte into a mudhole for all of the campaign. In the meantime, Japanese water-borne reinforcements arrived at the port of Ormoc.

The ground campaign began with high drama and great elation when Krueger's four divisions seized two major beachheads (separated by 14 miles, another touch of MacArthur's optimism) without facing serious resistance at the waterline. The one Japanese division then defending eastern Leyte had withdrawn to prepared positions in Leyte's Central Mountain range, some 20–30 miles from the beaches. Local covering forces caused some anxious moments, but not enough to prevent MacArthur from landing on Red Beach, where the 24th Infantry Division had found the most determined Japanese resistance. Leading his entourage through the low surf, MacArthur waded ashore for the first of several times at Leyte in front of Tacloban, the site of his first duty station after his graduation from West Point in 1903. "It was a full moment for me." He then made a radio broadcast to the Filipinos that he had kept his pledge to return and that "the hour of your redemption is here." He had no special regard for his foe, General Yamashita, whom MacArthur characterized as a braggart for suggesting (so MacArthur had been told) that he would take MacArthur's surrender just as he had Percival's at Singapore. Yamashita might be "an able commander," MacArthur admitted, "but . . . he talked too much."[4] In his message MacArthur urged all true Filipinos to rally and "strike" in the name of Philippine patriotism, Christianity, and the United States. He did caution the Filipinos that they should "strike" when American troops got close enough to rescue them from Japanese retaliation, but the guerrillas had already digested that bit of tactical counsel. Those present at this Columbiad moment felt its power, but remembered it more as a photo opportunity than as a great speech.

Even as the U.S. Navy took the measure of the Japanese Combined Fleet, the Sixth Army found that much of the striking would come from the Japanese. American heavy artillery could influence the battle where the infantry met, but only the Fifth Air Force could stop the flow of reinforcements from the north, and it could not do so while hampered by foul weather and the struggle against the Fourth Air Army. Within a week of the landings, Japanese bombers attacked Tacloban air field, the landing beaches, and the anchorages with shocking regularity, turning American aircraft into junk. The air forces had not experienced such devastation since the darkest days on New Guinea. Attacks on logistical shipping also proved worrisome; before the completion of operations in the Philippines the following year, 46 cargo ships were sunk or damaged in Philippine waters, an inordinate number of them carrying ammunition and aviation gasoline. Even if the suicide aircraft, now identified as the new *kamikaze* aviation corps, could be shot down with relative ease, any air defense was likely to leak—with catastrophic results. One direct result of the attacks on the American air and logistical bases was that Whitehead had to strengthen his interceptor force on Leyte, thus sacrificing his offensive air capability. Locked with the Japanese in Leyte's mountains, the Sixth Army's embattled divisions could not expect much air support. Nevertheless, the American infantry pushed forward into the slippery slopes and struggled over the mountain roads toward the Ormoc valley and the ports that welcomed Japanese reinforcements. Basically, only the northern third of Leyte became the battle zone.

For more than a month, the lines of contact between the Japanese Thirty-Fifth Army and the U.S. Sixth Army stalled from Leyte's north coast road south along the difficult Central Mountain range. Krueger tried a couple of small amphibious envelopments, none of which changed the stalemate. When he planned more ambitious landings, MacArthur told him that the landings planned for Luzon got first priority. The Sixth Army continued its dogged forward movement, drawing essential combat power from its abundant artillery and limited tank force. Nevertheless, it entered the northern edge of the Ormoc valley and turned south against Ormoc itself, only to discover another system of Japanese defenses that crossed the valley. Three more weeks of battles of attrition were required before the Japanese defense weakened. Faced with the prospect that his Leyte defense force would collapse, Yamashita accepted a plan from Fourth Air Army to stage a commando raid, supplemented by the drop of an entire crack parachute regiment on Leyte's air fields. For almost a week in early December, Japanese raiders bedeviled Sixth Army's rear areas and confounded the base forces of Fifth Air Force, but they did not change the tactical balance. Instead, the ground attack designed to support the raid exposed one Japanese division to punishing artillery fire. Krueger delivered the coup de grâce by landing the entire 77th Infantry Division near Ormoc itself. By late December the two American forces met, and the campaign, for all purposes, ended. The Japanese Thirty-Fifth Army had lost about 60,000 dead, while inflicting only 3,500 dead and 12,000 wounded on the U.S. Sixth Army.

Conclusion

The campaign for Leyte represented the last struggle between the American and Japanese armed forces within the parameters of conventional warfare. It fully engaged every element of the air, ground, and naval forces the belligerents had deployed to the Pacific War. It also forced the highest degree of interservice cooperation (or lack thereof) of the Pacific War. Even if Japanese air-ground and army-navy cooperation had retained its inherent tensions, the defense of the Philippines demonstrated that the Japanese armed forces still possessed not just a willingness to die but considerable skill to fight within the operational limitations imposed by American fire superiority and growing strength in numbers. The U.S. armed forces themselves showed a new willingness to work together, whatever the ego problems and organizational loyalties of their senior commanders. During the Leyte campaign, for example, the Marine Corps had sent a composite air group to Tacloban to help Fifth Air Force with its air superiority and ground close air support missions. Army-navy cooperation and understanding had expanded beyond the Seventh Fleet to influence operations throughout the entire Pacific Fleet.

While the American armed forces perfected their conventional military operations, the Japanese—in actions fueled by desperation—sought to abandon the traditional definitions of how war should be waged. As the Pacific War approached the Home Islands, no one on either side could know for certain whether modernized or traditional Japanese values would shape the empire's ultimate opposition to foreign subjugation.

14

THE KILLING TIME

1943–1944

In the last half of 1943, as U.S. forces went over to a full-scale offensive in the Pacific, the war in Europe inexorably swung against Nazi Germany. During the summer, Allied operations exerted a growing, interrelated pressure across the European theaters. Hitler's decision to call off the Kursk battle on the Eastern Front resulted not only from tactical defeats but from the Anglo-American invasion of Sicily and the threat of Italian collapse. The Germans were no longer masters of events. No matter how skilled their conduct of defensive battles, the weight of Allied military power was wearing away the Wehrmacht's tactical advantages.

Still, from our perspective and with our knowledge of the crimes Hitler's henchmen were inflicting on Europe's defenseless civilians, Allied operations at times seem hesitant and flawed. The Holocaust was in full course in 1943; the great killing camps of Auschwitz, Sobibor, and Treblinka daily received their cargoes of victims, primarily Jews, but also significant numbers of other "undesirables." The pogroms of 1939 against Jews in Poland—accompanied by the systematic murder of Polish intellectuals and leaders—had escalated by 1941 into organized massacres of hundreds of thousands of Jews in places like Babi Yar. There, SS Einsatzgruppen had executed old, young, men, and women by firing squad and had thrown the bodies into great pits. By 1942 Himmler's executioners had moved on to organized, industrialized killing of Europe's "inferior" races in great extermination camps whose sole mission was the murder of hundreds of thousands of innocents. Slowly but inexorably, the great ghettos set up by the German conquerors in 1939 and 1940 emptied. The chimneys of the crematoria belched their ashes into the atmosphere, while Adolf Eichmann and other bureaucrats searched far afield for new victims.

By 1943 Franklin Roosevelt and Winston Churchill had seen refugee reports suggesting that the Nazis were systematically slaughtering Jews as a "final solution" to the "Jewish question" in Europe. But Roosevelt, Churchill, and Allied commanders concluded that the only hope of ending the atrocities was military victory over the Wehrmacht; only by defeating and occupying Nazi Germany with ground troops could they bring these crimes against humanity to an end. There was no moral equivalence between killing Germans—civilians as well as soldiers—and the crimes they committed or condoned.

The killing of Germans by every means available in order to win the war became the Allies' goal. But Allied armies could accomplish that goal only at heavy cost to themselves. Their opponent was tenacious, well-trained, highly motivated, and determined to postpone the day of reckoning as long as possible. As the massive upswing of arms production throughout the world reached the combatants, the level of fighting intensified. It would not cease until May 1945.

The Italian Campaign, September 1943–May 1944

In July 1943, Anglo-American forces had landed in Sicily. Despite considerable squabbling among Allied commanders, their forces had driven the Germans back on Messina. These Axis defeats were sufficient to bring about the collapse of Mussolini's regime, the possibility of which the Germans, unlike their opponents, had considered. From the German perspective, the operative word was when, not if, Italy would abandon the war. Rommel had received command of Army Group B in Austria in order to funnel German troops into Italy as rapidly as possible and assume command of the theater. On the Italian side, King Vittorio Emanuele II had appointed Marshal Badoglio as Mussolini's successor with the charge to take Italy out of the war. Given Badoglio's record—corps commander at Caporetto, overseer of the military buildup in the 1930s, head of Commando Supremo during the disasters of 1940—the marshal was the last person capable of leading Italy out of the war without wrecking the country. The cast of generals surrounding him was no better prepared for the business of resisting German troops, who were already flooding Italy and moving south.

Neither the Allied high command nor the Italian leadership acted quickly enough. The first Italian emissary to the Allies arrived in Portugal without authority to negotiate. Instead, he carried a message urging the Allies to land as soon as possible. Further discussions occurred in August, as Allied forces prepared to invade the mainland. Not until 1 September did

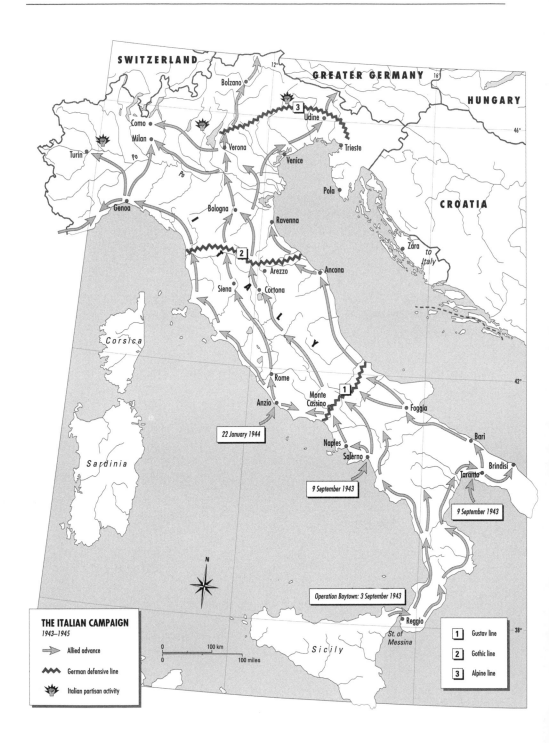

THE ITALIAN CAMPAIGN
1943–1945

→ Allied advance

〰 German defensive line

💥 Italian partisan activity

1 Gustav line

2 Gothic line

3 Alpine line

SWITZERLAND

GREATER GERMANY

HUNGARY

CROATIA

Bolzano

Como
Milan
Turin
Verona
Venice
Trieste
Pola

Po

Genoa
Bologna
Ravenna

Corsica

Siena
Arezzo
Cortona
Ancona

Zara
to Italy

Rome

Anzio
Monte Cassino
Foggia
Bari

22 January 1944

Naples
Salèrno
Brindisi
Taranto

9 September 1943

9 September 1943

Sardinia

N

Operation Baytown: 3 September 1943

Reggio
St. of Messina

Sicily

Udine

0   100 km
0   100 miles

the Italians accept the Allies' armistice conditions. Initially, General Sir Harold Alexander, ground forces commander, considered landing the U.S. 82nd Airborne Division in Rome to help hold the Italian capital, but a quick visit to the city by the assistant division commander, Brigadier General Maxwell D. Taylor, convinced the Allies that the Italians were not ready to fight the Germans. The drop was canceled just as the aircraft were loading.

As the Salerno landings began in southern Italy on the morning of 8 September, Eisenhower announced that Italian leaders had agreed to an armistice. In Rome, the king, crown prince, Badoglio, and other luminaries decamped for southern Italy. They left no orders for subordinates. As a result, the Germans quickly and easily disarmed the Italian forces and immediately shipped off most of the unfortunates to work in Nazi slave labor camps. In those instances when the Italians resisted, the Germans gave full vent to their fury at the betrayal of the Axis alliance. On the Greek island of Cephalonia, where Italian forces held off repeated assaults of the Wehrmacht's 1st Mountain Division, the Germans captured and executed 155 officers and 4,750 soldiers.

The fact that the governmental party slipped through German roadblocks on their way to southern Italy, despite Hitler's order that German troops round up the king and those who had betrayed the Axis alliance, suggests that Italian leaders had made a deal with "Smiling" Albert Kesselring, commander of German forces in the Mediterranean. They probably exchanged a safe conduct south for a betrayal of their duty, people, and country. Meanwhile, military events set the stage for a long, discouraging campaign. The landings at Normandy on 6 June 1944 have tended to overshadow events in Italy. Yet from September 1943 to April 1945 the Allies suffered 312,000 casualties in the Italian campaign, while inflicting 435,000 on their Nazi opponents. In this grim and bitter struggle, the combatants wreaked destruction on Italy from north to south.

Unwilling to risk his forces beyond the range of fighter cover, Alexander landed Montgomery's Eighth Army at the tip of the Italian boot, while Lieutenant General Mark Clark's Fifth Army came ashore at Salerno. Many of Clark's contemporaries believed he possessed one of the best minds in the U.S. Army. Others believed his character consisted of equal parts vanity and slipperiness. Both views were right. In the end, it was character that Clark lacked. In late December 1942 Clark received command of the Fifth Army and spent most of the next six months keeping an eye on Spanish Morocco, in case Franco should come into the war on the Axis side. Because Clark had refused an additional appointment to serve as the chief

American adviser to Churchill, Bradley took command of the U.S. First Army in England in September 1943, while Clark led Fifth Army into Italy. Meanwhile, George Patton, the most competent U.S. operational commander in the European Theater of Operations, who should have received one of those two appointments, still lurked under a cloud due to his unprofessional behavior in slapping two soldiers in Sicilian hospitals.

For all of his brilliance as a staff officer, Clark proved one of the more disappointing U.S. commanders in the war. Ambitious, ruthless with subordinates, profligate with the lives of his soldiers, unsympathetic to the difficulties of other Allied armies, and more impressed with style than substance, Clark possessed little of Eisenhower's empathy or capacity to put the interests of the alliance ahead of his own. For Clark, military effort was directly proportional to the number of casualties. Moreover, he understood little of the tactical and operational framework within which his forces waged war. And he displayed the worst qualities of the "looking-good general" GIs detested; when he learned that Marshall might visit his theater on the way to Yalta in February 1945, Clark had every Bailey bridge in Italy whitewashed.

Over Clark was Alexander, Auchinleck's successor as Middle Eastern Theater commander after the disasters in the desert in 1942. Now as ground force commander in the Mediterranean under Eisenhower, he was one of the great, courageous gentlemen in the British Army, a guardsman of proven valor in World War I and commander of the rearguard at Dunkirk. In his command positions Alexander displayed great tact as well as the capacity to work within an Allied framework. But he was never able to control Montgomery effectively, and Clark proved no more cooperative. Consequently, the Anglo-American armies in Italy fought their own battles.

The campaign's beginning was less than auspicious. Montgomery's forces crossed the Straits of Messina on 3 September. But his advance up the toe slowed to a crawl because the bridges on the roads leading north had been demolished by German combat engineers. Five days later, as American and British troops came ashore at Salerno, Montgomery was nearly 100 miles away. Kesselring had believed that the Allied landings would probably occur at Salerno, and—ever the smiling optimist—he believed that his forces possessed sufficient strength to defend German-held territory south of Rome. Rommel, by contrast, argued that the Wehrmacht's strength was insufficient for this task and that German strategy should focus on preventing an Allied amphibious move farther up the peninsula. Caught between these two powerful voices, Hitler remained uncertain, but Allied troubles with the Salerno landing convinced him that Kesselring was right. Thus,

Kesselring remained in command in Italy, while Rommel moved on to prepare the defenses of northwest Europe.

The Allies' Fifth Army plan for Salerno projected a landing on two beaches, one by the British X Corps and one by the American VI Corps, separated by a distance of 10 miles as well as the River Sele. When briefed on the plan, Patton, as Clark's backup, had suggested that if the Germans knew their business they would find the gap between the two corps and attempt to exploit it. Clark paid no attention. The Italian surrender had given too many Allied planners a false sense of optimism; some had even predicted that the attacking force would be in Naples within three days. What they did not take into account was Kesselring's prescience. In the days immediately before the landing, he moved the 16th Panzer Division into the Salerno area and positioned two more divisions just south of Naples.

Despite these preparations, the Germans reacted rather slowly to the actual invasion. The landings occurred at 0330 hours on 9 September, the morning after Eisenhower announced the Italian surrender. On the south side of the invasion, the U.S. 36th Infantry Division, a green division largely consisting of Texas National Guardsmen, ran into heavy German fire on the beaches, but destroyers provided covering fire that smothered many of the German strong points. Brigadier General John O'Daniel, commandant of Fifth Army's amphibious warfare school in North Africa, provided firm direction and organization in getting the troops and supplies sorted out on the American beaches. On the 36th Infantry Division's left wing, some units managed to drive five miles inland; but on the right, the 141st Regimental Combat Team had a much harder time in front of Paestum, as local German resistance and counterattacks created considerable difficulties.

At the British landing to the north, Allied forces also ran into substantial resistance from strong points defending the beaches; again, naval gunfire support was crucial in helping the troops establish a beachhead. But the British fell into considerable confusion when part of the 46th Division landed in the wrong area. The Royal Navy reported that a number of units dumped their extra loads of ammunition without waiting to exit the landing craft; another unit landed with a piano for the sergeant's mess; and one regiment even brought along a pig for its officers' victory dinner in Naples. The British could have used a general like O'Daniel on their beaches.

The outcomes from the British landings were mixed. Units of Brigadier L. O. Lyne's brigade in the 56th Division advanced on Montecorvino air field, where, to their astonishment, they found a number of German aircraft still on the field; they destroyed 39, along with an assortment of tanks, assault guns, and half-tracks. By contrast, the infantry of the Hampshires in the 46th Division, advancing with considerable noise in expectation of no serious German resistance to their front, collided with a company-sized force of panzer grenadiers. After the shooting died down, the battalion had lost 100 men killed or wounded and 300 captured.

By the end of the day, when both Allied landing forces were ashore, a seven-mile gap remained between them. Moreover, Luftwaffe opposition had been surprisingly strong. Over the period 9–11 September, German air attacks badly damaged the British battleship *Warspite* and the cruiser *Uganda*, while sinking one cruiser, four transports, and seven LST/LCTs (landing ship tanks/landing craft tanks). By 10 September, German reinforcements were flowing into the area surrounding the beachhead; over the course of the next several days the 29th Panzer Division, a battle group from the Hermann Göring Division, and the 3rd and 15th Panzer Grenadier Divisions arrived. Luckily for the Allies, the Germans had too many corps and army headquarters mixing in the planning, and so the main attack of the 11th was uncoordinated and failed to stop the British. But the Germans succeeded in putting increasing pressure on the entire landing force.

One of the Allies' major advantages was vastly superior firepower. Battleships, cruisers, and destroyers pummeled any target that their spotters could identify, while Allied air power now targeted the immediate area around Salerno almost exclusively. In one case, during the landing phase, a British destroyer was able to demolish a German Tiger tank. The fact that a *Brooklyn*-class cruiser could fire 1,500 5″ shells in ten minutes underscores the level of firepower Allied naval forces provided the landing forces.

By 12 September, Clark was worrying—quite correctly—that the Germans would attack the inner flanks of either the British X Corps or American VI Corps. The Germans lived up to his expectations. On the 13th a skillfully prepared German counterattack by the 16th Panzer and 29th Panzer Grenadier Divisions hit the American left flank. Although the Germans lacked sufficient strength to threaten the beachhead, the skill and fierceness of their attack wrecked one U.S. battalion. Vainly attempting to exploit their success, the Germans advanced along an Italian military road that led nowhere but to a cul-de-sac. Two American artillery battalions then pumped nearly 4,000 shells onto the hapless Germans. Nevertheless, Clark was alarmed enough at the severity of the German counterattack to consider a withdrawal. But after reinforcements arrived on the scene—including a regiment from the 82nd Airborne Division that parachuted into the bridgehead near midnight on the evening of 13 September—the Allies finally stabilized the landing. The Germans made one last major attack on the 16th, but Allied sea, air, and ground firepower smothered it. Kesselring now drew his forces off, his retreat unhindered by Allied pursuit.

By pulling back into the mountains, the Germans gained sufficient time to fortify the carefully chosen Gustav Line position, which was anchored on the Rapido River in the west and crossed the Apennines to the Adriatic near Ortona. By early November, German resistance, added to snow, rain, and a sea of mud, halted the already painfully slow Allied advance. As the king of Italy had suggested the previous spring, the one way *not* to conquer Italy was to drive from south to north up the peninsula. At least the Allies gained Naples and the air fields around Foggia, which would prove of great value for air attacks on southern Germany and Romanian oil fields in 1944. Nevertheless, despite a continuing stalemate, Allied commanders never contemplated abandoning the campaign. They hoped to pin down sufficient German forces in Italy to ease the path of the invasion forces in France. With Rome barely 80 miles to the northwest, it seemed inconceivable that Allied military forces could not capture the Eternal City before D-Day.

Clark's conduct of operations in January 1944 displayed him at his worst. Under considerable pressure from Churchill, the Joint Chiefs of Staff agreed to an amphibious landing behind German lines at Anzio, barely 40 miles south of Rome. The operation would take place on 22 January. In the meantime, Clark scheduled a series of attacks for the British and American divisions in Fifth Army. Unfortunately, the dates he chose were far enough apart that the German Tenth Army found sufficient time to reply to each attack. Clark's offensive opened on 17 January with an attack against the Gustav Line. The British X Corps achieved a limited tactical success, but Clark refused to support it. With only enough assault boats for one brigade, the British 46th Division then failed in its attempt to cross the Garigliano River, and British commanders, refusing to reinforce failure, called the attack to a halt.

The U.S. 36th Infantry Division, already seriously depleted due to heavy fighting in the mountains, suffered an even bloodier repulse on the Rapido. From the start, the crossing was a shambles. The river was in full flood; the troops were tired and dispirited; the infantry and engineers had not coordinated their work; and there was no concerted fire plan. But Clark—who viewed the British failure to cross the Garigliano with nothing but contempt—ordered the American troops to try again, and the results were equally disastrous. By the time the Allied VI Corps landed at Anzio on 22 January, 1,000 men from the 36th Infantry Division were dead or missing and 600 wounded. The German after-action report laconically noted that their forces had "prevented enemy troops crossing at S. Angelo."[1] The operation was so badly executed that the Germans subsequently believed they had faced only diversionary attacks.

The only Germans on the beach at Anzio when the Allied forces came ashore were four drunken officers in a Volkswagen Kübelwagen, who proceeded to drive up through the open doors of an LST. The landing had caught the enemy by surprise; German military intelligence, the Abwehr, living up to its standards, had just delivered a report indicating there was no prospect of an amphibious landing behind the Gustav Line. The response of Allied commanders reflected their over-cautious approach to war. The corps commander, Major General John Lucas, after comparing his situation to the Battle of the Little Big Horn, noted in his diary that such battles "aren't much fun, and a failure now would ruin Clark, probably kill me and certainly prolong the war."[2] Instead of breaking out and aggressively advancing to the Alban Hills and thus cutting off one of the main supply routes running near the coast from Rome to the German Tenth Army, Lucas hunkered down and established a solid defensive perimeter. On a visit to Anzio on the first day, Clark reinforced Lucas's caution by remarking that he "was not to stick his head out."[3] In retrospect, Lucas's response may well have been correct. First, Clark had scheduled Fifth Army's attacks too early, with the result that the Allied attacks failed to put pressure on the Germans. But the real justification for Lucas's actions came from the swiftness with which the Wehrmacht responded to the landing behind their line. Within a day, scratch German units were arriving in Anzio, and the OKW immediately released reserve divisions throughout the theater. Within eight days the Germans had part or all of eight divisions around the Anzio perimeter. The swift response represented a warning from the Führer of what the Allies could expect should they attempt to land on the French coast.

Churchill remarked that he had expected the Anzio invasion to pounce on the shore like a "wildcat," but instead it beached like "a stranded whale." The VI Corps did not attempt to break out until 30 January, well after the Germans had established their defenses. Not surprisingly, the effort failed, and casualties were heavy. A major German counterattack on 16 February achieved some success, but as the Germans exploited the initial break against the U.S. 45th Infantry Division, the weight of Allied firepower wrecked the advancing units. A renewed attempt two days later was less successful, as was an attack on 28 February. The fighting inflicted heavy casualties on the Germans, reducing their operational reserves. But

Hitler wanted the landing force destroyed, and his subordinates had little choice but to obey his unrealistic orders.

Meanwhile, the Allies again attempted to breach the Gustav Line, this time at Cassino, in a series of costly and ineffective attacks. In one of the most inexcusable bombings of the war, Allied air forces destroyed the ancient home monastery of the Benedictine Order at Monte Cassino. The result served only to provide defending Luftwaffe paratroopers better defensive positions in the ruins.

While the Allied advance stalled short of Rome, the Germans brought their special brand of order to the portions of Italy still under their control. Rescued by SS commandos in September, a grateful Mussolini established "The Republic of Salo" to provide legitimacy for the hard fist of German rule in Italy; but no one, including the former dictator, was fooled. The SS began the business of ferreting out Jews from within the Italian population; in hiding and protecting their fellow citizens, the Italians exhibited a degree of conscience not seen in much of the rest of occupied Europe. For one of the few times in the war, the Catholic Church, at the direction of Pope Pius XII, devoted substantial efforts to saving Jews. In the end, four-fifths of the Jewish population of Italy escaped slaughter—a remarkable record of moral courage.

Nazi rule proved equally harsh in other areas. A vicious war between anti-Fascist partisans and Mussolini's Fascist militia, backed up by German forces, was soon under way throughout much of Italy. On 23 March 1944, Italian terrorists in Rome exploded a series of bombs along the route where the 3rd Battalion of the SS Police Regiment paraded daily. When the smoked cleared on the Via Rasella, 32 German policemen were dead and more were wounded. Hitler furiously demanded that his military authorities in Italy execute 10 Italians for every German killed by the bombs. With the compliance of Kesselring, SS authorities in Rome rounded up 320 victims and transported them to the Ardeatine caves on the outskirts of Rome, where SS policemen murdered them all. German Army engineers then dynamited the entrance to the caves, but news soon leaked out from eyewitnesses. The slaughter at Ardeatine was only one of a series of reprisals inflicted with great enthusiasm on the Italian population. In one late-September 1944 incident at Marzabotto in the Apennines, Fascist militia and the SS murdered 1,830 civilians, with, as usual, the full knowledge of senior German military leaders.

By late winter it was clear to the Allies that a successful breakthrough to link up with Anzio and move on Rome and northern Italy demanded careful planning by all of Fifth Army. Such an offensive could not come until May, a date that jeopardized the proposed Allied landing in southern France, now called Operation Anvil. The British argued against Anvil, because they hoped to use the Italian campaign as a springboard to drive into southern Austria and perhaps even the Balkans. Eisenhower, already in England to command the invasion of northern France, agreed with them, but largely because he wanted the amphibious resources available in the Mediterranean for his attack. But the U.S. Joint Chiefs of Staff remained solidly behind Anvil, even though the landings would have to be postponed until at least July.

The Italian Campaign, May–September 1944

The offensive in Italy that began in mid-May represented the pinnacle of Allied strength in the theater. Substantial French and Polish forces, trained and equipped by the Americans, proved a crucial addition. The French troops came from North Africa and other colonies. The Poles had found their way to the Middle East after release from Stalin's camps; despite the certainty that either the Germans or the Soviets would control their homeland after the war, they still fought with extraordinary bravery.

Plans called for Eighth Army, which had taken over the front at Monte Cassino, to make a major thrust up the Liri valley; to its left, Fifth Army would break through to Anzio, while the six divisions in the pocket would, at the appropriate time, break out toward Valmontone. There, Route 6 represented both the main logistic link for the German Tenth Army as well as its main escape route. The campaign intended to destroy German forces south of Rome. However, Clark never accepted this fundamental goal of Allied operations. He was much more interested in ensuring that *his* Fifth Army and *his American* troops would liberate the Eternal City and bask in the international publicity a grateful press would shower on this moment in history.

With an overwhelming superiority in firepower, the Allies plastered German frontline positions on 11 May. The firing of 1.2 million heavy shells suggests the Allied advantage. At first the offensive achieved little. Eighth Army gained minimal ground, while the Poles suffered heavily in attacks on Monte Cassino. Fifth Army's veteran units had no greater success. But in the middle of the Allied lines, the four French colonial divisions proved startlingly effective. Because the mountainous terrain seemed impassable, the Germans covered the sector in front of General Alphonse Juin's divisions with one weak division. Clark himself had little respect for the French, which is why they drew a sector with such formidable terrain. For his part, Juin showed a mutual disrespect for Clark's plans and, in French fashion, proceeded to march off on his own line of attack.

After heavy fighting, the North African troops destroyed the German defending force, broke through the Gustav Line, and proceeded across the mountains. Unlike many other Allied generals, Juin understood and accepted his operational goal: to penetrate the rear of the German Tenth Army and allow the breakout of Fifth and Eighth Armies. The French success opened the way for the American II Corps. Equally important, Juin's Goums (his Moroccan mountain infantry) crossed the escarpment and broke into the Liri valley before the Germans could man the backup Hitler Line. Thoroughly taken in by Allied deception efforts, Kesselring responded slowly. Adding to his troubles were the absence of his competent Tenth Army commander, General Frido Senger von Etterlin (who was home on leave), and the failure of commanders on the scene to respond quickly.

The plans of Alexander's chief of staff, Major General John Harding, called for Fifth Army to link up with the six divisions in the Anzio bridgehead. The combined force was then to drive north to Valmontone on Route 6 and cut the main avenue for any German withdrawal. With Valmontone in Allied hands, Fifth Army would possess good prospects for encircling much of the German Tenth Army. The Germans expected a drive out of the Anzio bridgehead northwest toward Rome, an expectation VI Corps cultivated. However, on 23 May the Americans struck out of the beachhead due north toward Valmontone, and in two days of heavy fighting achieved a breakthrough. The road was open to Route 6. At this point Clark's G-3 (operations officer), Brigadier General Donald Brann, arrived at VI Corps headquarters, where Major General Lucian Truscott was in command. Clark, defying Alexander's orders, sent only one division toward Valmontone, while the whole weight of VI Corps was to push straight toward Rome. Truscott demanded to see Clark, but the Fifth Army commander had conveniently taken himself out of circulation.

In fact, Alexander had some intimation that Clark might disobey his orders, but he was not prepared to call his American commander on the carpet. In some ways Clark's insubordination was similar to Montgomery's disobedience in 1944 in not making the opening of Antwerp his first priority. But the difference was that Montgomery's disobedience reflected the field marshal's operational analysis of the situation, while Clark's disobedience reflected a vainglorious pursuit of publicity and prestige.

The Germans held Valmontone long enough to allow most of Tenth Army to escape. As Fifth Army pushed on toward Rome, it immediately ran into strong German defenses. However, the German I Airborne Corps failed to cover the steep slopes overlooking Velletri, and troops of the U.S. 36th Infantry Division seized the position. Kesselring now had to admit that he could not hold Rome, and German troops pulled north in good order. On 4 June Clark and his troops marched into an undefended city—whereupon the Pope highlighted his ambiguous record by asking that the Allies keep black troops out of the Eternal City. For a few brief moments, Clark basked in publicity on the front pages of American newspapers, but within two days Operation Overlord—the invasion of northern France—subsumed events in Italy, and Clark found his army and himself relegated to the back pages.

Still, the fighting in Italy did not cease. The Germans fell back toward their new Gothic Line in front of the Po River valley just north of Florence. There, they intended to take a strong stand, since industrial production in northern Italy, largely untouched by Allied bombing, was supplying weapons and other materiel in considerable quantities to the Reich. Over the course of the summer, Kesselring fought a series of delaying actions as his troops withdrew, and for once Hitler—distracted by events elsewhere in Europe—did not object to withdrawals. Kesselring was merely retreating to a line that Hitler had considered holding in fall 1943.

As their advance ground slowly northward, the Allies pulled seven divisions out of the theater for the invasion of southern France (its codename now changed from Anvil to Dragoon). Clark gave up three veteran U.S. divisions, his special forces of divisional strength, and all six of his French divisions. He was probably not sad to lose the last, since the French not only had proved cavalier in following his instructions but then had been successful in their disobedience to boot. After the war, a number of British commentators suggested that removal of these divisions from the Italian theater prevented Alexander from capturing the Po River valley and driving on to Trieste and Vienna. Given the record of Allied Armies Italy, it is possible that they might have captured the Po River valley, but the idea that they might have pushed on over the Alps to Vienna is inconceivable. After all, the Austrian Army had managed to use the mountains to hold off innumerable Italian attacks in World War I (and kill 600,000 Italians), and this time the defenders in the Alps would have been Germans, not Austrians. Moreover, Dragoon's contribution in opening up the ports of southern France proved crucial in meeting the Allies' supply crisis in France in fall 1944, especially after Montgomery's failure to open the Scheldt. Even more to the point, it hardly seems reasonable that France would leave its troops in Italy, while its own countryside was being liberated from the Germans.

In late August, Alexander's forces tried to break through into the Po with the remaining 18 Allied divisions. The Canadians delivered a skillful blow that came close to penetrating German defenses near the Adriatic and gaining the Po River valley. But the Eighth Army commander, General Oliver Leese, failed to position his reserves to take advantage of such a possibility. A plodding infantryman, Leese had been the XXX Corps commander at El Alamein, where his performance had been less than spectacular. As always, the Germans responded more quickly than did the Allies, and the possibilities opened up by the Canadian success disappeared. Moreover, the rainy season arrived to turn the battlefield into a morass that slowed movement to a crawl.

Clark's drive on Bologna opened on 10 September; the sterling U.S. 88th Infantry Division, one of the best in Italy, attempted to outflank the city to the east but failed. Clark followed up that effort with a series of straight-ahead attacks that bled his divisions white. In fact, the U.S. Army was facing a worldwide crisis in manpower, and the Italian theater was well down on the priority list for infantry replacements. This crisis finally brought home to Clark why the British were so much less willing than he to drive their divisions to exhaustion. As a result of their failures, the Allies could maintain only a weary watch on the Po River valley over the winter of 1944–45.

Mark Clark would move up to take command of the Allied army group in Italy, but that could hardly have assuaged his thirst for glory. In April 1945, Allied forces in Italy finally broke their German opponents, but largely as a result of the collapse of German forces elsewhere. To Allied strategists, the Italian theater had been a major disappointment; but to the troops who fought there it had been a horror, and for the Italian people it was nothing short of a catastrophe.

The Eastern Front, Summer–Fall 1943

The defeat of Operation Zitadelle at Kursk in early July 1943 had underscored how much the correlation of forces on the Eastern Front had changed since summer 1942. In that offensive, the Germans had attempted a limited military operation to bite off the Kursk salient and destroy the defending Soviet forces. Suffering frightful casualties, German attackers barely made a dent in Soviet defenses. As Hitler shut down the Kursk battle in mid-July, the German commanders in the theater had no idea what would transpire next in the east. Their worst imaginings could not have approached the terrifying reality that ensued. A series of stunning defeats far beyond their most pessimistic calculations unfolded over the next two years.

By now in summer 1943, the Red Army enjoyed a significant numerical superiority over its German opponents: 5,755,000 Soviet soldiers, 7,855 tanks, and 21,050 anti-tank guns, against 3,064,000 German soldiers with 2,088 tanks and 8,063 anti-tank guns. The Soviets also possessed considerable advantages in intelligence-gathering, deception, and the execution of operations. If Soviet attacks at times displayed tactical rigidity, a cavalier attitude toward logistics, and an over-reliance on firepower (the latter a reaction to the manpower losses the Red Army had suffered in the war's first two years), Soviet commanders executed their offensives with growing competence and confidence as the war on the Eastern Front ground on.

A good portion of the Soviet military's success in 1943 reflected the impact of the Lend-Lease program. Allied foodstuffs covered the gap between the Soviets' current production and the levels formerly produced in the vast grainbelt of the Ukraine. Western machine tools and raw materials supported the production of arms and ammunition. Military equipment from the West was probably of less significance; by 1943 the Soviets were producing rugged, easily maintained aircraft, though American and British aircraft were useful to the Red Air Force, particularly for transport. Lend-Lease's greatest impact undoubtedly was felt in the realm of logistics. Over the course of the war, the Western Allies shipped 11,800 locomotives and railroad cars to the Soviets, along with 409,000 cargo trucks, many of them with four-wheel drive, and 47,000 jeeps, all of which proved of inestimable value in maintaining the forward impetus of Soviet offensive operations. Could the Soviet Union have survived without Lend-Lease? Most probably. But the cost of the war for the Soviets would have been considerably higher.

Before Kursk, the Soviets had stationed powerful reserves near the battle zone. These reserves would have been flung into the battle if the Germans had made major gains. In fact, some of General Ivan Konev's forces had been drawn off to handle the attack of Field Marshal Erich von Manstein (commander of Army Group South) on the southern side of the Kursk salient. But the secondary purpose was to enable the Red Army to switch to the offensive in the south and center, once its forces in the Kursk salient had handled the immediate threat and worn down the Germans. On 12 July 1943 the Soviets felt confident enough to launch their first blow. The Bryansk and Western fronts opened with a series of attacks on the

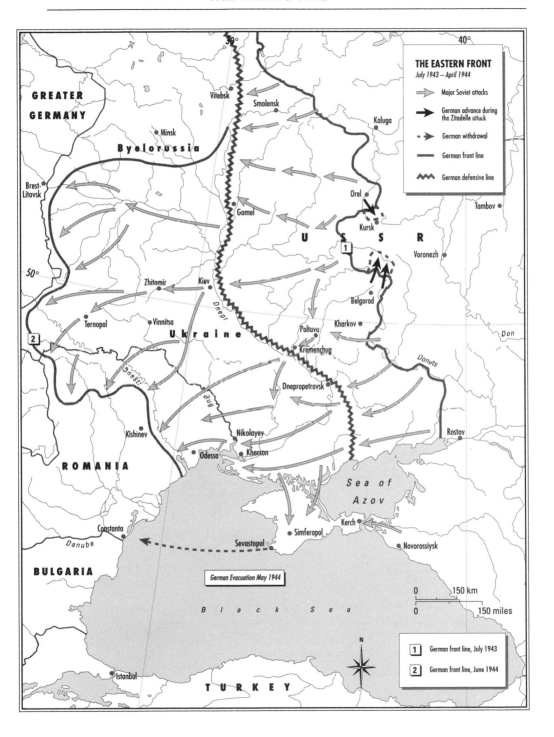

THE EASTERN FRONT
July 1943 – April 1944

⇨ Major Soviet attacks

➡ German advance during the Zitadelle attack

⇢ German withdrawal

— German front line

⋙ German defensive line

GREATER
GERMANY

Byelorussia

U   S   S   R

Ukraine

ROMANIA

BULGARIA

TURKEY

Vitebsk
Smolensk
Kaluga
Minsk
Orel
Tambov
Brest-Litovsk
Gomel
Kursk
Voronezh
Zhitomir
Kiev
Belgorod
Ternopol
Vinnitsa
Poltava
Kharkov
Don
Kremenchug
Donets
Dnepropetrovsk
Kishinev
Nikolayev
Rostov
Odessa
Kherson
Sea of
Azov
Constanta
Simferopol
Kerch
Danube
Sevastopol
Novorossiysk

German Evacuation May 1944

Black   Sea

Istanbul

Dnepr

Dniester

Bug

50°
30°
40°

0   150 km
0   150 miles

N

1 German front line, July 1943

2 German front line, June 1944

northern side of the Orel salient. Almost immediately they scored a major breakthrough in the north that threatened the entire German position in the salient. Field Marshal Günther von Kluge, still Army Group Center commander, immediately diverted two divisions scheduled to go to Generaloberst Walter Model's Ninth Army and called on the latter to release two of his panzer divisions. The next day Model received command of the entire Orel salient.

Soon to emerge as the Wehrmacht's expert on defensive war, Model had a knack for extracting uncharacteristic concessions from the Führer. For example, Hitler allowed Model to begin construction on defensive positions west of Orel, and then at the end of July, after a skillful German defensive effort and bad weather had taken the sting out of the Soviet offensive, to pull out of the Orel salient entirely. Hitler's agreement reflected his confidence in Model, one of the most ardent Nazis among the senior generals and one of the more competent ones as well. But it also reflected Hitler's need to release additional divisions to meet Germany's growing difficulties in Italy and in the Ukraine.

Manstein had been the only commander on the Eastern Front to urge Hitler to continue Zitadelle; the relative success of Manstein's forces convinced the field marshal, even after the cancellation of Zitadelle, that his operations had gutted much of Soviet offensive capabilities. Thus, he moved a substantial portion of his armored reserves south to handle Soviet diversionary attacks along the lower Dnepr and Mius rivers. Manstein urged the OKW in late July either to give him reinforcements or to allow him to pull back from the Donets River to the Dnepr River. Given the situation elsewhere, the former was impossible, while Hitler refused to allow any loss of territory where active operations were not under way.

Manstein's problem was that Army Group South was defending a long front along the Donets with inadequate forces; moreover, the terrain lying behind the Donets offered outstanding territory for Soviet exploitation, but minimal advantages for defensive purposes. In operational terms, a breakthrough on Army Group South's left flank between the Kursk salient and Kharkov would open up clear avenues for the Soviets to exploit through to the Dnepr and allow them to cut German supply lines supporting the forces along the Donets. On 3 August the Soviets struck. Immediately, the Germans were in trouble, their difficulties exacerbated by the fact that Manstein's overconfidence had led him to place his troops in positions seized in the Kursk offensive rather than to pull them back to their old, more defensible positions. Nevertheless, the Soviets faced a hard fight, and it was not until late afternoon of 5 August that they broke through German defenses. By nightfall, Soviet troops were 60 kilometers behind German lines, while Belgorod fell on the same day.

Caught by surprise, the Germans responded with dispatch. Hitler immediately released Großdeutschland and 7th Panzer Divisions from Army Group Center, although Kluge and Model persuaded him to limit the call on their forces. The OKH ordered SS Divisions Das Reich and Totenkopf, which had been about to depart for Italy, to Army Group South. However, Hitler refused Manstein's urgent pleas to pull back from the Donets Line, despite the fact that no additional reserves remained in the area. Meanwhile, the Soviets had achieved a major breakthrough that split Fourth Panzer Army and Army Detachment Kempf apart and created a 35-mile gap through which a whole Soviet front (the equivalent of a German army) began to pour. The only forces standing between the Soviets and the Dnepr was a single German division at Poltava. With reinforcements arriving in piecemeal fashion, Manstein had to place them at the shoulders of the breakthrough. Limited German counterattacks failed to master a deteriorating situation: over the period 13–17 August, Soviet forces fought SS panzer units to a draw near Bogodukhov. Meanwhile, Hitler stridently demanded that Kempf hold Kharkov. Kempf's prediction that another Stalingrad was in the making contributed to his relief on 14 August. Army Detachment Kempf received the new title of Eighth Army several days later.

As the war on the Eastern Front deteriorated, Hitler did order construction to begin on a defensive line, but throughout the remainder of the summer he displayed no disposition to authorize retreats to more defensible positions or to shorten lines. With strong German forces on his flanks, Colonel General N. F. Vatutin turned in against Eighth Army to force the Germans out of Kharkov. Heavy fighting by Vatutin's forces allowed Konev's front finally to liberate Kharkov over the night of 21–22 August. Nevertheless, the Soviets' concentration on that city gave Manstein an opportunity to plug the gap between Fourth Panzer Army and Eighth Army. A new Soviet drive in the south now counterbalanced Manstein's success in the north. By the end of the month, the Soviets had driven First Panzer and Sixth Armies (reconstituted since Stalingrad) out of the Donbas and back to the so-called Panther Line. Thus, while the Soviets had achieved a major breakthrough at the beginning of the month, they had failed to exploit their advantage. But the heavy fighting had further worn down German divisions and increased the imbalance between the opposing forces. And Hitler's refusal to make any hard decisions on preemptive withdrawals exposed German forces to further attack at the hands of the Soviets.

In late summer 1943 the Soviets were following a pattern in operations quite different from the deep-encirclement operational concept the Germans had used in 1941 or their own effort in January–February 1943 to exploit the breakthrough on the Don. Undoubtedly, the serious setback precipitated by Manstein's late winter counterattack introduced an element of caution into the Soviet conduct of operations. The overall pattern represented a series of fluid offensives in which, when thwarted in one area, Soviet fronts rapidly shifted the axis of advance or reinforced areas where their forces had been more successful. This continual pressure kept the Germans permanently off balance, always responding to one desperate situation after another and never able to prepare an operational response of their own.

In the center and north, the Soviets proved less adept. A major offensive against Army Group North in late August failed dismally. A series of attacks on Army Group Center were no more successful, since the Germans had fallen back to a fairly well-prepared defensive position. But these attacks kept the Germans pinned down and prevented either army group from providing reinforcements to the rapidly deteriorating situation in the south. In its initial attack on 26 August, Colonel General Rokossovsky's Central Front failed to gain operational advantage as the German Second Army, informed by aerial reconnaissance where the main attack was likely to come, put up an effective defense. But instead of reinforcing failure—the trademark of Soviet operations in 1941—Rokossovsky transferred two of his corps 60 miles to the south and then threw them into a subsidiary attack that soon made significant progress against Second Army's southern flank. By the third week in September, three of the Central Front's armies, supported by the two mechanized corps, had sundered the connections between Army Group South and Center and were approaching Kiev from the northeast.

While Manstein's left flank was now up in the air, he was confronting equally disconcerting news on his right. First Panzer Army, pulled back from the Donets River line as Sixth Army fell back on the Kalmius River, lost its grip; the open steppe simply could not provide defensible positions. Having closed rapidly on the retreating Germans, Southwest Front hit First Panzer and Sixth Armies with a major attack three days after they had arrived in their new positions. Within two days, Colonel General Rodin Malinovsky's XXIII Tank Corps and I Guards Mechanized Corps were 100 miles behind German front lines. The desperate situation finally forced Hitler to order a pullback of Army Group South to the Dnepr and Army Group Center to the Panther Line. The latter move should have freed up a number of divisions. However, almost immediately the Führer reneged on the agreement, while Kluge persuaded the Führer to go slow on the pullback in Army Group Center, thus allowing the army group to keep most of its divisions.

For Manstein and Army Group South, the retreat back to the Dnepr came too late. By waiting so long to make a sensible operational decision to retreat to more defensible positions, Hitler had produced two negative effects. The ferocious fighting in July, August, and early September severely reduced most of Army Group South's divisions. Even more important, the Germans had been badly beaten, and if the Führer and his generals did not understand this fact, the troops certainly did. The retreat to the Dnepr did not result in a complete collapse—Malinovsky's two spearhead corps, for example, received a thorough beating as they reestablished contact with their supporting forces, and in most areas the Germans were able to make an organized withdrawal—but in some areas the German forces did become unglued. One soldier in the Großdeutschland remembered a crossing near Kiev in the following terms: "We heard the sounds of gunfire and explosions coming closer, punctuated by bloodcurdling screams. Men suddenly plunged out of the pale, enveloping [fog], and disappeared like ghosts into the black water. From the sounds of the splashing, we guessed they were trying to swim. We felt petrified by fear, and stayed where we were. A terrible growling mass of machines passed by close to us, shaking the earth and water, and a penetrating headlight pierced the fog. We couldn't see where it was going, only that it was moving . . . We could hear the sounds of machine guns ripping into the air very close to us, over the grinding roar of the tank treads. And always, terrifying screams, as the tanks drove a bloody furrow through the tightly packed crowds paralyzed by terror and darkness. A little higher up, two other lights, barely visible in the gloom, were seeking out other victims."[4]

The Germans recrossed the Dnepr at a relatively small number of places. While the Soviet forces pursuing them had also suffered heavy losses in the fighting, they could aim at the Dnepr across its entire length. Thus, as the Germans pulled back through their major crossing points, the Soviets bounced the Dnepr and established several bridgeheads on the river's left bank. The Steppe Front, for example, seized three small bridgeheads between Kremenchug and Dnepropetrovsk, which it then expanded into a single major enclave on the west bank 30 miles wide and 10 miles deep. Across the length of the Dnepr River Line, the Soviet bridgeheads meant that to all intents and purposes the Germans had lost control of the Dnepr before they even had a chance to hold it. The Soviets did call a short halt to operations in early October to reorganize, refit, and resupply units involved in constant fighting over the past three months. For the rest of October into early November, the northern portion of the Dnepr front settled into an uneasy calm.

By now STAVKA had decided that Soviet operations would focus on driving the Germans out of the Ukraine and would leave Army Group Center for a later reckoning. A major breakout attempt from the Kremenchug bridgehead allowed Konev's forces to take Krivoi Rog in mid-October, only to lose that Ukrainian town to a German counterattack. But the major Soviet break in October came in the far south. Fourth Ukrainian Front began a major attack on 9 October against Sixth Army's defenses surrounding Melitopol. Despite overwhelming superiority in numbers and firepower (15,000 shell bursts in two German divisional sectors in a two-hour period), Soviet attackers required two weeks to capture the city and create a breakthrough. On 25 October, Twenty-Eighth and Fifty-First Armies broke into the open.

Once again Hitler refused to make a hard decision, this time whether to pull Seventeenth Army out of the Crimea. By 3 November the Soviets had reached the Black Sea and cut off Seventeenth Army. The remnants of Sixth Army fell back on the southern reaches of the Dnepr, but Hitler demanded that First Panzer Army hold Nikopol as a jumping-off point for a counterattack to recreate links to the Crimea. By the end of October, Manstein had succeeded in bringing some order to his right flank, but almost immediately a new crisis blew up on Army Group South's left near Kiev. Vatutin attempted to take Kiev from the Bukrin bridgehead, but the German defenders thwarted the breakout attempt. Vatutin immediately shifted to the Liutezh bridgehead. Only by buttoning T-34 tanks up and running them through river crossings at full speed (many of them did not make it) were the Soviets able to assemble sufficient armored forces in the swampy bridgehead. The Germans never expected the Soviets to strike from such an area, but strike they did, achieving a clear breakthrough that almost immediately led to the liberation of Kiev.

It also wrecked whatever chance the Germans had of making a stand on the Dnepr. Once again Manstein had to rush his weary mechanized forces to stem another crisis. Vatutin's spearheads captured Fastov—the crucial center on which much of the logistical system of Manstein's Army Group depended—before German defenders could arrive. On 10 November XLVIII Panzer Corps gave the lead Soviet spearheads a severe beating near Fastov but failed to retake the city.

Manstein's hopes of gaining another success by a counterattack similar to his victory at Kharkov in March 1943 foundered on greater Soviet sophistication at the tactical and operational levels. The Germans gained some local successes in heavy fighting throughout the rest of November and into December, and in one case they managed to destroy a portion of 1st Guards Cavalry Corps, which had liberated Fourth Panzer Army's liquor supply and was not exactly in fighting trim. But the Dnepr Line was no longer defensible.

The Eastern Front, Winter–Spring 1944

Winter provided no let-up in the pounding the Germans received at the hands of their Soviet tormentors. The blunting of an offensive in one area was almost immediately followed by major attacks elsewhere, after the Germans had denuded the area of reserves. The disparity in forces was even greater than in the summer. At the end of 1943 the Germans possessed approximately 2.5 million troops on the Eastern Front, supported by 700,000 satellite soldiers. Nazi forces included 26 panzer divisions with approximately 2,300 tanks; artillery tubes numbered slightly over 8,000, nearly 2,000 under the numbers of high-velocity guns that were defending German skies against the depredations of the Combined Bomber Offensive. Finally, the Luftwaffe possessed approximately 3,000 aircraft. On the other side of the hill, the Red Army mustered nearly 6.4 million soldiers, 5,800 tanks, and 13,400 aircraft.

But what gave the Red Army an even larger edge than the three-to-one ratio suggested by these figures was that Soviet *maskirovka* (deception) consistently misled the Germans as to where the Red Army would next strike. One might have thought the Germans could have picked up what Soviet *maskirovka* was doing to their intelligence estimates, given the continuing series of operational surprises. But as was the case with Ultra, the Germans' fanatical belief in their own superiority made the idea that Slavs could manipulate German intelligence with such consistency utterly inconceivable. As the situation became more and more desperate, Manstein could only issue platitudes like: "He who holds his positions for a minute longer will have won."[5]

Operations at the end of December suggest the extent of German self-deception. Manstein launched a major counterattack along the Korosten-Kiev Line and destroyed what turned out to be Soviet *maskirovka* forces covering for another major offensive by Vatutin's First Ukrainian Front. On Christmas day, the real Soviet offensive began. First Guards and First Tank Armies, led by 14 infantry divisions and 4 mechanized corps (each equivalent to a full-strength German panzer division), blasted through German defenses and headed southwest toward Berditchev and Kazatin. This move threatened Army Group South's entire left flank. The offensive ended German illusions that Soviet forces were as exhausted by the summer and fall battles as German forces were. Manstein desperately requested permission to pull back the remaining troops along the Dnepr to free up reserves. The OKH at Hitler's direction did allow some pullbacks and promised reinforcements, but it failed to give Manstein the kind of operational freedom the grave situation demanded. On 28 December the lead spearheads of First Ukrainian Front reached Kazatin, a major supply center, and destroyed hundreds of German trucks; by evening the Germans held only half the city, while Fourth Panzer Army appeared on the brink of collapse.

Exacerbating Manstein's difficulties was the fact that the OKW, which held responsibility for the western and Mediterranean theaters, had recognized that Anglo-American forces would make the long-advertised invasion of Europe in the spring or early summer of the coming year. Thus, Keitel and Jodl persuaded Hitler not to withdraw the refitted, reorganized German divisions from France and Belgium but rather to build up German forces in the west to defeat the invasion. Such a German victory would then allow the Wehrmacht to turn its full military power against the Soviet Union. Thus, over the course of the winter fighting in the Ukraine, the OKW lost only one division (from Norway) and three regiments of recruits from its theaters, while considerable reinforcements flowed out of the Reich to the western and the Mediterranean theaters.

In early January 1944, Vatutin's First Ukrainian Front, which had initially concentrated on Fourth Panzer Army, worked its way around the Germans' right flank and suddenly positioned itself to threaten again the security of Army Group South. On the 4th, Manstein visited Hitler and requested permission to abandon the Dnepr bend; however, knowing Hitler's predispositions, he was unwilling to suggest that his army group pull all the way back to the Bug River. The German position certainly appeared desperate enough. Besides the threat to the German forces remaining near the Dnepr, the gap between Army Group Center and Army Group South had grown to over 100 miles. Only the existence of the Pripyat Marsh prevented the Soviets from destroying the entire Nazi position on the Eastern Front.

Sustained fighting over the past six months had decimated the German divisions. In early January, XIII Corps reported that its divisions were down to less than 300 infantrymen, and the whole corps had a frontline strength equivalent to that of a single regiment. So desperate was the manpower situation that reinforcing divisions from the west often were committed to the fight without time to acclimatize to theater conditions and in some cases before all their equipment and weapons had arrived. The appalling attrition of combat infantry raises the question of why German soldiers persevered. It certainly could not have been group cohesion alone, given the losses suffered.

The explanation seems to be that at every level German officers inculcated their troops with the values and assumptions of Nazi ideology and the mortal menace of the racial-Communist threat. By early 1944, ideological indoctrination was playing a major role in combat preparation on both the Eastern and Western Fronts. After the war, German generals claimed that neither they nor their troops had taken ideological instruction seriously, but the evidence suggests otherwise. Not only do the letters and diaries of combat soldiers indicate that ideology was a considerable factor in German combat effectiveness, but unit commanders from the division level on down consistently picked highly decorated combat officers to serve as "leadership" officers in charge of troop indoctrination. Such assignments underline the seriousness with which the army as a whole was taking ideological motivation.

All of this Nazi indoctrination was then backed up by a military justice system whose ruthlessness only the Soviets exceeded. In World War I the German Army had executed only 48 of its soldiers for breaches of military discipline. In World War II, by contrast, the German Army executed somewhere between 13,000 and 15,000 soldiers as a direct result of courts-martial for subversion, desertion, or disobedience in the front lines. And that total does not include the tens of thousands ordered to serve in penal battalions—assignments which for all intents and purposes were equivalent to death sentences.

Hitler still refused to allow Army Group South to pull back from the growing salient that Vatutin's advance was creating by its drive past First Panzer and Eighth Armies. Throughout mid-January, Manstein struggled to reknit the front between Fourth Panzer and First Panzer Armies. German counterattacks enjoyed even less success than Army Group South's attacks in December; there would be no replay of the second battle of Kharkov. On 24 January, the second Soviet hammer dropped on Army Group South. Fourth Guards and Fifty-Third Armies, assigned to Konev's Second Ukrainian Front, broke through German defensive positions east of Korsun-Shevchenkovskii. Vatutin's front attacking from the west had a harder time, but by 3 February 1944 Soviet forces had linked up and trapped XI and XLII Corps in the Cherkassy pocket. Manstein quickly assembled a rescue force consisting of three understrength army panzer divisions and the Waffen SS panzer division Leibstandarte Adolf Hitler. The rescue force never quite broke through to the pocket, owing to intense Soviet resistance, but those in the pocket launched a desperate breakout attempt after abandoning and destroying their heavy equipment. The survivors of the SS Wiking Division of Nordic Fascists had to swim the Gniloy Tikich River, where hundreds drowned in the icy waters.

There is some question about how many troops escaped. The Germans claimed 30,000, while the Soviets reported 55,000 Germans killed or wounded in the operation and 18,000 captured. Whatever the claims, those who did escape were in such desperate shape that they had to be shipped to Poland for reconstitution. Stalin rewarded Konev with promotion to the rank of Marshal of the Soviet Union. Vatutin might have received a similar promotion, but at the end of the month Ukrainian partisans, engaged in a hopeless effort to free their homeland from both Hitler and Stalin, had killed him.

Throughout March, terrible weather on the Eastern Front, wavering between freezing and thawing, heavy snow and rain, turned the Ukraine into a glutinous sea of mud. Nevertheless, the Soviets were able to maintain their uninterrupted assault on Army Group South because of two key advantages, the first in tank design and the second in support vehicles. The conventional explanation for the cross-country maneuverability of Soviet armor, particularly that of the exceptional T-34, has been the wider treads of the tanks. However, the Soviet advantage in tank mobility resulted largely from the fact that the center of gravity of the T-34 resided in the center rather than the front of the vehicle. German tanks, particularly the heavy Tigers and Panthers, with centers of gravity well forward, tended to go nose down in mud, whereas the T-34s rode smoothly cross-country or over muddy roads. Soviet naval engineers had suggested this crucial change in the 1930s, when they participated on tank-design teams. Added to the Soviets' advantage in tank maneuverability was an influx of American four-wheel drive vehicles which helped move supplies to spearhead units. German mobility during the spring mud season *(rasputitsa)*, by contrast, depended to a great extent on peasant *panje* wagons.

The STAVKA aimed to drive the Germans out of the Ukraine by spring and position the Red Army for a drive into the Balkans. The Germans continued to hope that the *rasputitsa* would halt operations, but they would have no pause until May. Having cleaned up the Cherkassy pocket, the Soviets redeployed, again aiming to break loose on Fourth Panzer Army's left. Three Soviet tank armies moved to the northwestern flank of Army Group South in the last days of February and first days of March. Manstein had attempted to strengthen Army Group South's front in the north, but his forces remained largely rooted halfway between the Dnepr and the Bug in an indefensible sea of mud. Most dangerous to the Germans was the fact that the Soviets had not yet committed all their reserves; even after the winter's heavy fighting, they still retained substantial numbers of fresh troops.

First Ukrainian Front, with Zhukov in command as Vatutin's replacement, now indicated how idle were German hopes that the *rasputitsa* would stop military operations. On 4 March, Zhukov launched his forces in a sledgehammer attack at the gap between First and Fourth Panzer Armies. Third Guards Tank Army broke cleanly through and headed south. Subsequent Soviet attacks followed in the next several days, but the thrust by the Third Guards Tank Army was definitely the most dangerous. Manstein hoped to lop off its lead spearheads with an attack from Ternopol in the west by Fourth Panzer Army and with an attack from Proskurov in the east by First Panzer Army. But as Soviet forces drove south, First Panzer Army's counterattack force of four panzer divisions was just beginning to entrain. For the moment, Manstein stitched together sufficient forces to hold the front between Ternopol and Proskurov, but Zhukov was clearly bringing up further reinforcements to reopen the way south. Moreover, Army Group South was confronting equally serious threats to its right flank.

The drive by Third Guards Tank Army was only the first of a number of emergencies that confronted Manstein in his last month of command. On 6 March, Sixtieth and First Guards Armies achieved breakthroughs that soon isolated the German LIX Corps at Staro Constantinov. Meanwhile, Konev's Second Ukrainian Front had struck in the east. No less than three Soviet armies hit Eighth Army north of Uman; within two days that city was in Soviet hands. As Konev's drive gathered steam, its objective was clearly to link up with Zhukov's forces—a move which would encircle the entire left wing of Army Group South. German units, with most of their equipment mired in the mud, struggled south toward the Bug. Hitler's continued refusal to withdraw meant that there was no hope of holding the line on that river, and it was even doubtful whether the Germans could hold on the Dnestr. To add to the confusion, the Führer declared a number of cities and towns as fortresses, in which the troops, from commanding general on down, would fight to the death. The honor of commanding such positions was soon known within the army's senior ranks as Himmelfahrtskommandos or "trip-to-heaven commands." Hitler's belief was that such strong points would slow down the onrush of Soviet forces; in fact, they represented one more excuse to delay making decisions in crucial operational situations.

As Manstein struggled to restore the collapse on Army Group South's right flank, Zhukov brought up additional reinforcements. On 21 March, he unleashed three tank armies, backed up by First Guards Army on the German defensive line between Ternopol and Proskurov. The attackers drove 200 tanks through German defenses on the first day and never looked back. Once again a Soviet attack had blasted First and Fourth Panzer Armies apart. By the 23rd, Soviet pressure had pushed German forces behind Ternopol. Since Hitler had refused to make a decision to withdraw, a substantial body of troops remained in the "fortress" of Ternopol. Meanwhile, Zhukov's spearheads had reached Chortkov 60 miles to the south on their way to meeting up with Konev's forces south of the Dnestr. The latter's forces had just crossed the Dnestr at Yampol. For the moment it appeared the Soviets had put all of First Panzer Army in the bag; the loss of its single-track railroad had entirely isolated the panzer army between the two great Soviet drives.

On 25 March, after an all-day series of arguments, Manstein persuaded Hitler to order First Panzer Army to break out, while at the same time he received II SS Panzer Corps (the Hohenstaufen and Frundsberg panzer divisions) along with two army infantry divisions. In effect, the decision touched a significant portion of the reserves the OKW and Hitler were planning to use for the defense of the west in the spring. Thus, Soviet attacks in the Ukraine played a significant role in the Allied success in Normandy by denying German commanders in the west use of four first-class divisions in the opening days of the battle (the two SS divisions would arrive late).

For its breakout, First Panzer Army attacked toward Fourth Panzer Army, directly across the lines of communications of Zhukov's Fourth and First Tank Armies. The Germans had to reverse their front and attack to the rear, while at the same time keeping a sufficient rearguard to prevent the Soviets from exploiting the retreat. A heavy blizzard masked the movement; when the snow cleared, Zhukov rushed forces to prevent the Germans from crossing the Seret River. He failed. Supported by Ju-52s flying in ammunition and fuel, the Germans forded the river. Two days later, II SS Panzer Corps, arriving from Germany, opened up a major attack and broke through to First Panzer Army. By 10 April the survivors, in considerably better shape than those who had escaped the Cherkassy pocket in February, were back behind German lines.

While First Panzer Army fought for its life, the Soviets administered a series of stinging blows against Eighth Army and Army Group A (Sixth Army). Nevertheless, while the Soviets had broken through German defenses in a number of places, they never achieved the kind of operational

64. American troops come ashore in North Africa on 8 November 1942 as part of Operation Torch. One of the soldiers carries a large American flag in the hope that the French would not fire. In fact, the Vichy French put up fierce resistance against the Allies in Algiers and Morocco but none against German paratroopers in Tunisia.

65. British light armor lines up along the waterfront in Tripoli after the fall of Libya's capital to Montgomery's Eighth Army.

66. In Tunisia in spring 1943, the rival prima donnas Montgomery and Patton prepare for the invasion of Sicily.

67. A long line of LSTs (landing ships tanks) prepare to take on board their complement of Sherman tanks from a U.S. armored unit for Operation Husky.

68. A British sniper in Cupa, Italy.

69. British troops work their way through a Sicilian town in July 1943.

70. Hap Arnold, commander of U.S. Army Air Forces, visits the Italian front in December 1943. Here he is receiving a briefing from Fifth Army Commander Mark Clark.

71. Guarded by police and SS troops, Jews from the Warsaw Ghetto wend their way through the city streets to the trains that will take them to Auschwitz.

72. In January 1943 Soviet troops fight their way into Rostov for the second time in a year as they liberate the city.

73. Hitler and Manstein discuss the possibilities for Army Group South to counterattack Soviet spearheads in February 1943.

74. During the Battle of Kursk—the climatic battle of World War II on the Eastern Front—
Soviet infantry follow in the wake of T-34s in ferocious close fighting.

75. German panzer grenadiers jump from their armored half track as they come under
heavy Soviet fire during the failed drive from the Orel salient.

76. Soviet rocket launchers lay down a heavy barrage on German positions during the early stages of the Battle of Kursk. The Red Army's artillery was one of its major advantages during the last half of the war.

77. Soviet troops pass by a burning German tank in fighting that liberated Kiev in fall 1943.

78. One of the Soviet Union's most effective military leaders, Marshal Ivan Konev looks somewhat bemusedly at the camera.

79. A B-17 formation heads to the Reich in summer 1943. In deep penetration raids, the B-17s suffered "unacceptable" casualties as a result of U.S. and British air leaders' general lack of interest in long-range escort fighters.

80. The results of precision bombing show clearly in this Eighth Air Force raid on the French Hispano Suiza aircraft engine repair depot near Paris on 31 December 1943.

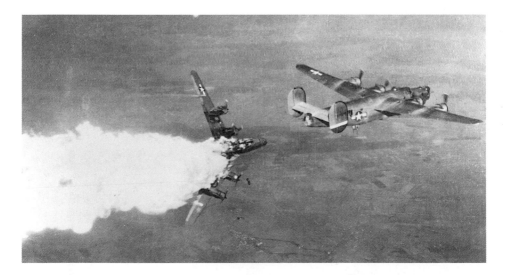

81 & 82. During the battle for air superiority in summer 1944, a B-24 breaks in half and is engulfed in flames as the result of a direct hit by German flak, and a Bf 109 pilot bails out of his aircraft.

83. A FW 190 blows up at low altitude in summer 1944, as captured in the gun camera film of a U.S. fighter.

84. In February 1945, bodies line the streets of Dresden awaiting disposal after the firestorm that resulted from one of Bomber Command's most successful raids.

85. The catapult officer of the *Enterprise* rescues the pilot of a Grumman F6F fighter after a raid on Makin Island, Central Pacific, in November 1943. Carrier aviation allowed the U.S. Navy to destroy the Combined Fleet.

86. Soldiers of the U.S. 27th Infantry Division wade ashore on Butaritari Island, Makin Atoll, on 20 November 1943 as part of a campaign to eliminate Japanese reconnaissance airbases in the Gilbert Islands.

87. Marines of the 2d Marine Division seal a Japanese command bunker on Betio Island, Tarawa Atoll, Gilbert Islands, on 20 November 1943. The assault on Betio cost the marines more than 1,000 men but produced lessons on how to use naval gunfire against fortifications.

88. Profiting from the lessons of Tarawa, the 4th Marine Division captures Roi-Namur Atoll, Marshall Islands, in January 1944 and wipes out the Japanese garrison with minimum casualties. Marine artillery firing from neighboring islets and naval gunfire sealed the fate of these Japanese defenders.

89. Kwajalein Atoll, Marshall Islands, provides an anchorage and fleet logistics base for future naval operations after its capture in February 1944. Extemporized advanced naval bases and ship-to-ship underway replenishment allowed the Pacific Fleet to operate at a tempo the Japanese could not match.

90. Soldiers of the U.S. 37th Infantry Division work with a Sherman medium tank to eliminate a Japanese bunker on Bougainville, Northern Solomons, March 1944, in the last phase of the campaign to isolate Rabaul. Tank-infantry coordination proved essential in jungle warfare.

91. African-American soldiers of the 25th Infantry Regiment go into battle on Bougainville in the Americal Division, April 1944. One of the earliest experiments in limited racial integration in the army, the 25th Infantry proved its battle-worthiness on Bougainville.

92. General Douglas MacArthur and Admiral Chester W. Nimitz discuss Pacific war strategy in a meeting at MacArthur's headquarters in Brisbane, Australia, in March 1944. With Rabaul isolated, MacArthur redirected his Southwest Pacific forces toward western New Guinea and the Philippines, while Nimitz enlarged and sped up his naval campaign in the Central Pacific.

93. Marines of the 2nd Marine Division land in intense shellfire at Saipan, the Mariana Islands, in June 1944. The V Amphibious Corps of two marine and one army divisions required four weeks of intense combat to eliminate a Japanese garrison of 32,000. The capture of Saipan allowed the subsequent capture of Tinian and Guam.

94. Dead marines mark the Saipan beaches. A large agricultural island with mountains and caves, Saipan gave Japanese mobile artillery and tanks room to maneuver and hide until destroyed by marine close air support.

95. Lieutenant General Holland M. Smith, commander V Amphibious Corps, tours Saipan. The campaign for the Marianas lured the Combined Fleet out for the Battle of the Philippine Sea—a catastrophic defeat for Japanese naval aviation—and provided bases for American air and submarine attacks on Japan's economic lifeline to Southeast Asia.

96. Infantry battalions of the 4th Marine Division spearhead the amphibious assault on Tinian, the Marianas, in July 1944. The marines are riding an amphibian tractor or Landing Vehicle Tracked-4 (LVT-4). The capture of Tinian provided a base for B-29 heavy bombers from which to bomb the Home Islands.

freedom that Zhukov and Konev had achieved to the north. As a result, both German armies successfully retreated from the Ingulets River to the Bug. Then, on 28 March, both began a withdrawal to the Dnestr without the threat of catastrophic defeat that had hung over German forces farther north. Nevertheless, a major Soviet breakthrough on 2 April that reached the Dnestr behind Odessa hastened the two Nazi armies back toward the Romanian frontier. Although the Germans reached the Dnestr Line, the Soviets had already seized a number of bridgeheads they would use to good effect when their offensive into the Balkans began in late August.

The distressing series of defeats and retreats finally led Hitler to decide on major command changes. On 30 March, Manstein and Kleist flew to Hitler's headquarters to receive the Knight's Cross to the Iron Cross and then to be summarily dismissed. Hitler told Manstein that the time for great operational maneuvers had ended and Germany now needed commanders more capable of defending to the last man. After Manstein became convinced the Führer would not recall him to save the Reich, he displayed his grasp of strategy and politics by taking the substantial honorarium he received from Hitler as well as the family savings and buying an estate in East Prussia in October 1944.

Manstein and Kleist's replacements would be the thoroughly Nazi generals Model and Ferdinand Schörner. The latter's military capabilities are best suggested by the remark he had made when he was a corps commander in northern Lapland: "The Arctic does not exist."[6] Manstein's replacement, Model, had recently restored the situation in Army Group North after a major Soviet success in that theater. At the time Model received his assignment, he was writing a memorandum suggesting why Army Group North could only afford to give up two divisions to Army Group South. After dispensing with that draft, he wrote a new one which indicated that Army Group North could, in fact, afford to lose six divisions to support Army Group South. Hitler was persuaded, but the OKH's chief of staff, Kurt Zeitzler, intervened to reduce the number of divisions transferred to one.

Hitler decided to rename Army Group South and Army Group A as Army Group North Ukraine and Army Group South Ukraine. But all of his reorganizing and renaming did not end German troubles in the south. Despite the pleas of the Romanian dictator, Antonescu, that the Führer permit a withdrawal from the Crimea to save seven Romanian divisions on the peninsula, Hitler demanded that Axis forces stand firm. He still worried that the Crimea would serve as a base from which Allied air power could attack the Romanian oil fields. There was some irony in this position, because beginning in March 1944 American bombers, flying out of the Foggia fields in Italy, opened up an offensive aimed at destroying the Romanian oil fields. By spring Hitler had also pushed considerable German resources onto the Crimea to defend the Perekop isthmus and Kerch peninsula, where the Soviets had again established themselves. Over the course of the winter, the Crimea received four German divisions as reinforcements. In addition, two self-propelled assault gun brigades, almost the equivalent of a panzer division, had also arrived. Hitler had ordered these reinforcements despite the desperate situation in Army Group South. The Germans and Romanians did have time to build substantial defenses on the Perekop isthmus and Kerch peninsula, but beyond those positions there were no other defensible positions on the Crimea until one reached Sevastopol.

On 7 April, Schörner arrived to inspect the Crimea's defenses. Displaying extraordinarily bad timing as well as little ability as an analyst, the general pronounced the fortifications outstanding and defensible "for a long time." The next morning Fourth Ukrainian Front attacked and within two days had destroyed the 10th Romanian Division holding a portion of the Sivash bridgehead. German commanders on the scene had no choice but to authorize a withdrawal to Sevastopol. Hitler was furious, but since Schörner confirmed the need for a retreat urged by the Seventeenth Army commander, the Führer acquiesced.

Nevertheless, Hitler demanded that German forces hold Sevastopol indefinitely even though denying the Soviets air bases on the Crimean peninsula was no longer a possibility. By 12 April the Soviets had broken through an interim line the Germans had established, and by the 16th the Germans had fallen back into Sevastopol's defenses. Unfortunately for the Germans in the Crimea, the Luftwaffe and navy painted a rosy picture of their ability to supply the "fortress," thus reinforcing Hitler's determination that Seventeenth Army hang onto Sevastopol. As he explained to Schörner, he needed to hold onto the Crimean city for six to eight weeks until he had defeated the Anglo-American invasion in the west. In an extraordinary piece of moral courage, the Seventeenth Army commander, General der Pioniere Erwin Jaenecke, requested that his army be directly subordinated to Hitler, thus making the looming disaster the Führer's responsibility. For his honesty, he was immediately relieved. In early May, Antonescu again sent a desperate message requesting a withdrawal so that the Romanian formations could return to defend their borders, where Soviet forces were already gathering. So tense was the atmosphere that Hitler's headquarters staff refused even to show the Führer the message.

Thus, Seventeenth Army remained in Sevastopol. The Red Army now ended the debate. On 5 May, a feint attack focused German attention on the north side of the city's defenses. Two days later the main offensive surged over the Balaklava heights where the British Light Brigade had ridden to its death nearly a century before. By the end of the first day, the Soviets had seized the Sapun heights. German counterattacks failed to drive them back, and in the face of certain defeat Hitler finally authorized withdrawal. The German Navy bungled the effort, and 26,700 Axis soldiers fell into Soviet hands out of a garrison that had numbered over 64,000 at the beginning of May. Given the high casualty rate in the fighting, the Germans probably rescued barely 20,000. Hitler's callous disregard for Romanian interests destroyed what little support remained for Antonescu and set the stage for Romania's complete collapse at the end of August.

Army Group North, Winter 1944

For the period after the end of the Soviet winter offensive in April 1942, Army Group North had suffered few of the travails that had marked the terrible fighting on the Eastern Front farther in the south. The Soviets launched a number of attacks over the course of 1942 and 1943, but they had achieved minimum success. Meanwhile, in response to directions from the OKH and Hitler in September 1943, Army Group North began construction of a defensive line, called the Panther position. But unlike Manstein's desperate efforts in the south, Army Group North was under no pressure and hence could undertake major engineering work on the line. German engineers, helped by thousands of slave laborers, built 800 concrete bunkers and over 5,000 field bunkers, laid 125 miles of barbed wire, and dug vast trench systems and anti-tank ditches. The new line stretched from the Baltic up the Narva River and along the western shores of Lakes Peipus and Pskov, and then into the swamps south of Pskov. Besides the advantage to the Germans of falling back to a carefully prepared position with which the Soviets were unfamiliar, the new line was 25 percent shorter than the old line and would free up substantial numbers of troops.

Army Group North's staff planned to begin a pullback in mid-January. But at the end of December the OKH began redeploying units from the north to help in the south. At that time, the army group commander, Field Marshal Georg von Kuechler, actually persuaded Hitler to authorize a retreat to the Panther position. Unfortunately for the Germans, the Eighteenth Army commander, Generaloberst Georg Lindemann, reported to Hitler that his corps and division commanders believed they could hold their present positions. That was enough for Hitler, and Army Group North, including Eighteenth Army, remained in place.

In mid-January the Soviets struck, this time with better prepared and stronger forces, while the Germans had already lost three divisions. The Soviets possessed the equivalent of over 60 divisions, against 20 Nazi divisions; they also possessed a six-to-one advantage in tanks. And, as was now happening on a regular basis, *maskirovka* threw a solid cloak over Soviet preparations. Leningrad Front immediately placed great pressure on German forces still close to the city, while on Eighteenth Army's right Volkhov Front threatened Novgorod. One of the Luftwaffe field divisions—created from surplus air force personnel whom Hitler and Göring had refused to turn over to the army—collapsed on the second day of the Soviet attack. Within four days the situation in front of Leningrad had become desperate for Eighteenth Army. At Novgorod, Hitler authorized a retreat at the last moment, and most of the troops escaped. In the north, however, Soviet spearheads reached the czar's former summer residence at Krasnoye Selo and cut off two German divisions. Kuechler desperately pleaded for permission to retreat to the Panther Line, even though his considerable losses already would leave him barely enough men to hold the line. Hitler again refused to authorize a retreat, this time by claiming that a retreat would allow the Soviets a straight road to the Panther Line with all their forces. The German troops were to fight where they stood in order to inflict heavy casualties on Soviet forces. "The battle must be fought as far away as possible from the German border."[7]

By the 25th the Soviets had taken Krasnogvardeysk, thus compromising much of Eighteenth Army's supply situation. Not until 30 January, with Lindemann's army now broken into three pieces, did Hitler finally allow a retreat to the Luga River. But even then he demanded that Eighteenth Army restore its contact with Sixteenth Army and close off all Soviet penetrations, one of which was already 30 miles wide. On 31 January, Hitler dismissed Kuechler and assigned Model to restore the deteriorating situation. Model set the tone of his command with the message that no one would authorize a retreat at any level of command without his direct permission. Eighteenth Army had suffered terrible losses; while nearly 58,000 combat infantrymen had been on its rolls on 10 January, that number had fallen to an infantry strength of 17,000 even with the reinforcements that reached the army in the intervening period.

Throughout February the German position in the north remained tenuous. Ironically, Model suggested risky offensive operations to restore Eighteenth Army's situation along the Luga. Hitler, however, turned uncharacteristically cautious and favored a complete withdrawal to the Panther Line. His motivation was undoubtedly the worsening situation in the Ukraine; thus, he was more disposed than usual to free up troops and divisions that might take the pressure off Army Group South. Moreover, Soviet commanders, once their forces had blasted the Germans out of their initial positions, displayed none of the operational effectiveness that Vatutin, Konev, and Zhukov demonstrated in the south. As a result, the Germans were gradually able to pull back to the Panther Line. By the beginning of March they were largely in that position. Soviet efforts to break through came to naught, as an early spring thaw severely affected movement. Once again German forces had survived, but at an exorbitant cost. Had Hitler taken Kuechler's advice in early January, the Germans could have pulled back in good order and saved substantial reserves for use in the south.

The Resistance

In Britain's darkest hour in summer 1940, Winston Churchill persuaded the British Cabinet to establish the Special Operations Executive (SOE). Churchill made clear his vision from the organization's first moments as he told SOE's new head: "And now set Europe ablaze."[8] The resistance never quite met the prime minister's hopes for a revolution on the Continent that would engulf the Nazis, and yet the contributions of the various resistance movements in every independent occupied nation, except for Austria, were dramatic.

The varied conditions of geography, national experience, the nature of German rule, the degree of urbanization, and amount of outside support all helped to guide the many resistance movements in different directions. The most important trait possessed in common by resisters was that of character; neither class nor nationality nor age determined who would contribute significantly to the resistance. Two cases underscore this point. The first involved Andrée de Jongh, the 24-year-old daughter of a Belgian schoolmaster, who showed up at the British consulate in Bilbao, Spain, in August 1941 with a British soldier and two young Belgian men in tow. She noted to the startled consulate officials that she needed only to be recompensed for their fare, and she would provide a steady supply of future escapees. She and her comrades brought out more than 700 over the next two years, until the Germans destroyed her network. After two years in a German concentration camp, she was working in a leper hospital in Addis Ababa as late as the 1970s.

Jean Moulin came from the privileged sector of French society. As the prefect of Chartres at the age of 41, he was the youngest prefect in France. In 1940 he attempted suicide rather than sign German propaganda statements alleging French atrocities. After recovering from his self-inflicted wounds, he threw himself into organizing the resistance in the Rhone River valley. In fall 1941 he came out from France to London, where he put himself and his influence completely at General de Gaulle's disposal. Early in January 1942 he parachuted back into occupied France, and by March 1943, after persuading all the non-Communist groups to unite (no mean accomplishment), Moulin put together an umbrella organization, Conseil National de la Résistance, over the entire resistance. Less than a month later the Germans caught him and killed him while inflicting excruciating torture on his body. He never talked. His body was never found, but in Chartres Cathedral a tightly clamped fist enclosing the hilt of a broken sword commemorates his extraordinary contribution and bravery.

The path to resistance was quite different in Eastern and Western Europe. In the West, the Germans arrived on the flood of their overwhelming victories. A dazed and seemingly broken population was willing at first to seek accommodation with the victors. Moreover, the Germans masked their intentions with a veil of skilled propaganda. Only in the course of the succeeding year did the mendacity of German aims become clear. Military resistance in Western Europe confronted the fact that few places existed where one could safely build up large guerrilla forces. The carefully plotted farmlands of France and Belgium, with their innumerable small villages and excellent roads, provided the Germans and their underlings with both the bureaucratic means to control the population and the transport access to crush even the slightest agitation. Nevertheless, the French did mount several serious military rebellions. In March 1944 on the Glières plateau in the Savoy region, the Germans, with the support of French collaborators, had to mount a major military operation to destroy a large number of guerrillas. In July an even bigger military defeat befell an open rebellion near Grenoble. But in Brittany in summer 1944, SAS (Special Air Service) and Jedburgh teams of Allied special forces received sufficient support to wrest much of the region from the Germans, who not surprisingly had other things on their minds.

In Eastern Europe, resistance was never in question; from the first moment, the Germans were recognized as the murderers and villains they truly were. Consequently, those who eventually embarked on resistance had a somewhat clearer choice: either slavery followed by almost certain death, or resistance. Yet, even in the East, resistance had a limited military impact. Admittedly, in areas such as the Balkans, particularly in Yugoslavia, military units of partisans immediately formed, their birth considerably assisted by the rapid withdrawal of German units to participate in Barbarossa, which left large numbers of young, fully armed men hiding in the mountains with nobody to round them up.

But there was the rub. The areas where bands of partisans and resisters could gather in numbers sufficient to be militarily significant were precisely the areas of the least interest to the Germans. While the Ukraine and Belorussia lacked mountains, they did possess swamps and great forested regions that provided the necessary cover for Soviet partisans. But again, those areas had no strategic or operational importance for the Wehrmacht. By 1943 Soviet partisans were carrying out extensive sabotage of German supply lines, but they rarely struck at targets of great military importance. In late June 1944, partisans carried out 14,000 attacks on the rail lines supporting Army Group Center. But by then the Soviet superiority probably made the partisan contribution less significant in the overwhelming Soviet victory.

Even if its overall military impact was not decisive, resistance could cause the German occupiers enormous problems in terms of sabotage, delay, and other logistical difficulties. Aided by SOE operatives, 150 Greek partisans blew up the viaduct that carried the Salonika-Athens railroad across the Gorgopotamos gorge on 10 October 1942. They thereby shut down Rommel's main supply line to North Africa and El Alamein at the time and significantly contributed to the defeat of the Afrika Korps in November. But sabotage and military resistance were not always so spectacular. When the Allied invasion came at Normandy on 6 June 1944, the Waffen SS division Das Reich was located in the neighborhood of Toulouse. It immediately moved out on a journey that was supposed to take three days to the invasion front. Its tanks, which were on railroad cars, hardly moved at all. Members of the French resistance had already lubricated the railroad transporters for the tanks with abrasive grease, supplied by SOE, which immediately burned out the ball bearings. Then, as the Germans proceeded north, they came under fire from resistance units which covered the countryside; though ill-trained and ill-led, the French nevertheless inflicted casualties on the Waffen SS units.

Infuriated, the Germans then spent days hunting down their attackers and executing thousands of Frenchmen, including all the inhabitants of Oradour sur Glane; they shot down the men in the fields surrounding the village, while herding the women and children into the church, which was burned down around them. Das Reich took almost two weeks to reach Normandy, and by that time a very different situation obtained than would have been the case had the division arrived on the third day. But the difficulties that Das Reich ran into represented only a portion of the wholesale sabotage of railroads and power and telephone lines that members of the resistance carried out in the days after the landings in Normandy. For example, on the night of the landing, the resistance managed to make 950 cuts in rail lines throughout France.

Even in the slave labor camps of the Third Reich, some chose to resist. One American bomber crew, upon return from a mission over Germany, found a message of hope from its makers in an empty cannon shell stuck in the body of their aircraft: there was no powder in the shell to explode. Similarly, the products of Germany's slave laborers hardly measured up to the exacting standards of German workmanship. In 1942 the Swiss bought 50 Bf 109s from Germany and found them so well made that they were used in the Swiss Air Force until the early 1960s. In 1944 the Swiss (being nothing if not loyal customers of the Reich) bought a further 50 Bf 109s, but these aircraft were so badly made that the lot had to be junked in the late 1940s.

Intelligence was also a major contribution of the resistance. In April 1942 French linemen tapped into one of the two main German communications cables that ran between Paris and Berlin. For the next eight months they were able to pass along invaluable intelligence to London, intelligence that was particularly important because where the Germans had land lines they did not use radio and hence were not vulnerable to British intercepts.

In the east, Soviet partisans were particularly good at transmitting order-of-battle intelligence information on the Germans to their controllers in Moscow. Such information was particularly useful to the Soviets in the conduct of *maskirovka* to shield their own operational intentions. Nevertheless, the resistance did not always obtain the intelligence that the Allies really needed. For example, its agents failed to pick up the movement of the German 352nd Division into the area that was to become the Omaha beach landing. But sometimes even when the resistance passed along crucial information, such as the arrival of SS tank formations in the area where Operation Market Garden—the Allied airborne invasion of southern Holland in September 1944—was to occur, skeptical receivers refused to believe the intelligence.

The resistance provided other important services. The networks that helped downed fliers to escape from Western Europe were invaluable to the Allied air forces. Perhaps the resistance's most significant contribution lay in the sense of honor and national pride that the liberated peoples could feel in 1944 and 1945. Not surprisingly, many stepped forward and claimed participation in 1944, whereas far too few resisted in 1940 and 1941, when their efforts—though extremely dangerous—might have made a significant difference to the course of the war. But that should not detract from the fact that resistance in 1944 was still an exceptionally dangerous occupation, as thousands of Frenchmen found at the hands of the Waffen SS and the Wehrmacht. The participation in the clandestine press, in passing messages, in protecting or passing along downed Allied airmen or Jews, in daubing the walls of cities with painted slogans, and in carrying out the thousand little missions on which the resistance depended for its survival provided Europeans across the Continent with a sense that they at least had not been craven subjects of the Third Reich.

For the extent of the resistance and its contribution to the Allied cause the Germans had only themselves to blame. The pitiless nature of their occupation provided more than enough reason for those with a shred of decency and courage, and above all character, to resist. The Nazi policy of shooting hostages for "crimes" against the Wehrmacht or for sabotage redounded against the occupiers in the end. The occupiers' economic policy also contributed to the spread of resistance. Over summer and fall 1941, the Germans looted Greece of virtually all its foodstuffs; mass famine was the immediate consequence. By spring 1942, over 40,000 Greeks had died of starvation, most in the cities. By then no self-respecting Greek was willing to cooperate with the Nazis. The Germans' looting of their subject populations continued right to the end of the war. Over the winter of 1944–45 in Holland, 16,000 Dutch died of starvation, a tragedy made ironic by the fact that the Dutch had gone to extraordinary lengths to feed starving German children over the winter of 1918–19.

In Germany itself, a few citizens resisted the Nazis. Perhaps the noblest of those were the "white rose" circle of idealistic young Germans who attempted to publicize the crimes of the regime in Munich in early 1943 and met their end gruesomely under the executioner's axe. The military conspirators reached closer into the heart of the regime. Count Claus von Stauffenberg, a colonel so badly wounded in Tunis that he had only a few fingers left, set off a bomb in one of Hitler's staff conferences on 20 July 1944. The bomb killed a number of officers, but Hitler survived to wreak terrible vengeance on those who had participated in the plot. In the end it was probably to Europe's advantage that Hitler survived, because his survival made it impossible for the Germans to blame their defeat in the war on anyone other than the Führer.

Conclusion

The conduct of operations by Soviet military commanders after the Battle of Kursk displayed an approach to war that relied increasingly on more-complex methods and concepts. The initial set of operations after Kursk involved a series of attacks aimed as much at keeping the Germans off balance as in achieving overarching operational objectives such as encircling large German formations. In effect, the Soviets were counting on their superiority in numbers of men and equipment to batter the Germans back to the Dnepr and then beyond. Those operations, besides liberating substantial territory, also inflicted losses on the Germans that they could ill-afford, while the Soviets could replace their losses. By mid-winter, Soviet commanders were able to control operations that isolated and then wrecked two German corps at Cherkassy. The operational competence translated into an even more ambitious effort that involved two fronts, Konev's and Zhukov's, in a wide-ranging effort that almost destroyed First Panzer Army. The fact that the Germans escaped showed that the Soviets still had a few things to learn. But they were making every effort to benefit from their mistakes. In the coming summer offensive, they would raise their operational performance to a new level; the result would be the complete destruction of Army Group Center in the most devastating display of operational art in World War II and the most impressive victory of that conflict.

In May 1944, operations on the Eastern Front came to a temporary halt, before resuming at the end of June. Two reasons explain the tailing-off of Soviet offensive operations during this brief period. The first was that the fighting had to a great extent exhausted the Soviet armies in the Ukraine. But even more importantly, Stalin was now awaiting the opening of a second front in the west. The long-promised great amphibious offensive by the Western powers was about to occur. The Soviets would now wait to see whether the Anglo-American effort would succeed. If it did, they would launch their great summer offensive against Army Group Center. If the invasion on the Western Front failed, the Soviets could then wait to see whether the Germans would attempt to regain the initiative they had lost at Kursk.

THE INVASION
OF FRANCE

1944

In a radio speech to the French in October 1940, Winston Churchill ended with a promise: "Good night then: sleep to gather strength for the morning. For the morning will come. Brightly will it shine on the brave and the true, kindly upon all who suffer for the cause, glorious upon the tombs of heroes. Thus, will shine the dawn."[1] Dawn finally came on the 6th of June 1944, four long years after the Germans had expelled the British Army from the Continent. Operation Overlord, the cross-Channel landing on the shores of Normandy, represented four long years of preparation. The scale of its success placed the democratic powers back in Central Europe, a political position of critical importance in the second half of the century. The invasion of France was to be the most operationally complex offensive of World War II, and on its results hung the political and strategic outcome of the war.

The Opposing Sides

Although the Wehrmacht had sustained crippling losses on the Eastern Front for three years, its soldiers remained formidable opponents. Through to the end of 1943, the Germans had believed that an invasion of France was unlikely. As a result, they embarked on relatively few defensive preparations, mostly along the Pas de Calais on the Channel coast north of the River Seine. In 1942 and 1943, German units occupying France were either divisions recuperating from fighting on the Eastern Front or third-line, badly equipped divisions with little mobility. But by early 1944, the OKW and Hitler had recognized that a major cross-Channel invasion would soon occur, and they proceeded to upgrade the western theater of operations. Now, units reconstituting from heavy losses in the east or newly forming units would remain in the west to meet the invasion. Field Marshal Gerd von Rundstedt held overall command in the west; but to energize and control defensive preparations in France and the Low Countries, Hitler appointed Erwin Rommel as commander of Army Group B, in charge of defending the most threatened coastal areas from the Bay of Biscay to Denmark.

Both Rommel and Rundstedt believed that the Pas de Calais was the probable target for an Allied invasion, but there was a key difference in their views on how to defend Fortress Europe. Rundstedt believed the panzer forces should remain back from the coastal regions in order to execute a powerful counterattack. Rommel, recognizing the overwhelming air and logistical superiority of the Anglo-American powers, argued that German defenders must defeat the Allies on the beaches or the campaign and war were lost. Typically, Hitler refused to decide between the differing concepts and placed the mechanized reserves under OKW control so that they could move only with his permission. Because neither Rommel nor Rundstedt would command the operational reserve, the chance of a prompt response to the invasion evaporated.

Nevertheless, Rommel brought his ceaseless energy to the challenge of meeting the Allied threat. He oversaw a massive construction program that sowed millions of mines, built thousands of bunkers and field fortifications, placed tens of thousands of poles ("Rommel asparagus") in fields to interfere with glider landings, and installed huge numbers of anti-boat obstacles along the beaches. So successful was the beach-obstacles program that the Allies were forced to land at low rather than high tide, so that they could spot and avoid this peril. And since they also needed to land at dawn, the Allies were left with only a few days each month to execute their complex plans. Given his personality, Rommel brought the training of the defending German divisions to a high pitch—even third-line coastal divisions received a thorough dose of realistic work-ups. France was no longer a vacation spot for weary, burned-out troops from the Eastern Front. It was now a beehive of ceaseless exercises, training days and nights, and construction work.

Reinforcing the preparation of German units was the same potent doctrine of combined arms, decentralized leadership, and small-unit initiative that had made the Wehrmacht such a formidable opponent throughout the war. Moreover, the ideology of Nazism reinforced the competence of the troops on the battlefield. But none of this preparedness could compensate for the Wehrmacht's fundamental problem in the months preceding June 1944—namely, its inability to uncover the precise location of the coming

Allied invasion. Lacking this knowledge, the Germans had to waste much of their work on beaches the Allies would not attack. Nor could they count on the Luftwaffe for support, given the terrible losses the Combined Bomber Offensive had inflicted on Luftwaffe fighter squadrons over the course of the spring air battles in the skies over the Reich. Finally, they would not receive adequate warning of an invasion and thus would have to fight and maneuver against Allied landing forces while under massive air attacks—one more indication of the dismal failure of the German intelligence system in World War II.

But the Allies struggled with their own problems. Initial planning for an amphibious assault on Fortress Europe had rested on the assumption that the invasion forces must capture a major port in the initial days of the campaign. The Dieppe debacle in August 1942, when third-class German troops crushed an Anglo-Canadian amphibious raid, exploded that hope. Defeat at Dieppe made clear that a successful landing would have to occur not at a harbor but over open beaches, which allowed enough space for men and equipment to come ashore and build up to an invasion-strength force. Overlord was not the largest amphibious landing of the war—during the attack on Sicily, more divisions landed on the first day. But in Normandy, German resistance would be substantially tougher. Moreover, once the Allies achieved a lodgment, they had to build up their forces faster than the defenders in succeeding weeks—a daunting problem since reinforcing troops and supplies would have to come ashore over open beaches, whereas the Germans could move their reinforcements on the excellent French rail and road network.

In answer, Air Marshal Sir Arthur Tedder, Eisenhower's chief deputy, developed a plan to use Allied air power, including strategic bombers, to destroy the French transport system before the landings. Despite considerable arguments from the bomber barons, the Combined Chiefs of Staff placed the strategic bombers at Eisenhower's disposal from 1 April 1944 until September 1944. Because Allied air attacks could not concentrate on Normandy lest the Germans deduce the site of the planned invasion, the interdiction campaign ranged across the length and breadth of France. At night, Bomber Command hammered French marshaling yards, while Eighth Air Force and swarms of British and American fighter bombers strangled the French transportation system during the day. In late May, the Allies began a sustained campaign to destroy the Seine bridges. By that time, rail traffic in France had declined to 55 percent of January's totals; by 6 June, it had fallen to 30 percent; and by early July, to barely 10 percent. Attacks on rail movement in western France were particularly effective; by mid-June,

Alderney E n g l i s h   C h a n n e l

Cherbourg

Cotentin

Peninsula

Guernsey

Sark

Channel Islands
German occupied

St. Mère-Église

Jersey

Gulf d e St. M a l o

Coutances

St. Lô

Bayeux

Villers-
Bocage

Caen

Quiberet

Baie de la Seine

XXXXX
21

XXXX
1 US

XXXX
2 BRITISH

XXX
VIII

XXX
V

XXX
XXX

XXX
I

1

2

3

4

5

XXXXX
21
Montgomery

XXXXX
12 U.S.
Bradley

XXXX
2
Dempsey

XXXX
1
Crerar

Falaise

N o r m a n d y

Orne

Granville

Vire

Flers

Argentan

St. Malo

Dinard

Dinan

Avranches

Mortain

Domfront

XXXX
1 U.S.
Hodges

Rance

Fougère

Mayenne

B r i t t a n y

XXXX
3 U.S.
Patton

Rennes

Vitré

Mayenne

48°

Vilaine

Sarthe

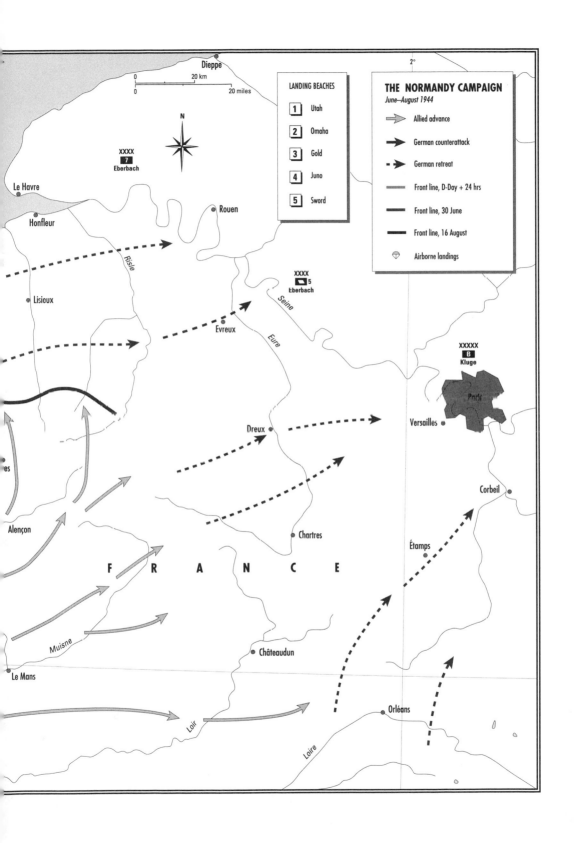

Dieppe

0   20 km
0   20 miles

N

XXXX
7
Eberbach

Le Havre

Honfleur

Risle

Lisieux

Rouen

Evreux

Seine

XXXX
◤5
Eberbach

Eure

XXXXX
B
Kluge

Paris

Versailles

Dreux

Corbeil

Alençon

Chartres

Étamps

F   R   A   N   C   E

Muisne

Châteaudun

Le Mans

Loir

Orléans

Loire

LANDING BEACHES

1	Utah
2	Omaha
3	Gold
4	Juno
5	Sword

2°

THE NORMANDY CAMPAIGN
June–August 1944

⇒ Allied advance

➤ German counterattack

┅➤ German retreat

Front line, D-Day + 24 hrs

Front line, 30 June

Front line, 16 August

⊕ Airborne landings

the trains that might have supplied the defenders of Normandy were no longer operating. The campaign to dismantle the transportation system led to significant loss of French lives, but even Charles de Gaulle, leader of the Free French, was willing to tolerate the suffering imposed on his people.

Until late 1943, planning for the invasion rested in the hands of the British Army's Lieutenant General Frederick Morgan. His staff proposed an amphibious landing of three divisions, supported by one airborne division. At the end of 1943, virtually the entire Allied senior high command from the Mediterranean—Eisenhower, Montgomery, Tedder, Spaatz, Bradley, and Patton—arrived in London and rejected this strategy. Eisenhower and Montgomery demanded and obtained a five-division assault force, along with three airborne divisions to secure the flanks of the landing areas. To support the invasion, the Allies had already created a number of engineering marvels—in particular, two great artificial harbors, called "Mulberries," which they would move across the Channel and install off the Normandy beaches to ensure that the lodgment would receive sufficient support and reinforcements.

In choosing a site for the landing, the Allied commanders recognized that the Pas de Calais offered better terrain and was closer to the Reich. But this operational advantage made it equally accessible to the Germans, who could counterattack from three different directions. Normandy, by contrast, would be more difficult for the Germans to reinforce, and the geography of the region would limit German attacks to one direction—from the south. By landing at Normandy, the Allies also hoped to deceive the Germans into believing that a second, even larger, invasion was coming against the Pas de Calais; this threat might freeze substantial enemy forces north of the Seine.

The Allied high command represented one of the few instances in history where allies truly cooperated in achieving larger objectives. Much of the credit was Eisenhower's. If Ike deserves the accolade of "great," it rests on his performance in managing the generals under his command, as fractious and dysfunctional a group of egomaniacs as any war had ever seen. Moreover, as the Supreme Commander Allied Expeditionary Forces, Eisenhower had to withstand countervailing pressure from Washington and London, which held diverse perspectives on the conduct of the war, not to mention the not-always-helpful advice of the senior Allied military leaders, General George Marshall of the United States and Field Marshal Alan Brooke of the United Kingdom. At the operational level, only Patton understood how best to utilize Allied ground mobility to exploit German weaknesses; the emphasis elsewhere, particularly in the British Army, focused on firepower rather than on maneuver.

Allied weaknesses were especially glaring in the areas of weaponry, tactics, and training. Despite the bountiful production of Anglo-American industry, many of the mass-produced weapons—machine guns and tanks, among others—proved distinctly inferior to their German counterparts. The Sherman tank was a wonderful armored fighting vehicle in some respects—more reliable than anything in the German inventory—but with the exception of an upgunned British version (called the Firefly), it possessed a low-velocity 75mm gun that could not penetrate the armor of the German Panther and Tiger tanks, or even Mark IVs at close range.

A more serious weakness in the Allies' preparations for the invasion lay at the tactical level. British and Canadian troops had had four years to prepare themselves for Normandy; not all units did a good job. At lower levels, British troops possessed no common doctrine; as a result, training rarely reached a high level of consistency or effectiveness. Even basic infantry tactics displayed considerable problems. The British relied on little more than a straightforward rush and the hope that their artillery had already smashed the Germans to bits.

Part of the problem lay in the unwillingness of the British Army to base officer promotion on effectiveness rather than social class. Too many senior officers found employment after failure in the field. The higher military leadership was also weak, except Montgomery. The hero of El Alamein was a gifted commander, who understood the limitation of his troops and generally refused to take risks that would expose their weaknesses. In many ways, the battle Montgomery fought at Normandy was his most skilled, given the limitations of the forces at his disposal and his own predisposition to caution; only his habit of smug self-congratulation robbed him—at least in the eyes of many Americans—of his due.

Coming into the war last, the Americans experienced their own weaknesses. In 1939 the U.S. Army had ranked seventeenth in the world. As compared with the Germans, who by 1939 had been preparing themselves for war for six years, the Americans had barely three years before their troops were committed to combat. Consequently, many units that fought in Normandy displayed a depressing lack of tactical sophistication. Nevertheless, most U.S. formations exhibited greater adaptability than their British counterparts, and their learning curve was steady and steep. Such improvements owed much to the flexibility of a citizen army, as well as to the ruthlessness with which Eisenhower sacked senior officers who failed.

Yet, here, too, problems emerged. Eisenhower's U.S. subordinates often proved as frustrating to work with as their British counterparts. Particularly troublesome was the senior U.S. ground force general, Omar Bradley. Jealous of Patton, suspicious of the British, unimaginative and dour, Bradley was not at all the soldier's general of media legend. A soldier's general saves their lives; he doesn't just dress like them. None of Bradley's frontline soldiers ever wrote of him in terms like those a veteran of the Burma campaign used to describe his general, William Slim: "Slim emerged from under the trees by the lake shore, there was no nonsense of 'gather round' or jumping on boxes; he just stood there with his thumb hooked in his carbine sling and talked about how we had caught Jap off-balance and were going to annihilate him in the open . . . You knew, when he talked of smashing Jap, that to him it meant not only arrows on a map but clearing bunkers and going in under shell-fire; that he had the head of a general with the heart of a private soldier . . . And afterwards when it was all over and he spoke of what his army had done, it was always 'you,' not even 'we,' and never 'I.'"[2] Only hacks among American journalists called Omar Bradley a soldier's general.

Patton, on the other hand, possessed a solid grasp of war at the operational level, but he had seriously damaged his reputation and position by his lack of self-discipline in Sicily. He also exhibited throughout his career a penchant for sticking his feet into his mouth—cavalry boots, socks, and all. Only Eisenhower's patience and recognition of Patton's extraordinary operational talents kept him in the fight, despite Bradley's efforts to remove a more gifted subordinate (one of Bradley's bad habits). Adding to the difficulties in the Patton-Bradley relationship was the fact that Patton had a way of looking good before the cameras. Bradley also had a tendency to pose, but more often than not he looked downright silly.

The Allied conception for the landing and the campaign was relatively straightforward. The initial amphibious attack of five divisions—supported by three airborne divisions—would achieve a lodgment from which Allied forces would drive inland. On the eastern flank, the British 6th Airborne Division would seize the high ground on the east bank of the Orne, thus shielding the invasion from a counterattack from the east. Similarly in the west, the 101st and the 82nd Airborne Divisions were to prevent the Germans from interfering with the landings at Utah Beach at the base of Normandy's Cotentin Peninsula. Thus, the only direction from which the Germans could counterattack with effect on the first day would be the south. Of the beaches, only Omaha, with its long shelf and dunes over which cliffs rose upwards of 200 feet, represented a forbidding natural obstacle. But the seizure of Omaha Beach, positioned between Utah Beach in the west and the British beaches in the east, was essential if the Allies were to succeed.

In fact, the Omaha Beach landing was almost a failure, largely due to Bradley's unwillingness to address essential tactical problems confronted by an amphibious assault on prepared defenses. In the spring, Marshall had sent Major General Charles Corlett from the Pacific, where he had led the successful assaults on Attu and Kwajalein, to advise Bradley and the other senior U.S. generals in charge of the landing on the obstacles the army and marines had run into in conducting opposed landings in the Pacific. Corlett was astonished by the reception that he got in Europe. None of the senior U.S. commanders, including Eisenhower and Bradley, displayed the slightest interest in learning anything about his experiences in the Pacific. In fact, the prevailing attitude was that "anything that had happened in the Pacific was strictly bush league stuff" of no use to those planning operations in the European Theater.

Not only was Corlett alarmed by the lack of fire support for the Normandy landings, but he warned that the ammunition allocations for the upcoming battles had been significantly underestimated. On both counts he was completely correct. Admiral Kent Hewitt, the U.S. Navy's leading practitioner of amphibious warfare in the Atlantic, admitted to Corlett that the army in Europe was six months behind the practices of the Pacific, but that there was nothing he could do to educate its leaders, given their attitude that they had nothing to learn. Only General Alexander Patch, who would command the Dragoon landings in August in southern France, sought Corlett out to learn from his experiences in the Pacific.

The most significant lesson from the Pacific that Bradley and his senior planners passed up was the critical importance of naval gunfire support for troops storming the beach. As a result of Bradley's obtuseness, U.S. troops at Omaha and Utah beaches would receive direct support from only 2 battleships, 4 light cruisers, and 18 destroyers. By comparison, at Kwajalein the 7th Infantry Division alone had attacked with the support of 7 battleships, 3 heavy cruisers, and 18 destroyers over a far longer bombardment period. After making this inexcusable tactical error, Bradley next turned down the specialized armored fighting vehicles developed by the British for clearing beach mines and obstacles, a decision that would add significantly to U.S. losses throughout the Normandy fighting.

On the British side, Montgomery hoped to capture Caen on the first day and then pivot on the city to swing up to the Seine. In the meantime, the Americans would first capture the Cotentin Peninsula and Cherbourg and then drive south to open the Breton ports. But as Brooke explained to U.S.

generals in April 1944, the coming campaign would not be a war of wide-ranging movement but rather a steady, implacable advance along the lines of the British drive into Belgium in fall 1918. Certainly, the phase lines drawn up by logistical planners suggested such an approach. But while the Allies meticulously planned the amphibious landing and the buildup of logistics and follow-on divisions, they did relatively little thinking about the fighting required to expand the bridgehead.

The Norman countryside of thick hedges, stone walls, and farmhouses proved ideal for the Wehrmacht to conduct its tactics of defense in depth—a tactical framework in which German strong points of machine guns and anti-tank weapons extended far into the rear, while reserve forces deployed deep in the defensive zone to counterattack and destroy any Allied penetrations. Only Patton knew the area well, and in June and July he was far from the area, leading a phantom army in England that was supposedly preparing to land on the Pas de Calais. Thus, the one officer who knew the terrain was entirely removed from the conduct of operations. Nevertheless, Patton did have an important role: the Germans fell for the deception hook, line, and sinker.

The Invasion

The Allied forces poised for the invasion of France represented four years of mobilization to address the Nazi threat. Five American, British, and Canadian divisions along with three British armored brigades would make the amphibious assault on D-Day, the 6th of June. Three U.S. and British airborne divisions would precede them and drop troops behind the German beach defenses. Putting over 150,000 soldiers onto the European Continent in a single day required a vast armada of ships and aircraft. Over 7,000 naval vessels contributed to the invasion effort: 138 warships, from battleship to destroyer, provided fire support for the landing forces; 221 escort vessels protected the great convoys of ships; and 287 minesweepers and 495 light coastal craft executed various naval missions. Added to the naval ships were landing ships, landing craft, and other amphibious vessels totaling over 4,000. Carrying the bulk of the Allied ground forces and their support were 805 cargo vessels, from tankers to ammunition ships, while 59 blockships would eventually form the breakwater obstacles for the two great artificial harbors.

In the air, the entire panoply of strategic bombers, tactical bombers, photo-reconnaissance aircraft, fighters, fighter-bombers, and transports that made up the Allied air forces were at Eisenhower's disposal. The total number of military aircraft supporting the invasion was 11,590. Nearly 1,400 troop transports would drop the Allied airborne forces and their equipment on the far side of the beaches, while 3,700 fighters would cover the invasion beaches themselves as well as the great fleet in the Channel. Overlord was indeed an impressive military operation, one entirely beyond the comprehension of the Germans, who awaited the blow.

The weather in May 1944 in Britain had been unusually good. After taking the tides into account, Supreme Headquarters Allied Expeditionary Forces (SHAEF) scheduled the landing to take place between 4 and 6 June. But the weather turned rainy and windy at the beginning of the month, and on the 4th Eisenhower had to postpone the landing scheduled for 5 June. But Allied weather forecasters divined a short break in the weather and on the evening of the 4th Eisenhower, with Montgomery's support, decided to go on the 6th of June. As dusk settled over the English air fields on 5 June, paratroopers from the three Allied airborne divisions clambered on board their aircraft.

The first paratrooper pathfinders were down on the ground before midnight to mark the drop zones. Helped by a superbly executed glider operation that captured Pegasus bridge across the Orne, the British 6th Airborne landed its paratroopers within its planned drop zones. In the west, however, a combination of clouds, heavy flak, and inexperienced transport pilots spread U.S. paratroopers across the length and breadth of the Cotentin Peninsula. That dispersion turned out to have one advantage: the Germans found it impossible to divine the objectives of the American amphibious assault. While German attention focused on the U.S. paratroopers behind the beaches, the 4th Infantry Division made a successful landing on Utah Beach.

The American landings at Utah were also helped considerably by the fact that the paratroopers from the 101st took out a number of the German artillery positions looking directly toward the beaches. But the 4th Infantry Division was also well-trained and -led—its assistant division commander, Theodore Roosevelt, Jr., would be awarded a Medal of Honor—and took care of its share of Germans. Roosevelt would die of a heart attack within the month and eventually be buried in the Omaha Beach Cemetery beside his brother Quentin, who had been killed 26 years earlier in France while flying for the U.S. Army during World War I.

As for the British and Canadian landings, despite some local impediments, the British had firm control of Gold and Sword beaches by mid-day, while the Canadians were equally successful on Juno Beach. Units of the British 50th Infantry Division advanced to within three miles of the ancient Norman city of Bayeux. Still, the clutter and confusion of the beach-head, the complexities of moving off the beaches and through the cleared exits, as well as German resistance, made it impossible for the British or Canadians to capture Caen.

It was on Omaha Beach that the Normandy invasion almost foundered. Virtually everything went wrong. Clouds obscured the beaches at dawn. Consequently, the heavy bombers that were scheduled to plaster German defenses dropped late in order to avoid killing Allied troops; and when they finally did drop, they missed their targets. Therefore the bombing attack contributed little to silencing the enemy.

The navy botched its job by dropping the amphibious tanks for the 1st Infantry Division well beyond the drop-off point; only 5 out of 34 reached the beaches. More of the 29th Infantry Division's tanks reached the beach, only to be destroyed by German anti-tank guns. The artillery fared no better; few howitzers survived the movement through the rolling surf, their DUKWs (amphibious vehicles) capsizing at sea.

Finally, Allied intelligence failed to pick up the fact that the Germans had moved their 352nd Infantry Division, a first-class unit, into the area back in May. The subsequent slaughter of attacking U.S. infantry totaled twice that of Tarawa (a battle that army partisans have unfairly used to suggest marine ineptitude). For much of the morning, American survivors barely made it to the dunes below the cliffs. The soldiers huddled along the shoreline amid their burning vehicles scattered all over the beach. The German officer commanding the fortifications overlooking Omaha reported to his superiors that the U.S. landing had failed. Similar reports reached Bradley, who considered shutting Omaha down and funneling all reinforcements into Utah.

But gradually the attackers prevailed. Naval gunfire, particularly by destroyers, took an increasing toll on the German defenders, while the 352nd Division received no reinforcements—undoubtedly because of its favorable reports and the deteriorating situation elsewhere. U.S. troops on the shattered beach took matters into their own hands and gradually fought their way up the draws that led through the cliffs to the plateau above. By afternoon, they had established a foothold on the heights, driven the Germans back from their seemingly impregnable positions, and captured the blocked beach exits from the rear. The cost was terrible. On the first day, approximately 2,500 Americans died on Omaha Beach.

Still, by sunset on 6 June the Allies had secured a successful lodgment on the coast of Western Europe. They had landed over 155,000 men onto French soil by aircraft and ship—75,215 across the beaches in the British sector, 57,500 in the American sector, and 23,000 paratroopers and glider-borne infantry. Altogether, eight divisions and three armored brigades were ashore. Most importantly, the Allies were in a position to push the Germans inland so that the buildup of Allied forces and supplies could begin.

If D-Day at Omaha was bad for the Americans, it was worse for the Germans. To begin with, they were misled by their weather reports and entirely missed the possibility that the weather might break. As a result, Rommel had driven back to Germany to give his wife a birthday present. Other senior officers went off to attend a war game at Rennes, while German defenses, which had been at full alert in May during good weather, relaxed their guard as rain and wind pounded the Norman coast. Without Rommel's presence, the response to the invasion stalled. Rundstedt asked for release of mobile reserves in the early morning, but Jodl, OKW operations officer, demurred that the Führer was asleep and could not be awakened, and only Hitler could give the permission required. Thus, the Germans failed to respond with their reserves until early afternoon of D-Day, and then only 21st Panzer Division, located near Caen, launched a major counterattack. Late in the afternoon a panzer task force (Kampfgruppe) almost reached the Channel between Sword and Juno beaches. Luckily, British Fireflies in the area blunted the attack, and over the course of the day 21st Panzer Division lost 70 of the 124 tanks it had possessed that morning.

That night German reinforcements in the form of the 12th SS Panzer Division (Hitlerjugend) arrived in Caen and deployed north of the city. The teenage soldiers of this formation quickly established a firm hand on what proved to be the focus of the battle for the next six weeks. Hitlerjugend drew its membership from the most fanatical members of the Nazi youth movement, whom battle-hardened veterans of the Eastern Front then trained and led. The division was one of the most ideologically driven and murderous formations of the war. The next day, Hitlerjugend panzers and panzer grenadiers under Kurt Meyer piled into the Canadians. "Panzer" Meyer had joined the SS Leibstandarte Regiment in 1934 despite having to wear orthopedic shoes due to a severe injury earlier in life. By 1944 he had already amassed an extraordinary combat record and been decorated in France, Greece, and the Soviet Union for heroism under fire. In Greece when his soldiers had displayed some reluctance to advance directly against Greek machine gun fire, he had rolled live hand grenades from behind in order to encourage them to move forward and attack. He would soon take over command of Hitlerjugend when the division commander was killed in the ferocious fighting of early June. A skilled and effective tactical commander, he was also a fanatical Nazi, fully committed to the most ruthless conduct of the battle. In heavy fighting the Canadians came off second best; but supported by naval gun fire, they held—barely. Several hundred Canadians surrendered, many soon to be murdered in cold blood by their captors. In one incident, Hitlerjugend troopers machine-gunned Canadian prisoners and then drove their tanks over the bodies.

While the Germans were attempting to batter the British and Canadians back from Caen, the Allies had time to consolidate their beachheads into one defensive perimeter. Hitler still hoped for a massive counterattack to drive the Allies into the Channel, but the arrival of German reinforcements was painfully slow, owing to the destruction Allied air forces had wrought on the French transportation network. The 2nd Waffen SS Division (Das Reich) was supposed to take only two days to reach Normandy from Limoges, but it was nearly two weeks before the division and its equipment began to arrive. Air attacks and ambushes by the French resistance made the move a nightmare. Along the way, the division's frustrated soldiers murdered the French indiscriminately; the worst incident occurred at Oradour-sur-Glane, where enraged SS troopers killed nearly 600 hostages because partisans had kidnapped their battalion commander.

To add to German woes, senior commanders persisted in the belief that the main attack would come at the Pas de Calais; they would hold that delusion until the collapse in Normandy of their forces in August. Thus, a substantial portion of German reserves remained tied to Fifteenth Army north of the Seine, while Rommel was left holding the dike in Normandy with only Seventh Army. The Allied success in breaking German message traffic exacerbated the situation. Ultra intercepts on 9 and 10 June indicated the precise location of Panzer Group West's headquarters, which was about to take charge of the mobile battle. Obligingly, the Germans, straight off the Eastern Front, placed their tents and vehicles in an open field, where Allied fighter-bombers wrecked the entire site and killed a number of highly trained staff officers. Panzer Group West was thus effectively out of the battle.

However desperate their position, the Germans had excellent terrain from which to wage a defensive battle. Using that advantage, they proved a nightmare to dig out. British officers found it disconcerting to come over the top of a ridge only to discover the Germans dug in on the reverse slope—"something we had never envisioned"—an extraordinary admission, since reverse-slope positions had been a basic principle of German doctrine since 1917.

At times the Allies were their own worst enemy. On 12 June, General Sir

Miles Dempsey, commander of British Second Army, and Montgomery recognized that German positions west of Caen had an open flank—a result of the heavy fighting around that city as well as the slow arrival of German reserves. The British switched the 7th Armored Division's axis of advance to the west of Caen. That division's spearhead brigade was soon through German lines, and its lead elements reached Villers-Bocage on the way to outflanking Caen from the west. But the advance units moved as if on peacetime maneuvers; there was no reconnaissance to the front, and the British forces bunched up on the main road stretching through the village. Unfortunately for the 7th Armored Division, the Waffen SS 501st Heavy Tank Battalion (Tigers) had arrived as the advance guard of the I SS Panzer Corps; its commander was the great tank ace Michael Wittman. With a handful of Tigers, he shredded 7th Armored's advance brigade by knocking out 25 British tanks and 28 other armored vehicles. Wittman had plugged the dike long enough for the 2nd SS Panzer Division to arrive. But the British failure at Villers-Bocage was more than the result of sloppy tactics at the front; the corps commander handled the situation badly by failing to reinforce 7th Armored while the Germans were in trouble. As Dempsey noted after the war, "The whole handling of that battle was a disgrace."[3]

The unexpected slowness of their advance confronted Allied commanders with a significant problem. Although they were winning the battle of the buildup, the lodgment area was severely overcrowded. Even after one of the worst storms in Channel history (18–22 June) shut down movement of Allied forces ashore for three days (and wrecked the Mulberry at Omaha), the Allies still managed to land over 500,000 troops (20 divisions) within the first two weeks. By early July, a million men had come ashore, supported by 190,000 vehicles. But the Germans still prevented a breakout, despite the destruction of the French rail system. Crucial to their logistic support was barge traffic on the Seine—inexplicably not a major target of Allied interdiction efforts. Thus, the farther west the Germans moved along the front and away from the Seine, the more critical their supply situation became.

By 18 June, the Americans had cut the base of the Cotentin Peninsula and reached the Atlantic Ocean at Barneville. Major General J. Lawton ("Lightning Joe") Collins, VII Corps commander, handled the drive north to Cherbourg. The Americans quickly fought their way into the city; by 27 June, Nazi resistance there had ended, but the Germans had destroyed the port facilities. Despite massive efforts to repair the damage, the Americans would not use Cherbourg until September, and then only on a limited basis. Elsewhere, the Americans had an even harder time driving forward than did the British. Bradley's forces were in the heaviest portion of the bocage—a landscape of intermingling woods and heath, small fields, and orchards whose tall hedgerows and stone farm compounds provided the Germans with excellent defensive positions. Bradley added to the difficulties of the terrain by attacking all along the front—a series of weak jabs rather than a solid strike. This approach, so reminiscent of Douglas Haig's British offensives in 1916 and 1917, failed to achieve anything but local, tactical success. The Germans seemingly had less to fear from the Americans. Given British pressure, which at times threatened to break out onto more open ground beyond Caen, the bulk of the German reinforcements concentrated on the eastern flank of the lodgment.

German commanders at every level recognized that Allied superiority was wearing their forces down. On 28 June, Rommel and Rundstedt journeyed to Berchtesgaden to report to the Führer. The resulting blow-up did nothing to improve relations within the German high command. Shortly thereafter, Rundstedt, drawing on pessimistic reports from army and Waffen SS generals, demanded a free hand to conduct defensive operations; he did not help his situation by suggesting to Keitel that Germany should make peace. Forthwith, Hitler removed Rundstedt and replaced him with Field Marshal Günther von Kluge, who mirrored the Führer's optimism but possessed no experience in fighting the British or Americans. Kluge arrived full of enthusiasm and immediately accused Rommel of defeatism. But it did not take long for the new commander to alter his own attitude in accordance with reality.

In late June, Montgomery and Dempsey launched a major attack west of Caen. This attack, codenamed Epsom, failed, although at battle's end the British did draw in and maul the last of the fresh armored units the Germans possessed—a result that was largely fortuitous. Nevertheless, Montgomery's optimism was placing him in an increasingly uncomfortable position with his superiors and colleagues. Just as at Villers-Bocage—and with less reason—the British senior generals abandoned crucial terrain advantages, largely because they were unwilling to take risks. The British were little closer to capturing Caen than they had been before Epsom, and the increasingly heavy attrition of infantry confronted British generals with the probability that they would soon have to break up units to provide replacements. Montgomery followed Epsom with two additional attacks in July. The first, codenamed Charnwood, used Bomber Command to blast the way into Caen, but that blow largely missed the German positions. At considerable cost, the British infantry then fought their way into the northern half of Caen, but the failure to make any significant advance suggested that a stalemate had settled over the front.

Worried by his infantry losses but with a large number of tanks available, Dempsey then concentrated three armored divisions to break through German defenses after another major attack by Bomber Command. British forces would drive over the Bourguébus ridge overlooking Caen and reach the good tank country to the south. Dempsey seems to have focused on the attractiveness of the end rather than the weaknesses of the attacking force. To begin with, the Germans had an outstanding observation post from the top of the great Colombelles steelworks in Caen; thus, the British would have to redeploy units for the attack only at the last moment. But there were larger problems. Montgomery made serious alterations to Dempsey's plans and followed a more cautious approach; the result was considerable confusion within the British command structure as to the operational goals for the coming attack. Montgomery's caution in planning the Caen offensive, codenamed Goodwood, reflected his assessment of the weaknesses of his troops. Yet in dealing with Eisenhower, SHAEF, and the RAF, whose Bomber Command would deliver the opening salvo, he remained tight-lipped about his plan and over-optimistic about its prospects.

Another serious impediment came on the intelligence front. Ultra provided fewer indications than usual of German plans and preparations; and on the other side, German tactical intelligence divined the coming attack. As a result, the Germans established an intricate defense system with four separate defensive lines. The Germans dug their anti-tank guns in and awaited the next blow. Thirty-six hours before the attack, Ultra finally warned that the Germans expected to fight a battle "decisive for the course of the war." That warning, however, had little impact on those preparing the offensive.

At dawn on 18 July, the full weight of the Allied strategic bomber forces fell on German front lines along the Orne. Bomber Command dropped 15,000 1,000-pound and 500-pound bombs. An hour and a half later, Eighth Air Force dropped an additional 13,000 100-pound and 76,000 20-pound fragmentation bombs. Vast devastation greeted the survivors as they crawled from their lairs: smashed-up trees, Tiger tanks flung upside down, and soldiers dazed or half-crazed. Nevertheless, a number of tanks and anti-tank guns survived, and the Wehrmacht's discipline and battle drills took hold. Moreover, the main German artillery positions behind Bourguébus ridge remained unscathed by bombing, while four Luftwaffe anti-aircraft 88s survived in Cagny, directly in the path of British armor. When the Luftwaffe battery commander suggested that his 88s did not do tanks,

Oberst (Colonel) Hans von Luck put a pistol to the Luftwaffe officer's head and suggested he reconsider. Over the course of the 18th, the British armored divisions lost well over 200 tanks in heavy fighting. They failed to breach German positions laid out in depth; by evening, enemy reinforcements were flowing into the battle area, and further fighting only brought the British to the ridge line, which had been their minimal objective.

On 20 July, Montgomery called the attack off—it had been a clear failure that might have resulted in his relief had not German defenses in the west crumbled before the Americans. Nevertheless, one must give Montgomery and British forces their due; whatever their tactical weaknesses, they fought the best formations in the German Army to exhaustion. The fighting around Caen pinned German armor to the eastern battlefield and prevented Rommel from gathering the mechanized units for a counter thrust. By late July, 14 divisions, including 6 panzer divisions, faced the British and Canadians; 11, including only 2 battered panzer divisions, confronted the Americans. Ironically, the failure to achieve a breakthrough beyond Caen worked to Allied advantage. Any breakthrough in June or July might well have resulted in a mobile battle in central France—where the Germans could have fallen back on supply dumps, extracted their forces in relatively undamaged condition, and inflicted heavier casualties on Allied forces.

The Breakout

On 3 July, the U.S. VII Corps launched a drive on St. Lô. Initially, the American offensive fared no better than had British attacks, for Bradley again spread his effort across too wide a front. Nevertheless, though suffering heavy casualties, the Americans pushed the Germans back on St. Lô, an attritional process that weakened German defenses. During late June and early July, U.S. units gradually came to terms with the bocage both tactically and technologically. American combined-arms tactics, emphasizing firepower with maneuver, steadily improved in the harsh classroom of war. Moreover, GIs designed a variety of devices, the most famous of which was Rhino, to handle the hedgerows. The Americans took steel beams (most of them from German obstacles on the Normandy beaches), cut them into jagged teeth, and welded them to the front of Shermans. With these hedgerow cutters, the tanks could smash from one field into the next. By mid-July, hundreds of U.S. tanks had achieved cross-country mobility with these devices, while German tanks remained bound to the roads.

At the end of July, Bradley unleashed the decisive offensive. Always a slow learner, he finally concentrated Operation Cobra on a narrow front-age. Collins's VII Corps would strike on a front of only 7,000 yards. To pre-pare the way, Bradley, like Montgomery, asked for Allied strategic bomb-ers. Air commanders agreed but refused his request that the bombers make their runs parallel to the front. Instead, attacking bombers flew perpendic-ular to U.S. lines. The results were predictable to everyone but the airmen. Bad weather precipitated a cancellation on 24 July, but a number of aircraft dropped anyway, with many bombs falling short onto U.S. troops; 25 Americans died, and a further 131 were wounded. The next day dawned clear; the raids swept in with 1,000 bombers and fighter-bombers blasting German positions. Only the more accurate fighter-bombers were to hit German positions on the front line, but another error by the B-17s resulted in a heavy bombardment of American positions. This time 111 American soldiers, including Lieutenant General Leslie McNair, died; another 490 soldiers were wounded. Nevertheless, the bombardment, while it did not entirely break enemy resistance, hurt the Germans badly.

The American attackers, though severely shaken, discovered that Ger-man defenses now contained holes through which they could press. For the Germans, the fighting after the bombardment destroyed what was left of many units, while the supply situation, particularly in terms of artillery ammunition, was desperate. After receiving an order from Kluge that his division, Panzer Lehr, must hold, General Fritz Bayerlin replied: "Out in front everyone is holding out. Everyone. My grenadiers and my engineers, and my tank crews—they're holding their ground. Not a single one is leav-ing his post. They are lying silent in their foxholes for they are dead."[4] At first the Americans failed to achieve a breakthrough. But Collins pushed his reserves forward before German troubles were entirely clear; thus, VII Corps picked up speed as pockets of German resistance crumbled.

Moreover, there were few German reserves in the west, while a local attack by British forces on the eastern end of the battlefield focused Ger-man attention away from the unraveling situation to the west. Collins's troops advanced to the southwest, cutting behind German defenders, who were holding in front of VIII Corps. Collins recognized that the situation of-fered the possibility for a complete breakout of U.S. forces, while Bradley was still emphasizing a breakthrough. The capture of Coutances, followed shortly by Cérences and La Haye-Pesnel, signaled the collapse of German positions in western Normandy. U.S. attacks were now forcing German de-fenders away from the coast; their flank hung in the air. On the 30th, U.S. troops captured Avranches, which sits on great bluffs overlooking the Bay of Mont St. Michel; the next morning, they seized bridges just south of the town. The roads of France beckoned; the German line, which had stretched from the western shores of Normandy to the Channel near Caen, had finally cracked.

Unfortunately, senior U.S. leaders had focused so much attention on achieving a breakthrough in June and July that they failed to consider whether plans to liberate the Breton ports were still relevant. The German demolitions in Cherbourg should have suggested that the ports in Brittany would not be of much use. Montgomery—and Eisenhower to a lesser extent—recognized that the situation had changed in fundamental ways; but Bradley clung to "the plan," and the plan called for an advance into Brittany. The 4th Armored Division's commander, Major General John Wood, vigorously challenged the order to head west. On 1 August, Third Army under George Patton was finally activated to conduct the breakout. Patton sympathized with Wood's objections, but considering his delicate position, particularly his relations with Bradley, he was hardly in a position to argue. Thus, the first two U.S. divisions through Avranches, the 4th Armored and 6th Armored Divisions, swung west into Brittany. The Americans executed a brilliant exploitation of the breakthrough, but in the wrong direction. Eventually, even Bradley awoke to the fact that the pre-invasion plan should not dictate a move into Brittany. It suggested, rather, that in the case of a German collapse U.S. forces might dispense entirely with Brittany, turn the enemy's flank, and drive east to push the Wehrmacht out of France. The next corps moving through Avranches turned south and east toward Le Mans and the German supply dumps behind the Normandy battlefields.

With their operational situation worsening, the Germans at this point made a disastrous mistake. Looking at the narrow joint of the breakthrough, the Führer ordered a determined counterattack at Avranches to cut off the lead American units and to restore the front through to the Atlantic. What appeared obvious on the map, however, looked quite different to those on the spot. Avranches itself dominated the surrounding countryside, while terrain to the east and north provided favorable defensive positions. Moreover, Patton, as his newly constituted Third Army flowed through Avranches, had added depth to U.S. positions. Allied fighter-bombers maintained absolute control of the air and consistently brought massive firepower to bear on enemy troop and armor concentrations. Finally, Ultra had warned of the coming German attack, although it seems to have played little or no role in the American dispositions when the German attack began. When the Führer's order arrived to move German panzer divisions west from the British sector into what was clearly a potential encirclement, the Allies received the order as well.

Kluge was in no position to argue, however. Involved in the 20 July assassination attempt on Hitler's life, the field marshal knew that his life hung in the balance. By using reserves that were reaching the theater to replace panzer divisions already in the line, Kluge cobbled together four panzer divisions to launch the counterattack. The U.S. 30th Infantry Division, defending the position through which the Nazi counterattack would come, was a solid outfit, while the terrain favored the defenders. The initial attack, although ragged—only three of the assault groups jumped off at the correct time—achieved some local successes. Yet, at St. Barthelmy north of Mortain, the 1st Battalion, 117th Infantry Regiment, blunted the attack of the 1st SS Panzer and 2nd Panzer Divisions until the sun burned through the fog on the morning of 7 August.

Meanwhile, the German advance had isolated four companies of the 2nd Battalion, 120th Infantry Regiment, on Hill 317, while approximately 70 tanks broke through Mortain and headed west. But they did not get far. From their vantage point on 317, the Americans called in massive artillery fire on the enemy columns. German attacks on Hill 317 failed to take out the Americans, while Allied fighter-bombers and artillery ceaselessly battered the Wehrmacht troops. By 12 August, when relief finally arrived, only 357 of approximately 700 men on Hill 317 were able to walk off under their own power. The four company commanders received Distinguished Service Crosses. The Mortain counterattack had failed. Nevertheless, Hitler flirted with the idea of resuming the counterattack and ordered two more panzer divisions facing the British to move west.

Meanwhile, Patton's exploitation to the south and east was throwing an encircling arm around German forces in Normandy. USAAF fighter-bombers played an essential role in breaking up pockets of German resistance and allowing Patton's flying columns to maintain their mobility. Here, Major General Elwood "Pete" Quesada's innovative leadership of IX Tactical Air Command represented one of the brighter spots in U.S. air-ground cooperation during World War II. By putting pilots with radios into the lead armor columns as forward air controllers, Quesada was able to provide advancing U.S. troops with responsive, effective air support when needed. Ultra intelligence indicated that the German heads were in the noose. Not until the Americans had reached Alençon on 11 August did Hitler react to the growing encirclement of his forces in Normandy and authorize a counterattack to hit the Americans on the flank—the first move toward escape.

Neither Montgomery nor Bradley grasped the possibility of encircling the German forces. On 11 August, Montgomery determined that Argentan would remain the boundary line between his forces driving from the north and the Americans from the south. Admittedly, U.S. forces were farther away, but there were no Germans in front of them, while the remains of Hitlerjugend still blocked British and Canadians approaching from the north. The Canadians displayed all too much of the cautious, unimaginative training they had received at British hands from 1940 through 1944. Moreover, the British corps supporting the Canadians was led by General Neil Ritchie, who had presided over the disaster of the Gazala battles in May and June of 1942 and had not improved with age. Only the Polish First Armored Division showed a consistent willingness to grapple with the Germans on their front, and they would lead the slow advance on Falaise.

Patton was the only Allied commander who grasped the fleeting opportunity. On the evening of 12 August, he pressed Bradley to let Major General Wade Haislip's XV Corps go all the way to Falaise, which would have completely encircled German forces in Normandy. But Patton met obdurate rejection. After the war Bradley blamed the stop order on Montgomery, but the record underlines his responsibility. As the British advance ground southward, and as Bradley procrastinated, Patton suggested a more ambitious and operationally imaginative solution. On 17 August, he urged Bradley to allow Third Army to turn northeast and sweep down both banks of the Seine to entrap Germans escaping from Falaise. The problem was that Bradley and Montgomery were focusing on the gaining of territory rather than on the destruction of German forces in France. Not surprisingly, Patton again met with a curt refusal.

Meanwhile, the Germans kept the jaws of the Falaise pocket open sufficiently to extricate approximately 50,000 soldiers from the wreckage. From 13 through 20 August, when the Allies finally closed off escape, the toughest soldiers in the German Army made their way through the destruction wrought by incessant Allied fighter-bomber attacks. The wrecked equipment, slaughtered horses, and smashed body parts resembled a scene from Dante's inferno. But those who escaped through the bottleneck survived to fight another day; and they provided the framework to rebuild the German Army in the west. Admittedly, they had lost most of their equipment, but back in the Reich, Albert Speer's factories were producing vast quantities of armaments that would reequip the battered formations escaping from Normandy.

As the Falaise battle reached a crescendo, the German high command went through another crisis. Kluge had proven no more successful than Rundstedt and Rommel. Moreover, as the Gestapo worked its way through the evidence from the 20 July conspiracy to assassinate Hitler, the investigators identified a core of resistance within Army Group Center, Kluge's command in 1942 and 1943. On 15 August, Hitler's suspicions of his commander in the west reached the boiling point. On that day, Kluge had gone to visit subordinate commanders to gain a firsthand view of what was happening at the front. Due to a communications breakdown, the OKW could not reach Kluge for most of the day; the Führer concluded that the field marshal was negotiating a surrender with the Americans. Hitler's response was immediate; he sacked Kluge and ordered Field Marshal Model to assume command in the west. Sensing his fate, Kluge wrote the Führer a long letter of self-justification and then, on his way home from France, committed suicide.

After the war, many German generals argued that they had followed Hitler's obtuse orders to the letter, as a way not to prolong the war but to hasten its end. In fact, almost to a man they consistently tried to mitigate Hitler's instructions and to improve on them whenever possible. By doing so, they lessened the extent of German defeats and contributed to the war's continuation into 1945. Had Kluge followed Hitler's orders to the letter, he would have ensured the destruction of Army Group B, a result that might have ended the war in 1944. But as with the great majority of generals, Kluge did his duty to the "bitter end," whatever the consequences for the German people.

The Falaise disaster was not the only problem confronting the Germans in mid-August. On 15 August, the Americans launched Operation Dragoon, their landing in southern France with the French-American Sixth Army Group. That decision, which pulled much of the U.S. Army's strength out of Italy, caused considerable bad blood between the American and British chiefs of staff. The latter, strongly supported by Churchill, had argued that major prospects still existed in Italy for Allied troops to push the Germans back on the Alps, capture the Po River valley, and seize Italy's northern industrial region. But the Americans insisted that Italy was a side show and that crucial strategic and operational gains could be made by landing in southern France and then driving north to link up with the Allied breakout from Normandy.

The Americans were right. Dragoon cleaned up southern France and provided the Allies with an unbroken front that ran from the Channel to Switzerland. More important, the capture of the great port of Marseilles in southern France proved a logistic godsend to the supply of U.S. forces fighting on the German frontier in fall and winter 1944–45, especially since the Allies could not use the port of Antwerp until December. Dragoon captured Marseilles' facilities in undamaged condition, while the French rail network up the Rhone River valley remained intact because Allied air forces had concentrated mostly on destruction of the French railroad network in northern, western, and central France.

Meanwhile, Model, having replaced Kluge, threw himself into directing the defensive battle with his accustomed energy, but his efforts were not enough to restore the collapse. With heavy losses in Normandy, there was no chance of a defense on the Seine, as Hitler proposed; the real question was whether the Germans could save enough forces to defend the Franco-German frontier effectively and prevent the Allies from bouncing the Rhine. For Allied leaders, the German strength in France had collapsed with startling suddenness, and the focus on achieving a breakthrough prevented them from fully exploiting the hard-won victory. In the largest sense, Montgomery, Bradley, and Eisenhower missed the opportunity to destroy Wehrmacht forces in the west.

Bradley consistently interfered with Patton's exploitation of the developing situation. On 15 August, arriving at Third Army Headquarters, the First Army commander ordered a halt all along a line that stopped Patton's army on the Seine and at Chartres and Orléans. Only reluctantly did he allow Patton to keep his bridgehead across the Seine. On the other hand, Patton stands out as the exception among Allied commanders; on the 24th he again pressed Bradley to allow Third Army to launch a great, sweeping encirclement to cut deep ahead of the oncoming British and Canadian forces to entrap German forces in the west. Bradley would have none of it.

Failure on the Frontier

As the Allied drives across France gathered steam, Montgomery began arguing for a single great drive into the Reich on the northern flank of the Allied advance—an advance that would, not surprisingly, come under his command. Montgomery's suggestion possessed no real operational focus, except to grab more territory. Moreover, had British forces reached the Rhine without the logistical support of Antwerp, they would have confronted insurmountable supply shortages, while the Germans would have been fighting in their own backyard. After the war, the British military pundit Basil Liddell Hart argued that a single drive was the only hope the Allies had to end the war in 1944, but that Patton, not Montgomery, was the general most suitable to lead it! But at the end of August, Patton was unfortunately focusing on Metz, which was, ironically, one of the few areas in the west where the Germans were capable of putting up effective resistance. Patton's misplaced emphasis was the result of the distortions that Pershing had inculcated in the American official histories and lessons-learned analyses of World War I. Metz was not a crucial logistical center but rather a formidable fortress city, quite simply not worth a major attack.

In fact, Eisenhower's concept of a broad front advance, as opposed to a

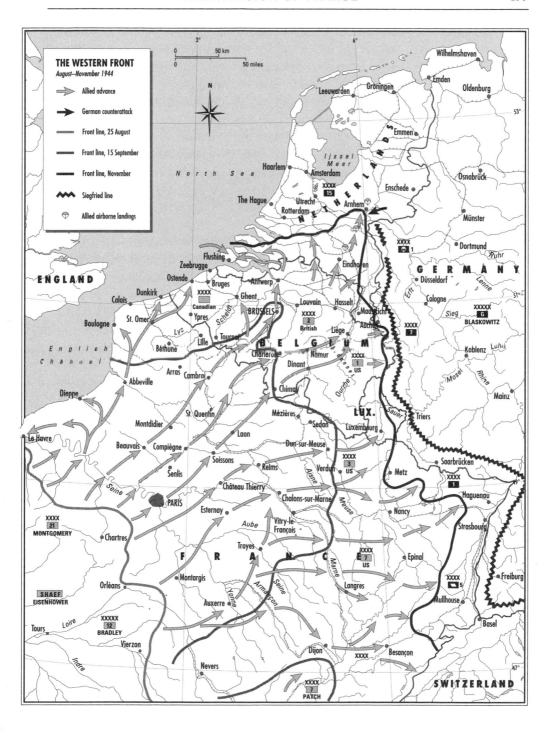

THE WESTERN FRONT
August–November 1944

Allied advance

German counterattack

Front line, 25 August

Front line, 15 September

Front line, November

Siegfried line

Allied airborne landings

single drive, possessed the greatest chance of breaking down German defenses in the west, but to do so required an assertive leadership style that the supreme commander never practiced—and one that probably would have backfired, given the egotism that characterized most of the leading Allied generals. The largest objection to a single, major drive—by either the British or Americans—is that such an approach would have thoroughly disrupted alliance politics. Eisenhower understood this, but Montgomery and Brooke refused to recognize that political reality and continued to advocate a single drive. One makes war as one can, not as one would like.

Much of the argument over the single-drive versus the broad-front approach has reflected the general appearance of German collapse in August 1944. As the Allied pursuit gathered steam, driving across the Seine, liberating Paris, and then approaching the Low Countries, euphoria gripped Allied soldiers from generals on down. Eisenhower's deputy, Walter Bedell Smith, commented in Paris in early September that in a military sense the war was won. But it was not. Given the personalities of those in command and the logistical realities, the failure to win in 1944 was predetermined from the beginning of the campaign.

As the pursuing Allied divisions hit the Seine, Eisenhower considered bypassing Paris, so that his logisticians would not have to feed the city's population. However, the citizens of Paris rose in revolt, while military reality argued that the Allies could not leave a Wehrmacht-occupied Paris behind them in their drive to the German frontier. General Phillipe Leclerc's 2nd French Armored Division received the honor of reinforcing the French resistance partisans and liberating the capital. Luckily for civilization, the newly appointed German commandant of Paris, General Dietrich von Choltitz, disobeyed Hitler's orders to destroy the city; rather, for one of the few times in the war, a German general followed the course of decency and conscience. Nevertheless, Leclerc's division was rendered *hors de combat* as hordes of enthusiastic French, mostly women, engulfed their liberators with wine and affection; the unit would not reappear as combat ready for the next several weeks.

As August shifted into September, Allied drives continued at full speed, while a desperate Model attempted to revitalize German defenses. On 1 September, Eisenhower assumed control of the ground battle from Montgomery, who continued to lead Twenty-First Army Group. But Bradley now became Montgomery's equal in command of Twelfth Army Group. To assuage Montgomery's ego as well as public opinion, the British government promoted him to field marshal. But Eisenhower's movement of SHAEF to Paris also involved the movement of Lieutenant General John C.

Lee's Communication Zone logistical headquarters, including the general's personal piano, in direct contravention of Eisenhower's orders. Lee executed his move by utilizing much of the C-47 transport fleet, just as supply shortages, especially fuel, were appearing throughout the European Theater of Operations.

Two factors were now coming into play as the Allies approached the German border. First, at the end of July, SHAEF's logisticians had increased the ammunition allocation to Allied forces fighting in Normandy and lowered the fuel allocations on the basis of troop demand thus far in the fighting. The second factor was that the advance placed Allied ground forces on the far side of a transportation wasteland created by Allied air forces when they isolated the Germans from their supplies. The French railroads no longer ran on time, or at all.

On 1 September troops of the British Second Army took Amiens and crossed the Somme, passing by memorials to Germany's previous attempt to rule Europe. The main British drive was now heading in a northeasterly direction. Meanwhile, the U.S. First Army had captured Laon and was approaching the Meuse at Mézières. On its left, Patton's Third Army had just taken Verdun and was heading due east toward Metz. Thus, the Allied drives were diverging—Montgomery toward the north and Patton toward the east. But nowhere did the Germans yet display signs of stiffening in their flight from France. Instead, weary Nazi troops made their way back to the German frontier, while a few rearguard *Kampfgruppen* attempted to delay the Allied advance. Throughout this period, Montgomery badgered Eisenhower to put the Allied effort into his drive onto the north German plain. Eisenhower, however, declined to turn the whole show over to Montgomery. But he was willing to provide substantial additional support to the British.

The major factor in Ike's decision, which soon led to Operation Market Garden, lay in his belief that Antwerp, because of its port facilities, represented *the* crucial objective in the puzzle for the coming fall and winter campaigns. His directives to Twenty-First Army Group emphasized that capturing Antwerp and opening the Scheldt River were Montgomery's most important priorities. However, for one of the few times in his career, Montgomery had his eyes fastened on a sweeping, risk-taking approach to operations. He decided to throw everything he had into striking for the north German plain, leaving Antwerp for solution at a later date.

Montgomery's failure to open the Scheldt may have been deliberate—so that there would be sufficient supplies to support only his drive over the Rhine. Then, for logistical reasons, SHAEF's forces would have had to support his single thrust onto the north German plain. The obstinate refusal of Twenty-First Army Group to support the Canadian First Army, who were supposed to clear the banks of the Scheldt of German forces, as well as Montgomery's directions that they focus instead on the capture of the Channel ports, provides circumstantial evidence for this interpretation. Not until mid-October, and then only after pressure from the Royal Navy as well as Eisenhower, would Montgomery give priority to supplying the Canadians with artillery ammunition and thus provide them with the support necessary to open the Scheldt.

In early September, the British drive reached its culmination. On the evening of 3 September, the Guards Armored Division pressed through Brussels; two days later, the 11th Armored Division reached Antwerp and to its astonishment captured the port in undamaged condition. Moreover, by capturing Antwerp, the British had almost entirely isolated the German Fifteenth Army, which was desperately trying to escape up the Channel coast. Yet, because Antwerp lies a considerable distance up the Scheldt estuary, the Allies needed to capture both river banks, particularly the Dutch islands of Walcheren and South Beveland, in order to use the port. An advance of only 18 miles from Antwerp would have cut off the entire estuary, thus trapping Fifteenth Army in southern Holland and northwest Belgium. Inexplicably, the British advance stopped. The division commander refused to act, while Montgomery was already looking toward the north German plain rather than concentrating on the seemingly unrewarding task of securing Antwerp. After the war, Montgomery's supporters used the excuse that the British spearheads were out of fuel; in fact, XXX Corps near Brussels had sufficient fuel for another 100 kilometers.

The decision to halt at Antwerp had a number of fateful consequences. First, the German Fifteenth Army largely escaped. On 6 September, with covering support from flak batteries on both sides of the Scheldt, the Germans began ferrying 80,000 troops across to Walcheren Island on the north side of the Scheldt estuary. For the second time in the 1944 campaign in France, the Allies had allowed a major German force to escape encirclement and destruction. From there, Fifteenth Army's troops deployed across South Beveland and back into Holland directly to the north of British forces. This action had a twofold effect. It provided the Germans with solid control of the Scheldt estuary, a hold British and Canadian troops would not be able to break until late November. Equally important, the escaping Germans provided a crucial reserve for defending southern Holland.

And so the British halted on the Dutch frontier, as Montgomery planned what would soon become Operation Market Garden—the thrust of the

British Army and its supporting cast over the Rhine. Such a move, he hoped, would draw the support required for the one-drive strategy he so strongly advocated. At this point Eisenhower provided Montgomery with virtually everything he asked for, including the highest priority for fuel. By the end of the first week in September, Montgomery had settled the details for the upcoming attack, beginning with an airborne assault by the U.S. 82nd and 101st Airborne Divisions and the British 1st Airborne, supported by the Polish airborne brigade.

It was at this point that the failure to destroy German forces in Normandy exercised a second baneful effect on upcoming operations. Almost concurrently with Antwerp's capture, and just as planning for Market Garden was beginning, Ultra revealed that the Germans were transferring the 9th and 10th SS Panzer Divisions for "rest and refit" in the "Venloo, Arnheim [Arnhem], Hertogenbosch" areas.[5] There they were to receive new drafts and equipment to make up for heavy losses in Normandy. The 9th SS Panzer Division would eventually entrain for the Reich to carry out its refit near Koblenz, but many of its units were still in the area when the airborne attack came.

To add to Allied bad luck, the Germans located a number of key headquarters in the area immediately north of Antwerp. Model, now number two in the west as commander of Army Group B—Rundstedt had returned to overall command—located his headquarters near Arnhem. In addition, General Kurt Student, the paratrooper general who had led the assault on Holland in 1940, had arrived from his training billet in the Reich and received command of a ragtag force, with the imposing title of First Parachute Army, confronting the British along the Albert Canal. Finally, an SS corps headquarters under Wilhelm Bittrich remained near Arnhem to oversee refitting of 9th and 10th SS Panzer Divisions. Thus, the Germans had a number of experienced commanders in the area who by training and inclination would respond effectively to Market Garden.

The reconstituting of German forces north of Antwerp would play a major role in the coming battle, but Allied carelessness and planning mistakes would prove equally costly. The significance of the Ultra messages concerning the 9th and 10th SS Panzer Divisions was lost to Allied intelligence due to breakdowns in Montgomery's staff. Moreover, within a few days, confirming intelligence about the presence of German armor in the Arnhem area came out from the Dutch underground. That warning too was ignored, this time not only by Montgomery's Twenty-First Army Group but by the British airborne commanders as well. Montgomery's plan was simple enough; ironically, it was similar to the German plan that had broken down the Dutch defenses around Fortress Holland in 1940. But back then, the Germans had committed the equivalent of only a single reinforced airborne brigade and a single panzer division. In this new attack, Montgomery would use three and a half airborne divisions to capture the bridges leading across southern Holland toward the Rhine at Eindhoven, Grave, Nijmegen, and Arnhem, where the bridge over the Rhine provided access to the north German plains. The supporting force would be XXX Corps, led by Lieutenant General Brian Horrocks. It would drive straight up the airborne corridor to reinforce the Arnhem bridgehead. Once that position was secure, Montgomery believed his forces could strike out onto the north German plain.

The commander of the Allied First Airborne Army was Lieutenant General Louis Brereton, who possessed an undistinguished war record but was clearly a survivor. Brereton had been involved in a number of disasters, including the destruction of the B-17 force at Clark Field in the Philippines in December 1941. But like MacArthur, Brereton displayed considerable skill in deflecting blame onto shoulders other than his own. His most recent command of Ninth Tactical Air Force had not exactly cloaked him in glory, but he had many friends in high places, and he displayed an array of qualities beloved by the Army Air Forces—with hard-drinking, golf-playing, and womanizing foremost. With little knowledge of airborne or ground operations, Brereton found himself in command of the Allied Airborne Army. Nevertheless, despite the fact the British contributed only one division, they dominated Market Garden's planning as well as command positions.

The man selected to plan and command Market Garden was an immaculate guardsman, Lieutenant General Frederick "Boy" Browning. It is not entirely clear why Browning received command of the operation over the more experienced American general Matthew Ridgway, commander of the newly constituted XVIII Airborne Corps. Undoubtedly, the fact that the attack was in support of Twenty-First Army Group had much to do with the choice. Browning's celebrity included his marriage to the novelist Daphne du Maurier. He appears to have received his corps command because Brooke felt the guards establishment needed an appointment at corps level. Browning had been involved with airborne units for a relatively lengthy period of time, but he had never jumped in combat. He now decided to accompany the operation with his entire corps staff, a decision that diverted 34 gliders from the number available to the British 1st Airborne Division in its attack on Arnhem. When his intelligence officer, Major Brian Urquhart, confronted him with aerial photographs confirming Dutch reports of German armor in the Arnhem area, Browning declared, "I wouldn't trouble myself about these if I were you . . . They're probably not serviceable at any rate."[6] Browning then sacked Urquhart and sent him off for a rest, while at the same time failing to inform 1st Airborne Division of this vital information. By then it was probably too late to cancel the operation, but British paratroopers could certainly have adjusted their loads to take along additional anti-tank mines and weapons.

The determination of where the divisions would drop underscores the mistakes made in the planning. The easiest drops would involve the experienced U.S. 101st and 82nd Airborne Divisions, while the inexperienced British 1st Airborne Division would execute the most dangerous drop at Arnhem. The latter division's commander, Major General Roy Urquhart, a tough Scots infantryman, had no experience with airborne operations. The division staff's initial plan placed the bulk of its landing force in the immediate vicinity of the Arnhem bridge. But the air transport commander, Air Vice Marshal L. N. Hollinghurst, rejected the drop zones south of the bridge, because they required his aircraft to pass over heavy concentrations of flak. He also insisted that the ground was too soft for gliders and their vehicles. Urquhart acquiesced and settled for another drop zone more than six miles from the objective. General Richard N. Gale, who commanded the British 6th Airborne Division in Normandy, later commented that he would have resigned as divisional commander had he been in Urquhart's position. After the war, General James Gain, commander of the 82nd Airborne, commented that he would have taken the RAF's refusal to drop the paratroopers on their chosen drop zone all the way to Eisenhower.

The 1st Airborne Division's acceptance of a distant drop zone put the operation in jeopardy for another reason: airlift planners refused to consider more than one drop per day. Urquhart would have to wait until another day for much of his division, and then two days for the Polish Airborne Brigade. Much of the first day's force would have to guard the drop zones for the next day's wave of paratroopers. The subtraction of 34 gliders from the 1st Airborne Division's lift to support Browning's corps, combined with Urquhart's need to guard the drop zone *and* take the Arnhem bridge, meant that the British attack, despite being the deepest and most exposed drop, would be seriously short of fighting power. The cascading consequences of such shoddy planning guaranteed that Market Garden's flaws would prove fatal.

One additional mishap plagued the operation. None of the British radios taken into the bridgehead worked upon arrival. Thus, for much of the fight, the British airborne remained out of touch with the Allied command structure, and no one outside of the perimeters around Arnhem bridge and

Oosterbeek—the drop zone where the bulk of 1st Airborne Division fought and died—had a clue as to the desperate situation.

If Market Garden suffered from faulty assumptions at the outset, its actual execution quickly revealed larger strategic and operational weaknesses in Montgomery's thinking. From the first, German resistance was tenacious and effective. The commanders on the spot—Model, Student, and Bittrich—reacted in the coordinated, aggressive fashion called for by German doctrine. They were considerably helped by the capture of Market Garden's plans, when an American officer, in direct disobedience to orders, took a full set of plans along with him to his death in a glider crash. Within hours, Student—a man eminently qualified to understand airborne operations—had the Allied plans in his hands.

The 101st and the 82nd Airborne Divisions captured most of the bridges that were their targets or replaced them when blown. The British pushed a battalion onto the north side of the Arnhem bridge. But then things went very wrong very quickly. In Arnhem, Waffen SS troopers, whose presence in the area Browning had so casually dismissed, blocked movement into the town from every direction after one British battalion had slipped past. Thus, the Germans had isolated the 1st Airborne Division from its target. Urquhart, the division commander, was cut off inside the town. Moreover, the weather turned foggy, so that the Poles, scheduled to drop south of Arnhem on day three, did not arrive until day five.

Farther south, XXX Armored Corps' troops made an exceptionally slow advance up the airborne corridor. German troops in the area, many of whom were escapees from Fifteenth Army, launched a series of savage and effective counterattacks as the troops of XXX Corps crawled their way north toward Arnhem. On a number of occasions the Germans succeeded in cutting the corridor, which forced the British to backtrack and regain positions captured earlier. Dempsey, as commander of the Second Army, had ordered the XXX Corps to make as rapid an advance as possible. The advance was anything but that. After they had captured the bridge at Nijmegen at great cost, paratroopers from the 82nd Airborne Division watched—infuriated—as tankers from the Guards Armored Division stopped to brew up tea. By the time British armor reached the south bank of the Rhine at Arnhem, all that remained was to rescue the survivors from across the river. The 8,000 casualties suffered by the British 1st Airborne Division stands in stark contrast to the 1,500 casualties suffered by *all* the units in XXX Corps.

Undeniably, Nazi ideology contributed to the fighting effectiveness of Wehrmacht units; but German military doctrine, with its emphasis on exploitation, speed, decentralized decision-making, and above all discipline, also contributed to the response at Arnhem. At every juncture the Germans proved that any assumptions about the Wehrmacht's defeat were premature. Perhaps the saddest comment on the British failure lay in an all-too-successful effort by Browning, with the connivance of Dempsey and Montgomery, to blame the Polish Airborne Brigade's commander, Brigadier General Stanislow Sosabowski for the failure. His only mistake had been to warn his superiors against overconfidence.

Market Garden's dismal showing reflected the systemic and conceptual mistakes of Allied leaders, their inability to grasp the conduct of war on the operational level, and the inherent difficulties of the Western Front in September 1944. In the largest sense, Montgomery's strategy was territorial in nature, aimed at gaining a bridgehead over the Rhine and then fighting a battle on the north German plain. But there were no discernable operational objectives such as the cutting off of German forces or the isolation of the Ruhr, one goal of Eisenhower's operational approach. The irony was that in stopping the advance of his troops on 6 September so that he could prepare to jump to the Rhine, Montgomery closed off the possibility of trapping and destroying the German Fifteenth Army, which was not yet in position to fight a sustained battle at the mouth of the Scheldt River.

Eisenhower at least had the foresight to recognize Antwerp's crucial importance to the resolution of a looming logistical nightmare. The one time in his career that Montgomery refused to play his usual cautious game, the outcome was tragic. Instead of opening the Scheldt and taking advantage of Antwerp's capture, the new field marshal dreamed of a distant decisive victory. Brooke, who rarely found fault with Montgomery, returned from the Quebec Conference in early October to note in his diary that Allied setbacks were entirely the result of Montgomery's September mistakes.

Montgomery's halt allowed the Germans time to cobble together military forces sufficient to hold the Allies at bay. But if his plan to strike over the Rhine and fight a decisive battle on the far bank had succeeded, it might in fact have resulted in an even more serious defeat. With the Scheldt still closed, any effort to fight a major battle on German territory with tenuous supply lines reaching back all the way to Normandy was a recipe for serious trouble. And American forces to the south, immobilized by Montgomery's drive, would have been incapable of pressuring the Germans. The support Montgomery received for Market Garden represented a substantial portion of what he was demanding for his single-thrust strategy. In the end, the field marshal failed to deliver either the Rhine crossing or Antwerp.

Meanwhile, the withdrawal of the C-47s to get ready for the airborne operation ended the airlift of gas to Patton's forces. By the time Third Army's advance resumed, German forces defending Metz were already established. Whatever opportunities existed for further exploitation on the Western Front were rapidly disappearing. But Patton, directed by Bradley and Eisenhower and misled by the U.S. Army's reading of European geography in the interwar period, was already driving at the wrong objective in moving against Metz, even before he lost his fuel. He might have had a better chance to reach the Rhine had he pushed toward the Ardennes, the very area through which the Germans had stormed in 1940. Equally useful to the Allied cause, Patton might also have closed up with the forces of Sixth Army Group which were advancing up the Rhone River valley. The failure to close that gap allowed much of Army Group G to escape despite a clear warning from Ultra that sizeable numbers of Germans (more than 50,000 troops) were eluding capture.

By mid-September, Allied ground forces were facing the harsh realities of a supply crisis, occasioned by their rapid advance across France. The problem lay not only in the distance from Normandy but in the damage their own air campaign had inflicted on the French railway system. The Allies not only had to funnel supplies to their forces on the German frontier but also had to feed much of the Belgian and French civilian populations—a task rendered more difficult by the four years of extensive expropriations made by the occupying Germans. What prevented the Allies from suffering a major strategic or operational defeat in late 1944 was Operation Dragoon, which opened up the only undamaged section of the French transportation network. Through the rest of 1944, Marseilles was responsible for carrying nearly 40 percent of the supplies used by Allied armies fighting on the Western Front.

Conclusion

In the largest sense, Operation Overlord achieved its objectives: to return the armies of the Western powers to the European Continent. It was the most complex and difficult military operation of World War II because the Allies had not only to achieve a successful lodgment but also to match the flow of German reinforcements onto the Normandy battlefield. The initial airborne and amphibious assaults succeeded, despite Bradley's botching of the Omaha Beach landing. But once ashore, Anglo-American forces found themselves engaged in an intractable battle against a skilled and effective foe. In the ensuing confrontation, they fought the Germans to exhaustion and collapse. While Allied armies adapted according to the actual operational and tactical situation they faced, the stalemate in June and July reflected a failure to give sufficient forethought to the problems in fighting through the bocage region of western France. Perhaps that was inevitable, given the logistic and tactical difficulties that amphibious operations create.

But it also reflected a general lack of intellectual preparation for war at the operational level. Throughout much of 1944, Allied generals focused on the immediate tactical problems of the landing and buildup, without paying sufficient attention to longer-range operational possibilities. When Allied armies broke out in early August, senior commanders had failed to think through the possibilities offered by a breakout. The uncoordinated pursuit into Brittany prevented an effective initial exploitation. Even when the Germans cooperated by moving their armor deeper into the emerging Mortain pocket, Bradley, with little intervention from Eisenhower, refused to accord Patton's ideas serious attention. Thus, significant German forces escaped. Within a few weeks, Montgomery—dreaming of decisive victory on the north German plain—allowed another significant German force to survive to fight again.

For those who walk the silent cemeteries of Normandy, the cost of victory may seem steep indeed. The fighting between 6 June and 29 August cost the Twenty-First Army Group (consisting of British, Canadian, and Polish troops) 83,045 casualties. American ground troops suffered a further 125,847 casualties. In addition, the RAF and the USAAF each lost over 8,000 men, while preinvasion maneuvers cost the Allies a further 12,000 killed or wounded. Altogether, Allied losses were approximately 225,000. On the other side, the Germans suffered over 200,000 casualties, with an additional 200,000 captured. By any standard, the summer campaign of 1944 was a bloodbath, on a par with the battles of the First World War— the only difference being that the losses were spread over much of France rather than concentrated in a small area.

In the end, though, the Allies won a great victory that liberated France and set the stage for the final destruction of Nazi Germany. That strategic achievement brought the armed might and the ideals of democracy back onto the Continent and eventually into Central Europe, establishing preconditions not only for the postwar peace but for eventual victory over Communism in the Cold War. Thus, the invasion of France was a triumph of great significance for the political future of Europe in the last half of the twentieth century, as well as for the eradication of Nazi Germany.

16

THE END IN EUROPE

1944–1945

As summer 1944 waned, victory over the Third Reich was certain. Among the Allies, the question was not "if" but "when." For a brief moment in late August and early September, the Nazi regime, under siege from all directions, teetered on the verge of defeat. But the end did not come. Despite their seemingly hopeless situation, and in the face of unremitting Allied pressure, the Germans fought on with grim ferocity and palpable fanaticism, reinforced by knowledge of the crimes for which they must answer in defeat—crimes all too familiar to civilians as well as the military. During every day that the war ground on, tens of thousands died—in slave labor camps, on the front lines, as the victims of military operations, and in German cities pounded by Allied air forces.

For the Allies, a second looming question was how military operations in the final days of the war would reconfigure the postwar world. Stalin in particular shaped the conduct of Soviet military campaigns to gain political control over Eastern Europe and the Balkans. His aim was not to end the war as quickly as possible but rather to ensure that the Red Army physically controlled those territories he regarded as lying within his sphere of influence at the conflict's termination.

The Soviet Summer and Fall Offensives

For two years, the fighting on the Eastern Front had raged in the south, while in the north the Soviets had finally driven the Germans back from Leningrad over the winter of 1943–44. But in the center, the Germans remained in control of much of the Belorussian territory they had seized in 1941. The Soviets now set about to rectify that state of affairs. Yet the great offensive against Army Group Center was only one of five the STAVKA

planned for summer and fall 1944; the larger objective of these campaigns
was to push Soviet forces deep into the Balkans and position them for the
kill in Central Europe.

The first Soviet blow hit Finland on 10 June 1944. Soviet forces possessed overwhelming superiority in numbers and firepower—nearly half
a million troops and 10,000 artillery pieces and mortars against Finnish
forces of 268,000 troops and less than 2,000 artillery pieces. Given their
previous experience with the Finns, the Soviets took no chances. Soviet
maskirovka failed to fool Finnish intelligence, but Finland's high command
disregarded the warnings. The Twenty-First and Twenty-Third Soviet Armies struck north from Leningrad toward Viipuri and almost immediately
broke through. Eleven days later, a second attack hit the front in Karelia.
By 21 June the Soviets had captured Viipuri, but by mid-July, with considerable German help, the Finns had stabilized the front. Nevertheless, their
heavy losses and the collapse of German forces elsewhere led Finland to
sue for peace in late August. Soviet terms were harsh, but at least they preserved Finnish independence—a reflection of Stalin's long-term worries
about the postwar balance in the Baltic and his recognition of American
sympathies for the Finns.

The offensive against Finland, as well as the invasions of Italy and Normandy, drew the Reich's attention away from Army Group Center. There,
maskirovka disguised Soviet preparations. Foreign Armies East under Colonel Reinhard Gehlen, later the head of the Bundesrepublik's intelligence
services and adviser to the American intelligence agencies on the Soviet
Union, predicted that the Red Army's main efforts would come in the
north and south, not against the center. The distribution of panzer divisions on the Eastern Front underlines the success of Soviet deception.
Army Group Center possessed only three panzer divisions, while Army
Group North Ukraine and Army Group South Ukraine had eight each. By
1944, the Soviets had become masters of deception; false signals, dummy
positions, misleading troop movements behind the front lines, and highly
skilled camouflage all covered Soviet operational intentions from the prying eyes of German intelligence. Moreover, the lack of Luftwaffe aircraft on
the Eastern Front meant that German intelligence received little support
from aerial reconnaissance.

Over May and June 1944, the Soviets gathered their forces. Marshals
Zhukov and Vasilevsky each commanded two fronts—the former with five
armies, the latter with seven. These tactical preparations caused some disquiet among German frontline units; Ninth Army in particular became
alarmed. But Army Group Center's commander, Field Marshal Ernst

Busch, a thoroughly undistinguished soldier, remained under Hitler's thumb and refused to initiate any action not in accord with the Führer's wishes. So blind was the German high command that even during the first three days of the actual attack, Busch and the OKH failed to recognize the extent of the Soviet offensive and its goals. By then, they were witnessing the complete collapse of Army Group Center.

Operation Bagration began on 22 June 1944, just 12 days after the invasion of Finland and 16 days after D-Day. But more significant to the Soviets, it began on the third anniversary of Barbarossa—the German invasion of the Soviet Union. The first stroke hit Third Panzer Army hard on both sides of Vitebsk. Almost immediately, Soviet forces trapped five German divisions. Not until the 24th did Busch persuade Hitler to allow a breakout, but by then it was too late. Meanwhile, on 23 June, Third and Second Belorussian Fronts ripped into Fourth Army and threatened Mogilev and Orsha. And on the 24th, First Belorussian Front struck Ninth Army and quickly ruptured its front in a number of places. Army Group Center's front dissolved along its entire length as Soviet spearheads pushed ever deeper into Army Group Center's rear. Everywhere, Busch attempted to hold his forces to a linear defense, while refusing pleas to allow withdrawals. When the Fourth Army commander, General Kurt von Tippelskirch, ordered a retreat, Busch countermanded the order and demanded that Tippelskirch's troops retake the abandoned ground. Within four days, Army Group Center had lost operational control of its forces.

Ninth Army was first in the bag. Refused permission by Busch and the OKH to retreat, XXXV and XLI Corps were trapped in the area of Bobruysk. Meanwhile, Rokossovsky's spearheads were pointing toward Minsk and bigger game. Much of Fourth Army escaped Mogilev despite Hitler's orders, but the Soviet drive on Minsk soon enveloped the escapees. On the 28th, Busch admitted to Zietzler that little remained of Third Panzer, Fourth, and Ninth Armies. Nevertheless, he ordered his subordinates to hold a line running due north and south of Beresino, a line that Hitler had drawn with the aid of a ruler on an OKH situation map at Rastenburg. At last the OKH and Hitler had finally awakened to the extent of the Soviet offensive.

Hitler then fired Busch and turned Army Group Center over to Model, who remained commander of Army Group North Ukraine as well. Now having command of both army groups, Model could more easily move reserves north from the south to close the yawning gaps in Army Group Center's line. On 3 July, Soviet troops took Minsk, while rear echelon units cleaned out pockets of Germans. In a 12-day period, the Soviets had destroyed Army Group Center and its 25 divisions. Barely a quarter of the

THE EASTERN FRONT
June–October 1944

⟹ Russian advance

▬▬ Front line, June 1944

━━ Front line, mid-October 1944

⋀⋀⋀ German defensive line

── Borders shown, late 1944

German troops survived the catastrophe, and those few who returned to combat had to be reformed into entirely new units. The Soviets' exploitation of these breakthroughs stands in stark contrast to Anglo-American generals' failure to exploit their operational advantages at Avranches, Falaise, and the Scheldt. Bagration was the most impressive ground operation of the war.

After the Soviets captured Minsk, Army Group Center expected them to halt, given that the advance had carried spearhead units over 125 miles. However, the Soviet logistic system, now comprising large numbers of Chevrolet, Ford, and Dodge trucks received through Lend-Lease, could finally support what Soviet theorists of the 1930s had only dreamed about: the conduct of deep operations—offensive movements that could paralyze the enemy by striking deeply into his rear areas. The tempo of the Soviet advance did not abate. While some units completed destruction of the Minsk pocket, others were already on the road to Vilnius and Baranovichi, thus opening up a route through the heavily wooded and swampy areas of western Belorussia. Such was the speed of the Soviet advance that the Germans had little prospect of halting it until their opponent's logistical system could no longer support the forces far down the dusty roads of Belorussia. By 8 July, Soviet spearheads had surrounded Vilnius, although the city would not fall until the 13th. To the north, the Soviets were already close to severing links between Army Group Center and Army Group North.

The next stage of the Soviet summer offensive unfolded on 13 July in the south, as Marshal Ivan Konev's forces attacked Army Group North Ukraine. Initially, the Soviets ran into heavier resistance than expected, but the Sixtieth Army effected a small breakthrough. Konev pushed First Guards Tank Army into that narrow gap. That push soon broke the connection between First and Fourth Panzer Armies. The Germans had prepared a fallback position, the Prinz Eugen Line, but the Soviets almost immediately splintered that line as well. By 18 July, Konev had encircled the XIII Corps east of Lvov, which First Panzer Army still covered. The situation north of Lvov rapidly deteriorated as Konev committed fresh forces as the gap between the panzer armies widened.

While Konev's forces wrecked the German Army Group North Ukraine, events in the Third Reich set off reverberations that were felt on all fronts. A bomb set by Colonel Claus von Stauffenberg exploded in Hitler's headquarters in East Prussia. The fallout for the German Army was immediate. Guderian assumed the position of chief of the general staff and lent his enthusiasm and talents to purging the officer corps as well as providing ideological guidance to those fighting at the front. He warned general staff officers they should display "exemplary attitude[s]." The desperate situation then confronting German forces in southern Poland occasioned another outburst from Guderian: "We must take the offensive everywhere! To retreat any farther is absolutely not tolerable."[1] But the communication, sent by Schörner, the new commander of Army Group North, to one of his division commanders best sums up the nature of Nazi leadership on the Eastern Front: the general was "to restore his own and his division's honor by a courageous deed or I will chase him out in disgrace. Furthermore, he is to report by 2100 which commanders he has had shot or is having shot for cowardice."[2] In the face of the Soviets' relentless advance, the German response degenerated into blind self-sacrifice.

Fourth Tank Army was soon approaching the crossings over the San River between Jaroslaw and Przemysl; it passed that obstacle on 25 July. That night, units of Second Tank Army closed on Siedlce, within 50 miles of Warsaw, while Fourth Panzer Army had both its flanks in the air. But the situation of Second Army was the most desperate; the refusal of Guderian and Hitler to countenance a retreat out of Brest resulted in the Soviets encircling another German corps. By the 26th, Soviet pressure and advances to the west forced First Panzer Army to abandon Lvov. By the end of July, Soviet forces neared Warsaw and threatened to bounce the Vistula in a number of places. On the 30th, Second Tank Army units had advanced to within seven miles of the Polish capital. Farther north, the situation was almost as bad for the Germans; on 31 July, Soviet forces reached the Baltic southwest of Riga and thereby cut Army Group North off from the Reich.

At this point the Soviet advance suddenly slowed. Western analysts have long accused Stalin of halting the advance to allow the Germans to crush the Polish uprising, which was just beginning in Warsaw. Whether or not that was a factor, it is clear that the Soviets had outrun their logistical tether. Ironically, the halt came precisely at the moment when American units began the breakout from Normandy at Avranches. Northeast of Warsaw, the III Soviet Tank Corps, low on fuel and ammunition, halted in an exposed position where a counterattack by the SS Wiking, the Hermann Göring, and the 19th Panzer Divisions destroyed it. The German attack also badly battered VIII Guards Tank Corps, which was unsupported by other Soviet units. Nevertheless, Second Tank Army shifted its focus to establishing a bridgehead well south of Warsaw, where it could provide no support to the Poles.

On 1 August, the Poles had risen against their oppressors. No doubt they hoped to accomplish something of political value before the Red Army arrived. Nevertheless, the German plans to make a stand on the Vistula did little to improve Polish prospects. The Polish Home Army fought desperately, largely unsupported because the Soviets refused to allow the Western powers access to their air bases for supply missions. In heavy fighting that eventually descended into the sewers, the Germans retook Warsaw block by block. The worst sort of SS units conducted much of the fighting, and the atrocities were extraordinary, even by German standards. Heroic courage was simply not enough against superior firepower. Virtually nothing remained of Warsaw when the fighting finally subsided. The German destruction of the Polish resistance would make Stalin's job that much easier at the war's end; few remained to oppose his tyranny.

In a strategic as well as an operational sense, the Soviets now went over to the defensive in the center and north. Their armies were positioned deep in the Baltic states and Poland, and they were within easy reach of Eastern and Central Europe. The Red Army's success in these two offensives had been extraordinary. Bagration had largely destroyed Army Group Center, along with 30 Nazi divisions (not including Army Group North Ukraine); it had also pushed Soviet-held territory nearly 200 miles to the west and inflicted over half a million casualties on the Germans. But victory came at a heavy cost. The Soviets lost 243,508 dead, with a further 811,603 wounded in these two offensives.

With their armies poised to drive into Central Europe after the successes of Operation Bagration, the Soviets could turn their attention to the Balkans. Back in June and July, the Soviets had begun preparations for their southern campaign, whose aim was as much strategic as operational. Two Soviet fronts, Second and Third Ukrainian, would conduct the operation; their strength was over 1,314,000 men against slightly over 900,000 Romanians and Germans. But tank strength would tell the real story: the Soviets possessed 1,874 tanks and assault guns, the Germans barely 170. The front on the Dnestr had remained quiescent since the spring thaw, after the terrible battering Romanian and German forces had taken over the winter. By summer 1944, Marshal Antonescu's dictatorship had lost all credibility. Nevertheless, the German ambassador and the head of the military mission in Bucharest were charter members of the Kesselring school of optimism. Those at Hitler's headquarters in Rastenburg had little sense of the disillusion in the Romanian population and army; the ever-optimistic Keitel suggested that Romania would stick with Germany in the most desperate of circumstances. But even Germans who were in direct contact with the Romanian Army often missed the signs of dissatisfaction with Antonescu's dictatorship and with Germany's conduct of the war.

Meanwhile, the OKH and Guderian had been rapidly pulling divisions from Army Group South Ukraine to rebuild Army Group Center and hold the Vistula Line. Five panzer and six infantry divisions moved north—one-third of Army Group South Ukraine's strength. Thus, by the time of the Soviet invasion of the Balkans, the forces along the Dnestr were left with only one panzer, one panzer grenadier, and one Romanian armored division to conduct counterattacks. Still, Army Group South Ukraine's commander, Generaloberst Johannes Friessner, newly arrived, was optimistic. There had been some talk at higher staff levels of a retreat from the Dnestr to a defensive line on the Carpathians and lower Danube, but Antonescu had no trouble persuading Hitler, who never liked the idea of abandoning territory, that such a move would destroy Romanian morale. To hold Romania in the war, the Germans forswore any realistic hope of forming a defensible line on the Carpathians and lower Danube. Sixth Army, reconstituted since Stalingrad, would defend the Dnestr Line, with Fourth Romanian Army on its left flank and Third Romanian on its right (both also reconstituted since Stalingrad).

The fourth major Soviet offensive of the year began on 20 August. In some places, particularly against the Germans, the Soviets ran into tenacious opposition. But the flanks of Sixth Army dissolved as most Romanian units simply collapsed in flight or surrender. By 24 August, Soviet spearheads had trapped Third Romanian Army along the Black Sea; on the following day it surrendered, and within a matter of weeks many of its units found themselves fighting on the Soviet side. As the front on the Dnestr broke, the government in Bucharest collapsed. On 23 August, in circumstances similar to those in Italy in July 1943, Antonescu was called to the palace, where he was arrested. The king then broadcast to the nation that Romania was switching sides and at the same time denounced the 1940 Treaty of Vienna that ceded much of Transylvania to Hungary.

German ineptitude once again took its toll. Hitler ordered Army Group South Ukraine to smash the anti-Antonescu coup and put the military dictator back in control. Early on the morning of 25 August, General der Flieger Alfred Gerstenberg, commander of flak troops in Romania, reported from Bucharest that the Romanian leadership lacked toughness and that 6,000 German troops were moving on the capital from Ploesti. In fact, the Nazi force was far too small to break through Romanian troops deployed on the road to the capital. Heavy fighting continued throughout the day; Hitler then ordered the Luftwaffe's Fourth Air Force to attack government buildings throughout Bucharest.

Meanwhile, with the collapse of Romanian forces on its flanks, Sixth Army was in desperate straits; it soon broke into two pockets, the largest of which contained the fighting strength of four corps. The Soviet advance west of Sixth Army was so rapid that the Germans almost broke through to safety. But the Soviets finally blocked the escape routes and destroyed Sixth Army for the second time on the far side of the Siret River. Elsewhere in Romania, German units desperately attempted to escape, as Soviet spearheads—with Romanian support—advanced. The Soviets swept up nearly 300,000 Germans in another great operational disaster for the Wehrmacht. So extensive was the German defeat that Soviet forces were able to swing through Romania and then sweep north to seize the passes leading through the Carpathians and Transylvanian Alps onto the Hungarian plain.

The Romanian collapse brought the Red Army down on Bulgaria. Although the Bulgarians had refused to declare war on the Soviet Union, they were German allies and were at war with the Western powers. The arrival of Soviet troops on their frontier on 2 September led the Bulgarians to renounce their alliance with Germany and return to full neutrality. That declaration bought little time. The Soviets declared war, and three days later the Bulgarians switched sides to join the Soviets. Soviet troops flooded over the countryside on the way to Macedonia; this advance put the entire Nazi position in the western Balkans and northern Greece in question, while Yugoslav partisans continued to harass the Germans.

Army Group E under Field Marshal Weichs still deployed approximately 300,000 German troops in Greece; the problem now was how to get them out before the Soviet advance and Yugoslav partisans closed off the escape routes. By early November, Weichs had removed a substantial portion of German forces, but only because the Soviets focused on reaching Budapest instead of cutting German escape routes through Macedonia. Linking up with Tito's partisans, Soviet forces "liberated" Belgrade and ejected the Germans from southern Yugoslavia. Although Soviet troops found themselves crossing countryside over which their socialist Yugoslav brothers had fought and died in great numbers, they looted, burned, and raped their way forward. Such behavior outraged the puritanical partisans; Milovan Djilas even complained to Stalin about the widespread raping of Yugoslav women by Soviet soldiers. The dictator, however, replied that one could hardly deny men who had sacrificed so much in the war a little "fun with a woman."[3] The criminal acts of Soviet troops against the civilian population drove the first wedge in the Soviet-Yugoslav rift that opened up in the late 1940s.

While the Germans scrambled to escape from Greece and the southern Balkans, the Hungarians were looking for a way to exit the war. But the Germans had a firmer grasp on the Hungarians than on the Romanians.

Alarmed by Hungarian overtures to the West, the Germans had forced Admiral Horthy, the regent, to install a pro-Nazi government in Budapest in March 1944. That government had then cooperated in shipping off to Auschwitz a substantial portion of Hungary's Jewish population until Allied threats forced a cessation of transports. Romania's collapse caused the OKW to position two SS divisions within striking distance of Budapest. In early September, rumors circulated in the Hungarian capital that the Soviets were only 140 miles away. The government immediately demanded that the Germans provide five panzer divisions within 24 hours.

On 10 September, Friessner, still commander of Army Group South Ukraine and thus intimately acquainted with Balkan countries attempting to bail out of the war, reported that matters were tenuous in Budapest. He was right: that same day Horthy tried, but failed, to persuade the Cabinet to support a request for an armistice. A visit by the Hungarian chief of staff on 12 September to Rastenburg only aggravated German suspicions—justifiably, as matters turned out. On his departure, Guderian presented the Hungarian with a new Mercedes, which, several weeks later, he used to drive over to the Soviets.

Initially, the Hungarians put up stout resistance, mostly against Romanian units fighting on the other side. But contact with Soviet forces quickly revealed how little stomach the Hungarians had for the fight. On 21 September, they lost Arad, and panic gripped Budapest. Guderian ordered a strong panzer force to the vicinity for rest and refit. In fact, Hitler was assembling panzer forces for a major counterattack to trap Soviet forces north of the Transylvanian Alps. But Marshal Malinovskys Second Ukrainian Front struck first. Initially, the Soviets made significant gains, but a German counterattack by two panzer divisions trapped three Soviet corps near Debrecen. However, most of the Soviets soon escaped by breaking out. As the fighting approached Budapest, Horthy again attempted to abandon the alliance. But the majority in parliament and a substantial number of senior officers remained loyal to Germany.

On 15 October, Horthy broadcast his acceptance of Soviet terms for an armistice, but by then the Germans were ready. SS General Erich von dem Bach-Zelewski, recently in command of Warsaw's destruction, and SS commando leader Otto Skorzeny almost effortlessly removed Horthy's supporters, shipped the regent to Germany, and established the leader of the Arrow-Cross Party, Ferenc Szalasi—remarkable for his stupidity—at the head of a new government. The internal conflict destroyed what remained of Hungarian resistance: many generals and their units deserted, while the rest were hardly willing to fight to the end.

The Germans, however, fought on. In the last days of October, near

Nyiregyhaza, they trapped three Soviet corps that had rashly advanced too far and too fast; this time the Soviets did not escape. Nevertheless, Soviet attacks ground steadily forward toward Budapest, as attacks by Malinovsky battered the Germans back on the Hungarian capital. Not until December did the Soviets finally drive into the city, largely owing to German mistakes. Friessner took the two reinforcing panzer divisions and divided the armor and the supporting infantry into separate forces. The infantry went to defend the northern approaches to the city, while the armor, without supporting infantry, moved to bolster the defenses south of the city. On 20 December, Malinovsky launched two massive blows, one south and the other north of Budapest. This time the Soviets broke through and trapped the IX SS Mountain Corps and a number of Hungarian units in the capital. Budapest was almost in Stalin's hands.

The Soviet offensive into the Balkans was an impressive achievement—a masterful marriage of military operations to the goals of politics and grand strategy. It destroyed much of Army Group South Ukraine and laid the foundation for Soviet domination of the Balkans in the postwar period. Yet, the Balkan campaign diverted significant Soviet military forces away from central Poland, where a renewed offensive might have led to the defeat of Nazi Germany in late 1944. But then Stalin might not have gained his strategic objectives.

The Fall Battles in the West

With Market Garden's failure in southern Holland, the swift Anglo-American advances in the west abruptly halted. Some of the difficulties now besetting British and American commanders were of their own making, some the unintended effects of sensible decisions, some the inevitable outcome of military miscalculation. Allied armies were now on the far side of a supply desert created by the air campaign to shut down French transportation. No matter how fast or how hard engineers worked to rebuild bridges and marshaling yards, logistics confronted Allied commanders with a nightmare in projecting forward the hundreds of thousands of tons of supplies that Allied armies required. Moreover, the Allies also confronted the logistical difficulty of feeding substantial portions of the Belgian and French populations.

Montgomery's refusal to open Antwerp in September represented a calculated decision to forced Eisenhower to support Twenty-First Army Group in its drive onto the north German plain. Had the Allies followed the British strategy in 1944 of launching a single drive under Montgomery across the Rhine, the results might well have been a disaster for Anglo-American forces. Montgomery's idea of pushing 40 divisions onto the north German plain with no clear operational goal could have resulted in a major Allied defeat, especially since American forces to the south, deprived of logistic support by Montgomery's proposal, could not have rendered any significant support to the British. Luckily for the Allies, Operation Dragoon and the opening of the Rhone River valley allowed the Allies to funnel supplies through Marseilles and transport them up the valley to their forces on the German frontier.

Two other difficulties faced Allied commanders. First, the British, Canadian, and American armies had suffered far heavier infantry casualties than precampaign estimates had forecast. Thus, the replacement pool was rapidly drying up. The situation in the British Army was so bad that Montgomery resorted to the expedient of breaking units up to provide replacements—an almost unheard-of act of desperation. In every respect, the British had reached the end of their manpower resources. That was not the case with the Canadians, whose government refused to ship conscripts overseas, or the Americans. In the U.S. case, the manpower problems were precipitated by the decision to settle for an 89-division army; this prevented the Americans from pulling divisions off the front line for rest and refit, because every division was required to hold the line—there was virtually no reserve. Thus, American divisions remained in battle for the duration of the fighting in Europe, while individual soldiers joined them directly in combat after a brief stay in replacement depots—"repple depples," in the lingo of the victims. In their new units, these fresh replacements remained friendless and alone during their initial combat experience. The American manpower shortage was exacerbated by the army's retention of too many support troops, who could easily have served in combat without a serious impact on the logistical structure.

But the greatest manpower mistake the Allies made in 1944 was their underestimation of their opponents' strength. The German collapse in France had been so sudden and complete that Allied generals found the notion of a revival of Wehrmacht forces inconceivable. By this point in the war, senior Soviet generals could certainly have warned their Western counterparts that the Germans were all too effective in resurrecting their military forces. And the effective German resistance to Market Garden should certainly have raised warning flags. But optimism prevailed in the Allied senior ranks. The senior leaders, despite logistic shortages, looked for that one final push to drive the Germans over the edge into defeat—as had occurred at the end of July. It was to prove a long wait.

After the failure of Market Garden, Montgomery boasted that the operation had been 90 percent successful. However, the long thin penetration pointing toward the Rhine added over 120 miles to the front that Montgomery's Twenty-First Army Group had to defend. To bolster his demands for further support, Montgomery focused the Canadian First Army on a mission to clear the Channel ports and other operations inland, while ignoring German positions along the Scheldt River. Thus, instead of clearing the approaches to Antwerp, British and Canadian troops took Le Havre, Boulogne, Calais, and the Cape Gris Nez batteries. In every case, the Germans thoroughly wrecked the port facilities during their retreat, as they had at Cherbourg. But even in undamaged condition, none of these small ports could have significantly relieved the overall supply shortages.

With the pause in British operations required by Market Garden, the Germans had strengthened their defensive positions in the Breskens pocket south of the Scheldt, along the access routes to South Beveland and Walcheren Islands as well as on the islands themselves, which formed the northern banks of the Scheldt estuary. In mid-September, the Canadian 4th Armored and Polish 1st Armored Divisions attacked German positions on the south bank. Both efforts resulted in heavy casualties, and in the end they failed—too much of the First Canadian Army was involved elsewhere, while the Canadians remained at the bottom of Twenty-First Army Group's priorities even for artillery ammunition. In early October, Admiral Bertram Ramsey reported to Eisenhower that Montgomery had relegated the Canadians to the lowest priority for supplies, despite the importance of clearing the Scheldt. After a major confrontation at the highest levels of command, Montgomery received a direct, explicit order to clear the Scheldt immediately, and he complied by supplying the Canadians adequately, but whined all the while about Ramsey's disloyalty.

On 6 October, the Canadians launched a heavy attack against fierce German resistance on the north side of the Leopold Canal. Not until 2 November did they finally clear the south bank of the Scheldt of German positions. South Beveland proved less of a problem. Over the last week of October, Canadian troops attacked the Germans and liberated the area. Walcheren Island, site of a disastrous British expedition during the Napoleonic Wars, proved a tougher nut. Bomber Command attacks broke the dikes and flooded much of the area that lay below sea level. This allowed Canadian and Royal Marine amphibious units to use the flooded fields inside the islands to attack German defenses from the opposite direction from where they were positioned.

The Germans had a number of heavy coastal batteries guarding the Scheldt that air attacks could also have taken out, but Montgomery backed up Bomber Harris in his refusal to support the attacking ground forces. In early November, under the violent storms the North Sea can brew up, Royal Marine Commandos and Canadian troops took these coastal batteries during a week of heavy fighting and extraordinary heroism. Casualties were heavy. But after Walcheren fell, Allied minesweepers could finally clear the Scheldt. On 28 November, the first convoy entered Antwerp—85 days after British troops had captured the port in undamaged condition.

The failure at Arnhem in mid-September finally forced Montgomery to secure his rear. To the west of the Scheldt, the British Second Army—with American help—drove through Breda and pushed the Germans back on the Maas, creating a solid flank to the west of Market Garden's narrow salient. But bad weather and the sodden fields, flooded plains, farms, and towns of southern Holland blocked any rapid advance. The most that Twenty-First Army Group could accomplish was to drive the dogged German defenders from their defenses and give Antwerp breathing room.

If Montgomery confronted significant problems, Bradley's Twelfth Army Group was in little better shape. The delay caused by the U.S. supply situation in mid-September provided the Germans with just enough time to reknit their defenses on the *Westwall*. Moreover, Twelfth Army Group spread its attacks over too wide an area. There was, in German terms, no *Schwehrpunkt* (concentrated focus) to its efforts, while the logistical situation was never fully resolved; more often than not, the American divisions were living a hand-to-mouth existence with insufficient time to build up significant reserves for a sustained drive.

In operational terms, the great weakness in the American approach in September lay in Eisenhower's decision to direct Courtney Hodges's First Army away from Patton's Third Army. Thus, the American effort divided into two drives, separated by the Ardennes and thus not mutually supporting. Hodges's First Army turned its support to Montgomery's Twenty-First Army Group, with its focus on the north German plain. Hodges soon found himself involved in intense fighting with first-class German units north of the Ardennes. Surprisingly, given the Ardennes' role in the 1940 campaign, SHAEF planners rejected the possibility of using that region as an avenue of approach into the heart of Germany—an area where the Germans had virtually no forces until early November. For a brief moment in mid-September, 5th Armored Division cleanly broke through the scanty fortifications of the *Westwall,* just north of the Ardennes. But neither Major General Leonard Gerow, the corps commander, nor his superiors grasped the possibilities.

Meanwhile, 80 miles to the south, Third Army found itself embroiled in driving the Germans over terrain that had featured prominently in the Franco-Prussian War. Patton attempted to seize the fortifications surrounding Metz—an area that the enemy knew in intimate detail, since during both the First World War and the current conflict it had been the center of major training areas. While Patton failed to replicate his August successes owing to constrained logistics, Third Army's attacks disrupted German plans for launching a major counterattack in the area. Third Army, however, took heavy casualties. The summer fighting had exhausted both sides, but the Germans were in a position to use the terrain and the cold, rainy fall weather to their advantage. The limited American offensive actions in October served only to underline the logistical and manpower constraints under which U.S. commanders were operating.

During October, Hodges's First Army carried much of Twelfth Army Group's effort. On 2 October, XIX Corps, led by the 30th Infantry Division and followed by the 2nd Armored Division, launched an attack aimed at encircling Aachen from the north; attacking forces planned to meet VII Corps advancing from the south at Würselen and envelop the ancient Roman city. Initially, the attack went well despite intense German resistance. By 7 October, the 30th Infantry Division was within three miles of Würselen, where the 1st Infantry Division was waiting. But the Germans prevented the Americans from closing the encirclement until 16 October. The garrison surrendered five days later, after the Americans, liberal in their use of firepower, had reduced what was left of the bombed-out city to complete ruin.

Farther south, First Army had launched a series of ill-fated attacks into the Huertgen Forest. The initial objective was strictly limited: to provide flank protection for Collins's VII Corps. Unfortunately, from the beginning, operations in the Huertgen reflected little credit on American commanders at any level except the front lines. Senior American generals failed to recognize that dams south and east of the forest on the Roer River would allow the Germans to flood any advance U.S. forces made in the north. The 9th Infantry Division's G-2, who did recognize the danger the dams represented before the attack, was too junior to have any influence. To the Germans, the Huertgen Forest was an essential piece of real estate, the loss of which would threaten their entire position in front of the Rhine. Ironically, an easier avenue of approach to the southeast of the Huertgen Forest would have allowed the Americans to capture the dams and then clear out the forests and difficult terrain lying down-river. Thus, the effort to protect VII Corps' flank by clearing the Huertgen placed American forces at great disadvantage in terms of terrain and avenues of approach. In effect, they were heading into a cul-de-sac until other forces had captured the dams lying upstream.

With only logging trails leading across its deep gorges, the Huertgen Forest put the attackers at a critical disadvantage, especially since on the far side the Germans possessed roads that would allow them to move in reinforcements quickly. In every respect, the location represented a tactical nightmare. First Army exacerbated its difficulties by feeding units into the fighting piecemeal. The attack began on 6 October. Five days of fighting pushed two attacking regiments a mile into the forest to the first clearing. Ten days of ferocious combat won the 9th Infantry Division another mile of worthless terrain—its two-mile advance cost the attackers nearly 5,000 casualties, and they did not yet hold the whole forest.

In November the pace picked up across the front. Eisenhower and Bradley believed that a series of major attacks would, as in Normandy in July, eventually rupture the enemy's front line. In the north a new American army, the Ninth, under Lieutenant General W. H. Simpson, made its debut. Simpson's forces, possessing a density of troops and artillery per kilometer not typical of Allied forces in fall 1944, launched a limited offensive that carried them through to the Roer River. But as long as the Germans held the dams, there was no possibility of crossing, since the Germans could isolate any successful lodgment by flooding.

Unfortunately, Hodges persisted in his efforts to clear the Huertgen Forest rather than capture the dams. Irascible and truculent, he possessed few operational or tactical abilities despite standing high on Bradley's list. In early November he turned the battle over to the 28th Infantry Division, commanded by Major General Norman "Dutch" Cota, one of the heroes of D-Day. Troops and a few tanks from the division crossed the Kall River gorge and reached the crossroads town of Schmidt in the first attacks. From there they threatened the dams. The Germans reacted vigorously, and with better roads available they drove two American battalions out of Schmidt after heavy fighting. In spite of these failures, Hodges continued placing impossible demands on his troops. He did not relieve the 28th Infantry Division until 13 November, after it had suffered over 6,000 casualties.

Reflecting Bradley's demands for renewed efforts to rupture the German defenses, Patton launched a major attack against Metz south of the Ardennes. Third Army had attempted to take Metz by a *coup de main* in September. American troops had actually stormed onto the top of Fort Driant, a major fortress guarding the city, but German defenders had fought tenaciously within the fort and called down heavy artillery fire on themselves.

Over the night of 12–13 October, the Americans had abandoned their foothold on the fortress, while Patton reconsidered how to take the city. Third Army resumed its attack on 8 November.

South of Metz, XII Corps attacked toward the Maginot Line. Heavy rains led the corps commander, Major General Manton Eddy, to argue for postponement. When Patton suggested that Eddy might want to name his successor, XII Corps attacked as ordered. The weather may have helped, since the Germans hardly expected the Americans to attack without the support of the ubiquitous fighter-bombers. But a heavy artillery bombardment plastered the enemy and caused severe dislocation among the defenders— as in Normandy, artillery was an American strong point. While no breakthrough occurred, XII Corps committed its armor on the second day, and the Americans made major gains. But the slashing rains continued, and casualties due to noncombat causes, such as trench foot, almost equaled those due to combat.

A pincer arm consisting of the 95th and 90th Infantry Divisions swinging from the north to meet the 5th Armored Division driving from the south encircled Metz on 19 November. However, much of Metz's garrison escaped before encircling forces linked up east of the city. Patton's attack might have gained more had the weather been better. But Twelfth Army Group had refused to take into account the normal weather patterns for Western Europe in late fall.

To Patton's south, General Jacob Devers, commanding the newly created Sixth Army Group, which was formed from forces landing in southern France in August, successfully attacked in support of Third Army. French troops drove through the Belford gap and within four days reached the Rhine. General Leclerc's 2nd French Armored, fighting under Lieutenant General Alexander Patch's Seventh Army, liberated Strasbourg. But Devers lacked the troops and artillery to create a significant breakthrough in the north, while any crossing of the Rhine in the south would only lead into the interminable depths of the Black Forest. Eisenhower sanctioned a move northward, which merely brought Seventh Army up to the *Westwall*. In the south, the Germans still maintained a sizeable bridgehead on the Rhine's west bank at Colmar.

Over the course of October and November, as weather conditions steadily deteriorated, Bradley emphasized bringing up fuel and ammunition, but winter clothes and boots failed to appear in sufficient quantities. Equally inexcusable were the failings of the supply system under the callow leadership of Lieutenant General John C. Lee, who was more concerned with his own comforts than in supporting hard-pressed frontline troops. The cost to American units for the overconfidence of their superiors can be read in the casualty figures: 118,698 in November, as compared with 51,424 in July, 42,535 in August, 42,183 in September, and 31,617 in October. The combat casualties suffered in November (62,437) were 20 percent higher than those suffered in July's ferocious fighting, while the noncombat casualties (56,261) were mostly due to the conditions under which the troops were fighting. Although a portion of these losses stemmed from problems associated with the army's individual replacement system, the major villain of the piece was Bradley's policy of launching ill-thought-out and ill-prepared attacks across Twelfth Army Group's front. Without clear, large-scale operational objectives for these attacks, the best the Americans could expect were local successes, hard-won over a cold, rain-sodden terrain that inflicted almost as many losses as did the enemy.

American losses in equipment were equally heavy in November. In its attack toward Werth and the Roer River on 16 November, 3rd Armored Division lost 48 out of 64 attacking tanks in the first 26 minutes. But combat and maintenance support for American armored divisions was so strong that by nightfall 40 of the damaged tanks were under repair. The real scandal in U.S. equipment was the decision of senior armored officers, including Patton, to stay with the M-4 Sherman tank instead of the new M-26 Pershing with its 90mm gun, improved silhouette, and thicker armor, which was ready to go into full production in early 1944. The result for an armored division like the 3rd was a trail of wrecked and burned-out tanks from engagements American tankers had little chance of winning. By the end of the war, 3rd Armored Division, with a table of organization of 232 tanks, had lost 648 tanks destroyed in combat, with a further 700 damaged but repairable.

The Battle of the Bulge

The German success in restoring the Western Front in September 1944 allowed Hitler to consider a major effort to regain the initiative. The question was where. To the east, the Soviets remained quiescent in Poland. While their drive into the Balkans caused the Germans heavy losses in troops and equipment, that advance represented no immediate threat to the Reich itself. Even during the desperate struggle to rebuild the Western Front in September, Hitler considered the possibility of a major counteroffensive. He rejected a strike against the Soviets, since there appeared to be no operational objective that would undermine Stalin's political will. But Hitler held the Anglo-Americans in considerably less respect. Perhaps a major attack could divide them or even drive the British from the war. Given the atmosphere in the Reich, as Himmler's agents pursued those responsible for the 20 July assassination plot, there was little opposition to the Führer's dreams among his senior military leaders. Guderian, the OKH's new chief of staff, did urge Hitler to give priority to the Eastern Front, but Hitler, minimizing Soviet strength as he had so often in the past, discounted the advice and turned to the west.

Hitler was almost immediately tempted to repeat the success of May 1940 by a drive through the Ardennes. Eisenhower had demonstrated that Allied military leadership thought the Ardennes of little importance by sending First Army to its north and Third Army to its south. By October, the Americans were using the area to introduce new divisions to the war and to rest badly battered divisions. Hitler therefore concentrated on preparing to launch all the forces he could rebuild in a major strike through the Ardennes to capture Antwerp. This would achieve two operational objectives: it would divide Allied forces in France and defeat them in detail, and it would retake Antwerp. The Western powers, realizing the impossible logistic situation Hitler had put them in, might then finally quit the war and allow the Wehrmacht to concentrate its entire strength on defeating the Soviets. Yet, the fact that the Germans had only enough fuel to get halfway to Antwerp underlines the constraints that the bombing of the German oil industry had placed on the German Army.

At the end of September, the OKW began pulling SS and army panzer divisions off the Western Front, including both Sixth and Fifth Panzer Armies. Speer's industrial empire was still producing considerable amounts of military equipment, while convalescent soldiers and new conscripts filled up the ranks. In addition to the refitting of panzer and panzer grenadier divisions, Ultra provided a number of clear warnings of unusual German activity in October. The disappearance of the firstline units as well as Fifth Panzer Army and Sixth SS Panzer Army should have been worrisome enough, but there were other indicators. The Luftwaffe received the task of protecting the major Rhine bridges lying behind the Ardennes. Ultra also indicated that the Reichsbahn was shuttling large numbers of trains into the region. Similarly, at a time when every German army fighting on the Western Front was desperately short of food, fuel, and ammunition, Ultra reported that the Germans were building up huge dumps in the Ardennes, the one area where the Allies were not attacking.

Yet, despite overwhelming evidence—including air reconnaissance and reports from frontline divisions—SHAEF and Twelfth Army Group clung to the delusion that the Germans could not launch a major offensive. Only Patton among Allied commanders divined that the Germans might take such a huge risk. On 24 November, he noted: "The First Army is making a terrible mistake in leaving the VIII Corps static, as it is highly probable that the Germans are building up east of them."[4] Some junior officers were also less optimistic than their senior commanders. Only in the north around Monschau, where the 99th Division was supporting an attack against the Roer River dams, did the Americans possess adequate strength in the Ardennes. From Monschau south, VIII Corps held a weak line: the 106th Infantry Division, recently arrived from the United States, deployed to guard the Schnee Eifel along a 20-mile front. Next in line, the badly battered 28th Infantry Division, which had suffered over 6,000 casualties in the Huertgen, held a 25-mile front along the Our River. Finally, the 4th Infantry Division, almost as badly battered in the Huertgen, guarded a 20-mile stretch of front to the boundary with Third Army south of Luxembourg City. Major General Troy Middleton, VIII Corps' commander, did have the 9th Armored Division in reserve, but one of that division's combat commands was moving north to support the attack on the Roer dams.

By 16 December, the Germans enjoyed a three-to-one advantage in manpower, a two-to-one advantage in tanks, and general superiority in artillery. But they did have a significant disadvantage in air power, and that is precisely why Hitler launched the offensive during a period of bad weather. The strongest German force, Sixth SS Panzer Army, under SS Generaloberst Sepp Dietrich, was to strike in the north. A competent division commander at best, Dietrich had the services of a highly trained staff. Fifth Panzer Army, under General der Panzertruppen Hasso von Manteuffel, would attack from St. Vith to the south. Under the clouds, rain, and snow of late fall, the Germans had assembled an impressive force, but in no way was it comparable to the armies they had launched through the Ardennes in May 1940. Nor were the Germans up against the ill-trained and incompetently led French forces that had collapsed on the banks of the Meuse four years before.

Before dawn on 16 December, a massive artillery bombardment hit U.S. positions throughout the Ardennes. Within hours, heavy infantry and armor attacks hit the hard-pressed American positions. For the most part, American units responded with skill, courage, and determination and, when outflanked, fought until they were out of ammunition. In the north of the front, Dietrich's Sixth SS Panzer Army had aimed to break through American positions and then drive along four major arteries leading west to the Meuse. But the 99th Infantry Division, despite its greenness, put up tough resistance over the course of the first day. While many of its units broke on the next afternoon, the 2nd Infantry Division, involved in the attack on the Roer dams, had time to switch fronts and form a strong defensive position in front of the Elsenborn Ridge. There, the Americans held over the course of the next two days despite ferocious German attacks. Not

BATTLE OF THE BULGE
16–24 December 1944

→ German attacks

⛉ German paratroop drop

~~ U.S. front lines

| 1 | Allied front line, 15 December 1944 | | 3 | Allied front line, 20 December 1944 |
| 2 | German paratroop drop zone, night of 16 December 1944 | | 4 | Allied front line, 24 December 1944 |

until the evening of the 19th did the 2nd Division pull back to the ridge, where the reformed 99th Division and two reinforcing divisions were in place. And there Americans would hold the northern shoulder of the growing German salient for the remainder of the battle.

But the Germans did slip an armored task group of the 1st SS Panzer Division under a hard-bitten veteran of the Eastern Front, Obersturmbannführer Joachim Peiper, through the gap that opened up almost immediately between the 99th and 106th Infantry Divisions. Nevertheless, with that exception, Dietrich's army failed to achieve its objectives. Farther south, Fifth Panzer Army, which was to support Dietrich's advance, gained a greater measure of success. Its attack struck the inexperienced 106th Infantry Division and two depleted regiments of the 28th Infantry Division. Over the course of the first day, the 106th Division held the Germans to limited gains. But an inexperienced division commander, Major General Alan Jones, failed to recognize the strength of German attacks and the seriousness of the enemy's penetrations. As a result, Jones ordered his troops to hold in their exposed positions. On the 17th, the front collapsed and the Germans engulfed two regiments of the 106th Division. By the 19th, they had captured nearly 8,000 Americans.

South of the 106th Infantry Division, a depleted regiment of the 28th Infantry Division concentrated in front of the key road junction at St. Vith. There, the Americans held until 21 December. The Germans had hoped to capture St. Vith by the second day in order to use the roads through the central Ardennes. The tenacious American defense denied the panzers use of the roads for over five days. The neighboring regiment of the 28th Division was even more dispersed. Nevertheless, it held the town of Clervaux and blocked the roads leading toward Bastogne until late on the 17th. While there was considerable dislocation and even panic among American service units as frontline positions unraveled under German pressure, for the most part U.S. soldiers reacted with discipline and initiative. Engineers blew up bridges to delay the Germans; artillery batteries remained at their posts until the situation became untenable; and ad hoc units held out until they had exhausted their ammunition or fallen in battle. By their courageous resistance, American troops, most of whom either had little combat experience or were badly battered by the fall fighting and were spread across the length of the Ardennes, robbed the Germans of the tactical and operational fruits of strategic surprise. It was a soldier's victory.

At Trois Ponts on 18 December, American engineers blew up the bridges in the face of Kampfgruppe Peiper, while enterprising Belgian guards created a wall of fire in front of a million-gallon dump on the Stavelot-Spa road. Such random but heroic actions prevented Peiper's force from reaching the Meuse that night. Peiper was already running out of fuel. Not surprisingly, the SS troopers acted with savage ruthlessness. Behind Peiper's advance lay a trail of dead and raped Belgian civilians and murdered U.S. POWs. The Malmedy massacre was the worst of several incidents: 86 American soldiers were killed in cold blood. After the war, an American tribunal sentenced Peiper and a number of his fellow war criminals to death. But Senator Joseph McCarthy of Wisconsin used his influence to get the sentence commuted to life imprisonment because of Peiper's "anticommunism." After serving minimum time, the West German authorities let Peiper off for good behavior. He then moved to France, where a few Frenchmen with memories blew him up.

Initially, the American high command missed the significance of the German attack. Eisenhower and Bradley did not even find out what was happening in the Ardennes until the evening of the 16th. Bradley's immediate reaction was that the German offensive represented only an attempt to disrupt the ongoing attack on the Roer dams. Further intelligence, particularly from Ultra, disabused him of that notion. Closer to the scene, Hodges persisted throughout the 16th in refusing to shut down First Army's attack on the dams. But by the next day the extent of the threat was clear to everyone in the U.S. high command. Already on the evening of the 16th, Eisenhower had ordered the two armored divisions in reserve to move to the Ardennes to bolster a deteriorating situation. The 101st and the 82nd Airborne Divisions were also in reserve, both preparing for a divisional football game that undoubtedly would have been the bloodiest in history. Several of the most important airborne commanders were elsewhere. The XVIII Airborne Corps commander, Major General Matthew B. Ridgway, was in England, while the 101st Airborne Division's commander, Major General Maxwell D. Taylor, had gone to Washington to look for a more prestigious command. Thus, Major General James M. Gavin, commander of the 82nd Airborne, assumed command of XVIII Airborne Corps. The soldiers of the 82nd Airborne Division embarked by truck to Werbomont on the north side of the growing bulge, while the 101st, under Brigadier General Anthony McCauliffe, as the acting division commander, moved toward Bastogne, where other American units were gathering to defend the crucial crossroads that ran through the town.

On the 19th, Eisenhower met with his senior commanders to devise a coherent response to the growing German penetration through the Ardennes. Patton had his own ideas: "Hell, lets have the guts to let the sons of bitches go all the way to Paris. Then we'll really cut 'em up and chew 'em up."[5] Because the situation appeared to be stabilizing in the north, the most significant problem was how to dam up Manteuffel's advance. Patton had already prepared three possible responses by Third Army. Thus, he was able to telephone his staff the codeword for one of those alternatives at the conclusion of his meeting with Eisenhower and Bradley. Third Army immediately sprang into action. Patton's instinct was to drive at the base of the salient, but Eisenhower, astonished at the speed with which Patton promised to respond, decided on an advance on Bastogne. Besides this operational decision, Eisenhower made one major command decision. To Bradley's considerable dismay, Eisenhower asked Montgomery to assume temporary command of First Army units along the northern side of the German breakthrough. Twelfth Army Group would conduct the battle on the southern side of the bulge.

In fact, by now the Germans had no chance of reaching their goals. By the 19th, the 101st Airborne Division and an assortment of other units were in firm control of Bastogne. Of the two armored divisions in Manteuffel's army headed for the Meuse, the 2nd Panzer Division found its way blocked by an American force at Noville just north of Bastogne. It was not until the 20th that the Germans fought their way through that obstacle. Meanwhile, an ad hoc force, including Canadian foresters, blew the bridges up along the Ourthe River and effectively halted the 116th Panzer Division. In the north, American resistance around St. Vith and the Elsenborn Ridge had stymied Dietrich's advance, while efforts to redistribute German forces to take advantage of Manteuffel's success foundered on bad weather and fuel shortages. These shortages, a direct result of the Combined Bomber Offensive, also slowed 2nd Panzer Division's advance to the Meuse after it had finally cleared Noville.

By the 22nd, the Americans had recovered their balance. As good as his word, Patton had rearranged Third Army's boundaries with Seventh Army so that he could pull two full corps out of line. Within three days he had three divisions redeployed in a 90-degree shift not only in their operational direction but in their logistic support as well. Under dreadful winter conditions, Third Army's divisions were in a position to strike north by 23 December. By this point in the battle the Germans had completely cut off Bastogne and were applying intense pressure on the defensive positions that surrounded the town. Nevertheless, McCauliffe gave a laconic reply to German demands that he surrender: "Nuts!" On the 23rd, Hitler's luck ran out; a weather front from Russia pushed the scudding clouds out of Central Europe, and the skies over the battlefield cleared. The drastically improved weather allowed Allied tactical air forces to savage the Germans across the breadth of the front. Meanwhile, C-47s and C-46s carried out massed drops of ammunition and supplies to the beleaguered garrison in Bastogne.

The position at the tip of the bulge, where the German spearhead units were approaching the Meuse, still remained uncertain for the Americans. The 2nd Panzer Division slipped past the flank of the U.S. 84th Infantry Division and moved on toward the Meuse. Montgomery had ordered Hodges to hold the reinforcements he was receiving for the eventual counterattack, which was already in the planning stages. Nevertheless, on 25 December, First Army allowed Collins to commit the recently arrived 2nd Armored Division to attack the Germans before they reached the Meuse. With the support of Allied fighter-bombers, the Americans smashed the lead Nazi spearheads just two miles from the Meuse; by evening on Christmas day, a day Patton described as "a clear cold Christmas, lovely weather for killing Germans," the enemy was withdrawing, abandoning over 80 tanks in the wreckage of defeat.[6]

The Germans had reached their high-water point. That is not to say they would not launch further attacks; for the rest of the month, they battered Bastogne despite the fact that Third Army had driven a relief column through to the besieged town on 26 December. German attacks that attempted to take the city and cut its lifeline failed because Third Army had so rapidly supported its forces in the Ardennes. By 31 December, Patton had six divisions committed; the result was a savage series of battles that steadily ground Manteuffel's forces down and limited German options elsewhere—in particular in the south, where a limited German attack had threatened Strasbourg for a short time.

With the defeat of the German counteroffensive, the question confronting the Americans was what objectives their own counterattack should seek. Montgomery, commanding U.S. forces in the north, had been astonishingly tactful in handling his American subordinates—a performance he soon ruined entirely by an arrogant press conference in early January. In contrast to Bradley and Patton, Montgomery favored a counteroffensive later rather than sooner. Patton, with his keen grasp of operational possibilities, argued for deep enveloping attacks at the base of the salient by First and Third Armies to put German forces in the bulge in the bag. But Bradley had no stomach for risks, while Hodges argued that the primitive road network in the north would hamper his troops. Not surprisingly, Montgomery supported the more limited solution of pushing the Germans out of the bulge rather than attempting to cut them off. Thus, the collective wisdom of the other Allied senior commanders overruled Patton, as it had so many times. First and Third Armies would attack toward Houffalize in the center of the bulge rather than toward the east. They would then sweep on to the German frontier.

The defeat of the Germans in the Battle of the Bulge was a victory for the U.S. soldier. He had stood the test of everything the Wehrmacht could throw at him, particularly early in the battle, when he was outnumbered and unprotected by air cover. It was not, however, a victory for the American high command. At the start, the strength and ferocity of the Nazi attack caught the American generals completely by surprise, despite plenty of indications that a massive buildup was under way. Thereafter, with the exception of Patton, they reacted as though the balance of the war had dramatically changed to favor the Germans. Eisenhower, stunned and disheartened, requested that the Joint Chiefs of Staff send every soldier available in the Continental United States to Europe; he even entertained the idea that 100,000 marines might be put at his disposal—an astonishing admission of pessimism, given his prejudices against the Marine Corps. In a gesture of desperation—disastrous because of its impact on the Anglo-American bargaining position at Yalta—Allied commanders begged the Soviets to begin their long-awaited winter offensive in Poland. And finally, when the Germans had been stopped, the American high command, led by Bradley and Hodges, chose merely to drive the enemy out of the Ardennes rather than to destroy him.

U.S. casualties suggest the battle's toll. Over a month and a half, American units suffered 81,000 casualties, 19,000 of them killed, 15,000 captured (more than half from the 106th Infantry Division), and 47,000 wounded. The Germans suffered approximately 100,000 casualties; but the loss of over 800 tanks and vast amounts of other military equipment hurt the Wehrmacht more than the loss of manpower. By now the Combined Bomber Offensive had nearly shut down the entire German transportation system. The Germans could no longer move to the combat units the meager weapons and ammunition Speer's remaining factories were grinding out under the terrible conditions of winter 1944–45. In effect, the offensive in the Ardennes used up Germany's strategic reserve not only in the west but throughout the Reich as well. The Germans had nothing left except enemies, and they were poised for the kill.

The Collapse of the Reich

In an air of unreality, the German high command responded late, if at all, to the disasters confronting it. Hitler remained optimistic about prospects in the west until late December, and even then he proved unwilling to sanction anything but last-minute withdrawals. Thus, the German response to a deep envelopment of the Ardennes might have led to another Falaise. But as the Wehrmacht pulled back from the Ardennes, it confronted its worst nightmare in the east. There, Hitler refused to believe the Soviets were preparing a massive offensive on the Polish front. In early January 1945 Guderian attempted to warn the Führer about the looming disaster; a furious row ensued, as Hitler declared insane the OKH's estimates about Soviet strength. Moreover, what panzer divisions the OKH still maintained in the east were poorly distributed. Of 18 panzer divisions in that theater, 7 were involved in the fighting around Budapest, 2 were in the isolated garrison of Courland (Latvia), 4 were in East Prussia, and only 5 were in reserve covering central Poland.

Meanwhile, the Soviets had spent four months rebuilding their forces and establishing vast stockpiles along the Vistula. Four massive fronts—(from south to north) First Ukrainian Front (under Konev), First Belorussian (Zhukov), Second Belorussian Front (Rokossovsky), Third Belorussian Front (I. D. Chernyakhovsky)—had bedded down and prepared to launch the largest blow of the war. Soviet forces numbered just under 4 million men, 9,800 tanks, and over 40,000 artillery tubes and heavy mortars. The weight of the offensive would lie in the south and center in Konev's and Zhukov's forces; there, Soviet superiority was five-to-one in troops, five-to-one in armor, and seven-to-one in artillery. Moreover, the Soviets possessed vast fleets of Lend-Lease trucks which ensured logistical support for deep operations, while the Germans, deprived of most of their fuel by the Combined Bomber Offensive, had been rendered practically immobile.

The major thrust of the offensive came from Warsaw to the Carpathians and aimed to capture Silesia, with its considerable industrial strength. The two fronts in the north were to take out German forces defending East Prussia and cover the advance to the Oder. Since the Western powers had requested Soviet assistance in diverting German reserves away from the Ardennes in early January, the Soviets moved up the attack by approximately a week.

In the early morning hours of 12 January, Konev's First Ukrainian Front opened the offensive. A massive artillery barrage blew XLVIII Panzer Corps' three divisions out of their positions. Within nine hours, the Soviets had unleashed their armored forces to exploit the holes opened up by the initial attacks. So fast was the Soviet advance that their spearheads overran the 16th and 17th Panzer Divisions in their assembly areas. By evening of 12 January, Konev's divisions had moved forward 20 miles from their starting point. By the end of the next day, the base of the salient Konev was driving

COLLAPSE OF NAZI GERMANY
February–May 1945

- ⇒ Allied advance
- ▸▸ German retreat
- —— Front line, April 1945
- ━━ Front line, May 1945
- ▪▪▪ German pockets
- ▨ Axis territory at surrender, 8 May 1945

1 Remnants of Eleventh Army surrender 19 April

2 Remnants of Army Group B surrender 21 April

3 Axis forces withdraw from Balkans January–May 1945

100 km
100 miles

56°

NORWAY

SWEDEN

Stockholm

Gothenburg

Aarhus

Copenhagen   Malmö

DENMARK

North Sea

Baltic Sea

Königsberg

Danzig   Elbing

East Prussia

Kolberg

Stettin

SECOND BELORUSSIAN FRONT ROKOSSOVSKY
XXXXX

Poznan

Vistula

Bremen   Hamburg

Amsterdam

NETH.

Hanover

Berlin   Kustrin

FIRST BELORUSSIAN FRONT ZHUKOV
XXXXX

Warsaw

Oder

Elbe

Dresden

Lodz

Poland

XXXXX
21
MONTGOMERY

Brussels

BELGIUM

Cologne
Ruhr
2

Bonn

Remagen

Koblenz

Frankfurt

Leipzig

1

Breslau

FIRST UKRAINIAN FRONT KONEV
XXXXX

Cracow

XXXXX
12
BRADLEY

Bohemia

Prague

GERMANY

Metz

XXXXX
6
DEVERS

Nuremberg

Danube

Brünne

SLOVAKIA

FOURTH UKRAINIAN FRONT PETROV
XXXXX

Stuttgart

Rhine

Strasbourg

48°

Dijon

Munich

Salzburg

Vienna

Bratislava

Debrecen

Budapest

HUNGARY

Zurich

Berne

Innsbruck

Austria

Graz

SECOND UKRAINIAN FRONT MALINOVSKY
XXXXX

Geneva

SWITZERLAND

Pécs

FRANCE

Milan

Ljubljana

Trieste

3

Zagreb

Sava

THIRD UKRAINIAN FRONT TOLBUKHIN
XXXXX

Belgrade

Venice

Genoa

ITALY

Adriatic Sea

Bologna

Zara

CROATIA

Sarajevo

16°

into German lines was 40 miles across, while Soviet armor in some places had driven 30 miles behind the original front line.

On 14 January, Zhukov's First Belorussian Front began its attack. A devastating artillery bombardment fell on the defenders, while Hitler once again refused to countenance any withdrawals to better defensive positions. The German Ninth Army collapsed so rapidly in face of the initial bombardment and reconnaissance in force that the Soviets canceled follow-up artillery preparations. Some of Zhukov's advancing divisions pushed forward 14 miles on the first day; even more importantly, 26th Guards Rifle Corps seized a bridge over the Pilitsa River that could support tanks. Thus, the Second Tank Army's advance was well ahead of schedule.

In most places German defenses entirely collapsed. Soviet air attacks broke a counterattack by the XL Panzer Corps almost before it began. From Warsaw to the Carpathians, the situation unraveled hour by hour. In Silesia, the Germans had a significant number of tanks but virtually no fuel to conduct a mobile defense. A desperate Guderian requested that all reinforcements go to the raging battle; but on 16 January, Hitler informed him that while two panzer corps from Sixth SS Panzer Army would leave the Ardennes, they would go to Hungary to continue the attacks the Germans had mounted north of Budapest.

By 18 January, First Belorussian and First Ukrainian Fronts were heading toward the Oder; Konev's advance swept up the XLII Corps and, after destroying the corps headquarters, wrecked the isolated and panic-stricken units. Hitler finally responded to the worsening situation in southern Poland, already threatening to engulf Silesia, by ordering Großdeutschland Panzer Corps transferred from East Prussia. But that move was certainly a case of robbing Peter to pay Paul. Against German forces defending East Prussia, Third Belorussian Front had begun its attack on 13 January. Here, the Germans utilized the defenses prepared in the 1920s and 1930s, as well as additional work carried out during heavy fighting in fall 1944. There was no rapid advance, just a terrible slogging match in which casualties were heavy on both sides. However, the removal of Großdeutschland and other reserves to the south lightened the task of Soviet troops advancing on Königsberg. On 21 January, the Soviets captured the area where the great Tannenberg memorial, commemorating Marshal Paul von Hindenburg's victory in August 1914, had stood. But the Germans had already dynamited the memorial and transferred Marshal Hindenburg's body to the west.

The difficulties Soviet forces were experiencing in East Prussia resulted in a considerable change in the axis of advance for Second Belorussian

Front. Rokossovsky began his offensive on 14 January with the aim of driving to the Oder on Zhukov's right flank. But the STAVKA ordered Second Belorussian Front to shift from a northwestern to a northern drive in order to cut East Prussia off from the rest of Germany and drive in behind East Prussia's defenders. By 24 January, Soviet spearheads, driving straight through Elbing with their headlights on, reached the Baltic. They had cut off East Prussia from the rest of the Reich, while, under pressure from Third Belorussian Front, the troops defending East Prussia pulled back into Königsberg's outer defenses. Nevertheless, Rokossovsky's new direction uncovered Zhukov's northern flank.

For the moment, it did not seem to matter. Warsaw, Lodz, Cracow had all fallen in short order. On 22 January, Eighth Guards Army, led by Colonel General V. I. Chuikov, the hero of Stalingrad, surrounded Poznan and 60,000 Wehrmacht troops. By 31 January, spearhead units from Bogdanov's Second Guards Tank Army had reached the Oder River by the fortress of Kustrin, over 250 miles from their starting point. At the same time, Konev's forces were moving northwest along the Oder and driving through German Silesia; Fourth Tank and Thirteenth Army even managed to seize a bridgehead across the Oder just north of Breslau. Meanwhile, Third Guards Tank Army turned south at Oppeln and then swung south along the Oder to take much of Silesia's industrial region.

By now this massive force of Soviet armies was fighting on German territory. Three and a half years of German occupation, of deprivation and destruction, of aggression and annihilation, had provoked murderous rage among Soviet troops. Egged on by Stalin's propagandist Ilya Ehrenburg, Soviet troops unleashed a reign of terror over German territory, marked by mass rapes, the brutal murders of tens of thousands of civilians, looting, and wanton destruction. In but one example of Red Army atrocities, Soviet tanks consistently drove straight down columns of refugees at full speed, while gunners shot any Germans who escaped being crushed under the tracks. In the long run, these crimes against German civilians would undermine Soviet efforts to establish a Communist regime in East Germany. And yet no matter how savage the atrocities committed by Soviet troops or how innocent some of the victims, the German people and their regime, through their own crimes, had sown the wind, and now they were reaping the whirlwind.

Soviet forces on the Oder near Kustrin were barely 50 miles from the German capital. In early February, the STAVKA believed that only a short halt to refit Zhukov's and Konev's fronts would be necessary before Soviet forces resumed their advance on Berlin. But a number of factors intervened to delay the attack across the Oder. Zhukov's flank remained exposed to the north. Moreover, significant German reinforcements were finally beginning to arrive along the Oder and especially in Pomerania, where the Eleventh SS Panzer Army was assembling—seemingly a threat to Zhukov's flank. The second factor was that Konev's strength lay on his southern flank. Consequently, he would have to make substantial redeployments to support Zhukov. That redeployment in turn demanded that Konev clean out the rest of Silesia, including the "fortress" city of Breslau.

Since Zhukov's forces were now well positioned on the Oder, the STAVKA determined to clear out the flanks first, before resuming the advance on Berlin. Since the Western powers were still on the far side of the Rhine, risk-taking seemed unnecessary. German actions clearly helped the Soviets to make up their minds. On 8 February, Konev began his assault out of his bridgeheads on the western bank of the Oder; it quickly became apparent that German defenses were stronger than anticipated. While Soviet troops encircled Breslau, the defenders were positioned and equipped for a prolonged siege. In the north, with so much of its force drawn off to the fighting in East Prussia, Second Belorussian Front made little headway in Pomerania. Moreover, Eleventh SS Panzer Army attacked Zhukov's flank. A swift redeployment of Zhukov's and Rokossovsky's forces then allowed the Soviets to begin their offensive against West Prussia and Pomerania on 24 February. The Soviet strike again caught the Germans flat-footed. By the end of the first week in March, the Soviets had taken all of Pomerania and driven the Germans—those who survived—across the Oder.

Astonishingly, given the extent of the Soviet successes from the Baltic to the Carpathians and the fact that Zhukov was already within striking range of Berlin, Hitler persisted in his efforts to drive Soviet forces back on Budapest. Sixth SS Panzer Army made the difficult move across the wreckage of the German transportation system to redeploy on the Hungarian plain while catastrophe was occurring in the north. Perhaps only Hitler's Austrian ancestry and a desire to protect Vienna and the Hapsburg lands from Soviet ravages distracted his attention from East Prussia, Pomerania, and Silesia. Whatever the reason, in early March, Sixth SS Panzer Army launched its offensive, at best a spoiling attack with no prospect of a major operational success. The Soviets were ready; and, as during the Zitadelle offensive, they refused to commit their reserves; after the Germans had expended their strength in a 20-mile advance, the Soviet counteroffensive simply swamped the German defenders across the front. As the German defenses dissolved, the road to Vienna lay open.

These Soviet successes occurred immediately before and concurrently with the Yalta Conference in February 1945, during which the principal Allies divided up the soon-to-be-conquered German nation. Given that Stalin's armies were in the full flood of success, that Anglo-American armies remained firmly stuck on the far side of the Rhine, and that Soviet troops were within 50 miles of the German capital of Berlin, it was a major diplomatic achievement for Britain and the United States that they gained all of western Germany and a significant portion of central Germany for their occupation zones. At Yalta, Brooke continued the British campaign to turn the ground war over to Montgomery and launch a single drive north of the Ruhr. But the Americans resisted; for military as well as political reasons, they were not about to give command of the ground war over to Montgomery. And as events soon proved, to have done so would have been a strategic as well as an operational error of enormous magnitude.

As American troops pushed the Germans out of the Ardennes at the end of January, Eisenhower set as his operational goal closing on the Rhine. He was willing to allow Bradley and Patton considerable leeway, but he warned them that his main emphasis would lie on the British drive to the north of the Ruhr, which Simpson's Ninth Army would support. Nevertheless, Ike turned down another tiresome request from Montgomery that Hodges's First Army remain under Twenty-First Army control.

In early February, First Canadian Army launched Operation Veritable from the north to push the Germans back behind the Rhine. At the same time, Ninth Army launched Operation Grenade across the Roer to push north and link up with the Canadians. While the dams finally fell into American hands on 9 February, the Germans had destroyed the spillways and control machinery, thus unleashing a flood down river. Not until 23 February did the Roer drop sufficiently for Simpson to attack.

Nevertheless, the effect of the combined offensive by the U.S. Ninth Army and the Canadian First Army put the German Fifteenth and First Parachute Armies in a desperate situation. Despite pleas from Rundstedt and Model, Hitler refused permission for withdrawal. By early March, Simpson's troops were cleaning up the Rhine and searching for a bridge over the river that the Germans had yet to destroy. The Germans managed to blow up all the bridges. Nevertheless, Simpson requested permission to cross near Ürdingen where the Germans had few troops and where he thought the open terrain on the northern side of the Ruhr offered considerable potential for exploitation. Montgomery's response indicates why he was unsuited for the position of overall commander of Allied ground forces: he turned Simpson down cold in order to wait two weeks for his own massive, ponderous, carefully planned, and long-advertised crossing of the Rhine to take place.

While Bradley had to relinquish several divisions to Ninth Army, he still possessed 22 divisions in his two armies. Thus far in 1945, First Army and Third Army had made relatively little progress. Collins's VII Corps had supported Simpson's attack across the Roer; that crossing had now opened the way for Collins to strike at Cologne. By 5 March, the great Cathedral was in U.S. hands. Meanwhile, III Corps had reached the Rhine at Bonn and then turned south against Germans more interested in crossing the Rhine than in defending the Rhineland. Hitler was, of course, standing by his no-retreat order, so that the units available in the Eifel remained in place with their northern flank increasingly vulnerable.

To the south of Bonn along the Rhine lies the relatively small town of Remagen, important only because the Ludendorff railroad bridge spanned the river at that point. In midafternoon on 7 March, a task force of the American 9th Armored Division, led by several new Pershing tanks, advanced through the flotsam of escaping Germans. As the Americans approached the bridge from the west, a large explosion greeted them. An even larger explosion followed, clearly designed to drop the bridge into the Rhine. To the astonishment of Germans and Americans alike, when the smoke cleared, the bridge still stood—the charges had lifted the bridge straight up in the air instead of twisting it, and the bridge had come back down on its pillars.

The Americans reacted without orders; infantrymen, supported by heavy machine gun and tank fire, rapidly crossed and drove the Germans back. By night the Americans had pushed a small force of tanks across the river—and within 24 hours they had 8,000 men across. Over the course of the next ten days, Hodges pushed a substantial force across the Rhine River in the face of desperate German efforts to destroy the bridge. The bridge's capture had delighted Eisenhower and Bradley, although neither showed much interest in exploiting the advantage. To Hodges's fury, Eisenhower limited First Army to a maximum of five divisions in the bridgehead, while Bradley ordered First Army to limit its advance to 1,000 yards per day and to hold in place once it reached the Frankfurt autobahn.

While First Army was achieving this success, Patton made his own crossing of the Rhine. On 3 March, Third Army had gone over to the offensive in the Eifel. So tenuous had the German position become that the defenses collapsed on the first day. Within three days, 4th Armored Division had advanced 44 miles and reached the Rhine. Patton then turned south behind the German First and Seventh Armies, which were still holding in place along the Moselle and *Westwall*. By 14 March, Patton had a corps across the lower Moselle near Koblenz, and the threat was real that Patton's troops would roll down the Rhine and cut off the remainder of German troops on the west bank. In a drive reminiscent of August 1944, Third Army cleaned up the west bank of the Rhine all the way south to Worms and Speyer; Third and Seventh Armies claimed well over 100,000 German prisoners in the victory.

Hitler's demand that German forces stand on the far side of the Rhine had played a major contributing role in the American successes. All told, Model and Rundstedt lost upwards of a quarter of a million prisoners and a third of their strength in defending the indefensible. The Germans were now back on the Rhine, and they had nothing but badly battered units to hold the front. Patton was, of course, thinking of crossing the Rhine as soon as his troops had cleaned up the west bank. Over the night of 22 March, Third Army secured two crossing points, and its engineers immediately went to work constructing pontoon bridges. The next evening Bradley informed the press that without any artillery bombardment, air support, or paratrooper drops, Third Army had successfully crossed the Rhine—a sharp dig at Montgomery's massive offensive. Four days later, troops of Patch's Seventh Army had seized a bridgehead at Worms, soon to be followed by Lattre de Tassigny's French First Army.

In stark contrast, Twenty-First Army marshaled vast resources, prepared everything to the *n*th degree, laid on massive artillery and air bombardments, and dropped a host of paratroopers against exhausted and weak German defenses. In fact, Twenty-First Army Group could have made the crossing north of the Ruhr weeks before, as Simpson had urged. In a visit to Eisenhower's headquarters shortly after exploitation had begun, Brooke admitted that the broad-front strategy was now working, but only because the Allies had sufficient ground strength. What, of course, the CIGS did not admit was that as recently as February he had urged in the strongest terms that Montgomery command all Anglo-American ground forces. In fact, to have done so would have resulted in a far more labored advance—one, moreover, that would have confined Allied operations to the north German plain.

In early April, the armies of the Western powers spread across the heartland of Nazi Germany. On 26 March, having finally received permission to exploit its bridgehead, First Army began its drive to encircle the Ruhr from the south. Hodges's orders were to drive around the Ruhr to meet up with

Simpson's Ninth Army northeast of Paderborn. In two days Hodges's lead division, 3rd Armored, had reached 45 miles around the southern outline of the Ruhr. First Army's race to Paderborn picked up even greater speed, and on the 30th, the 3rd Armored Division advanced 45 miles in a single day. Yet, for all the rapidity of advance, countless small and medium encounters with German troops left hundreds of Americans and even more Germans dead and turned entire villages and towns into smoking ruins. Unlike the British—perhaps because of very different experiences in the last war—U.S. commanders were willing to take heavy casualties in fighting their way through German villages to keep the drive going. Just short of Paderborn—a major tank training center for the Wehrmacht and the Waffen SS—one of 3rd Armored Division's lead columns ran into a force of Tigers and Panthers manned by students and instructors. The encounter turned into a chilling repeat of Villers-Bocage. The Germans shot up the front and rear of the column and then proceeded to destroy everything in between. The maintenance crews later counted 1 M36 tank destroyer, 2 jeeps, 3 trucks, 17 Shermans, and 17 half-tracks destroyed.

The heavy fighting around Paderborn raises the larger question of when German resistance actually finally collapsed. Certainly the long sharp arrows covering all of western and central Germany in late March and early April would assign the date of the collapse to mid-March. That would be an incorrect assumption. Robbed of its fuel and much of its ammunition, the German Army still conducted a fierce defense with little control or order. The Germans had no reply to the fluidity and mobility that had returned to the battlefield after six long months. But they did stand in innumerable locations and fight to the last. The number of Americans killed in the European Theater of Operations in April 1945 was 10,677, almost the same number as had died in June 1944 and 1,500 more than had died in February 1945; the number was only 3,000 under the grim totals for January and March 1945. The simple truth was that the real German collapse did not come until the last week of April. As long as the Germans had guns and ammunition, they died for the Führer and took all too many American, British, and Soviet soldiers with them.

On the strategic level, Eisenhower decided that capturing Berlin was simply not worth the candle. He was right. The Soviets were far too close to the German capital, while Allied politicians had already decided the postwar occupation zones. Thus, there seemed no reason to conquer territory at great cost, merely to have that territory turned over to the Soviets. Montgomery's Twenty-First Army Group received the task of advancing to the Elbe and Baltic. The aim was to position Allied forces for a possible campaign into Scandinavia, should German troops in Denmark and Norway refuse to surrender. Interestingly, it took considerable prodding from Eisenhower to push Montgomery into closing on the Baltic despite the German collapse on his front. Ninth Army and First Army were to envelop German forces in the Ruhr. At noon on Easter Sunday, 1 April 1945, Ninth Army's 2nd Armored Division linked up with First Army's 3rd Armored Division; between the encircling arms of those two armies lay the remnants of Army Group B, Fifteenth Army, Fifth Panzer Army, and First Parachute Army. In mid-April, Model dissolved his remaining forces and blew his brains out in a secluded woods. When the Americans finally totaled the number of prisoners taken in the Ruhr pocket, they counted 317,000. Simpson, Hodges, and Patton were soon free to continue advancing deeper into central Germany. Ninth Army quickly gobbled up Hanover, Brunswick, and Magdeburg. By mid-month, it held a bridgehead across the Elbe. But poised to advance on Berlin and Potsdam, Simpson was told by Bradley and Eisenhower to stand down.

To Simpson's south, First Army bypassed the Harz mountains and reached Nordhausen. Third Army was soon close to the Czech frontier. On Marshall's orders, Patton remained on the German side of the frontier, and the Soviets gained the honor of liberating Prague. It is possible that an American liberation of the Czech capital might have saved the Czechs from the 40 years of darkness that enveloped their nation in 1948. But one must remember that their leader, Eduard Beneš, had surrendered to the Germans without a squeak in 1938 and would do the same to the Soviets in 1948.

While a portion of Patton's army remained at Chemnitz, other units sliced southward along the Sudetenland's frontier to finally end the war at Linz. In the south, again at times against fanatical resistance, Patch's Seventh Army searched for the mythical Alpine redoubt. What they found instead was the same patchwork of surrender and fanatical resistance. But the collapse of command, the rapidity of the American advance, and a lack of fuel prevented the Germans from putting up a coherent defense. The 101st Airborne ended the war in Berchtesgaden with more liquor from Göring's private cellar than any American soldier could have considered possible in his wildest dreams.

The American advance was soon uncovering the gruesome evidence of the slave labor camps. Third Army captured the slave labor camps that surrounded the V-2 production site at Ohrdruf, but the capture of the larger slave labor camp at Nordhausen provided an even grimmer indication of what the Allies would uncover throughout Germany: "Rows upon rows of skin-covered skeletons. Men lay as they had starved, discolored, and lying in indescribable human filth. Their striped coats and prison numbers hung to their frames. One girl in particular I noticed; I would say she was about seventeen years old. She lay as she had fallen, gangrened and naked."[7]

The last act occurred in the east. For the past month, Soviet forces had prepared for it, and by mid-April they were ready. Three fronts led by Konev, Rokossovsky, and Zhukov were to deliver the death blow. Soviet forces consisted of no less than 2.5 million soldiers, 6,250 tanks and self-propelled guns, and 41,600 guns and heavy mortars. The storm broke on 14 April. Particularly in front of Zhukov's forces, the Wehrmacht put up a tenacious resistance. By now the Germans understood that the Soviets were extracting a full measure of revenge. But the disparity in forces was too great for the Germans to do anything but delay their enemy's wrath. Egged on by Stalin's open encouragement of a race to Berlin, Soviet forces soon broke into the clear. The Red Army's spearheads first enveloped the Ninth and Fourth Panzer Armies fighting along the Oder. On 19 April, German defenses completely collapsed. Konev's Third Guards Tank and Fourth Guards Tank Armies advanced nearly 60 miles and swept up on Berlin from the south. Zhukov's First Belorussian Front was closing in on Berlin from the north and east. On the 26th, with the city now isolated, Zhukov began the final assault on the German capital. With no coherent direction except Hitler's exhortations, German defenses slowly crumbled throughout the city. Using massive firepower, the Soviets destroyed what little Allied bombers had left untouched.

In his gloomy bunker on 26 April 1945, Hitler celebrated his 56th birthday, married his mistress, and then wrote a maudlin, bitter last testament, blaming the Jews and the German people for the final, shattering collapse of the Third Reich. Later that day, as the Soviet advance lapped ever closer to the ruins of the Reich's Chancellery, Hitler killed himself with a bullet to the head.

The price the Red Army paid for its final victory in taking Berlin was monumental: 361,367 Soviet and Polish soldiers fell in the effort—an indication of the kind of casualty bill the Western powers would have received had they attempted to take Berlin before the Soviets. Even by the standards of the preceding winter, the victorious, vengeful Soviets carried out an extraordinary orgy of rape and murder in the former capital of the Reich. In May 1945, World War II in Europe had finally come to a close.

Conclusion

To the end, the Germans fought with fanaticism. Their crimes in Poland and the Soviet Union, as well as those the Soviets unleashed against German civilians in reply, provide a partial explanation for the tenacity of the defense in the east. But the Germans were hardly less tenacious in the west. A fuller explanation lies in the ideological commitment throughout the Wehrmacht. That commitment, that belief in Adolf Hitler and the Third Reich, remained strong to the final days of the war.

American commanders had shown considerable improvement in the conduct of military operations in 1945. The drive to the Rhine displayed a willingness to exploit every advantage the enemy provided. Montgomery's refusal to allow Simpson's Ninth Army to cross the Rhine merely confirmed his inability to understand the conduct of operations beyond the setpiece battle. By contrast, U.S. commanders in this campaign, and not just Patton, displayed a superior understanding of exploitation and maneuver warfare that led to the greatest American victory of the war: encirclement of the Ruhr by First and Ninth U.S. Armies.

But the Soviets displayed the greatest abilities at the operational level of war. From Bagration, which took out virtually all of Army Group Center in summer 1944, to the operations that destroyed German forces in East Prussia and Poland in winter 1945, Soviet commanders exhibited outstanding capabilities in deception, planning, and the conduct of operations. Their victories were far superior to anything the Germans had achieved early in the war. And yet the casualties Soviet forces suffered, while completely within the perceptions of Stalin's ideology, carried political and social consequences that were to burden the Soviet Union to its demise.

On the other side of the hill, the German generals waged their war with total disregard for the long-range prospects of their people. A major theme in the postwar memoirs of some German generals followed the line, "If the Führer had only listened to me"; they clearly implied that if he had, the Wehrmacht would have fought more successfully and for longer. In reality, if Hitler had listened to his generals more often, and if the war had stretched into summer 1945, the Americans would have dropped the first atomic bomb on Germany, a fact the generals were still incapable of seeing decades after the war. In the end, the German military, by its skilled resistance, managed to wreck most of the Reich and Europe as well, a horrific accomplishment.

17

THE DESTRUCTION
OF THE JAPANESE EMPIRE

1944–1945

As Allied forces deployed for their final drive on the Third Reich, the political and military leaders of the Anglo-American coalition reviewed the war with Japan. In strategic memoranda drafted in summer 1944, the planners reflected an optimism born of the fall of the Marianas and the collapse of the German defenses in France. From the American perspective, Roosevelt and Churchill faced three chores when they met again in Quebec in September 1944: (1) to review the Allies' general approach to defeating Japan; (2) to determine the level and nature of British participation in the air-naval war in the Western Pacific; and (3) to assess the need to move American troops from the European theater to the Pacific and to schedule their release.

The Joint Chiefs (with the exception of Admiral King, who still wanted to invade Formosa) had already reached a consensus on how to defeat Japan. They thought that the key to destroying Japan's economy and industrial strength was to refocus their geographic objectives northward, by placing air and naval bases in the Bonins and Ryukyus just south of the Home Islands. The final defeat of Japan might ultimately require invasions of Kyushu and Honshu islands themselves. The planners saw no immediate value in liberating the southern Philippines or the Netherlands East Indies farther to the south, though perhaps American forces might seize bases on China's southeastern coast.

The flaw in this plan (JCS 924, "Operations Against Japan Subsequent to Formosa" and its revisions) was its failure to deal with the Japanese on the Asian mainland. Neither the British nor Roosevelt was inclined to go along with a plan that "forgot" Asia—though for different reasons. FDR still believed that the Chinese Nationalists might tie down Japanese ground forces and that Chiang Kai-shek's regime might fill the void left by the collapse of

European and Japanese imperialism. As a practical matter, this wishful thinking gave Roosevelt some political relief from the "Asia Firsters" in the Republican Party as he entered his fourth presidential election campaign. The British position on Asia also had its roots in politics, in this case Churchill's conviction that the British Empire's survival was essential to Britain's postwar rehabilitation. With the exception of Admiral Lord Mountbatten, Churchill found no fellow visionaries among the British high commanders, whose main worry was a premature departure of American forces from the European theater. When pressed to commit new resources to Asia, no British or American senior officer volunteered to weaken operations elsewhere. General Marshall refused to divert two European-bound infantry divisions to Burma, while the British chiefs would not send enough air and naval units to avoid an overland conquest of Burma. When some grand scheme for a widened campaign in Southeast Asia was proposed, inevitably the commanders would raise insurmountable logistical problems as an excuse for inaction. The only agreement reached in autumn 1944 was that the United States would provide greater air support for General William Slim's Fourteenth Army, which would take control of the road to Mandalay, a rough tract of jungles and broad rivers. For the Americans, such a campaign had only one attraction: it would drive the Japanese away from the road to China.

Roosevelt and Marshall reluctantly concluded that the only hope for any improvement in Chiang Kai-shek's willingness to fight lay in reassigning General Stilwell and in reorganizing the U.S. command in the region. The first change they made was to put a distinct American commander, subordinate to Mountbatten, in the Southeast Pacific theater; the officer chosen for this role was Lieutenant General Daniel I. Sultan, an air-minded engineer. Next, a separate China theater went to Lieutenant General Albert C. Wedemeyer, a Marshall protégé and a noted military planner with broad international experience. Wedemeyer's opening move was to have Marshall "retire" Brigadier General Chennault, Chiang's most ardent American fan. To give political cover to these rearrangements, FDR made Patrick Hurley, a Republican favorite and World War I hero, his ambassador to China. With Lend-Lease aid flowing in increasing quantities, Wedemeyer planned for a modernized Nationalist army that would recover the territory lost to Japan in 1944 and establish bases on the coast of south China.

Within only a few weeks, this October optimism gave way to the sober conclusion that there would be no major challenge to the Japanese Army in Asia by a Chinese-American ground and air army. The obstacles were many. The first one came from unexpected developments in Europe,

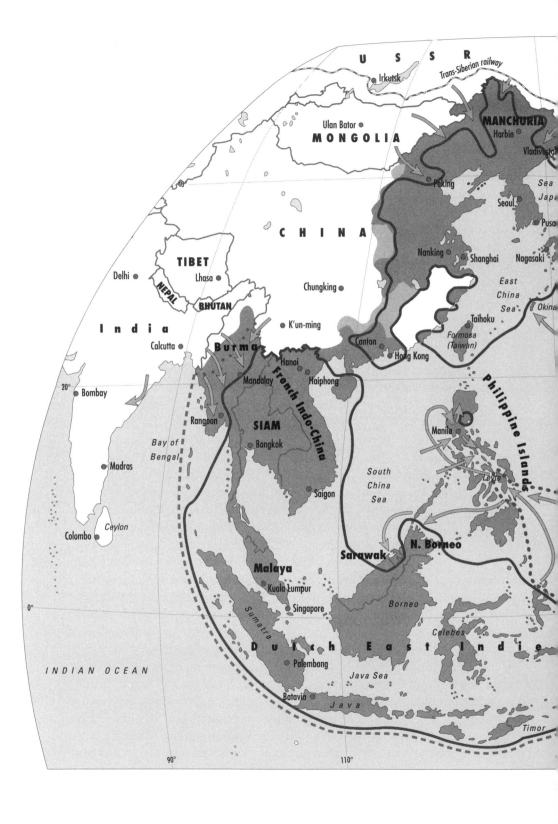

END OF EMPIRE
1944 – 1945

- Japanese empire mid-1944
- Japanese gains by December 1944
- Japanese losses by December 1944
- Japanese territory August 1945
- Major lines of Allied advance

Khabarovsk

Sakhalin

Aleutian Islands

Hokkaido

JAPAN

Kyoto   Honshu

Tokyo

Iwo Jima

PACIFIC OCEAN

Midway Is.

Hawaiian Islands

Wake Is.

Saipan
Tinian
Rota
Guam   Mariana Is.

Yap   Ulithi

Eniwetok   Marshall Is.

Truk   Ponape

Kwajalein

Caroline Islands

Majura

Jaluit

Palau

Tarawa

Gilbert Is.

Bismarck
Arch.   Rabaul

New Guinea

Salamaua

Solomon Is.

Guadalcanal

Arafura Sea

Port Moresby

Coral Sea 150°   170°   190°

where the Allied army groups had reached the borderlands of Germany west of the Rhine only to stall in bloody battles from Arnhem to the Alps. Under these circumstances, no transfer of American troops from Europe to Asia could be planned. Second, the battle for Leyte suggested that many more GIs would have to wade ashore before MacArthur's return to the Philippines was secure. In China itself, civilian diplomats and military missions (one army, one navy) continued to cast about for some way to get the Nationalist forces back in the war, but with little success. One group became intrigued with Communist guerrilla forces in northern China and encouraged Mao Tse-tung and Chou En-lai to accept a secondary role in a coalition government in exchange for American military assistance. Neither the Communists nor Chiang liked this arrangement, however, and it had no backing from Ambassador Hurley, who regarded his professional subordinates as a nest of Communists. Another faction backed Commodore Milton Miles's OSS-supported Sino-American Cooperation Organization, which evolved from weather watchers to guerrilla bands in collaboration with Chinese partisans and the Nationalist secret service run by General Tai Li. This shadowy figure wanted to start an anti-Communist crusade that would take him to Chiang's office, not fight the Japanese. Northern China, where the largest numbers of Chinese and Japanese faced one another, remained inactive, in part because the Nationalist generals spent their resources hounding the Communists, not the Japanese.

The stalemate in China forced American diplomats and military planners (against their judgment) to look to the Soviets to pressure Mao into cooperating with Chiang and to enter the war themselves with a campaign in Manchuria. By the time Roosevelt and Churchill met Stalin at Yalta in February 1945, the Combined Chiefs of Staff were urging their political masters to arrange Soviet participation in the Asian war. A Soviet army in Asia might deliver the coup de grâce to the Japanese Army, and at a minimum Russian air and naval forces could help halt exports and the deployment of reinforcements from Manchuria and Korea to Japan. The Americans even proposed that they use Soviet bases for their own air and naval operations.

Although some navy analysts argued that the Soviets were more trouble than they were worth, army planners focused only on when the Soviet entry would occur, not whether it was ultimately necessary or wise. One proposal brought the Russians into the war 90 days before the Kyushu invasion; another brought them into the war 90 days after the defeat of Germany. Roosevelt and Stalin agreed on the latter timing at Yalta. FDR promised to increase Lend-Lease weapons and equipment shipments through Persia to the Red Army and accepted Soviet claims to concessions in Manchuria and restoration of territories lost to Japan in 1905. Chiang Kai-shek also accepted this arrangement, since he still regarded the Soviets as good allies and a leash on Mao Tse-tung despite their ideological ties. Husbanding his armies for the postponed civil war, the Generalissimo was perfectly willing to fight the Japanese to the last Red Army soldier.

The effect of the China tangle on the course of the war was simple: throughout 1945 the Japanese were able to redeploy their armies from Asia to continue their hopeless struggle. As long as the Japanese generals had even a trickle of supplies and reinforcements from the continent, their duty to fight for the Emperor knew no limits other than death itself.

The China-Burma Theater

General William Slim's skilled and determined campaign to drive the Japanese Burma Area Army back to the border of Thailand showed how one non-European army might defeat the finest Asian army to take the field in modern times. In 1945, the Fourteenth Army, divided into three corps, was British in name only. Seven of its twelve infantry divisions were part of the Indian Army, and three drew their troops from the British colonies in Africa; only two divisions were predominately European. Protecting Slim's northern flank was the two-regiment U.S. composite brigade (Mars Force) that replaced the Marauders, but the bulk of the ground forces in northern Burma consisted of six Chinese divisions and the native partisan battalions raised by OSS and SOE. The Royal Air Force (with other Commonwealth contingents) and the U.S. Army Air Forces provided critical support, especially firepower and supplies, for the bold, sweeping movements that Slim's units would execute.

Exploiting the Japanese Fifteenth Army's defeat at Imphal-Kohima and withdrawal, Slim saw that he could now take the initiative. The mobility and logistical capability of the Japanese, even after they fell back on established lines of supply, were no match for his own. Evidence of his opponent's desperation was everywhere on the battlefield. Slim saw Japanese soldiers executed by their comrades because they were too badly wounded to evacuate, and Japanese corpses showed signs of disease and malnutrition; he saw troops abandon half their artillery because ammunition had run out. An army in such dire straits could not maneuver, but it could certainly fight and die in place. Slim had no intention of giving the Japanese generals that option.

The battered Burma Area Army could at best muster 100,000 combatants unless reinforced—an unlikely prospect, Slim knew, in the face of

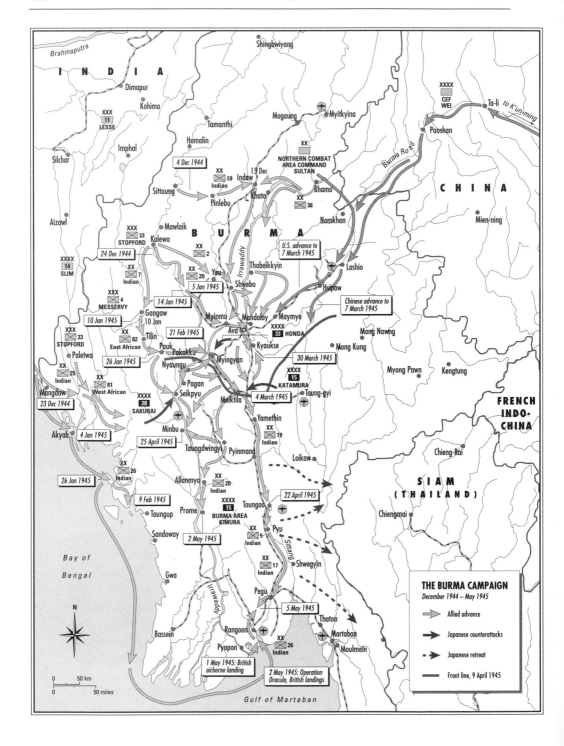

THE BURMA CAMPAIGN
December 1944 – May 1945

Allied advance
Japanese counterattacks
Japanese retreat
Front line, 9 April 1945

Allied air and naval superiority. The Fifteenth Army numbered only 21,000 men. Slim's Fourteenth Army, by contrast, began its campaign in January–March 1945 with 260,000 officers and men in 12 divisions, plus two separate infantry brigades and two armored brigades. Slim could also count on 183,000 Americans and 72,000 Chinese for supporting operations in northern Burma. His RAF and USAAF squadrons had approximately 800 operational combat aircraft of many types and about 250 transports. The Japanese at best could put approximately 250 aircraft in the air. Slim's campaign plan took advantage of this superiority in troop numbers, firepower, mobility, and logistical sustainability. By shifting divisions between his two corps in central Burma, he allowed his troops some respite from combat without sacrificing the tempo of his advance, and yet he made sure that his fighting troops did not outpace his engineers and service units. With adequate reserves for rear area security missions, aided by Burmese irregulars, he could take offensive risks, but he could quickly change plans if muddling ahead might bring unwarranted casualties. He had no intention of squandering his foot soldiers, especially the irreplaceable British and Gurkha battalions, when he had so much artillery and tank support at his command. He also established an unusually close bond with his officers and men because he respected their courage and skill. "I was, like other generals before me, to be saved . . . by the resourcefulness of my subordinate commanders and the stubborn valour of my troops."[1]

Fourteenth Army started its campaign with two corps headed east toward Mandalay and the third edging south by road and short amphibious envelopments down the Arakan coast toward Rangoon. When Slim learned that the Japanese intended to defend Mandalay from the eastern shore of the Irrawaddy, a river wider than the Rhine, he decided to cross with one corps well south of Mandalay at Meiktila, while the other faked a main attack north of the city. In March 1945, Fourteenth Army crossed the river and flanked the Japanese, who decided to fight only a rearguard action, not a decisive battle. Nevertheless, Slim's troops had to dig the Japanese out from a maze of pagodas and colonial fortifications before the city fell on 20 March 1945. Although the total casualties were almost equal, the Japanese lost more than four times as many dead as Slim's army: 6,500 to 1,600.

Now racing the monsoon, Slim ordered the Arakan corps to seize the mouth of the Irrawaddy and advance on Rangoon, while another corps moved south from Mandalay. In May 1945, the two forces met and invested Rangoon, but the Japanese again slipped away after losing another 7,000 soldiers (most of them dead) to Slim's 2,500. Assuming that the rains would hinder Slim's air support, artillery, and tanks, the Japanese attacked with the remnants of two field armies and were ambushed by an Indian division; another 11,000 soldiers were lost, almost all dead. The rout became a massacre, as 10,000 more Japanese soldiers died along and in the Sittang River, while Commonwealth forces lost only 435 dead and 2,000 wounded. In 1942, the Japanese had conquered Burma and Malaya at the cost of about 5,000 lives; in September 1945, they surrendered with more than 50,000 dead since the ill-fated Imphal-Kohima offensive had begun 12 months before.

Part of Slim's success in 1945 stemmed from the assistance he received from the Chinese divisions engaging Japanese forces in north-central Burma between the Irrawaddy and Chinese-Thai border. In addition, Aung San's Patriotic Burmese Army, defecting from its alliance with the Japanese, provided effective semi-guerrilla operations in the hill country to the north. Slim found a way to get everyone into the fight—the key difference between his generalship and that of Chinese and American commanders in China. Through careful tactics and painstaking logistical arrangements, especially his provisions for casualties and food, he raised the morale of his Indian and African soldiers to the point where they lost their fear of the Japanese. Although Slim characterized his force as an "Indian Army," Fourteenth Army actually represented the multinational, multicultural character of the entire British Empire. Except in reconnaissance, mechanized cavalry, and armored units, Indian units did not provide the majority of the troops in combat arms. In his two British divisions, Slim commanded 16 British infantry battalions and only 3 of other nationalities. In the 7 Indian divisions, all but 2 of 21 infantry brigades had a regular British battalion; a battalion of Gurkha Rifles served in 17 infantry brigades. Slim, however, managed to build the esprit and effectiveness of his Indian troops so they could assume more difficult combat missions as the British and Gurkha battalions shrank in size from lack of replacements, another example of Slim's superior leadership. The two African divisions had all-African infantry battalions.

While Fourteenth Army battled to liberate Burma, the Australian army, consolidated into 6 divisions and 2 armored brigades in 1945, conducted campaigns of irregular intensity against the Japanese stranded on New Guinea, Cape Britain (Rabaul), and Bougainville. Following the policy of using Australian troops to recapture areas under Commonwealth administration in 1941, General Sir Thomas Blamey cautioned his division and brigade commanders not to risk lives with hurried operations, but also not to use "live and let live" tactics that allowed the Japanese Army to counterattack. MacArthur prodded Blamey to stay on the offensive by threatening to redeploy some Australian divisions to the Philippines. To many Australians, even pointless battles in the New Guinea jungles seemed preferable to returning to MacArthur's control.

The Combined Chiefs of Staff, however, saw little reason for the Australians either to stay in the Southwest Pacific or to go to the Philippines. In early 1945, they asked the Australians to plan a series of landings on Borneo, an island divided into four sovereignties, two Dutch, two British. MacArthur approved the Borneo campaign as the first step to liberating the Netherlands East Indies, especially Java, since he did not believe Mountbatten's forces would ever break out of Burma. Air fields, oil fields, and refineries gave the island added luster as an objective. Borneo also attracted Allied attention as the site of the strongest resistance movement in the East Indies—a union of Chinese refugees and Allied military survivors of 1942 with the Dyak tribesmen.

In May 1945, an Australian corps with Allied air and naval support made its first landing on Borneo and continued with amphibious envelopments until the war's end. Guerrilla units urged prompt action in Borneo because they knew the Japanese planned to kill Australian POWs and civilian internees. Fewer than 600 Australian soldiers died in liberating the Dutch territories; they killed approximately 6,000 Japanese in the process. Unfortunately, in marching their POWs to new sites, the Japanese killed more than 3,500 POWs and civilian internees on Borneo and Ambon Island before Allied special forces could rescue them.

MacArthur and the Philippines

Not distracted even by annoying bombing raids on his quarters at Tacloban, Leyte, MacArthur pondered the campaign that offered his ultimate revenge and vindication: the liberation of Luzon, the island at the political and cultural heart of the Philippines. Throughout the battle for Leyte, MacArthur prodded his subordinates to move ahead with ambitious plans and timetables for a return to Luzon, especially to the capital city of Manila. In light of the ferocious air attacks on Leyte and the flow of reinforcements to its Japanese defenders, MacArthur's subordinate commanders, especially Kenney and Kinkaid, questioned whether MacArthur could make his return without changes in the prevailing pattern of operations. They argued that Japan had sufficient conventional and *kamikaze* air power to stop a naval charge straight for Lingayen Gulf.

Kenney's and Kinkaid's concerns did not reflect inordinate caution. Kenney's engineers doubted whether they could build expeditionary air fields quickly in northern Luzon, which was one of MacArthur's cherished assumptions; their experience at Leyte had jarred their confidence in the Allies' ability to establish land-based air operations in the face of enemy attack and bad weather. But Kenney did not believe a Luzon expedition could proceed without air superiority provided by his P-38 and P-47 fighters and offensive air capability provided by his B-25 and A-20 bombers, all part of his Fifth Air Force. Admiral Kinkaid shared this assessment, since it was now clear that *kamikazes* would seek out American naval carriers for special attention. Halsey's Third Fleet still ranged far and wide to strike enemy air fields throughout the Philippines and on Formosa, but these raids did not go unchallenged. On 30 October, *kamikazes* struck three carriers of Task Force 38 so severely they had to suspend flight operations and retire to Ulithi for repairs. A month later, four more carriers suffered substantial damage from *kamikaze* strikes. The losses convinced Halsey to call off another round of attacks and retreat to Ulithi.

However wise the navy's withdrawal, MacArthur railed about his lack of naval support to all within hearing distance. Kinkaid thought that his escort carriers might cover part of the advance northward, but only with army air cover. Kinkaid and Kenney presented MacArthur with an alternative: an assault on lightly defended Mindoro to convert it into an advanced base for Kenney's fighter squadrons, which could then provide combat air patrols over the Luzon invasion fleet. The Mindoro operation would require a postponement of the Luzon expedition until mid-January 1945, but MacArthur now thought the delay reasonable. He approved the Mindoro operation, which would begin with an amphibious assault on 15 December.

In the meantime, Halsey and the navy's air admirals had not been inactive. They changed the structure of each carrier's air group, adding at least one fighter squadron and reducing the number of scout-bombers and torpedo planes from 42 to 30. This change strengthened the combat air patrols. The Marine Corps provided F4U Corsairs for duty on selected carriers with the understanding that "all-Marine" escort carriers should be used for close air support missions as well as fleet protection. In addition, the navy changed the anti-aircraft armament on its ships, bolting down as many dual- and quadruple-mounted 40mm rapid-fire anti-aircraft cannon as they could find space for; these replaced 20mm guns that had been unable to stop *kamikazes*.

As Kinney and Kinkaid predicted, the Mindoro operation proved easy only for the landing force, two reinforced army infantry regiments of 12,000 soldiers backed by 16,000 army engineers and service troops. Well within range of Japanese aircraft in the northern Philippines, the invasion force endured its first air attacks on 13 December. A *kamikaze* smashed the bridge of the flagship-cruiser *Nashville,* killing 133 officers and men (including several high-ranking army and navy officers) and wounding over 200 more. Damage to an escorting destroyer made it inoperable. Despite the best efforts of army and navy fighters, Japanese aircraft still penetrated the anti-aircraft screen. Although the Japanese may have lost as many as 500 aircraft, they sank three LSTs and five Liberty ships off Mindoro. Still, the engineers somehow managed to produce an air field on 24 December, with others to follow. The fact that army aviators and navy PT boats could drive off an attack by 2 cruisers and 6 destroyers represented a new low for Japanese warships.

As MacArthur waited for the completion of the Mindoro operation and the deployment of 7 fighter and bomber groups to their new bases, he continued his impatient planning for the liberation of Luzon. He made clear he wanted to declare Manila liberated on his sixty-fifth birthday, 26 January 1945, and free as many POWs and civilian internees as he could find. In addition to decrying the navy's limited ardor, he wondered if he should not replace Krueger, whose command of the Sixth Army he regarded as dilatory. His own household was in some disarray, since MacArthur and his abrasive chief of staff, Richard K. Sutherland, had argued heatedly over the status of Sutherland's mistress, an army secretary he had secretly brought to Leyte against orders. The lady in question rapidly departed, along with Sutherland's power. Unfortunately, Sutherland's not-unwelcome fall did not redound to the advantage of the long-suffering professional officers around MacArthur but only strengthened the power of his two top courtiers, General Charles Willoughby and General Courtney Whitney.

This internal tempest would have been of no military importance except that Willoughby and Whitney went on to wield inordinate influence in shaping MacArthur's vision of the coming campaign. Like good court jesters, they fed their king's humor. Rational operational planning received secondary attention. They also continued the bad habit they had exhibited in the Southwest Pacific, which was to underestimate Japanese opposition and confuse press releases with truth. As planning for Luzon developed, MacArthur's staff assumed that Yamashita's Luzon army had shrunk to 158,000 soldiers and sailors because of the reinforcements sent to Leyte, although they adjusted this figure upward to 195,000 in January 1945. Using the same sources, plus a broader assessment of agent reports from

Luzon, Krueger's staff started with a baseline force of 234,500 and raised the number to 287,000. Yamashita's actual strength in January 1945 was 267,000, much closer to the latter estimate.

General Yamashita deployed his forces in order to prolong the battle for Luzon and inflict as many American casualties as possible. His conduct of the defense was one of the most brilliant of the Pacific War and one for which MacArthur eventually hanged the Japanese general. Yamashita knew better than to contest the landing, which he predicted would occur at Lingayen Gulf, exactly where the Japanese campaign had started in 1941. American firepower guaranteed that Sixth Army would land in force; in fact, Krueger planned to put 6 of his 10 divisions ashore as quickly as possible. Yamashita also believed correctly that MacArthur would drive down the central valley to Manila, exposing his flanks to damaging counterattacks. Yamashita, in fact, had an entire armored division (150 tanks) set aside for just such an operation. In addition to MacArthur's personal reasons for liberating Manila, which Yamashita understood, the Americans needed to recapture Manila harbor as well as Clark Field and other established air bases. Japanese engineers doubted that the soil of the Lingayen area would support expeditionary air fields. Yamashita assumed that the Americans would, nevertheless, achieve air superiority, since he had little faith that the *kamikazes* would do more than slow supply operations over the Lingayen beaches.

With these considerations in mind, Yamashita divided his forces into four operational groups, three of them army, the fourth under the control of Rear Admiral Iwabushi Sanji. The weight of the Japanese defense lay in Luzon's eastern mountains. The Shobu Group of 150,000 men would start in defensive positions in the Caraballo Mountains and look for opportunities to assault Sixth Army's left flank at Lingayen Gulf; it could then fight delaying actions back to the north in Luzon's rugged mountains. The Shimbu Group of 80,000 men would establish its operational base in the Sierra Madre mountains east of Manila and deploy detachments to the south of Laguna de Bay to block the southern approaches to Manila. The third army force, the Kembu Group, would set up a base area in the rugged western Zambales Mountains, to prevent the easy recapture of Clark Field and stop any force that landed on Bataan from taking Manila from the west. The fourth operational group, largely Japanese naval base forces and extemporized units drawn from surviving ships crews, would hold Manila long enough to destroy the port facilities and any supplies the Japanese Army could not transport into the mountains.

Yamashita had no intention of making Manila an "open city," thus free-

97. On D-Day, 6 June 1944, U.S. troops wade ashore from their landing craft at Omaha Beach. Paratrooper landings inland considerably eased the combat situation confronting the troops on this beach.

98. An M-1 rifle with a helmet above marks the initial burial place for an American GI— the price of Operation Overlord.

99. British soldiers of No. 4 Commando, supported by amphibious tanks, engage in heavy fighting on D-Day, as they drive inland to link up with the British 6th Airborne Division.

100. Canadian troops, covered by a Sherman tank, fight their way south toward Falaise in early August 1944. The failure to close the Falaise-Argentan Gap allowed a significant number of German soldiers to escape the encirclement.

101. American soldiers examine the wreckage of the German panzers' counterattack at Mortain. In the foreground sits a damaged German half track surrounded by panzer grenadiers killed by American artillery fire.

102. U.S. paratroopers from the 101st Airborne Division disarm captured German paratroopers near Eindhoven at the start of Operation Market Garden. Begun with great optimism, this operation led to the greatest defeat suffered by the Allies in the last year of the war.

103. Ike, in a moment of repose, Belgium, November 1944. Behind the grin lay an understanding of the political and strategic framework that largely escaped the grasp of his American and British subordinates.

104. A young member of the Waffen SS pauses to look back at the camera, while he and his comrades loot a supply convoy during the Battle of the Bulge. Around his neck loops additional ammunition for his squad's machine gun.

105. Two dead American soldiers, stripped of all their equipment by their killers (one even of his shoes), lie in the snow of the Ardennes.

106. A sign provided by that most hated branch of all military organizations, the military police, adds a bizarre touch to Bastogne's main square after the Battle of the Bulge had finally ended.

107. Field Marshal Walter Model talks with one of his young soldiers in late winter 1944. Unlike most of his colleagues, Model believed that he should not survive the war with honor after sending so many soldiers to their deaths. He committed suicide as the Ruhr pocket collapsed in April 1945.

108. The big three at Yalta pose for a photograph. The effects of ill health on Roosevelt are apparent. Field Marshal Brooke stands to the far left. Admiral King is directly behind Churchill; Admiral Leahy and General Marshall are behind Roosevelt.

109. Allied commanders in the West pose for the cameras in late March 1945. Brooke, Eisenhower, and Montgomery stand on the left. Bradley stands on the far right, trying to look like Patton.

110. American soldiers take cover in the railroad tunnel leading up to the Remagen bridge, while German artillery falls. The American success at Remagen underlined the fact that the Wehrmacht, though still a tenacious opponent, no longer possessed the capacity to respond to Allied mobility.

111. Spearhead units of the 6th Armored Division advance through a German village in April 1945. One dead American soldier lies in the foreground. A bed sheet, indicating surrender, hangs from a farmhouse window.

112. Hitler once claimed that future generations of Germans would not be able to recognize their country. An American soldier looks over the wreckage of Nuremberg.

113. Starved victims of the Nazi concentration camp at Ebensee, Austria, gaze at their American Army liberators.

114. Jews who labored at the SS camp at Neunburg lie dead after being executed in the forest.

115. African-American Marines of the 7th Ammunition Company, 1st Marine Division, move forward from the beach at Peleliu, the Palau Islands, Western Pacific, in September 1944. By fighting to the death from deep caves and manmade fortifications, the Japanese defenders halted a marine division for the first time in the war.

116. Soldiers unload two Landing Ships Tank (LSTs) at Leyte, in the first phase of the American reconquest of the Philippines, October 1944. Poor weather, Japanese air and naval attacks, and a stubborn ground defense upset MacArthur's ambitious timetable for his triumphal "return."

117. Task Group 38.3 of the U.S. Third Fleet returns to Ulithi, the Palaus, after air strikes against the Japanese airfields on Luzon, the Philippines. Two carriers are followed by three fast battleships and four cruisers, especially armed for anti-aircraft defense.

118. MacArthur greets Filipino guerrillas in Banambang, Luzon, after the American landing at Lingayen Gulf in January 1945. Filipino guerrilla forces played a significant role in the liberation of the islands.

119. A Filipino refugee family flees downtown Manila, as the battle between the Americans and Japanese destroys the central city and kills 100,000 Filipinos.

120. Army and navy beach parties unload 50-gallon drums of gasoline at Lingayen Gulf to fuel the U.S. Sixth Army's drive on Manila. Logistical support ensured the liberation of Luzon, but the skillful Japanese defensive campaign designed by General Yamashita Tomoyuki continually frustrated MacArthur's army.

121. A patrol from the 2/11th Infantry Battalion, Australian Imperial Force, crosses the flooded Danmap River in New Guinea in January 1945. The Australians continued to press back isolated Japanese forces on New Guinea and New Britain islands until the war's end, while MacArthur's two American armies drove westward to the Philippines.

122. British soldiers of Lieutenant General William Slim's Fourteenth Army cross the Irrawaddy River in Burma in March 1945, on a makeshift raft powered by outboard motors. By the war's end the Fourteenth Army had retaken all of Burma and virtually wiped out the Japanese Burma Area Army.

123. Marines of the 5th Marine Division move forward on terraced volcanic beaches of Iwo Jima in February 1945. The Japanese cave-and-bunker defensive system took a deadly toll of marines in the seven-week-long battle.

124. Marine stretcher-bearers evacuate wounded comrades on Iwo Jima. More than 25,000 American servicemen fell in the battle (about 6,000 dead), but the air campaign against Japan gained an important base, and 24,000 airmen eventually found a safe haven from an ocean crash.

125. Navy landing craft unload gasoline and supplies for the U.S. Tenth Army's slow campaign to take Okinawa, April-July 1945. Attacks by kamikaze aircraft and several types of suicidal naval forces placed the American fleet in constant danger and inflicted crippling casualties.

126. The carrier U.S.S. *Bunker Hill* (CV-17) sends columns of smoke from the fires on its hanger deck started by a kamikaze aircraft crash on 10 May 1945. More than 400 crew members died, but the survivors kept the carrier afloat. Kamikaze aircraft inflicted the greatest damage on the U.S. Navy in World War II.

127. The distinctive mushroom cloud of a nuclear explosion rises from Nagasaki, Japan, on 9 August 1945. The impact of two atomic bombings and Russian intervention persuaded the Japanese leadership to accept surrender terms on 14 August.

128. Although the principal Japanese capitulation occurred on the battleship *Missouri* in Tokyo Bay on 2 September 1945, Japanese garrisons all over Asia and the Pacific awaited Allied expeditionary forces before surrendering. Aboard the HMAS *Moresby*, Colonel Kaida Tatsuichi of the Imperial Japanese Army turns over Timor, Netherlands and Portuguese East Indies to the Australians. With the surrender, the Allies disarmed and repatriated more than five million overseas Japanese.

ing it from combat, but he also did not intend to turn it (as some of his sub-ordinates suggested) into a second Stalingrad. Iwabushi's operation would render the city useless for military purposes and then he would join the Shimbu Group. At that point, the three groups would use the mountains to hold MacArthur in the central valley, trapped among the Philippine popu-lation whose needs would slow the Americans.

Given their recent experiences at Leyte and Mindoro, Kinkaid and his admirals focused on putting Krueger's Sixth Army ashore with acceptable losses. They did so on 9 January 1945 under harrowing circumstances. Pressed by MacArthur and Nimitz, Halsey's carrier battle groups of TF 38 returned to the war on 10 December for more raids on Japanese air bases, but on 19 December the task forces ran into a typhoon whose course Halsey had misjudged. Task Force 38 lost 3 destroyers and 18 other war-ships damaged. After another period of reorganization, it sortied again from Ulithi to support the Luzon landings. Striking air fields on Luzon as well as Formosa, TF 38 did its best to reduce Japanese air power. Halsey's airmen claimed more than 150 kills, mostly on the ground, but lost 86 air-craft in the process, more than half through accidents.

The suppression effort had its holes, since the *kamikazes* still attacked Seventh Fleet in early January. Successive attacks on 4, 7, and 11 January sank 5 ships (one an escort carrier) and damaged 16 more. One *kamikaze* almost struck MacArthur's flagship cruiser *Boise*, and another killed a group of senior officers on the bridge of battleship *New Mexico*. The Japanese sup-plemented the *kamikazes* with a new weapon, suicide speedboats, which struck the amphibious task force on 8–9 January and sank or damaged 9 landing ships and craft. Nevertheless, after a massive naval bombardment that killed primarily Filipinos, Sixth Army landed with 4 divisions abreast on 9 January and established a permanent lodgment by day's end. The American armed forces had returned to Luzon—but at what cost in time and lives? On 29 and 31 January, two divisions of Lieutenant General Rob-ert Eichelberger's Eighth Army landed at Bataan and south of Manila Bay, both as a diversion and as an alternative force to take Manila should Sixth Army move too slowly.

For most of January 1945, MacArthur fought to liberate Manila, while Krueger and Eichelberger fought to avoid Yamashita's "fire sack" around the central Luzon plain. MacArthur's intelligence experts gave him a good understanding of Yamashita's plans, but MacArthur remained obsessed with Manila. Three American divisions held the eastern edge of the plain and fought the stubborn defenses and occasional counterattacks of Shobu Group; three more divisions closed on the four air fields of the Clark Field complex from both the east and west but met heavy resistance from the Kembu Group. The two corps of the Sixth Army in the central plain seized Clark Field and beat back the Shobu Group toward Yamashita's headquarters at Baguio. However, MacArthur's birthday and his plans for a triumphal parade into Manila had come and gone. The commanding general could not conceal his unhappiness and flitted from battlefront to battlefront, bypassing Krueger and his corps commanders and issuing orders directly to division commanders. Convinced from Willoughby's accommodating analysis that Manila was ripe for the taking, MacArthur personally intervened on 30 January to send a three-division charge toward the capital city.

The battle for Manila raged almost a month and yielded one of the most costly victories for American arms in the Pacific War. The only reason it set off no furor on the Home Front was that the thousands who died were not American soldiers but Filipino civilians and Japanese sailors. Most of the Filipinos died from American shells and bullets. MacArthur took no responsibility for the slaughter because he had prohibited air strikes on the city. He told Kenney that air strikes would kill too many innocent civilians. "The world would hold its hands up in horror if we did anything like that."[2] There were plenty of civilians in Manila to worry about, since of Luzon's eight million inhabitants, almost a million had fled to the shelter of the city's strong walls and modern buildings.

Excited by the first daring rescues of small groups of POWs and internees in Luzon, MacArthur ordered a "flying column" (two reinforced regiments) of the fresh 1st Cavalry Division to drive for Manila directly from the north, flanked by a regiment of the 37th Infantry Division to the west; the rest of both divisions followed to take the city, while the 11th Airborne Division of the Eighth Army attacked from the south. Within five days from the start date on 30 January, elements of all three divisions had reached the city's outskirts. One 1st Cavalry Division column liberated 500 internees at Santo Tomas University on 3 February. Yet, much to MacArthur's surprise, the battle for the city had just begun.

Still in the process of transferring supplies and destroying bridges and other military sites, Iwabushi's defenders took to no-withdrawal positions—the admiral's preference, but not Yamashita's orders. Anticipating an American thrust from the south, the Japanese had turned the modern concrete and stone buildings south of the Pasig River, as well as the old Spanish town of Intramuros, into one vast fortified bunker. The sailors armed themselves with naval guns and rapid-fire anti-aircraft cannon and machine guns. To make matters worse, Japanese army demolition teams set off raging fires around the city that consumed many of the residential areas, rich in flammable buildings. Thousands of refugees fled toward the central city and directly into American artillery fire. Meanwhile, the Japanese raped, shot, and stabbed the refugees.

Still smarting from MacArthur's criticism of his caution and yet anxious to minimize casualties among his soldiers, Krueger took Manila his way, and MacArthur never intervened. The 11th Airborne Division fought north toward the modern city while the 37th Infantry Division and 1st Cavalry Division advanced methodically from the north and east across the Pasig River and into the northern industrial areas and the walled Intramuros. In the ten-day battle, American artillery fired almost 10,000 shells into the central city, while tanks, tank destroyers, and anti-tank guns provided close, direct fire for the infantry. The sites of the major battles suggest the nature of the urban fighting, which replicated that of Stalingrad and Warsaw on a smaller scale; one by one the Americans captured the city stadium, the post office, the government buildings, the central police station, the city power plant, the University of the Philippines, the Manila Club, the Cathedral, and the Manila Hotel, where a dispirited MacArthur visited the wreckage of his former private suite, vandalized, burned, and littered with dead.

Cut off from a half-hearted relief attack by the Shimbu Group, Iwabushi's sailors perished in place. Probably 16,000 Japanese died in the hecatomb; American losses in the street fighting numbered more than 1,000 dead and 5,600 wounded. Frustrated and maddened by their inescapable fate, one group of Japanese took 3,000 Filipino hostages with them into the thick-walled buildings of the Intramuros; there they slaughtered a thousand before releasing the survivors. Like the Poles, the Japanese took to the sewers, where they perished in a rain of gasoline and grenades. Filipino political leaders rallied relief work within the city, aided by American hospital units and service troops, but the depth of the tragedy overwhelmed everyone. Carlos Romulo, a renowned journalist on his way to becoming a distinguished political leader, shuddered at the murder and pillage of the inner city. He collected evidence that the Japanese had designed a plan to murder the *americanista* elite and militant Catholics, but he also knew that American artillery had taken its toll. "Wherever I went I felt like a ghost hunting its way in a vanished world."[3] Manila had died as a city, and within its ruins rested the bodies of as many as 100,000 Filipino civilians, or six times the number of dead combatants. MacArthur returned to the city on 27 February to reestablish the Commonwealth government under President Sergio Osmeña. Overcome by the devastation, MacArthur could not complete his prepared speech and ended the ceremonies with the Lord's Prayer.

Even as the battle for Manila raged, MacArthur diverted attention by sending the rest of the Sixth Army and part of the Eighth Army to fight the Japanese on three fronts. If that were not enough, MacArthur launched most of Eichelberger's remaining divisions into a rapid, complex series of amphibious operations to liberate the islands south of Leyte. What made the southern Philippines campaign notable was that the Joint Chiefs of Staff did not know it was under way until it was too late to stop it. Once again MacArthur showed that when a major campaign was not going well, a minor campaign full of excitement and heroics could be a useful distraction—in this case staged by some ardent army infantry regiments and marine fighter-bomber squadrons. Some 50,000 Filipino guerrillas, especially the colorful and ruthless Moros, surged from the hills to take revenge on the isolated Japanese garrisons of the Visayans, Mindanao, and the Jolo archipelago. Aided by Japanese prisoners who realized that any GI was a better risk than a Moro, the Americans and their allies killed an estimated 13,000 Japanese at a cost of less than a thousand American lives and a comparable number of Filipino guerrillas. At war's end, the Eighth Army was about to make physical contact with the Australian divisions that had conducted a similar campaign in Borneo. In both campaigns the Allies rescued European POWs, found the bodies of thousands of others who had been massacred, and saved countless Japanese soldiers and civilians from the wrath of the local people.

Thanks to Yamashita's skill, the Luzon campaign continued, to the embarrassment of the Sixth Army except at the tactical level. The shrinking American infantry divisions did their best, again aided by the Filipino guerrillas, to execute the unimaginative orders of their generals. Even after Manila's fall, MacArthur's obsession with the city forced Krueger to fight a series of high-profile, high-risk operations around Manila Bay—including the drop of an entire parachute regiment on Corregidor—to recapture American coastal fortifications. Without adequate reserves or infantry replacements and with inordinate casualties, the GIs drove the Japanese deep within the tunnels of the fortified islands, where they died under engineer assaults with demolitions and flame weapons. In several cases the explosions of stored munitions killed defenders and attackers alike. In almost every case, MacArthur's intelligence staff underestimated the size of the Japanese garrisons.

Outside of Manila Bay, the campaign in the Luzon countryside proceeded with less finesse and higher cost, since Yamashita's generals understood and followed their commander's concept of protracted resistance. The Kembu Group in the Zambales Mountains had the most difficult task. In addition to being the smallest army unit, it contained a high proportion of aviation personnel, service troops, and too few heavy weapons; after a good stand to block the roads from Bataan to Manila, the group fell back into the mountains, where it presented no major threat. The most immediate problem for the Americans was the Shimbu Group, a well-supplied force of regular army divisions. Shimbu soldiers could move munitions and supplies into the mountains just east of Manila far more easily than Yamashita could build his own caches in northern Luzon. They also held something the Americans wanted badly: the reservoirs, dams, and aqueducts that supplied water to Manila and the heavily populated lower central valley. General Yokoyama deceived the Americans (probably by mistake) by massing his defense forces around the Wawa dam, which the 6th Infantry Division assaulted to the point of ineffectiveness while losing its division commander to enemy fire in the front lines. A cavalry brigade had no more success with the Wawa dam and the Ipo dam and lake—unlike Wawa, an essential source of water to Manila. It required three more American divisions to put the Shimbu Group out of action and capture Ipo dam.

The battles to eliminate the Kembu and Shimbu Groups ensured that while the Americans could not ignore Yamashita's Shobu Group, skulking in the mountains east of the Lingayen beaches and supply lines to American divisions in the south, they had insufficient strength to attack Yamashita. The result was some of the most bitter and least productive fighting on Luzon. Krueger put the Caraballo Mountains "front" under the responsibility of Major General Innis P. Swift of I Corps, who had three divisions to secure the army's left flank in January 1945. Swift then saw his divisions diverted to Manila and the other operations to the south, which left him to face Yamashita with only the 43rd Infantry Division. Krueger, however, brought three more divisions to northern Luzon in late February; in addition, he could depend on a Filipino force of almost 60,000 to aid the I Corps. Commanded by Colonel Russell W. Volckmann, a survivor of 1942 and a legendary partisan commander, the Filipino guerrillas of northern Luzon also included the Communist Hukbalahaps. Many of the pro-American Filipino leaders of the postwar period (like Ramon Magsaysay) won their military honors in U.S. Army Forces in the Philippines–Northern Luzon.

Swift's corps, even with enthusiastic guerrilla support, had to fight its way north—and uphill—on a three-division front to capture the passes and road network that ended at Yamashita's headquarters at Baguio. Yamashita made the passage as difficult as possible, turning his tanks into pillboxes and using his limited infantry and artillery to force the Americans into an attritional advance, even if American artillery and armor eventually destroyed each Japanese strong point. Although Japanese fire did not inflict dramatic American casualties in any one battle, the daily skirmishing and the toll of disease and exhaustion reduced the I Corps to a slow and disheartened pace. Baguio did not fall until late April, and even then Yamashita withdrew with more than half his army.

Although reduced by the lack of food, munitions, and heavy weapons to a light infantry force, the Shobu Group remained cohesive and battle-worthy until the end of the war. In early September, Yamashita himself arranged the surrender of his 100,000-man army. His enemy since May 1945 had been primarily the Filipino guerrillas, since the I Corps could no longer mount an effective attack, having suffered about 10,000 casualties in two months. Yamashita refused to commit suicide, since he believed his own execution for war crimes might spare the lives of his subordinate officers and soldiers. Even in defeat, the Tiger of Malaya set a standard for generalship seldom matched by the American commanders he faced in the Philippines, since he focused only on ways to spend his soldiers' lives wisely.

The campaign for Luzon revealed the growing peril of fighting a war of attrition with the Japanese, however imbalanced the ratios of battle deaths might be. Starved for infantry replacements, the divisions of Sixth Army— and to a lesser degree Eighth Army—shrank close to ineffectiveness by the time Krueger halted the advance into northern Luzon. Battle casualties were tolerable, and the army's medical services set new records in saving the badly wounded and returning the wounded to duty, in part because of a new system of evacuating the badly wounded with light planes and the army's first helicopters.

The doctors, however, lost the battle against disease. The permanent loss to duty of army personnel from disease in the Philippines in 1945 (51 per 1,000) rivaled those of MacArthur's army in New Guinea in 1943, the worst record of any theater. As for hospitalizations and outpatient treatment combined, only the African–Middle East theater (at 917 per 1,000) had a worse record than MacArthur's theater (at 807 per 1,000) for the wartime period. From January to September 1945, army hospitals in the Philippines admitted 92,000 soldiers for a variety of diseases. At numbers far above army rates worldwide, MacArthur's soldiers and airmen became hospital or limited-duty patients. Even more troubling, U.S. forces could have curbed the four worst diseases with better troop discipline and sanitation; these offenders were venereal diseases, malaria, hepatitis, and skin infections. A soldier's responsibility for a self-inflicted wound was difficult to hide, but blame for a self-inflicted disease could be diffused. A soldier could argue that frontline conditions precluded using preventive measures that would have kept him well and in the line of fire.

MacArthur's expeditionary force found itself fighting in a media void after the liberation of Manila, as the campaigns to capture Iwo Jima and Okinawa captured the attention of the American press. MacArthur also escaped the scrutiny of the Joint Chiefs of Staff. Disarray at the highest levels in Washington ensured that MacArthur would not have to answer for his misjudgments in the Philippines. Roosevelt died on 12 April 1945. Harry S. Truman, his successor, remembered MacArthur as a prima donna from his well-publicized service in France in 1918—a campaign in which Truman had also served respectably as a captain of artillery. Unlike Roosevelt, Truman was "an army man," a peacetime reserve colonel and great admirer of George C. Marshall, his most trusted military adviser. Although Marshall was no admirer of MacArthur, whom he regarded as a political opportunist and overrated commander, he still could see no profit to the army or the nation in criticizing the Luzon campaign. There was still a war to be won.

The Air and Sea War Against Japan

In 1944 the war closed in on the people of the Home Islands like the clouds of Mount Fujiyama and enshrouded them the following year. The first systematic blows against public morale and the Japanese economy came from U.S. submarines early in 1944. Their raiding of merchant ships reached catastrophic proportions in 1945. Even with an increase in escorts and a single-minded focus on moving oil to the Home Islands, Japanese industry and the armed forces found it increasingly difficult to produce war materiel and then train men to use it. The attack on the Japanese merchant marine now included strikes by American carrier aircraft along the narrow passages of the Inland Sea, while submarines and aircraft mined the same waters. In autumn 1944, B-29s began to appear over Japan, but they were too few in number and their bombardments too imprecise to be more than a nuisance. Yet, despite the efforts of Japanese interceptors and anti-aircraft fire, the great silver machines came back again and again.

The American submarines started the economic strangulation of the Home Islands. They reduced the Japanese merchant marine from 2.5 million tons at the start of 1945 to half that tonnage at war's end. American submariners also conducted a crueler sea war than they intended, for they sank ships they wished they had not. When the Japanese began to shift able-bodied Allied prisoners, mostly Americans and Australians, to slave labor assignments in the Home Islands in late 1944, the submarines sank four transports bearing POWs (which had not been identified as such by the Japanese) and killed more than 4,000, saving fewer than 300. Before the war's end, submarines and planes had killed 11,000 POWs of the 50,000 shipped to the Home Islands. Only the deaths of POWs on the Burma-Thailand railroad were more numerous. At least one-third of all POWs who died in Japanese custody died as a result of friendly fire, including POWs who perished in Tokyo, Hiroshima, and Nagasaki.

In one incident, an American skipper sank the *Awa Maru*, a large transport granted free passage by the U.S. State Department because it was supposed to be evacuating diplomatic personnel from Southeast Asia as well as distributing Red Cross supplies to POWs and internees. In truth, the *Awa Maru* had also picked up scarce contraband supplies and skilled naval personnel. Holed by four torpedoes, the *Awa Maru* carried almost all its 2,000 crew and passengers to the bottom, thus setting off a legal and political controversy that continued for 30 years after the initial event on 1 April 1945, the very day the Americans invaded Okinawa. Despite such incidents of miscalculation and wasted lives, Vice Admiral Charles Lockwood and his submariners enjoyed a place of honor in September 1945 when the Japanese surrendered in Tokyo Bay, an honor they richly deserved.

As the Allies' economic objectives widened from maritime commerce, Japan's industrial infrastructure took center stage as a target for aerial attacks. The B-29 attacks from China by summer 1944 had produced few results that justified further investment in Operation Matterhorn. Almost every imaginable catastrophe that could be linked to crew ineptness, technological failures, and operational factors had plagued the XX Bomber Command. As the Japanese offensive of 1944 forced the bombers deeper into China, the unfriendly skies through which the bombers must fly to reach the Home Islands widened. Except for the heroism of the aircrews, Arnold could find nothing about Matterhorn to like. He relieved the commander of XX Bomber Command, a personal favorite, and replaced him with Major General Curtis E. LeMay, no one's favorite but a bomber general who had proved his courage and expertise by leading deep strikes into Germany in 1943. A poor boy from Columbus, Ohio, LeMay entered the prewar Army Air Corps through the ROTC program of The Ohio State University. He had no patience with either personal relationships or poor bombing, but even he found the conditions confronting XX Bomber Command daunting. In 1944 Arnold wanted the strategic bombing of Japan fixed quickly, so he heeded LeMay's recommendation that the weight of the air war shift to XXI Bomber Command, just starting operations in the Marianas.

Mounting a strategic bombardment campaign against the Home Islands from the Pacific, as opposed to China, brought its own special set of problems that Arnold and his first Marianas commander, Major General Heywood Hansell, a courageous and intelligent bombardment pioneer, did not understand. With one hurriedly prepared B-29 wing, Hansell sent his first raid against Japan in November 1944. A group of 110 bombers left Saipan to destroy an aircraft factory on Honshu; less than a quarter of the bombers reached the primary target, and their bombs did little damage. The move to the Marianas simply transferred the B-29's ongoing problems to a new location, while adding a few extra twists. The Japanese air defense system, weak on radar, did not yet pose a major obstacle, so losses to active defense were manageable. What made the B-29 missions a nightmare was range and weather.

First, the industrial cities of Kyushu and Honshu lay at the limit of the B-29's range of 1,600 miles, so to reach these targets an aircraft needed almost 9,000 gallons of gasoline; consequently it could carry only two to three tons of high-explosive bombs out of a ten-ton maximum load. Even with so few bombs, the fuel load made take-off accidents frequent and still allowed the pilot only a 30-minute margin of error during flights that lasted 15 hours. Once the Home Islands were reached, the airmen found cloud cover over the targets almost 70 percent of the time. Moreover, Hansell, following his European experience, wanted the missions flown at high altitudes and against specific industrial targets, a concept that enlarged pilot and navigator errors and exposed the B-29s to perilous weather conditions.

The winds did the Americans no favors. At 25,000 feet, a northwest headwind of between 150 and 200 miles an hour meant that the B-29s had to struggle ahead, using up their precious fuel, and bomb at almost stall speeds through layers of winds of varying directions and intensity. The only alternative initially conceived was to fly west of the Home Islands, then turn eastward for the bomb run, riding a strong tailwind. This technique meant B-29s would roar over their targets at ground speeds of almost 550 mph, pushed by the Arctic jet stream. Such speeds, slow or fast, made precision bombing laughable. Then, short of fuel, the bombers had to fly back to the Marianas over miles of open ocean still unpatrolled by ships other than submarines. In the opening months of the bombing campaign, more aircrewmen perished at sea after ditchings than fell to Japanese air defenses. In addition, Japanese air forces remained in range of the Marianas, and strikes on American bases there destroyed or damaged 54 aircraft in December 1944 and January 1945.

Facing a second B-29 embarrassment from his decision to move operations to the Marianas, Arnold—a sick and bitter man—took the standard military option: change commanders. Sending Hansell off to a respectable new assignment and early retirement, Arnold again called for LeMay, who arrived at XXI Bomber Command in January 1945. Knowing LeMay's record, one squadron commander wrote that LeMay had arrived "and he will get us all killed."[4] Chomping his hallmark cigar, LeMay made it clear that he might kill all his aircrews, including himself, but they would put bombs on target. For three months he tried to make Hansell's approach work, through better training and planning, but not even LeMay could intimidate the jet stream. The bombs still fell everywhere but on the target, and airmen still fell in the Pacific. LeMay had, however, conducted some experiments in reducing the bombers' altitude and changing bomb loads to incendiaries. At lower altitudes, the B-29s could carry a heavier bomb load, as much as six tons. LeMay now decided that XXI Bomber Command would duplicate the RAF's bombing campaign on Germany. His bombers would fly most of their missions at night and attack their targets well under the jet stream at 8,000–10,000 feet. Night attack would make Japanese anti-aircraft fire and interceptors less effective than they might be during daylight. The organization of Japanese industry supported the area bombing concept. Unlike German industry, which ringed major cities, Japanese factories had grown up willy-nilly and well-dispersed by accident, fed by equally dispersed secondary suppliers. To destroy most of Japanese industry required a campaign that destroyed complete cities. By 1945, the lives of Japanese civilians played no role in anyone's planning.

In fact, Arnold and many of his senior staff officers, as well as LeMay's subordinate commanders, believed that only a dramatic change in operations against Japan would save strategic bombing and at the same time promote the major item on their postwar agenda, which was establishing an independent air force. Even if their loyalty to the air force and their racism toward the Japanese made these changes easier, their major concern remained the destruction of Japan's war industry. But they also wanted to make a statement about Japan's unhappy future, and so they selected Tokyo as the first target of a massive fire raid. In one of the most carefully orchestrated bombing operations of the war, XXI Bomber Command put over 300 B-29s into the air from the Marianas on 9 March 1945. In the early morning darkness, 1,665 tons of incendiaries fell on Tokyo from B-29s flying at between 5,000 and 10,000 feet and criss-crossing the city on different flight paths. When the fires finally burned out days later, more than 80,000 Japanese had died, and 250,000 buildings lay in ruin. Twenty-two major industrial targets disappeared in the holocaust.

The raid was not bloodless for the bomber force: 14 B-29s fell in the operation, 12 from enemy fire or operational failures, but no one knew for certain. The Japanese night-fighter and flak effort had been real enough, but of limited effectiveness. The raid set the pattern for future B-29 operations over the Home Islands.

From March until August 1945, LeMay's B-29s covered Japan with a "blanket of fire." Twentieth Air Force, the independent command for all B-29 operations in Asia, made Japan's 60–70 industrial cities and associated military installations the target set. The fire raids continued throughout March, destroying Nagoya, Osaka, and Kobe. At the end of March, LeMay's air forces in the Marianas had run out of incendiaries, but in April the B-29s had put their fire raids into a general operational context that now included daylight raids with mixed bomb loads. Through this phase of the campaign, XXI Bomber Command enjoyed a surge of new advantages: P-51 escort fighters based in the Bonins, a large and active sea-air rescue organization, more and better bombs and crews, and much-improved radar navigation and target identification.

The raids were not without cost. The Japanese mounted a determined night-fighter program, based primarily on the twin-engine Nakajima Ki-45 Dragon Killer, which, armed with 20mm upward-firing cannon, duplicated the Luftwaffe's deadly Messerschmidt 110G-H. The Americans countered with a two-engine night-fighter of their own, the P-60 Black Widow. Bombing operations became more sophisticated and devastating with every incremental improvement in weather forecasting, terminal guidance, and weapons effects. Bombers still fell, and the campaign eventually cost the army almost 500 bombers, lost to all causes, and nearly 3,000 lives.

Conclusion

Twentieth Air Force's strategic bombardment campaign had a staggering impact on the fabric of Japanese urban society. The most careful count, done by the Japanese themselves, produced fewer losses than the Americans estimated, but either number is horrific: 240,000 to 300,000 dead (mostly civilians), approximately 2.5 million homes destroyed, and more than 8 million refugees. Of 71 Japanese cities, only 5 escaped substantial damage—and two of these were Hiroshima and Nagasaki. About half of the bomb tonnage dropped on Japan (about 170,000 tons, but still only one-

ninth of the tonnage dropped on Germany) fell on specific industrial targets. In Tokyo, Osaka, and Nagoya alone, the areas leveled by fire-bombing
(almost 100 square miles) exceeded the urban areas destroyed in all German cities by the army air forces and RAF combined (an estimated 79
square miles). Without argument, the bombing crushed the Japanese aviation industry and contributed to the decline of power generation and
industrial production within Japan. In secondary missions, the B-29s conducted a successful mining program that turned the Inland Sea into dangerous waters. The fire-bombing brought the war home to the Home Islands in ways no other Allied operation could have, but it alone did not
persuade the Japanese political elite to give up the war.

18

THE END OF THE
ASIA-PACIFIC WAR

1945

Having lost his argument with General MacArthur over the good of liberating the Philippines, Admiral King remained convinced that isolating Japan required the elimination of the air and naval stronghold of Formosa and the subsequent movement of U.S. forces into maritime enclaves in north China. For King and the planners of every U.S. service, the ultimate objective was the Home Islands. By late 1944, neither commerce raiding nor bombing had produced any hint of surrender. King believed that the American armed forces would have to besiege Japan without substantial assistance from the British and Russians. Indeed, King sought no allies. He believed the capture of Formosa should be the first real attack on the inner defenses of the Home Islands, followed by additional operations to secure the western approaches of Shantung, China, and Korea. King also knew that committees of the JCS had turned their attention from grand strategy to postwar planning and the conditions for Russian entry into the war with Japan. He wanted strategic decision and action, not unpredictable debate.

In October 1944, King met representatives of the Central Pacific commands. Admiral Nimitz, as commander of the Pacific Ocean Areas Theater, was there, along with his naval staff and his army and air forces commanders. MacArthur did not attend, for King had not invited him. This meeting was to review plans only with Nimitz and his subordinates, and King intended to sell his Formosa plan to them. Instead, he found that the ever-cautious Nimitz, with the unanimous support of his commanders from the other services, questioned whether he could put together a ground force adequate to take Formosa. He could expect no help from MacArthur's two field armies, dedicated as they were to the liberation of the Philippines.

Nimitz and his generals also knew that MacArthur had already floated a proposal that would give him command of all army forces, ground and air,

509

committed to the war with Japan—a proposal anathema to Lieutenant General Simon Bolivar Buckner, Jr., commander of the new U.S. Tenth Army, and every airman not already under MacArthur's thumb. Nimitz spoke for all when he suggested that Iwo Jima in the Volcano Islands and Okinawa in the Ryukyus were the places to start the siege, since their seizure would deny the Japanese important air bases and open their use to American air and naval forces. The Pacific Ocean Areas flag officers believed that the forces at hand, especially their six marine and six infantry divisions, could do the job. Recovering the Third Fleet from Halsey, Spruance—trusted by all except the carrier admirals—would command the joint task forces built from the Fifth Fleet in both operations.

Although he did not surrender the idea that the capture of Formosa would follow Iwo Jima and Okinawa, King returned to Washington for consultation with the Joint Chiefs, who rapidly endorsed Nimitz's plan and set the dates for Iwo Jima (19 February 1945) and Okinawa (1 April 1945). MacArthur even approved the plan, probably to sink the Formosa option and to gain cooperation from the Joint Chiefs for the Leyte campaign, which would start only two weeks after JCS approval of the Nimitz plan on 3 October 1944.

Iwo Jima and Okinawa

None of the senior commanders thought Iwo Jima or Okinawa would be easy, but at least they would have weeks to bombard both islands while they waited for Nimitz and Spruance to reorganize their naval task forces after the Philippines landings. Carrier aircraft on wide-ranging raids and B-24s based in the Marianas would ensure air superiority. Arnold reassured the admirals and marine generals that Iwo Jima would be worth the price of an estimated 10,000 marine casualties, since its seizure would eliminate a Japanese fighter base and radar station. In American hands, Iwo Jima would provide an emergency landing site for B-29s, an air field for escort fighters, and a base for air-sea rescue operations. Okinawa's value as an air base and anchorage close to the Home Islands and the East China Sea needed no explanation or justification.

The invasion of the Philippines only accelerated plans in Imperial General Headquarters, now dominated by senior army officers, to transfer the army's best units and commanders from Japan and China to the outworks of Fortress Japan. To Iwo Jima, only 625 miles north of the Marianas, the army sent Lieutenant General Kuribayashi Tadamichi from a command in Manchuria to organize the island's defense; Kuribayashi's force of 21,000 officers and men consisted of one crack infantry regiment, a mediocre mixed brigade, a mediocre under-strength infantry division armed with ample artillery and mortars, and a good tank regiment. About 7,000 members of the defense force were sailors who brought gunnery skills as well as heavy weapons for base defense.

American submarines whittled away at the transports bearing fortification materials, but Kuribayashi, who knew Americans well from two tours in North America, pressed forward with his major construction plan to transform Iwo Jima into a massive system of caves, tunnels, bunkers, and covered trenches. In essence, he turned a volcanic island of ten square miles, seething with hot sulfur gases, into a Japanese Maginot Line that could not be flanked. His concept of defense left no room for interpretation: all Japanese defenders would hold their positions and fire their weapons until they died. Kuribayashi did not outlaw honorable suicide, but he forbade futile *banzai* attacks that merely wasted lives and ammunition.

The defense of Okinawa went to the Thirty-Second Army under Lieutenant General Ushijima Mitsuru, who assembled two infantry divisions from China and Manchuria, a brigade from Japan, and a tank and three separate artillery regiments. Again, the weight of the defense went to machine guns, mortars, and artillery. The Japanese Army provided aviation and service units, while the navy added more troops to the command. In addition, Ushijima absorbed the local Okinawan militia and many civilians into his army. His force soon numbered over 100,000, shielded by a native population of 450,000, of whom 150,000 eventually died. Like Kuribayashi, Ushijima adapted his defense concept to the terrain and enemy. He decided not to contest the landing, which he predicted would come over the broad Hagushi beaches at mid-island; he also rejected a major defense effort in the mountainous northern part of the island. Instead, his forces would defend the southern third of the island, site of two out of the island's four air fields as well as many sturdy buildings, including ancient castles. The steep, rocky ridges and draws were ideal for positional defense. He placed the first belt of defenses along the Uraseo-Mura escarpment, which ran from one side of the island to the other. The second line started at the west coast city of Naha, ran uphill to the magnificent Shuri castle, then followed another ridge line to Yonabaru on the east coast. All the hills, ravines, and pockets in this difficult terrain became centers of resistance, especially reverse slope defenses safe from American heavy weapons except close air support.

Ushijima's defense plan for Okinawa had a naval dimension that Kuribayashi's plan for Iwo Jima did not. Aircraft, submarines, and high-speed motorboats, all on suicide missions, would assault the American invasion fleet while the Thirty-Second Army fought to the death. In the weeks following the extemporaneous creation of the *kamikaze* flying corps during the Leyte campaign, Japanese aviation commanders had concluded that their young martyrs would do better if they simply plunged their aircraft into American warships rather than perish in inept attempts to drop bombs and torpedoes. Experienced pilots did not join these "Divine Wind" squadrons; instead, they flew interceptors over Japan or escorted the *kamikaze* raids, blasting holes in the American combat air patrols for their young charges.

The *kamikaze* pilots fell under the command of the Fifth Air Fleet's Vice Admiral Ugaki Matome, who organized them into the Thunder Gods Corps. His young army and navy pilots viewed their role as an unparalleled opportunity to give their lives for the Emperor, which 3,913 of them did. The Imperial Navy also assembled a small task force of suicide submarines (some just submersible torpedoes with riders) and motorboats, jammed with explosives, to attack American transports. The battleship *Yamato* and its escorts also prepared for a one-way attack on the American invasion fleet.

The planners of the Fifth Fleet's amphibious force and the V Amphibious Corps, composed of three marine divisions and reinforcing marine and army corps troops, knew that Iwo Jima would be no day at the beach. Nevertheless, even Major General Harry S. Schmidt, corps commander and a veteran of two earlier landings, had no idea how bad Iwo would actually be. Only Holland M. Smith, now reduced to spectator status, argued that the island would require weeks, not days, of naval bombardment, since the bombings that started in October 1944 had only driven the Japanese underground and unmasked the extent of their fortifications. The naval gunfire plan—four days of both pinpoint and area fire from battleships' main batteries down to special rocket-armed landing craft—would have leveled any atoll or cleared the beaches of another Saipan and Guam. Unfortunately, Iwo Jima was neither. It was one huge, fortified volcanic rock. Throughout the four days of naval shelling, the Japanese sat tight and held their fire.

The actual invasion occurred on 19 February 1945, with four regiments of the 4th and 5th Marine Divisions landing abreast. As eight assault battalions—roughly 10,000 marines—struggled up the terraces of black volcanic gravel for fifteen anxious minutes, they did not draw fire. Then a rain of death came to Iwo Jima. Crossing the terraces under relentless explosions, a veteran sergeant felt his mind shrivel at the sights about him: "Somewhere deep inside—inside his brain somewhere, wherever that voice is that talks when one is alone and in deep trouble—in that inner room of the mind, from that dark, mysterious place, the voice said to him: *Carnage.*"[1]

Kuribayashi turned Iwo Jima into a giant fire sack in which three marine divisions were trapped and almost destroyed, especially their infantry regiments. His plan spared no one; the rough landing sites, where the terraces met the raging surf, received a deluge of shells as well. Artillery, tanks, service units, and headquarters felt the weight of the bombardment for days, and landing craft turned to blasted wreckage as they brought ammunition and supplies to the beach and evacuated casualties. By the time survivors reached hospital ships, they often had more wounds than they took at the front; corpsmen and stretcher-bearers (bandsmen and service troops) fell alongside the frontline combatants. No one escaped. Of 24 infantry battalion commanders who began the battle in the three divisions, only 7 were still in command at the end of the campaign; the 17 others had died or been evacuated with wounds.

When a marine patrol raised an American flag atop Mount Suribachi on 23 February, the Battle of Iwo Jima had already achieved photographic immortality and looked over. But three more long weeks of flame-throwers, dynamite in satchel charges, grenades, millions of shells and bullets, and the lives of hundreds of good men would be expended before the last Japanese died. Nimitz did not exaggerate when he said that on Iwo, "uncommon valor was a common virtue."[2] After the battle, 27 marines and sailors received the Medal of Honor, a wartime record. Thirteen medals were posthumous.

As Kuribayashi predicted, he and his defenders died before the senior American admiral declared the island secure on 16 March 1945. Organized Japanese resistance went on for ten more days. Kuribayashi had made an impressive point: for the first time in the Pacific War, a Japanese garrison had inflicted more casualties on a landing force than it had suffered (21,000 Japanese casualties, versus almost 30,000 American casualties from all services). More than 6,000 Americans died on Iwo Jima, five times the number of deaths on either Guadalcanal or Tarawa.

The compensating statistic from the American perspective was that more than 25,000 army and naval airmen would find a safe haven on Iwo for their crippled aircraft before the war's end. As part of the bombing campaign against Japan, Iwo proved every bit as valuable as Arnold predicted. But as an omen for the future siege of Japan, Iwo Jima dampened any incipient American "victory disease" contracted during the conquest of the Marianas.

If Iwo Jima was a trial for the marines, Okinawa became an ordeal for almost everyone who came to the Ryukyus to celebrate April Fool's Day 1945. As Ushijima planned, his protracted defense, lasting from 1 April to 22 June 1945, with two more weeks of "unofficial" combat, proved harrowing for the Fifth Fleet as well as the Tenth Army. In the Fifth Fleet alone, almost 5,000 died and more than 7,000 were wounded—more casualties than the U.S. Navy had suffered during the entire Pacific War over the preceding two years. The numbers for the Tenth Army were even more horrendous. To kill more than 110,000 Japanese soldiers and Okinawan auxiliaries, the Tenth Army lost 7,613 dead and missing and almost 32,000 wounded, while 26,000 men fell to accidents and disease. What made the carnage at Okinawa so different from Iwo Jima, and so much worse, is that Simon Bolivar Buckner's flawed generalship contributed to the slaughter.

Operation Iceberg began with a coolness befitting its name, as assault regiments of two marine and two infantry divisions stormed the Hagushi beaches and walked inland, their formations untouched by fire. The 1st and 6th Marine Divisions secured central Okinawa and turned left to ensure that no surprises awaited to the north. After a nasty fight with a Japanese regiment on the Motobu peninsula, the III Amphibious Corps under Major General Roy S. Geiger accomplished its mission. The XXIV Corps, under Major General John R. Hodge, turned south with the 7th and 96th Infantry Divisions abreast and in four days ran into Ushijima's first belt of defenses.

The Japanese defense scheme was chillingly professional and efficient. Within a week, the Japanese had stopped two very good army divisions in their tracks. Assisted by drenching monsoon rains, the Japanese turned every hill, every ridge into a muddy deathtrap. Japanese infantry well-armed with machine guns and light mortars defended the forward slopes, but with only enough strength to force the Americans to disperse and go to ground; after sharp firefights, the Americans would finally conquer the crest, only to be smashed with artillery and fire from the reverse-slope positions. Reeling from the ambushes, the Americans would then fall back onto the forward slopes, smashed by mortar fire and showers of grenades.

After nine days of such chastening battles, Buckner admitted that XXIV Corps needed help and sent for the 1st and 6th Marine Divisions. He also brought in the 27th and 77th Infantry Divisions to strengthen XXIV Corps. The reinforcements made little change in the situation until Ushijima's chief of staff, intoxicated with the defensive success, ordered his best Japanese infantry to counterattack on 4 May. American artillery fire and solid infantry defense ruined the last great *banzai* charge of the Pacific campaign and cleared the first Japanese defense position, which fell on 5 May.

After such an initiation into Japanese defensive warfare, Buckner might have sought an alternative to his World War I offensive against the Naha-Shuri-Yonabaru Line. His admirals as well as marine and army generals associated with the campaign gave him intelligent advice, the essence of which was that Buckner should use the reserve 2nd Marine Division to make a second landing on Okinawa's eastern coast, thus flanking the Japanese defenses. The landing site had been explored and designated an alternate landing site for the 1 April assault. Buckner, however, concluded that logistical support was problematic and the landing too risky.

Sadly for his troops, Buckner did not have the experience to make such a critical decision. He had graduated from West Point in 1908 and advanced to command a field army on the basis of retaking the Aleutians, his first combat. Compared with his subordinates, Buckner was hardly fit to command a corps, let alone a field army. Yet he held the lives of over 100,000 soldiers and marines in his hand. He rejected every suggestion that he revise the concept of the campaign, ignoring the advice of the four marine generals who had captured Guadalcanal, Cape Britain, Guam, and Peleliu. Only Spruance and Nimitz had the authority to order Buckner to change his plan, and once again the admirals shrank from conflict with the army. On 28 June, as the bloody campaign neared its close, Buckner himself died from a shellburst while watching the final assaults on Okinawa's southern tip. But by then it was too late to commit the 2nd Marine Division to a landing.

Tenth Army's deathly slow advance into southern Okinawa forced substantial portions of the Fifth Fleet to remain in Ryukyuian waters to ensure a steady flow of supplies and troops into the battle. In addition, Fifth Fleet had to supply close air support until marine and army squadrons became operational on Okinawa. The threat of a conventional attack by the remnants of the Japanese Navy kept the fleet alert, and air attack remained a constant threat. On 6 April, the *Yamato* group sortied from Japan, covered by 355 *kamikazes* and escorts. The *kamikazes* struck first; they sank 7 ships and damaged another 17, seven so seriously that they had to leave the battle. The next day American naval aircraft sank the *Yamato* and 5 of its escort vessels at a cost of 10 aircraft and 12 aircrew. The naval battle for Okinawa had been joined, and it raged on with appalling results.

Between 6 April and 22 June, Admiral Ugaki sent out 10 large *kamikaze* raids that cost his *kamikaze* and escort force 1,500 lives and aircraft. Yet the toll he exacted from the Fifth Fleet beggared the losses in the Solomons. The U.S. Navy lost 64 ships sunk or so badly damaged they never returned to the war; another 60 took enough damage to force extensive repairs.

Even before landing, five American carriers had been so badly damaged that they had to withdraw. Admiral Spruance lost one flagship to Japanese aircraft, and Admiral Marc Mitscher of Task Force 58 shifted his flag three times in four days (11–15 May) when *kamikazes* ruined two more of his fleet carriers. The only thing that made the ordeal marginally bearable was that Japanese pilots had severe problems in ship identification and confidence. Instead of ignoring the gauntlet of destroyers and destroyer-escorts, they tended to attack the first ship they saw. For the courageous sailors on these small vessels, the result could not have been worse, for they absorbed the *kamikaze* rage. The destroyer *Laffey* took six *kamikaze* hits, lost almost half its crew, and remained afloat to retire as a gallant wreck, but many other anti-aircraft destroyers and destroyer-escorts sank immediately, in a torrent of flaming fuel and exploding ordnance. On the night of 24–25 May, the Japanese air forces mounted their heaviest *kamikaze* and bombing attack of the campaign and kept up the assault for four days. By the time the attacks withered away in a hail of anti-aircraft fire, Fifth Fleet had lost three destroyer transports, a destroyer minesweeper, and two destroyers. Three of these ships sank outright; the others were towed off to the naval junkyard at the Kerama Retto anchorage and never repaired.

Not all *kamikazes* hit the first line of ships. Some pressed on toward the carriers and struck them with distressing regularity. As the campaign slogged on, the number of ruined carriers climbed: *Bunker Hill*, *Franklin*, the new *Wasp*, the new *Yorktown*, and *Enterprise*. Fifth Fleet never lost control of the seas around Okinawa, but it paid a high price for its mastery. No American admiral, however, could find much comfort in the Okinawan campaign, since intelligence reports suggested that the Japanese still could muster an air force five times larger than the one they sacrificed to defend Okinawa.

To eyes in Washington, the Pacific War looked won, since the capture of Okinawa breached the wall of the Home Islands. The Japanese, however, failing to appreciate the clear-sightedness of the West's logic, continued to fight.

The Atomic Bomb

The Asia-Pacific war ended in August 1945 not with a whimper but with two very large blasts—explosions of nuclear weapons that sent shock waves deep into the second half of the twentieth century. Among the many burdens that suddenly fell on Harry S. Truman's shoulders on 12 April 1945 was the news that the United States had a "superweapon" under development—an "atomic bomb"—and that scientists would soon test it in a bleak piece of desert near Alamogordo, New Mexico. The historical name of the region, La Jornada del Muerto, seemed especially appropriate, for the weapon would certainly set many on the road to death. Two weeks after becoming president—an office for which he admitted he possessed only the qualifications of decency and responsibility—Truman received a briefing on the Manhattan Project, the droll name for the Anglo-American effort to harness the energy released from atomic fission and create a military explosive device. The effort to create an atomic bomb had been under way for more than three years, cloaked in a leaky mantle of secrecy and security and funded by over $2 billion hidden in the War Department's complex budget. On 2 May 1945, Truman charged an Interim Committee, headed by his briefer, Secretary of War Henry Stimson, to provide a recommendation on just what the bomb might mean to a war in the Pacific that refused to end.

Like his fellow countrymen, Harry Truman needed much tutoring on just how the atomic bomb, with its roots in the esoteric field of particle physics, had mushroomed to become a piece of ordnance. As scientists explored the mysteries of radiation at the end of the nineteenth century, several had speculated that radioactivity might provide an incalculable source of energy. In 1904 two British scientists argued that this energy might be harnessed into a bomb and then unleashed as a military explosion. Highly theoretical but successful work on the manipulation of atomic nuclei continued into the 1930s, combining pioneering developments in particle physics, physical chemistry, and laboratory engineering. The mathematics underlying this basic and applied research remained in the hands of a few gifted men. The difficulty was that such men could be found in Nazi Germany, Japan, and the Soviet Union as well as the West.

Fortunately for the Allies, in the 1930s a critical mass of scientific genius left the Continent for the pioneer community of nuclear physicists in Britain, and then moved on to the United States, the only country with the resources and interest to sponsor further research. These scientists came from Denmark, Germany, Hungary, Italy, Austria, and France, and their names have since become legendary in the annals of modern science: Niels Bohr, Enrico Fermi, James Franck, Otto Frisch, Lew Kowarski, Leo Szilard, Edward Teller, and others. The Anglo-American leaders included James Chadwick, Arthur H. Compton, Karl Compton, Ernest O. Lawrence, J. Robert Oppenheimer, Norman Ramsey, Ernest Rutherford, Harold Urey, and John Wheeler. In 1939 three of the expatriates enlisted Albert Einstein, who by that time had become a living icon of science, to warn Roosevelt of the possibility that Nazi Germany, the home of the gifted physicist Werner Heisenberg, could develop nuclear weapons and would certainly use them. FDR showed enough interest to order one of his aides to look into the matter, and the result was a Uranium Committee which granted Enrico Fermi $6,000 for research. In 1941 the alarmed nuclear physicists found an important patron, Dr. Vannevar Bush, head of the new Office of Scientific Research and Development (OSRD). Bush, in turn, enjoyed the confidence of the War Department, which backed his demands for scarce manpower, raw materials, and money to fund research and development of war-winning inventions.

With America's entry into the war, Congress opened the coffers for OSRD–War Department projects. At the basic-research level, the nuclear weapons program hardly required massive funding. In 1942 these studies took place in particle physics laboratories in universities—Columbia, Chicago, and California-Berkeley—and were comparatively inexpensive to carry out. The results they produced were significant, however, especially when a Fermi-Compton "pile" of graphite (carbon) beneath Chicago's football stadium went critical in December 1942. The experiment showed that uranium 235 could produce plutonium (an attractive substitute for uranium) and harness uranium and plutonium for a controllable explosion. Fermi made all the critical calculations with a slide-rule. This breakthrough gave a direct push to the Manhattan Engineer District, which was renamed the Manhattan Project—the U.S. Corps of Engineers' codename for nuclear weapons research.

The enterprise took final shape in 1943, and soon required massive funding. Two government-industrial complexes at Hanford, Washington, and Oak Ridge, Tennessee, produced the fissionable material and associated ingredients required for nuclear warheads. Industrial contractors—such giants in the machine tool and electrical business as Allis-Chalmers and General Electric—also participated in fabricating the bomb's exacting components, many of which demanded cutting-edge advances in metallurgical engineering. At the site of an Indian school at Los Alamos, New Mexico, the War Department built a special city where all the weapons experts (and their families) could be brought together to explore the feasibility of actually making an atomic bomb.

Brigadier General Leslie Groves, an ambitious if unpleasant engineer, became the administrator for the project, but J. Robert Oppenheimer, head of the Los Alamos Laboratory, provided the essential leadership for the scientists and engineers. Not until autumn 1944 did the Manhattan Project show signs that a bomb might actually be constructed, even though the basic science indicated that a fission explosion was possible. Among the largest obstacles was finding uranium and producing plutonium that could be safely shaped into a weapon. (Consistent with its wartime mission, the Manhattan Project produced its own casualties—eight fatalities during experimentation and testing, one by radiation poisoning.) Another challenge was designing a dependable triggering mechanism.

In early 1945 Groves and Oppenheimer judged they could (and should) fabricate a prototype nuclear device and explode it. Under highly suspenseful and considerably dangerous circumstances, the Los Alamos team set off a plutonium device, Fat Man, on 16 July 1945. Among the observers were Groves, Bush, Oppenheimer, and Fermi. A huge fireball enveloped the desert, sending out blinding waves of light and crushing air pressure; a column of cloud pushed upward, forming the shape of a mushroom. The blast registered a force of 17,000 tons of TNT. The observers felt jubilant but chastened by the destructive power that now rested in mankind's hands.

The only people in the War Department who had a clear picture of Manhattan's progress and the course of the war were Secretary Stimson and General Marshall. They had enough confidence that in 1943 they began preparing for atomic bombs to enter the American arsenal. Roosevelt and Churchill, of course, followed the Manhattan Project closely, and Britain continued as a partner by mutual agreement in sharing the scientific findings and talent, even if it did not bear the project's cost. The British worried about nuclear security and accused some of the expatriate scientists of dangerous sympathies with the Soviets; but in fact, the real Russian agents were a British-sponsored émigré German scientist at Los Alamos (Klaus Fuchs), a handful of deluded young Americans like Theodore A. Hall and Saville Sax, and four Communist members of the British intelligence and foreign services.

Groves took the lead in 1943 in organizing a small group of the faithful, the Military Committee, to explore the employment of nuclear weapons within the war's context. The group examined both German and Japanese targets, some military, some urban-industrial. No one questioned that the bomb would be used. In 1944–45, the Americans learned that the Germans would not be able to develop the bomb and, in fact, would lose the war. Attention then turned to Japan, the only remaining belligerent when Fat Man vaporized or crystallized everything in its blast.

In the meantime, the army air forces prepared a special unit, the 509th Bombardment Group (Composite), commanded by Colonel Paul W. Tibbets, a 29-year-old bomber pilot in the war over Germany. A gifted test pilot and aeronautical engineer, Tibbets became a key member of the team working on the B-29 project. In September 1944 he suddenly received orders to attend an interview linked to a special command. He found it puzzling that the selection committee had so many engineer officers. After his assignment, he learned that his special B-29 group would someday drop atomic bombs.

In May–June 1945, Tibbets's group—a wondrous collection of talented people and special equipment—deployed to a secure part of Tinian, one of the Marianas. Throughout the period of preparation in the United States and deployment in the Pacific, Tibbets learned everything he needed to know to train his group, and he even won some skirmishes with Curtis LeMay over training and support requirements. The one thing he did not know was when he would have a weapon, a target, and a mission.

At the highest levels of policy and strategy, the United States and Japan grasped at any faint promise that the war would end short of a full-scale invasion of Kyushu (codenamed Operation Olympic) in November and Honshu (Operation Coronet) the following spring. Linked as Operation Downfall, the two invasions would require landing forces of 1.3 million men and the entire Pacific Fleet, reinforced by the Royal Navy, and 5,000 combat aircraft. Strategic planning in Washington, supplemented with studies from MacArthur and Nimitz, began to assess the growing redeployment of the Japanese divisions from Asia to the Home Islands, the husbanding of suicide squadrons of planes and boats, and the mobilization of the Japanese population (especially displaced industrial workers and farmers) for service in construction and home-defense units. In the Homeland Operations Plan of January 1945, and again in the Volunteer Military Service Law of June 1945, the Japanese Cabinet essentially called the entire population to military service, while propagandists began "The Glorious Death of One Hundred Million" program to whip up enthusiasm for dying for the Emperor.

Faced with this level of defensive preparation, American planning included estimates of casualties, prepared by personnel specialists, medical planners, and logistics staffs. Although Truman, Stimson, and others confused the estimates then and later, usually mixing "deaths" with "casualties," the numbers were shocking in any case: the estimated total American casualties predicted for Operation Downfall, based on the recent battles in the Pacific, might number as many as 500,000. Planners noted that Pacific War casualties, measured by days of combat and losses per 1,000 soldiers, were already three times higher than American casualties in Europe in 1944–45. The most incalculable part of the process was considering what suicide ships and planes might do to transports carrying troops. King and other navy planners wondered whether the better part of wisdom would be to cancel Operation Downfall and continue the program of economic strangulation and fire-bombing until Japan surrendered. But Stimson, Marshall, and Arnold, as well as their advisers, did not find much appeal in a protracted war of uncertain termination.

Part of the urgency to finish the war came from problems of America's making. Although FDR did not follow his own pronouncements on unconditional surrender in dealing with Italy, Truman had embraced the policy and demanded the unqualified capitulation of the Third Reich in May. America's late-war casualties and the newly revealed horrors of the liberated death camps in Germany and the Philippines made any concessions to the Axis powers political dynamite. Conditioned to regard Hirohito as a war criminal, the public might greet any capitulation that allowed him to remain Emperor as a betrayal of trust for which Harry Truman stood responsible. Experts on Japan within the State Department, however, urged the government to save Hirohito and make him a key figure in controlling the occupied Japanese people, who would be totally disarmed, stripped of their empire, deprived of their traditional leaders, and subjected to unavoidable economic and emotional reconstruction. Even though some experts suspected that Hirohito had been an active force in Japan's aggression, they saw him as an essential instrument in rebuilding and reforming Japan.

Another consideration in the endgame was the Soviet Union's role in Asia after the war. At the Yalta Conference in February, FDR had won Stalin's promise to enter the Asian war at the price of the return of "lost lands" and special concessions in North Asia. If the Soviets now demanded an active role in the occupation, including massive reparations, Japan's rehabilitation would stand in danger. Some of Truman's advisers had also concluded that the Soviet Union had its own designs on Europe that could not be stopped by the new United Nations or the existing alignment of broken European states. Taking any action that might give the Soviets pause—such as introducing the atomic bomb—seemed worthwhile to some.

The main concern of those planning to drop the bomb, however, remained to reduce American casualties in a war nearing its end. Some advisers even thought that sparing Japanese lives would pay later dividends. In the meantime, the Japanese government—at least parts of it—searched for a negotiated settlement for the same reasons: to escape the bombing and economic strangulation and avoid the final blood-letting that would surely come with an American invasion. A handful of courageous diplomats in the dark corners of the Foreign Ministry started to make contacts with the Soviet Union, to ask whether Stalin might influence FDR and

Churchill to settle for something less than unconditional surrender. Their search took on new urgency when the Russians announced on 5 April that they would not renew their neutrality treaty. In April the general serving as prime minister gave way to retired Admiral Suzuki Kantaro, age 78, and hope grew among the peace faction in the Emperor's court. Even as the war and navy ministers pressed ahead with their Home Island defense plans, Suzuki played "the Russian card," but to no effect. When Okinawa fell, he and the peace faction understood that their nation faced not just defeat but extinction.

The Japanese Surrender

Against a background of more slaughter, Truman went to Potsdam in July to meet Stalin and Churchill; the latter was replaced in mid-conference by the Labour Party's leader, Clement Attlee. Stalin showed no special remorse over FDR's and Churchill's absence, and he did not react when Truman hinted that the United States had a "super bomb." In fact, Stalin probably knew more about U.S. nuclear weapons than Truman did, since he had been tutored by Igor Kurchatov, the Soviet Oppenheimer, who had organized the Soviet nuclear weapons program and had access to espionage reports from Los Alamos.

Stalin suggested to Truman that nothing would persuade the Japanese to surrender unless they received concessions—confirming what American intelligence officers had already concluded from intercepted communications. On 26 July, Truman approved a public message to Japan that it could avoid a final solution only if it surrendered now. The Potsdam Declaration did not mention the Emperor or his future, however, except to say that the Japanese government must remove "all obstacles to the revival and strengthening of democratic tendencies among the Japanese people." Truman thought he had authorized a text hinting that Hirohito's status was negotiable, but several translations and cultural filterings so distorted the message that it became no message at all. The Suzuki regime rejected the Potsdam Declaration on 27 July, but did so thinking it had left the door open for further communications on the Emperor's status.

Truman did not listen very hard for such a signal. On 24 July he had already directed the Twentieth Air Force to drop a nuclear weapon on one of four target cities, with the target choice and timing to depend on the weather and other local considerations. U.S. Navy warships had already brought two devices to Tinian, one a second plutonium Fat Man, the other a uranium Little Boy. Both weapons had been virtually hand-made and used much of the fissionable material available to the United States. Truman, of course, could have canceled the mission if he so chose, and Stimson gave him that chance on 27 July. Truman ordered the mission to go forward.

General LeMay selected Hiroshima because it had some military value, its T-shaped bridge made a perfect aiming point, and it contained no Allied POW camps as far as he knew. This last assumption turned out to be wrong. On 6 August, Paul Tibbets himself, flying the *Enola Gay,* dropped Little Boy above Hiroshima and blew the city and its citizens apart. Three days later, another B-29 dropped Fat Man on Nagasaki, with slightly less horrific results. No one could ever count the total casualties with accuracy, but 180,000 immediate deaths in the two cities is not an overestimate, while other deaths followed from radiation poisoning and, in later generations, from genetic damage. As though to drive the point of their defeat home to the Japanese, the Soviet Union declared war on Japan on 8 August and launched its armored forces of 1.6 million men into Manchuria.

One of the hundreds of thousands of Japanese caught in Hiroshima on 6 August was Sasaki Kazuji, an instructor at an army school for paymasters. Sasaki survived the collapse of his classroom building, where he was proctoring an examination. Despite serious internal injuries and radiation poisoning, he struggled to his home outside the city. He arrived on 12 August, already close to death. However, he started a report to the chief of the paymasters school, describing the damage to the school and the efforts to rescue the staff and students. Raging fires had driven him away from his office and the examinations and other records. He wrote on 18 August that his current condition forced his report to be incomplete: "My physical symptoms were localized pain, intense headache, high fever, frequent vomiting, complete lack of appetite. Although I exerted every effort, I allowed the documents to be ultimately destroyed by fire. I deplore exceedingly the vast difficulties in the admission of new students induced by this outcome. I am deeply aware of the gravity of my responsibility and find no way that I can excuse myself." As Sasaki dictated these words to his wife, he died—a loyal soldier to the bitter end.[3]

On 9 August, even before they learned of the bombing of Nagasaki that same day, the six most important men directing the Japanese war effort met in conference to consider their nation's future. Three of the six, one admiral and two generals, wanted continued resistance and reviewed their plans to pitch 2.3 million servicemen and 28 million male and female home guards into defense of the Home Islands. Three men, two admirals and a diplomat, wanted to pursue direct negotiations with the Americans.

Even when the prime minister expanded the group to include the entire Cabinet, the meeting remained deadlocked. During the arguments, the Japanese learned of Nagasaki's destruction, but War Minister Anami Korechika led a die-hard minority that rejected surrender. Suzuki scheduled another conference that night and then urged Hirohito to attend and break the impasse. The invitation also included Hirohito's personal staff and revered members of the *genro*, senior statesmen without official positions.

Around midnight all the conferees had assembled, and the debate for and against surrender raged on. Sometime in the darkest hours, Hirohito stood and silenced his advisers. In a thin voice, he told all of them that the only remaining hope for the Japanese people was to surrender as soon as possible, even if it cost him the throne. He wanted all the cabinet members to sign a new, official response to the Potsdam Declaration in which Japan surrendered on the condition that the Emperor retain his symbolic position as the representative of the Japanese people. By mid-morning 10 August, his message had reached Washington and all the world's capitals.

Once again Truman faced a problem he could not solve alone, and he happily embraced his advisers' recommendation that he accept the Japanese terms, even if it meant keeping Hirohito (stripped of his divinity) in office. Henry Stimson carried the debate, and no other adviser contradicted him. Marshall, Arnold, and King were not present, but they had no serious problems with the decision. In fact, all the Allied governments except the Soviet Union counseled peace now; the Russians felt cheated of a campaign they knew would revenge the defeat of 1905. In compensation for this lost opportunity, Stalin demanded new power over the occupation of Japan and the dismemberment of its empire. On 12 August, the Allies accepted Japanese terms with the caveats that the Emperor would be held responsible for a cooperative surrender but the "ultimate form" of a future Japanese government would depend on "the freely expressed will of the Japanese people." Since no one thought that Japan had converted to Jeffersonian republicanism, this condition seemed pro forma to the Allies.

Some Japanese thought differently. Inside the army a group of junior officers, fantasizing that the 1930s had never passed, planned to assassinate the peace faction and force the Emperor to fight to everyone's death. The immediate focus of their plot was to stop the public announcement of Japan's surrender. Once again Japan faced a national crisis, and even Prime Minister Suzuki wavered under the threat of a military coup. The minister of war and the chief of staff of the Japanese Army would not support the rebels; instead, they suggested that the officers follow their example and commit suicide.

With the threat of a coup still very much alive, Hirohito gathered his principal cabinet officers and advisers on 14 August and demanded that they all accept his decision to surrender. He also ordered General Umezu Yoshijiro, Army Chief of Staff, not to join War Minister Anami in suicide but to take personal responsibility to ensure a peaceful capitulation. He then recorded a surrender message for both the Allies and the Japanese people. Even so, a cabal of army officers attempted to stop the broadcast, only to be foiled at the last minute by loyal troops. The last Japanese killed between war and surrender was the general commanding the palace guard, who was slain by a rebel major.

In his message the Emperor ordered his troops to lay down their arms, to cooperate with Allied forces, to preserve order and discipline, and to join with the Japanese people in bearing their unbearable burden of defeat and disgrace. The cries of rage and relief that greeted the Emperor's message throughout Japan almost drowned out the sound of gunshots, as rebels and loyalists alike began to commit suicide.

The surrender message went out to a grateful world. In Washington, Truman announced, without elaboration, that Japan had accepted his demand that it surrender without conditions.

Conclusion

On 2 September, Japan's capitulation to the Allies was officially marked by a handful of Japanese diplomats and officers on the deck of Admiral Halsey's flagship *Missouri*, a new fast battleship dear to Truman. This final act of the Asia-Pacific war fell under the direction of the general-dramatist MacArthur, who had enlisted Halsey to stage a great naval-aerial demonstration in Tokyo Bay for the media and the victorious Allies. Among the major actors were Generals Jonathan Wainwright and Sir Arthur Percival, recently released from captivity.

The ritual on the *Missouri* merely symbolized acts of surrender already occurring across the wreckage of the Japanese empire: the Soviets accepted capitulations in Manchuria and northern Korea; the Commonwealth, forces in Southeast Asia and the East Indies; and the Chinese Nationalists, the Japanese armies in between. American troops first landed at Home Islands air fields on 28 August without incident, while more divisions, their lives spared by the atomic bombs, sailed for their assigned destinations to disarm the Japanese armed forces.

To make the *Missouri* a suitable site for the Japanese surrender, the ship's skipper, Captain Stuart S. Murray, arranged to have a special flag brought to his ship to fly on 2 September 1945. The media later reported that the American flag hoisted aloft over the *Missouri* was the very one flying over the Capitol on 7 December 1941. It was not. The American flag that shared the main staff that day with the five-star flags of General MacArthur and Admirals Nimitz and Halsey came directly from the ships' flag locker and had no lineage. Captain Murray's special flag was hung in front of the passageway to his cabin, a place the Japanese would have to face as they reached the maindeck from the gangway. Murray's flag would surely attract their attention, for it was worn and had only 31 stars. It had flown from the masthead of Commodore Matthew C. Perry's flagship when it entered Tokyo Bay in 1853, opening the door to Japan.[4]

Led by the new foreign minister, the feeble and crippled Shigemitsu Mamori, the Japanese surrender delegation of nine military and foreign ministry officers played out its part in MacArthur's bit of *kabuki*. Under a dull gray sky and cool breeze, the Japanese delegates took inconspicuous cars from Tokyo to Yokohama just in case some army rebels planned an ambush. Traveling through the devastated port city, Kase Toshikazu, a young diplomat skilled in English, saw little to cheer him: "The desolation was enough to freeze the heart." The delegation reached the *Missouri* by admiral's barge, "diplomats without flag and soldiers without sword, morose and silent." Their progress up the gangway was slow, since Shigemitsu climbed with great difficulty on his wooden leg, which had replaced a limb lost to a Korean terrorist's bomb. Kase looked with discomfort at the ranks upon ranks of Allied admirals and generals, mustered under a live canopy of journalists and photographers perched monkeylike from every possible place on the superstructure. Kase recognized the American flag in front of Captain Murray's stateroom since he had seen it once in the U.S. Naval Academy museum. He felt little but dread at the possible surrender terms.[5]

Shortly after 9:00 A.M., Foreign Minister Shigemitsu signed the surrender documents, and the Asia-Pacific war officially ended. One after another, the Allied representatives signed, Admiral Nimitz doing the honors for the United States. MacArthur presided with dignity and grace, setting the tone of the ceremony with one of his sermons on abolishing war and restoring Japan to the community of peace-loving nations. He promised that the Allied occupation, which he would command, would bring relief, recovery, and reform to Japan. The "day of infamy" had now been replaced by a time in which "the hope of mankind" would be "that a better world will emerge out of the blood and carnage of the past."[6] It would be the duty of the survivors of the Asia-Pacific war to make 2 September 1945 the first day in an era of healing.

19

PEOPLES AT WAR

1937–1945

Unlike their pre–twentieth-century counterparts, with the possible exception of the early Roman Republic and revolutionary France, the belligerents in World War II had unprecedented power to turn economic resources into military capability. Those resources fell into five broad categories: (1) raw materials from which to fabricate munitions; (2) foodstuffs to keep military forces and civilians alive and functioning; (3) a national infrastructure of factory systems and transportation that could expand and reorganize to increase productivity; (4) a labor force of sufficient size and skill to meet the needs of all productive sectors; and (5) the political will—exercised through coercion, propaganda, and appeals to civic duty—to enforce civilian sacrifices even when they became intolerable.

A War for Resources

One great geoeconomic fact looms over the history of World War II: the Axis powers could not eliminate the entire Western Hemisphere and sub-Saharan Africa as a resource domain available to the Allies. The enormous industrial and agricultural productivity of the United States and of the British Commonwealth, including its nonwhite colonies, which largely deferred their demands for independence, remained outside Axis reach.

World War II was a conflict of resources as well as ideologies, in both its causes and conduct. No natural resource was as essential as fossil fuels. Raw petroleum was the critical ingredient in gasoline and plastics, and coal fed the furnaces that made steel and turned turbines for electrical power. The Allies won the war because they had fossil fuels and because they prevented the Axis powers from turning the fossil fuels of occupied countries into war-winning resources. On the eve of Pearl Harbor, the United States produced two-thirds of the world's petroleum, largely because it could pump and deliver that oil at a price ($1.15 a barrel) that discouraged its competitors. Moreover, petroleum companies that were not American-owned belonged to U.S. allies, the British and the Dutch. The Soviet Union produced 10 percent of the world's oil and used it for its own needs; its reserves were significant. The rest of the actual and potential oil producers of the world operated within an economic sphere of interest dominated by prewar market patterns and geography that worked to the Allies' advantage. These nations were Mexico, Canada, Venezuela, Iraq, Iran, and Saudi Arabia. The Allies also controlled about two-thirds of the world's coal supplies.

The view from the Axis perspective was quite different. Already dependent on foreign oil when they went to war, Germany and Japan coopted or captured oil fields in Romania, Russia, and the Netherlands East Indies. Allied air attacks and naval interdiction campaigns by surface fleets and submarines reduced the flow of oil imports to Germany and Japan to such a degree that by mid-1944 gasoline shortages crippled parts of the industrial base and did serious damage to the Axis armed forces. Although the Axis had plentiful coal resources, they had to transport that coal to their power plants and factories, which made the coal vulnerable to air and naval attack.

Both the Allies and the Axis attempted to impose oil and coal rationing on their economies, and both experimented with synthetic fuels with some success. The access to almost unlimited fossil fuels, however, allowed the Allies to pioneer in the production of synthetic rubber, durable plastics, and synthetic fibers that substituted for raw materials in short supply such as cotton and silk, both of which were important military fabrics.

Similar patterns of abundance and scarcity could be found in the strategic minerals sector: the Axis had the emptier bins. Of 21 critical minerals, Germany had significant access to only 4 when the war began. It gained access to 6 more critical metals by conquering western Russia. By contrast, even after the Allies lost Malaya to Japan (its most important mineral conquest), the British Commonwealth and the United States could maintain their prewar dominance of strategic metals by turning to Latin America, where Anglo-American corporations dominated copper and tin mining. Canada expanded its mineral production, as did British colonies in Africa, where the Allies counted on cheap labor.

Another fortuitous development was the fact that the United States and the British Commonwealth tended to complement one another in strategic raw materials; where one was short, the other filled the void. The British had virtually no sulfur or phosphates, but the United States had plenty. The United States had limited supplies of tin and nickel, whereas the British had ample sources. The Axis enjoyed virtually no such complementarity, and any exchanges between Germany and Japan even in small amounts of rare minerals depended on submarines for transportation. The Russians fell into an intermediate category. Although the Soviets found some supplies of all 21 strategic minerals somewhere in the Soviet Union, weather and geography limited the wartime development of these resources. The Soviets did not, for example, use alloys much because alloys required minerals in short supply. Nevertheless, they had what they really needed to build and maintain a massive arms industry: coal, iron ore, chrome, phosphates, and manganese.

Feeding War

As Napoleon observed, armies march in tune with their stomachs, and nations-in-arms are no different. Allied farmers did their part to win the war, especially American farmers, who fed not only their civilian and military countrymen but every ally except China. The fortunate combination of soil, water, technical knowledge, mechanization, superior animal husbandry, and experience with land use (recently reinforced by the Dust Bowl trauma of the 1930s) prepared the United States to be "the Granary of Democracy." At the beginning of the war, it had a smaller agricultural work force than in 1918 and only 5 percent more acreage under production; this left plenty of room for expansion, and American farmers met the challenge. They increased their output in every major category of grain and livestock, in some cases as much as 25 percent. Government policy allowed farm prices to rise as much as 100 percent, and federal subsidies (like those for the tobacco and cotton industries) encouraged production.

Food rationing, especially of meat, kept domestic consumption low enough to feed the American armed forces and the British. The number of people an American farmer could feed per acre increased from 10 to 15 during the war. Even with the inevitable black market, war-workers got the food they needed to function, estimated at a minimum of 3,500 calories a day with ample proteins and carbohydrates. (By comparison, a typical American woman working in a sedentary job needs approximately 2,000 calories per day, and a typical sedentary American man needs about 2,500 calories per day.) Personnel in the armed services received a minimum standard of over 4,000 calories per day. It is a telling comment that the standard GI complaint was that the food did not look and taste as good as home cooking—not that there wasn't enough of it. Starving Asian and European civilians often survived on the garbage thrown out by American servicemen.

Subjected to bombing and submarine interdiction for almost two years before the United States entered the war, Britain was losing the struggle to feed itself while still maintaining its own crucial war industries and civilian morale. British farmers had made impressive improvements in the amount of land brought into cultivation and the amount of grains and potatoes they grew, while British fishermen had kept their catches at or above peacetime levels. In the end, however, the British could reduce their dependence on imported foodstuffs from 40 percent to only about 30 percent. For example, British dairy herds stayed stable in size during the war, but all categories of edible livestock declined, despite the fact that thousands of British families started their own family chicken and pig farms. Food animals—beef cattle, sheep, pigs, and chickens—used too much land and feed to justify the investment. Latin American suppliers made up some of the shortages in meat, as they had in World War I. Only severe rationing of all meats, sugar, eggs, and dairy products, as well as sugar-based foods like jams and pastries and even tea, could ensure that British servicemen and war-workers received adequate nourishment. Fortunately, fish, bread, potatoes, fruit, and vegetables remained plentiful, and after the defeat of the U-boats in 1943, imported American foodstuffs helped some.

What may have helped most, however, was the arrival of the massive American invasion forces in 1943–44, for the GIs brought their food and charity in abundance. British men might grouse about the Yanks being overpaid, oversexed, and over here, but the GIs were also overfed, and they knew it. They shared their food with many Britons, especially women and children. The army demonstrated its confidence that it could provide GIs with food in abundance by calculating the allowance of toilet tissue per soldier stationed in Britain at 22.5 sheets per day. The comparable British ration was 3 sheets.

Generosity of the sort practiced by many American GIs was not to be found among Axis armies. Where they occupied the nations of Eurasia, the Germans and Japanese confiscated foodstuffs and shipped them to their homelands to support their civilian populations—after the military had taken its self-defined requirements. Nazi policy dictated that German civilians would be well-fed; and every *real* German—which meant non-Jewish Germans living within the prewar boundaries of Germany and Austria—needed 2,600 calories a day. One of the major responsibilities of Nazi occupation authorities was to ensure that foreign foodstuffs flowed back to Germany, which they did with regularity until 1944, when territorial losses in Russia and the effects of Allied bombing began to disrupt the food distribution system.

From its earliest conception, Hitler's policy of conquest assumed that the rest of Europe should feed the German people. As Joseph Goebbels put it, "Our food is not here to be eaten by the people we have conquered—they have to take the consequences of the war they forced upon us."[1] France alone lost 500,000 draft horses and 400,000 farm workers to the Third Reich. Nazi officials—hardly economic geniuses in any sector—knew little about agriculture, and by 1944 farm output collapsed after German farmers and their neighbors ate their own livestock and draft animals. Since the Nazis had to reduce civilian food consumption, they starved their slave labor force rather than cut the consumption of nonproductive Germans. In 1944, when the Germans made their last effort to regulate food supplies, they established a daily standard of less than 1,000 calories for non-German captive workers. The caloric intake of the occupied French and Dutch fell well below 2,000 calories. The official caloric standard for all Germans, however, remained at around 2,000 calories until 1945.

When the Anglo-American armies landed on the Continent and liberated France and Belgium, they faced the same problem they had encountered in Italy the year before. They inherited a starved and sick civilian population that had to be fed somehow while the war still raged. Churchill and Eisenhower recognized that the Europeans expected the United States and Britain to provide food and medical supplies. Operations in France and Belgium in 1944 not only advanced the Allies' plans to envelop portions of the German Army but also to liberate ports, opening a flow of relief supplies from the United States. From D-Day to VE-Day (Victory in Europe Day), American and international agencies, using army facilities, provided about $1 billion of food, medicine, and clothes to Northern Europe.

No such concerns shaped Russian operations when the Red Army entered Eastern Europe. The Soviets saw no reason to spare German civilians from starvation or violent death; rather, the Russian Army's political commissars and senior commanders reminded their soldiers how much the Russian people had suffered in the defense of Mother Russia. In two years of war, 1941–1943, the Russians had lost almost half of their arable land and more than half of their grain production and livestock. They did not return to prewar agricultural production levels, which were miserable at best, until the 1950s. Two million farm workers went into the Red Army or to their deaths at the hands of the German invaders during that two-year period; they had to be replaced by new workers, 1.5 million of whom were unskilled women who had to learn to run farm machinery. In the first two years of the war, the cities of Leningrad, Moscow, and Stalingrad fell under German siege. In the first year of the siege of Leningrad, perhaps as many as a million Russians died from starvation; the Russians ate every living thing except one another. The civilians of Moscow and Stalingrad fared only slightly better.

The Soviets' plight was partially of their own making. In 1941, when the Germans first invaded, Stalin had ordered a scorched-earth policy rather than attempt to move foodstuffs to the east. While this policy might have defeated Napoleon in 1812, it made little difference to the Wehrmacht of 1941. Instead of slowing down the Germans, it starved Russians. At a time when the Soviet Union lost one-third of its people through death and occupation, its food resources dropped by 60 percent. Only soldiers and war-workers received adequate calories and proteins; older people, teenagers, and bureaucrats received the lowest rations. Even vodka was in short supply—a national crisis. Starvation may have indirectly fostered the partisan movement behind German lines in north-central Russia, since the Russian peasantry had plenty of incentives to raid German supply lines, if only to get food. When the Americans opened up maritime and land routes for Lend-Lease Aid to Russia in 1942, they learned that the Soviets wanted food and transportation (trucks and locomotives), not weapons. In dollar value, the Soviets received less than one-quarter of the $42 billion distributed to the Allies, but they received about one-third of the $5 billion of agricultural supplies sent abroad by the United States. Only the British received more food, about $3 billion.

The Japanese government fed its armed forces and civilian population with imported foodstuffs until American submarines cut those supplies in 1944. The rice supply remained adequate until 1945, largely because the Japanese put almost all of their arable land into rice cultivation. Japanese fishermen provided protein, but shortages of soybeans and sugar started the slide into malnutrition. Japan's demands for rice from its economic dependencies pushed these countries to the brink of starvation; Korean farmers doubled their rice production during the war, but the rice consumption of Koreans themselves fell by half in order to feed their Japanese masters. In both Japan and Korea, tofu had been deemed a poor person's food; by 1945 this protein-rich beancurd paste had reached the status of a popular and essential substitute for rice.

Meanwhile, in Germany, by the time the war ended, bakers were lacing black bread with sawdust. The roar of the guns ceased in both Europe and

Asia, only to be replaced by the growing rumble of the starving millions for whom peace meant nothing until they found something to eat.

The Industrialization of Warfare

World War I provided a vision of what a future war between the world's industrial powers might become. The distinguished British economist E. M. H. Lloyd, who served as an economic planner in both world wars, saw the future clearly in 1924: "Another great war will plunge the world into a sort of military communism, in comparison with which the control exercised during the recent war will seem an Arcadian revel."[2] Four of the seven major belligerents of World War II—Italy, Germany, Japan, and Russia—moved to planned economies even before 1939, in part to respond to the Depression but also to increase their economic autonomy during a period of rearmament and probable war. France, Britain, and the United States remained market economies, but even they began to rearm in the late 1930s and to forge bonds between government and industry that grew stronger with the war's coming. After France quickly fell into Germany's economic orbit in 1940, it contributed little to the Allied industrial war effort. The Russians could and did mobilize their industry for warfare but lost much of it to the Germans in 1941 or destroyed it themselves. Nevertheless, in 1942–43 their factories were back in business, feeding weapons to a resurgent Red Army. The Soviet miracle of production rested on the ruthless allocation of resources and the draconian use of human labor. Britain, probably the most efficient manufacturer in the conflict, and the United States produced prodigious amounts of war materiel and also accepted the additional burden of producing enough merchant ships to move the materiel across two broad and dangerous oceans. Even Italy and Japan surprised themselves and their enemies with their industrial effort, especially since their limited war industries had to endure bombing for almost a year and a half. Never in the history of warfare have so many made so much for such destructive purposes.

A major dimension of the industrialization of warfare was the commitment to develop and deploy new weapons that would give one's own armed forces distinct operational and tactical advantages over the enemy. Aerial weapons especially evolved rapidly; Germany set the pace in the development of strategic missiles (the V-1 and V-2) that could reach and ravage cities in Allied hands in 1944–45. The Germans also pioneered in the development of jet engines that could be mounted in the Me-262 interceptor, a bomber-killer. Allied strategic planners thanked Hitler for deciding not to mount the same engines in long-range bombers as well, since some planners knew that the Germans had begun to develop nuclear warheads for these bombers to deliver but that a V-2 could not, because of its payload weight limits.

Germany, Britain, and the United States all counted on fielding weapons with qualitative technological advantages over their opponents, and all of them succeeded in some areas. But the weapons that proved dominant on the battlefield were the ones that could be mass-produced, operated by trained and motivated fighters, kept in action with adequate fuel and spare parts, used with devastating and appropriate ordnance, and employed in concert with other weapons. By the end of the war, German and Japanese leaders began the losers' lament: we were beaten by more materiel, not good soldiers nor the highest-quality weapons. But the war's outcome proved that Allied weapons were good enough, and men, not robots, made them work in battle. Although the types of weapons systems differed from nation to nation, some impression of the success of the industrial mobilization can be drawn from the numbers of major weapons the Allies and Axis powers produced (see Table 2).

For the United States, wartime manufacturing rebuilt a heavy industry sector badly damaged by the Depression; most indices of capital investment and plant expansion showed increases double and triple prewar levels. The United States also pioneered in institutionalizing research and development by encouraging the collaboration of universities, industrial laboratories, and government research agencies through the Office of Scientific Research and Development, established in May 1941. Although much of the technical development began in Britain and Germany, the United States became equal (if not superior) to the two traditional technological giants in the development of radar, sonar, aerial weapons, ordnance, shell fuses, medicine, navigation systems for ships and aircraft, and radio communications.

So vast was American war production that the United States not only armed itself but shared its output with the other Allies—thus reversing its role from World War I, when the United States had fought with British and French weapons. In addition to becoming the "Granary of Democracy," the United States became the "Arsenal of Democracy." About half of the $42 billion in Lend-Lease aid to the Allies took the form of finished munitions, while another quarter took the form of petroleum and other industrial-essential raw materials and machine tools. The British Commonwealth received roughly half of this output. Congress required Lend-Lease recipients to pay for economic assets received from the United States that could be

Table 2. Major Weapons Produced by Allies and Axis Powers, 1940–1945

Weapons	1940	1942	1943	1944	1945
Aircraft					
Germany	10,247	15,409	24,807	39,807	7,540
USA	12,804	47,836	85,898	96,318	49,761
UK	15,049	23,672	26,263	26,461	12,070
USSR	10,565	25,436	34,900	40,300	20,900
Japan	4,768	8,861	16,693	28,180	11,066
Tanks and Self-Propelled Artillery					
Germany	2,200	9,200	17,300	22,100	—
USA	400	24,997	29,497	17,565	11,968
UK	1,399	8,611	7,476	4,600	—
USSR	2,794	24,446	24,089	28,963	15,400
Japan	1,023	1,191	790	401	142
Artillery Pieces					
Germany	5,000	12,000	27,000	41,000	—
USA	1,800	72,658	67,544	33,558	19,699
UK	1,900	6,600	12,200	12,400	—
USSR	15,300	127,000	130,000	122,400	93,000
Japan	—	2,250	2,550	3,600	1,650
Warships					
Germany	2	8	3	7	—
USA	28	108	369	330	89
UK	26	65	71	77	64
USSR	33	19	13	23	11
Japan	30	49	122	248	51
Submarines					
Germany	40	244	270	288	139
USA	2	33	56	85	35
UK	15	20	39	39	14
USSR	42	2	16	18	18
Japan	7	61	37	39	30

— no data

applied to postwar economic advantage, but Britain and most of the other Allies sought and received financial forgiveness of this requirement during or after the war. The exceptions were China and the Soviet Union; the latter argued that American aid did little to help its war effort, and it refused to pay even a fraction of its wartime debt until 1990 when, desperate for new economic assistance, the doomed Soviet Union paid about $600 million of its $2.5 billion Lend-Lease bill.

One of the most critical industrial achievements of the war was shipbuilding. Merchantmen and their anti-submarine escorts received the highest priority in the United States and Britain until late 1943, when the U-boats were defeated. For Britain, keeping a merchant fleet moving across the world's oceans became a matter of national life or death. By building new ships and incorporating Commonwealth and expatriate European merchant fleets into its convoys, Britain barely maintained its prewar level of about 19 million deadweight tons (dry cargo) of capacity. Over the course of the war, 4,700 British-flagged merchantmen went to the bottom. In the meantime, the need for more ships to deploy the Allied air and land forces around the globe rose dramatically, as did the industrial and consumer demands of Britain. Ships could not be built or found fast enough, despite the heroic efforts of British shipbuilders, often working under German bombing of steel factories and shipyards within range. The United States, thus, had to become the "Shipyard of Democracy," an assignment it executed with dispatch.

The American wartime shipbuilding program began in 1938 with a goal of producing 50 ships a year in a modest effort to rebuild the American merchant marine. It was largely the work of the War Shipping Administration and the U.S. Maritime Commission, directed by Admiral Emory S. Land. By 1945 Maritime Commission–sponsored American shipbuilders had produced some 5,800 vessels, mostly tankers and large cargo carriers, with 56 million deadweight tons capacity. The Axis sank 733 American-flag merchantmen, but the United States quintupled its merchant fleet in numbers and carrying capacity. In order to carry 64.7 million tons of oil and gasoline around the world, the Americans built more than 600 new tankers and increased tanker capacity from 560,000 to 10.7 million deadweight tons. It did so by increasing its shipyards to 70 and by shortening the time it took to build a standard merchantman (the Liberty or Victory ship of 10,000 tons) from 105 to 56 days.

The single most important shipbuilding innovation for the Allies was the switch from bolting to welding hull plates, a timesaver that eventually produced a hull of adequate strength, even if cracks remained a continuing problem. Other innovations in modular construction, materials substitution (plastics for metals), and electrical and marine-engineering inventions, many pioneered by Kaiser Shipbuilding, cut production times and improved ship serviceability.

The structure of American army divisions made shipbuilding miracles essential, since the War Department counted on high firepower and high mobility to compensate for the relatively few combat divisions (89) the army created and deployed. Higher firepower and mobility meant that more munitions and vehicles had to be shipped to the front. An American division included between 2,322 and 3,698 vehicles. The minimum satisfactory supply of gasoline and lubricants for a division was 6,700 tons, and the minimum satisfactory supply of 105mm artillery shells (a ten-day supply) weighed 5,582 tons. Just the gasoline and 105mm shells (not counting all other ammunition) of *one* deploying division required three or four ships, assuming they all survived the crossing. Even before its major deployments in 1943, the army shipped 23 million tons of dry cargo abroad; and when the war reached its height in 1944, the shipping load for that year alone was 48 million tons.

This logistical effort did not stop when the shipments arrived overseas, since the army had to build and man ports, build or rebuild railroads, and build and maintain roads and all the associated storage facilities for its supplies. In March 1945, when the army had about 2 million soldiers in combat units, it also had 1.5 million in combat-support jobs, with another 500,000 credited to "theater overhead." Without an extraordinary effort to make logistics a blessing rather than a burden, the American armed forces would have sunk themselves in their supply requirements.

At the same time that the United States and Britain were battling Germany to keep their merchant ships afloat, they also had to create a fleet of amphibious ships and landing craft. The British made important contributions in the design of beaching ships (the Landing Ship Tank or LST) and beaching craft (the Landing Craft Infantry or LCI), but the United States carried the burden of actually building the "Alligator Navy" that was so essential to every Anglo-American land campaign except the one in Europe after August 1944.

Amphibious ships fell into two broad categories: those large enough for ocean travel and those used principally for short shore-to-shore runs like the Normandy landing and many operations in the Southwest Pacific. In the former category were assault troop transports, troop and vehicle carriers like the LST and the Landing Ship Dock (LSD), and amphibious cargo ships. Ships used principally for short runs were the Landing Ship Infantry,

Landing Ship Mechanized, and Landing Craft Mechanized. These landing craft were designed to be carried across the ocean on the decks of amphibious ships or inside the well-decks of the LSD. Although the LST bore the major responsibility for putting tanks and heavy equipment ashore, the LSDs carried pre-loaded vehicular weapons and engineering equipment in the landing craft that were deployed in the early stages of an opposed landing, when the LSTs (dubbed "Large Slow Targets") had to remain off the beach for safety's sake. Beginning the war with virtually no "Alligator Navy," the United States eventually produced 845 amphibious ships, 1,051 LSTs and LSDs, 1,725 intermediate-size beaching ships, and 60,148 landing craft.

If the United States became the world's master shipbuilder, the Soviet Union became its master builder of tanks, artillery pieces, and ground-attack aircraft. Although marked by the chaos and brutality characteristic of Stalin's Russia, the Soviet industrial mobilization set wartime records for the production of these weapons. What is more remarkable is that this munitions extravaganza occurred despite two successive mass evacuations of plants and people from western Russia and away from German hands. The people and materiel abandoned and surrendered reached catastrophic proportions, but, nevertheless, some 10–20 million Russians, many of them skilled industrial workers, managed to move eastward, along with the relocation of around 1,500 major plants and 1,000 minor ones. The eastward movement put the plants closer to raw materials and hydroelectric power but nearly ruined the overused Soviet railroads, which were operating at half their prewar capacity despite the Russians' Herculean efforts. At one point, the Russian steel industry's highest priority product was rails.

The perilous condition of the Russian transportation system made Allied assistance crucial. Through the Lend-Lease Program and lesser measures, the Allies sent 2,000 locomotives and 11,000 railway cars to Russia. The Red Army also received 450,000 trucks and other vehicles, which were used to close the gap between the railheads and the fighting forces. When the Red Army went on the offensive in 1943, it had to conquer the same wide distances that had confounded the Wehrmacht the year before. Trains and trucks were critical to both the retreat and the advance. The Russian transportation system was not pretty, but it worked.

The quantities of weapons the Soviets produced early in the war reflected weaknesses in their war mobilization that simple efficiency measures could not correct. The heart of the Russian dilemma was a manpower shortage caused by the Red Army's defeats of 1941–42 and the people lost to German occupation; in one two-year period the Russian work force lost 30 million people. The voracious demands of the Red Army for infantry and tank crews kept consuming skilled manpower; slave laborers and con-scripted Muslims and other minorities could hardly become dependable skilled factory workers. Consequently, the production of consumer goods virtually ceased, and Russian rural workers (drawn by the promise of food and meager wages) had to reinforce the urban work force, thus slowing any agricultural expansion. Poor factory and military repair and mainte-nance standards added to the staggering demand for heavy weapons. The operational life of an artillery piece was five months, for a tank four months, and a combat aircraft three months. The Red Army had to replace about 20 percent of its heavy weapons roughly *every month*.

Like the Soviet Union, the Third Reich continued to perform prodigious feats of munitions production well into 1944, and it too faced a dire man-power shortage; Germany ran out of trained warriors and fuels before it ran out of tanks and planes. Concurrent with this industrial effort, how-ever, Hitler also built military fortifications in Germany on a scale un-known in Europe since the demise of the Roman Empire. Most of the fortifications faced the Anglo-American air forces and armies, economy-of-force measures that allowed the deployment of mobile forces to the East-ern Front. This strategic choice reflected the Führer's confidence in Fritz Todt, a 47-year-old architect-engineer whose technical skill and manage-rial expertise equaled his taste for power and flattery. Having won Hitler's confidence prior to the war, Todt took the challenge of building the *West-wall* (also known as the Siegfried Line) on Germany's trans-Rhine frontier with France. Todt even gave his own name to the organization he formed, something only the Führer did with the Hitler Youth. Organization Todt (OT) pushed 500,000 young workers (8 percent foreign) into the task of building a 300-mile belt of fortifications in three years (1938–1941). By 1939–40 the *Westwall* was already massive enough to deter the French; and despite having been neglected in 1940–1943, the *Westwall* still posed a major barrier to the Allied armies during their invasion of Germany in 1944–45.

The *Westwall* proved to be only a preliminary for OT's greatest construc-tion project, the building of the Atlantic Wall: 1,670 miles of fortifications along the coast of the English Channel, around the ports of Normandy and Brittany, and along the Bay of Biscay. *Festung Europa* also included OT-built submarine pens, aircraft shelters, underground factories and storage areas, and shelters for the "revenge weapons," the V-1 and V-2 rockets. At its peak strength of 1.4 million workers (most of them slave laborers and pris-oners by war's end), OT continued to set records for pouring concrete. The Atlantic Wall system required 17.3 million cubic tons of concrete—equal to two-thirds of all Germany's concrete production from 1942 to 1944. In their month of peak pouring for the Atlantic Wall, April 1942, OT's workers used 2 million cubic tons of concrete.

Although Todt died in an air crash in early 1942, OT still prospered under Albert Speer, who inherited OT along with the Ministry of Armaments and Munitions, also under Todt's direction since 1940. Speer used OT to repair railroads and factories damaged by air attacks; even under bombardment, his industrial plants tripled munitions output until 1945. Native Germans performed only the industrial tasks that required loyalty and skill; all the rest was done with slave labor. OT provided a thin cadre of technical experts, planners, managers, and overseers who manipulated a captive labor force by offering minimal rations and the slight hope of survival.

The Labor of War

The main gate of the prison camp at Dachau still bears the sign "Arbeit Macht Frei" or "Work Makes Freedom." Opened in 1933 for the first prisoners of the Third Reich, Dachau lies hidden in woods only 12 miles from Munich in the heart of Bavaria, not in some distant Polish forest. The workers' barracks are gone, but the gibbets and the crematoria still stand for the curious tourist. Dachau is awful, but by the standards of the Third Reich it was practically a resort, maintained for Western Europeans, not the *Untermenschen* and *Juden* who perished by the millions in Poland. Dachau provides one of the keys to the productivity of the Third Reich. The Germans would enslave millions of Europeans and exploit their labor to underwrite German industrial production until the end of the war. Freedom had no place in the Third Reich's economic system.

On either side of the English Channel, there are memorials to other kinds of war-workers. From the Normandy coast to the Netherlands, in London and the southern ports of England, monuments celebrate the sacrifices of the Allied merchant seamen who sailed and died, most of them victims of German U-boats. Allied merchant ships that escaped the Germans, primarily Norwegian- and Dutch-flagged vessels, also joined the Allied cargo fleets that plowed the North Atlantic and other waters. Before war's end, almost 30,000 sailors on British-flagged ships (probably a third of them Asians and other nonwhites) had perished. Another 6,000 Norwegian and Dutch sailors died. Behind Utah Beach in Normandy stands a statue of a lone Norwegian sailor looking out toward the sea. He is a long way from the fiords of his native land, but he and his messmates put the Allied armies on the beaches of France.

The impulses that created Dachau and the Allied merchant marine may represent opposite poles in human values, but they represent the same desperate need to spare no worker from the insatiable demands of the war. The trend in every belligerent nation was toward compulsory labor, whether in the redirection of workers from agriculture into war industries, the recruitment of women and marginalized minorities into the main labor force, or the manipulation of rewards (including the faint promise of survival itself) to spur workers to greater productivity, regardless of the human cost. The shortage of men represented only one source of social strain. Keeping the munitions factories running day and night meant moving workers of both sexes from place to place within their native lands (and often out of them), the disruption of family lives, a rise in alcoholism and sexually transmitted diseases, the near-collapse of public school systems as youths went into the work force or took to the streets, and the increase of theft and black-marketeering. Propagandists for the Allies might wax rhapsodic about their righteous cause, but even their war effort required governmental intrusion into people's lives on an unprecedented scale.

The German economic mobilization depended on three factors: (1) Nazi Party supervision, (2) travel and occupational controls on the native German labor force, and (3) the exploitation of slave laborers and prisoners of war by Heinrich Himmler's Reich Security Main Office (RSHA). Also under Himmler's control, the Gestapo became the dominant instrument of law enforcement and repression in Germany and the occupied countries and thus provided close supervision over the entire work force. At full mobilization in 1944, the Third Reich's work force numbered 29 million native Germans (half of whom were women), supplemented by more than 5 million imported slave laborers, the majority of whom were Russian and Polish young women, and nearly 2 million prisoners of war, the largest group of whom were Russians.

The German work force fell under the supervision of the German Labor Front (DAF) and the Reich Foodstuffs Corporation; about 36 million people of many nationalities worked under these two agencies, which took their directions from Albert Speer. The supervisors were almost exclusively members of the Nazi Party, whose membership increased from 4 million in 1939 to 6.5 million in 1945. By the war's end, joining the Nazis became less a matter of ideological conversion than access to scarce jobs and essential commodities: Nazi Party members received food and medical supplies denied others in Germany, including the army.

In Japan, the burden of war was light until 1944; but during that year, defeats abroad and attacks by submarines and bombers squeezed the Japanese labor force to produce more with fewer skilled male workers, who now went into the armed forces (as did college students) in larger numbers. Although the wartime work force did not increase much beyond the prewar 28 million, the changing make-up of the work force led to declining productivity; the shortages of workers brought an increasing number of unmarried young women, aging farmers, and unskilled and unhealthy youths into Japan's factories, while labor-intensive agriculture absorbed more than a million workers. The industrial work force included more than 800,000 Koreans. Married, middle-class Japanese women were spared from paid war work, but the Greater Japan Women's Association (1942) organized these women for volunteer work, civil defense duties, and paramilitary training. The Imperial Rule Assistance Association, reinforced by a million neighborhood associations, provided an administrative structure for social control and basic human services, channeling the communal self-discipline of the Japanese for wartime purposes. If protest and resistance seemed a problem, the government had ample authority to dictate economic employment and social behavior, and it controlled several civil and military police agencies that felt no restraints in imposing the Imperial Way.

Eventually, however, the stress of war came close to dissolving Japan's social cohesion. During the American bombing of 1944–45, the Japanese work force in Tokyo, Osaka, and other major cities had to move to find shelter, food, and safety for children and the aged. Refugees numbered 2–3 million by 1945. The Special High Police (Tokkotai), which enforced conformity, obedience, and reverence for Imperial institutions, reported to the Home Ministry that seditious opinions had flowered like the cherry blossoms—and had the same color. Obsessed with the threat of Communist revolution, the Special High Police found prerevolutionary attitudes far too common in the industrial work force. Despite their hard-handed repression of dissidents, the police could not stop growing absenteeism, workplace violence, worker flight from the cities to search for food, and a flood of underground graffiti and pamphleteering. The police blamed it on Chinese and Korean revolutionaries; but in truth, a significant minority of the Japanese people had lost confidence in the Imperial Way. One aristocrat in the peace faction reported with alarm a bit of doggerel he had heard a drunken worker sing on a Tokyo trolley:

> They started a war
> they were bound to lose
> Say we'll win, we'll win

> The big fools
> Look, we're bound to lose
> The war is lost
> and Europe's turned Red
> Turning Asia Red
> Can be done before breakfast
> And when that time comes
> Out I'll come.[3]

Outside the Home Islands, Asian conscript laborers and POWs strengthened the Japanese war effort. Most of these captive workers remained close to the mines and ore pits where they worked and far away from the scarce Japanese rice supply. The number of Asians (less the Koreans) who labored under compulsion abroad was estimated at over a million. About 20,000 Commonwealth and American POWs were eventually moved to the Home Islands as workers to keep them away from potential liberators. Like all other slave laborers, they suffered under a regime of treatment based on an old Japanese military concept for slave laborers: *ikasazu, korasazu* or "Don't let them live, don't let them die."

For Britain, the war brought "the best of times, the worst of times," to use Charles Dickens's phrase. In terms of national solidarity, the British set the standard for the Allies; more than half its population of 47 million served in the armed forces (around 5 million) or in essential industrial or agricultural jobs (21 million). British women filled in the work force, adding 1.5 million first-time workers by 1945 and moving from service jobs into heavy industry in unprecedented numbers. The proportion of women in the work force was around 38 percent, lower than the percentage of women working in Germany but about the same as the United States. The remaining portion of the population was divided among children, the aged, and the "unemployed" half of British women who split their time between volunteer work and caring for those that needed care. A report of 1944 captures the extent of the pressures that weighed on the British people:

> The British Citizen has had five years of blackout and four years of intermittent blitz. The privacy of his home has been periodically invaded by soldiers or evacuees or war workers requiring billets. In five years of drastic labor mobilization, nearly every man and woman under fifty without young children has been subject to direction to work, often far from home. The hours of work average fifty-three for men and fifty overall; when work is done, every citizen who is not excused for reasons of family circumstances . . . has had to do forty-eight hours a month in the Home

Guard or Civil Defense. Supplies of all kind have been progressively limited by shipping and manpower shortage; the queue is part of normal life. Taxation is probably the severest in the world, and is coupled with continuous pressure to save. The scarce supplies, both of goods and services, must be shared with hundreds of thousands of United States, Dominion, and Allied troops; in the preparation of Britain first as the base and then as the bridgehead, the civilian has inevitably suffered hardships spread over almost every aspect of his daily life.[4]

The war blurred British class distinctions, allowed unprecedented government regulation ("war socialism"), and gave the Celtic minority unusual access to skilled and managerial jobs. Even though the government received broad authority in the Emergency Powers (Defense) Act of 1940, it avoided repression by stimulating public participation in the war with a sense of shared risk and deprivation (aided by the Luftwaffe) and the influence of 10 million civil defense and Home Guard volunteers upon community life.

The British media and entertainment world became virtually an extension of the war cabinet for raising public morale. The British sang their way through the war, preferring "Doing the Lambeth Walk" to "Land of Hope and Glory." The British developed a tolerance for economic regulation and a civil service of over 2 million members. They also developed a faith that government economic intervention would provide more social services at bearable cost after the war. The ordeal of the British probably fell somewhere between the best and the worst that could be expected, largely because they escaped hostile occupation and muddled through with their historic capacity for enjoying the little things of life.

In terms of relative deprivation, the Americans gained most and lost least in their industrial mobilization. World War II provided individuals and families of virtually every social position and ethnic background new opportunities for employment and material accumulation, even if the latter had to be deferred. From 1939 to 1945 the United States increased its annual gross national product from $91 billion to $166 billion, and all indices of its industrial productivity doubled. The American work force added 14 million workers in a total population of 130 million; men and women who during the Depression had never been able to find a job replaced the 16 million workers who served in the armed forces. By 1946, 48 million Americans paid federal income tax, whereas only 7.8 million had done so in 1940.

Of the 54 million working Americans, only 8 million participated directly in war work. The government's caution about creating a large armed force at the expense of industry and farming, combined with its generous definitions of dependency and essential occupations, meant that the Roosevelt administration could keep adult males in two-thirds of all U.S. jobs. Like their British counterparts, women escaped from menial service jobs to higher-paying defense jobs and added 5 million more workers to the total work force. Recent European immigrants and African-Americans made impressive employment gains; large-scale farm producers persuaded the government to import 220,000 Mexican farm laborers *(braceros)*, and more than 100,000 Mexicans eventually entered the American armed forces. The only U.S. group to suffer severe economic loss during the war was the interned Japanese-Americans, who lost jobs and property assessed later to be worth $350 million in 1942.

Even though the United States spent almost $350 billion on its war effort, about 60 percent of its economic activity went into long-term capital investment, industrial infrastructure expansion (especially in electricity), and consumer production. Through governmental controls and incentives, American wages increased 68 percent while the cost of living rose only 23 percent. The people of the United States enjoyed an *increase* of domestic consumption during World War II, which helps explain why it remains "the good war" in the American historical imagination. Every other major belligerent consumed more than half of its economic productivity to fight the war, and for Germany and Russia the cost of the conflict was even higher. Only the United States emerged from World War II stronger in both absolute and relative terms than it was when it entered the war.

The effect of the war on American society cannot be captured in a few economic indicators, although gains in income and savings were real enough. Internal immigration toward the war industries on both coasts and in the traditional northern industrial cities set the stage for a new and often unhappy era in race relations that could not be solved by increases in family incomes. Three major groups found themselves in unwanted closeness at the factory worksite and in housing: dispossessed Anglo-American country folk, southern and eastern European immigrants, and African-American tenant farmers. All three groups were largely rural and held strong communal values; none found it easy to adjust to an urban life of limited housing, few satisfactory services, confusing business and personal relationships, high prices, and easy victimization at work or on the streets. The American labor movement moved reluctantly to use the unions as a means of social assimilation. The American Federation of Labor (AFL) still had an elitist, high-skill organizational bias, and the Congress of Industrial

Organization (CIO) faced the continued hostility of Big Steel and the auto industry as well as the new workers' dislike for regimentation of any sort.

The potential for American social disruption during the war—devoutly predicted by Adolf Hitler—remained real enough until VJ-Day (Victory over Japan Day). The labor movement walked a thin line between respectability and public condemnation. Since strikes were never outlawed in wartime America, labor leaders such as John L. Lewis of the United Mine Workers could bluster about striking and actually order his workers out, as he did several times in 1942 and 1943. Other war industries experienced work stoppages, too, although intervention by the National War Labor Board usually shortened the walk-outs. Nevertheless, the United States lost 36 million man-hours from strikes during the war. The heart of the problem could not be denied: inequities in the distribution of wealth. Corporate profits after taxes increased even more rapidly than wages.

The tension in the labor movement was exacerbated by racial tension in wartime cities, often rooted in clashes between African-American servicemen and workers and their white counterparts. Detroit, for example, became home for 500,000 black migrants during the period 1940–1943. In 1943 alone, racial violence flared in states as widely separated as Michigan, New York, Massachusetts, Texas, and California. Keenly aware that the migration of southern blacks to the North and the politicization of the new immigrants would add strength to the Democratic Party, FDR and his party chieftains had no stomach for cracking down on unrest but left the task to local authorities, who bore the onus of urban peace-keeping. But while the war increased social strife in some sectors, it weakened division in others. Anti-Semitism and anti-Catholicism faded in the armed forces and workplace except among the most violent bigots.

Probably the most corrosive effect of the war on American society stemmed simply from the strain of long working hours, occupational hazards in mining and heavy industry, urban crowding, and the boom-town living around military bases and large industrial complexes. Relations between women and men showed special strain. Although the divorce rate remained about the same in the 1940s, the incidence of sexually transmitted diseases, unwanted pregnancies, and extramarital sexual relations dramatically increased among young people who escaped family and community supervision, had money to spend on unrationed carnal experiences, and found ample chances to celebrate the end of Prohibition. As policemen and social workers already knew, liquor fueled violence and sexual appetites. On the other hand, many women welcomed escape from the drudgery of housework and the pressures of motherhood, assisted by prepacked frozen foods and a government-supported child daycare program.

The accelerated shift in gender relations that occurred during the war is captured in a letter Edith Speert of Cleveland, Ohio, wrote her soldier-husband in 1945: "I'm not exactly the same girl you left. I'm twice as independent as I used to be and to top it off, I sometimes think I've become hard as nails—hardly anyone can evoke any sympathy from me. I've been living exactly as *I* want to live and I do as I damn please. You are not married to a girl that's interested solely in the home. I shall definitely have to work all my life. I get emotional satisfaction out of working; I don't doubt that many a night you will cook supper while I'm at a meeting. Also, dearest, I shall never wash and iron—there are laundries for that!"[5]

Until the great campaigns in Europe and the Pacific in 1944, American casualties did not cast a pall on the Home Front population, and victory followed soon enough to prevent the nation from feeling the losses of the war as intensely as all the other belligerents did for years to come. Still, aware of the stark difference between the experience of its servicemen, especially the combat veterans, and the general public, Congress rushed to pass a GI Bill in June 1944 to provide educational benefits and other veterans programs to dampen postwar grievances against those who had profited from war work. Two-thirds of American veterans used their educational benefits and repaid the $4 billion investment four times over with their increased income taxes.

Among the Allies, the burden of war fell most heavily on the Soviet Union. For all its heroic industrial effort and the staggering mobilization and deaths in its armed forces (at least 11 million of the 30 million who served), the Soviet Union still fought the war as an imperial confederation divided against itself and consumed with a distrust that mocked the ideals of Karl Marx. The nationality division was real enough: only 58 percent of Soviet citizens were Russians. In the disaster of 1941, Stalin blamed everyone but himself, and he unleashed Lavrenti P. Beria's NKVD on the army and the people. By year's end, more than 2 million Soviets had been imprisoned in the slave labor camps of the NKVD's Main Administration of Camps (Gulag). Tens of thousands of deserters, stragglers, and discredited officers died in front of firing parties and executioners.

The director of the People's Commissariat of Armament, General B. L. Vannikov, knew the capricious nature of Stalinist defense policy from personal experience. He found himself in prison for disagreeing with Stalin's crony, A. A. Zhdanov, who supported Stalin's preference for an antiquated tank gun and Stalin's cancellation of two crucial artillery production programs. Two weeks later, the Germans began Operation Barbarossa. Panic-stricken officials and military officers stampeded to Vannikov's cell, asking for his advice on production problems and factory removal "despite the fact that I was in solitary confinement in a maximum security prison and had been accused of all grievous crimes."[6] Released without explanation in July 1941, Vannikov returned to his post as ordnance czar of the Soviet Union and became one of the most decorated managers of the Russian war effort.

When Stalin learned that thousands of citizens of the Baltic states and Ukraine had welcomed the Germans as liberators—and some had joined paramilitary groups that served German purposes—he deepened the repression of all untrustworthy ethnic groups (like many of the Cossack clans) and Asian minorities in the central Soviet republics. More than two million minority Soviets—Volga-Germans, Balts, Chechens, Turks, Armenians, Tartars, and Georgians—found themselves in workers barracks or miserable refugee camps. Stalin had reason for such fears, since Slavs and Muslims formed eight Waffen SS divisions. Sheer desperation forced Stalin in 1942 to reconsider his repression. Though every significant policy-making body remained under his personal leadership, including the armed forces and the general staff, Stalin suddenly discovered the power of Mother Russia to mobilize the masses; he ordered his people to show the same dedication and sacrifice that had repulsed Napoleon in 1812.

The short holiday from Communism that followed produced major reforms throughout the Soviet war effort. Professional military commanders received greater freedom from supervision by their political officers; Stalin's military deputy became Marshal Georgi Zhukov, an outspoken professional officer of great skill and drive and even more dangerous ambition. Victims of the purges of the late 1930s could not be reinstated since they were dead, but their families and kin could be rehabilitated and allowed to rejoin the army and state economic organizations. Almost a million Russians left the Gulag to fight the war. Some of the restored Russians later led the attack on Stalinism and undermined the Soviet Union in the 1980s.

Stalin ordered his propagandists to sell the Great Patriotic War. He encouraged the Russians to fight a holy war to prevent the extermination of all Slavs everywhere, and he even restored some of the Orthodox Church's autonomy. Authors and artists turned their considerable talents to patriotic themes. Sergei Prokofiev and Dmitri Shostakovich produced music that rivaled Tchaikovsky's for its Russian fervor. On film, the war brought new meaning to past wars against the Germans, the most memorable being

Sergei Eisenstein's *Alexander Nevsky,* an epic in which the Muscovite militia slaughters the Teutonic Knights to a score by Prokofiev.

As soon as the fortunes of war shifted for the Red Army in 1943, Stalin rebuilt his police state and the Communist Party, which had lapsed into passivity at the grassroots level. As the Red Army returned to western provinces of the Soviet Union, the NKVD and other special police screened the liberated populations for collaboration and executed or deported people with any taint of anti-Stalinism. The Red Army provided a haven for superficial Communists, but not for anti-Fascist partisans, who were often rewarded with execution and imprisonment because they had tasted the heady wine of popular resistance to oppression and had, therefore, become "enemies of the people." This policy continued when the Red Army entered Poland and Germany's erstwhile allies such as Hungary, Romania, and Bulgaria. Within Germany proper, everyone qualified as a Fascist worthy of extermination, and survival became more capricious than death for Germans caught by the Red Army.

Women in Warfare

Victims of war since the dawn of history, the women of Europe, North America, and northern Asia passed from noncombatant status to warworkers and then into direct military service in World War II to an unforeseen degree. In World War I, women worked only as civilian volunteers, workers, nurses, and paramilitary auxiliaries. Senior military officers, regardless of nationality, shared common assumptions about the role of women in war: they should not be in uniform in the first place, but they might have service and clerical skills that would free male soldiers for field duty. Given their experience in the civilian telecommunications industry, women could play a similar role in the military communications systems. In navies, women in the shore establishment would free male sailors for sea duty; and in air forces, women could perform technical tasks on the ground that would conserve male members for flight duty. No regular military establishment in 1939 anticipated that women would play a major role in a future war or that they would ever participate in combat.

World War II confounded the prophets on the future of women in modern warfare. For one thing, bombs did not discriminate by gender, and the political leadership of the belligerents, however conservative they all were on women's roles, had to admit that strategic bombing had rendered the question of special protection of women moot. The international laws and practices that encouraged soldiers not to rape and murder women (nine-teenth-century concessions to the quaint notion of "civilized" warfare) could hardly be applied to bombardiers. Another major change was the concept of racial warfare or genocide, first practiced by the Japanese in China and the Germans in Poland and Russia. If the annihilation of whole peoples had become an expressed purpose of war, then women as the po-tential bearers of "undesirable" offspring took on special strategic signi-ficance. The last factor was the changed attitudes of women themselves. Hardened by the struggles for political rights and socioeconomic assistance from the state, women understood that wartime participation, especially in uniform and in traditionally male roles, might advance the cause of women's rights in the postwar era. This attitude was held not only in Brit-ain and the United States but in revolutionary Russia as well.

The United States and the British Commonwealth nations created uni-formed women's branches for each of their services and recruited women as nurses (but very few as doctors) for their medical services. The British maintained a separate nursing corps, but the United States allowed the army and army air forces to create one nursing corps and the navy another to serve sailors and marines in naval hospitals. American female nurses (commissioned as officers) numbered 74,000; the officers and enlisted per-sonnel of each service auxiliary numbered 330,000. About 5 percent of these women served overseas, and about 30 women died from enemy ac-tion. Although denied official military status, the U.S. Women's Airforce Service Pilots (WASP) allowed women to become ferry pilots; about 1,000 women qualified as WASPs and proved that women had a future as com-mercial and military aviators—provided they could get men to accept not just their flying skills but their ability to command male subordinates from the left seat.

Britain also depended on volunteerism to fill its women's auxiliaries, but the low response convinced Parliament to pass a law in December 1941 that required unmarried young women to join up, although they could go into a war industry, civil defense, or full-time Home Guard positions as well as the armed services. Under this law, the British women's service compo-nents expanded to a wartime high of 470,000. Women made up about 10 percent of the British armed forces, a proportion five times larger than their American sisters. As participants in the British air defense system, British servicewomen were particularly vulnerable to enemy action, and more than 700 of them died in uniform while others perished as fire-fighters and air-raid wardens.

Despite the Nazis' conservatism about women's roles, all the German armed forces and the SS recruited women for their auxiliary services or Helferinnen. Wehrmacht regulations prohibited women from bearing arms, but in 1944 the Luftwaffe's ground-based flak system accepted 100,000 single women called up for military duty. Most of them were assigned to communications billets, thus releasing Luftwaffe ground airmen for combat duty in Russia, but some died serving flak guns. Women who joined the army and navy did so primarily as nurses and secretaries. The exception was a women's communications organization. The SS Helferinnen not only performed administrative duties but served as supervisors and guards of women in concentration camps. Some of these SS guards matched their male counterparts in sadism and, at the war's end, in imprisonment and execution for war crimes—a dubious achievement in the cause of equal treatment for women.

In the crisis of 1941–42, the Soviet armed forces turned to Russian women to fill their savaged ranks, and eventually 400,000 women served in the Red Army as tank crewmen, artillery and anti-aircraft gunners, snipers, combat fighter pilots, and light bomber pilots and aircrew. An additional 400,000 worked in a wide range of supporting services such as drivers, mechanics, clerks, and medical personnel. Although statistics about service in Soviet-sponsored guerrilla units are elusive, perhaps one in five partisans (200,000 of one million) was a woman. The basic rationale for female service in the Soviet forces was the same as it was in the Western Allied nations: women replaced men who could go to frontline tank and infantry units. Largely for propaganda purposes, the Soviets allowed the creation of three all-female aviation regiments and a few all-female ground combat units, but most Russian women served in integrated units. The Soviet Navy fulfilled its propaganda role by putting female sailors on a handful of auxiliary vessels. Russian women had little future in the "no quarter" warfare of the Eastern Front, and they reciprocated German brutality, as described, for example, in Willi Heinrich's autobiographical war novel, *Cross of Iron*, where Russian women seek revenge for sexual assaults by German soldiers with appropriate countermeasures.

Women combatants also emerged as leaders and killers in the resistance movements that challenged the German occupation of Western Europe and on and behind the Eastern Front. Polish women fought and perished in the two Warsaw uprisings of 1943 and 1944, and Tito's Communist partisans in Yugoslavia included 100,000 women soldiers, of whom 25,000 died. For Western Europe, the French Resistance (Communist or Free

French) offers a good example of the range of activities women played in the war of subversion against the Third Reich, roles duplicated on a smaller scale in Belgium, the Netherlands, Denmark, and Norway.

Until the two invasions of France in 1944, the French Resistance tried to avoid direct combat with the Wehrmacht and German intelligence-police agencies, both to survive and to follow the guidance from the Anglo-American SOE/OSS headquarters in England and the Gaullist Bureau Central de Renseignements et d'Action (BCRA). The Allied intelligence effort needed information, not sabotage or guerrilla warfare. The Allies also wanted some sort of escape system that would return downed airmen. As the French intelligence and escape networks *(réseaux)* grew, women, who probably made up 20 percent of the 150,000 network members, took over leadership roles because of their proven competence. The escape networks rescued 5,000 Allied airmen and 1,600 other servicemen, while French intelligence cells provided crucial information for the invasion planners on the status of fortifications and the Wehrmacht order-of-battle that would not have been revealed in Ultra intercepts. Certainly the Abwehr and Gestapo appreciated the internal threat, for their agents and Vichyite collaborators pursued the French operatives with vigor and cruelty. The Germans executed 200–300 French women for resistance activities, and they sent around 8,500 suspected resistance workers to the female concentration camp at Ravensbrück. Of this group of women, only about 400 survived the war.

French women also participated as both leaders and rank-and-file guerrillas in the Forces Françaises de l'Intérieur (FFI) and the Communist Franc-Tireurs et Partisans. Identified as the *maquis,* the French partisans took the field in 1944 with a vengeance, and with women in conspicuous roles. Two leading FFI chieftains, for example, were women. Women fighters participated in guerrilla operations in northern France that accompanied the Normandy invasion and joined the partisan bands in the Paris uprising in August 1944. Women *maquisards* fought and died in the Massif Central and the Haute Savoy in the uprisings of March–July 1944. For these guerrillas as well as the members of the escape and intelligence *réseaux* and the women who wrote and published the major clandestine newspapers, the legacy was the grant of full suffrage in the French Constitution of 1946 and a permanent place in the French armed forces.

Women served in less dramatic but dangerous roles as well. Sheer survival in occupied countries pushed women into virtual concubinage as the "girl friends" of occupying soldiers, the only people with reliable access to food and the basics of daily living. Caught between the flow of battle in 1944, for example, French women had to switch loyalties rapidly if they had been consorts to Germans; only GIs were likely to protect them from the retribution of the resistance. Every army except the United States took a relaxed attitude toward organized prostitution; the Free French colonial troops and the Japanese even took their bordellos with them from post to post. In the case of the Japanese, the Imperial Army simply conscripted 200,000 *ianfu* or "comfort women" from Korea, China, the Philippines, and Malaya to indulge its sexual samurai. Although military prostitutes might get some medical care, if only to prevent them from infecting their soldier-clients, they were especially vulnerable not only to sexually transmitted diseases but other contagious diseases, violence, starvation, and various forms of mistreatment.

As workers, farm laborers, and military personnel, the women of the world in 1937–1945 found themselves in the middle of a conflict created by the male-dominated political systems of their respective nations. Larger participation in politics did not encourage pacifism, as feminists now and then have argued, since women showed just as much chauvinism and aggressiveness as their male peers when they had a chance to mete out violence and not just endure it. Yet the women of World War II were doomed to suffer more violence than they caused. The available statistics on the strategic bombing of Great Britain, Germany, and Japan, for example, suggest that more than half the 1.3 million fatalities were women. The same division of death probably applies to the 15 million Russian civilians who perished. Another telling statistic is the world relief agencies' estimated number of European orphans in 1945: 13 million children survived the war without a living parent. With the coming of mass, industrialized warfare, culminating in the creation of nuclear weapons, no one could assume that he or she could avoid being part of any war. As a legacy of World War II, everyone became a potential warrior or victim.

20

THE
AFTERMATH
OF WAR

World War II was the most undiscriminating destroyer of peoples and re-sources in modern history. It is impossible to travel in Europe and Asia and not find memorials and mass gravesites for the civilian dead of World War II, whether one stands in Volkovo Cemetery in St. Petersburg, Russia, or before the soaring cenotaph built in memory of the Singaporean Chinese executed by the Japanese. Under the shadow of the Industry Promotion Hall in Hiroshima, one of the most photographed ruins of the war, one finds the grass-shrouded mounds of the mass graves from the first nuclear explosion. Whole nations bled and burned.

Fifty years of study by a legion of demographers have produced only esti-mates of civilian losses for the war years, 1937–1945, but this much is known: World War II killed at least twice as many innocents as soldiers, of whom at least 21 million died. The Axis states lost more than 3 million ci-vilians, and the Allies at least 35 million, more than 28 million of whom were Russians and Chinese. (Some Russian and Chinese demographers now put their combined civilian dead at over 40 million.) Any such calcu-lations are heavily Eurocentric; only Japan of the Asian belligerents made a careful study of its civilian losses, and the Japanese probably understated theirs (at 350,000 dead) in the name of postwar harmony with the United States. Imperfect though they are, these chilling statistics capture the es-sential truth of the war: no one was immune from death in its most wretched forms.

The worst single killer was the German concentration camp and slave la-bor system, in which at least 12 million people perished. Of these victims, 6 million were European Jews, deported from every occupied and Axis country in Europe for the purpose of ethnic cleansing and, in the last years of the war, genocide. The other victims were slave laborers gathered by the Germans from throughout Europe to work on construction projects and in factories until starvation and disease took their toll. Strategic bombing inflicted another 1.5 to 2 million deaths in Germany, Japan, France, and Great Britain—a horrible enough number, but smaller than the number of civilian deaths inflicted by the Wehrmacht as it rolled across Eastern Europe. During the 1939–1943 campaigns in Poland and Russia, over 2 million civilians died as victims of military operations and the repression by the German occupation forces, who killed resisters, local leaders, hostages, and bystanders.

The Soviet armies took their revenge during the last two years of the war, killing a comparable number of German civilians, at least 1.5 million. So terrible was the Red Army's vengeance as it swept westward that Germany actually *gained* 8–10 million new citizens in the war's last year and in the immediate postwar period. Even in defeat, however, the Axis powers could not stake a claim to greater suffering. Twice as many Jews died in the Holocaust as did Axis civilians from all causes. Among nation-states, Poland can justifiably claim that the Wehrmacht brought its people (of all religious persuasions) close to the brink of extinction. From its prewar population of 34 million, Poland lost over 6 million people to the German war machine. An additional 10 million Poles were deported or fled, and only 1.5 million of them returned to their homeland after the war. Many of those who did not return had died in slave labor or concentration camps. Of the 8 to 9 million war-related deaths among civilians in occupied Asia, hundreds of thousands were Chinese massacred by the Japanese in the 1937–1942 period. Chinese and other Asians who were worked to death in Japanese slave-labor projects throughout the Greater East Asian Co-Prosperity Sphere certainly numbered in the hundreds of thousands.

As the Chinese example shows, defining "war-related" deaths is not easy, and it is especially problematic in dealing with deaths from diseases, whether caused by epidemics or malnutrition. In the Soviet Union and much of China, for example, the rural populations in the 1920s and 1930s had already been ravaged by disease and starvation-related deaths, due in no small measure to the malevolence of Stalin's regime and the Chinese warlords. Interstate warfare certainly deepened the population's misery, but their preexisting condition makes it difficult to construct a firm number for war-related deaths. In nations like Britain and Germany, where the population was healthy at the beginning of the war, the distinction between deaths from disease and deaths from war-related causes like bombing and naval blockade is much clearer. In Britain, food rationing and evacuation of cities made disease-related fatalities negligible. In Germany, the Nazi Party's policy of caring for ethnic Germans while allowing everyone else to starve postponed malnutrition-related deaths among the German population until 1945 and the immediate postwar period. Among the worst sufferers from this policy were the Dutch, who spent the catastrophic winter of 1944–45 under German occupation. At least 16,000 Netherlanders died of starvation that winter, in a nation of only 9 million that had already lost almost 200,000 people to bombing by both sides and to incarceration by the Third Reich.

The slaughter of civilians in World War II reflected changes in military technology and the capacity of twentieth-century nation-states to direct their vast resources toward waging mass, industrialized warfare. The specter of "total war," glimpsed in the last two years of World War I, moved from the imaginative fiction of Jules Verne and H. G. Wells into wretched reality after 1937. The technology of warfare, especially the refinement of aerial attack, made it possible to strike concentrated civilian populations in industrialized cities, refugee-swollen transportation centers, and agricultural villages. The ordnance that could wreak havoc on civilians came in more varied forms than just high explosives; civilians perished from poison gases, bacteriological agents, and incendiary bombs of white phosphorus and jellied gasoline (napalm). The effects of the two atomic bombs dropped on the Japanese combined all the horrors of high explosives, incendiaries, and chemical-induced cellular collapse. Among survivors, radiation also produced genetic damage in children yet unborn.

Strategic bombing did not exhaust the ways that modern warfare could destroy the fabric of civil society. Whether engaged in battle or occupation, mass armies routinely leveled buildings, wrecked machinery, slaughtered farm animals, confiscated vehicles and fuels, stripped foodstuffs from fields and shelves, monopolized hospitals, disrupted electric systems, and destroyed sewage and water works. Modern armies did not invent these methods of depopulating whole countries, but the efficiency of military ordnance and transportation systems brought genocide within the realm of the possible. While one might rationalize the death of innocents as an unavoidable consequence of attacking the economic infrastructure of the enemy, as the British and Americans did, there was nothing unavoidable about the creation of the thousands of slave labor camps and 20 extermination factories that dotted the countryside throughout the German Reich and its occupied territories—a demonstration in the starkest terms of how the technology of modern civilizations can facilitate a descent into barbarism.

Modern military capability alone does not explain the slaughter of innocents in World War II. Germany's postwar protestations notwithstanding, for much of the German population the destruction of European Jewry had deep roots in fantasies cultivated since the Middle Ages that Jews were responsible for Germany's repeated failure to assume its rightful place of power in Europe. The imputed offenses of the Jews ranged from economic exploitation and financial manipulation to cultural depravity. These racist ideas were not confined to Germany but were pervasive in other countries that capitulated to or collaborated with the Third Reich, countries like France, Switzerland, and Yugoslavia. Although religious persecution of many faiths had a long history in Europe, heretics did not lose their human status in the eyes of their oppressors, who usually afforded their victims the option of salvation through recantation. In secular genocide, by contrast, the perpetrators' first act was to reduce their victims to nonhuman status as a justification for their slaughter—an intellectual fusion of social Darwinism, crackpot genetics, and racialism in its worst form with the politics of the mob. A preoccupation with ethnic characteristics and a tendency to attribute behavior to inherited and immutable racial genetics made it much easier for the Nazi Party to see genocide as merely social engineering and to sell that vision to ordinary Germans through its propaganda machine. But as the Japanese had already proved in China, the Nazis had no monopoly on rationalizations for their policies of military aggression, occupation, and murder.

Anti-Semitism and anti-Communism fused in the twentieth century to widen the categories of intolerable minorities to be eradicated. Resisters in Nazi Germany, Fascist Italy, and the occupied countries all got similar treatment at the hands of the Gestapo and its national police collaborators. The status "enemy of the regime" was not confined to the Axis powers in Europe, however. All the belligerent governments, especially Russia, were keenly aware that the armed forces in the field could not function without the economic productivity of their civilian populations. So governments could hardly ignore dissent, real or imagined, that might undermine civilian morale by calling into question the government's distinction of friend from foe. The result was an assault on the life and liberty of civilians everywhere, including the United States, which imprisoned 110,000 Japanese immigrants and Japanese-American citizens for most of the war and ruined them financially. It also detained or exchanged 14,000 enemy aliens from Europe (Germans, Italians, Hungarians, Bulgarians, and Romanians) from a potential pool of almost 1 million suspects—a ratio which suggests a racial double standard.

Although the civilian deaths of World War II reflected the war's egalitarian horror, the military fatalities cut deeply into a second generation of European males and gave Japan unprecedented losses. The Axis powers lost 8 million service personnel—Germany almost 5 million and Japan 2 million dead, with the six other co-belligerents and Fascist auxiliaries accounting for the balance. Italy lost 200,000 servicemen as an Axis power and 100,000 soldiers and partisans as an ally after 1943. On the Allied side, the Soviet Union lost at least 11 million soldiers; recent estimates add 1 or 2 million more. Nationalist China's armies suffered an estimated 2.5 million killed. Britain, Yugoslavia, the United States, France, and Czechoslovakia each had between 250,000 and 300,000 servicemen die from enemy action. Poland followed with 123,000, and the other Allies lost another 125,000 dead to Axis arms. In proportion, the Allies lost twice as many service personnel as the Axis, with the Russians alone losing more soldiers than all the Axis nations combined.

Of all the military establishments that fought World War II, the Red Army was the most dangerous in which to serve, the American armed forces the least. The Wehrmacht occupied the second-deadliest position. An estimated 25 million men and women served in the Soviet armed forces, and 11–13 million died in uniform. Of the nearly 16 million who served in the American armed forces, 405,399 persons died during their service, 291,557 directly from enemy action. Of the 18 million Germans and other nationalities who served the Nazi cause, 6 million died. In terms of military functions in ground warfare, infantry and tank crewmen suffered disproportionate casualties, but the growth of importance in naval and air warfare created new categories of mortality for service personnel. The German submarine service lost (killed or missing) 32,000 of the 38,000 officers and men it sent into war against Allied commerce; the airmen of the RAF Bomber Command and the U.S. Army Air Forces strategic bomber force proved only slightly less vulnerable. Bomber Command lost almost half of its aircrewmen (60,000 of 125,000), and the U.S. Eighth Air Force lost 18,000 pilots and aircrewmen killed in the war against Germany, with an additional 7,000 deaths in training and operational mishaps from an aircrew strength of 210,000 (1942–1945). Only after mid-1944 could the majority of Eighth Air Force bomber crews expect to complete 25 missions—the magic number for rotation home.

Postwar Europe

In summer 1945, Europe could only be described, in Winston Churchill's elegant prose, as "a rubble heap, a charnel house, a breeding ground of pestilence and hate."[1] Europe also had become a continent of disoriented and demoralized people on the move. An estimated 50 million people found themselves in places they had not known in 1939; 16 million were "displaced persons," a euphemism that covered refugees and forced laborers wandering outside their homelands. Although the Western Europeans generally wanted to return to their traditional homes, many Eastern Europeans (especially the million or so Jewish survivors) and Russians (meaning all those the Soviets claimed as citizens) did not. According to an agreement made at Yalta, the Western Allies promised to return anyone who might be classified (without much care) as a Russian, especially those who had served in the Wehrmacht. Using force when necessary, American and British troops placed more than 2 million Russian military prisoners and civilians on ships and trains bound for the Soviet Union; the British rounded up 44,000 Cossacks in Austria and Italy and shipped them off to certain death as "enemies of the people." In all, something like 6 million Russians returned, willingly or not, to the Soviet Union; Soviet sources later estimated that 10 percent of the repatriated Russians were executed as traitors, 20 percent were cleared and released, and 70 percent went straight to labor camps for political education and work that would make them free, provided they survived years of captivity.

Fearing the wrath of the Red Army and a future likely to be dominated by the Soviets' political allies, the Germans who lived outside Germany (*Volksdeutsch*), Poles, Latvians, Estonians, Lithuanians, Hungarians, Croats, Slovenes, and Romanians flooded into the Allied occupation zones of Germany and Austria until probably 6 million refugees joined the displaced persons (DPs) already in Germany. As the Soviet occupation forces placed hard hands on the people, property, food, and political power they found in Eastern Europe, more Poles, Czechs, and Slovaks headed west. French DPs headed back to France, but officials of the United Nations Refugee Administration estimated that 20 percent of the French population would emigrate if jobs became available elsewhere. Although the United States eventually accepted 200,000 DPs (after 1948) and Canada and Australia welcomed comparable numbers, most of the DPs remained in Europe, an added burden to prostrate societies. Most of the surviving Jews headed for Palestine.

Like the Soviet Union, Germany had lost more than half of its homes, factories, transportation system, and agricultural production. Its great cities lay in ruins, with corpses buried beneath the rubble, while survivors, in the grasp of starvation and illness, stumbled through the streets. Almost 6 million German soldiers surrendered to the Allies in 1945, preferring American to Russian captors. In one case the Americans immediately served justice by turning the SS 3rd Panzer Division (Totenkopf) leaders over to the Soviets after their surrender. In the initial weeks of peace, British and American commanders were happy to use German military organizations themselves to maintain order and discipline. The Germans obeyed, even shooting a number of their own soldiers foolish enough to declare themselves socialists or Communists.

One family's story—a lucky family at that—provides some insight into the postwar chaos. Returning to his native Luxembourg after 14 years as an immigrant to the United States, First Lieutenant John E. Dolibois, a military intelligence officer and German-language interrogator, arrived in May 1945 to find everything and everyone in his home town of Bonnevoie "worn, drab, abysmally poor, despondent." Although his official assignment was to question the highest-ranking Nazi war criminals, his personal mission was to find his two sisters and three brothers. He first found one sister-in-law, who told him that his brother Karl had been beaten to death by the Gestapo. Using his military connections, Dolibois learned that none of his other four siblings still lived in Luxembourg. He found his two married sisters and their families in Germany, one in Frankfurt, the other in northern Germany. He then continued his hunt for his missing brothers and eventually found them, too. Both had been drafted into the Wehrmacht and had survived campaigns in North Africa, France, and Russia to be imprisoned safely by the French and the British. The Dolibois family could hardly believe its good fortune in suffering only one death in the war. Forty years later, John Dolibois, a vice president of Miami University, returned again to Luxembourg, this time as the American ambassador.[2]

The first requirement of European reconstruction was food. Only the Allied occupation forces had assured rations, which found their way to the black market and starving civilians hired to do menial work for the Allied armies. About the only things the Europeans had to barter were sexual favors (discouraged by anti-fraternization orders), war souvenirs, and *objets d'art*. American army leftovers could not feed the 100 million people who depended on some sort of relief food distribution and who had to live on 1,500 calories or less a day. (In 1946 occupation authorities reduced the standard German ration to 900 calories per day.) All over Europe, production of dairy products, meat, corn, wheat, and eggs had fallen to half or less of prewar levels. Only vegetables were more plentiful, and local consumption by rural communities and the ravaged state of the railway and roads prevented timely distribution of raw foodstuffs. The fastidious Dutch ate tulip bulbs and sugar beets. In northern France, the campaign of 1944 had practically wiped out the dairy herds; in the Norman Department of Manche, 105,000 milk cows died, their bloated corpses resting among the shattered trunks and branches of more than 300,000 apple trees, thus destroying the region's cash crops. A winter drought in 1945–46 was then followed by a cold, wet winter in 1946–47 that created severe fuel shortages in Britain and on the Continent. Public morale remained close to despair.

To the best of their ability, the Allies (which realistically meant the United States) attempted to hold the line against starvation and epidemic disease. The American armies in Europe began their relief mission even before the shooting stopped. Civil affairs units, medical service units, and the whole logistical structure of the American expeditionary force started the distribution of relief supplies in France and Belgium in autumn 1944. The funds for the relief work came directly from the War Department's civil affairs budget or from Lend-Lease or from religious groups. One part of the food support program brought thousands of pregnant heifer dairy cows to France and Belgium, where their progeny graze peacefully today. Other cows and draft animals went to Poland, Czechoslovakia, and Greece.

Public health took the highest priority, and Allied occupation authorities established demanding sanitation regulations, enforced quarantines with detainment camps if necessary, and gave more DDT baths than water baths. In May 1945, relief work faced its greatest challenge, since by law the Lend-Lease program ended with the war, causing funding to dwindle at just the time that POWs and DPs flooded the land. Into the breach came the United Nations Relief and Rehabilitation Administration (UNRRA), established in late 1944 and funded largely by the United States. In 1945–46 UNRRA provided 25 million tons of food, agricultural revival supplies, clothing and textiles, and industrial rehabilitation equipment at a cost of $1 billion. Two-thirds of the money and tonnage went to feed and treat Europeans. When commodities were available in Europe, they were purchased there to stimulate economic revival, but in such critical categories as grains and cereals (half of the total foodstuffs distributed), the major supplier was the United States. A peculiarity of the UNRRA operation was that it did not help Britain, France, the Low Countries, and occupied Germany as much as other countries; the former Allies had to rely on loans for purchases, and the Germans fell under the management of the Allied zonal occupation authorities. UNRRA's emergency relief operation simply dramatized the fact that French and German economic recovery was essential to European rebirth and that neither could prosper until the Allies accelerated the reconstruction of Germany.

Germany's wartime policy of stripping its occupied victims of public and private assets to enrich the Nazis and pay for the Wehrmacht left Europe destitute, with no easy way to finance a recovery program. The Germans had spared no one; all the countries they occupied lost financial and material resources estimated at half or more of their national wealth. The first postwar estimates put the Nazi confiscations at $26 billion. Germany had entered the war in 1939 with monetary reserves of around $200 million. Over the course of the war the Germans converted their foreign currency reserves and the wealth of private German businesses and individuals into gold-based monetary reserves worth $1 billion in 1945,* so even after wartime expenses Germany had quintupled its "international wealth" by the end of the war. Almost half the money had been transferred to Swiss banks in order to finance trade with neutral nations such as Portugal, Sweden, Spain, and Turkey, but the Allies had set up a preemptive buying program that limited German overseas spending. After the war the Allies established a Tripartite Gold Commission to identify and recover Nazi overseas assets, which amounted to about three-quarters of Nazi gold reserves, and direct them toward refugee relief and economic reconstruction. Largely because of Swiss intransigence, the commission and its successors recovered little Nazi gold until the late 1990s.

Nazi Germany was one of history's greatest kleptocracies, fed by foreign loot and property stripped from Jews at the extermination camps. The Nazis had encouraged Jews to bring their personal valuables with them to the camps and then had confiscated them. Some of this wealth became "official" gold, but much of the currency, nonmonetary gold, jewels, and other valuables simply went into storage in the Reichsbank and into accounts controlled by the SS. During the Allied occupation of Germany, the United States government collected unclaimed private property whose value was estimated at $400 million. About $260 million of this loot was found within the Allied occupation zones, and much of it eventually was restored to governments and individuals by a U.S. agency, the Foreign Exchange Depository, by 1950. None of the responsible officials believed, however, that their restitutions or distributions represented more than a

---

*To convert to 1990s dollars, these wartime estimates should be multiplied by a factor of nine or ten.

fraction of the property and valuables taken from Europeans, especially Jews. The SS account in the Reichsbank, for example, for death camp confiscations showed only $1.6 million, but the number of missing and incomplete records suggested unaccounted-for loot of millions more, and that figure does not include the property Jews left behind in ghettos or their original homes. Unclaimed accounts in Swiss banks amounted to an estimated $177 million—some, no doubt, owned by the thousands of Jews who were denied sanctuary in Switzerland and returned to German hands.

Another measure of Nazi Germany's economic rape of Europe is the amount of money paid by the Federal Republic of Germany to the 4 million claims filed against it and settled between 1949 and 1999. These payments totaled $55 billion. When the provisions for Bundesentschädigungsgesetz or "Federal Law for the Compensation of the Victims of National Socialism" payments expired, the German government made block grants of $720 million to the governments of twelve Western European countries and to Poland, Belarus, Ukraine, and Russia of $1.2 billion so that these governments could continue to meet the needs of Nazi victims. As with the gold and other unclaimed property, a true measure of the Third Reich's crimes against humanity is how few family members survived to make any claim at all.

Negotiations to compensate forced laborers for their ordeals and lost income continued into the 1990s. In 1999 Germany offered a settlement of $4.1 billion from its government and 36 German companies that used forced laborers during World War II. Representing the laborers are their current nations of residence: the United States, Israel, Poland, Ukraine, Russia, Belarus, and the Czech Republic. The Germans estimate that those who qualify for compensation number no more than 250,000, but the seven-nation negotiators believe that the number is larger and justifies an additional settlement of $1 billion.

The capitalization of European recovery thus could not be limited to the redistribution of surviving German assets or reparations. The United States took the leadership in developing a plan for long-range recovery and economic reform, not just for its own self-interest in encouraging market economies and free international trade but because it saw the danger in planting the seeds of European extremism once again. In 1944 the United States and its Western Allies met at the United Nations Monetary and Financial Conference at the Bretton Woods estate in Washington, D.C. The Bretton Woods agreements established the International Monetary Fund, an organization to shore up inflation-plagued national monetary systems and to curb currency speculations fed by the movement of gold reserves. They also founded the International Bank for Reconstruction and Development to improve trade and international economic integration. Since Britain was now the world's greatest debtor nation, it profited most by these arrangements, but these new international organizations aided the Continent as well. They could not, however, create more credit than someone was willing to extend, and that "someone" was the United States government.

Troubled by the rise of leftist parties (socialist and Communist) in France and Italy and the threat of both Soviet aggression and internal upheaval, the Truman administration and a bipartisan coalition of internationalists in Congress joined forces to create the European Recovery Program in 1947, usually known as the Marshall Plan to honor its sponsor, George C. Marshall, the general turned secretary of state. The priorities of the program struck at the heart of Europe's greatest shortages: food, coal, electrical power, oil, steel, and transportation infrastructure. Sixteen nations and Allied-occupied Germany eventually received $13 billion between 1947 and 1951. In addition to improving public morale in Europe, the Marshall Plan provided additional and critically targeted funding for modest economic growth and the creation of new wealth from domestic and foreign trade. In 1948 the per capita income of the United States ($1,755) was four times that of Britain, France, West Germany, and Italy combined ($441). Ten years later the ratio was $2,538 to $1,017. Growing productivity and wealth strengthened the hand of the economic integrationists of Europe, who eventually established the European Economic Community in 1957.

The end of the European interstate war did not stop the civil wars that Axis occupation had encouraged. In some cases the violence took the obvious form of urban warfare and guerrilla and counter-guerrilla rural operations. Armed with weapons traded by the Germans for safe passage and also equipped with Soviet arms, Tito's Communist partisans made short work of their main opponents, the Serbian Chetniks of Draza Mihailovic, as well as the Slovene and Croatian forces that had served as German allies in attempting to crush the Yugoslav resistance. Tito's victory in 1946 and a similar success by the Albanian Communists the same year assured the resurrection of a civil war in neighboring Greece. Outraged by the British-Royalist alliance that brought a British expeditionary force to Athens in October 1944, the Communist-dominated republican guerrilla movement mounted an uprising in Athens that lasted until February 1945. After killing 4,000 hostages, the Greek Communists fled to the northern borderlands with Albania, Yugoslavia, and Bulgaria. Reorganized and rearmed, the Communists returned to guerrilla warfare and terrorism until, 160,000 deaths later, the insurgents faded away, crushed by the Greek Army (with American advisers) and abandoned by Tito, who needed American protection from Russia.

The Greek civil war, a Communist coup in Czechoslovakia in 1948, and the threat that the legal Communist parties of France and Italy would dominate the weak parliamentary governments of their respective countries alarmed American and British political leaders and their proto-democrat allies on the Continent. Economic assistance alone might not prevent postwar radicalization, especially through the end of the 1940s. The most immediate challenge to public order was a continental thirst for vengeance against anyone of German descent and anyone minimally associated with the Axis occupation regime.

Nazi War Criminals

In the wake of liberation, French and Italian partisans—both rich in dedicated Communists—murdered as many as 8,000 suspected collaborators, often with Allied troops nearby. The war had polarized both nations. In France, for example, the Germans had killed some 60,000 French resisters, but the Allies had killed even more Frenchmen with bombs and artillery shells, even if done without malice. The French also believed that Britain had abandoned them in 1940, and the Americans appeared to be merely new pawns for the British. The French Vichyites, however, had even been more perfidious—becoming willing tools of the Nazis in betrayal, deportation, and death. American and British authorities in Germany tried to buy some French forgiveness by rounding up suspected collaborators—such as French members of the Waffen SS—and delivering them to French justice. Courts operating under the draconian Code Napoléon had no trouble convicting 200,000 Frenchmen for collaboration and executing 2,000, including the Vichy premier, Pierre Laval. Unhindered by statutes of limitations, French courts tried and convicted Vichyites into the 1990s.

Throughout Europe, the national court systems and governmental commissions of inquiry and investigation turned over the rubble in search for collaborators, both to punish them for past crimes and to decapitate any neo-Fascist political movements that sought to capitalize again on postwar disorder, as had happened in the 1920s. Norway took legal action against 18,000 people and hanged Vidkun Quisling. The Dutch investigated 150,000 persons held in captivity and convicted 66,000 for collaborationism and assorted crimes. The Belgians sent members of the royal family into internal exile and convicted 77,000 of its 87,000 suspects for pro-Nazi acts. The Austrians, eager to prove they were really a conquered people and thus should be spared from a long Allied occupation, tried 9,000 Nazis and executed 85 of them. Even the British hanged two of their citizens for treason.

As the Europeans settled their own accounts, the Western Allies attempted to punish the crimes of the Third Reich and dismantle every remnant of the Nazi civil-political organization to prove that Communists had no monopoly on retribution. In the Soviet zone, the Russian authorities carried out their own version of denazification, simply executing suspects or shipping them to terminal assignments in the Gulag work camps. The Western Allies proceeded with more decorum and growing leniency, but under American and British leadership, denazification proceeded with uncommon haste. After screening almost 14 million suspects, American occupation authorities ordered more than 600,000 Germans to trial, almost all of whom were convicted. Some 31,000 Germans went to prison, while the others endured some combination of property confiscation, fines, loss of government employment, and some sort of occupational prohibition. General George Patton also lost his job—command of the U.S. Third Army—because of his vocal lack of enthusiasm for denazification.

The Allies, following their agreement in the Moscow Declaration of October 1943, prosecuted the surviving Nazi leadership for their criminal responsibility in starting the war and conducting it with barbarism. In August 1945 the United States, Britain, France, and the Soviet Union agreed on the categories of crimes and a structure for prosecution, the International Military Tribunal, which convened at Nuremberg in October 1945. Twenty-two Nazi leaders' names were on the charge sheets and 21 were physically present in the defendant's dock. The one leader tried in absentia was Martin Bormann, Hitler's closest political adviser. (Already a suicide in 1945, Bormann's remains went undiscovered until 1972.) After a year of testimony and legal niceties, the four judges—one representing each of the convening powers—found 19 defendants, including Bormann, guilty of at least one of the four categories of crimes: (1) conspiring to start a war of aggression; (2) starting the war by committing "crimes against peace"; (3) engaging in criminal behavior in the conduct of the war; and (4) committing "crimes against humanity." It turned out to be less politically embarrassing and easier to prove the Germans guilty of counts 3 and 4, since they did not raise serious questions about Allied appeasement and temporary collaboration, as in the Nazi-Soviet Non-Aggression Pact of 1939.

The judges, prosecutors, and defense attorneys also knew that they were setting precedents for international law in creating expanded concepts of criminality in the use of force for state purposes. Given the clear genocidal policies of Nazi Germany—executed by all agencies of the Nazi security system and the entire Wehrmacht—the defendants' collective guilt still appears justified in moral (if not strictly legal) terms. Eleven Nazis went to the gallows, and the remaining seven went to jail for terms ranging from life to ten years. The best-known defendant, Hermann Göring, committed suicide with a poison capsule hidden in his teeth and thus cheated his American hangman. Those who received the lightest sentences—Albert Speer (20 years), Karl Dönitz (10 years), and Konstantin von Neurath (15 years)—were all free men by 1966 and lived into the 1980s. Rudolf Hess, Hitler's political adjutant until his quixotic flight to Great Britain in 1941, remained imprisoned until his death in 1987 at the age of 93, largely to appease the Russians.

Even as tension with the Soviet Union mounted after 1946, the British and Americans continued to exercise their powers to try war criminals under international law within Germany while France held more trials within its own courts. Many of the prosecutions proceeded on counts 3 and 4, but the American trials, also held at Nuremberg in 1946–1949, still attempted to hold leaders of the Wehrmacht and German industry criminally responsible for acts that violated counts 1 and 2, including service in organizations that carried out criminal acts. This aggressive prosecution produced mixed results. Of the 185 defendants, 54 could not be convicted, 24 more went to the gallows, and 107 received prison terms.

The Cold War soon distorted and foreshortened efforts to cast a wider net over German society to catch more of those responsible for Nazi atrocities. After 1949 the new West German government, supported now by the Western Allies as a bulwark against Communism, received jurisdiction for overseeing imprisoned war criminals. Eager to forget the past, West German politicians proved lenient in accepting pleas of officers and civil servants that they had only followed orders or had had no knowledge of the crimes committed by others. The Americans even accepted General Reinhard Gehlen and his intelligence organization, Foreign Armies East, which had so consistently misestimated Soviet intentions, as the basis for their espionage effort against the Soviets.

Few of those given jail terms by Western courts served their full sentences—except those convicted by the Trial of Major War Criminals at Nuremberg, and then largely as a result of Soviet intransigence. Some of those sentenced to die had their sentences commuted. "Reasons of state" ensured that the unpleasant past soon sank from public consciousness, as the Western powers sought to make the German Federal Republic a functioning political and military member of NATO. And so the great majority of the guilty—the little men who had made it all possible—lived out their lives as civil servants, businessmen, doctors, farmers, workers, or even soldiers. Justice succumbed to expediency.

The decline in the official Anglo-American search for Nazi war criminals did not, however, guarantee safety for the most notorious German fugitives. Allied authorities calculated that as many as 20,000 German war criminals escaped in the chaos of 1945, eventually turning up in Latin America and the Middle East—and even American cities—with new identities. Some, like Heinrich Müller, head of the Gestapo, remain unaccounted for. Others survived to die of old age. Dr. Josef Mengele, whose medical experiments on Auschwitz inmates disgraced his profession, died in Brazil at the age of 68. SS Colonel Otto Skorzeny, Hitler's favorite commando, escaped from a prison in Germany and organized Odessa, the network of Nazis that smuggled their comrades out of Europe. Skorzeny lived in affluence in Spain until his death in 1975. Other Nazi notables found no sanctuary absolute. Working with Simon Weisenthal, the Javert of Nazi pursuers, Israeli intelligence agents found and kidnapped Adolf Eichmann from Argentina to stand trial in Israel for his leadership in implementing "the Final Solution." Eichmann went to the gallows in 1962. SS Lieutenant Colonel Joachim Peiper, whose troops executed 71 GIs during the Battle of the Bulge, died in a mysterious house fire in France well after the war. Head of the Gestapo in Lyons, France, Klaus Barbie earned the title "butcher" for his love of torture. Among his victims was Jean Moulin, a resistance leader with a reputation only slightly less heroic than Joan of Arc. Barbie's loyal assistant was a Lyons Vichyite police captain named Paul Touvier. French authorities tracked Barbie to Bolivia, brought him back to France, convicted him of war crimes, and put him in prison in 1987 for the rest of his short life. After Barbie's death in 1991, French agents found Touvier, and he was convicted of crimes against humanity in 1994 and sent to prison for life. Even 55 years later, there are still people who want to settle outstanding accounts with the Nazis.

Postwar Asia

Japan's surrender in Tokyo Bay provided a false finale to the war in Asia. The people of the Home Islands might obey the Emperor's orders to bear the unbearable pain of American occupation, but 5 million Japanese, more than half of them armed soldiers, still defended the shrunken East Asia Co-Prosperity Sphere. Of all the occupied countries, only Burma, Manchuria, and the Philippines had been liberated by Allied armies before Japan's surrender. Four million Japanese still inhabited China. Already aware of the plight of the 220,000 Allied POWs and civilian internees from the rescues in the Philippines and Netherlands East Indies, Anglo-American expeditionary forces rushed to the political centers of Asia to rescue POWs and accept Japanese surrenders. Their mission was to ship the Japanese back to the Home Islands as quickly as possible before wars of revenge broke out all over Asia. Even the occupation of Japan might not proceed as smoothly if the repatriation process became consumed in a retributive bloodbath. In Hong Kong, for example, a Chinese mob assaulted the disarmed Japanese as they marched to their ships and killed hundreds—without firearms.

The extemporized, urgent Allied effort to make the surrender work and save the overseas Japanese also saved the local Asian populations. Any incident might have sparked a repetition of the rape of Nanking, not at all improbable in cities like Shanghai, Canton, and Singapore, where Communist-dominated labor unions could easily control the streets and force the Japanese to do battle. The Japanese proved quite capable of protecting themselves until they could claim the protection of American or Commonwealth troops. In China, the postsurrender political arrangements produced alliances of a kind between the Japanese Army, the Chinese Nationalists, and the surviving warlords. The Western Allies had designated Chiang Kai-shek the official agent for accepting Japanese surrenders, but the Nationalist armies were still cowed by the Japanese and too poorly armed and too small in number to keep order. Therefore, the Japanese Army remained armed and dangerous throughout the coastal areas of China, while other Japanese forces backed toward the sea and repatriation. Thousands of Japanese soldiers faded into the Chinese population or hired themselves out to warlords in the interior. Many Japanese brought out as much wealth as they could convert into gold and jewelry or other portable, concealed property.

In pursuit of surviving prisoners and the Japanese authorities and guards who had killed or tortured to death almost 40 percent of Allied POWs, the victorious expeditionary forces also rushed to their occupation zones to halt the growth of native independence movements. Only the fear of a war for which they were unprepared stayed the hands of the revolutionaries—as well as their residual fear of a premature clash with the Europeans or Japanese. Commonwealth troops returned to Malaya and found the resistance leaders cooperative, in part because the Malayan Communists (largely Chinese) feared a Malay counter-revolution. In Indochina, the national leader, Ho Chi Minh, declared a Vietnamese socialist republic but ordered his Viet Minh forces to cooperate with the Commonwealth and Chinese Nationalist forces that split his country into occupation zones. He even said that he would welcome the French back just to replace the Chinese and Indians, since he felt confident that he could later drive the French back to Europe. Nevertheless, Vietnamese terrorists attacked Japanese and French civilians, only to be driven off by Japanese soldiers.

In the Netherlands East Indies, the liberating British, Australian, and Dutch forces found the Indonesians of Java and Sumatra unwilling to surrender their new republic and return to Dutch rule. The armed Japanese protected themselves from the Indonesians, but Commonwealth and Dutch soldiers fought several bloody battles with the Indonesians until President Achmet Sukarno agreed to accept a cease-fire, provided the Commonwealth troops would leave Indonesia and the Dutch would meet with all the Indonesian factions to negotiate some peaceful path to independence. The last British and Indian troops to die in World War II perished fighting in the streets of Surabaya, Java, in November 1945.

The Japanese and Koreans faced great peril from the Soviet armies of 1 million that poured into Manchuria in August 1945 and did not stop until they reached the 38th Parallel in mid-Korea and the territories north of the Great Wall in northern China. The vaunted Kwantung Army, now a force of only 400,000 collaborationist Chinese, Koreans, and third-rate Japanese troops, quickly folded. The refugees sought the protection of Chinese Nationalist forces and the 46,000 marines of the U.S. III Amphibious Corps, which had established safe havens around Peiping and in Hopeh and Shantung provinces. Nevertheless, the Soviets took 600,000 soldiers and civilians prisoner and packed them off in boxcars to the slave labor camps in Siberia; of these human reparations, only 224,000 survived to return to Korea and Japan in 1949.

Soviet troops, many of them Mongolians and Central Asian Muslims, looted, raped, and murdered their way through Manchuria. Behind the Soviet forces came work crews who dismantled and removed as much Japanese machinery and property as they could take. They turned the captured weapons over to the Chinese Communist guerrillas they met marching east from their base areas in western China. In front of the new occupiers, thousands of Japanese occupiers fled or died. One young Japanese refugee came across a woman sitting along a mountain path and tending a small fire: "As I attempted to pass by, I caught my breath. Four little legs were sticking out from underneath the dried grasses. Unable to comprehend this odd scene, I went over to her and asked, 'What happened?'

Keeping her face averted, she replied, 'They can't move any more. I've killed them and I'm burning them.'"[3]

As the Soviet armies swept into Korea, the soldiers continued their campaign of pillage and mayhem despite the fact that Moscow had plans to turn Korea into a model socialist state. The Red Army did not discriminate between the Japanese and the Koreans, a subject people who wanted nothing more than to leave the Japanese empire. Shops and stores were looted for cheap watches and other souvenirs; any office that appeared part of the local government became a trash heap. Enthusiastic Soviet engineers sawed telephone poles off at the ground for fires or for logs to corduroy the roads. Factories of every sort came apart with the thud of hammers and the screech of great wrenches and went aboard railcars bound for Vladivostok. Filled with terror, Korean refugees packed all the belongings they could carry and headed south for the 38th Parallel and the American occupation zone.

Panicked by the growing cooperation between the Soviets and the Chinese Communists in Manchuria and northern China, Chiang Kai-shek ordered his generals to patch together local alliances that would keep the Japanese armed and the Chinese Communists at bay. In defeat, the Japanese discovered that the Americans and the Chinese Nationalists could be more malleable victors than the Japanese could ever have imagined, given their own perception of the rights of conquerors. Despite political confusion throughout Asia, the Allies, primarily with American money and Japanese shipping, evacuated 5 million overseas Japanese, all but 500,000 in the first 10 months after the surrender. In so doing, the Allies saved thousands of lives and ensured a peaceful occupation and rehabilitation of Japan. The United States' postwar political aggressiveness placed American troops throughout the Home Islands to guarantee the peace and blunt Stalin's arguments that the Soviet Union should send troops to Japan. The American occupation, nominally shared with the British Commonwealth, did not, however, make peace without shedding more Japanese blood.

Japanese War Criminals

Although the Truman administration, the American media, and the European colonial powers had scores to settle with Japan's wartime leaders, General Douglas MacArthur, appointed the Supreme Commander Allied Powers (SCAP) in Japan, played the central role in pursuing Japan's most celebrated war criminals. He meted out his own brand of justice in two major postwar trials of Japanese leaders. Legal considerations had little to do with either event, but subduing the Japanese and impressing other Asians had a great deal to do with bringing Japanese politicians and military leaders to the dock.

Deflecting cries of vengeance away from Emperor Hirohito and distracting attention from his own errors of judgment that had doomed thousands of Filipinos in 1942 and 1945, MacArthur set the tone for his witch hunt by trying, convicting, and executing Generals Yamashita Tomoyuki and Homma Massaharu. On 7 December 1945, in a show-trial in Manila, Yamashita faced charges that he failed to control Japanese troops who had murdered thousands of Filipinos in Manila earlier that year—an imaginative reading of Yamashita's real span of command. Homma's conviction stemmed from his distant association with the atrocities of the Bataan Death March. Both Japanese shared a common crime: they had displayed more generalship in Luzon than the convening authority. Their conviction and death sentences received only cursory review all the way to the U.S. Supreme Court, which confirmed the proceedings with a seven-to-two vote. Despite pleas from many Japanese, MacArthur ordered Yamashita hanged—a humiliating death borne with grace by Japan's greatest field commander. MacArthur then relented to family pleas and allowed Homma to be executed by firing squad.

MacArthur also arranged the trials conducted by the International Military Tribunal Far East, a court of eleven judges from as many different countries who tried and convicted 25 of 28 indicted Class A war criminals, that is, Japanese policymakers identified with the decisions for war between 1937 and 1941. Two defendants died during the proceedings, while another became too insane to try. Many other potential defendants, including Minister of War Anami Korechika, had already committed *seppuku*. As with the Yamashita and Homma trials, the verdicts produced no surprises. Seven defendants died by hanging and sixteen were given life imprisonment; only two received lesser sentences. Poised and unrepentant, Tojo Hideki went to his death after writing delicate verse and observing Buddhist rituals. Temple bells rang in reverence all over the city.

Ten nations pursued more conventional war criminals, Japanese Class B and C suspects who had committed atrocities against POWs or civilians. The first category of defendants had committed the crimes; the second category were responsible officers who had failed to prevent the crimes or had encouraged them. Over a period of six years, Allied tribunals tried 5,700, convicted more than half, and executed approximately 1,000. Although legal standards did not always prevail, these trials at least had roots in established international law on the conduct of war, and they considered the evidence with some care. As tempers cooled, many sentences were reduced.

More controversial were all those Japanese who escaped retribution, especially those who had abused fellow Asians. The most unacceptable failure to prosecute focused on Lieutenant General Ishii Shiro, a medical doctor and the evil genius behind Unit 731 and other organizations dedicated to bacteriological warfare research and other medical "challenges." This "research" had involved human subjects (some of them European POWs) and almost always produced death for the laboratory "animals" or *marutas* (logs), as the Japanese termed the human beings on whose bodies they were experimenting. Other human subjects were used to study the effect of hypothermia, extreme gravitational pressure, and hazardous drugs and medical procedures. Some experiments involved vivisection. Doctor Ishii and his associates, however, bargained all their "scientific findings" in return for amnesia on the part of U.S. war crimes investigators. Ishii lived fourteen years after the war as a free man because Americans wanted to keep his research accessible but secret, away from the prying eyes of the Soviets and Chinese Communists.

Building his Japanese constituency with his own regal performance and his use of the Emperor to endorse the reform process, MacArthur presided over a set of dramatic reforms actually designed by American diplomats, technocrats, and Japanophiles. The imperial armed forces were dissolved; more than 200,000 "undesirables" left the government ministries; and the industrial conglomerates received orders to divide their operations into smaller, independent corporations. Abandoning his role of Virginia tidewater patrician, which his mother—a Norfolk belle—had encouraged, Douglas MacArthur revealed that at heart he was a Wisconsin progressive, in the tradition of his father's home state. He advocated women's suffrage, the protection of labor unions, land reform, regulation of public services, educational restructuring, and the sanctity of the vote. This political diet proved too rich for the Japanese, but at least it created an alternative to the authoritarian and militarized modernization that had taken them to war. Prey to self-delusion and self-congratulation, MacArthur and the other American reformers believed that they had created a new Japan, often unaware of the fact that many Japanese regretted only their unsuccessful methods, not the national goals they sought in the 1930s.

Conclusion

Although the effects of World War II varied from country to country, few who lived through the 1930s and 1940s would deny that the war defined their lives and shaped their worlds for decades to come. Many of World

War II's belligerents faced other unpleasant conflicts in the future: the British in Northern Ireland, the French in Algeria, the Russians in Afghanistan, the Chinese in Korea, and the Americans in Vietnam. But World War II has been *the war* for half a century, and in Europe and Asia it will retain that status well into the twenty-first century.

Once asked to describe the role of the North Atlantic Treaty Organization, Hastings Lord Ismay, Churchill's wartime secretary and adviser, quipped that NATO's mission was to keep the Americans in, the Russians out, and the Germans down. Ismay's droll characterization of NATO was even more true of World War II's impact on Europe, with the major difference that the war put the Russians "in" too, until the collapse of the Warsaw Pact in the 1990s. World War II brought an end to the great power rivalries of Europe, to the extension of those rivalries to much of the world through imperialism, and to European dominance of the world's economic development and culture. After the war, analysts of various ideological persuasions argued whether the twentieth century was the American century or the Russian century or the Japanese century. Behind this argument was the assumption that, in any case, it would not be the European century. World War II ensured that in the decades to follow most varieties of imperialism would collapse, the economies of the Western Hemisphere and Eurasia would become more interdependent, and populist nationalism throughout the non-European world would flourish. Fifty years after its founding, the United Nations has more than three times the member nations that it had when its charter was signed in San Francisco in June 1945. World War II is past, but it continues to shape the present and the future.

EPILOGUE:
IN RETROSPECT

One cannot look across the long, seemingly endless rows of headstones that mark the military cemeteries throughout Europe and the Pacific or the great memorials and earthen mounds memorializing the dead of Eastern Europe without a sense of the terrible cost of victory in World War II. The cold stones underscore the brevity of those lives cut short in early adulthood—men who never again saw their families and homes. And as each year passes, fewer and fewer elderly visitors come to these lonely corners of France, Britain, Belgium, Poland, Hawaii, the Philippines, Malaya, and other foreign lands. The generation that fought World War II is now fading into the shadows of history. By 1999 in the United States, those who served during the war were dying at the rate of 1,000 per day. By the third decade of the twenty-first century, they will all be gone.

As the past recedes from memory and takes form on the printed page, historians and other commentators have begun to depict victory in that terrible conflict in soft words. A number have suggested that the Allied war effort was nothing more than the opposite side of the same coin—that the Allied cause was as morally bankrupt as the Axis cause, that an American or British war crime can be found for every one committed by the Germans or Japanese. Across the ledger from Nanking, Rotterdam, Belgrade, Oradour-sur-Glane, or Malmédy, they place the Allies' refusal to bomb the rail lines to Auschwitz, the starvation of German POWs at war's end, and the incineration of Hiroshima—that worst of all "crimes against humanity."

These advocates for moral equivalence are wrong. In considering the war's human cost, those of us privileged to live at the dawn of a new millennium should renew our effort to remember why the war was fought and why so many were called to pay the ultimate price for victory. The wars unleashed by the Japanese in 1937 and by the Germans in 1939 came close to destroying the two great centers of world civilization and to imposing in their stead imperial regimes founded on racial superiority, slavery,

575

and genocide. They did not succeed because of the extraordinary efforts and sacrifices made by Allied soldiers, sailors, airmen, and marines from around the world—Americans, Australians, Britons, Chinese, French, Indians, Poles, Russians, Ukrainians, and innumerable other nationalities.

The words Pericles uttered in his funeral oration memorializing the Athenian dead in the Peloponnesian War and recorded by that greatest of all historians, Thucydides, best capture the debt of remembrance and respect we owe:

> To me it seems that the consummation which has overtaken these men shows us the meaning of manliness in its first revelation and in its final proof. Some of them, no doubt, had their faults; but what we ought to remember first is their gallant conduct against the enemy in defense of their native land. They have blotted out evil with good, and done more service to the commonwealth than they ever did harm in their private lives. No one of these men weakened because he wanted to go on enjoying his wealth; no one put off the awful day in the hope that he might live to escape his poverty and grow rich . . . In the fighting, they thought it more honorable to stand their ground and suffer death than to give in and save their lives. So they fled from the reproaches of men, abiding with life and limb the brunt of battle; and in a small moment of time, the climax of their lives, a culmination of glory, not of fear, were swept away from us.

APPENDIX 1

MILITARY ORGANIZATION

By the twentieth century, the major industrialized powers of Eurasia and the Western Hemisphere had created standing armed forces based on some combination of voluntary and coerced service by their male populations. These forces divide by mission and operating environment into three *services:* (1) ground forces (armies); (2) air forces; and (3) naval forces (navies). Marines are naval forces designed for amphibious operations and are considered a fourth service in some countries such as the United States. Air forces—the most recent creation—might or might not have full status independent of a nation's army and navy, depending on interservice politics, strategic imperatives, and other nonmilitary factors. Germany, for example, had an autonomous air force, the Luftwaffe, that controlled airborne divisions, air base defense forces of ground divisions, massive anti-aircraft artillery forces, and its own prisoner-of-war camps for Allied aircrewmen. Britain had an independent air force—the Royal Air Force—but in 1937 allowed its navy to recreate its own air force for fleet operations, the Fleet Air Arm. Yet the RAF, with its Coastal Command, still conducted its own naval campaign against the German U-boats. The United States and Japan created separate air forces as part of both their armies and navies, while the Soviets created one air force subdivided into two functional air forces—one to support ground forces, the other to provide air defense.

In the field, military services might or might not operate under a single commander. The Germans and Japanese kept their services separate and their allies subservient, while the Anglo-American Allies created a framework for coalition warfare that strengthened national and service cooperation. The highest level of coalition command was the *theater,* defined principally by geography but influenced by the preponderance of national interest and commitment of national forces. The theater commander had both *combined* (multinational) forces and *joint* (multiservice) forces. The only exceptions were strategic air forces (see Air Forces, p. 581), which took their missions from a higher authority, the Combined Chiefs of Staff (the united American and British service commanders and general staffs). The strategic air forces were too important for theater commanders to control. To demonstrate combined and joint organization: the Allied theater commander in the Mediterranean from 1943 to 1945 commanded air, naval, and ground forces from

Britain, Canada, Australia, New Zealand, India, South Africa, the United States, France and its African colonies, Italy, Poland, and Brazil.

Ground Forces

Before men fought on horses or from boats, they attacked one another with their feet planted on the ground and thus defined war as the combat of foot soldiers or *infantry*. Even in World War II most infantrymen walked into battle, even if they reached the front by train or truck. Infantrymen did not inflict the most casualties, but they certainly suffered the majority of them (often 80–90 percent in any army) in their effort to destroy enemy ground forces, seize key terrain, capture air and naval bases, occupy farmlands and cities, and generally represent the permanent conquest of an enemy by coming onto his land to stay unless driven off. By World War II infantry had joined forces with mobile *artillery* and gasoline-powered *mechanized* and *motorized* forces to increase the destructiveness and tempo of operations. This combination imposed cascading requirements for specialized service and support units, which might appear in small detachments in an infantry battalion or regiment but became a major part of an infantry division or larger formations like corps and field armies. By the time one counted all the ground forces in a national army, the percentage of infantry might be less than half the size of the entire ground forces establishment, but foot soldiers still carried an inordinate burden of the fighting.

Ground combat forces of division strength normally included more than infantry units; the minimum additional unit would be an artillery unit armed with mortars and cannon. The other standard organic or attached units included reconnaissance (scouting) forces, armor or tank forces, anti-tank forces, and engineer combat forces capable of creating or destroying barriers with demolitions, mines, and specialized equipment. If a division was designated armor, mechanized, or motorized, it meant that all or almost all of its units had their own organic tracked or wheeled vehicles.

Ground forces followed this general pattern of organization (all numbers of men are approximations):

Platoon	20–50 men
Company	100–200 men in three to five platoons
Battalion	600–1,100 men in four to six companies
Regiment or Brigade	1,800–3,200 men in two or more battalions
Division	10,000–20,000 men in three or more brigades or regiments, with combined-arms capability
Corps	50,000 men in two or more divisions and corps troops
Army	100,000 men in two or more corps with army-level units
Army Group or Front (USSR)	500,000 men in two or more armies

Air Forces

The *squadron* was the essential tactical aviation unit during World War II. A squadron might rate as few as 6 and as many as 24 aircraft. Squadrons tried to have more pilots and aircrewmen than aircraft so that a squadron could always man whatever aircraft were operationally ready at any given time. Thus a fighter squadron might have 20 or more pilots for 15 aircraft.

When various ground support units were added to a squadron, it became a *group*. Groups might be aggregated as *wings* with two or more flying and support squadrons that provided personnel administration, base support and security, ordnance handling, transportation, fueling, aircraft maintenance, and communications/air control. The Soviets, holding firmly to the past, called wings *aviation regiments*.

Larger aviation formations were called *divisions* and *air forces*. Naval aviation formations were designated *carrier air groups* (one for each carrier) and *air fleets* (Japanese) or *naval air forces* (United States) for land-based naval aviation. The largest functional group might be a *command* like RAF Bomber Command or a *force*, for example, Far Eastern Air Force (U.S.) or U.S. Strategic Air Forces (USAAF strategic bombers in Europe, 1944–45).

Naval Forces

Naval forces of World War II had two essential components: (1) operational *fleets* of ships and aircraft, such as the Imperial Japanese Combined Fleet, and (2) shore establishments. Operational fleets tended to be organized as *type commands* of similar ships and aircraft for administrative and training purposes and *task forces, task groups*, and *task units* organized for actual operations. Sometimes there was no difference between a type command and a task force; for example, a squadron or flotilla of destroyers might deploy intact. Submarine forces were type commands that often conducted their own campaigns of commerce raiding but might also form part of task forces in fleet engagements. Major combatants like battleships and carriers seldom sailed except as task forces, with accompanying escorts of cruisers and destroyers for anti-air and anti-submarine defense.

A *fleet* might be a combination of operational ships and aircraft in task forces, type commands, and a shore establishment. For example, in 1944–45 the United States Navy in the Pacific War had a Pacific Fleet, three numbered fleets (Seventh, Third, and Fifth), many type commands (such as Submarine Force Pacific, Service Force Pacific), and an extensive shore establishment, subdivided by geographic location and function.

Special Forces

During World War II the political leadership of all the belligerents (with the possible exception of Japan) found the existing service organizations unresponsive to what they conceived as their needs for *special forces*, defined by mission and politics. Adolf

Hitler never trusted the traditional German Army, so he supported SS Reichsführer Heinrich Himmler's efforts to create within the multifunctional SS (Schutzstaffel) empire a corps of elite combat ground units, the Waffen SS. The rest of the Schutzstaffel ran the Third Reich's national police, secret police, concentration camp, slave labor, and extermination organizations. The Waffen SS remained a conventional ground force of 27 divisions that conducted land campaigns with the army.

Reflecting Winston Churchill's fascination with special forces, the British blended civilians and personnel from several services into large and effective special organizations: (1) MI-5, counter-intelligence; (2) MI-6, foreign intelligence; (3) the Special Operations Executive (SOE), an agency to encourage and support native partisans against the Axis; and (4) Combined Operations Command, which developed amphibious operations forces and equipment and provided elite raiders known as commandos (British Army) or Royal Marine Commandos (Royal Marines). The British organized other elite units such as the Long Range Desert Group (LRDG), the Special Air Service Regiment (SAS), and the Royal Marine Special Boat Squadron (SBS), all infiltration groups for reconnaissance and raiding missions.

The American armed forces resisted such expedient organizations, fearing that special units would only weaken the regular field forces. But Franklin Roosevelt insisted on the creation of the Office of Strategic Services (OSS), which had wide-ranging responsibility for foreign intelligence gathering and assessment, propaganda and psychological warfare, subversion and sabotage, partisan warfare, and clandestine spying and negotiations. The American armed forces did provide an Air Commando (special operations wing) in Burma, marine raider and parachute battalions, army ranger battalions, and navy underwater demolition teams ("frogmen").

All the major belligerents fielded special forces of many kinds, but most of them remained part of an existing service, for example, the German Army's Brandenberg Regiment, Otto Skorzeny's SS commandos, Italian naval commandos, the British Army "Chindits" or Long Range Penetration Groups, Japanese Special Naval Landing Forces, and Soviet airborne deep penetration forces. Special forces also included guerrilla and terrorist forces supported and often advised or led by Allied teams from SOE and OSS. Some, like the underground Polish Home Army, functioned autonomously. Special units might be formed of refugees and immigrants who might pass for Axis forces on the basis of a common language; these included German-Jewish commandos in British service and Japanese-American *(nisei)* scouts and interpreter-translators with the American forces in the Pacific. Special forces always seemed to offer cheap and dramatic victories, like Skorzeny's rescue of Mussolini in 1943, the Czech assassination of SS General Reinhard Heydrich in 1942, and the British raid on the great dock at St. Nazaire in March 1942. But many of their missions aborted or resulted in catastrophic losses and betrayals.

APPENDIX 2:

THE CONDUCT OF WAR

Policy

Policy is a government's position, statement, or plan of action designed to influence and determine future decisions and actions in the polity's interest. During times of war, policy reflects a government's war aims and embodies its understanding of the war's causes, its conduct, and the circumstances of its conclusion and consequences. A government's policy is usually complex and subject to changes in timing and emphasis, as are the shared policies of coalitions of belligerents.

Members of coalitions often have both common and conflicting war aims, based on different national interests and expectations. In World War II, for example, the United States, Britain, and the Soviet Union agreed that they would destroy Nazi Germany's political institutions and the German armed forces, and this shared war aim dictated an "unconditional surrender" policy. The Allies did not, however, agree on the nature of postwar Germany and therefore could come to no mutual policy for dealing with such matters as prisoners of war, economic reparations, and territorial changes. Not surprisingly, national policies for the purposes of a war often change once an enemy is defeated and ceases to be a military threat.

Strategy

Strategy is a general plan for the creation, deployment (geographic movement), and employment (use) of coalition and national armed forces to achieve war aims by destroying the enemy's will and ability to wage war. In theory, war aims should determine strategy, but often other factors such as geography and distance, coalition relations, and the speed with which decisive armed forces can be created shape strategy as well. Strategic plans attempt to identify the combination of enemy forces, war-waging potential, and geography that represent the essential enemy strengths that a nation must overcome. An enemy weakness or vulnerability (such as dependence on overseas oil) might be of strategic importance, but often it is not.

In World War II, differences in geopolitical perspectives and disparities in military power determined strategy-making among the Allies and the Axis powers. The Americans and British came closest to designing a global strategy that accommodated their war aims, some of which they held in common (to regard Germany as a worse threat than Japan), some of which they did not (to liberate Malaya). Franklin Roosevelt and Winston Churchill shared advice and plans prepared by their Combined Chiefs of Staff, which tried to weigh different theater priorities, assess military forces, and encourage the political leaders to deal with realities.

No such support system served Adolf Hitler and Joseph Stalin, who regarded many of their own senior officers as treasonable, incompetent, or both. With interservice plans seldom in balance, coalition cooperation, especially between Germany and Italy, became virtually impossible, even at the level of sharing intelligence or technological-operational data. Early in the war (1939–1942) Axis cooperation might have played a decisive role, for example, if Germany and Japan could have cooperated to launch a two-front war on Russia or an attack on the British in the Middle East. But Anglo-American weaknesses early in the war made unilateral planning more tempting to the Axis than cooperation.

Strategic and Operational Planning

The principal belligerents of World War II shared a common legacy at least two centuries old: that military organizations could plan and test their operational plans before a force tried to execute those plans in battle. The oldest type of activity for testing likely combat performance was the maneuver or mock battle, often an extension of a formal parade in eras when marching and maneuvering were one and the same. Once restored in seventeenth-century armies, drill was actually tactical rehearsal and testing. When extended to formations in the thousands, such drills became maneuvers, and with the appearance of formal staffs in the Napoleonic era, exercises might become war games in which nominally opposing forces faced each other in mock battle. When general staffs appeared in the nineteenth century, they built their expertise through professional military education and training in various levels of officer schools, which soon specialized in strategic and operational planning of all sorts and in designing tests of new weapons and operational concepts.

By the end of the nineteenth century, modern naval establishments had also formed planning staffs at the service and fleet level and linked these staffs with the faculties and students of naval war colleges. The duties of naval planners included the design of fleet exercises, usually held annually, in which opposing forces went to sea and participated in simulated naval battles, usually constrained by considerations of weather and safety. The same pattern of exercising forces accompanied the creation of air forces in the early twentieth century. By the 1930s all the prospective belligerents of World War II had service general staffs and advanced officer schools that specialized in strategic and operational planning and testing.

The foci of military exercises were: (1) the testing of an actual contingency plan for war with a likely opponent, one of the best-known examples being War Plan

Orange, the American plan for a war with Japan; and (2) the testing of new capabilities that might not be directed at a specific opponent, for example, the joint German-Russian tests of armored war fare in the 1920s. These two purposes were not necessarily incompatible. The methods of testing, however, could be quite different. Military staffs could not test strategic contingency plans on the actual ground, but they could examine the possibilities in a war game, usually done with maps, boards, and representational counters in precomputer days. Usually two teams "fought" each other while a third team played "control" or "God" and made decisions about the outcome of movements and combat on the basis of mathematical tables and personal experience. The "control" team ensured that both sides followed the pregame scenario or rules or refereed "free-play" games. Another variant was the "staff ride," in which teams analyzed an actual battle in the field and played different roles in assessing the decisions of the actual generals and their staffs.

The German Army led the world in creating regular war games and staff rides, which all other military establishments copied in varied forms. A variant of the staff ride was the tactical exercise without troops or the command post exercise (CPX) in which commanders and staffs actually went to the field and worked from extemporized headquarters but did not command actual field formations. This technique could train staffs without wasting the time of the troops and wearing out equipment. All these economical substitutes for full exercises had their place in military planning but could not replace some field and fleet exercises, since they all contained inherent artificialities.

Exercises of all sorts provided critical information to strategic and operational planners. They forced a realistic appraisal of enemy capabilities and intentions—or at least should have. They clarified critical decisions across the dimensions of time and space and forced some consideration of the logistical supportability of various schemes of maneuver. They might reveal shocking limitations in methods of command, control, and communications or clarify problems in task organization, weapons performance, and unit training. Even if never completely successful, precommitment planning and exercising tried to reduce the inherent complexities and uncertainties of twentieth-century warfare.

Operations

Military operations are the violent actions undertaken by armed forces in the pursuit of strategic objectives (which are, in turn, based on policy and war aims). Operations might take the form of a specific mission, such as landing an Allied expeditionary force in northern France, or they may be generic in nature, such as conducting amphibious assaults throughout the Pacific. Operations entail armies, fleets, and air forces numbering in the tens or hundreds of thousands of personnel and operating over vast distances and extended periods of time (a *campaign*) or activities of smaller forces for shorter periods of time. Operations usually have codenames like Overlord (the Normandy invasion, 1944), Zitadelle (the German offensive at Kursk, Russia, 1943), and A-Go (the Japanese naval attack on the U.S. Fifth Fleet off Saipan, 1944).

The principles that shape military operations are based on centuries of experience and institutional refinement and are used almost universally. When codified and applied in training and wartime operations, such principles are called *doctrine*. Doctrine usually applies to operations (by specifying how to conduct campaigns and extended battles) and to tactics (how to conduct a single engagement or series of similar engagements), but not to strategy. "Strategic doctrine" is an oxymoron since strategy is defined by contingent war aims.

Because most operational concepts developed through the experiences of armies, they often do not transfer easily or completely to naval and air warfare. Air and naval leaders insist that their forces operate in a unique physical medium and should not be judged by inappropriate ground combat concepts. While this position contains some truth, it has been used to argue that naval and air forces should operate autonomously, detached from the operational concerns and supervision of officers unfamiliar with air and naval operations. In fact, many operational concepts from naval warfare found their way into the language of air operations for no other reason than that they were different from the principles of ground combat operations. The true challenge of operational planning, however, is not just to reach agreement on interservice semantics but to use one's forces effectively against the enemy's forces in the face of uncertainty.

Offensive action: A military action such as a battle or a campaign in which a combatant makes a forward movement to engage the enemy, and in so doing takes the initiative in choosing the time, place, strength, and type of forces committed, as well as the objectives and general deployment and employment concepts for the commitment of offensive forces.

Defensive action: A military action that usually combines some form of positional defense such as the defense of an ocean area or airspace or a ridgeline, with some form of mobile defense in which deployed forces seek opportunities for a *counteroffensive* once the enemy's offensive intentions are clear. A defender may trade time and space in order to minimize losses or to take advantage of changing terrain and weather to disrupt the enemy's forward movement. Giving up air, sea, or land space may also complicate an enemy's supply arrangements as well as his ability to control his forces or to conserve one's own forces for offensives elsewhere.

Combined arms: A permanent combat or a task force that integrates units of different combat capabilities to improve combat effectiveness. The concept usually suggests an ability to operate with surprise, shock action, overwhelming firepower, and mobility against an enemy. A ground-combat combined-arms force, for example, would include infantry, artillery, armor, engineers, and communications elements along with some logistical sustainability.

Schemes of maneuver: Types of movement by attacking forces that aim to produce high enemy casualties, destroy his unit cohesion, and demoralize his forces. The simplest such action is a *frontal attack* or *assault,* which pits an attacker directly against a defender's strength but may have the advantages of surprise and superiority of combat power. An *envelopment* seeks to place overwhelming combat power on a vulnerable flank (side) of the enemy's deployed forces. Although the term comes from ground combat, it can apply to air and naval forces that attack the flank of enemy forces at an angle different from their direction of movement. An envelopment seeks to apply fire to enemy forces that cannot bring all their own firepower to bear on the attacker. Sometimes attackers attempt a *double envelopment,* which means two simultaneous flank attacks from different directions.

Turning movement: A flanking action that aims to change a strategic relationship by opening a new campaign theater or adding a new area of engagement (a *front*) to an ongoing campaign. A successful turning movement forces a decisive change in the way an enemy deploys his troops; this change may take the form of a withdrawal or redeployment of forces as an alternative to destruction or surrender. The Allied landing at Anzio in 1944 was planned as a turning movement designed to alter the Italian campaign, but it was unsuccessful.

Penetration: An essentially linear action in which an attacking force ruptures enemy defensives, usually by massing forces with superiority in numbers, mobility, and firepower. A successful penetration allows the attacker to destroy enemy reserves behind the defensive line and to disrupt enemy command and logistical organization (see Logistics, page 590). In German and Soviet operations especially, penetrations usually led to exploitation operations (or *deep operations*) that attempted to *encircle* (surround) major enemy forces.

Infiltration: The undetected movement of attacking forces through enemy advanced (or security) positions and main defenses, for the purpose of opening an engagement in an enemy's rear areas or against more distant (and less alert) reserve forces. Such operations involve ambushes, road blocks, and surprise attacks. A concept born in ground operations, infiltration is usually the first phase of a major ground force operation and is closer to tactics (see page 589) than operations. Dropping parachute infantry onto road junctions would be a type of infiltration-from-above.

Airborne operation: An action in which parachute infantry drop from transport aircraft, followed by air-landing units that are flown to the secure drop zone or landing area in towed (unpowered) gliders or transport aircraft. All the major World War II belligerents developed airborne operations forces, ranging from companies to armies, to conduct airborne operations (later known as *vertical envelopments*). Since parachute infantry had no sustained defense against tanks or artillery, air-landing units were essential sources of anti-tank and counterbattery support, but the lack of heavy weapons in all airborne formations restricted the distance they could be used away from friendly heavy ground forces, essential to stopping a mechanized enemy. The difficulty in resupplying airborne forces by parachute and dropped bundles also limited their usefulness. In Burma, for example, resupply and medical problems blunted the operations of the Long Range Penetration Forces, not just Japanese counterattacks.

Amphibious operation: An action in which seaborne ground combat forces land on beaches defended by the enemy in order to seize an island or a continental entrant. In World War II, the first requirement was air and naval superiority in the objective area so that amphibious shipping could conduct undisrupted landing operations. If the landing forces could not avoid an enemy ground defense force, the landing became an *amphibious assault* by the ship-to-shore movement of troops carried in amphibian tractors or beaching ships and craft. The lightly armed assault troops required fire support from naval guns and aircraft to overcome enemy beach defenses and mobile reserves. Sometimes airborne operations complemented amphibious operations to *interdict* (block) the routes of mobile reserve forces attempting to counterattack a landing force. Amphibious planners in Europe most feared German panzer counterattacks, while in the Pacific theater the major concern was Japanese air and naval attacks on amphibious shipping.

Air warfare: A broadly defined military activity consisting of two components: (1) *strategic air campaigns,* waged by aircraft that bomb urban populations, industrial centers, transportation systems, domestic military bases, power-generating facilities, and agricultural infrastructure such as fertilizer plants and irrigation systems, in order to crush an enemy's will and capability to wage war by destroying his homeland; and (2) *tactical air campaigns* targeted at enemy military bases and air, sea, and ground forces engaged in an active campaign, wherever they may be. The targets and the desired outcomes of air strikes defined the difference between strategic and tactical air operations, not the types of aircraft and ordnance used. Heavy bombers might strike ground troops, as they did in France in 1944; carrier tactical aircraft might drop mines to destroy merchant shipping, as they did in Japan in 1945.

Both strategic and tactical air warfare might require reconnaissance missions, air combat against enemy planes, and attacks on enemy air bases and radar systems. Offensive tactical air operations, however, include attacks on enemy formations and supplies moving toward the battle *(interdiction)* or attacks on enemy forces already locked in battle *(close air support).* Aircraft also provided important services to ground forces such as artillery spotting, emergency resupply, casualty evacuation, electronic warfare, reconnaissance, and transporting personnel and high-level commanders. World War II was the first war in which air power played a significant part in a war's outcome.

Naval operation: A military action fought by navies against other navies for control of the sea, against land targets in range of naval aircraft and guns, and against seaborne commerce. Sea control—comprehensive or limited—is essential to naval operations. In World War II, naval operations involved attacks on fleets by carrier aircraft, land-based aircraft (usually long-range bombers), and warships firing naval guns and torpedoes, and ships that laid mines.

After the United States took command of the Western Pacific in 1945 by defeating the Imperial Japanese Navy (sea control), it had the opportunity to sever Japan from its overseas resources through blockade and commerce raiding and to conduct operations against land targets by shelling, air attacks, and amphibious landings. Destroying merchant ships by submarines did not require traditional command of the sea, as German and American submarines proved. Submarine warfare, however, did require complex supporting operations by air and surface forces to weaken the enemy's anti-submarine operations.

Tactics

Tactics are the discrete actions taken by ground combat units, aircraft, and ships and their personnel to defeat the enemy in battle. Tactics kill people and destroy things. Tactics can be situation-specific, that is, shaped by a single engagement. Tactics may also refer to *tactical doctrine*—institutionally recommended ways of fighting used to train individuals and units before they enter combat. Successful combat leadership and unit performance usually results from a combination of sound tactical doctrine with the flexibility to apply and adapt that doctrine under fire, according to the conditions of the battlefield. Tactical performance depends on a thorough understanding of both weapons systems and human factors like morale, training, enemy capabilities, fatigue, unit cohesion, and small-unit leadership.

Each type of combat has unique tactical characteristics. For example, aerial combat by fighter aircraft in World War II depended on pilot gunnery with machine guns and cannon. A few pilots were superior marksmen, but most were unable to choose the proper range and angle of attack against an elusive foe. Moreover, pilots had to be alert to their oxygen supply, which was affected by both altitude and gravity in steep, fast dives and sharp turns. Blacked-out pilots, deprived of blood flow to the brain, did not fly well. In naval combat, surface warships made radical changes of direction (zigzag maneuvers) to avoid enemy shells, torpedoes, and aerial bombs; such maneuvering, however, had to be adjusted to allow a ship's batteries to make accurate target-laying for their own salvos. In tank-against-tank warfare, maneuverability, firepower, and armor had to be balanced. From 1942 to 1945 American and Soviet tanks tended to be more maneuverable, but German tanks took the lead in main gun (turret cannon) lethality, measured by range, sighting, and gun-shell penetrating characteristics. German tanks also carried heavier frontal armor. Therefore, even with better main guns, Allied and Soviet tank crews had to look for side angle and rear shots at close range to destroy or at least cripple German heavy tanks, whose crews placed a high premium on driver-gunner coordination and the clever use of terrain for cover and concealment. It also meant that Allied and Soviet tanks fought and survived best when engaged as pairs and threes so that one tank could engage while others moved, especially since gyro-stabilized tank guns did not exist or were in early development.

Logistics

Logistics refers to the material support and movement of armed forces. It always influences, and often determines, the outcome of warfare. Beans, bullets, bandages, and brake fluid make or break armies; oil keeps ships at sea; and spare parts for engines put aircraft in the sky. Logistics applies to military actions at the global, theater, operational, and tactical levels of warfare. In World War II, the United States and British Commonwealth required thousands of ships to supply their forces around the world (an example of global logistics). Germany relied on railroads to serve its continental forces on three fronts, and Japan moved supplies by sea to its Pacific bases and by sea and rail to China (theater logistics). During specific ground operations, the distribution of supplies focused on rail-truck combinations, sometimes supplemented by cargo aircraft as a last resort. At sea, operational logistics depended on replenishment ships, some of which (in the U.S. Navy) could transfer supplies while under way. Ground forces in battle received supplies by trucks, light vehicles, wagons and carts pulled by animals, pack animals (mules in Italy, elephants in Burma), bicycles, hand-carts, and human porters. A can of machine gun ammunition carried by hand is an example of tactical logistics.

Logistical activity entails more than transportation. Someone must manufacture or grow the bullets and beans, package them, and send them on their way through a series of depots and other storage facilities. Some things are durable goods such as tanks; others such as tank shells and gasoline are consumables. For military equipment (durable), important considerations are mass production, standardization, and simplicity. By focusing on these factors, the United States and the Soviet Union reduced the need for skilled workers and technicians and allowed the rapid replacement of destroyed weapons. American ground forces classified goods according to their characteristics of manufacture, function, and durability and adopted a system of supply classification that combined the question of consumables/durables and the ability to predict routine requirements: (1) food, water, and living supplies; (2) regular organizational equipment and weapons; (3) petroleum, oil, lubricants, and related maintenance supplies; (4) special equipment and nonissue supplies; (5) ammunition. The flow of supplies varied depending on calculations of need (for training, routine combat, or emergency combat) and by distribution system. Requirements might come from providers ("push" logistics) or from requests by users ("pull" logistics). Planners in World War II became intimately familiar with concepts like "days of fire" for shell consumption, steaming miles for warships, and flying hours for aircraft.

In addition to procuring and distributing supplies, military forces try to keep their durable goods in use through maintenance and repair, supplemented by recovery and salvage operations. A tank that blows up may leave a salvageable track; a tank with an inoperable track can be recovered and repaired. Maintenance of major weapons systems—crucial in warfare—may be performed by various people and organizations, depending on the time and complexity of the work and the source of parts and skilled technicians. A sailor can chip and paint a deck, but specialized maintenance men in a secure naval base are needed to change a damaged propeller for an aircraft carrier.

Maintenance logisticians responsible for bomber wings and tank battalions have to calculate their ability to provide adequate numbers of aircraft and tanks for their organizational missions and provide these statistics (operational readiness rates) to their commanders. Individual weapons systems and units can be fully mission-capable, mission-capable, or not mission-capable, depending on their state of maintenance and repair. Such calculations may rest, for example, on the barrel life of a machine gun (how many bullets can it fire before it is so worn that it is no longer accurate?) or the number of flying hours for a gas-piston fighter engine (how long can it fly without a severe risk of malfunction?). Major weapons may be "deadlined" (declared not operational until repaired or given replacement parts) or "written off" as nonrepairable and hence available for the stripping of usable parts (cannibalization) or change of mission (such as turning a tank turret into part of a concrete defense bunker).

Medical services are logistical requirements, at least until the wounded are out of a combat zone. At the operational level, military medical services focus on the emergency treatment, collecting, classification (triage), and evacuation (clearing) of casualties. No matter how horrible wounds may appear, they all kill through shock, heart and respiratory failure, brain damage, or catastrophic bleeding. The quicker the treatment and evacuation to emergency surgical units, the more likely a patient's survival, so planning and coordination between transportation officers and medical services officers is crucial. Medical treatment has a direct effect on troop morale, as does the speedy removal and disposition of dead comrades by graves registration and mortuary units.

Successful commanders are almost always skilled logisticians or have expert logistical staffs and service force commanders. As one military adage goes, amateurs talk tactics, but professionals talk logistics.

APPENDIX 3:

WEAPONS

The arsenals that the belligerents of World War II turned upon one another brought a new level of lethality to warfare. Although many types of weapons made their first appearance in World War I—or even before—the arsenals of 1937–1945 made combat between conventional armed forces more deadly (but not more efficient) than ever, while the development of aerial weapons made attacks on civilians in cities horrific. Most of the war's destruction came from masses of bullets, shells, and bombs that were "aimed" in only a loose sense of the word. *Area fire*—whether streams of machine gun bullets or tons of high-explosive bombs from a B-29 bomber—characterized World War II combat. The mass, industrialized, assembly-line production of weapons made such deluges of firepower possible. The exploration of nuclear energy for destructive purposes by both coalitions represented another path of advanced research and technology turned toward weapons design. Given the limitations of 1940s technology, the limited time for training combatants, the sheer size and complexity of the armed forces, and the demand for mass-produced weapons, the belligerents could hardly afford to push technological innovation too far. The one nation that did—Nazi Germany—lost.

Nevertheless, World War II armed forces did make halting steps to improve the accuracy and effectiveness of weapons, largely through electromagnetic technology. Probably the single most effective killer in ground combat was the artillery and mortar forward observer (FO) team—a group of soldiers armed with binoculars, compasses, good maps, and—the critical element—dependable radios. These teams—used by all armies in some form—could call for fire from full battalions of artillery, could rapidly correct and adjust concentrations of shells, and could kill soldiers and destroy all military vehicles except the heaviest tanks and assault guns. Often infantry companies (especially Anglo-American units in Europe in 1944–45) functioned as if their purpose was not "to close with and destroy the enemy" but to protect the FO teams as they went about their deadly work.

In air and naval combat, the greatest electronic advance was *radar* (*radio direction and ranging*), which propagated radio waves through the atmosphere at known distances, altitudes, and speed and then measured the "return" when the waves met resistence from solid objects and bounced back. The underwater variant was *sonar* (*so*und *n*avigation *a*nd *r*anging) or *asdic* in British terms, in which ultrasonic waves penetrated water at calculable ranges and depths. An operator using radar or sonar could "see" or "hear" anything from a flight of enemy bombers to a hostile submarine.

Electronically powered or passive acoustic listening devices supplemented radar/sonar target identification by capturing and focusing sounds like the turning of ships' propellers or the rush of bubbling water (cavitation) made by a ship's bow. Radar and other electronic aids had many aerial applications: simple navigation by flying along preset radio beams from ground stations, guiding air defense artillery, directing interceptors toward attacking aircraft, locating large ground targets such as cities, and, in the experimental stage, providing guidance to bombs bound for ground targets. Radar and sonar were the essential improvements for directing World War II firepower.

The exploitation of the electromagnetic spectrum found many other World War II applications that enhanced destructiveness. One was the use of many types of radios for military communications, from the theater to the company level of command, which radically increased the volume and speed of information (and misinformation) available to a commander. Telephones, which were widely used in World War I, might be more secure and dependable, but wire systems took time to deploy and were vulnerable to artillery fire or bombs. Radios minimized these risks but also brought their own problems. Radio messages might be intercepted and "read" by the enemy, even if encoded. Moreover, radio intercepts might lead to the discovery of the transmitting station, which was usually linked to an operational headquarters. Woe to the talkative general who kept a stationary radio transmitter within the range of enemy artillery.

Lethality of another sort came from miniaturized transmitters in the fuse of a shell, which detonated the shell not by contact but by the return from a radio beam, hence the name *proximity fuse*. Such fused shells, exploited most by the United States, caused havoc with German ground forces and Japanese aircraft in 1944–45.

Ground Forces Weapons

In broad terms, ground combat forces—infantry, artillery, armor, anti-tank, and combat engineer units—employed weapons that served their missions and means of mobility, but all also had weapons for personal and vehicle protection that did not principally serve offensive purposes.

Infantry: Infantrymen had to carry their own weapons, often in difficult terrain like jungles and mountains and in all sorts of unpleasant weather. Infantry used rifles, submachine guns, automatic rifles, light and heavy machine guns, hand grenades, and mortars. Leaders and members of crew-served weapons (machine guns and mortars) carried pistols (handguns) and light rifles (carbines) or submachine guns.

The only officers who consistently carried swords were the Japanese, although infantrymen carried a wide variety of bayonets, knives, machetes or bolo knives, and entrenching tools that proved useful for close combat as well as digging.

Infantrymen fought with rifles that carried five to ten bullets and were fired from the shoulder. Bullets came in different sizes, ranging from 6.5 millimeters (mm) to 7.92mm or, in Anglo-American usage, .30-caliber bullets of several slight variants. The best mass-produced rifle was the U.S. M-1 (Garand), which fired eight rounds from a clip, one round with each trigger pull without working a manual bolt to reload the chamber. This feature made the M-1 a semiautomatic rifle with a gas-propelled bolt when all other standard models were hand-powered bolt-action rifles. Mauser (German) and Enfield (British) rifles had better workmanship, but the M-1 fired faster and just as accurately and could be maintained under virtually any battlefield condition. The Germans produced limited numbers of similar assault rifles late in the war. Pistols (revolvers and automatics) ranged from 7mm to 9mm (.35 caliber, with some up to .45 caliber) and came in many dependable models: Luger, Mauser, Sauer, Webley, Walther, Browning, Colt, Beretta, and Tokarev.

Submachine guns and carbines were for individual protection, but the automatic fire and heavy bullets of submachine guns made them popular for close combat in jungles, forests, and houses where, paired with hand grenades or "bombs," they were deadly killers. The German MP40 and Russian PPsH Model 1941 (both called "burp guns") shared the field with the American Thompson ("Tommy"), the Australian Owen, and the British Sten (Shepherd/Turpin-Enfield) guns. The Italian Beretta was also good, while the American M3 "grease gun" was heavy and accurate only at close range. Submachine guns used magazines (spring-activated bullet feeding) that contained up to 30 rounds or drums up to 50 rounds.

As infantry tactics developed during the war, foot soldiers grouped around air-cooled light machine guns in what became known as fire teams or sections. The Americans had two such weapons: the Browning Automatic Rifle (a two-man team) and the Browning .30-caliber M1919A4 and M1919A6 light machine guns (a five-man team). Other armies normally had similar weapons such as the German MG34 and MG42 machine guns and the British Bren (Brno-Enfield) gun. Whether the gun was mounted on a bipod or tripod—and some could use either—the team fired the gun from the prone or crouching position. Heavy machine guns (from water-cooled .30 caliber to air-cooled .50 caliber) were tripod or vehicle mounted on a pedestal or ring and required five men or a small vehicle to move. These machine guns were deadly long-distance (1,000-plus yards) defensive weapons and could also deliver heavy suppressive fire to support attacking infantry. The machine guns of World War II were improved weapons based on 1918 models: Degtyarev, Hotchkiss, Maxim, Vickers, Browning, and Nambu Types 97 and 99.

Infantry battalions and regiments had two types of artillery: lighter variants of cannon and howitzers found in artillery battalions or anti-tank (AT) cannon, and mortars of bore size from 60mm to 100mm. (Heavier mortars were classified as artillery.) A mortar was a metal tube mounted on a bipod and baseplate that sent a shell on a high trajectory down upon enemy infantry. Skilled mortarmen could fire shells distances of under 100 yards. Mortar shells were visible in flight but made almost no noise until they burst. Infantrymen did not like mortar fire.

Infantrymen did not like tanks, either, or any other type of armored fighting vehicle. They had some defensive weapons against tanks, but none gave infantry much advantage. High-velocity towed cannon had some utility, but late-war German tanks had too much frontal armor even when Allied AT cannon went from 37mm to 57mm to 75mm in bore size and with complementary shell improvements. The Germans made the best adjustment, using the deadly 88mm gun, an anti-aircraft cannon, as their key AT defense weapon. The "eighty-eight" was large, relatively immobile, and difficult to conceal, but for all that a superior tank-buster. Russian AT towed guns proved as limited as Allied models and were largely abandoned, except for the M44 100mm gun, modeled on the German Panzerabwehrkanone (PAK) 75, also a good gun.

Infantry often had to depend on anti-tank mines (stationary, concealed explosives) or light anti-tank weapons that fired an armor-penetrating rocket. The German Panzerschreck used an 88mm shaped-charge rocket that could penetrate eight inches of armor plate, ample to destroy Allied tanks with frontal shots. The American version was a 2.36-inch rocket also fired from a shoulder-held launcher or "bazooka," named for an odd comic strip musical instrument. The British had the Projectile Infantry Anti-Tank or PIAT, which could launch its anti-tank "bomb" for a high-angle, armor-avoiding shot. The German Panzerfaust was probably the best of the lot because of its large warhead and simple one-man launching tube. (A bazooka required a two-man crew.) Infantry also used various hand-carried explosives or gasoline bombs (the Molotov cocktail) to attack tank track systems or rear-mounted engines, a tactic of desperation most often used by the Russians and Japanese.

In World War II, land mines became a staple economy-of-force weapon (supplemented by boobytraps), used with great effectiveness by German and Russian armies in their many defensive operations of 1942–1945. A mine is an exploding device that is planted in the ground or concealed in some other "host" like a barbed-wire fence or a house wall. Originally developed for naval warfare, mines for ground warfare were generally categorized as anti-tank (or anti- any other vehicle) and anti-personnel mines. Anti-tank mines had to be powerful enough to at least blow off a track; since tank armor was thinnest at a tank's floor, a mine might do even more damage when it exploded beneath a tank.

Any mine designed to cripple a tank would destroy any lesser vehicle. Mine designers had to produce pressure-plate exploders that could not be set off by light vehicles, reserving their blasts for their main victims. The Germans developed a family of Teller mines for a wide range of targets; these mines were fused to blow up any enemy engineer who tried to clear and disarm them. The Japanese and Americans soon developed similar anti-tank mines. The major limitation of such mines was that they had to be planted by hand or simply laid in the open (perhaps concealed by snow or sand), which made minefield laying a labor-intensive, time-consuming activity.

The Germans and Japanese excelled in using anti-personnel mines and booby-traps of many sorts, some sophisticated, others extemporized from small shells and hand grenades. The German S-mine made infantrymen miserable by popping into the air before exploding between the victim's knees and chest; its activator could not be easily seen in rough ground. Wooden box mines, detonated by a trip-wire or pressure devices, could not be found by a metal mine detector and could be adapted to many "hosts." Small mines made searching dead soldiers for intelligence materials dangerous; the most ruthless soldiers had no compunction in boobytrapping the wounded. Mines of any sort always slowed an enemy force, making it vulnerable to artillery and mortar fire.

Mine clearance depended on the identification of a mined area, an assessment of the mines' locations and characteristics, and the use of appropriate countermine equipment and techniques. For large fields, engineers preferred to blow up the mines in place with various types of line-charges (linear explosives) or armored engineer vehicles like a flail tank. Cleared lanes through fields could then be marked. Anti-personnel mines usually required location by a mine detector and then hand digging and disarming. If speed was of the essence, mines were marked and left in place, still a threat to the unwary.

Artillery: After the dominance of artillery on the battlefields of World War I, no major army ignored the need for a wide variety of guns in massive numbers. Artillery pieces can be classified by several characteristics. One measure is barrel length. A short-barreled cannon is a howitzer; a long-barreled cannon is a gun. Generally, a howitzer could fire a heavier shell more accurately than a gun, but at reduced range. A howitzer shell travels a high trajectory, a gun shell a flatter trajectory. A gun fires shells at a higher velocity and has greater penetrating power against tanks, fortifications, and buildings. Artillery pieces can also be classified by source of mobility. Siege guns and railway guns moved on railway cars or could be pulled only by the most powerful tractors. The heaviest field guns (175mm–240mm and above) moved behind tractors—slowly. Medium artillery (105mm–175mm) was normally towed by dual-drive trucks, but such guns also served as self-propelled artillery in armored formations, which meant that 105mm howitzers and some heavier guns (150mm and 155mm) were mounted on tank chassis. Another World War II variant was the assault gun, designed to blast fortified positions. The best was the German tracked Sturmgeschütz with its high-velocity 100mm gun, also a tank killer. By war's end the Russians had a reliable family of self-propelled guns for armored warfare: the Su76 general-purpose cannon, the Su100 anti-tank gun, and the Su122 assault gun with the type designators indicating cannon bore width in millimeters. Light artillery came in sizes from 57mm to 105mm, with the most common the 75mm howitzer. Some of these cannon could be disassembled and packed on animals for mountain and jungle operations. Others could be easily pulled by light vehicles, which made them attractive for airborne and amphibious operations.

The types of shells and their fuses made artillery pieces more effective than their World War I equivalents. The basic shell was high explosive (HE), which destroyed people and structures with concussion, blast effects, and shell fragments. A shrapnel shell upon detonation produced a shower of fragments much like a giant shotgun; when exploded above ground among trees ("air burst"), this shell and HE shells multiplied their fragmentation effects on troops. Some cannon—usually guns—used anti-tank rounds (HEAT) with high-velocity, "shaped charge" shells to bore holes through armor plate and destroy a tank's interior. White phosphorus (WP) shells started fires. Some shells provided screening smoke, and others flares to brighten the night for defenders. Shells also could carry propaganda leaflets, which provided enemy troops with scarce paper for varied purposes.

Armored and mechanized vehicles: Invented during World War I, the tank was essentially an armored caterpillar tractor with guns, designed to cross terrain by the movement of its tracks. Tanks provided mobile fire support for infantry, but their principal missions came from a horse cavalry heritage: reconnaissance, screening and counter-reconnaissance, the penetration of enemy defenses ("the charge"), and rapid exploitation operations in depth against enemy reserve forces and installations. These missions became integrated as armored warfare, conducted by combined-arms units of tanks, self-propelled artillery, anti-aircraft guns, mounted infantry and combat engineers, communications vehicles, and truck convoys of refuellers and maintenance vehicles.

As World War II continued, tanks became larger, more heavily armed and armored, and more powerful, but not faster. Their basic components never changed. Tanks carried a main, high-velocity cannon in a turret that could usually traverse 360°, supplemented by one or two internal, forward-firing machine guns (one a coaxial machine gun, turret-mounted and aligned with the cannon) and an external heavy machine gun mounted near the turret-hatch for anti-aircraft defense. Tank crews numbered three to five men to drive the tank and fire its weapons, two or three in the turret, and one or two inside the hull. Main guns went from 37mm in the 1930s to 88mm and 90mm by the war's end, the former mounted in some German Panther and Tiger tanks and the latter in the U.S. M-26 Pershing. The Russian T-34 at first mounted a 75mm short gun, then switched to 76mm and 85mm long guns of greater penetrating power and long-range accuracy. American and British tanks mounted a short 75mm gun, but both armies changed some tanks to a long 76mm gun or 17-pounder (UK) in 1944 to close the "gun gap" and "armor gap" created by the German Panthers and Tigers. Most American and British tanks, however, were undergunned until the Pershing arrived in 1945 or the conversion to the Firefly Sherman with the long 17-pound gun. The Stalin (JS II) Russian heavy tank carried the heaviest gun at 122mm when it appeared in 1944.

Tank design involved trade-offs between shape (wider and lower was better), engine choice, amount of armor on the bow/frontal plane and turret, gun size, and maneuverability over soft and steep terrain. Another consideration was the ease of mass production and field maintenance—a factor that weighed heavily with the Americans and Russians. Although on-road tank speeds could reach 40–50 miles per hour (mph) in some models, tanks seldom needed to run at more than 30 mph even in exploitation operations because of fuel usage (1–4 gallons per mile), track wear, and mechanical breakdowns in the engine and powertrain to the sprocket wheels. Main battle tank weights varied, but Allied, Russian, and German medium tanks fell in the 30–35-ton range. The Panthers and Tigers started at 44 tons and reached 69 tons while the Soviet Stalin reached 53 tons. The heavier the tank, the less effective its rough-terrain speed and maneuverability. (A tank's ability to cross moist ground was calculated by matching total weight against track width in pounds-per-square-inch overpressure, an operational concern tankers fully understood but infantrymen often did not.) All tanks faced common problems: the crews' limited visibility, fuel consumption, vulnerability to catastrophic fires and ammunition explosions, and mechanical breakdowns. Design changes sometimes helped (switching from gas to diesel engines), but design changes to increase survivability meant more weight and thus reductions in maneuverability, speed, and the ability to cross extemporized military bridges.

Armored formations employed light tanks, which reached high speeds (50–60 mph) by sacrificing armor (one-half inch was standard) and mounting light guns (37mm to short 75mm). Light tanks (often the main battle tanks of the 1930s) performed best in reconnaissance roles by supporting scouting vehicles, but required medium tank support if engaging enemy tanks. The American armored forces in Europe in 1944–45 created cavalry groups of medium and light tanks and armored cars to scout ahead of corps-sized formations. Attached medium tank battalions (usually only one) provided armored support for infantry divisions.

Tank chassis and modified tanks produced armored vehicles that supported armored warfare. The British were especially inventive in creating tracked engineering vehicles to breach barbed-wire and minefields, assault fortifications with flame-throwers, fill trench lines, and bridge canals and ditches. It became common for British and American tank battalions to include tanks with mounted bulldozer blades. Tank chassis could mount howitzers; the U.S. M-7 Priest with a 105mm howitzer became a mainstay for American armored divisions. Another variant was to mount a heavier high-velocity gun in a lighter turret or another mounting arrangement and make it a self-propelled anti-tank weapon. The Germans, for example, put a long 75mm gun on a panzer MkIV chassis without a turret, but provided 3-inch armor and 30-plus mph speed. The U.S. used the M-3 and M-4 tank chassis for the M-10 and M-36 tank destroyers, which mounted 3-inch and 90mm cannon in open turrets.

The armored forces included mobile reconnaissance forces and mounted infantry (or Panzergrenadiers) to make the tank battalions less vulnerable to ambushes. Reconnaissance vehicles could be wheeled (armored cars) and ranged from unarmored jeeps and Kübelwagens to multiwheeled (six or eight) cannon-armed cars like the Allied M-8 Greyhound or the German eight-wheeled M234 Panzerspähwagen. Accompanying infantry rode in vehicles with wheels in front and tracks in the rear. These "infantry fighting vehicles" or "half-tracks" could mount light cannon, but more often carried multiple heavy and light machine guns. Most common were the German 9-ton Schützenpanzerwagen (SPW) and the U.S. M-3 10-ton half-track, designed to carry one infantry squad. Mechanized infantry employed the usual infantry weapons, plus their vehicle machine guns and vehicle-mounted mortars and assault guns. Other half-tracks carried .50-caliber anti-aircraft machine guns in multiple mounts or towed artillery pieces.

The nontactical vehicles of armored formations were largely trucks or vans on truck chassis, although commanders often used half-tracks jammed with radios and maps and bristling with antennas as forward command posts. Trucks also towed field artillery and anti-tank guns in armored divisions.

Aerial Ordnance

Without weapons, an aircraft is not a military instrument except for administrative and auxiliary services. Although aircraft themselves reached new levels of capability in terms of range, speed, engine-power, maneuverability, survivability, payload, and navigation accuracy, none of these improvements would have brought military advantage without complementary improvements in aerial ordnance. Such developments were, in fact, uneven and came relatively late (1944–45) in the war. Most of the damage in air warfare in World War II came from "iron" or unguided bombs filled with high explosives (HE) and directed at ground targets and from wing-mounted machine guns used in air-to-air combat.

The most dramatic attempt to escape the limitations of manned aircraft (air defenses and weather) came from the Germans, who developed two operational unpiloted rockets, the revenge weapons (Vergeltungswaffen) known as the V-1 buzz bomb and the V-2 ballistic missile. First employed in June 1944, the V-1 was a cruise missile powered by a jet engine, capable of carrying a high-explosive warhead of almost a ton. Launched from canted ground rails, the V-1 had a primitive navigation system and autopilot that could not be jammed, but its accuracy was equally primitive, since only three-quarters of the buzz bombs would fall within an eight-mile radius around the theoretical aim point. Moreover, the V-1 could be tracked by radar and shot down by interceptors and anti-aircraft artillery, since its speed was approximately 350 mph. Nevertheless, over 6,000 V-1s fell on Allied territory (mostly in Britain) and inflicted more than 50,000 casualties. Some 10,000 were shot down or failed in flight.

Having begun their rocket program in the 1930s, the Germans developed a short-range (about 200 miles) ballistic missile, the V-2, 46 feet long and carrying a ton-plus of high explosives. It was even less accurate than the V-1, but it could not be shot down since it reached 2,200 mph in its downward plunge. The Germans fired some 3,000 V-2s at targets in Britain, France, Belgium, and western Germany, causing nearly 13,000 casualties. The relatively light payload and gross inaccuracy spared crowded cities and mass military bases from catastrophic damage, but the lack of defense against the V-2 gave Allied leaders pause. Allied air and ground operations gave a high priority to destroying V-1 and V-2 rocket sites. Savaged by air attacks and overrun by ground forces, the launch sites and production and test facilities fell to the Allies with 7,000 V-2s still unlaunched. The V-2 had to be attacked on its open launch pads during fueling (alcohol and liquid oxygen), for once launched the Allies could only hope for failures (quite common) in the inertial guidance system or overheating and disintegration during the reentry process. One benefit of the V-2 program was that its development starved several promising surface-to-air anti-aircraft missile programs of scarce engineering talent and technology.

The other belligerents counted on manned aircraft—bombers—to carry ordnance to industrial cities, power-generating complexes, and military factories and depots. Gravity or free-falling bombs followed predictable (more or less) flight parabolas to earth and could be fused to explode above ground, upon contact, or after penetrating the ground or concrete buildings. The high explosives in a bomb were about one-third to half its total weight, which might range from 250 pounds to 2,000 pounds or higher for special missions like attacking underground fortifications and concrete dams. The Tall Boys dropped by Bomber Command weighed six tons and were in use by 1944. In March 1945 Bomber Command's Lancasters dropped 11-ton Grand Slam bombs that took out the Bielefeld aqueduct merely by their shock effect. Dive-bombers carried much lighter bombs but could achieve great accuracy, provided they avoided anti-aircraft fire.

The high explosive content of a bomb was state-of-the-art in the 1940s, but airmen knew that HE bombs alone would do limited damage. Instead, they counted on "secondary explosions," which could mean bombing and igniting gas mains in a city, stockpiled ammunition, oil and gasoline inside a storage tank or an aircraft carrier, or a factory that made artillery shells. Fires and collapsing buildings killed people and wrecked production facilities with greater lethality than bursting bombs. An alternative to the HE bomb was the incendiary bomblet, which weighed only six pounds; it was loaded with white phosphorus or some other chemical mixture that reached high temperatures and could not be extinguished with water. For battlefield targets, the Allies developed napalm, a naphtha-jellied gasoline that burned or suffocated enemy personnel with its searing fires.

From the perspective of an ordnance explosives expert and warhead designer, the development of a nuclear warhead provided an exciting liberation from the physical limitations of chemical explosives. The blast effects of uranium 235 and plutonium isotope fission could be measured in TNT equivalents of tens of thousands of tons. One bomb could substitute for several thousand bomber raids. In addition to its immense blast, the heat of a nuclear explosion brought instantaneous incineration or spontaneous fires to anything burnable within several miles of ground zero. Blast and fire could create human casualties like conventional weapons, if on a greater scale, but a nuclear explosion also released radiation that destroyed human cellular systems and brought death through organic failure.

All the belligerents developed rockets to be fired from aircraft at either ground or aerial targets. Rockets could also serve in the ground-to-ground artillery role, used most extensively by the Soviets. Since terminal guidance systems for rockets did not reach common operational use, military rocketry sought to join light but potent warheads with high-velocity rockets fired in salvos that would go roughly where they were aimed with crude sighting devices and the Mark I eyeball. The Americans, British, and Soviets pioneered in the use of rockets ranging from 2.36 inches to 5 inches for aircraft attacks on tanks and found that rocket attacks from above brought massed armored attacks to a confused halt. Aerial rockets also proved deadly against railroad locomotives and railcars.

Confronted with raid after raid by Allied bombers, the Germans and then the Japanese tried to use air-to-air rockets to shoot down heavy bombers, a tactic that allowed the interceptors to operate outside the range of the bombers' machine guns. The Germans had some success with aerial rockets against bombers, but American escort fighters blunted their use against day bombers. Luftwaffe night-fighters, however, found aerial rockets deadly against the RAF and even dropped aerial mines on parachutes as effective anti-bomber weapons.

Like air-to-air rockets, aircraft machine guns and cannon were useful against ground or air targets. Machine guns, which might range from one to eight on a fighter-interceptor, started in the .30-caliber range at the war's beginning but shifted into the .50-caliber range by war's end. Cannon often replaced machine guns as the basic air weapon, especially for ground attack fighter-bombers. The Germans and the Russians even found ways to mount a 75mm cannon in an under-carriage pod as a tank-buster. To attack armored vehicles and armored bombers, the Russians and Germans led the race to rearm single- and dual-engined fighters and fighter-bombers with 20mm cannon, which had more killing power than machine guns. Usually wing strength and aerodynamic handling limited the number of cannon to one per wing, so it was not unusual to find aircraft (except American and British) with a combination of cannon and machine guns in the wing mounts. Some heavy German night interceptors carried a cannon in a topside turret, another effective bomber-killer. On the other hand, the standard armament for strategic bombers remained a combination of .30-caliber and .50-caliber machine guns. These weapons switched from one to two guns in the powered ball turrets of American bombers until the U.S. Army Air Forces armed the B-29 Superfortress with 20mm cannon as well as .50-caliber machine guns. Aerial cannon still required sighting and close-range firing, but their shells had greater destructiveness than machine gun bullets because they carried an explosive warhead.

Aerial ordnance in World War II reflected incremental changes in the ordnance introduced in 1914–1918, but the development of rocketry, missilery, and nuclear warheads hinted at the potential destructiveness of new forms of weapons for all types of warfare.

Naval Ordnance

The surface warships of World War II depended on naval guns as their main armament and torpedoes as supplementary weapons. In addition to their main batteries, which carried a ship's offensive punch against other ships and land targets, large warships carried light guns (5-inch and 3-inch) and 40mm and 20mm rapid-firing cannon as well as heavy machine guns to defend themselves from aircraft and small surface combatants. Usually the armament of a warship represented a combination of arms for offensive naval missions and defensive weapons.

The heaviest guns a ship carried were called its main battery, even if the main battery consisted of one or two 3-inch guns in an open gun tub. Main batteries, however, usually meant one to three guns mounted in a turret, either alone or paired fore and aft of a warship's superstructure. Some battleships and cruisers carried turreted guns amidships for additional firepower, but such a position limited turret traverse (turn) both fore and aft. For a battleship, the common arrangement was six guns in two turrets forward and three guns in one turret aft, but other arrangements might be four turrets of two or three guns each. The bore size might vary from 18 inches (Japanese superbattleships) to 12 inches in older models in almost every navy. The standard British and German gun was 15 inches, for American battleships 16 inches. The maximum effective range of a battleship's main batteries fell between 20,000 and 30,000 yards or 15–20 miles. Actual engagements occurred at 10–15 miles. American battleships at Surigao Strait engaged at 12 nautical miles. Heavy and light cruisers (usually divided as vessels above or below 10,000 tons) might carry a variety of main battery guns in numbers (some as high as eight or ten, others as few as six), but most of the guns were either 8-inch or 6-inch long naval guns, smaller versions of the main batteries on battleships. Cruisers usually mounted torpedoes in launchers amidships, as part of their offensive punch. Some classes of heavy cruisers in several navies carried a suite of 12 torpedo tubes. Both battleships and cruisers carried 14–20 dual-purpose 5-inch and 3-inch guns (or some equivalent) for defensive roles against aircraft. They also carried one or two floatplanes that could be used for naval gunfire spotting and scouting, lowered and recovered by giant cranes mounted on the stern.

The gradual adoption of radar to naval gunnery in World War II provided a welcome escape from the historic tyranny of aiming naval guns by eyesight. The gap between the range of shells and the powers of the eyeball—however enhanced by magnifying optical sights and rangefinders—widened early in the twentieth century. Providing battleships with airborne spotters helped some, at least during daylight. The most advanced modern navies used sophisticated optical sighting systems. One reason the Japanese specialized in night naval battles was to offset Anglo-American sighting systems and aerial reconnaissance. The use of radar provided a welcome alternative to optical sighting and made accurate night-shooting a real possibility at long ranges. Careful plotting with radar also allowed a naval commander or ship's captain to keep track of friendly warships, often the unintended victims of friendly fire in battles at night or in reduced visibility. Radar-based navigation allowed warships to take evasive action with a reduced risk of collision or running aground. The central functions of naval command shifted from the bridge to the combat information center, where the radars and radios did their magic.

Destroyers, destroyer escorts, frigates, and corvettes had main batteries that might be six 5-inch turret guns on a heavy destroyer to one or two 3-inch guns on the smallest escort vessels. Destroyers, which also mounted torpedo tubes, participated in offensive fleet actions as the naval equivalent of scouts and skirmishers, but the lighter vessels worked primarily to protect convoys from air and submarine attack and possessed rapid-firing guns of various types and depth charges (undersea bombs). Destroyers also performed the escort role for submarine and air defense.

Weapons on destroyers and lighter warships often were identified by their bore diameter and barrel length (caliber) as in 5-inch/38 or 3-inch/50 since such designators gave the analyst some sense of the gun's range and accuracy, with the longer barrel being the more capable. Barrel length in inches equaled bore width (5-inch) multiplied by caliber (38), which meant that a standard American destroyer carried main battery guns approximately 15 feet long.

The ammunition fired from main battery naval guns, stored in armored magazines below the turrets, came in several types, dictated by target. Armor-piercing shells were fired against other warships and coastal fortifications, high explosives against land targets (fixed or moving), and flare shells to light up the night above any target. Like artillery shells, naval shells might be fused for different bursting effects or maximum penetration. The size of heavy naval guns demanded that the actual shell be loaded separately from the bagged powder charges, which came into the turret on lifts and trolleys and were rammed into the breech separately from the shell; lighter guns like 6-inchers and 5-inchers used fixed ammunition with a brass cartridge.

Rapid-firing cannon (called pom-poms in many navies) came from Scandinavian-British designers like Oerlikon and Bofors and could be mounted in pairs or as single weapons in a variety of open gun mounts. Potent against any sort of target, these guns came in 40mm, 25mm, and 20mm bore sizes and included large magazines that allowed rapid loading and firing. A Bofors 40mm gun could fire 120 rounds a minute, the 20mm gun double that number. The Swedish Bofors saw service in virtually every navy in some sort of adaptation or copy. Pom-poms could be found on every warship type, from battleship to submarine. The Japanese battleship *Yamato* carried 174 rapid-fire guns, the American *South Dakota* 148 such guns. Late-war American destroyers employed 12 to 16 of the heavy Bofors cannon against attacking Japanese aircraft that slipped past the rapid-fire 5-inch/38-caliber dual-purpose guns that engaged targets at the higher altitudes.

The most dramatic change in naval warfare, especially fleet battles, came from the use of land-based and carrier aircraft to attack warships. The threat of enemy air attacks, for example, made night actions much more attractive to a force operating with aerial inferiority, whether self-inflicted or unavoidable. Naval commanders knew that their own carriers would always be more vulnerable than their battleships and cruisers, since aircraft carriers carried aviation gasoline and aerial ordnance that had to be handled on the modestly protected flight and hangar decks. With damage-limiting structural design like hull compartmentalization, the use of bilge pumps and counter-flooding systems, and the employment of skilled and valiant fire-fighters and damage-control parties, large warships proved difficult to sink. If enemy aircraft could deliver several bombs and torpedoes on an enemy warship, however, it might float but not fight. Carrier-based dive-bombers proved potent attackers in terms of bombing accuracy, but their bombs were too light to inflict crippling structural damage on a battleship. The same bombs exploding in a hangar deck, however, created a nautical hell no survivor ever forgot and sent carriers out of the battle. Air-dropped torpedoes carried enough high explosive to crack the strongest hulls, but a single torpedo seldom put a large warship out of action. Bombs, shells, and torpedoes in the tens sank large warships, so air planners knew that they needed many carrier air groups to wage naval air offensive operations.

The torpedo was the greatest ship-killer of World War II. It sank more warships and merchantmen than any other piece of ordnance. Although naval torpedoes of the era carried more destructive warheads than their World War I predecessors, torpedo effectiveness depended on complementary developments in fusing, propulsion systems, and target acquisition. Torpedoes could be adapted to several launching platforms: submarine torpedo tubes, the launchers of cruisers and destroyers, a variety of aircraft from carrier-based planes, and large, long-distance naval reconnaissance and anti-submarine bombers. Torpedo fuses became more sophisticated with the introduction of magnetic or influence exploders, which proved unreliable in actual operations, but the attention to fusing produced reliable contact fuses, usually after a period of combat. The development of electric motors for torpedoes added a few knots to torpedo speed, but the real advantage of the electric torpedo (available early in the war to all but the Soviet Union's submarines) was that it left no telltale wake of bubbles en route to its target. The world-class torpedo in terms of speed, range, and lethality was the Japanese Type 93 or Long Lance, a killer with a 1,000-pound load of explosives that could travel 10 to 12 miles at a speed of almost 40 mph. Only its accuracy limited its effectiveness, but firing a spread of "fish" on different bearings gave compensatory coverage.

The most dramatic improvements in torpedo lethality came from sighting and guidance systems in submarines. First, submarines and surface ships adopted automated calculators to produce firing solutions that could match the speed and direction of the submarine, the torpedo, and the victim. Instead of having to launch on a direct line to a target, a submarine could make long-distance, stand-off launches that made its position difficult to calculate without radar and sonar. The next major improvement, in which the Germans led the field, was to give torpedoes some terminal guidance capability, that is, to match homing capabilities in the warhead to the characteristics of the target. One option was to guide the torpedo by wire from the submarine with the aimer using sonar or periscope sightings to make course adjustments, but such a system tied the submarine to the torpedo too long and increased the submarine's vulnerability to retaliatory attack by convoy escorts. A preferable system was "fire and forget," an approach that made the torpedo do its own homing without help from the parent submarine. The German began to test various homing systems in 1941–42 and used homing torpedoes in 1943–1945. Basically the homing torpedo listened to the noise created by the turning propellers of its target, adjusting course to follow the noise of the revolving screws and the wake the ship created. The U.S. Navy employed the same principle in developing anti-submarine torpedoes that could be dropped from a patrol aircraft or used as mines planted in the waters used by German and Japanese submarines as they left and returned to their bases. Such anti-submarine torpedoes had to compensate for the slower speed and reduced noise made by submarines.

Depth charges and mines rounded out the family of naval weapons used in World War II. Depth charges were barrels of explosives fused to explode at different depths to crush submarines' hulls; depth charges could be rolled off the stern racks of destroyers and other escorts or fired from launchers (Y-guns) to give greater coverage to a pattern of depth-charge attacks by an escort vessel. Mines had been available to naval forces for centuries, but in World War II they reached a new level of sophistication. Mines had always been detonated by contact with a ship or by human activation, decidedly dangerous to the intrepid miner. The modern mines of the 1940s could be detonated by the noise of a passing ship or by the magnetic field created by a hull in the ocean or simply by changes in water pressure caused by a passing ship. The most advanced mines could be dropped from a ship or aircraft, sink to the bottom of the sea, and then wait for an unsuspecting victim to pass overhead. The mine could then detonate in place or be released to close the distance to the hull before it exploded. Although such mines had their greatest application against merchantmen, they contributed to the war on Axis submarines. Often disdained by the naval commanders of every nation, mine warfare was one of the most effective naval weapons systems of the war. Mines were inexpensive to manufacture, could be placed in dense fields in natural choke points and harbor approaches, and did not require large, sophisticated mine-laying ships. They could be placed—according to design and purpose—from almost any ship or naval aircraft. Their only major drawback was that they could not discriminate between enemy and friendly ships, which meant that mine-clearance forces had to clear enemy waters that had been previously mined before they became safe for other ships.

APPENDIX 4:

EXPLORING WORLD WAR II

The investigation of World War II sprawls across a world of research and writing shaped by a range of literary, political, and intellectual tastes. There are more than 4,000 books alone about the war in print and available today—and that number undoubtedly excludes many publications not in English. In the United States only the Civil War produces more words on paper—and now words and pictures on electronic communicators. This appendix is only a portal to the information available to the student of World War II and represents advice rather than a statement of authoritativeness.

For the determined investigator, the place to start is an organization: the U.S. World War Two Studies Association, which is part of an international World War Two studies federation founded in 1967. The current secretary is Professor Mark Parillo of the Kansas State University history department, who may be reached electronically at parillo@pop.ksu.edu. Professor Parillo publishes the association's quarterly newsletter, which is the single best source on archival holdings and publications on World War II. For the *Newsletter*'s September 1999 issue, Professor Parillo compiled a major finding aid, "World War II on the Web," a guide to the use of electronic sources on the war. In addition, the *Newsletter* publishes bibliographical descriptions of current books and articles in several languages. Using his links with the other national commissions, Professor Parillo is an aggressive investigator of World War II subjects. The *Newsletter* publishes archival developments, meeting announcements, news of museums and historical sites, private papers availability, declassifications, audio-visual media news, and virtually anything else one might imagine useful as a World War II finding aid.

A second point-of-entry for identifying World War II literature, especially the publications of the historical divisions of the European armed forces, is the annual bibliography of the International Commission of Comparative Military History (ICMH). Founded in 1972, the ICMH is a confederation of 35 national commissions. One of the principal missions of the ICMH is to publish an international bibliography to which any member commission can contribute. The *Bibliographie Internationale d'Histoire Militaire* (BIHM) first appeared in 1978 and has now reached 20 volumes; each annual volume includes some 300 entries in English, French, and sometimes the language of the book or article cited. Twenty-six nations make annual submissions on a regular basis, and others contribute on an occasional basis. Of the major belligerents of World War II, only the Soviet Union (now the Russian Republic) fails to make submissions, but many of the earlier volumes include many Soviet entries on World War II, thanks to the aggressive leadership of the late Pavel A. Zhilin and the late Dimitri Volkogonov, both Red Army generals, heads of the Russian State Military Archives, and chiefs of military history of exceptional dedication to international historical collaboration. The BIHM is assembled and produced by an able group of Swiss historians, sponsored by the ICMH, the Swiss Federal Military Library, and the Service Historique of the Swiss Army, Berne.

The annual BIHM also now contains "scientific reports" that are essentially essays on the state of research and writing on military history in one or two of the member states. These essays combine historiography and bibliography as well as describe archival holdings and official history publication programs. For military historians, one of the benefits of the end of the Cold War and the collapse of the Warsaw Pact is new access to the military records of the Eastern European nations, all of whom have World War II materials. The most active participants are Poland, Hungary, the Czech Republic, and Romania. Bulgaria is also a member of the ICMH, but the devolution of the former Yugoslavia has destroyed its national commission and participation in the ICMH. On the other hand, both the People's Republic of China (the Academy of Military Sciences) and Japan (National Institute for Defense Studies, Tokyo) are active members of the international commission.

Anglophone nations that have national commissions are the United States, Britain, Canada, and Australia. Official military historians in all these nations played critical roles in founding the International Commission and guiding its activities, so it is not surprising that World War II themes and publications programs have been a central concern of each national commission. The Australian Commission, for example, led by Professors Peter Dennis and Jeffrey Gray of the Australian Defence Force Academy, can provide expert guidance to the exceptional major collection of World War II papers related to the war with Japan held by the library and archives of the Australian War Memorial, Canberra. The Australians also can provide guidance to the study of World War II in India and Southeast Asia. The United States Commission on Military History, which maintains a web site, can provide suggestions on whom to contact abroad for information or archival sources and publications, but it does not provide answers to substantive questions of fact and interpretation on World War II.

The number of general histories of World War II available in English defy easy analysis. There are two books, however, that stand out for their breadth and insight. One is Gordon Wright, *The Ordeal of Total War, 1939–1945*, part of the Rise of Modern Europe series edited by William L. Langer of Harvard University. Wright's book is all the more remarkable since it appeared in 1968. Because it takes advantage of the most recent international scholarship and deals with the war with Japan, the new benchmark for all other books is Gerhard L. Weinberg, *A World at Arms: A Global History of World War II* (Cambridge, 1994). Both books provide extensive bibliographies. (See Gerhard L. Weinberg, "World War II Scholarship, Now and in the Future," *Journal of Military History* 61 [April 1997], 335–346.)

To the winners belong the documents, provided fire and flood have not claimed the papers first. It is no accident that the non-Continental belligerents (the United States, Britain, and Japan) managed to preserve the most records as well as the materials they captured during the course of the war. The Japanese, of course, had to surrender their holdings to the Allies, although they have since been returned, as have those of Germany, at least those seized by the Americans and British. Only the Russians know what they have and do not have, although Professor John Erickson (University of Edinburgh) and Colonel David Glantz, USA (Ret.) have enjoyed unusual access to the Russian military records, as their books show. There is no easy way to ascertain the existence and availability of World War II's documentary detritus. One place to start is James E. O'Neill and Robert W. Krauskopf, eds., *World War II: An Account of Its Documents* (Washington, DC, 1976). The best way to start a documentary investigation is still to consult the back issues of the *Newsletter* of the World War Two Studies Association.

The single largest group of World War II experts is the international community of historians who produced the official histories of the war. The first comprehensive review of their work is Robin Higham, ed. and comp., *Official Histories: Essays and Bibliographies from around the World* (Manhattan, KS, 1970). Professor Higham, a key figure in encouraging World War II studies, is also the author of a book on the British Commonwealth official history program. An anthology of assessments and reports on the official history projects is Jürgen Rohwer, ed., *New Research on the Second World War: Literature, Surveys, and Bibliographies* (Stuttgart, 1990).

After World War I the armed forces and defense ministries of Britain, France, and Germany organized a pioneering effort to write multivolume, multiauthored, multiservice histories of the war. For obvious reasons, only Britain could make a similar commitment in producing an official history of World War II. Profiting from the organizational mistakes of the first effort, which put too much editorial power in the hands of Brigadier General Sir James E. Edmonds, Jr., the British official history projects of World War II are notable for their careful research and superlative maps and appendices. They are divided by service and working "syndicate." James R. M. Butler and other senior historians, aided by such proven soldiers and professional historians as Michael Howard, wrote six volumes on British grand strategy in World War II. These books are the foundation of The United Kingdom Military Series (1952–1969). Other volumes examined subjects as diverse as the 1940 campaign in Norway, the campaign in France in 1940, the defense of the United Kingdom, and the campaign in northwest Europe, 1944–45. F. H. Hinsley headed the team that wrote four volumes on intelligence (1979–1988), and Michael Howard completed the five-book series with a study on deception (1991). I. S. O. Playfair and his group of authors covered the war in Africa, the Near East, the Balkans, and the Mediterranean. S. Woodburn Kirby and his group wrote *The War against Japan*, 5 vols. (1957–1969). All these books were released by Her Majesty's Stationery Office.

The British air and naval services did their histories as separate enterprises. The Royal Air Force's effort comes in two official histories: Charles Webster and Arthur Noble Frankland, *The Strategic Air Offensive against Germany*, 4 vols. (London, 1961), and Dennis Richards and Hillary St. George Saunders, *The Royal Air Force*, 3 vols. (London, 1953–54). The Royal Navy recruited Stephen W. Roskill, a naval officer and experienced historian, to write *The War at Sea, 1939–1945*, 4 vols. (London, 1954–1961), but Roskill's fine work should be supplemented by the semiofficial books of Captain Donald Macintyre, RN, whose work on the Battle of the Atlantic still merits study.

The British official history programs had their counterparts in the other Commonwealth belligerents, with World War II series completed or still in progress. Canada's series is the Official History of the Canadian Army in the Second World War, thus far two volumes on the campaigns in northwestern Europe and Italy, 1943–1945. New Zealand has eight volumes on its war effort. Australia published ten volumes on the Middle East and the Pacific campaigns as well as home front mobilization, written under the editorial direction of Gavin Long. The editorial directors of the Canadian and Australian official history projects both wrote comprehensive histories of their nation's role in World War II: C. P. Stacey, *Six Years of War: The Army in Canada, Britain, and the Pacific* (Ottawa, 1955), and Gavin Long, *The Six Years' War: A Concise History of Australia in the 1939–1945 War* (Canberra, 1973).

Like their British counterparts, the historians of the Office of the Chief of Military History (now the Center of Military History), U.S. Army began working on the official history of World War II while the war raged. Professional historians served in ranks that ranged from colonel to sergeant, with others participating as civilians, either as War Department employees or later as contract historians. The U.S. Army in World War II series employed the most historians, produced the most books, and went on for the longest period of time, 1949–1993. These "Green Books" still serve as essential sources for the American war effort and were reprinted (not all volumes) in the 1990s upon the war's fiftieth anniversary. Recruited and organized by Professor Kent Roberts Greenfield of Johns Hopkins University, the army historians included authors who became the "founding fathers" of civilian military history in the United States, including Forrest Pogue, Louis Morton, Philip Crowl, Maurice Matloff, Martin Blumenson, and James MacGregor Burns. The books themselves are still available from Government Printing Office stores and its mailing service and are listed in full in Center of Military History publications and electronic information sites.

The U.S. Army in World War II series is best understood as a group of subseries volumes. The perspective of the War Department General Staff is captured in four volumes on grand strategy and four on global logistics and home front mobilization. These eight volumes present the most comprehensive and integrated account of the army's global role in the war, supplemented with two volumes of studies of the organization and training of the Army Ground Forces and one on the role of the Army Service Forces. The strategic-operational volumes are divided by geographic theater: Western Hemisphere (2 vols.), Pacific (11 vols.), North Africa–Mediterranean (4 vols.), Northern Europe, 1944–45 (10 vols.), Persian Gulf (1 vol.), and the China-Burma-India theater (3 vols.). There are 24 volumes on the accomplishments of the army's technical services, all of which provide essential information on ordnance, transportation, communications, supply, engineering, the atomic bomb, and medical services. There are an additional eight special studies of the army medical effort, including a full volume on urological problems. In addition, the army published nine special studies of such issues as racial integration, women's roles and missions, military government, and military assistance to the Allies. It published two large photograph albums and provided separate folios of its exceptional maps. There are also shorter monographs on specific military operations, including some on the Eastern Front. In fact, the Center of Military History even published its own three-volume history of the Russo-German war, by Earl F. Ziemke, largely from German sources with the assistance of the surviving German commanders. The scope of this program is described in Louis Morton, "Sources for the History of World War II," *World Politics* 13 (April 1961), 435–453.

The other American services surrendered nothing to the army in terms of quality official history, but their publishing programs had more modest goals in terms of volume numbers, and they developed their own peculiarities. The U.S. Army Air Forces found two academic historians of high repute, Wesley Frank Craven and James Lea Cate, to organize and edit the seven-volume *The Army Air Forces in World War II* as well as write part of it, but the series also involved several other historians, some of whom contributed to the army series, too. The USAAF official history was published by the University of Chicago Press, 1948–1958, and reprinted by the GPO in the 1990s. In addition to wartime monographs, operations reports, and special studies, the air force historians profited from the massive data collection of the U.S. Strategic Bombing Survey, whose purpose was to show the essential contribution of the American strategic bombing campaign. It is not surprising, therefore, that Craven and Cate suffer from "bomber-centrism" and that other, later studies had to capture the full range and significance of the U.S. air war.

The historical projects of the U.S. Navy and the U.S. Marine Corps not only differed from those of the Army and Army Air Forces but also from each other. The navy bowed to the pressure of President Roosevelt and sent his favorite historian, Samuel Eliot Morison of Harvard University, to sea in uniform. Since Morison could not be everywhere at once, he formed a team of researchers, translators, document collectors, and writers that included some of the navy's finest wartime intellectuals. This team effort made it possible for the navy to publish its official history in record time and through a major commercial publisher (Houghton Mifflin): Samuel Eliot Morison, *History of the United States Naval Operations in World War II*, 15 vols. (1947–1962). A reissue of the series became available in hardback and paperback in the 1990s and can now be found at bargain prices in cut-rate bookstores along with the reissued volumes of the U.S. Army in World War II. True to its heritage, the Marine Corps did its five-volume series in the straightforward, old-fashioned way; its staff historical division of civilian historians and uniformed officers produced *History of Marine Corps Operations in World War II* (Washington, DC, 1958–1968) under the direction of chief historian and editor Henry I. Shaw, Jr., a Marine Corps veteran.

The cornerstone of the Soviet official history effort, written by a committee of 29 officer-historians (IVOVSS [Soviet Institute of Military History]) is *Istoriya Velikoi Otechiestvennoi Voiny Sovetskogo Soyuza SSR (History of the Great Patriotic War of the Soviet Union)* (Moscow, 1960–1965), originally published in 6 volumes and then expanded to 12 volumes in A. A. Grechko et al., *Istoriya Vtoroi Mirovoi Voiny, 1941–1945 (History of the Great Patriotic War)* (Moscow, 1973–1982). A companion piece is M. M. Kozlov, ed., *Veklikaya Ostchestvennaya voina: Entsiklopediya (Encyclopedia of the Great Patriotic War)* (Moscow, 1985). A condensed English-language version (Moscow: Progress Publishers, 1974) appeared in one volume.

The Axis side of the history of World War II reflects Germany's increasing willingness to face the horrors of the Third Reich and the relative lack of interest in Japan in seeking a forthright accounting of Japan's war effort and an international understanding of Japan's conduct of the war. The Italians have also mounted a serious effort that has grown increasingly critical of the Italian officer corps as its volumes have been published. The historical office of the Bundeswehr is the Militärgeschichtliche Forschungsamt (MGFA), once hidden away in bucolic Freiburg am Breisgau but now displaced to Potsdam upon the unification of Germany, while the military archives remain in Freiburg. The Bundesarchiv/Militärarchiv has taken control of all the German military records that survived the Third Reich and those left by the departed Democratic Republic of Germany. The historians of the MGFA, uniformed and civilian, are schooled and credentialed to the highest professional standards, and they have needed every bit of professional skill and moral courage to complete *Das Deutsche Reich und der Zweite Weltkrieg (The German Reich and the Second World War)*, which has won them many friends abroad but few among the wartime generation at home. Of the projected ten volumes, seven have been published (1979–1999), and of these four have been translated and published by Oxford University Press. The published German-language volumes carry the war to 1943 and the translations to the end of 1941. There are also a number of other important volumes on World War II published by various members of the MGFA's staff.

The Japanese War History Office/Defense Research Center, Japanese Defense Agency, has completed its official history in the *Senshi Sosho* (War History) series of 104 volumes (1966–1980). No volume is available in English-language translation, although the books have been selectively used by Western scholars in English-language books, because the authors either read Japanese or have had portions of the *Senshi Sosho* translated. The best substitutes are the historical monographs written during the occupation of Japan by teams of American and Japanese historians on selected aspects of the war, available in part in Donald S. Detwiler and Charles B. Burdick, eds., *War in Asia and the Pacific, 1937–1945*, 6 vols. (New York, 1980).

The two Chinas have two sets of official histories on the war with Japan. The Nationalist perspective appears (in English and Chinese) in *War Resistance against Japan*, which is volume 4 in an anthology sponsored by the Compilation Committee, *Symposium on the History of the Republic of China* (Taipei, 1979), and in Chin Hsiao-yi and the Editorial Committee, Principal Historical Source Materials on the Republic of China, eds., *Documents of the Republic of China: The Period of the War of Resistance against Japan* (Taipei, 1981–1987). The Academy of Military Sciences, People's Liberation Army, Beijing, has published several monographs on the Communist partisan war with Japan, including a book on Japanese atrocities, and the AMS Historical Division included a volume on the Anti-Japanese Liberation War in its multivolume *Chinese Military Encyclopedia*.

The official histories can only create a baseline for surveying the literature. The advantage of commercially published bibliographies is that they bring together the official histories of World War II with all the other categories of literature, a process improved in the last decade by the collection and compilation programs of the electronic information industry. On the assumption that the libraries and individual readers in the United States offer the most likely customers, publishers tend to define the market in American terms for English-language publications. The most comprehensive bibliography and commentary is Robin Higham, ed., *A Guide to the Sources of United State Military History* (Hamden, CT, 1975), which includes three *Supplements* (vols. 1–3) published in 1981, 1986, and 1993 in collaboration with Donald J. Mrozek. A more recent entry into the historiography-bibliography field is the work of Professor Lloyd E. Lee (SUNY–New Paltz), *World War II* (Westport, CT, 1999), and *World War II in Asia and the Pacific and the War's Aftermath* (Westport, CT, 1998). Lee's anthologists include experts on Asian literature and sources as well as authors of separate essays and bibliographies on technology, science, the arts, propaganda, popular culture and social history, and the impact of the war. Earlier works that still have reference value are John J. Sbrega, comp., *The War against Japan, 1941–1945: An Annotated Bibliography* (New York, 1989); ABC/CLIO (n.a.), *World War II from an American Perspective* (Santa Barbara, CA, 1983); and Arthur L. Funk, *The Second World War: A Select Bibliography of Books in English since 1975* (Claremont, CA, 1985).

NOTES

1. Origins of a Catastrophe

1. Albert Speer, *Inside the Third Reich* (New York, 1970), p. 162.
2. Quoted in Martin Gilbert, *Winston Churchill,* vol. 5, *1922–1939* (London, 1976), p. 550.
3. John Milton, *Paradise Lost,* book V.
4. *History of the Times,* p. 78.
5. Gordon Craig, *Germany, 1866–1945* (New York, 1978), p. 635.
6. Public Record Office (PRO) CAB 23/92, Cab 12 (38), Meeting of the Cabinet, 12.3.38, pp. 349–350.
7. Telford Taylor, *Munich: The Price of Peace* (New York, 1979), p. 884.
8. Winston S. Churchill, *The Second World War,* vol. 1, *The Gathering Storm* (Boston, 1948), p. 292.
9. Quoted in Wilhelm Deist et al., *Das Deutsche Reich und der Zweite Weltkrieg,* vol. 1, *Ursachen und Voraussetzungen der Deutschen Kriegspolitik* (Stuttgart, 1979), p. 329.
10. *Documents on German Foreign Policy,* Series D, vol. VII, Doc. #192.
11. PRO CAB 23/100, Cab 47 (39), Meeting of the Cabinet, 1.9.39, p. 443.

2. The Revolution in Military Operations, 1919–1939

1. F. Scott Fitzgerald, *Tender Is the Night* (New York, 1933), p. 66.
2. Quoted in James S. Corum, *The Roots of Blitzkrieg: Hans von Seeckt and German Military Reform* (Lawrence, KS, 1992), p. 37.
3. Chef der Heeresleitung, *Die Truppenführung* (Berlin, 1933), p. 1.
4. PRO CAB 63/14, Letter from Sir A. Robinson to Sir Thomas Inskip, Minister for the Coordination of Defense, 19.10.36.
5. Bernard MacGregor Knox. "1940: Italy's 'Parallel War,'" Ph.D. Dissertation, Yale University, 1976, p. 27.
6. MacGregor Knox, *Mussolini Unleashed, 1939–1941: Politics and Strategy in Fascist Italy's Last War* (Cambridge, 1982), p. 121.
7. "Bombardment Text," Air Corps Tactical School, Langley Field, Virginia, 1930, p. 109, Air Force Historical Research Center, Maxwell Air Force Base, AL.

3. German Designs, 1939–1940

1. Franz Halder, *The Halder War Diary, 1939–1942,* ed. Charles Burdick and Hans-Adolf Jacobsen (Novato, CA, 1988), p. 73.
2. OKW files: "Denkschrift und Richtlinien über die Führung des Krieges im Westen," Berlin, 9.10.39, National Archives and Records Service (NARS) T-77/775.
3. H. R. Trevor Roper, ed., *Blitzkrieg to Defeat: Hitler's War Directives* (New York, 1965), p. 13.
4. Telford Taylor, *The March of Conquest: The German Victories in Western Europe, 1940* (New York, 1958), p. 158.
5. Ibid., p. 74.
6. Trevor-Roper, *Blitzkrieg to Defeat,* Directive #8, 20 November 1939, p. 16.
7. Halder, *Halder War Diary,* pp. 95–96.
8. Ibid., p. 106.
9. Alistair Horne, *To Lose a Battle: France 1940* (Boston, 1969), p. 132.
10. Ibid., p. 126.
11. Public Records Office (PRO CAB) 84/16, M.R.(J)(40)(S)2, 11.4.40, Allied Military Committee, "The Major Strategy of the War, Note by the French Delegation."

4. Germany Triumphant, 1940

1. Alistair Horne, *To Lose a Battle: France 1940* (Boston, 1969), p. 170.
2. Quoted in F. H. Hinsley et al., *British Intelligence in the Second World War,* vol. 1 (London, 1979), p. 127.
3. John Costello, *Ten Days to Destiny: The Secret Story of the Hess Peace Initiative and British Efforts to Strike a Deal with Hitler* (New York, 1991), p. 35.
4. Heinz Guderian, *Panzer Leader* (New York, 1957), p. 84.
5. Erwin Rommel, *The Rommel Papers,* ed. B. H. Liddell Hart (New York, 1953), pp. 21–22.
6. Ibid., p. 26.
7. Robert Doughty, *The Breaking Point: Sedan and the Fall of France, 1940* (Hamden, CT, 1990), p. 100.
8. Horne, *To Lose a Battle,* pp. 334–335.
9. Halder, *The Halder War Diary,* pp. 147–149.
10. Antoine de Saint Exupéry, *Last Flight to Arras,* tran. Lewis Galantière (New York, 1942), p. 56.
11. Winston Churchill, *The Second World War,* vol. 2, *Their Finest Hour* (Boston, 1949), p. 46.
12. Horne, *To Lose a Battle,* p. 478.
13. Halder, *The Halder War Diary,* p. 167.
14. Major General Sir Edward Spears, *Assignment to Catastrophe,* vol. 1, *Prelude to Dunkirk, July 1939–May 1940* (New York, 1954), p. 250.

15. Halder, *The Halder War Diary*, p. 172.
16. Hansard, 4 June 1940.
17. General Major Erich Marcks, 19 June 1940, quoted in MacGregor Knox, *Foreign Policy and War in Fascist Italy and Nazi Germany* (Cambridge, forthcoming), chap. 5, epigraph.
18. PRO CAB 65/7, War Cabinet, Confidential Annex, 27 May 1940, 4:30 P.M.
19. PRO ADM 205/4, undated and unsigned memorandum.
20. Chef WFA, 30.6.40, "Die Weiterführung des Krieges gegen England," International Military Tribunal (IMT), *Trial of Major War Criminals (TMWC)*, vol. 28, pp. 301–303.
21. Chef WFA, 30.6.40, "Die Weiterführung des Krieges gegen England," IMT, *TMWC*, vol. 28, pp. 301–303.
22. Francis K. Mason, *Battle over Britain: A History of German Air Assaults on Great Britain, 1917–1918 and July–December 1940* (New York, 1969), Appendix K, OKL, 16.7.40, Operations Staff Ic.
23. BA/MA RL 2II/27, "Algemeine Weisung für den Kampf der Luftwaffe gegen England," ObdL, Führungsstab Ia Nr. 5835/40, 30.6.40.
24. *Documents on German Foreign Policy*, Series D, vol. 9, Doc. #471, 18.6.40.

5. Diversions in the Mediterranean and Balkans, 1940–1941

1. Quoted in MacGregor Knox, *Mussolini Unleashed, 1939–1941: Politics and Strategy in Fascist Italy's Last War* (Cambridge, 1982), p. 137.
2. Galeazzo Ciano, *The Ciano Diaries, 1939–1943*, ed. Hugh Gibson (New York, 1956), p. 285.
3. Knox, *Mussolini Unleashed*, p. 164.
4. *Documents on German Foreign Policy*, Series D, vol. XI, Document #84.
5. Ciano, *The Ciano Diaries*, p. 300.
6. Martin Gilbert, *Winston S. Churchill*, vol. 6, *Finest Hour, 1939–1941* (Boston, 1983), p. 1013.
7. Percy E. Schramm, *Kriegstagebuch des Oberkommandos der Wehrmacht (Wehrmachtführungstab)*, vol. 1, 1 August 1940–31 December 1941 (Munich, 1982), p. 368.
8. BA/MA, RL 7/657, Luftflottenkommando 4, Führungsabteilung Ia op Nr 1000/41, Wien, 31.3.41, "Befehl für die Luftkriegführung Jugoslawien."
9. Thucydides, *History of the Peloponnesian War*, trans. Rex Warner (New York, 1972), pp. 242–244.

6. Barbarossa, 1941

1. R. J. Sontag and J. S. Beddie, eds., *Nazi-Soviet Relations, 1939–1941: Documents from the Archives of the German Foreign Office* (Washington, DC, 1948), p. 324.

2. Ibid., pp. 345–346.
3. Gustav Hilger and Alfred Meyer, *The Incompatible Allies* (New York, 1953), p. 336.
4. Halder, *The Halder War Diary*, p. 232.
5. Ibid., p. 311.
6. Ibid., p. 346.
7. Ibid., pp. 15–16.
8. Klaus Reinhardt, *Die Wende vor Moskau: Das Scheitern der Strategie Hitlers im Winter 1941/42* (Stuttgart, 1972), p. 21.
9. Halder, *The Halder War Diary*, p. 232.
10. Ibid., p. 245.
11. Ibid., p. 233.
12. Ibid., pp. 293–294.
13. H. R. Trevor Roper, *Blitzkrieg to Defeat: Hitler's War Directives, 1939–1945* (London, 1964), pp. 48–51.
14. *Documents on German Foreign Policy,* Series D, vol. XIII, Doc. #154.
15. John Erickson, *The Soviet High Command* (London, 1962), p. 587.
16. Halder, *The Halder War Diary*, p. 410.
17. Quoted in John Erickson, *The Road to Stalingrad*, vol. 1, *Stalin's War with Germany* (New York, 1975), p. 134.
18. Halder, *The Halder War Diary*, pp. 446–447.
19. Theodor Plievier, *Moscow* (New York, 1953), pp. 44–46.
20. Quoted in David M. Glantz and Jonathan House, *When Titans Clash: How the Red Army Stopped Hitler* (Lawrence, KS, 1995), p. 60.
21. Halder, *The Halder War Diary*, p. 506.
22. BA/MA, RL 8/49, Rußland-Feldzug 1941: VIII Fliegerkorps.
23. Martin Van Creveld, *Supplying War: Logistics from Wallenstein to Patton* (Cambridge, 1977), p. 171.
24. BA/MA, RH 19III/656ID, "Der Feldzug gegen die Sowjet Union: Kriegsjahr 1941: Bearbeitet in der Führungsabteilung des Oberkommandos der Heeresgruppe Nord."
25. Reinhardt, *Die Wende vor Moskau*, p. 77.
26. Ibid., p. 71.
27. Ibid., pp. 139–140.
28. Earl F. Ziemke, *Stalingrad to Berlin: The German Defeat in the East* (Washington, DC), 1968, p. 63.
29. Holger H. Herwig, *Politics of Frustration: The United States in German Naval Planning, 1939–1941* (Boston, 1976), p. 228.
30. Earl F. Ziemke and Magna E. Bauer, *Moscow to Stalingrad: Decision in the East* (Washington, DC, 1987), p. 282.
31. Halder, *The Halder War Diary*, pp. 596–600.
32. Ziemke and Bauer, *Moscow to Stalingrad*, p. 102.
33. Ibid., p. 131.

34. Ciano, *The Ciano Diaries*, p. 411.

35. Christian Streit, *Keine Kameraden: Die Wehrmacht und die Sowjetischen Kriegsgefangenen, 1941–1945* (Stuttgart, 1978), p. 90.

36. International Military Tribunal (IMT), *Trial of Major War Criminals (TMWC)*, vol. 34, pp. 84–86.

37. Ibid., pp. 129–132.

38. Horst Boog et al., *Das Deutsche Reich und der Zweite Weltkrieg*, vol. 4, *Der Angriff auf die Sowjetunion* (Stuttgart, 1983), p. 1038.

7. The Origins of the Asia-Pacific War, 1919–1941

1. Quoted in Tsunoda Jun et al., *Japan's Road to the Pacific War: The Final Confrontation*, vol. 5, *Japan's Negotiations with the United States*, ed. James William Morley, trans. David A. Titus (New York, 1994), p. 105.

2. Quoted in John Toland, *The Rising Sun: The Decline and Fall of the Japanese Empire* (New York, 1970), p. 50.

3. Evans F. Carlson, *Twin Stars over China* (New York, 1940), p. 168.

4. "Problems of Guerrilla Warfare," May 1938, in *Selected Military Writing of Mao Tse-tung* (Peking, 1967), p. 160.

0. The Japanese War of Conquest, 1941–1942

1. Memoir of Earl M. Schaeffer, Jr., on 7 December 1941, quoted in James Stokesbury, ed., *World War II: Personal Accounts* (Austin, TX, 1992), p. 66.

2. Memorandum of conversation, Secretary of State Cordell Hull with Japanese diplomatic delegation, 7 December 1941, *Foreign Relations of the United States of America: Japan, 1931–1941* (Washington, DC, 1943), vol. 2, p. 787; Cordell Hull, *The Memoirs of Cordell Hull* (New York, 1948), vol. 2, pp. 1095–1100; Dean Acheson, *Present at the Creation: My Years at the State Department* (New York, 1969), p. 35.

3. Lieutenant Harry G. Lee, USA, quoted in John Toland, *But Not in Shame: The Six Months after Pearl Harbor* (New York, 1961), p. 94.

9. The Asia-Pacific War, 1942–1944

1. Quoted in Eric Bergerud, *Touched with Fire: The Land War in the South Pacific* (New York, 1996), p. 218.

2. Account of the Battle of Savo Island by Captain Ohmae Toshikazu, IJN, in David C. Evans, trans. and comp., *The Japanese Navy in World War II*, 2nd ed. (Annapolis, 1986), p. 242.

3. Undated notebook entry, 1944, in Theodore White, ed., *The Stilwell Papers* (New York, 1948), p. 251.

10. The Battle of the Atlantic, 1939–1943

1. OKM, Berlin, 3.9.39, "Gedanken des Oberbefehlshabers der Kriegsmarine zum Kriegsausbruch," NARS T-1022/2238/PG33525.
2. Quoted in Correlli Barnett, *Engage the Enemy More Closely: The Royal Navy in the Second World War* (New York, 1991), p. 196.
3. Winston Churchill, *The Second World War*, vol. 3, *The Grand Alliance* (Boston, 1949), pp. 100–101.
4. Patrick Beesley, *Very Special Intelligence: The Story of the Admiralty's Operational Intelligence Centre, 1939–1945* (Garden City, 1978), pp. 114–115.

11. Year of Decision for Germany, 1942

1. "The Diaries of Lord Alanbrooke," Brooke Papers, Liddell Hart Archives, Kings College, London, 5/5/1, 28 June 1942.
2. General Sir Leslie Hollis, *One Marine's Tale* (London, 1956), p. 66.
3. Lord Hastings, *The Memoirs of General the Lord Hastings* (London, 1960), p. 269.
4. Quoted in David Fraser, *Alanbrooke* (New York, 1982), p. 297.
5. Walter Warlimont, *Inside Hitler's Headquarters* (New York, 1966), p. 272.
6. Quoted in Earl F. Ziemke and Magna E. Bauer, *Moscow to Stalingrad: Decision in the East* (Washington, DC, 1987), p. 282.
7. Quoted in David M. Glantz, *Zhukov's Greatest Defeat: The Red Army's Epic Disaster in Operation Mars, 1942* (Lawrence, KS, 1999), p. 200.
8. Earl F. Ziemke, *Stalingrad to Berlin: The German Defeat in the East* (Washington, DC, 1968), p. 55.
9. Richthofen diary entry for 25.11.42.
10. Ibid., entry for 26.12.42.
11. Johannes Steinhoff, *Messerschmitts over Sicily* (Baltimore, MD, 1987), pp. 59–60.

12. The Combined Bomber Offensive, 1941–1945

1. John Terraine, *The Right of the Line: The Royal Air Force in the European War, 1939–1945* (London, 1985), p. 259.
2. Ibid., p. 175.
3. Richard J. Overy, *The Air War, 1939–1945* (New York, 1980), p. 105.
4. Sir Charles Webster and Noble Frankland, *The Strategic Air Offensive against Germany*, vol. 1, *Preparation* (London, 1962), p. 177.
5. Martin Middlebrook, *The Battle of Hamburg: Allied Bomber Forces against a German City in 1943* (London, 1980), p. 268.
6. Martin Caiden, *Black Thursday* (New York, 1981), pp. 209–211.
7. "Hitler zur Frage der Gegen maßnahmen zur Beantwortung der alliierten Luftangriffe," 25.7.43, AFSHRC K 113.312–2, vol. 3.
8. David Irving, *Hitler's War* (New York, 1977), pp. 574–575.

9. BA/MA, RL 3/61, "Stenographische Niederschrift der Besprechung beim Reichsmarschall am 28.11.44 in Karinhall," pp. 94–95.

10. A. S. Milward, *The New Order and the French Economy* (Oxford, 1970), p. 77.

11. Friedhelm Göluke, *Schweinfurt und der Strategische Luftkrieg, 1943* (Stuttgart, 1980), p. 115.

12. Arthur Harris to Winston Churchill, 3.11.43, PRO/PREM/3/14/1.

13. Joseph Goebbels, *The Goebbels Diaries, 1942–1943*, ed. and trans. L. Lochner (New York, 1948), pp. 532–535.

14. Oral interview with D. C. T. Bennett, RAF Staff College Library, Bracknell, England.

15. Frank Futrell, *Ideas, Concepts, Doctrine: A History of Basic Thinking in the United States Air Force* (Montgomery, AL, 1965), p. 139.

16. Wesley Frank Craven and James Lea Cate, *The Army Air Forces in World War II*, vol. 3 (Chicago, 1951), p. 53.

17. Air Historical Branch, "Air Attacks against German Rail Systems during 1944," Luftwaffe Operations Staff/Intelligence, No. 2512/44, "Air Operations against the German Rail Transport System during March, April, and May 1944," 3.6.44.

18. PRO 31/20/16, "The Handling of Ultra Information at Headquarters Eighth Air Force," Ansel E. M. Talbert, Major, U.S. Army Air Corps.

19. PRO DEFE 3/166, KV 6673, 6.6.44., 2356Z.

20. "Heimatverteidigungsprogramm 1943, Besprechung beim Reichsmarschall am 7.10.43, Obersalzberg, Fortsetzung," AFSIIRC: K 113.312–2, vol. 3.

13. The Destruction of Japanese Naval Power, 1943–1944

1. Robert W. Love, Jr., "Ernest Joseph King," in Robert W. Love, Jr., *The Chiefs of Naval Operations* (Annapolis, 1980), pp. 137–179.

2. Quoted in Theodore Taylor, *The Magnificent Mitscher* (Annapolis, 1991), p. 237.

3. Memoir of Vice Admiral Koyanagi Tomiji, IJN (Ret.), in "The Battle of Leyte Gulf," in David C. Evans, ed. and trans., *The Japanese Navy in World War II* (Annapolis, 1986), p. 371.

4. General of the Army Douglas MacArthur, *Reminiscences* (New York, 1964), pp. 215, 217, 221.

14. The Killing Time, 1943–1944

1. Shelford Bidwell and Dominick Graham, *Tug of War: The Battle for Italy* (New York, 1986), p. 149.

2. Ibid., p. 141.

3. Ibid.

4. Guy Sajer, *The Forgotten Soldier* (New York, 1967), p. 261.

5. Earl Ziemke, *Stalingrad to Berlin: The German Defeat in the East* (Washington, DC, 1968), p. 188.

6. Ibid., p. 238.

7. Ibid., p. 256.

8. M. R. D. Foot, *SOE in France* (London, 1966), p. 11.

15. The Invasion of France, 1944

1. Winston S. Churchill, *Blood, Sweat, and Tears* (New York, 1941), p. 403.

2. George MacDonald Fraser, *Quartered Safe Out Here: A Recollection of the War in Burma* (London, 1995), pp. 36–37.

3. Quoted in Carlo D'Este, *Decision in Normandy: The Unwritten Story of Montgomery and the Allied Campaign* (London, 1983), p. 196.

4. Max Hastings, *Overlord: D-Day and the Battle for Normandy, 1944* (London, 1984), p. 256.

5. Public Record Office, DEFE 3/127/XL 9188, 5.9.44., 1152Z, and DEFE 3/128, XL 9245, 6.9.44., 0103Z.

6. Cornelius Ryan, *A Bridge Too Far* (New York, 1977), p. 131.

16. The End in Europe, 1944–1945

1. Earl Ziemke, *Stalingrad to Berlin* (Washington, DC, 1968), pp. 335–336.

2. Ibid., p. 342.

3. Milovan Djilas, *Wartime* (New York, 1977), p. 429.

4. Charles B. MacDonald, *A Time for Trumpets: The Untold Story of the Battle of the Bulge* (London, 1984), p. 68.

5. Ibid., p. 420.

6. Carlo D'Este, *Patton: A Genius for War* (New York, 1995), p. 691.

7. Charles B. MacDonald, *The Mighty Endeavor: The American War in Europe* (New York, 1985), p. 529.

17. The Destruction of the Japanese Empire, 1944–1945

1. Field Marshal the Viscount Slim, *Defeat into Victory* (New York, 1961), p. 263.

2. Quoted in D. Clayton James, *The Years of MacArthur*, vol. 2, *1941–1945* (Boston, 1975), p. 635.

3. Carlos Romulo, *I See the Philippines Rise* (Garden City, NY, 1946), pp. 216–229.

4. Quoted in Kenneth P. Werrell, *Blankets of Fire: U.S. Bombers over Japan during World War II* (Washington, DC, 1996), pp. 139–140.

18. The End of the Asia-Pacific War, 1945

1. T. Grady Gallant, *The Friendly Dead* (New York, 1981), p. 84.

2. CINCPOA Communique 300, 16 March 1945, OPI, *Pacific Fleet Communiques, 1943–1945* (Washington, DC, 1945).

3. Testimony of Wada Michiyo, daughter of Mr. Sasaki, with a reprint of Mr. Sasaki's report in Frank Gibney and Beth Cary, ed. and trans., *Sensō: The Japanese Remember the Pacific War* (London, 1995), pp. 213–214.

4. Admiral Stuart S. Murray, USN, "A Harried Host in the *Missouri,*" in John T. Mason, Jr., *The Pacific War Remembered: An Oral History Collection* (Annapolis, 1986), pp. 353–354.

5. Kase Toshikazu, with a foreword by Daniel Nelson Rowe, *Journey to the Missouri* (New Haven, 1950), pp. 1–14.

6. MacArthur's remarks reprinted in ibid., p. 8.

19. Peoples at War, 1937–1945

1. Quoted in Lothan Burchardt, "The Impact of the War Economy on the Civilian Population of Germany during the First and Second World War," in Wilhelm Deist, ed., *The German Military in the Age of Total War* (Dover, NH, 1985), p. 50.

2. Quoted in Alan S. Milward, *War, Economy, and Society, 1939–1945* (Berkeley, 1979), p. 99.

3. Quoted in John W. Dower, "Sensational Rumors, Seditious Graffiti," in Dower, *Japan in War and Peace: Selected Essays* (New York, 1993), pp. 146–147.

4. W. K. Hancock and M. M. Gowing, *British War Economy* (London, 1949), p. 519.

5. Edith Speert to Victor Speert, quoted in Stephen E. Ambrose, "The War on the Home Front," *Timeline* [Ohio Historical Society] 10 (November–December 1993), pp. 2–21.

6. Quoted in Seweryn Bialer, ed., *Stalin and His Generals* (New York, 1969), p. 158.

20. The Aftermath of War

1. Quoted in Douglas Botting, *World War II: The Aftermath: Europe* (New York, 1983), p. 23.

2. John E. Dolibois, *Patterns of Circles: An Ambassador's Story* (Kent, OH, 1989), pp. 80–83, 105–109, 138–139, 155–158.

3. Testimony of Tamada Jin'o in Frank Gibney and Beth Cary, eds. and trans., *Sensō: The Japanese Remember the Pacific War* (London, 1995), p. 268.

SUGGESTED READING

GENERAL REFERENCES

Brown, David, comp. *Warship Losses of World War Two*, rev. ed. Annapolis, 1995.

Browning, Robert M., comp. *U.S. Merchant Vessel Casualties of World War II.* Annapolis, 1996.

Chandler, David G., and James Lawton Collins, Jr., eds. *The D-Day Encyclopedia.* New York, 1994.

Crow, Duncan. *Tanks of World War II.* New York, 1979.

Dear, I. C. B., and M. R. D. Foot, eds. *The Oxford Companion to World War II.* New York, 1995.

Dunnigan, James F., and Albert A. Nofi. *Victory at Sea: World War II in the Pacific.* New York, 1995.

Ellis, John, comp. *World War II: A Statistical Survey.* New York, 1993.

Fahey, James C., comp. *The Ships and Aircraft of the United States Fleet.* 4 vols. Annapolis, 1939–1945, rpt. 1973–1976.

Griess, Thomas E., ed. *The West Point Atlas for the Second World War: Europe and the Mediterranean and Asia-Pacific.* Garden City, NY, 1994.

Halevy, Yechiam, et al., eds. *Historical Atlas of the Holocaust.* New York, 1996.

Hata, Ikuhiko, and Yasuho Izawa. *Japanese Naval Aces and Fighter Units in World War II.* Don Cyril Gorham, trans. Annapolis, 1989.

Hogg, I. V. *Dictionary of World War II.* London, 1994.

Ireland, Bernard. *Jane's Naval History of World War II.* London, 1998.

Jentschura, Hansgeorg, Dieter Jung, Peter Mickel, David Brown, and Anthony Preston, trans. *Warships of the Imperial Japanese Navy.* Annapolis, 1976.

Keegan, John, ed. *Who's Who in World War II.* New York, 1975, rev. 1998.

Lenton, H. T. *British and Empire Warships of the Second World War.* Annapolis, 1998.

Leverington, Karen, and Tim Senior, eds. *Fighting Aircraft of World War II.* Shrewsbury, UK, 1995.

Mollo, Andrew, with Malcolm McGregor and Pierre Turner. *The Armed Forces of World War II: Uniforms, Insignia and Organization.* New York, 1981.

Niestle, Axel. *German U-Boat Losses of World War II.* Annapolis, 1998.

Office of the Chief of Staff of the United States Army. *Biennial Report, 1943–1945: Supplement: Atlas of the World Battle Fronts.* Washington, DC, 1945.

ONI, with A. D. Baker III, comp. *German Naval Vessels of World War Two.* Annapolis, 1993.

Rohwer, Jürgen. *Axis Submarine Successes of World War Two: German, Italian, and Japanese Submarine Successes of World War Two, 1939–1945.* Annapolis, 1999.

Smurthwaite, David. *The Pacific War Atlas.* New York, 1995.

U.S. Army Service Forces, War Department. *Statistical Review: World War II.* Washington, DC, 1945.

U.S. War Department. *Handbook on German Military Forces, 1945.* Introduction by Stephen E. Ambrose. Rpt. Washington, DC, 1990.

U.S. War Department. *Handbook on Japanese Military Forces, 1944.* Introduction by David Isby. Rpt. Washington, DC, 1991.

Wynn, Kenneth, comp. *U-Boat Operations of the Second World War.* 2 vols. Annapolis, 1998.

Zabecki, David T., ed. *World War II in Europe: An Encyclopedia.* 2 vols. New York, 1999.

Zentner, Christian, and Friedman Bedurftig, eds. *The Encyclopedia of the Third Reich.* New York, 1997.

1. Origins of a Catastrophe

Adamthwaite, Anthony. *France and the Coming of the Second World War.* London, 1977.

Boyce, Robert. *Paths to War: New Essays on the Origins of the Second World War.* London, 1989.

Bullock, Alan. *Hitler and Stalin.* New York, 1992.

Cameron Watt, Donald. *How War Came: The Immediate Origins of the Second World War.* New York, 1989.

Deist, Wilhelm, et al. *Das Deutsche Reich und der Zweite Weltkrieg,* vol. 1, *Ursachen und Voraussetzungen der Deutschen Kriegspolitik.* Stuttgart, 1979.

Gibbs, Norman H. *Grand Strategy,* vol. 1, *Rearmament Policy.* London, 1976.

Hildebrand, Klaus. *The Foreign Policy of the Third Reich.* Berkeley, 1970.

Jäckel, E. *Hitler's Weltanschauung.* Tübingen, 1969.

Knox, MacGregor. *Foreign Policy and War in Fascist Italy and Nazi Germany.* Cambridge, 2000.

Murray, Williamson. *The Change in the European Balance of Power, 1938–1939. The Path to Ruin.* Princeton, 1984.

Murray, Williamson, and Allan R. Millett, eds. *Calculations, Net Assessment and the Coming of World War II.* New York, 1992.

Taylor, Telford. *Munich: The Price of Peace.* New York, 1979.

Thorne, Christopher. *The Approach of War, 1938–1939.* New York, 1967.

Ulam, Adam B. *Expansion and Coexistence: The History of Soviet Foreign Policy.* New York, 1968.

Wandycz, Piotr S. *The Twilight of French Eastern Alliances, 1926–1936: French-Czecho-slovak-Polish Relations from Locarno to the Remilitarization of the Rhineland.* Princeton, 1988.

Wark, Wesley. *The Ultimate Enemy: British Intelligence and Nazi Germany, 1933–1939.* Ithaca, 1985.

Weinberg, Gerhard L. *The Foreign Policy of Hitler's Germany: Diplomatic Revolution in Europe, 1933–1936.* Chicago, 1970.

——*The Foreign Policy of Hitler's Germany: Starting World War II, 1937–1939.* Chicago, 1980.

Weinberg, Gerhard L. *Germany, Hitler, and World War II: Essays in Modern German and World History.* Cambridge, 1995.

2. The Revolution in Military Operations, 1919–1939

Baer, George W. *The U.S. Navy, 1890–1990: One Hundred Years of Seapower.* Stanford, 1994.

Bond, Brian. *British Military Policy between the Two World Wars.* Oxford, 1980.

Coox, Alvin W. *Nomonhan: Japan against Russia, 1939.* 2 vols. Stanford, 1985.

Corum, James S. *The Roots of Blitzkrieg: Hans von Seeckt and German Military Reform.* Lawrence, KS, 1992.

Deist, Wilhelm. *The Wehrmacht and German Rearmament.* London, 1981.

Doughty, Robert. *The Seeds of Disaster: The Development of French Army Doctrine, 1919–1939.* Hamden, CT, 1985.

Evans, David C., and Mark R. Peattie. *Kaigun: Strategy, Tactics, and Technology in the Imperial Japanese Navy, 1887–1941.* Annapolis, 1997.

Glantz, David M. *Stumbling Colossus: The Red Army on the Eve of World War.* Lawrence, KS, 1988.

Hayashi Saburo and Alvin D. Coox. *Kogun: The Japanese Army in the Pacific War.* Quantico, 1959.

Homze, Edward. *Arming the Luftwaffe: The Reich Air Ministry and the German Aircraft Industry, 1933–1939.* Lincoln, NE, 1976.

Johnson, David E. *Fast Tanks and Heavy Bombers: Innovation in the U.S. Army, 1917–1945.* Ithaca, 1998.

Kiesling, Eugenia C. *Arming against Hitler: France and the Limits of Military Planning.* Lawrence, KS, 1996.

Knox, MacGregor. *Mussolini Unleashed, 1939–1941: Politics and Strategy in Fascist Italy's Last War.* Cambridge, 1982.

Maurer, Maurer. *Aviation in the U.S. Army, 1919–1939.* Washington, DC, 1987.

May, Ernest. *Knowing One's Enemies: Intelligence Assessment before the Two World Wars.* Princeton, 1984.

McFarland, Stephen L. *America's Pursuit of Precision Bombing, 1910–1945*. Washington, DC, 1982.

Millett, Allan R., and Williamson Murray, eds. *Military Effectiveness*, vol. 2, *The Interwar Period*. London, 1988.

Murray, Williamson. *Luftwaffe*. Baltimore, 1985.

Murray, Williamson, and Allan R. Millett, eds. *Military Innovation in the Interwar Period*. Cambridge, 1996.

Odom, William O. *After the Trenches: The Transformation of U.S. Army Doctrine, 1918–1939*. College Station, TX, 1999.

Rapoport, Vitaly, and Yuri Alexeev. *High Treason: Essays on the History of the Red Army, 1918–1938*. Durham, 1985.

Roskill, Stephen. *Naval Policy between the Wars*. 2 vols. London, 1976.

Smith, Malcolm. *British Air Strategy between the Wars*. Oxford, 1984.

Turnbull, Archibald D., and Clifford L. Lord. *History of United States Naval Aviation*. New Haven, 1940.

Winton, Harold R. *To Change an Army: General Sir John Burnett-Stuart and British Armored Doctrine, 1927–1938*. Lawrence, KS, 1988.

3. German Designs, 1939–1940

Bethell, Nicholas. *The War That Hitler Won: The Fall of Poland, September 1939*. New York, 1972.

Deutsch, Harold C. *The Conspiracy against Hitler in the Twilight War*. Minneapolis, 1968.

Guderian, Heinz. *Panzer Leader*. New York, 1952.

Halder, Franz. *The Halder War Diary, 1939–1942*. Charles Burdick and Hans Adolf Jacobsen, eds. Novato, CA, 1988.

Horne, Alistair. *To Lose a Battle: France, 1940*. Boston, 1969.

Kennedy, Robert M. *The German Campaign in Poland, 1939*. Washington, DC, 1956.

Maier, Klaus. *Das Deutsche Reich und der Zweite Weltkrieg*, vol. 2, *Die Errichtung der Hegemonie auf dem Europäischen Kontinent*. Stuttgart, 1979.

Taylor, Telford. *The March of Conquest: The German Victories in Western Europe, 1940*. New York, 1958.

Trevor Roper, H. R., ed. *Blitzkrieg to Defeat: Hitler's War Directives*. New York, 1965.

Westphal, Siegfried. *The German Army in the West*. London, 1951.

4. Germany Triumphant, 1940

Bell, P. M. H. *A Certain Eventuality: Britain and the Fall of France*. Boston, 1974.

Collier, Basil. *The Defense of the United Kingdom*. London, 1957.

Derry, T. K. *The Campaign in Norway*. London, 1952.

Doughty, Robert Allan. *The Breaking Point: Sedan and the Fall of France, 1940.* Hamden, CT, 1990.

Frieser, Karl-Heinz. *Blitzkrieg-Legende: Der Westfeldzug 1940.* Munich, 1995.

Gilbert, Martin. *Winston S. Churchill,* vol. 6, *Finest Hour, 1939–1941.* Boston, 1983.

Harvey, Maurice. *Scandinavian Misadventure: The Campaign in Norway, 1940.* Tunbridge Wells, 1990.

Jones, R. V. *The Wizard War: British Scientific Intelligence, 1939–1945.* New York, 1978.

Johnson, Brian. *The Secret War.* London, 1978.

Mason, Francis K. *Battle over Britain.* Garden City, NY, 1969.

Rommel, Erwin. *The Rommel Papers.* B. H. Liddell Hart, ed. New York, 1953.

Spears, Edward M. *Assignment to Catastrophe.* 2 vols. New York, 1954.

5. Diversions in the Mediterranean and Balkans, 1940–1941

Beevor, Anthony. *Crete and the Resistance.* London, 1991.

Blau, George. *The German Campaign in the Balkans, Spring 1941.* Washington, DC, 1953.

Butler, J. R. M. *Grand Strategy,* vol. 2, *September 1939–June 1941.* London, 1956.

Cervi, Mario. *The Hollow Legions: Mussolini's Blunder in Greece, 1940–1941.* Garden City, NY, 1971.

Ciano, Galeazzo. *The Ciano Diaries, 1939–1943.* Hugh Gibson, ed. New York, 1956.

Fraser, David. *Knight's Cross: A Life of Field Marshal Erwin Rommel.* London, 1993.

Jacobsen, Hans Adolf. *Kriegstagebuch des Oberkommandos der Wehrmacht: Wehrmachtführungsstab,* vol. 1, part B, *1941.* Munich, 1982.

Kiriakopoulos, G. C. *Ten Days to Destiny: The Battle for Crete, 1941.* New York, 1985.

Mazower, Mark. *Inside Hitler's Greece: The Experience of Occupation, 1941–1944.* New Haven, 1993.

Mühlesen, Hans-Otto. *Kreta 1941: Das Unternehmen 'Merkur,' 20.5. bis 1.6. 1941.* Freiburg, 1961.

Playfair, Major General I. S. O., et al. *The Mediterranean and the Middle East,* vol. 1, *The Early Successes against Italy.* London, 1954.

Roskill, Stephen. *The War at Sea,* vol. 1. London, 1954.

Schreiber, Gerhard, et al. *Das Deutsche Reich und der Zweite Weltkrieg,* vol. 3, *Der Mittelmeerraum und Südosteuropa.* Stuttgart, 1984.

Van Creveld, Martin L. *Hitler's Strategy: The Balkan Clue.* Cambridge, 1973.

6. Barbarossa, 1941

Bartov, Omar. *Hitler's Army: Soldiers, Nazis, and War in the Third Reich.* Oxford, 1991.

Blau, George. *The German Campaign in Russia: Planning and Operations, 1940–1942.* Washington, DC, 1955.

Boog, Horst, et al. *Das Deutsche Reich und der Zweite Weltkrieg*, vol. 4, *Der Angriff auf die Sowjetunion*. Stuttgart, 1983.

Erickson, John. *The Road to Stalingrad*, vol. 1, *Stalin's War with Germany*. New York, 1975.

Erickson, John. *The Soviet High Command*. London, 1962.

Fugate, Brian I. *Operation Barbarossa: Strategy and Tactics on the Eastern Front, 1941*. Novato, CA, 1984.

Glantz, David M., and Jonathan House. *When Titans Clashed: How the Red Army Stopped Hitler*. Lawrence, KS, 1995.

Hillgruber, Andreas. *Hitlers Strategie: Politik und Kriegführung*. Frankfurt, 1965.

Laqueur, Walter. *Stalin: The Glasnost Revelations*. New York, 1990.

Manstein, Erich von. *Lost Victories*. Novato, CA, 1982.

Overy, Richard. *Russia's War: Blood upon the Snow*. New York, 1997.

Reinhardt, Klaus. *Die Wende vor Moskau: Das Scheitern der Strategie Hitlers im Winter 1941/1942*. Stuttgart, 1972.

Seaton, Albert. *The Russo German War, 1941–1945*. New York, 1971.

Streit, Christian. *Keine Kameraden: Die Wehrmacht und die Sowjetischen Kriegsgefangenen, 1941–1945*. Stuttgart, 1978.

Sydnor, Charles. *Soldiers of Destruction: The SS Death's Head Division, 1933–1945*. Princeton, 1977.

Van Creveld, Martin L. *Supplying War: Logistics from Wallenstein to Patton*. Cambridge, 1977.

Werth, Alexander. *Russia at War, 1941–1945*. New York, 1964.

Whaley, Barton. *Codeword Barbarossa*. Cambridge, 1973.

Ziemke, Earl M., and Magna E. Bauer. *Moscow to Stalingrad: Decision in the East*. Washington, DC, 1987.

7. The Origins of the Asia-Pacific War, 1919–1941

Boyd, Carl. *The Extraordinary Envoy: General Hiroshi Oshima and Diplomacy in the Third Reich, 1934–1941*. Washington, DC, 1980.

Butow, Robert J. C. *Tojo and the Coming of War*. Stanford, 1961.

Chang, Iris. *The Rape of Nanking: The Forgotten Holocaust of World War II*. New York, 1997.

Chi, Hsi-sheng. *Nationalist China at War: Military Defeat and Political Collapse, 1937–1945*. Ann Arbor, 1982.

Cohen, Warren I. *America's Response to China*. New York, 1971.

Dorn, Frank. *The Sino-Japanese War, 1937–1941: From Marco Polo Bridge to Pearl Harbor*. New York, 1974.

Drea, Edward J. *In the Service of the Emperor: Essays on the Imperial Japanese Army*. Lincoln, NE, 1998.

Dwyer, Edward L. *China at War, 1901–1949*. New York and London, 1995.

Fairbank, John King. *China: A New History*. Cambridge, MA, 1992.

————*The United States and China.* New York, 1958.

Gibney, Frank, ed., and Beth Cary, trans. *Senso: The Japanese Remember the Pacific War.* Armonk, NY, 1995.

Harries, Marion, and Susie Harries. *Soldiers of the Sun: The Rise and Fall of the Imperial Japanese Army.* New York, 1991.

Hsiung, James C., and Steven I. Levine, eds. *China's Bitter Victory: The War with Japan, 1937–1945.* London, 1992.

Iriye, Akira. *Across the Pacific: The Inner History of American–East Asian Relations.* Chicago, 1992.

————*The Origins of the Second World War in Asia and the Pacific.* London, 1987.

Koen, Ross Y. *The China Lobby in American Politics.* New York, 1974.

Morley, James William, and Kamikawa Hikomatsu, eds. *Japan's Road to the Pacific War.* 5 vols. David A. Titus et al., trans. New York, 1976–1994.

Schaller, Michael. *The U.S. Crusade in China, 1938–1945.* New York, 1979.

Toland, John. *The Rising Sun: The Decline and Fall of the Japanese Empire.* New York, 1970.

Utley, Jonathan G. *Going to War with Japan, 1937–1941.* Knoxville, TN, 1985.

Wetzler, Peter. *Hirohito and War: Imperial Tradition and Military Decision-Making in Prewar Japan.* Honolulu, 1998.

Wilson, Dick. *When Tigers Fight: The Story of the Sino-Japanese War, 1937–1945.* New York, 1982.

8. The Japanese War of Conquest, 1941–1942

Drea, Edward J. *MacArthur's ULTRA: Codebreaking and the War against Japan, 1942–1945.* Lawrence, KS, 1992.

Dull, Paul S. *A Battle History of the Imperial Japanese Navy, 1941–1945.* Annapolis, 1978.

Evans, David C., ed. *The Japanese Navy in World War II.* Annapolis, 1986.

Holmes, W. J. *Double-Edged Secrets: U.S. Naval Intelligence in the Pacific during World War II.* Annapolis, 1979.

Lewin, Ronald. *The American Magic: Codes, Ciphers and the Defeat of Japan.* New York, 1982.

Lundstrom, John B. *The First South Pacific Campaign: Pacific Fleet Strategy, December 1941–June 1942.* Annapolis, 1976.

————*The First Team: Pacific Naval Air Combat from Pearl Harbor to Midway.* Annapolis, 1984.

Morton, Louis. *United States Army in World War II: The War in the Pacific: The Fall of the Philippines.* Washington, DC, 1953.

Prados, John. *Combined Fleet Decoded: The Secret History of American Intelligence and the Japanese Navy in World War II.* New York, 1995.

Prange, Gordon, with Donald M. Goldstein and Katherine V. Dillon. *At Dawn We Slept: The Untold Story of Pearl Harbor.* New York, 1981.

Spector, Ronald H. *Eagle against the Sun: The American War with Japan*. New York, 1985.

van der Vat, Dan. *The Pacific Campaign: The U.S.-Japanese Naval War, 1941–1945*. New York, 1991.

Willmott, H. P. *Empires in the Balance: Japanese and Allied Pacific Strategies to April 1942*. Annapolis, 1982.

———*The Barrier and the Javelin: Japanese and Allied Pacific Strategies February to June 1942*. Annapolis, 1983.

Winton, John. *ULTRA in the Pacific*. Annapolis, 1993.

9. The Asia-Pacific War, 1942–1944

Bergerud, Eric. *Touched with Fire: The Land War in the South Pacific*. New York, 1996.

Blair, Clay, Jr. *Silent Victory: The U.S. Submarine War against Japan*. Philadelphia, 1975.

Boyd, Carl. *American Command of the Sea: Carriers, Codes, and the Silent Service*. Newport News, VA, 1995.

Boyd, Carl, and Okihiko Yoshida. *The Japanese Submarine Force and World War II*. Annapolis, 1995.

Brown, David, comp. *Warship Losses of World War II*. Annapolis, 1995.

Condit, Doris, et al. *Challenge and Response in Internal Conflict*, vol. 1, *The Experience in Asia*. 3 vols. Washington, DC, 1968.

Dull, Paul S. *A Battle History of the Imperial Japanese Navy*. Annapolis, 1978.

Dunigan, James F., and Albert A. Nofi. *Victory at Sea: World War II in the Pacific*. New York, 1995.

Frank, Richard. *Guadalcanal*. New York, 1990.

Gannon, Robert. *Hellions of the Deep: The Development of American Torpedoes in World War II*. State College, PA, 1996.

Griffith, Thomas E., Jr. *MacArthur's Airman: George C. Kenney and the War in the Southwest Pacific*. Lawrence, KS, 1998.

Kenney, General George C. *General Kenney Reports*. Washington, DC, 1987.

Kimball, Warren F. *Forged in War: Roosevelt, Churchill, and the Second World War*. New York, 1997.

Leary, William M., ed. *We Shall Return: MacArthur's Commanders and the Defeat of Japan*. Lexington, KY, 1988.

Lundstrom, John. *The First Team and the Guadalcanal Campaign*. Annapolis, 1994.

Merrill, James M. *A Sailor's Admiral: A Biography of William F. Halsey*. New York, 1976.

Miller, John, Jr. *United States Army in World War II: The War in the Pacific: The War against Japan: Cartwheel: The Isolation of Rabaul*. Washington, DC, 1959.

Parillo, Mark. *The Japanese Merchant Marine in World War II*. Annapolis, 1993.

Potter, E. B., Jr. *Nimitz*. Annapolis, 1976.

Saburo, Hayashi, with Alvin D. Coox. *Kogun: The Japanese Army in the Pacific War.* Quantico, VA, 1959.

Tuchman, Barbara. *Stilwell and the American Experience in China, 1911–1945.* New York, 1970.

Turner, Lieutenant General William H. *Over the Hump.* Washington, DC, 1985.

Wheeler, Gerald E. *Kinkaid of the Seventh Fleet.* Washington, DC, 1995.

10. The Battle of the Atlantic, 1939–1943

Barnett, Correlli. *Engage the Enemy More Closely: The Royal Navy in the Second World War.* New York, 1991.

Beesley, Patrick. *Very Special Intelligence: The Story of the Admiralty's Operational Intelligence Centre, 1939–1945.* Garden City, NY, 1978.

Blair, Clay. *Hitler's U-Boat War: The Hunters, 1939–1942.* New York, 1996.

Boog, Horst, et al. *Das Deutsche Reich und der Zweite Weltkrieg,* vol. 6, *Der Globale Krieg, 1941–1943.* Stuttgart, 1990.

Cohen, Eliot A., and John Gooch. *Military Misfortunes: The Anatomy of Failure in War.* New York, 1990.

Gannon, Michael. *Operation Drumbeat.* New York, 1991.

Hinsley, F. H. *British Intelligence in the Second World War,* vols. 1–3, *Its Influence on Strategy and Operations.* London, 1979, 1981, 1984.

Ministry of Defense. *The U-Boat War in the North Atlantic, 1939–1945.* London, 1989.

Morison, Samuel Eliot. *The Two Ocean War: A Short History of the United States Navy in World War II.* Boston, 1963.

Roskill, Stephen W. *The War at Sea,* vols. 1–3. London, 1954, 1956, 1960.

Showell, Jak P. Mallman. *Fuehrer Conferences on Naval Affairs, 1939–1945.* Annapolis, 1990.

van der Vat, Dan. *The Atlantic Campaign: World War II's Great Struggle at Sea.* New York, 1988.

Winton, John. *Ultra at Sea: How Breaking the Nazi Code Affected Allied Naval Strategy during World War II.* New York, 1988.

11. Year of Decision for Germany, 1942

Bartov, Omar. *Hitler's Army: Soldiers, Nazis, and War in the Third Reich.* Oxford, 1991.

Bennett, Ralph. *Ultra and Mediterranean Strategy.* London, 1989.

———*Intelligence Investigations: How Ultra Changed History.* London, 1996.

Blau, George. *The German Campaign in Russia: Planning and Operations, 1940–1942.* Washington, DC, 1955.

Boog, Horst, et al. *Das Deutsche Reich und der Zweite Weltkrieg,* vol. 6, *Die Ausweitung zum Weltkrieg und der Wechsel der Initiative, 1941–1943.* Stuttgart, 1990.

Carver, Michael. *Dilemmas of the Desert War: A New Look at the Libyan Campaign, 1940–1942.* Bloomington, IN, 1984.

D'Este, Carlo. *Patton: A Genius for War.* New York, 1995.

Erickson, John. *The Road to Stalingrad,* vol. 1, *Stalin's War with Germany.* New York, 1975.

Fraser, David. *Knight's Cross: A Life of Field Marshal Erwin Rommel.* London, 1993.

Glantz, David M. *Soviet Military Deception in the Second World War.* London, 1989.

———*Zhukov's Greatest Defeat: The Red Army's Epic Disaster in Operation Mars, 1942.* Lawrence, KS, 1999.

Glantz, David M., and Jonathan M. House. *The Battle of Kursk.* Lawrence, KS, 1999.

Hayward, Joel S. A. *Stopped at Stalingrad: The Luftwaffe and Hitler's Defeat in the East, 1942–1943.* Lawrence, KS, 1998.

Hillgruber, Andreas. *Kriegstagebuch des Oberkommandos der Wehrmacht: Wehrmachtführungsstab,* vol. 2, *1. Januar 1942–31. Dezember 1942.* Munich, 1982.

Kehrig, Manfred. *Stalingrad: Analyse und Dokumentation einer Schlacht.* Stuttgart, 1974.

Playfair, Major-General I. S. O. *The Mediterranean and Middle East,* vols. 2–4. London, 1956, 1960, 1966.

Rommel, Erwin. *The Rommel Papers.* B. H. Liddell Hart, ed. New York, 1953.

Seaton, Albert. *The Russo-German War, 1941–1945.* New York, 1971.

Werth, Alexander. *Russia at War, 1941–1945.* New York, 1964.

Ziemke, Earl M., and Magna E. Bauer. *Moscow to Stalingrad: Decision in the East.* Washington, DC, 1987.

12. The Combined Bomber Offensive, 1941–1945

Beck, Earl R. *Under the Bombs: The German Home Front, 1942–1945.* Lexington, KY, 1986.

Bennett, Air Vice-Marshal D. C. T. *Pathfinder: A War Autobiography.* London, 1958.

Boog, Horst, et al. *Das Deutsche Reich und der Zweite Weltkrieg,* vol. 6, *Der Global Krieg.* Stuttgart, 1990.

———*The Conduct of the Air War in the Second World War: An International Comparison.* New York, 1992.

Crane, Conrad. *Bombs, Cities, and Civilians: American Airpower Strategy in World War II.* Lawrence, KS, 1992.

Craven, Wesley Frank, and James Lea Cate, eds. *The Army Air Forces in World War II.* 7 vols. Chicago, 1948–1958.

Davis, Richard G. *Carl A. Spaatz and the Air War in Europe.* Washington, DC, 1993.

Frankland, Noble. *Bomber Offensive: The Devastation of Europe.* London, 1970.

Greenhous, Brereton, et al. *The Official History of the Royal Canadian Air Force,* vol. 3, *The Crucible of War, 1939–1945.* Toronto, 1994.

Hastings, Max. *Bomber Command.* London, 1979.

Mets, David R. *Master of Airpower: General Carl A. Spaatz.* Novato, CA, 1988.

Middlebrook, Martin. *The Battle of Hamburg: Allied Bomber Forces against a German City in 1943.* London, 1980.

————*The Berlin Raids: R.A.F. Bomber Command, Winter 1942–1944.* London, 1988.

————*The Nuremburg Raid, 30–31 March 1944.* New York, 1974.

Mierzejewski, Alfred C. *The Collapse of the German War Economy, 1944–1945: Allied Air Power and the German National Railway.* Chapel Hill, 1988.

Muller, Richard. *The German Air War in Russia.* Baltimore, 1992.

Neufeld, Michael J. *The Rocket and the Reich: Penemünde and the Coming of the Ballistic Missile Era.* New York, 1995.

Steinhoff, Johannes. *Messerschmitts over Sicily.* Baltimore, 1987.

Terraine, John. *The Right of the Line: The Royal Air Force in the European War, 1939–1945.* London, 1985.

Webster, Sir Charles, and Noble Frankland. *The Strategic Air Offensive against Germany.* 4 vols. London, 1961.

13. The Destruction of Japanese Naval Power, 1943–1944

Alexander, Joseph A. *Storm Landings: Epic Amphibious Battles in the Central Pacific.* Annapolis, 1997.

Ballantine, Duncan. *U.S. Naval Logistics in the Second World War.* Princeton, 1947.

Buell, Thomas B. *Master of Sea Power: A Biography of Fleet Admiral Ernest J. King.* Boston, 1980.

————*The Quiet Warrior: A Biography of Admiral Raymond A. Spruance.* Boston, 1974.

Cannon, M. Hamlin. *United States Army in World War II: The War in the Pacific: Leyte: The Return to the Philippines.* Washington, DC, 1954.

Meulen, Jacob Vander. *Building the B-29.* Washington, DC, 1995.

Potter, E. B. *Nimitz.* Annapolis, 1976.

Schratz, Paul R. *Submarine Commander.* Lexington, KY, 1988.

Sherrod, Robert. *On to Westward: The Battles of Saipan and Iwo Jima.* Baltimore, 1990.

Woodward, C. Vann. *The Battle of Leyte Gulf.* New York, 1947.

14. The Killing Time, 1943–1944

Bennett, Ralph. *Ultra and Mediterranean Strategy.* New York, 1989.

Ehrman, John. *Grand Strategy,* vol. 5, *August 1943–September 1944.* London, 1956.

Erickson, John. *Stalin's War with Germany,* vol. 2, *The Defeat of Germany.* London, 1968.

Garland, Albert N., and Howard McGaw Smith. *United States Army in World War II: The Mediterranean Theater of Operations: Sicily and the Surrender of Italy.* Washington, DC, 1993.

Glantz, David M. *Soviet Military Deception in the Second World War.* London, 1989.

Graham, Dominick, and Shelford Bidwell. *Tug of War: The Battle for Italy, 1943–1945.* New York, 1986.

Hinsley, F. H., et al. *British Intelligence in the Second World War*, vol. 3, part 1. London, 1984.

Howard, Michael. *Grand Strategy*, vol. 4, *August 1942–September 1943*. London, 1972.

Hubatsch, Walter. *Kriegstagebuch des Oberkommandos der Wehrmacht: Wehrmachtführungsstab*, vol. 3, *1. Januar 1943–31. Dezember 1943*. Munich, 1982.

Kesselring, Albert. *A Soldier's Record*. New York, 1954.

Klink, Ernst. *Das Gesetz des Handelns: Die Operation "Zitadelle" 1943*. Stuttgart, 1966.

Mellenthin, F. W. von. *Panzer Battles*. Norman, OK, 1956.

Pogue, Forrest C. *United States Army in World War II: The Supreme Command: The European Theater of Operations*. Washington, DC, 1954.

Sydnor, Charles. *Soldiers of Destruction: The SS Death's Head Division, 1933–1945*. Princeton, 1977.

Tedder, Arthur. *With Prejudice: The War Memoirs of Marshal of the Air Force Lord Tedder*. Boston, 1967.

Vaughan-Thomas, Wynford. *Anzio*. New York, 1961.

Ziemke, Earl F. *Stalingrad to Berlin: The German Defeat in the East*. Washington, DC, 1968.

15. The Invasion of France, 1944

Ambrose, Stephen E. *D-Day, June 6, 1944: The Climactic Battle of World War II*. New York, 1994.

Bennett, Ralph. *Ultra in the West: The Normandy Campaign, 1944–1945*. New York, 1979.

———*Intelligence Investigations: How Ultra Changed History*. London, 1996.

Blumenson, Martin. *Patton: The Man behind the Legend, 1885–1945*. New York, 1985.

———*The Battle of the Generals: The Untold Story of the Falaise Pocket*. New York, 1993.

———*Breakout and Pursuit*. Washington, DC, 1961.

Copp, Terry, and Robert Vogel. *Maple Leaf Route: Caen, Falaise, Antwerp*. Alma, Ontario, 1984.

Ellis, Major L. F. *Victory in the West*, vol. 1, *The Battle for Normandy*. London, 1962.

D'Este, Carlo. *Decision in Normandy*. London, 1983.

———*Patton: A Genius for War*. New York, 1997.

Featherston, Alwyn. *Battle for Mortain*. Novato, CA, 1993.

Gelb, Norman. *Generals at War*. New York, 1994.

Harrison, Gordon A. *United States Army in World War II: European Theater of Operations: Cross-Channel Attack*. Washington, DC, 1950.

Hinsley, F. H. *British Intelligence in the Second World War: Its Influence on Strategy and Operations*, vol. 3, part 2. London, 1988.

Hastings, Max. *Overlord: D-Day and the Battle for Normandy, 1944*. London, 1984.

———*Das Reich: The March of the 2nd SS Panzer Division through France*. New York, 1981.

MacDonald, Charles B. *The Mighty Endeavor: The American War in Europe*. New York, 1992.

Ryan, Cornelius. *A Bridge Too Far*. New York, 1977.

Schramm, Percy Ernst. *Kriegstagebuch des Oberkommandos der Wehrmacht: Wehrmachtführungsstab*, vol. 4, *1. Januar 1944–22. Mai 1945*. Munich, 1982.

Thompson, R. W. *The 85 Days*. New York, 1957.

Weigley, Russell F. *Eisenhower's Lieutenants: The Campaign of France and Germany, 1944–1945*. Bloomington, IN, 1981.

Wilmot, Chester. *The Struggle for Europe*. New York, 1952.

16. The End in Europe, 1944–1945

Blumenson, Martin. *Patton: The Man behind the Legend, 1885–1945*. New York, 1985.

Ellis, Major L. F. *Victory in the West*, vol. 2, *The Defeat of Germany*. London, 1968.

Erickson, John. *Stalin's War with Germany*, vol. 2, *The Road to Berlin*. London, 1983.

Glantz, David M. *When Titans Clashed: How the Red Army Stopped Hitler*. Lawrence, KS, 1995.

Hinsley, F. H., et al. *British Intelligence in the Second World War: Its Influence on Strategy and Operations*, vol. 3, part 2. London, 1988.

MacDonald, Charles B. *The Battle of the Bulge*. London, 1984.

——*The Mighty Endeavor: The American War in Europe*. New York, 1992.

——*The Last Offensive*. New York, 1973.

Niepold, Gerd. *The Battle for White Russia: The Destruction of Army Group Center June 1944*. London, 1987.

Read, Anthony, and David Fischer. *The Fall of Berlin*. New York, 1992.

Toland, John. *The Last 100 Days*. New York, 1965.

17. The Destruction of the Japanese Empire, 1944–1945

Allen, Louis. *Burma—The Longest War*. London, 1984.

Aluit, Alfonso J. *By Sword and Fire: The Destruction of Manila in World War II, 3 February–3 March 1945*. Manila, 1994.

Baclagon, Uldarico S. *The Philippine Resistance Movement against Japan, 10 December 1941–14 June 1945*. Manila, 1966.

Bishof, Günter, and Robert L. Dupont, eds. *The Pacific War Revisited*. Baton Rouge, LA, 1997.

Connaughton, Richard, John Pimlott, and Duncan Anderson. *The Battle for Manila*. London, 1995.

Edoin, Hoito. *The Night Tokyo Burned: The Incendiary Campaign against Japan, March–August 1945*. New York, 1987.

Friend, Theodore. *The Blue-Eyed Enemy: Japan against the West in Java and Luzon, 1942–1945*. Princeton, 1988.

Hartendorf, A. V. H. *The Japanese Occupation of the Philippines*. Manila, 1967.

Reister, Frank A., comp. *Medical Statistics in World War II*. Washington, DC, 1975.

Smith, Robert Ross. *United States Army in World War II: The War in the Pacific: Triumph in the Philippines*. Washington, DC, 1991.

Steinberg, David Joel. *Philippine Collaboration in World War II*. Ann Arbor, 1967.

Tanaka, Yuki. *Hidden Horrors: Japanese War Crimes in World War II*. Boulder, 1996.

Werrell, Kenneth P. *Blankets of Fire: U.S. Bombers over Japan during World War II*. Washington, DC, 1996.

Woodburn Kirby, Major General S., et al. *The War against Japan*. 5 vols. London, 1957–1969.

18. The End of the Asia-Pacific War, 1945

Albright, Joseph, and Marcia Kunstel. *Bombshell*. New York, 1997.

Baxter, James Phinney III. *Scientists against Time*. Boston, 1946.

Butow, Robert J. C. *Japan's Decision to Surrender*. Stanford, CA, 1954.

Christman, Al. *Target Hiroshima: Deak Parsons and the Creation of the Atomic Bomb*. Annapolis, 1998.

Feis, Herbert. *The Atomic Bomb and the End of World War II*. Princeton, 1966.

Frank, Benis M. *Okinawa: The Great Island Battle*. New York, 1978.

Frank, Richard B. Dowfall: *The End of the Imperial Japanese Empire*. New York, 1999.

Hewlett Richard G., and Oscar E. Anderson, Jr. *The History of the Atomic Energy Commission*, vol. 1, *The New World, 1939–1946*. State College, PA, 1962.

MacEachin, Douglas J., ed. *The Final Months of the War with Japan: Signals Intelligence, U.S. Invasion Planning, and the A-Bomb Decision*. Washington, DC, 1998.

Hatsuko, Naito. *Thunder Gods: The Kamikaze Pilots Tell Their Story*. Tokyo, 1989.

Rhodes, Richard. *The Making of the Atomic Bomb*. New York, 1986.

Ross, Bill D. *Iwo Jima*. New York, 1985.

Sherwin, Martin J. *A World Destroyed: The Atomic Bomb and the Grand Alliance*. New York, 1975.

Sigal, Leon V. *Fighting to the Finish: The Politics of War Termination in the United States and Japan, 1945*. Ithaca, 1988.

Tibbets, Brig. Gen. Paul W. *Flight of the Enola Gay*. Reynoldsburg, OH, 1989.

19. Peoples at War, 1937–1945

Barber, John, and Mark Harrison. *The Soviet Home Front, 1941–1945*. London, 1991.

Blum, John Morton. *V Was for Victory: Politics and American Culture during World War II*. New York, 1976.

Calder, Angus. *The People's War: Britain, 1939–1945*. New York, 1969.

Crost, Lyn. *Honor by Fire: Japanese Americans at War in Europe and the Pacific*. Novato, CA, 1994.

Ellis, John, comp. *World War II: A Statistical Survey*. New York, 1993.

Garlinski, Jozef. *Poland in World War II*. London, 1985.

Goodwin, Doris Kearns. *No Ordinary Time: Franklin and Eleanor Roosevelt: The Home Front in World War II*. New York, 1994.

Harrison, Mark, ed. *The Economics of World War II*. Cambridge, 1998.

Hartman, Susan M. *American Women in the 1940s: The Home Front and Beyond*. Boston, 1982.

Leighton, Richard M., and Robert W. Coakley. *United States Army in World War II: The War Department: Global Logistics and Strategy*. 2 vols., *1940–1943* and *1943–1945*. Washington, DC, 1955, 1968.

Merryman, Molly. *Clipped Wings: The Rise and Fall of the Women Airforce Service Pilots: WASPs of World War II*. New York, 1998.

Mierzejewski, A. C. *The Collapse of the German War Economy, 1944–1945*. Chapel Hill, 1998.

Milward, A. S. *The German Economy at War*. London, 1965.

——*War, Economy and Society, 1939–1945*. Berkeley, 1977.

O'Neill, William L. *A Democracy at War: America's Fight at Home and Abroad in World War II*. New York, 1993.

Olson, M., Jr. *The Economics of Wartime Shortage*. Durham, 1963.

Polenberg, Richard. *War and Society: The United States, 1941–1945*. Philadelphia, 1972.

Rossiter, Margaret L. *Women in the Resistance*. New York, 1986.

Rupp, Leila. *Mobilizing Women for War: German and American Propaganda, 1939–1945*. Princeton, 1978.

Speer, Albert. *Inside the Third Reich*. New York, 1970.

Werth, Alexander. *Russia at War, 1941–1945*. New York, 1964.

Wilson, G. M. *Politics and Culture in Wartime Japan*. Oxford, 1981.

20. The Aftermath of War

Bishof, Günter, and Stephen E. Ambrose, eds. *Eisenhower and the German POWs*. Baton Rouge, LA, 1992.

Bower, Tom. *The Pledge Betrayed: America and Britain and Denazification in Postwar Germany*. Garden City, NY, 1982.

Cairncross, Alec. *Years of Recovery: British Economic Policy, 1945–1951*. London, 1985.

Dower, John W. *Embracing Defeat: Japan in the Wake of World War II*. New York, 1999.

——*Japan in War and Peace*. New York, 1993.

——*Empire and Aftermath: Yoshida Shigeru and the Japanese Experience, 1878–1954*. Cambridge, 1979.

Ellwood, David W. *Rebuilding Europe: Western Europe, America, and Postwar Reconstruction*. London, 1992.

Gimbel, John. *The Origins of the Marshall Plan*. Stanford, 1976.

Hogan, Michael J. *The Marshall Plan: America, Britain and the Reconstruction of Europe, 1947–1952*. New York, 1987.

Huston, James A. *Across the Face of France: Liberation and Recovery, 1944–1963*. West Lafayette, IN, 1963.

Interagency Group on Nazi Assets [Eizenstat Report], "U.S. and Allied Efforts to Recover and Restore Gold and Other Assets Stolen or Hidden by Germany during World War II," Office of the Historian, U.S. Department of State, May 1997.

Jones, Howard. *A New Kind of War: America's Global Strategy and the Truman Doctrine in Greece*. New York, 1989.

LaFeber, Walter. *The Clash: A History of U.S.-Japan Relations*. New York, 1997.

Maier, Charles. *A Search for Stability: Explorations in Historical Political Economy*. New York, 1987.

Maser, Werner. *Nuremberg: A Nation on Trial*. New York, 1979.

Milward, Alan. *The Reconstruction of Western Europe, 1945–1951*. London, 1984.

Minear, Richard H. *Victor's Justice: The Tokyo War Crimes Trials*. Princeton, 1971.

Piccigallo, Philip R. *The Japanese on Trial: Allied War Crimes Operations in the East, 1945–1951*. Austin, 1979.

Rioux, J. P. *The Fourth Republic, 1944–1958*. London, 1987.

Schaller, Michael. *The American Occupation of Japan*. New York, 1985.

Schonberger, Howard. *Aftermath of War: Americans and the Remaking of Japan, 1945–1952*. Kent, OH, 1989.

Taylor, Lawrence. *A Trial of Generals: Homma, Yamashita, MacArthur*. South Bend, 1981.

Tusa, Ann, and John Tusa. *The Nuremberg Trial*. New York, 1984.

Vincent, Isabel. *Hitler's Silent Partners: Swiss Banks, Nazi Gold and the Pursuit of Justice*. New York, 1997.

Williams, Peter, and David Wallace. *Unit 731: Japan's Secret Biological Warfare in World War II*. New York, 1989.

Zink, Harold. *American Military Government in Germany*. New York, 1947.

ACKNOWLEDGMENTS

We authors are children of World War II. One of us was born while the German Army and the Nazi Party consolidated their grip on Austria and the Japanese Army continued its advance into China. The other entered a world that wondered if the Germans would take Moscow before Christmas even after the first Russian snows flew or when a U-boat would sink another destroyer. It was also a world that speculated whether the latest Japanese mission to Washington had a real peace plan. World War II and its aftershocks have had a defining influence on the history of our world and our lives ever since. One of us contained Communism in the Caribbean, and the other took on the same mission in Southeast Asia, and neither of us would have had these experiences (one suspects) if the German Army had actually taken Moscow.

As our good friend the late Coach Woody Hayes often said, the responsibility of the successful is to "pay forward," so we hope our children and grandchildren will remember that their lives, peaceful or not, owe a debt to all those who fought and won World War II. We also want to thank our wives, Lee Smith and Martha Farley-Millett, for their understanding when work on this book ruined plans and strained patience. We are doubly fortunate since our wives are both academic historians whose counsel is invariably right. They also have been enthusiastic companions in our visits to many of the places in Europe and Asia where the events about which we write take place: Amsterdam, Athens, Beijing, Berlin, Brussels, Budapest, Cologne, Edinburgh, Hiroshima, Hong Kong, Leningrad, London, Melbourne, Oslo, Paris, Prague, Rome, Saigon, Singapore, Tokyo, and Vienna.

We have many people to thank for their contributions to this "mighty endeavor," as Winston Churchill characterized the D-Day landings of 1944. Although we authors bear the ultimate responsibility for this book, we are grateful to all those who stimulated our interest in history from our childhood. Probably the best place to start is with our undergraduate history teachers at Yale University and DePauw University, but our graduate school mentors deserve the pride of place for their patient attempts to deal with veterans who knew everything about war: Harry L. Coles, Andreas Dorpalen, Foster Rhea Dulles, Sydney Fisher, Hans Gatzke, Donald Kagan, Charles Morley, and Piotr Wandycz, all members of the faculty of Yale and The Ohio State University. Through the years other giants in the world of academic history shaped our thinking about war in general and World War II in particular: Stephen E. Ambrose, Brian Bond, Horst Boog, Andre Corvisier, Wilhelm Deist, Sir Michael Howard, Manfred Messerschmidt, Louis Morton, Forrest Pogue, Olav Riste, Jürgen Röhwer, Luc de Vos, and Russell F. Weigley.

We also profited beyond measure by our association with Dr. Andrew Marshall, the Director of Net Assessment, Office of the Secretary of Defense, the U.S. Department of Defense. Through Dr. Marshall's beneficence and confidence, we directed and wrote some of three group studies that advanced our understanding of world military affairs in the first half of the twentieth century: *Military Effectiveness* (3 vols., 1988); *Calculations: Net Assessment and the Coming of World War II* (1992); and *Military Innovation in the Interwar Period* (1996). We are indebted to all our friends and colleagues who participated in these studies, but we are particularly thankful for the wise counsel of those experts who knew several nations and their armed forces far better than we: Carl Boyd, Alvin D. Coox, Robert A. Doughty, Jürgen Förster, Holger H. Herwig, Ronald Chalmers Hood II, John E. Jessup, MacGregor Knox, Ian Nish, Steven Ross, Brian Sullivan, and Earl F. Ziemke.

This book also reflects some group learning in a course on the history of World War II we established at The Ohio State University more than twenty years ago. Although the leadership in this course has varied between us and many of our colleagues— especially John F. Guilmartin and Mark Grimsley—the course continues and serves as an inspiration to improve our grasp of the modern world's most influential war. In addition to the generations of students who passed through this class—which included a Rhodes Scholar and one of the NFL's best running backs— we especially owe a debt to another (if smaller) generation of graduate students who assisted us in this course or whose own research enriched our teaching and inspired us to keep up with our students. Others worked closely with us in additional courses on European and American military history in the twentieth century. Many of them hold their own places of honor as scholars of World War II: Michael Doubler, Allison Gilmore, Russell Hart, Peter Mansoor, Geoffrey Megargee, Bradley J. Meyer, Richard Muller, William Odom, Jeffrey Roberts, and Peter Schrijvers.

We also want to thank our colleagues of the history department of The Ohio State University for their advice and, in some cases, close reading of our analysis of domestic and home front politics of the countries of their expertise: James Bartholomew (Japan), Alan Beyerchen (Germany), Samuel Chu (China), Susan Hartmann (United States), David Hoffman (Russia), John A. M. Rothney (France), Leila Rupp (Germany), and David Stebenne (United States).

During the review process initiated by our publisher, this manuscript was read in its entirety by three experts on World War II, and we are in their debt for the constructive suggestions they made for corrections and revisions: Professor Holger H. Herwig (University of Calgary), Dr. Mark R. Peattie (the Hoover Institution and Stanford University), and Professor Russell F. Weigley (Temple University). Before and after this formal review process we profited from the advice (based on reading portions of the manuscript) of Professor Ray Callahan (University of Delaware), whose expertise on the British campaign of Southeast Asia proved invaluable, and from Professor Peter Maslowski (University of Nebraska–Lincoln) and Professor Mark Parillo (Kansas State University), who not only provided relevant knowledge of the war but examined portions of the book for its suitability for students in their own World War II courses. We also want to thank Brigadier Geneneral David A. Armstrong, USA (Ret.), a military historian with a doctorate from Duke University and a former Military Academy instructor, for his help with the three appendices on military organization, the conduct of war, and weapons. General Armstrong is the historian for the Chairman, Joint Chiefs of Staff. Lieutenant Colonel Michael Perry, Director, U.S. Army Military History Institute, also provided valuable support.

As on other projects, Ms. Beth Russell, Mershon Center, The Ohio State University, provided dependable and skilled secretarial and administrative assistance above and beyond the call of duty. We are also grateful for the continued support of the Mershon Center and especially its current director, Dr. Richard Ned Lebow, and the patronage of Major General Raymond E. Mason, Jr., USAR (Ret.), a generous alumnus and sterling example of "the Greatest Generation."

In our search for photographs that caught the global nature of the war and still had some freshness, we turned to our friends and colleagues of the International Commission of Comparative Military History. We want to thank Admiral Paolo Alberini and Admiral Tiberio Moro, Italian Armed Forces; Dr. Isobel Campbell, Historical Office, Canadian Armed Forces; Dr. Jeffrey Grey, Australian Defence Force Academy; Colonel Piet Kamphuis, Chief of Military History, Military History Section, Royal Netherlands Army; Colonel Jarl Kronlund, Office of the Chief of Military History, the General Staff, Finnish Army; Frau Kuhl, Bundesarchiv, Koblenz; Dr. Ioannis Loucas, Hellenic Naval Academy, Greek Navy; Dr. Bruce Menning, U.S. Army Command and General Staff College; Dr. Manfried Rauchensteiner, Director, Austrian Military History Museum, Vienna; and Dr. Luc de Vos, the Royal Military Academy, Royal Belgian Army. Mr. Malcolm Swanston provided an exceptional set of maps.

We have benefited from the work of our two senior editors at Harvard University Press, Ms. Joyce Seltzer (New York) and Ms. Susan Wallace Boehmer (Cambridge), whose active, critical, and creative participation in this project produced a better book.

   Williamson Murray   Allan R. Millett
   Burke, Virginia   Columbus, Ohio

ILLUSTRATION CREDITS

INDEX